For eleven years .... was a reporter for *The Wall Street Journal*, where his investigative work ranged over many fields, including white-collar crime and securities and tax frauds. It was in writing for the *Journal* that he broke the Columbia Pictures story.

He is the author of the much-acclaimed *Stealing From the Rich* and lives in New York City.

Indecent Exposure

A True Story of Hollywood and Wall Street

David McClintick

CORGI BOOKS

INDECENT EXPOSURE

A CORGI BOOK 0 552 12389 7

Originally published in Great Britain by Columbus Books

PRINTING HISTORY
Columbus edition published 1983
Corgi edition published 1984

Corgi Books are published by Transworld Publishers Ltd.,
Century House, 61-63 Uxbridge Road, Ealing, London W5 5SA

Made and printed in Great Britain by
Hunt Barnard Printing Ltd., Aylesbury, Bucks.

For Judy
and
For my parents
Dorothy and Dean McClintick

ACKNOWLEDGMENTS

I am grateful to a large number of people whose aid and comfort were crucial in the writing of this book— friends and acquaintances in the entertainment industry and the business world at large, as well as at my former professional home, *The Wall Street Journal*. They contributed time, encouragement, and various forms of more tangible help—sometimes when it was not convenient, and occasionally against their better judgment. Most of them would be uncomfortable if I named them, but they know who they are and how much they mean to me.

In the category of equally important people who can be identified, I should like to thank the management and staff of William Morrow & Company, especially my outstanding editor, James Landis, and of Dell Publishing Company, particularly Carole Baron and Susan Moldow.

Thanks also to Robert D. Sack, the finest libel lawyer in America and, not insignificantly, an astute editorial critic.

I owe the profoundest of gratitude to Kathy Robbins and Richard Covey, who have combined literary representation of the very highest quality with a deep and durable friendship that I cherish. They have, quite literally, changed my life.

Finally, Judith Ludlam McClintick, my wife. The period of this book's preparation, and the writing itself, have encompassed times of pain and anguish. Judy has seen me through all of them with strength, grace, wit, and love.

AUTHOR'S NOTE

Everything in this book is real—every episode, scene, weather reference, conversation, and name. The reader is urged to consult the source notes for a detailed explanation of the author's *modus operandi* and a delineation of his sources.

"It's the jungle. It appeals to my nature. . . . It's more than a place where streets are named after Sam Goldwyn and buildings after Bing Crosby. There's more to it than pink Cadillacs with leopard-skin seat covers. It's the jungle, and it harbors an industry that's one of the biggest in the country. A closed-in, tight, frantically inbred, and frantically competitive jungle. And the rulers of the jungle are predatory and fascinating and tough. L. B. Mayer is one of the rulers of the jungle. I like L.B. He's a ruler now, but he has to watch his step or he'll be done in. He's shrewd. He's big business. . . . L.B. is tough. He's never trying to win the point you're talking about. His aim is always long-range—to keep control of the studio. He loves Dore. But someday he'll destroy Dore. L.B. is sixty-five. And he's pink. And healthy. And smiling. Dore is about twenty years younger. And he looks old. And sick. And worried. Because L.B. guards the jungle like a lion. But the very top rulers of the jungle are here in New York. Nick Schenck, the president of Loew's Inc., the ruler of the rulers, stays here in New York and smiles, watching from afar, from behind the scenes, but he's the real power, watching the pack close in on one or another of the lesser rulers—close in, ready to pounce! Nick Schenck never gets his picture in the papers, and he doesn't go to parties, and he avoids going out in public, but he's the *real* king of the pack. And he does it all from New York! God, are they tough!"

JOHN HUSTON
1950

"The new Hollywood is very much like the old Hollywood."

—DAVID CHASMAN
Executive Vice President, MGM
1981

Part I

ONE

Evelyn Christel, a slim woman of forty-one with short blond hair, eased her brown Pinto from Van Nuys Boulevard into the rush-hour crawl of the Ventura Freeway and headed east. She squinted into the sun, which had just cleared the snow-covered San Gabriel Mountains on the far horizon straight ahead.

It was 8 A.M., Friday, February 25, 1977, clear and bracing—one of the chilliest mornings of the brief, subtropical Los Angeles winter.

Evelyn's drive would take thirty-five minutes if she was lucky, forty-five minutes if she was not. Like thousands of logs glutting a river, the traffic crept past Bullock's and I. Magnin, Coldwater Canyon Avenue and Laurel Canyon Boulevard. Twenty miles an hour, then fifty, then ten.

Evelyn negotiated a careful merge with the southeast-bound Hollywood Freeway. Universal Studios on the left. Cahuenga Pass through the scrubby hills, green from the winter rains. Hollywood Bowl on the right.

Off the freeway at Vine. South on Vine down the hill, stop-and-go, through Central Hollywood. The Capitol Records Tower. TAV Celebrity Theater Presents the Merv Griffin Show. Art City.

Vine becomes Rossmore at Melrose. Along Rossmore, gently curving, past the Wilshire Country Club and the grand old homes of Hancock Park, all the way to Wilshire Boulevard. A long light, then across Wilshire to the stone gates of Fremont Place, an elegant and very private residential enclave. Another wait while the guard located Evelyn's name on his list. Over the speed bump, around the corner to the right, and into the driveway of the first house, 97 Fremont Place West, where Evelyn's employer, Cliff Robertson, the motion-picture actor, was in temporary residence.

Evelyn might have preferred a commute as short as those during

Cliff's previous extended visits to Los Angeles. He had rented houses in Coldwater Canyon and Brentwood, which were much closer to her home in the working-class San Fernando Valley community of Van Nuys. But in nineteen years as Cliff Robertson's part-time secretary, Evelyn Christel had grown used to, and actually quite fond of, just about all of Cliff's eccentricities, mainly because they weren't really eccentricities at all but quite normal traits that seemed eccentric only in Hollywood. One of them was a strong preference for living near where he was working. Most movie celebrities, no matter how remote the location of the studio that might be employing them at a particular time, insisted on living in Beverly Hills or Bel-Air. Any other place would have threatened their self-image. Cliff Robertson, however, wasn't so insecure as most in Hollywood (another of his "eccentricities"). Although he sought out luxurious comfort wherever he went, it didn't necessarily have to have a chichi name like Beverly Hills. And since he was making a movie at Paramount that winter, the real-estate agent had suggested to Evelyn Christel that Cliff consider Fremont Place, which was only five minutes from the Paramount lot.

Most of the seventy-three houses in the half-century-old enclave were as elegant as many in Beverly Hills. But only three celebrities lived in Fremont Place—Muhammad Ali, the heavyweight boxer; Karen Black, the film actress; and Lou Rawls, the pop singer. The majority of the residents were lawyers, bankers, and businessmen who drove east to offices in the skyscrapers of downtown Los Angeles instead of west and north to the show-business factories of Beverly Hills, Hollywood, and Burbank. Fremont Placers tended mildly to disdain the entertainment industry; its products occasionally were amusing, but its people and ambience were too gaudy and often too vulgar for the modest and somewhat smug sensibilities of Fremont Place.

As it happened, this was an attitude which was privately shared by the new resident of Number 97 West—still another of Cliff Robertson's atypical traits. But as people close to Cliff were aware, his choice of temporary abode and his attitude toward his industry were not isolated quirks. They were broad hints of the kind of person Cliff Robertson was—a maverick, usually a benign one, but by Hollywood standards nonetheless a maverick, whose determined independence manifested itself multifariously, from the way he handled his money, to the way he handled his career, to the way he handled his life.

Although he had grown up in Southern California, Robertson had always found the Hollywood community somewhat claustrophobic and more than a bit tawdry, and had chosen to live in New York City for much of his adult life. He didn't depend on Hollywood for financial security, though he had earned a great deal of money there. He was independently wealthy in his own right and was married to one of America's richest women, Dina Merrill, the actress, socialite, and daughter of the late Marjorie Merriweather Post and the late E. F. Hutton. Unlike many movie people who found it chic to spend their money freely but ignore its management, Robertson watched his money and investments carefully. And instead of using one of the big, flashy financial-management agencies in Beverly Hills, which were status symbols themselves to many in the community, he chose to have his finances handled by a small, staid CPA firm on Sunset Boulevard in old Hollywood.

At deeper levels of personality and character, too, Cliff Robertson was something of an alien. In an industry populated by sizable numbers of loud, slick, bullying maneuverers, Robertson came across as the complete gentleman—kind, pleasant, deliberate, not especially temperamental, not unreasonably demanding toward people around him, a man who was never more content than when he was spending time with his family in the privacy of their home. ("The last of the hearth huggers," Dina called him.) Moreover, in a community where erratic and unethical human behavior were common enough to require constant vigilance, Robertson seemed to live by a traditional moral code—simple and staunch—forged in his strict Presbyterian upbringing.

Robertson's way of life, of course, endeared him to his friends, associates and employees—people like Evelyn Christel, for example, who had lived for two decades on the fringes of the Hollywood scene but centered her life on her family, their printing business in Van Nuys, and the Roman Catholic Church. But Cliff's qualities grated a little on a lot of Hollywood people. They found him self-righteous, old-fashioned, too bland to be much fun and, worst of all, too unpredictable ever to be fully acceptable in the world's ultimate company town.

In these people's eyes, Robertson was perpetually guilty of a serious and unforgivable offense: he didn't truly *need* Hollywood.

As a result, a number of his relationships in the entertainment community had always been a bit uncomfortable and had contained the seeds of friction. Although Cliff had never been a big enough star to dictate terms of film contracts and isolate himself from the hurly-burly of the business, the friction had usually been quiescent and had affected his career only occasionally and only in relatively minor ways.

But all of that was about to change. Cliff Robertson soon would be engulfed in a holocaust of controversy and pain that would maim several lives, including his own, wound hundreds of other people, and jostle the foundations of the world's most glamorous industry.

The institution of Hollywood, with all its staying power, would never be quite the same again.

Evelyn Christel passed through the white stucco Spanish-style house and out onto the large patio where Cliff Robertson, clad in slacks and a heavy sweater, was relaxing next to the pool with a mug of coffee and a lap full of mail.

Dina wasn't in evidence. Eight-year-old Heather Robertson was brought to the patio by her governess to kiss her father good-bye before leaving for school, and Cliff and Evelyn got down to work. When the Robertson family was away from New York for extended periods, their mail was collected in large envelopes and forwarded to them every few days. When it arrived in Los Angeles, Cliff would summon Evelyn, dictate replies to letters, give her bills to pay, and turn over any other matters which she appropriately could handle.

That morning in Fremont Place it took about an hour and a half to dispense with the two dozen or so pieces of mail that had just arrived. All but one were fairly routine. It was a windowed envelope from the Internal Revenue Service containing an IRS Form 1099, Statement of Miscellaneous Income, 1976. The form indicated that Cliff Robertson had been paid $10,000 the previous year by Columbia Pictures.

"Does this ring any bells with you?" Cliff asked Evelyn.

She examined the document. "No."

"Columbia Pictures. Ten thousand dollars," Cliff mused. "That's funny. I didn't do any work for them last year, and I certainly didn't get any money from them. At least I don't remember any. It's an odd figure, too, ten thousand. That's not what I get for a picture. Maybe it was supposed to be a residual payment of some kind, but whatever it was I'm quite sure I didn't receive it. Why don't you check with Michael or Bud and see if they know anything about it.''

By noon, Evelyn was back in Van Nuys and Cliff was at Paramount where, since late December, he had been filming a television movie to be entitled *Washington: Behind Closed Doors*, based on the John Ehrlichman novel about the Watergate White House and the CIA. Cliff played the director of Central Intelligence.

TWO

The inquiry into the matter of the $10,000 seemed no more urgent than the many other tasks that Evelyn Christel was performing for Cliff Robertson, and it was not assigned a unique priority. The following week, she telephoned Abraham ''Bud'' Kahaner, the senior partner of Prager & Fenton, Robertson's accountants. Kahaner had no record of the $10,000 payment from Columbia Pictures. Neither did Michael Black, Cliff's agent at the Los Angeles office of International Creative Management. Evelyn then phoned the Columbia accounting department in Burbank. After being passed among several clerks, she finally was told that the payment appeared to be related to the 1976 motion picture *Obsession*, a psychological thriller in which Robertson played a businessman who meets the double of his widow (Genevieve Bujold). *Obsession*, which director-writer Brian De Palma derived in part from Hitchcock's *Vertigo*, had not been made under Columbia Pictures' aegis; the studio had purchased the finished movie from an independent film company and distributed it. Evelyn confirmed with Kahaner and Black that all of Robertson's fees from *Obsession* had been paid by the filmmaker. He was owed nothing and had received nothing from Columbia Pictures.

Cliff told Evelyn to demand a written explanation, and on Tuesday, March 15, she dispatched a letter to Columbia's accounting department asking the details of the $10,000 payment.

                    *   *   *

Columbia Pictures' movie and television operations were situated at
The Burbank Studios, a 105-acre tract at the north foot of Cahuenga
Peak, one of the highest and steepest hills in the ridge separating the
San Fernando Valley from the rest of Los Angeles to the south. The
Burbank Studios, together with nearby NBC, Universal and Disney,
formed the northern point of a rough, fifty-square-mile diamond
within which were found just about all of the companies, facilities,
and people comprising what the world at large thought of as
"Hollywood," or the "Show Business Capital of the World." The
eastern point of the diamond, as one looked at a map, was formed
by Paramount Pictures and the ABC studios southeast of Burbank
across the hills in the eastern part of Hollywood proper. The western
point was the cluster of Beverly Hills, Century City, and the Twentieth Century-Fox studios southwest of Burbank across the hills in the
western sector of Los Angeles. The southern point of the diamond
was the Metro-Goldwyn-Mayer lot, housing MGM and United Artists,
a forty-five-minute drive south of Burbank in Culver City, not far
from the Los Angeles airport.

Columbia Pictures shared the thirty-eight sound stages and other
facilities of The Burbank Studios with Warner Bros. The Columbia
executive offices were housed in a striking two-story redwood,
tinted glass, and concrete building with a central atrium at the
northeast corner of the Burbank lot. The accounting department was
on the second floor at the back.

When Evelyn Christel's letter arrived, the accounts-payable
supervisor, Dick Caudillo, pulled the files and found that a check
payable to Cliff Robertson had been drawn on September 2, 1976, at
the request of the president of the Columbia studio, David Begelman,
the flamboyant former talent agent who had been running Columbia
for nearly four years. Caudillo informed Begelman's office of the
Robertson inquiry and was told that the money had been paid to
Robertson to cover his expenses for a personal-appearance tour that
he had made to promote *Obsession*. The inquiry took two weeks to
make its way from Caudillo to David Begelman's office and back.
Caudillo forwarded the information to Evelyn Christel on Monday,
March 28.

What he forwarded was not the full story, however. Dick Caudillo,
a stocky man in his early thirties, with thinning dark hair, did not
tell Christel a curious fact which he found amusing. Cliff Robertson's

inquiry was one of dozens of similar inquiries and complaints that had deluged the studio during those late winter and early spring weeks. The furor arose because Columbia, in tightening some of its accounting practices to conform to stricter rules of the Internal Revenue Service, had reported to the tax authorities, via the requisite Form 1099, a substantially greater number of "miscellaneous payments" for 1976 than it had reported for past years. Such payments—to actors, directors, producers, and a host of other people—were a way of life in the entertainment business. In addition to paying the salaries and fees prescribed in contracts for specific services such as directing or acting in a film, the studios also shelled out countless other payments under countless other labels, mostly to retain the goodwill of the recipients. A studio would give an actor $10,000 to cover his "expenses" on a promotional tour, knowing that the expenses would be only a fraction of the $10,000 but not asking for any accounting of unused funds. A director would do some extra work on a picture, and instead of being paid an additional fee, he would be given a new $30,000 automobile. Whether these payments were in cash, cars, or other tender, their tax status historically was in doubt. Theoretically, the payments were taxable, but the IRS never declared them so specifically and the studios rarely bothered to report them to the IRS. The aggregate result was the payment of millions of dollars of tax-free income that was widely taken for granted by those who received it.

In the seventies, however, the IRS explicitly ruled such payments taxable and also developed more sophisticated auditing methods to detect them. The studios, therefore, began reporting more of the payments to the IRS, with the result that income that had been tax-free suddenly became taxable. Many of the habitual recipients were incensed, and in the early months of 1977—the time for reporting 1976 income—angry letters poured into the Columbia Pictures accounting department. Of course, the recipients of 1099 forms couldn't officially berate the studio for obeying the law. So instead many people simply claimed that they had not gotten the payments indicated by the forms. Dick Caudillo would routinely locate the documentation for payments that were questioned and inform the recipients that they had, in fact, received the payments. Caudillo, a man who rather enjoyed pricking wealthy show business personalities with odious little government forms, assumed that the

Cliff Robertson inquiry was like the others and that a single letter of rebuff would end the matter, as it had in other cases.

When Evelyn reported to Cliff that Columbia claimed the $10,000 had been paid to him for his expenses on the *Obsession* promotional tour, he was mystified. Yes, he had traveled to three or four cities to promote *Obsession*, but he certainly hadn't been given $10,000 to pay his expenses. His accountants had been reimbursed after billing the studio directly, and the amount had come to far less than $10,000.

"What are you going to do?" Dina Merrill asked her husband one evening in the Fremont Place house shortly before he completed *Washington: Behind Closed Doors.*

"Jesus, I'm not going to pay taxes on ten thousand dollars I didn't receive," Cliff said. "I'll just have to keep pressing until I get to the bottom of this."

The mystery began to perplex Cliff. He didn't think about it constantly or even frequently, but it had ceased being a minor oddity and had become an issue to be resolved. He told Evelyn to keep needling Columbia. The Robertsons returned to New York in April, and Cliff soon left for Ireland to write a screenplay.

When Evelyn again telephoned the Columbia accounting department, Dick Caudillo was away, but she left a message that she wanted a copy of whatever document the studio claimed to have dispatched to Robertson. She received nothing. In late April, she called again, and again Caudillo was out. She left the same message to no avail. On Thursday, May 26, she wrote another letter requesting a copy of the front and back of the canceled check.

Dick Caudillo again called for the Robertson file and, for the first time, actually examined the check. It had been drawn on Columbia Pictures' general account at the main Hollywood office of the Bank of America; made payable to Cliff Robertson, 870 United Nations Plaza, New York City; and sent to the office of the studio president, David Begelman, presumably for forwarding to Robertson. The check bore the endorsement "Cliff Robertson," a bold, sweeping signature written with a felt-tipped pen, and also had been initialed with a ball-point pen. The check had been cashed on September 10, 1976—eight days after it was dated—at some branch of the Wells Fargo Bank in Los Angeles. It had cleared the Bank of America on September 13.

The more Dick Caudillo stared at the endorsement, the uneasier he became. Although he could not be sure, the endorsement looked very much like the handwriting of President David Begelman. Caudillo did not have anything else signed by Robertson with which to compare it, but he was intimately familiar with Begelman's writing, and this signature resembled it to a startling degree.

Choosing his words carefully, Caudillo phoned Evelyn Christel, apologized for the delay, and told her that a check payable to Robertson actually had been drawn and cashed. "The endorsement may not be Mr. Robertson's, though," he said. "It appears to have been endorsed by someone whose initials are right under the endorsement." He mailed her a copy of the check, and when she received it the next day she immediately phoned Caudillo and confirmed that the signature definitely was not that of Cliff, whose official signature was "Clifford P. Robertson" and whose handwriting was smaller and more delicate than that of the person who signed the check. Evelyn did not recognize the initials. Furthermore, no one had the legal authority to sign Robertson's name on his behalf. Caudillo and Christel agreed that there must be a reasonable explanation for the confusion and that they would investigate further and stay in touch.

Caudillo, however, had no intention of investigating further himself. He took the file to his immediate superior, the Columbia studio controller, Louis Phillips. Caudillo and Phillips had been close friends for years, and Phillips was the only person in whom Caudillo felt free to confide his suspicions.

"I think I know who signed that check, Lou," Caudillo said. "I think Begelman himself endorsed it."

Lou Phillips, a precise, careful man both in speech and manner, perused the check and correspondence. Without responding to Caudillo's fear, he said he would look into the matter and that Dick shouldn't concern himself with it any further.

THREE

James T. Johnson, the Columbia studio's vice president for administration, was fond of quipping that he and Frank Sinatra were Hoboken, New Jersey's principal contributions to American show business. Although Johnson savored his company title and the accompanying perquisites, it was his nature to twit his modest role in the entertainment world rather than inflate it. Unlike many eastern street kids who had gotten CPA licenses, come to Hollywood, and put on airs, Jim Johnson had never bothered to smooth all of his rough edges and become a noveau-snob. He owned a spacious four-bedroom house in Encino and drove a Cadillac provided by the studio. But at age thirty-eight, slender with dark hair, he retained, almost intact, the coarse, jocular, one-of-the-boys style of his working-class-Hoboken adolescence. It was't immaturity, just boyishness and irreverence, and he could restrain it when necessary. But it gave him a versatility of temperament that normally served him well in his main function as the vice president for administration, which was to know everything happening at the Columbia studio and keep it running smoothly. He wasn't a meticulous administrator, but he was savvy—as sensitive to the proclivities of clerks and janitors as to those of production vice presidents. Very little escaped his attention.

Therefore, he was surprised and annoyed on the morning of Friday, June 3, when Lou Phillips presented him with the Cliff Robertson problem. As Phillips's predecessor as studio controller and more recently as his boss, Johnson had handled the occasional snafus that inevitably arose in the dispatch and receipt of tens of millions of dollars in checks of all sizes. But he had never seen anything like the Robertson inquiry.

"Fuckin' weird," Johnson muttered as Phillips watched him examine the file. "*Somebody* sure cashed the fuckin' thing. No doubt about that."

Johnson and Phillips had never been close and Phillips was obsessively discreet in his conduct of studio business. So he didn't tell Johnson of Dick Caudillo's suspicion that David Begelman had forged the check. He merely indicated that Cliff Robertson's people seemed intent on getting to the bottom of the matter. Still, Johnson didn't have to be prompted to the possibility of embezzlement. He thought first of Begelman's long-time secretary, Constance Danielson, who had borrowed several thousand dollars from Columbia a couple of years earlier to make a down payment on a house. Jim had had qualms about the loan at the time, not because he didn't trust Connie but because the company normally didn't make loans to secretaries. But Connie had been with David Begelman for more than a decade. Begelman had brought her west with him when he had moved from the New York office of his talent agency to the Los Angeles office, and he had brought her with him to Columbia when he was made president of the studio in 1973. Thus, the loan had been approved as the exception to a rule. Could Connie later have mismanaged her finances and desperately needed money? Johnson doubted it, but it was conceivable.

It was inconceivable, however, that Begelman himself had embezzled funds. Jim was very fond of David, who had always treated him well and whom Jim credited with transforming a nearly moribund movie studio over the past four years into a lively, spirited place to work. With his huge salary and lavish expense account, David couldn't have needed $10,000. And even if he had, he easily could have obtained it in any number of legitimate ways. Presidents could borrow from their companies more easily than secretaries could.

But how could Johnson be absolutely sure of anyone, even Begelman? He decided he would have to take the problem to the next level of the company bureaucracy. Normally that would have been Begelman, to whom Johnson reported directly on most matters. But he naturally felt uncomfortable going to David with this, and luckily someone else was readily available.

Joseph A. Fischer, the balding, mustachioed senior vice president and chief financial officer of the Columbia studio's parent company, Columbia Pictures Industries, was in town from New York with other members of the corporate high command for quarterly budget meetings. Joe Fischer and Jim Johnson were friendly. Fischer had lured Johnson to Columbia from a New York CPA firm in 1968 and had made him controller of the film studio in 1972. Even though Begelman technically was Johnson's boss, Jim dealt directly and closely with Joe Fischer on many financial and administrative matters.

After listening to Johnson and Phillips's account of the Cliff Robertson problem, Fischer, an impassive and blunt man, examined the check through his steel-rimmed glasses, puffed on his slim Monte Cruz cigar, and looked up at Johnson:

"That's David's signature."

"What?"

"That looks very much like David's handwriting."

"You're outta your fuckin' mind," said Johnson, laughing derisively.

Fischer handed the check to Lou Phillips. "Doesn't that look like David's handwriting?"

"I suppose there's some resemblance," Phillips said cautiously.

"You're outta your fuckin' minds. You guys are fuckin' crazy," Johnson repeated. "It might be Connie copying David but it can't be David. What would he do something like that for?"

"Goddamned if I know—I'm just saying it looks to me exactly like David's handwriting," replied Fischer, who had never shared Johnson's affection for Begelman. Fischer agreed that it seemed most unlikely that David Begelman would embezzle $10,000 from the company. He thought perhaps someone in the Robertson camp had intercepted the check and managed to cash it before it could be entered on the books. But even that seemed farfetched. There had to be an innocent explanation. The three men discussed various possibilities. Finally, Fischer instructed Johnson to ask David Begelman if he recalled anything about the check.

After lunch, Johnson crossed the hall to Begelman's suite.

"David, I'm sorry to bother you with such a small and silly question, but do you remember requisitioning a check for ten thousand dollars for Cliff Robertson last September?"

"Yes, I recall it distinctly. Why do you ask?"

"Oh, Jesus, I'm so glad to hear that. I was afraid somebody might have done it without your knowledge. Robertson's people have been writing us letters claiming he never got the money." Johnson showed him the correspondence and check.

"Let me keep this file for a while. I'll handle it. I'll have to refresh my memory, but I'll take care of it."

"If there's anything I can do—"

"No thanks, Jim, I'll handle it myself."

Johnson reported back to Fischer and Phillips that Begelman remembered the Robertson check and would handle the inquiry himself. David hadn't recalled the details on the spot, but he had not seemed disturbed, and Connie obviously was not involved. Johnson was very relieved. Fischer and Phillips accepted the news with little comment.

That afternoon, during a break in a budget meeting, Joe Fischer was going over a list of minor business matters with his and Begelman's boss, Alan Hirschfield, the president and chief executive officer of Columbia Pictures Industries. Even though the Robertson matter was not on the list, Fischer mentioned there was some confusion in the studio accounting department over a check made out to Cliff Robertson that someone else might have cashed. Begelman and Johnson were handling it. Nothing to worry about. Hirschfield shrugged.

After Jim Johnson left his office, Begelman studied the Robertson file for a few minutes and then asked Connie Danielson to get Cliff Robertson on the telephone. Robertson wasn't at his United Nations Plaza apartment in New York, so Danielson left word for him to call. An hour later, and again two hours later, Begelman himself dialed Robertson's number and left messages for the actor to phone him at the office or over the weekend at home.

Columbia Pictures threw a splashy reception and dinner that Friday evening for its regional executives from the forty-seven nations and territories outside the United States where the studio exhibited its movies. The party, held in the private Chestnut Room of Chasen's, was the prime social event of an unprecedented four-day convention. Never before had Columbia convened and feted its foreign managers, who came from as far away as India, Egypt, and Finland. Many had never been to America before and hardly realized that they were part of a corporation which made phonograph records and pinball machines as well as motion pictures and television shows. Corporate camaraderie, however, was an integral part of the management style of Alan Hirschfield, the spirited forty-one-year-old show business maven from Wall Street who had taken command of Columbia Pictures Industries four years earlier. "Let's have a convention" seemed to be Hirschfield's answer to a gamut of corporate problems. While some of his colleagues worried that it sometimes seemed to be his *primary* answer—an insufficient one in view of the complexity of some of the problems—no one could deny that morale in the management ranks of the company under Hirschfield's regime had improved dramatically and had contributed substantially to Columbia's return to prosperity from the brink of financial disaster.

When Herbert Allen, Jr.,* scion of the New York investment firm of Allen & Company, had bought control of Columbia Pictures in the summer of 1973 and recruited his friend Alan Hirschfield to run it, Columbia's management was a collection of weary cliques with barely enough money left to fight each other, let alone make profits. The company had lost $50 million that year and its bankers were considering forcing it into bankruptcy. But Herbert Allen and Alan Hirschfield, together with David Begelman, the agent whom they hired to run the ailing movie studio, had turned the corporation around. It had become consistently profitable again and in 1977 was poised for new levels of prosperity. Perhaps more than at any time in its fifty-seven-year history, people enjoyed working at Columbia. Alan Hirschfield was very skilled at making people feel that they weren't just employees of a company but were valued members of a large, happy family. No single event signaled the new spirit more than the party for the foreign executives at Chasen's. It was a stellar evening.

Huge posters and color slides of scenes from *The Deep* and *Close Encounters of the Third Kind*, pictures scheduled to be released later in the year, and from *Police Woman*, Columbia's hit television series, adorned the paneled walls. Large stereo speakers blared the music of Barry Manilow, the Grateful Dead, and other artists whose records had made Columbia's Arista subsidiary the fastest growing record label in the nation. The music was punctuated by the jangle of four pinball machines installed for the occasion by Gottlieb, the

---

*Herbert Allen, Jr., whose full name is Herbert Anthony Allen, technically is not a junior; his father has no middle name. For the sake of convenience, however, the two men have been known for decades as Herbert junior and senior. And unless otherwise specified, the man known as Herbert Allen throughout this book is Herbert junior. In addition, it should be noted that the investment firm of Allen & Company actually comprises two entities: Allen & Company, a family partnership founded in 1922, and Allen & Company Incorporated, a corporation founded in the 1960s that performs investment banking services for clients. Distinctions between the entities, which share offices, commonly blur in practice. Herbert Allen, Jr. is both the president of the corporation and a general partner of the family partnership. Most references to the firm in this book are to the corporation.

large pinball machine manufacturer that Columbia had acquired for $50 million just six months earlier.

As Alan Hirschfield sipped a glass of wine and kibitzed Joe Fischer, who was playing pinball, David Begelman sidled over:

"Oh, Alan, by the way, did Joe mention the matter of the Cliff Robertson check?"

"Yes, he said something in passing. What's up?"

"Well, I just wanted to be sure you knew it was being taken care of and you needn't be concerned about it."

"What's being taken care of? What's the problem?"

"It apparently is just a minor misunderstanding. I'm not even sure myself yet of all the details, but I do know that it's nothing to worry about."

"Fine, if you say so, David, I'm not concerned."

The moment passed, swept away in the hubbub of the party, as three of the foreign guests approached to pay their respects to Hirschfield and Begelman, who then gradually separated and began working the room, greeting each of the guests individually.

FOUR

In East Hampton for the weekend, Cliff Robertson received David Begelman's three phone messages and telephoned him at home in Beverly Hills the next morning, Saturday, June 4.

"Cliff, I appreciate your calling me back. The reason I phoned is that I'm interested in knowing what you know about this ten thousand dollars."

"You're speaking of the ten-ninety-nine form?"

"Yes."

"I know only that I didn't get the money, and that I wasn't owed any money because I didn't work for Columbia in 1976."

"I'm very interested in following this up because apparently there's been some mistake or misunderstanding somewhere along the line. Will you do me a favor?''

"Okay.''

"Let me know personally if you hear anything further about this.''

"Sure, David, I certainly will.''

"And I'll keep you posted. I'm sure we'll have it clarified soon.''

"Fine.''

"Are you coming to California any time soon?'' Begelman asked.

"I have no immediate plans.''

"Well, if you do come, call me and let's have lunch. It's been too long.''

"Thank you, David, I'll do that.''

Robertson hung up. "I'm really impressed,'' he said to Dina, who had overheard part of the conversation.

"Why?''

"For an ex-agent, he's really minding the store. He's obviously dealing in millions at that studio, but he's not overlooking a relatively small matter of ten thousand dollars.''

The casual invitation to lunch amused Cliff. An entirely phony gesture of friendship so typical of Hollywood in general and Begelman in particular, he thought. David had been Cliff's agent until a few years earlier when they had quarreled bitterly over a film deal and, in effect, called each other liars. There had even been a lawsuit. The *Red Baron* suit. (The film was to have been about air combat in World War I.) Now Begelman is friendly again, Cliff mused. Only in Hollywood will an agent betray a client one year and cozy up to him the next as if nothing had happened.

On Tuesday, June 7, David Begelman telephoned Bud Kahaner, Robertson's accountant at Prager & Fenton.

"Bud, I wonder if I could ask you to relay word to Cliff that we've solved the mystery of the ten thousand dollars. We've looked into this very carefully and it turns out that a young man who was employed here at the studio last summer somehow managed to embezzle the money. We've confronted him with it and he's admitted it. His father has come to me on bended knee, promised full restitution, and begged us not to prosecute his son. So far as we can determine, this is his first offense, so we are not inclined to press charges. That seems to me to be the proper, fair, and compassionate thing to do, but I wanted to let you and Cliff know and make sure that you both agree with this approach.''

Begelman gave the same message to Michael Black, Cliff's ICM agent, with one elaboration: the young man who had stolen the money had been working in New York on the *Obsession* promotional tour and was supposed to have given the money to Cliff for his expenses.

"Sure," Cliff said when Bud Kahaner reported the conversation. "I don't want to send the kid to jail. It's a pretty heavy crime for a first time out, but if it's true, and if nobody's breaking any law by not reporting it, I don't see anything to be gained by prosecuting." Kahaner agreed, and assured Cliff that Columbia had sent a notice to the IRS canceling the errant Form 1099.

The next morning, Robertson flew to Chicago and drove to the home of friends in suburban Winnetka, Illinois. He and daughter Heather were scheduled to be there for part of the summer with Dina while she appeared in the Robert Altman film, *A Wedding*, which was being shot nearby. Cliff phoned Evelyn Christel that afternoon to confirm some travel arrangements. He was to fly to New Zealand in two weeks to make several appearances in a campaign to raise funds for the mentally ill. Since his 1968 Oscar-winning performance as a mentally retarded laborer in *Charly,* Robertson had given a lot of time and money to charities that help the mentally handicapped and in 1977 was serving as chairman of the National Mental Health Association. Evelyn confirmed that his plane and hotel reservations were in order.

"I guess the mystery of the ten thousand dollars has been solved," Cliff said.

"Yes, it appears to be," Evelyn said, having heard Begelman's "young man" story from Bud Kahaner's office. "Columbia sent me a copy of the check and I passed it along to Prager & Fenton," she added. "I thought they should have it."

"Check? What check?" Cliff asked.

"The check that was made out to you and this young man apparently cashed."

"I didn't know there was actually a check made out. Nobody told me how the kid got the money. You mean he forged my name on a check?''

"Yes, he signed your name on the back. It's a big splashy signature, 'Cliff Robertson.' Doesn't look at all like your signature."

"That's amazing. I had no idea there was an actual check. It's incredible that a young kid could get away with something like that. I wonder how he cashed it."

"I don't know. Prager & Fenton has the check. There's probably a stamp on it that tells where he cashed it."

When Dina arrived home from the *Wedding* set, Cliff exclaimed, "Jesus Christ, guess what! The kid who stole the ten thousand dollars actually forged my name on a check and cashed it. This wasn't some sophisticated bookkeeping manipulation. There was *actually* a check made out to me for ten thousand dollars and the kid forged my signature as the endorsement and actually took it out and cashed it! It's amazing!!"

Robertson still essentially believed Begelman's story. Even though he had distrusted David since their quarrel years before, there obviously was no connection between that episode and this one. Still, as Cliff relaxed at the sprawling Winnetka home over the next few days, the forgery preoccupied him. How could a kid—a menial temporary employee—simply scrawl a famous person's name on a check for $10,000 made out to that famous person, cash it, and walk away with the money? The more Cliff mulled over the question, the more it intrigued him. And then he learned something more that injected a note of implausibility into the intrigue. Someone at Prager & Fenton, describing the check to him over the phone, said that the stamp on the back seemed to indicate that it had been cashed at some branch of the Wells Fargo Bank in Los Angeles, perhaps the Beverly Hills office. It wasn't until Cliff hung up the phone that he asked himself how the young man could have cashed the check at a bank in Los Angeles if he had been employed at Columbia in New York. David Begelman had told Cliff's agent that the youth had worked in New York on the *Obsession* promotional tour. While it was possible that he lived in California or somehow cashed the check while traveling there, Cliff supposed, it seemed unlikely.

Cliff was sufficiently curious to ask Bud Kahaner to try to learn from the Wells Fargo Bank the circumstances of the check cashing. Kahaner agreed to do what he could, but with the potential IRS problem eliminated and the basic mystery seemingly solved, Cliff's fascination with how the check got cashed wasn't enough to prod Bud to immediate action during this busy mid-June week.

In the leisure of his Illinois retreat, however, with little else to occupy his mind, Cliff Robertson's curiosity turned gradually to concern, bordering on compulsion. He had to know whether the story of the young man was the complete account of what happened. *He had to know whether David Begelman was lying.* On Friday, June 17, not having heard from Kahaner, Robertson began dialing telephone calls from the Winnetka home into the vast bureaucracy of the Wells Fargo Bank in Los Angeles. His first call, to the Beverly Hills office, was transferred among several people, none of whom could or would help.

"We can't give out information like that by phone."

"You'll have to write a letter."

"Are you sure you're Cliff Robertson? Cliff Robertson, the actor?"

He got no further at Wells Fargo's regional headquarters for Beverly Hills and West Los Angeles, or at its Southern California headquarters in downtown LA.

Linda Bjork got Cliff's call as the frustrated afterthought of a switchboard operator who had run out of options. Bjork, an earnest, conscientious woman in her early thirties, was the operations officer of the Wells Fargo branch situated on the ground floor of the Wilshire Boulevard building which housed the Southern California headquarters of the bank. Although Linda Bjork thought it was odd that a celebrity himself would telephone rather than have a representative do it, she knew instinctively that the man on the line was *the* Cliff Robertson and that his concern was genuine.

"I have a problem and I don't know where to turn anymore."

"What's wrong, Mr. Robertson? I'll certainly try to help you."

In a voice revealing deep frustration, Robertson told Linda Bjork his story and said he suspected that Columbia Pictures had not given him a complete or accurate account of what had happened. From his description of the check, she deduced that it had been cashed at the main Beverly Hills branch office, which, like other banks catering to the show business community, occasionally bends procedures to accommodate the demands of its wealthy and eccentric clientele.

"I've already talked to about a dozen people there and got nowhere," Robertson said.

Bjork assured Robertson that the bank's Beverly Hills operations officer, Lorie Fitzsimmons (whom Cliff's calls had missed), could help him. Bjork offered to have Fitzsimmons telephone him. Cliff asked instead that Lorie Fitzsimmons call his accountant and said he would alert Bud Kahaner to expect her call.

The Wells Fargo Bank's Beverly Hills headquarters occupied a twelve-story building of gray-green glass and beveled mirror trim at Little Santa Monica Boulevard and Camden Drive opposite the Mandarin Restaurant and Dick Dorso's fashion boutique. Operations Officer Lorie Fitzsimmons governed her domain from a desk in a green-carpeted sector of the ground floor adjacent to the main retail banking arena. Fitzsimmons, an effusive and somewhat star-struck veteran of Beverly Hills banking, was delighted with the task that Linda Bjork gave her.

"Cliff Robertson? Really? Oh, wow!" she said to Bjork.

Lorie Fitzsimmons attempted to call Bud Kahaner that Friday afternoon but did not succeed in reaching him until the following Tuesday morning. She said she would need a copy of the check, and Kahaner sent it immediately by messenger. Because of the sensitivity of the inquiry, Fitzsimmons did the necessary research herself instead of assigning it to a clerk. Using the encoded numbers on the back of the check, she located the nine-month-old transaction on microfilm and displayed on a screen the bank's photograph of the front and back of the check. The endorsement "Cliff Robertson" appeared clearly, as did the initials "JRL," which Fitzsimmons recognized as those of Joseph R. Lipsher, the vice president in charge of the bank's entertainment-industry lending, who apparently had approved the cashing of the Robertson check.

On the screen opposite the check was its "offset entry"—the disposition of the proceeds from the check. The offset entry was a receipt for $10,000 in American Express traveler's checks. The receipt had been signed by David Begelman, the president of Columbia Pictures.

With Heather in tow, Cliff Robertson landed in Los Angeles shortly after noon that day, planning to lay over until Thursday morning before flying on to New Zealand. Before leaving the airport for the Bel-Air Hotel, he phoned Evelyn Christel to see if there were any messages or changes in his schedule.

"Bud Kahaner wants to see you right away. There's a problem with the Columbia Pictures check."

"What is it?"

"He told me not to say anything to you on the phone, but you'd better call him immediately. He sounded almost desperate."

Robertson phoned Kahaner.

"You've got to come up here right away, Cliff. I can't explain over the phone."

"But I've got Heather with me, Bud. We've got all our luggage. Can't I at least go check into the hotel first?"

"No, Cliff, this is urgent. I'd much prefer that you come directly here."

Cliff and Heather took a taxi to the RCA Building, a symbol of the new Hollywood amid symbols of the old on Sunset Boulevard. Just down the hill from the house where Nathanael West wrote *The Day of the Locust*, and just a few blocks from the crypts of Rudolph Valentino, Harry Cohn, Cecil B. De Mille, and Bugsy Siegel, the RCA Building mostly housed companies in the record industry. The CPA firm of Prager & Fenton, somewhat out of character, occupied a small suite of offices on the seventh floor. Leaving Heather and their luggage in the care of the receptionist, Cliff settled into a chair behind the closed door of his accountant's office. Bud Kahaner handed him photocopies of the front and back of the Columbia Pictures check, and for the first time Cliff was able to examine the document that had come to haunt him. His eyes immediately were drawn to the expansively scrawled endorsement, so different from his own.

Bud Kahaner, a serene white-haired man in his fifties with a high-pitched speaking voice, wasn't easily excited. Born and reared in Brooklyn, he had been an IRS agent in Manhattan for fifteen years and had grown accustomed to confronting fraudulent and bizarre financial transactions.

"Cliff, we may have a serious and somewhat alarming situation on our hands here. I've spoken with Miss Fitzsimmons at Wells Fargo Bank, but before we discuss what to do, I want you to hear the basic facts directly from her. She felt it was appropriate if she told you directly as the primary party rather than relay it through me." Kahaner dialed Lorie Fitzsimmons's direct number and Cliff picked up the extension.

"This is Bud Kahaner again, Lorie. Mr. Robertson has just arrived in town and is here with me. Would you be good enough to repeat the things you told me a while ago?"

"Certainly."

"The check appears to have been brought in last September tenth," Kahaner said, "and approved for cashing by the person whose initials appear on the front and back of the check."

"That's right, it was approved by Mr. Lipsher, Joe Lipsher, the head of our entertainment industry division."

"And it was cashed?"

"Yes, it was exchanged for ten thousand dollars in American Express traveler's checks."

"And who cashed it?"

"Mr. David Begelman, the president of Columbia Pictures. He apparently told Mr. Lipsher at the time that he was about to leave on a trip and would be traveling with Mr. Robertson."

"Thank you, Lorie."

Robertson and Kahaner hung up and stared at each other. Cliff was too shocked to speak.

"Let's review what we know, Cliff," Kahaner said. "We know the following things for sure: You never received this money and obviously were not owed it. Yet a check obviously was made out to you and cashed. We have it right here in front of us. Begelman's story about the young man—the 'mystery is solved' story—obviously was a lie. Begelman almost certainly forged your signature and cashed the check himself, and bought traveler's checks in his own name. I guess there's still a slight possibility of an innocent explanation, no matter how bizarre, but that appears extremely unlikely. We have to face the fact that David Begelman almost certainly used your name to embezzle ten thousand dollars from Columbia Pictures. It's possible that this is just the tip of an iceberg. You just may be sitting on a hydrogen bomb."

"What do I do now?"

"I think you should seek legal counsel. It's possible that you could just let it go and nothing more would come of it. But suppose something surfaces through another channel. Suppose somebody else catches Begelman stealing, and they investigate and trace this trans-action back to you. If you haven't reported it, or at least gotten legal advice, it's going to look like either you actually got the money or were covering up for Begelman."

Robertson and Kahaner discussed lawyers and decided Cliff should not use the attorney who normally handled his movie and television contracts, Gunther Schiff. Schiff, who had practiced law in the Hollywood community for a quarter of a century, had long been friendly with David Begelman, and Cliff felt that Schiff might feel awkward in a sensitive criminal inquiry that pitted him against Begelman. Instead, Cliff chose to call Seth Hufstedler, the senior partner of a distinguished Los Angeles law firm which did relatively little entertainment work but handled a number of nonentertainment matters for the Robertson family.* Nervous and agitated, Robertson phoned Hufstedler from Kahaner's office and explained the situation. Hufstedler asked Robertson to come to his office immediately. Another taxi was called, and Cliff and a confused, restless Heather Robertson headed several miles down the Hollywood Freeway to the Crocker Bank Plaza in downtown Los Angeles and the twenty-second floor suite of Beardsley, Hufstedler & Kemble.

The legal community in downtown Los Angeles differed sharply in appearance and atmosphere from its counterpart across town in Beverly Hills and Century City. The downtown firms served mainly banks and big corporations and functioned with the unspoken but firm conviction that they actually *practiced law* while their show business brethren merely made and unmade deals between childish people engaged in childish endeavors. While that was a considerable exaggeration, the contrasting tones of the two communities suggested at a minimum different styles. In Beverly Hills law offices, one saw open collars and gold baubles, *Record World* and *Daily Variety*, and bright—sometimes garish—decor. The chatter tended to be loud, urgent, and constant. Downtown, there were ties, three-piece suits, *The Wall Street Journal*, bland motifs and subdued, well-modulated conversations.

Seth Hufstedler, a former president of the California and Los Angeles County bar associations, was a slim, unassuming man in his middle fifties with white hair and a small beard and mustache. He spoke with a quiet resonance and his manner was calm, precise, and unemotional. After hearing Robertson's story, Hufstedler said he would report the matter to law enforcement authorities immediately. Cliff made clear that he did not want to spearhead any prosecution of David Begelman but would be willing to testify if the authorities began a legal proceeding. That seemed reasonable to Seth. Cliff remarked that he hoped he wouldn't have to interrupt his trip to New Zealand.

---

*Seth Hufstedler's wife, Shirley Hufstedler, was a federal appeals court judge in Los Angeles and later was named U.S. Secretary of Education by President Jimmy Carter.

"Where are you staying?"

"The Bel-Air Hotel."

"If I were you I wouldn't stay in a hotel," Hufstedler said. "Not to overdramatize this, but we have no way of knowing at this point how big this is, who else may be involved, or where it all may lead. Begelman knows you've raised questions. Until we have a better handle on the dimensions, and until we put it in the proper law enforcement channels, you probably should stay away from public places in this community where you'll be recognized."

"Well, I guess I'll have to call some friends and see what I can arrange. There aren't that many people here that I'm really close to."

"I'd stay away from people in the industry as much as possible."

Coming from Seth Hufstedler, perhaps the calmest man Robertson knew, the admonition to lie low worried him almost as much as the revelation of Begelman's crime. He walked out to the reception area where Heather was waiting.

"Gee, Daddy, when are we going to the hotel?"

"Honey, what was the name of your friend who went to Disneyland with us a couple of months ago? Do you have her phone number?"

Heather produced the number from a tiny address book. She and the other youngster had been classmates—and had become close friends—when Heather had attended school in Los Angeles during the filming of *Washington: Behind Closed Doors*. The friend was one of four daughters of a film editor and the family lived in a modest old home in Central Hollywood. Robertson got the man on the phone and explained that the hotel had misplaced his reservation. He was having difficulty reaching other friends, he said, and wondered if he and Heather could stay overnight. If the idea that a famous film actor could not get a hotel room in Los Angeles strained the man's credulity, he didn't show it, and welcomed the Robertsons warmly.

It was late afternoon by the time Cliff and Heather left Seth Hufstedler's office. The lawyer consulted his law partner, Samuel Williams, who was then serving as president of the Los Angeles Police Commission, a civilian oversight body. Williams telephoned the assistant chief of police, who sent to Seth Hufstedler's office the captain in command of the police department's bunco-forgery division and the lieutenant in charge of the specialized forgery unit. After hearing Hufstedler's account of the forgery, the captain said that the LAPD probably would have to refer the case to the police departments in Burbank, where Columbia Pictures was located, and in Beverly Hills, where the forgery itself apparently had occurred.

Cliff telephoned Dina in Illinois and told her the news, but he made only a few other calls and did not leave the house in Hollywood until it was time to go to the airport on Thursday morning. Although he kept up an amiable front—sitting in the living room reading, or playing with the girls, or just staring out the window into the hazy sunshine—he felt an upsetting mixture of worry, disbelief, resentment, and confusion. He felt like a fugitive, a spy in hiding, a witness in protective custody. "Tip of the iceberg" were the words Bud Kahaner had used. "Hydrogen bomb." Cliff conjured up notions of high crime and hit men. But that's silly, isn't it? Why me? Why did Begelman have to pick *my* name to forge?

Cliff mused a lot about David that day. What gall it must have taken to forge a check in as blatant a manner as this one had been forged! But perhaps he shouldn't be so shocked. Cliff had never particularly liked David, even when they were client and agent. They had different personalities, different backgrounds, different values. And since the episode that had come to be known as the *Red Baron* affair, Cliff actually had thoroughly despised and distrusted David.

The Red Baron had been a genuine fiasco.

Shortly after the success of *Charly*, Cliff had received a number of lucrative film offers but had declined them all because he wanted to write, direct, and star in a film centering on one of his hobbies—old airplanes. He had been approached by a man from Ireland who owned several World War I fighter planes in excellent condition. Cliff had persuaded Cinerama Incorporated, the company that had distributed *Charly*, to put up $150,000 to enable him to go to Ireland and film some aerial combat sequences. David Begelman had negotiated the deal on Cliff's behalf, and Cliff had written a treatment for a script tentatively titled *I Shot Down the Red Baron, I Think*. As Cliff understood the arrangement, if Cinerama liked the combat footage, it would finance the rest of the movie. If not, Cliff would have the option of reimbursing Cinerama its $150,000 and owning the project himself.

By the time the filming in Ireland was completed several months later, Cinerama was in financial difficulty, chose not to proceed with the movie, and demanded that Cliff refund its money immediately. Cliff claimed that while he had an option to buy the film, he had no obligation to buy it. He promised, however, to try to obtain financing for the film from another company and reimburse Cinerama when and if he was able to do so. The argument dragged on, and to Cliff's consternation, David Begelman sided with Cinerama. Begelman even went so far as voluntarily to swear out an affidavit saying that Cliff indeed had an obligation to repay the money to Cinerama immediately. Robertson was enraged.

"David, I want you to keep this straight and honest, this whole relationship, and I don't want you leading anybody down the garden path, and I don't want you in any way to indicate other than the truth. . . ." Cliff had warned Begelman at the time.

Robertson and Begelman had disputes, as well, over David's agent's commission from *Charly* and over other issues. The agent-client relationship was terminated, and subsequently Cinerama used David Begelman's affidavit against Robertson as the basis for suing Cliff for the *Red Baron* money. Defending himself in a sworn deposition, Robertson called Begelman a liar. "It was more and more apparent to me that something wasn't right in the dialogue between Begelman and Cinerama," Cliff testified. "I had the feeling that I was gradually being sandbagged. . . . I felt I had been completely subverted by my own agent in my moment of despair, anguish, and shock" (when Cinerama claimed Cliff owed the money).

After a year of bitter wrangling, Robertson reluctantly agreed to pay Cinerama $25,000 plus an additional $25,000 if the *Red Baron* picture ever was made. The suit thereby was settled, but Robertson never forgave Begelman. They didn't speak again until an inconsequential meeting on another topic a few years later. Cliff thought David might take that opportunity to express at least a little regret over the *Red Baron* episode. Begelman not only failed to mention the incident but was so unabashedly friendly that Cliff later remarked to Dina that he had been appalled at David's insensitivity. There had been one or two other brief encounters. David had even stopped Cliff on the beach at the Cannes Film Festival in May 1976, to compliment him on *Obsession*. The next time they had spoken, however, was two weeks ago Saturday when Begelman had telephoned to assure Cliff he would "clarify" the $10,000 "misunderstanding" and then had invited Cliff to lunch. Now, David stood revealed as a forger, an embezzler, and again, a liar of staggering proportions.

The man's gall is beyond all imagining, Cliff thought, as he nervously idled away the hours in the house in Hollywood.

Airborne for New Zealand the next morning, Cliff felt better. To the extent that he had been in hiding, he had escaped, at least temporarily. He was putting distance between himself and a difficult situation which was now in the hands of someone else. His past troubles with David Begelman were irrelevant. In this instance, he had simply witnessed a crime and reported it—the duty of any citizen. Surely the police would take appropriate action against Begelman.

To underscore the end of two difficult days, Cliff asked one of the first-class stewardesses to bring him a small bottle of champagne. Whether it was a tiny celebration or just a way to relieve tension was unimportant. He deserved it.

"What are you doing, Daddy? It isn't even noon yet," asked a surprised Heather.

"Sweetheart, there are times in everyone's life when he is inclined to have a little extra to drink."

FIVE

As the senior vice president in charge of "physical production," John Veitch was Columbia Pictures' highest ranking nuts-and-bolts man. Veitch had come to Hollywood from New York in the late forties, working first as an actor and then as a production manager. He had worked on *Some Like It Hot, The Greatest Story Ever Told, The Magnificent Seven,* and *Major Dundee,* among other films. Many years later, it was Veitch, an impeccably groomed man with white hair and a deep tan, who exercised daily scrutiny over the complex logistics and vast quantity of hardware involved in the making of Columbia's movies. He oversaw the securing of sufficient quantities of horses for Westerns and sufficient numbers of automobiles for chase scenes. He made sure that they did not cost too much and that they were transported to the right locations at the right time. He concerned himself with bad weather, faulty cameras and lights, temperamental people, and all the other impediments to on-budget, on-schedule movie making. He and his assistants monitored all of Columbia's films in progress, whether that required strolling across the Burbank lot to a sound stage, or flying to Africa.

On the morning of Tuesday, July 5, John Veitch was at an optical facility in the Marina del Rey section of Los Angeles watching technicians complete the elaborate special effects for *Close Encounters of the Third Kind*. His secretary telephoned and said that a Detective Elias of the Burbank Police needed to see him. Elias wouldn't say what it was about. It couldn't be handled on the telephone. Veitch asked that the detective come to his office in the Columbia executive suite at The Burbank Studios that afternoon.

Robert Elias turned out to be a short Mexican-American in his forties with curly salt-and-pepper hair, a round, fleshy face, and a small potbelly. He wore a bright, open-collared sport shirt outside his trousers to conceal the .38 caliber service revolver on his belt. Although he normally answered his phone, "Check Detail, Elias," check forgers did not confront him as often as small businessmen who cooked their books and used-car salesmen who stole credit cards. David Begelman was Bob Elias's first movie-mogul forgery suspect.

Elias showed John Veitch an LAPD memorandum on Seth Hufstedler's report of the forgery. Learning of the matter for the first time, Veitch said he was certain that there had been a mistake and that it was inconceivable that Begelman (who was then on a two-week trip to Europe) could have forged a check. Detective Elias said that if Columbia, as the apparent victim, wanted the police to conduct a formal investigation, the studio would have to file a complaint. Immediately after Elias left, Veitch telephoned David Begelman at the Plaza Athénée Hotel in Paris. Begelman asked Veitch to see if the detective could come to the studio on Friday, July 15, David's first day back in the office after his trip.

Instead of seeing Elias that morning, Begelman telephoned the detective and told him that what appeared to be a forgery actually had resulted from an error in the Columbia accounting department and had been rectified internally.

"Columbia appreciates the concern and interest of the police department," Begelman said, "but there will be no need for an investigation." David sounded sincere and truthful. His speaking persona, particularly on the telephone, had always been one of his assets. Assured and forthright, cultured and articulate, and without a trace of snake-oil resonance, his voice was youthful—the voice of a man at least two decades younger than his fifty-six years. Detective Elias thanked Begelman for his help in resolving the matter.

Caressed by Muzak, Begelman sat at his elaborate *faux marbre* desk and thought about the check and about Cliff Robertson. John Veitch's call to Paris had stunned David. In a quarter of a century as an agent and four years as a studio head, he had never encountered a situation quite like this one. David had been confident in June that he had assuaged Cliff's concern, but obviously he had miscalculated. Although he was relieved that he had deflected Detective Elias so easily, he suspected that he had not heard the last of the issue; that he might never hear the last of it; that even now it might be beyond his control. Why had Robertson gone to the police? Why had he gone to what must have been extraordinary lengths to investigate Begelman's story of the young man's embezzlement, when Bud Kahaner and Michael Black had accepted it without question? One thing certainly was clear. Using Robertson's name to steal the money in the first place had been a big mistake, even though it had seemed perfectly logical at the time. Robertson had, indeed, been making a promotional tour for *Obsession*, and giving expense money to actors was a frequent practice of the studio. The accounting department had no reason to question Begelman's request for the check. After having it drawn, he had kept it in his desk for nearly a week. Then, late one afternoon, he had telephoned his friend Joe Lipsher, who handled loans to the entertainment industry at the Wells Fargo Bank, and said he needed $10,000 in traveler's checks for a trip the next day. To accommodate Begelman, Lipsher sent an assistant from Beverly Hills to The Burbank Studios with the traveler's checks. The assistant accepted the Robertson check as payment without question, but when Lipsher saw it the next morning he telephoned Begelman and expressed concern about the absence of a second endorsement on the check. Begelman assured Lipsher that it was just an oversight; he was going to be traveling with Robertson and they both would be using the money. Lipsher, a veteran Beverly Hills banker who had learned long ago that it was poor diplomacy to enforce strict banking discipline on major studio clients unnecessarily, wished Begelman bon voyage and approved the check.

Begelman had an enjoyable and very restful vacation in Bermuda over the next several days, despite the fact that stolen money and lies were paying for it. He had stolen in the past without being caught and he would steal again. Although he didn't plan his embezzlements as carefully as a bank robber planned a complicated heist, he wasn't reckless either, always making sure he had a plausible alibi in case questions were raised. Until now, questions had not been raised and wouldn't have been in this instance were it not for the IRS Form 1099. The 1099, however, wasn't the heart of the problem. Cliff Robertson was. Almost anyone would have accepted Begelman's "young man" story without question. Why had Robertson bothered to challenge the explanation, especially since he hadn't lost any money?

Begelman thought back to the *Red Baron* episode. Surely that couldn't have anything to do with Robertson's state of mind in the summer of 1977. As intense as the dispute had been, Begelman had never looked upon it as anything more than an argument over a business deal—the sort of thing that inevitably happened occasionally in the jungle of contracts and deals in which the entertainment industry functioned. Begelman didn't take business disagreements personally and knew few people who did. Could it be that Robertson was one of those few? It hadn't seemed so. They had had one or two cordial encounters since the *Red Baron* incident.

However, Robertson's career hadn't gone well in recent years. He hadn't had a hit movie and was less and less in demand. Was it possible that he had become frustrated, and harbored deep resentment against Begelman all these years, and now was seizing the opportunity of a forged check to try to get even?

Begelman tried to telephone Robertson but couldn't locate him. His calls, however, prompted the Prager & Fenton office to warn Evelyn Christel: "Don't talk to David Begelman unless you talk first to Bud Kahaner. If Begelman calls, say Cliff is out of the country."

Concealing his concern over the Robertson matter, David Begelman kept a date that Friday afternoon with a *New York Times* photographer, who was preparing pictures for an article on "The New Tycoons of Hollywood" which the *Times* was planning to publish in August.

Begelman posed with his Rolls-Royce. With a prominent nose, puffy facial features, receding dark hair, and shallow eyes, David was a plain man, capable of appearing modestly handsome through meticulous grooming, stylish dress, and the assertion of his notably charming, ingratiating personality. Attired this day in dark blazer, polka-dot tie, light slacks, and loafers, he leaned against the left front fender of the Rolls with his ankles crossed and his hands in the side pockets of his blazer. The expression on his face was serene. He looked like a man at the top of his game.

Actually, Cliff Robertson was not out of the country. He was ensconced in the house on Hackberry Lane in Winnetka where Dina was still working on the Altman picture, *A Wedding*. He had returned with Heather after ten days in New Zealand raising mental health funds and another ten days in Tahiti vacationing, and now was studying the script of a motion picture which he was to begin filming in London with Jean Simmons in mid-September. He also had just agreed to direct and star in a movie based on Pulitzer Prize winner James Kirkwood's novel *Good Times, Bad Times*, a story of tragedy at a New England preparatory school.

It had been well over a month since he had reported Begelman's forgery and, so far as Cliff knew, the police in Los Angeles had done nothing except ask him to swear out an affidavit of forgery. Even such a simple, preliminary request as that—from a detective in Beverly Hills—hadn't come until early August. Cliff mailed the affidavit to attorney Seth Hufstedler, who also seemed mystified by the lack of police action. "They [the police] all seem a little at a loss about how to proceed in a matter where somebody reports something to them that appears to be a crime but nobody wants to be a prosecuting witness," Hufstedler told Robertson. "That confuses me because I thought the job of the police department was to investigate on its own."

Robertson's frustration grew. Even a sophisticated, influential lawyer like Seth Hufstedler, a law partner of the president of the Los Angeles Police Commission, didn't seem able to prod the authorities to action. There had always been a tacit assumption around Hollywood that the Los Angeles law enforcement agencies tended to take it easy on the movie colony. But how could they ignore a blatant case of forgery? Was some sinister force impeding the investigation? Cliff had not been able to shake off the fear planted by his accountant's comment that the check forgery might be the "tip of the iceberg," and by Seth Hufstedler's suggestion that he stay out of sight. The apparent inaction by the police fed his anxiety.

In the middle of August, while still in Illinois, Robertson decided on a new course of action. He telephoned Congressman Morris K. "Mo" Udall, the Arizona Democrat in whose 1976 presidential campaign Cliff had worked. The two had become friends. After hearing Cliff's tale, Udall said: "It sounds like you may have your own Watergate."

"Well, what can I do? I seem to be at the end of the road in Los Angeles."

"There might be some federal crimes involved, Cliff. The check appears to have gone through a couple of national banks. And Begelman may have IRS problems if he's stolen any money. I'd consider calling the FBI."

Cliff fretted through Labor Day. Dina finished *A Wedding* and the family returned to New York. There was no news from Los Angeles. Finally, through a friend of Dina's family, Cliff arranged an appointment with the FBI in Washington for Monday, September 12, two days before he was to leave for London. An agent met him at National Airport and drove him to headquarters where he told his story and stressed his feeling that he might be in some personal danger. The agents asked that he telephone the FBI office in London immediately after he arrived. ;

Washington telexed the pertinent details to London, and when Cliff was settled a few days later, he gave the local FBI office the address of the studio where he would be working and the address of the country house where he would be living. The London agent said that he would keep Cliff posted and that in any event Cliff should check in by telephone once a week but say nothing to anyone else in London about the matter. His chauffeur was told to be alert for anyone who might be following his limousine. The studio was asked, without explanation, to admit the limousine through a back entrance. And it was suggested to Robertson that as the vehicle approached the studio in the morning and left it in the evening he should lie down on the back seat and cover himself with a blanket.

He dwelt on the absurd array of possibilities that his state of affairs seemed to pose. Either he was paranoid and would be a laughingstock if anyone ever found out about the FBI, the back entrance and the blanket. Or he was in genuine danger from the "iceberg of fraud" and might be vulnerable despite the security measures. Or, lacking any knowledge of the fate of his now-three-month-old report of David Begelman's crime, which seemed to have vanished into a void of silence and inaction, he was merely taking judicious precautions.

Although he preferred to believe the latter, he felt very unsure of himself during those first several days in London. Things seemed to have gotten out of control since he discovered that odd little IRS form on his sunny patio in Fremont Place last February.

Never before had Cliff Robertson felt so frustrated, so helpless, so ridiculous.

SIX

After David Begelman mentioned the check inquiry to his boss from New York, Alan Hirschfield—the president and chief executive officer of Columbia Pictures Industries—at Chasen's on the evening of Friday, June 3, the subject did not come up again. Even though Begelman and Hirschfield were together in Los Angeles and New York at least half a dozen times through the summer, often in the company of Joe Fischer, the corporation's financial vice president, Begelman naturally avoided the issue and Hirschfield and Fischer soon forgot about it, having accepted Begelman's word that it was an innocent misunderstanding. In Alan Hirschfield's universe, the Robertson check was nothing more than a tiny scrap of information that was visible only partially and only momentarily, and then was quickly swept from sight and mind by much larger, more pressing matters that commanded his full attention.

In the four years that Alan Hirschfield had been at the helm of Columbia Pictures Industries, the corporation not only had regained its financial health but achieved the highest profits and revenues in its history. It had just completed a fiscal year (Columbia's year was

July through June) in which the motion picture and television operations had taken in nearly $300 million. Phonograph records, pinball
machines, broadcasting stations, and other smaller businesses had
added another $100 million, bringing the year's total to almost $400
million. Debt had been reduced to well below $100 million from the
more than $220 million that had nearly swamped the company just
before the new management took over in 1973. In the late spring of
1977 the banks had increased Columbia's line of credit and lowered
the interest rate they were charging.

Alan Hirschfield was delighted but not satisfied. Although Columbia was healthy again, it remained essentially what it had been since
the Cohn brothers and Joe Brandt founded it in 1920—one of the
smaller of the major entertainment companies. Its revenues were less
than half those of Warner Communications Incorporated, parent of
the vast Warner Bros. group of movie, television, and record
companies, and also less than half those of MCA Incorporated,
whose principal subsidiary, Universal Pictures, was supplemented
by a diverse cluster of other businesses, including major publishing
interests.

With a modest amount of luck, Hirschfield believed, Columbia
could double its size. Much depended on *Close Encounters of the
Third Kind*, the most expensive and ambitious film the company had
ever made. Hirschfield, David Begelman, and a growing number of
other insiders felt that *Close Encounters*, scheduled to open in
November, stood a chance of becoming one of the biggest box-
office hits of all time. If it did, Columbia's coffers would be
overflowing and the company would be in a position to make
another major acquisition or two. Alan Hirschfield had his eye on
several companies. They included Mattel Incorporated, the world's
largest toy company, which made Barbie dolls and Hot Wheels,
owned the Ringling Bros. and Barnum & Bailey Circus, and financed a
few movies. (Mattel had coproduced the award-winning *Sounder*
starring Cicely Tyson and Paul Winfield in 1972.) High on
Hirschfield's list as well was EMI Ltd., the huge London-based
entertainment conglomerate which owned Capitol Records and major
motion picture and television interests. If Columbia Pictures Industries somehow could get its hands on Mattel, and then the combined
corporation could go after EMI, Columbia would ascend to the ranks
of Warner and MCA where Hirschfield longed to be. For the time
being, however, he was willing to await the results of *Close Encounters*

and bask in the immediate glow of record corporate profits and revenues.

Alan Hirschfield gave several press interviews that summer, having always attracted good press, even before Columbia's new success was certified. Reporters, especially women, enjoyed interviewing him. He was an attractive man—a six-footer of medium build with an athletic bearing, hair that was expertly coiffed even though thinning and graying, and a countenance that revealed his droll, playful personality through twinkling eyes and the trace of a smile. Relaxed and informal, he laughed easily and often, and his speaking voice was the kind of soft, gentle adult voice that children find comforting.

In 1975, Hirschfield had been the subject of major articles in *The Wall Street Journal*, *Forbes*, and *Variety*. "Imagine!" exclaimed *Forbes*. "All but broke in 1973, Columbia under Alan Hirschfield suddenly has three hits: *Funny Lady* (Streisand), *Tommy* (Elton John), and *Shampoo* (Julie Christie, Warren Beatty)." In 1976, *Business Week* had published two articles portraying Hirschfield as a management wizard. Unlike those pieces, however, which were prompted by specific news events, the interviews in the summer of 1977 pointedly reflected Hirschfield's increasing visibility as a personality—a major figure in the entertainment business. Financial columnist Dan Dorfman, after interviewing Hirschfield, wrote in *New York* and *New West* magazines: "Twentieth Century-Fox, with its *Star Wars*, may be the hottest play in the stock market, but Columbia Pictures is on its way to stealing center stage." An article in *Women's Wear Daily*, carrying the headline, ALAN HIRSCHFIELD SETTING A PROFIT MOTIF AT COLUMBIA, was illustrated with a photograph of the Hirschfield children at a Gottlieb pinball machine, which was set up in the Columbia boardroom in front of a display case full of Oscars. "When I came to Columbia," Hirschfield was quoted as saying, "it just never occurred to me that we'd fail. . . . My wife gets angry with me. She says, 'You're a success. Why don't you show any emotion?' I tell her, 'That's what I'm supposed to be.' "

As Alan Hirschfield's press clippings accumulated, they began to raise eyebrows, especially in Hollywood, which had always been extremely sensitive to the nuances of acclaim. What was responsible for Columbia Pictures Industries' recovery? Was it Hirschfield's adroit management of the corporation's financial structure? Or was it David Begelman's adroit selection of profitable movie projects? Hollywood voted heavily in favor of Begelman, one of its own, and against Hirschfield, the intruder from Wall Street. Hollywood insiders were particularly rankled to see Alan Hirschfield applauded as broadly as he was in some articles, as if Hirschfield himself had made *Funny Lady* and *Shampoo* and *Tommy* and *Taxi Driver* and *Close Encounters of the Third Kind*.

It is Hollywood's nature to be touchier about such things than are other American industrial subcultures whose products are more tangible and prosaic than Hollywood's. This touchiness—hypersensitivity born of insecurity—is one of the differences between an industry which makes, say, refrigerators, and an industry whose principal product is, in essence, fantasy. The reasons for the success of a piece of fantasy—a movie or a TV show—rarely are as identifiable as the reasons for the success of a refrigerator. A movie is shaped by disparate and often indistinct collaborative elements, and represents an amalgam of highly subjective and even arbitrary creative and financial decisions.

The allocation of credit for a movie's success, therefore, is inherently imprecise, elusive, and subject to elaborate manipulation, particularly among people in the positions of David Begelman and Alan Hirschfield. Unlike the actors, the Begelmans and the Hirschfields are one or more steps removed from the actual making of the picture, and thus their contributions to the success of the venture are ambiguous. How much acclaim does the head of the studio deserve? Or the president of the parent corporation who put up the money and perhaps was instrumental in structuring the project? Or the key member of the corporate board of directors, who approved the expenditure of funds and the concept of the movie? Since it is difficult to evaluate their contributions by objective criteria, the executives normally vie with each other, even if only subtly, for the most acclaim they can garner, whether they deserve it or not.

Acclaim is as important to executives as it is to stars, for it is through acclaim that most show-business executives obtain and consolidate their power. The acclaim for making a successful movie or TV show, whether the executive deserves it or not, usually is accompanied by the power to make more movies and TV shows. The acclaim for making *several* successful movies or TV shows, whether the executive deserves the acclaim or not, often leads to the opportunity to run an entire studio or network. And whether it is deserved or not, the acclaim for rescuing a studio or network from financial ruin (the kind of acclaim that had begun to become an issue between David Begelman and Alan Hirschfield by the summer of 1977) usually opens even larger vistas—the chance to be a genuine mogul of show business, to become truly rich and famous, to play a major role in determining how the nation and indeed the world are entertained. For men like Hirschfield and Begelman, who long had aspired to power in show business, and who had achieved a lot but wanted much more, the stakes could hardly have been higher.

Every executive learns eventually, of course, that power in Hollywood can be as ambiguous, elusive, and ephemeral as the acclaim that leads to it. The power can even be mystical, just like the institution of Hollywood itself. Hollywood—its mores, its *modus operandi*, even its *raison d'être*—has been shrouded in myth since movies began and remains so today. And anyone who has held power for very long has found it necessary to fathom the truths behind the myths. They have had to learn where real power resides and where it does not. And they have had to accept and accommodate those aspects of the institution of Hollywood that are eternally mysterious and impenetrable by computer analysis.

Myth: The Hollywood of today is totally different from the Hollywood of a half century ago. *Truth:* Even with a more diverse group of power seekers, even with all the changes wrought by television in the fifties when it became a mass medium competing for audiences with movies, even with all of the impending changes posed by new forms of home entertainment, the institution of Hollywood has changed far less than is conventionally believed. More than a place, Hollywood is a state of mind. And the same elemental forces that drove it in the twenties and thirties still drive it today. In addition to the pleasures of power, there are money, fame, sex, a stake in creating American popular culture, and an opportunity to have a great deal of fun in the pursuit of these pleasures.

Myth: By the 1970s, movies had become a rational business, with much of the risk eliminated. *Truth:* Despite attempts to rationalize it—and even a modicum of success—the fundamental process of conceiving, producing, and distributing a motion picture is more arcane now than it was fifty years ago. There has never been any mystery about how a refrigerator is made. There has always been a mystery about how a movie is made. "Not half a dozen men have ever been able to keep the whole equation of pictures in their heads," F. Scott Fitzgerald wrote in 1940.* Fitzgerald's comment was still apt four decades later. And the presence of television only thickened the plot.

Myth: The spirit of the old moguls, with their consummate showmanship and their insistence on quality, even at the expense of profit, is gone forever. Hollywood today is run by accountants concerned about nothing but profit. *Truth:* The old moguls were far from homogeneous. Some were skilled showmen with good taste. Some were inept fools with bad taste. All of them, however, were in business for the money more than for the art. Pictures of high quality were the exception rather than the rule, just as they are today. And despite many obvious differences from their predecessors, the men who vie for power in Hollywood today are the direct cultural and psychological descendants of the men who founded and ran Hollywood from the early 1900s until the fifties, men whom Irving Howe has called "the dozen or so Yiddish-speaking Tammarlanes who built enormous movie studios [and] satisfied the world's hunger for fantasy, [men who were] bored with sitting in classrooms, too lively for routine jobs, and clever in the ways of the world." Contrary to popular notions about bland financiers, most important executive positions in the entertainment business today are occupied by high-spirited, entrepreneurial Jews who emigrated to Hollywood from New York and other points in the East and Midwest. Even though the incumbents are better educated and more urbane, they are colorful, creative, flamboyant—and in some cases outrageous—in many of the same ways as the old moguls. And Yiddish remains the second language of Hollywood.

Myth: The studio system is dead. Independent producers and agents now hold the power in Hollywood. *Truth:* Despite many structural changes, the power wielded by the major studios in the production of motion pictures and television programs remains formidable. The studios no longer directly employ large numbers of actors, directors, and writers. Instead, they normally contract with "independent" producers who in turn hire the talent. But the change is hardly revolutionary. The studios still put up most of the money for movies and retain the considerable power that resides with the money. With few exceptions, the studios still have a major voice—

---

*The statement actually was made by Fitzgerald's character Cecilia Brady in *The Last Tycoon*.

frequently veto power—in the producer's assembly of a film project and in the production of the film itself. Most "independent" producers in fact are dependent producers.

Myth: Studio bosses used to have absolute power but are impotent today. *Truth:* The heads of the film studios have—and always have had—less power to function independently of their corporate parents than has been commonly portrayed. Louis B. Mayer was one of the most famous figures in America from the twenties until the fifties, and was thought to have absolute power over his Hollywood domain, the Metro-Goldwyn-Mayer studio. Fewer people had heard of Nicholas M. Schenck (pronounced Skenk), the president and chief executive officer of Loew's Incorporated. Loew's Incorporated, however, owned MGM, and L. B. Mayer did not function in a vacuum. He reported to Nick Schenck. They talked by telephone two or three times a day in an age when coast-to-coast telephone calls were not made so casually as they are today. Nick Schenck was the "undisputed boss of the whole shebang," reported *Fortune* in 1939, and had an "uncanny eye for profitable pictures." It was Nick Schenck, not L. B. Mayer, who spoke perhaps the most prescient sentence ever uttered about the movie business: "There's nothing wrong with this business that good pictures can't cure." The two men railed at each other constantly. Mayer referred to Schenck variously as "the general," "Nick Skunk," and "the smiler and the killer."

"That Nick," Mayer once said to MGM production boss, Dore Schary, "he always has to be the big 'I am.' The big cheese. All he knows about movies you could stick in a cat's ass."

David Begelman and Alan Hirschfield were saying comparable things about each other in the seventies, although not to each other's face. Their rivalry was subtle and their relationship actually was quite cordial and reflected a strong mutual grasp of the truths of Hollywood. They understood that power in Hollywood resided where it always had—in the top echelon of the film studios and networks and their parent corporations; that power rarely was absolute and usually was shared among the two or three or four top people in each company; that a degree of rivalry and jockeying for position was inevitable;* and that when all the acclaim had been handed out, and

---

*Although they usually kept their feelings to themselves, it was mutually irritating to Hirschfield and Begelman that long-standing corporate nomenclature enabled each of them to call himself "the president of Columbia Pictures." Hirschfield's official title was president and chief executive officer of Columbia Pictures Industries Inc. He referred to the corporation's motion picture studio as "the picture

all the executive titles bestowed, *ultimate* power in Hollywood was financial power, vesting in the people who owned, or were perceived to own, the controlling interests in the big entertainment companies. Lew Wasserman at MCA-Universal. Bill Paley at CBS. Kirk Kerkorian at MGM. Herb Allen, Jr., of the Allen investment banking family, at Columbia Pictures. The power of ownership was not often exercised overtly, however, and the top hired executives like Hirschfield and Begelman wielded a great deal of authority.

Having been in the business longer, David Begelman's understanding of these truths perhaps was greater than Alan Hirschfield's. But Hirschfield presumably was learning.

No one questioned that David Begelman was Columbia Pictures' principal initiator and overseer of film projects. But Alan Hirschfield, more than some corporate presidents, felt it was his right as well as his responsibility to question his studio head's judgment. While Hirschfield normally went along with Begelman's wishes in the end, he occasionally vetoed him and the two men tangled frequently over the structure and dollar value of particular film deals, and even over the merits of scripts. Begelman wanted to make the movie version of *The Sunshine Boys* at Columbia but Hirschfield didn't. The producer took it to MGM. Begelman wanted to make a movie out of *That Championship Season*, the Pulitzer-prize-winning play by Jason Miller. Hirschfield felt strongly that the play would not convert well to film. Begelman gave up and it was not made. Begelman wanted to make *Shampoo*. Even though the script was offbeat and somewhat provincial, he had great faith in Warren Beatty, the producer and coauthor of the script.† Hirschfield hated the script and did not like the structure of the financial deal with Beatty. But he eventually relented and the film was made. Begelman had to talk hard to get Hirschfield to go along with the rock musical film *Tommy* until Hirschfield saw a rough cut and became the film's most enthusiastic proponent.

---

division," to its television production company as "the television division," and to Begelman as the "president of the picture and television divisions." Begelman actually had three titles: president of Columbia Pictures, the official name of the studio; president of Columbia Pictures Television, the official name of the TV production company; and senior executive vice president of Columbia Pictures Industries Inc., the parent of both the film studio and the TV company. The abbreviation "president of Columbia Pictures," therefore, was convenient for both men, each of whom was eager that his title convey his status as a major entertainment mogul.

†Asked a few years later why he had been so enthusiastic about *Shampoo*, David Begelman said, "Warren's one of the best producers ever. Warren doesn't come to lose. He comes to win. For instance, that line in the picture that Julie Christie gets off was not in the script . . . the party in the Bistro where she's a little bit tipsy because she's being neglected by her friend and his wife is putting

Hirschfield didn't mind his tussles with Begelman. He enjoyed being involved in the selection of movie projects. And he felt Begelman needed to be challenged. Hirschfield, at age forty-one, was coming to the conclusion by the summer of 1977 that Begelman, at age fifty-six, would soon be too old—if he wasn't already—to possess all of the vision required to guide the studio in the new era of video cassettes and discs, and cable and satellite television. Although Begelman still had few equals at the primary art of assembling and guiding particular movie and television projects—and still had a bright future at Columbia in that role—Hirschfield had begun to think of him as a member of the Hollywood old guard. Hirschfield felt that it would take men like himself—men whose careers encompassed Hollywood but were not enveloped by it—to lead Columbia and the industry at large into the new age.

So, while he was certainly willing to give Begelman his due, Hirschfield didn't object to the implication of his press clippings that he, more than Begelman, was responsible for the new success of Columbia Pictures Industries.

Hirschfield also welcomed the opportunity of the publicity to assert—slowly and strictly by implication—his independence of the Allen family and their investment banking house, Allen & Company. The Hirschfield and Allen families had been closely associated since the 1920s in Wall Street where Alan Hirschfield's father, Norman, and Charles Allen, the founder of Allen & Company, had become fast friends as struggling, would-be tycoons barely out of their teens. Alan Hirschfield himself had worked for or on behalf of Allen & Company almost continuously since graduating from the Harvard Business School in 1959. The firm had employed him as an investment banker, giving him a chance to make a lot of money in various business deals. When the Allens took effective control of Warner Bros. in the sixties, they sponsored Hirschfield for a year as Warner's vice president for finance. When they took control of Columbia, they sponsored him as president and chief executive officer of

---

her down, so a man in the restaurant asks her what she would like, thinking her answer might be 'a cup of coffee,' or 'a martini,' or something, and she says, 'I'd like to suck your cock.' Now, that wasn't in the script, but Warren knew that if he could get a major actress to say that line in a major film. . . . He called that his twenty-million-dollar line. When I heard it for the first time, I almost fell off my chair. I had to listen to it a couple of times and convince myself that it should stay in. So I knew that Warren was going to make a terrific film." (Actually, the Julie Christie character, Jackie, said to the man, "I'd like to suck his cock," referring to the Warren Beatty character, George.)

Columbia. But while Hirschfield appreciated all the Allens had done for him, he had gradually begun to feel unappreciated by the Allens for what he had done for them. In particular, Hirschfield considered himself superior in intellect and business acumen to Herbert Allen, Jr., the firm's scion and Charles Allen's nephew, who was four and a half years younger than Hirschfield and, unlike Hirschfield, born to great wealth. Herbert had entered the family firm straight from college without training, had been made its president only five years later at the age of twenty-seven, and by the 1970s was the firm's most visible symbol. Hirschfield had come to resent the control that Herbert exercised as the most powerful member of Columbia Pictures Industries' board of directors. As a practical matter, Allen & Company remained Hirschfield's boss with all that that implied about enforced loyalty to the Allen family. Apart from not particularly respecting Herbert Allen, Hirschfield felt that he had earned, by his outstanding performance as president of Columbia, a chance for more independence and freedom from Allen's control than he was accustomed to enjoying. He, not Herbert, had saved Columbia. He, not Herbert, was one of the brightest young show-business executives in the nation. Herbert knew relatively little about the entertainment business, and what he did know had given him old-fashioned views, Hirschfield felt, because it had come from old men—from Herbert's uncle, the patriarch of Allen & Company, seventy-five-year-old Charles Allen, who long had been a director of Warner Bros. and a pal of Jack Warner; and from sixty-two-year-old Ray Stark, the producer of *Funny Girl*, *The Way We Were*, and other films. Stark had become Herbert's closest friend in recent years and in many ways was idolized by the younger man.

None of Hirschfield's feelings was stated or even hinted in Herbert's presence, however. While never best friends, Alan and Herbert always had had a close, comfortable relationship which continued in the summer of 1977.

After the regular monthly meeting of the Columbia board of directors in New York on Thursday, September 8, Alan Hirschfield showed David Begelman the galley proofs of the company's latest annual report to shareholders, which was scheduled to go to press by the end of the month. Lavishly illustrated with color photographs, and printed on the finest paper, the report was the most expensive document that Columbia Pictures Industries had ever produced. In his introductory letter to shareholders, Hirschfield noted that the motion-picture division continued to be the major contributor to the corporation's profits. "The results are a tribute to David Begelman as he continued to provide the leadership and keen insight so vital to the continued success of our motion-picture program," Hirschfield stated. Begelman's photograph appeared on the first page of the movie section of the report, along with scenes from *The Deep,* and *Murder by Death.* On the facing page was Muhammad Ali's photograph, without his name, just the caption "The Greatest," the title of a film which the boxer had made for Columbia.

Pointing to the Ali caption, Hirschfield remarked to Begelman and other bystanders that "The Greatest" should be moved across and placed under David's picture. Everyone chuckled. Well-timed flattery was one of Hirschfield's most endearing traits, and on that occasion he really meant it. Despite his belief that he, not Begelman, was the center of the corporation's gravity and the wave of its future, and despite his eagerness to be perceived that way, Hirschfield fully recognized and appreciated Begelman's vital importance to the success of current movie and television operations.

Over lunch at La Côte Basque the next Monday, September 12 (the day Cliff Robertson briefed the FBI in Washington), Alan Hirschfield and Herbert Allen sketched the outlines of a new contract for David Begelman that would net him a million dollars in bonuses and stock options over the next four years. (It was understood, too, that when Hirschfield's contract came up for renegotiation in a few months, he would get a deal at least as good as Begelman's.)

Hirschfield spent Tuesday at home in Scarsdale in observance of Rosh Hashanah. He stayed home Wednesday as well to deal with an appraiser from the Parke-Bernet Galleries who came to estimate the value of Hirschfield's collection of Oklahoma Indian art. Arriving at Columbia's corporate headquarters at 711 Fifth Avenue just before noon, he took two routine telephone calls before having a leisurely lunch downstairs at La Côte Basque with Joe Fischer, the chief financial officer, and Victor Kaufman, the corporate general counsel.

When Hirschfield returned to his office, there was a message to call a Detective Silvey of the Beverly Hills Police Department. Had there been a lot of phone calls to return, Hirschfield might never have gotten back to the detective. But it was a slow day, the police call was the only one, and he was a bit curious. The first surprise was that Detective Silvey was female.

"Is this really Detective Silvey? This isn't a joke, is it?"

"No, this is really Detective Silvey. It's no joke."

"My friends in the picture business sometimes play jokes," Hirschfield said. "I thought maybe this was a Ray Stark special."

"I assure you it's no joke. It's a serious matter. We're investigating a possible case of check forgery involving Mr. David Begelman, the president of Columbia Pictures in Burbank. Are you authorized to speak for Columbia?"

"I guess so. I'm the president and chief executive officer of the parent company, but I can't imagine what you're talking about."

"Are you responsible for financial matters at Columbia?"

"Yes, in a general sense, but we're a large company. We have people who handle that sort of thing specifically."

"Are you aware that Mr. Cliff Robertson has reported to the police that David Begelman forged his name on a check?"

"No, I'm totally unaware of any such thing," Hirschfield said.

"We have reason to believe that Mr. Begelman took a Columbia Pictures check for ten thousand dollars payable to Cliff Robertson, endorsed it with Mr. Robertson's name and cashed it, and got ten thousand dollars in traveler's checks in return."

"Now that you mention it, some of this is beginning to sound a little familiar. I'll tell you what I do know about it, and this is all I know. Several months ago I was told that there was some problem with a check for Cliff Robertson. But I was assured that it had all been taken care of, and I've heard nothing about it since. You say Robertson reported it to the police?"

"Yes, he did, and I'm having trouble getting a straight answer from anybody at Columbia in Burbank."

"The man you should talk to is Mr. Fischer, Joe Fischer. He's our financial vice president here in New York. I'll have him call you right away."

Hirschfield, agitated and apprehensive, strode next door to Fischer's office.

"I've just had a very peculiar phone call. A detective from the Beverly Hills Police Department. A woman named Silvey. Something about an investigation of check forgery. Begelman forging Cliff Robertson's name. Do you have any idea what the hell this could be about?"

Fischer paled. "Oh, Jesus! Remember me telling you when we were out there for the foreign-managers meeting that something about a Cliff Robertson check had come up?"

"Vaguely," Hirschfield said.

"Johnson and Phillips had a complaint from Cliff Robertson's people about a ten-ninety-nine form for some money that Robertson never got. David said he'd take care of it. He mentioned it at Chasen's that night."

"Well, apparently Robertson has gone to the police. You better call this lady back and find out what the hell's going on. Then come and see me."

Detective Silvey briefed Joe Fischer and asked what Columbia intended to do. He said he was sure that the entire matter had resulted from a mistake of some sort but that he would fly to Los Angeles the next day and discuss it with her in person.

In Hirschfield's office seconds later, Fischer said: "Evidently, somebody signed the back of the check. Forged Robertson's name. The money was used to buy traveler's checks and evidently David got the traveler's checks."

"Did you know any of this?" Hirschfield asked.

"Christ, no! Absolutely not! This is the story I get from the detective."

"Jesus Christ! Call David! See what's going on."

"I think I better go out," Fischer suggested.

"I think you better go out, too. Get on the next plane. Jesus, this is unbelievable! It's like dynamite! Is she actually saying David forged a check?"

"I'm afraid that's exactly what she's saying."

SEVEN

The radical singularity of Beverly Hills, California, is evident not so much in its famous residents and lavish homes as in certain of its statistics. With an area of less than 6 square miles and a population barely exceeding 30,000—only 20,000 of whom are old enough to vote—Beverly Hills supports 35 banks, 20 savings and loan associations, 711 lawyers, 299 beauty salons, 651 medical doctors and psychoanalysts, and 761 gardeners. The banks and savings and loans hold deposits of more than $7 billion.

With wealth of that magnitude—the densest concentration of wealth of any self-contained residential-commercial community of its size anywhere—Beverly Hills naturally attracts multitudes of people from all over the world who are bent on learning how all that money got to Beverly Hills in the first place, why it stays there, and how they might get some of it for themselves. There are shopping-center tycoons who want to invest in the movies. There are Arab oil magnates who want to buy real estate. There are European bankers who want to open local branches of their banks. There are busloads of tourists who merely gawk. There are international socialites who can function satisfactorily in any number of places but who find Beverly Hills to be unusually congenial not only financially but psychologically as well.

Whether these people stay for brief periods, long periods, or settle permanently, their number inevitably includes a sizable contingent whose principal occupation is theft. These aren't street thugs who snatch purses on Rodeo Drive (such a thing is almost unheard of) but much more genteel thieves who steal much larger amounts of money—stock swindlers, tax manipulators, commodity-options scammers, securities counterfeiters, art forgers. Some of these people are members of organized crime, but most are not. Some of them live in

Beverly Hills, but most do not. Some swindle the local residents, and some use Beverly Hills as an address from which to swindle elsewhere. But they all make Beverly Hills their headquarters not only because of the presence of so much money but also because of the resonance of the city's name. Thus, they have made it one of the half dozen or so most important centers of "paper" crime in the world.

A burgeoning group of law-enforcement bureaucracies have been grappling with these criminals for years and, for the most part, losing. There is so much crime that the enforcement has to be extremely selective. At the top of the hierarchy are the local offices of the U.S. Securities and Exchange Commission and the Internal Revenue Service, who do what they can to combat the most sophisticated of the swindlers. One step down is the Federal Bureau of Investigation, which concentrates on more straightforward crimes such as bank embezzlements and international traffic in stolen securities. And at the bottom of the hierarchy, outmanned and overworked, is the bunco squad of the Beverly Hills Police Department, which deals with local and relatively petty activity such as stolen credit cards and forged property deeds. Even the local crimes can be very complex; a single scheme can involve several teams of con artists and a bewildering maze of stolen credit cards and forged documents.

Very little of this crime attracts much attention in Beverly Hills. Equity Funding, the largest insurance scandal in history, and Home-Stake Oil, the most spectacular celebrity tax-shelter swindle in history, were exceptions. The attitude of most Beverly Hills residents is cynical; they have so much money that they hardly notice if relatively small amounts of it are stolen. Most of the criminals are well-dressed and most of the crimes are carried out in silence, or the soft tones of subdued voices and the light scratch of pen on paper. The law enforcers are unobtrusive if not invisible. There is no sizable federal building in Beverly Hills; the SEC, IRS, and FBI cover the town from offices a few miles out Wilshire Boulevard in Westwood, or from downtown Los Angeles. The Beverly Hills Police Department is tucked away in the basement of City Hall, which—with its churrigueresque architecture; mosaic tile dome; and landscaping of palm, olive, and pepper trees—looks more like a college library somewhere in Spain than an American seat of local government. The entrance to the police department itself, were it not for a discreet sign, could easily be mistaken for the rare-books entrance to the Spanish library.

In such a milieu, the forgery of a solitary $10,000 check normally would command negligible interest in the public at large—if indeed it knew of the forgery—and would receive no more than perfunctory attention in law-enforcement circles. These nuances certainly were not lost on David Begelman, who lives on Linden Drive in Beverly Hills and forged Cliff Robertson's name rather casually. Joe Lipsher, Begelman's friendly banker at the Wells Fargo a few blocks away on Camden Drive, cashed the check rather casually. And the Beverly Hills police bunco squad, just a few blocks up Santa Monica Boulevard on Crescent Drive, received the referral from the LAPD downtown rather casually. The detective to whom the case was assigned was within a month of retirement, and his investigation was less than vigorous.

Nevertheless, in much the way that he was unlucky when he chose the name of Cliff Robertson to forge instead of someone more tolerant, Begelman was unlucky again when the forgery file finally came to rest, in early August of 1977, on the desk of Detective Joyce Silvey.

Perhaps it was Silvey's newness to the job and eagerness to prove herself; she had been made a detective only a year earlier after ten years as the police department's supervisor of records. Perhaps it was her upbringing in Oklahoma, where stealing is viewed perhaps a bit less cynically than it is in Beverly Hills. Perhaps it was her serious, intense personality, which made it difficult psychologically for her to let any case—no matter how trivial—lie dormant for long. Perhaps it was the extra streak of thin-lipped toughness that she had developed in the course of functioning as a female detective in a world of mostly male crooks and mostly male cops. Perhaps it was a combination of those traits. Whatever the explanation, Joyce Silvey made more progress on the Robertson case in August and early September than either her retiring colleague or her counterpart across the hills in Burbank, Detective Bob Elias, had made since the LAPD had forwarded the case to both police departments in late June. In the midst of handling approximately three dozen other cases—the normal load for the Beverly Hills bunco squad—Silvey had managed to obtain an affidavit of forgery from Cliff Robertson and to interview attorney Seth Hufstedler extensively. She had interrogated Joe Lipsher at the bank. She had talked with John Veitch, the senior vice

president of the Columbia studio, whom Detective Elias had visited
a month earlier. While the forgery certainly wasn't the crime of the
century, it was clear to Silvey that it was in fact a *forgery*, defined
as a form of felony grand theft by the Penal Code of the State of
California, and she refused to ignore it. She refused to take "yes"
for an answer ("Yes, we're familiar with it"; "Yes, it was just a
misunderstanding"; "Yes, we have rectified the error in the accounting department"). She placed one or two calls to David Begelman
himself but they were not returned. So she was surprised when Alan
Hirschfield not only returned her call on Wednesday, September 14,
but sent the second-ranking officer of the corporation, Joe Fischer,
to visit her personally and immediately.

Flying west on Thursday morning, Fischer was nervous, his usual
impassivity overcome by the *shpilkis*. Fidgeting in his seat, picking
at his food, meandering about the first-class cabin, he groped for an
explanation (and chastised himself for failing to press for an explanation three months earlier when Jim Johnson first brought the matter
to his attention). If Begelman were going to steal, surely he would
steal more than $10,000. It didn't make sense. Could the Cliff
Robertson check be one of many? Does Begelman have millions in a
Swiss account? Are other people involved? If a lot of money were
being stolen from the studio, wouldn't the auditors have caught it?
Were the studio's accounting procedures lax? Had auditors been paid
to look the other way? Fischer knew that if widespread theft were
discovered, several people's jobs, including his own, might be in
jeopardy. There might be lawsuits, prosecutions. Had he been
negligent? Could there still be an innocent explanation? There had to
be! Why did Cliff Robertson go to the police? Why didn't his
lawyers call Columbia's lawyers and try to clarify the matter internally?

Through their secretaries the previous afternoon, Fischer had let
Begelman know that he was coming but didn't tell him why. Immediately upon checking into the Beverly Hills Hotel, Fischer telephoned
Detective Silvey and was dismayed to learn that she was out of the
office on a case and wouldn't be in until eight the next morning.
That meant he would have to confront Begelman without any documentary material. He drove to the studio, and as he expected, their
conversation was inconclusive. Begelman was vague; he maintained
that there had been an error or misunderstanding—or perhaps a
series of errors or misunderstandings—which he thought had been

clarified but which he would now look into again. He acknowledged
having gotten the traveler's checks the previous September, just as
he did prior to all of his frequent trips. But his secretary put checks
and other documents in front of him to sign many times every day,
Begelman said, and he didn't always look carefully at what he was
signing. He couldn't imagine signing Cliff Robertson's name; perhaps there had been a Cliff Robertson check on his desk that day and
it had been given to the bank by mistake. (Begelman calculated that,
for the moment at least, Fischer didn't have enough information to
challenge the gaping holes in his story. What about the tale of the
errant young employee that Begelman had told to Robertson's
representatives? What about the handwriting similarity?)

Actually, Fischer had grave questions about Begelman's story, or
lack of one. For one thing, Begelman was too meticulous a person
by nature not to know exactly what he was signing, no matter how
many times a day he signed his name. For another, it had been
Fischer's experience that Begelman had an exceptional memory. He
retained the most minute details of the most complex motion-picture
contracts. It was inconceivable that he didn't remember the details of
the Robertson matter. But Fischer didn't press Begelman further that
afternoon; he wanted to see the police file first.

Begelman seemed markedly concerned about only one thing: Was
Alan Hirschfield aware of the police inquiry? Fischer said no—the
police had called him directly, and he had flown out in hopes he
could resolve the matter without bothering Hirschfield. Begelman's
relief was just the reaction that Hirschfield and Fischer had hoped
for when they concocted the story the previous afternoon. They did
not want to alarm Begelman unduly and prompt him to do something
rash before Fischer had a chance to investigate.

Fischer arrived at the Beverly Hills Police Department precisely at
eight Friday morning and found that the inside of the department—
like so many other things in Los Angeles—belied its sunlit, tranquil,
well-landscaped exterior. The detective squad room was like detective squad rooms everywhere—a bit intimidating, with glaring fluo-
rescent lights, constantly ringing telephones, holstered revolvers on
polyestered hips, and heavy steel filing cabinets and desks, piled
high with untidy stacks of files and jammed so close together that
one could hear the conversation at the next desk as clearly as the
conversation at one's own.

Joyce Silvey turned out to be a plain, slim, pantsuited woman in her middle thirties, with tired eyes and short, prematurely gray hair. Smoking a Marlboro 100, she greeted Fischer coolly and, without preliminaries, proceeded to display a convincing—and, to Fischer, shocking—array of documentary evidence supporting her assertion that Begelman had forged Cliff Robertson's name on a Columbia Pictures check and pocketed the money. She showed him the check itself (which naturally looked more incriminating in the detective's office in September than it had looked in Jim Johnson's office in June), Robertson's affidavit of forgery, a memorandum from the Los Angeles police summarizing its interview with Seth Hufstedler, and a statement from the Wells Fargo Bank that Begelman himself had cashed the check. Silvey said that she would need an official letter from Columbia Pictures stating whether it wanted to prosecute Begelman. Fischer had little to say. He took photocopies of her material and promised to be in touch with her soon.

Back outside in the bright, balmy sunlight, Fischer couldn't recall ever before having been so distraught. It was 11:45 A.M. in New York. He put a dime in a sidewalk telephone booth behind the City Hall and called Hirschfield.

"We're in deep shit," Fischer said. "You wouldn't believe the stuff this cop showed me. It's obvious that David did it. The cop wants to know whether we'll prosecute. They want something in writing. I said I'd get back to her. What we need now is a good solid local lawyer who knows how to deal with the police."

"I've already got a call in to Mickey," Hirschfield said. "He was somewhere in Nevada yesterday and hasn't gotten back to me. Why don't you try to reach him."

Milton A. "Mickey" Rudin, with offices five blocks away on Wilshire Boulevard, represented Frank Sinatra, Lucille Ball, and other entertainers, and on occasion over the years had represented Alan Hirschfield, whom Rudin had gotten to know when Hirschfield was Warner Bros.' investment banker in the sixties and Frank Sinatra had sold the controlling interest in his record company to Warner. Hirschfield considered Mickey Rudin one of the shrewdest and most perspicacious human beings he had ever met.

Fischer drove to the Beverly Wilshire Hotel, across the street from Rudin's office, and sipped coffee in the hotel snack bar while waiting for the law offices to open for the day. Rudin was still out of town, it turned out, so Fischer left a Columbia studio number and said it was urgent that Rudin telephone him as soon as possible. By 10:15 he was back in Burbank huddled with Jim Johnson and Lou Phillips. Instructing them to discuss the matter with no one else, he briefed them on the police investigation and asked that they think back over Begelman's tenure at the company to try to recall any other transactions—checks, contracts, transfers of money, and the like—which possibly could have been irregular. Nothing came immediately to mind.

Fischer then returned to Begelman's office and spread Detective Silvey's documentation on the coffee table in front of the sofa.

"What about that endorsement, David?"

"What about it?"

"It looks like your handwriting."

"It isn't my handwriting, Joe. It simply and unequivocally is not. I swear to you on the life of my child that it is not my handwriting and that I have done nothing wrong—nothing which merits the attention of the Beverly Hills Police Department. It's obviously a horrible chain of coincidences for which there must be an explanation. I will make every effort to trace it back and see what happened."

"What about this young man in the accounting department embezzling money?"

"At one time a few months ago, it appeared that such a thing might have happened. I haven't heard how it was resolved."

"David, I've never wanted anything so much in my life as I want now to believe you, but I gotta tell you that this police file looks depressingly conclusive."

Begelman shrugged, and the two men stared at each other. They had worked closely for four years—on the phone nearly every day and in person at least once a month. As terrifying as the prospect was, there was no question in Fischer's mind that Begelman was lying. And Begelman knew that Fischer knew. The beginnings of tears glistened in their eyes.

Without another word, Fischer gathered the papers, returned to the visiting-executives' suite, and got out a yellow legal pad. Sitting alone at his desk, he made two lists: the first of the evidence against Begelman, the second of possible mitigating circumstances, possible reasons for believing Begelman's contention that it was all a misunderstanding. The first list overwhelmed the second. Fischer didn't feel any better, but the act of writing it all down helped to calm him and clarify his thoughts.

His solitude was interrupted by Mickey Rudin, calling from beside the swimming pool at Frank Sinatra's compound in Palm Springs. Fischer gave Rudin a brief account of what had happened but said he was reluctant to go into detail over the telephone and offered to drive to Palm Springs. Rudin suggested instead that since it was already Friday afternoon they wait until Monday when, as it happened, he was planning to be in New York and could meet in person with Fischer and Hirschfield. Fischer agreed.

A few minutes later, controller Lou Phillips arrived with more news that potentially was ominous. In early 1975, he recalled, David Begelman had asked the studio accounting department to prepare a check for $35,000, payable to a man named Peter Choate, whom Begelman said he had hired as a special sound consultant to equip theaters around the country with new sound gear for *Tommy*, a film featuring music by the rock group The Who. Although Phillips had had the check drawn and sent to Begelman without question, he had thought it odd that the request had come from Begelman personally and not from the studio vice president in charge of such technical matters. Later, Begelman had asked Phillips repeatedly whether the auditors checking the financial records of *Tommy* had cleared the Choate expenditure. It was very unusual for Begelman to ask even once, let alone repeatedly, whether a particular transaction had been passed upon by the auditors. Phillips gave Fischer the file on the Choate matter, which listed an office address for Peter Choate in Santa Monica but gave no further identification.

Fischer phoned Hirschfield again, and told him of the possibly irregular Choate transaction. Then he caught the late afternoon American Airlines flight to New York, accompanied by Jim Johnson, who had business the following week at Columbia's New York headquarters. The two men worried their way across the country, their moods darkening as rapidly as the sky on eastbound flights at dusk. It seemed unlikely to Fischer that Begelman had stolen small amounts of money without also stealing larger amounts. There were many ways in which a studio president could steal. He could solicit kickbacks from producers whose motion pictures or television programs he had agreed to purchase or distribute. If money changed hands abroad, there was little chance of detection by internal auditors, the IRS, or anyone else. Fischer feared that in two days in Los Angeles he had barely scratched the surface, and knew there would have to be a full investigation. That almost certainly meant publicity—

bad publicity—just as Columbia Pictures Industries seemed headed into its finest hour.

As they were parting at Kennedy shortly after midnight, it seemed to Jim Johnson that Fischer was more disturbed than he had ever seen him in the decade they had known each other.

EIGHT

The week had been at least as frustrating for Alan Hirschfield as it had been for Joe Fischer. Conducting normal business and putting up an amiable front, while waiting for the telephone to ring with devastating and highly confidential news, seemed more aggravating to Hirschfield than actually conducting the investigation. Had it been an extremely busy week it would have been easier. But the pace of business had not yet come up to full speed following the summer doldrums and the Labor Day holiday.

Hirschfield attended a cocktail party on Thursday evening at the Fifth Avenue apartment of his friend Robert Bernstein, the chairman and president of Random House. He lunched at "21" on Friday with an acquaintance in the real estate business. As he did routinely two or three times daily, he spoke by telephone with his stockbroker, Stan Heilbronn, about personal investments, and with Herbert Allen about Columbia business. He spoke to Fred Silverman, the head of programming at ABC, and Herb Schlosser, the president of NBC; to Steven Spielberg, the director of *Close Encounters of the Third Kind*; to Jack Valenti, the president of the Motion Picture Association of America; and to several other people. He said nothing to any of them about the David Begelman problem. He even spoke twice to Begelman about routine business matters, but by prior arrangement with Joe Fischer, he did not mention the embezzlement issue. Begelman, of course, did not raise it either.

However, Hirschfield did reveal the problem to two people in

New York that Friday. One of them was Clive Davis, the president of Arista Records, Columbia's phonograph record subsidiary. Davis had become an intimate friend and confidant in the two years since Hirschfield had hired him to rejuvenate Columbia's ailing record operations. Hirschfield hadn't necessarily planned to confide in Davis so soon, but in the course of a telephone talk on another subject, he simply blurted out his consternation at being confronted with a sensitive, difficult, and unexpected crisis. Clive Davis knew something about such things. He had been fired four years earlier from the presidency of CBS Records for illegally charging personal expenses to CBS. The expenses included renovation of his Central Park West apartment and a reception at the Plaza Hotel following his son's bar mitzvah. Davis subsequently had been prosecuted for federal income-tax evasion and pleaded guilty.* However, Hirschfield and Herbert Allen had decided they could overlook what they considered minor law violations in order to obtain Davis's considerable talents as a record executive. Now, two years later, Davis expressed sympathy for Hirschfield and agreed to say nothing about the Begelman matter to anyone.

The other person whom Hirschfield told that day was Leo Jaffe, Columbia's aging board chairman. Jaffe, who had been with Columbia Pictures for nearly half a century, having started as a bookkeeper in 1930, had seen much of his authority removed when Allen & Company took control and installed Hirschfield as chief executive officer. Since then, Jaffe had functioned partly in a ceremonial capacity as an elder-statesman-ambassador-at-large in the Hollywood community, and as the contact man for various public events in which Columbia was obliged to participate. That week Jaffe was busily completing arrangements for a dinner to be held the following Tuesday evening in the Grand Ballroom of the Waldorf-Astoria Hotel, at which Brandeis University would present its "Distinguished Community Service Award" to Alan Hirschfield. The dinner was mounted annually in New York to raise funds for Brandeis, a number of whose graduates held prominent executive positions in the entertainment business. The recipient of the award didn't necessarily have to be a Brandeis alumnus or extraordinarily active in

---

*The charges to which Davis eventually pleaded guilty concerned questionable travel expenses and did not encompass the bar mitzvah or apartment renovation, which he has consistently denied involved any wrongdoing.

"community service." Hirschfield was neither, although he had given generously to a number of charities.

The dinner meant more to Hirschfield psychologically than it did to Brandeis financially. In a sense, the affair was a coming-out party for Hirschfield, a rite of initiation, a symbol that at age forty-one he had been accepted into the high society of show-business tycoons, the loose network of several dozen men who run the entertainment industry in America. The group encompassed not only the heads of the motion picture companies and television networks but also a number of investment bankers, financiers, and lawyers active in the business, and an assortment of other interested hangers-on. The cochairman of the evening, along with Leo Jaffe, was Steven J. Ross, the chief executive of the Warner Communications conglomerate. The "honorary chairmen"—who for the most part did not participate actively but permitted their names to be used—included Charles and Herbert Allen, Leonard Goldenson of ABC, Lew Wasserman of MCA-Universal, Arthur Krim of United Artists, Dennis Stanfill of Twentieth Century-Fox, Barry Diller of Paramount, Andrew Heiskell of Time Incorporated, Edgar Bronfman of Seagram's, Preston Robert Tisch of Loew's, and David Begelman. Among the "vice chairmen" were Joseph E. Levine and Ray Stark, the producers; Herb Schlosser of NBC, and David Mahoney of Norton Simon Incorporated (a major shareholder in Twentieth Century-Fox). The 120-member "dinner committee" included producers David Merrick, Walter Mirisch, Robert Chartoff and Irwin Winkler; Marvin Josephson, the head of International Creative Management, the world's largest talent agency; Fred Pierce, the president of ABC television; and the entire high command of Columbia Pictures Industries, including its legal counsel, Robert Todd Lang, a senior partner of the prestigious firm of Weil, Gotshal & Manges.

Hirschfield had always had mixed feelings about becoming a full, active member of this fraternity. He had spent most of his adult life, in fact, torn between the Manhattan and Beverly Hills high life, and his relaxed family life in Scarsdale. In four years at the helm of Columbia Pictures, he had decided, tentatively at least, that he could mix both lives successfully. Although he had not yet achieved the status of Steve Ross or Herbert Allen in Manhattan society, or Lew Wasserman in the upper stratum of Los Angeles, the Brandeis dinner demonstrated that he was on his way. He did not want anything to mar its success.

It was with some hesitation, therefore, that Hirschfield distracted Leo Jaffe with the Begelman problem late that Friday afternoon, only four days before the dinner. But he was afraid that Jaffe would hear about it from someone else. Actually, Jaffe was miffed at Hirschfield for not telling him immediately upon hearing the news himself, but he registered only a token protest and proceeded with his work on the Brandeis dinner.

Despite his dismay at the Begelman revelations and Fischer's confirmation of the details, Hirschfield maintained the hope that the incident would turn out to be an aberration which somehow could be contained—handled privately within the company. This hope was lessened considerably, of course, by Fischer's report late Friday of the possibility of a second embezzlement, the Peter Choate- *Tommy* contract. Although Hirschfield wanted to examine the material Fischer had gathered as soon as possible, he was committed to business meetings all day Saturday, so he asked Fischer to come to the Hirschfield home on Park Road in Scarsdale at eleven o'clock Sunday morning.

During a break on Saturday, Hirschfield decided to do a small amount of detective work on his own. He telephoned a man in Los Angeles who had recently left the Columbia studio after several years to take a post at another motion picture company. It was a man with whom Hirschfield had a close relationship and whom he could trust to keep a confidence.

"I want to ask you a yes-or-no question," Hirschfield said. "Your inclination is going to be to say no, so I'd really like you to think about it before you answer."

"All right, what is it?"

"In all your time at Columbia, did you ever have occasion to suspect Begelman of doing anything improper? Improper in a financial sense, that is. In his handling of funds?"

The man took only a few seconds to answer.

"There was one thing that seemed sort of odd. A couple of years ago he hired somebody—some outside contractor—to install special sound equipment for *Tommy*. I could never put my finger on what it was, but something about it smelled fishy. I was never sure he actually hired the guy. Nobody ever saw him."

Hirschfield's sigh was audible even over the hiss of the coast-to-coast telephone connection.

"What's going on? Do you have a problem?" his friend asked.

"I can't say anything right now. But can you remember anything more about this *Tommy* situation? Anything at all would be helpful."

"No, just that David seemed to take an unusual amount of personal interest in hiring the guy. It was handled pretty much out of the chain of command. And then nobody ever saw any trace of the fellow. It may have been nothing, but since you ask, it did seem odd at the time."

"Okay, thanks very much. And please don't say anything about this to anybody."

Hirschfield sat at his dining-room table sipping coffee and studying the material that Fischer had spread before him. He was beginning to feel as much anger toward Begelman as shock and dismay. Here was documentary evidence that one of the two or three most important officers of Columbia Pictures Industries—some felt *the* most important— was a thief—a man directly responsible for restoring the health of Columbia's ailing movie studio and more recently its lethargic television production company; a man with whom Hirschfield had worked closely for four years and had a warm personal and professional relationship; a man whom Hirschfield had defended two years earlier when a powerful Columbia board member and stockholder— Matthew Rosenhaus—had wanted to dump Begelman and replace him with Frank Yablans, a recognized figure in the industry who had just been fired as the head of Paramount Pictures.

A sense of dread enshrouded Hirschfield and Fischer like a thick, foul fog. The Begelman problem seemed surrealistic. Each question they asked themselves seemed to have no adequate answer and led only to a more perplexing question. Why did he steal? If he'd needed money he easily could have borrowed from any one of several friends and colleagues in the company, or from the company itself. He could have borrowed, that is, unless he needed a huge sum. Were the Cliff Robertson and Peter Choate transactions (assuming for the moment that the Choate matter was fraudulent) only a small part of the total? If they were, how much more had Begelman stolen, and by what means? Did Begelman have some secret, desperate need for a lot of money? Had he been gambling? Was he in hock to loan sharks? Mobsters?

How would the company be affected? It seemed clear to Hirschfield that if Begelman had done what he appeared to have done, he would at the very least have to resign from Columbia. Even if the company could avoid the embarrassing public spectacle of having him prosecuted for forgery, there was no way he could stay in the company.

On that Sunday, however, Hirschfield gave little thought to how he might replace Begelman. He still was intent on containing the problem, and still preoccupied with whom to tell next about the embezzlements. He longed to summon his friend Todd Lang, Columbia's chief legal counsel, who lived just around the corner. On the other hand, he dreaded telling Herbert Allen and the rest of the board of directors. Something like this reflected badly on the officers of the company above and around Begelman, including Hirschfield himself.

Finally, he and Fischer decided to confer with Mickey Rudin as scheduled the next day before letting anyone else in on their secret.

That evening, Hirschfield hosted a prerelease, VIP screening of the new Columbia film *Bobby Deerfield*, starring Al Pacino, at the Coronet Theater in Manhattan. Several Columbia board members, Allen & Company officers, and Wall Street brokers and investment bankers were on hand. At the film, and at the dinner afterward at Tavern-on-the-Green, Hirschfield managed to hide his gloom and show nothing but his usual gregariousness and good humor. He was adept at rising to such occasions. He genuinely enjoyed playing host at social events, and by the end of the evening he was in the best mood he'd been in since before Detective Silvey's Wednesday call.

Instead of going home to Scarsdale, Hirschfield spent the night at an apartment which Columbia maintained for visiting executives in the Carnegie House at Fifty-seventh Street and the Avenue of the Americas. The company leased the place—a spacious two-bedroom duplex complete with live-in butler—from Freddie Fields, David Begelman's ex-partner. Appropriately enough, the butler had worked many years earlier for Harry Cohn, who cofounded Columbia Pictures in 1920 and ran it until his death in 1958. When Hirschfield arrived, he found a wry note from Jim Johnson, who was occupying the smaller of the two bedrooms over that weekend: "Dear Alan. When you get in, please don't make any noise. I'm upstairs working. How about breakfast?"

Hirschfield left before Johnson awakened on Monday morning, but replied to his note in kind: "Jim. Sorry I missed you at breakfast. I wanted to discuss your becoming president of the studio."

NINE

Hirschfield juggled secrets all day Monday. After morning conferences about Begelman with Joe Fischer, he had to attend a luncheon
meeting on an entirely different subject that was just as secret and
sensitive in its own way as the Begelman affair. The IBM Corporation,
which had never been in the entertainment business, had quietly
been conducting research on a video system, involving laser and
optics technology, which promised to be more sophisticated than
other video-cassette and disc systems then being developed by other
companies. Hirschfield, along with a young Columbia senior vice
president, Allen Adler, had been trying hard to persuade IBM to let
Columbia Pictures be the exclusive supplier of programming—the
so-called "soft-ware"—for the IBM system. Security cloaking the
system and Columbia's potential role in it rivaled that with which
the Pentagon guards a new missile system, so it was in hushed tones
and cryptic language that Hirschfield and Adler discussed the latest
developments with two IBM executives at La Côte Basque, which
was situated on the Fifty-fifth Street side of the ground floor of the
Columbia Pictures building, and functioned during most noon hours
as the Columbia executive dining room.

Hopeful that they had advanced their cause with IBM, Hirschfield
and Adler returned to Columbia's eleventh-floor executive suite
where Hirschfield had a 2:30 meeting scheduled with Mickey Rudin
and Joe Fischer. Passing from one capsule of secrecy into another
was especially difficult for Hirschfield, a man uncomfortable with
secrets. Even more than most people, he loved to share good news
instantly, and was quick to seek the solace of friends in the event of
bad news. He had wanted to discuss the Begelman problem with
Adler, whose judgment he valued, but he had resisted the temptation
to do so, even though the two had been together a lot in recent days.

As they parted at the door to Hirschfield's office, Adler suddenly asked: "Is something brewing around here? Joe disappeared Thursday and Friday and has been walking around with a long face all morning."

Hirschfield rolled his eyes upward and sighed. "Please don't ask. You don't want to know, take my word for it. We'll fill you in some time this week, but I just can't do it now. And please don't say anything to anyone else." A confused Adler sauntered down the hall to his own office, and Hirschfield went into his meeting with Rudin and Fischer.

Whatever the problem of a particular moment, the presence of Mickey Rudin had always made Alan Hirschfield feel more secure. A heavy man with a deep voice made raspy by ten thousand cigars, Rudin moved slowly, talked slowly, and thought quickly and incisively. The son of a Russian-Jewish *shmatteh* manufacturer, he had grown up in a deteriorating section of the Bronx, moved to the Fairfax district of Los Angeles as a teenager, gone to Harvard Law School where he made law review, and practiced law in Beverly Hills since the late forties. Although he was best known for representing Sinatra, he served a varied clientele. There were few important people in the entertainment communities of Hollywood, Las Vegas, and New York whom Mickey Rudin did not know, few parts of the entertainment industry with which he was unfamiliar, few kinds of information to which he did not have access.

Hirschfield and Fischer showed Rudin the Cliff Robertson and Peter Choate documents and told him all that they had been able to learn. Rudin had a close business relationship with the Wells Fargo Bank and knew Joe Lipsher, the vice president who had approved the cashing of the Robertson check, so he assured Fischer and Hirschfield that he could easily obtain any information in the bank's possession. The name of Peter Choate, too, rang a bell, but for the moment Rudin could not recall why.

Rudin suggested the retention of a handwriting expert to compare the endorsement on the Robertson check with other examples of Begelman's handwriting. And, despite Hirschfield's eagerness to keep the Begelman problem quiet, Rudin urged him to inform other key Columbia people, including Todd Lang, the chief legal counsel, and Herbert Allen.

"You can't sit on this yourself," Rudin told Hirschfield. "You have an obligation to let the board in on it, or at least the executive

committee, and your corporate counsel. You certainly have a moral
obligation to tell Herbie Allen there's a problem. And you have to
think about the SEC. There are some potentially very serious facts
here, and I think you have to bring this to the attention of the SEC.
That's my opinion to you, Alan. I know you want to be protective of
the company and of the man [Begelman], but there's a limit, when
you're in a public company, of how protective you can be. My own
knowledge of Sporkin [Stanley Sporkin, the SEC's director of
enforcement]* is that he is rather decent and fair if you level with him
and tell him what your problems are. But if you hide scandals from
him, he can be relentless. I've never found him unreasonable in my
dealings with him. You're farther ahead if you level with him and
tell him your problems than if you let him discover your problems."

Hirschfield agreed with Rudin's comments and said he would
inform Todd Lang and Herbert Allen within the next day or so.

Suddenly Rudin placed Peter Choate. "What did you say his
address is?"

"Santa Monica."

"If it's the one I'm thinking of, he's an architect. When I drive
home in the evening, I go past a small office complex out near the
beach with a sign, Peter Choate, A.I.A. He's a well-known designer
around Beverly Hills."

"Does he do music or acoustics or theater work?" Hirschfield
asked.

"No, he's a house designer. His father's an architect, too. Did
Begelman have anything done to his house recently?"

"Jesus Christ, yes!" said Hirschfield. "He had a screening room
built, but thirty-five thousand dollars was a lot more than we authorized him to spend on it."

"I'll have my office look into it," Rudin promised.

Hirschfield had to begin a meeting with two advertising people

---

*The Securities and Exchange Commission, the federal agency that regulates the issuance, purchase,
and sale of securities in publicly owned corporations, and investigates irregularities that may affect the
value of the securities, was devoting a lot of attention in the mid- and late 1970s to malfeasance by
senior officers of major U.S. corporations. The SEC had been aggressive in bringing charges against a
large number of corporate executives who had authorized the payment of bribes overseas, contributed
illegally to political campaigns, abused their expense accounts and other perquisites of office, or
otherwise misused corporate funds. As the SEC's tough and relentless enforcement chief, Stanley
Sporkin was the symbol of this effort to every executive and corporate lawyer in the nation. Whenever
a corporation discovered a potential internal scandal, one of its first calculations was the way in which
the SEC, and Sporkin in particular, might react.

from the studio concerning preparations for the release of *Close Encounters of the Third Kind*. Mickey Rudin agreed to return the next day.

Herbert Allen was a few minutes late getting uptown Tuesday noon from his office in the Wall Street area, and Hirschfield awaited him at their regular corner table in the front room of La Côte Basque. On the phone that morning, Hirschfield had been brief: "We've got a serious problem. I can't talk on the phone. It's bad news—terrible news." At the table, over their usual light lunch, Alan quietly but urgently told Herbert the full story—the call from the detective, the Robertson check, Fischer's trip, the discovery of the possibility of a second embezzlement, the summoning of Mickey Rudin, the need for an investigation, the likelihood that more thefts would be discovered. In contrast to Hirschfield, who was ebullient when he was happy and agitated when he was upset, Herbert Allen didn't often display bursts of emotion in the face of good news or bad. Although he was trim and fit, he had slightly sunken eyes which gave him a somewhat gaunt, tired look and projected coolness, cynicism, nonchalance, and even indifference, much more often than joy or sadness. His reaction to the Begelman news was only slightly more acute than if Hirschfield had said that the company's first-quarter earnings would be lower than last year's.

"Do we know anything about his financial status that would explain why he would need money?" Herbert asked.

"No. He lives high, of course, and he's eager to get his new contract."

"It doesn't make sense. He could have borrowed from one of us. What about gambling?"

"I don't know of any gambling. Or women. I'm as close to him as anyone in the company, and I don't think he has a woman. He's devoted to Gladyce."

"Ten thousand, or even forty thousand, seems small for a man at his level," Herbert said.

"We feel there may be a lot more. This may be just the tip of the iceberg. We'll have to have a full audit. Mickey feels we should get a handwriting expert to look at the check before we do anything else."

"I can take care of that."

"Do you think we should tell Ray?" Hirschfield asked.

"Absolutely. He got me involved in this company. He helped get you your job and helped us hire David. We owe it to him to tell him there's a problem. He may even know something that will shed some light on what David's problem is."

"Would you mind calling him?"

"No, I'll do it right now."

Herbert Allen got up from the table and called Ray Stark from a pay phone just inside the mirrored door of the men's room near the restaurant's entrance. Stark, Hollywood's most consistent producer of commercially successful films for the past decade, a close associate of Allen & Company since the fifties, and the architect of its takeover of Columbia Pictures, had become Herbert Allen's closest friend in recent years, following Herbert's divorce and the death, apparently by suicide, of Ray's son, Peter.* Ray and Herbert spent a lot of time together and spoke by telephone at least once daily. Typically Ray would begin his day in Bel-Air between 6 and 7 A.M. by calling Herbert at his Broad Street office. They knew each other's every nuance, so Herbert required few words on the men's room phone at La Côte Basque.

"Something serious has come up. I can't tell you what it is, but can you get on the next plane?" It was 10:30 at The Burbank Studios. Stark was aboard a 1 P.M. flight from Los Angeles International.

Herbert Allen accompanied Hirschfeld back upstairs to the Columbia offices where Hirschfeld was to continue his meetings with Mickey Rudin and Joe Fischer and, for the first time, to confer with Columbia's chief legal counsel, Robert Todd Lang, who had been summoned from his office in the General Motors Building two blocks up Fifth Avenue. Lang, fifty-three years old, was a top partner at Weil, Gotshal & Manges, one of the largest and fastest-growing law firms in New York. A leading corporate and securities lawyer, Lang represented clients in a diversity of businesses including entertainment and publishing. He represented Barbra Streisand, and his practice had brought him into contact with Alan Hirschfeld and David Begelman several times over the years. He had been Columbia Pictures Industries' general counsel† since shortly after the Hirschfeld-Allen-Begelman team took over the company in

*Peter Stark, at the age of twenty-five, apparently jumped from his fourteenth-floor apartment in Manhattan in February 1970, according to the police.
†Like all big corporations, Columbia Pictures Industries used several lawyers for various purposes. The lawyers are of three general types. The first is the principal legal counsel, typically a senior partner of a

1973. A wiry, good-humored man, conservative in mien and dress, Lang was a vigorous weekend tennis player and a neighbor of Hirschfield in Scarsdale.

After hearing a lengthy recitation of the facts from Joe Fischer and Mickey Rudin, Lang fully endorsed Rudin's belief that the Begelman problem had to be reported to the Securities and Exchange Commission. The initial report could be informal and private, but it should be made as soon as possible. The longer Columbia waited, the greater the risk that someone outside the company might tip the SEC and arouse suspicion that Columbia was trying to conceal a scandal. If Columbia itself was the informant, Lang reasoned, it could assure the commission that an internal inquiry was being conducted in good faith and thus reduce chances that the SEC staff would launch its own investigation.

While not disputing the need to consider the SEC, Herbert Allen was antagonistic—the reaction of an entrepreneurial businessman who had clashed more than once with the SEC and felt that the agency had far too much power to interfere in the affairs of corporations. Just two weeks earlier, in fact, Allen & Company had won a court battle stemming from fraud charges the commission had made and failed to sustain against the Allen firm in a case unrelated to Columbia Pictures. Still feeling confident and combative, Herbert wanted to tell the SEC as little as possible about the Begelman affair and to avoid letting concern about SEC reaction govern the way in which Columbia handled the matter.

"The SEC is a runaway agency, but they're not going to run over this company as long as I'm here," he said.

Hirschfield sided with Todd Lang's preference for candor and promptness. The possibility of a leak of information increased daily. Although the number of people who knew about the Begelman problem remained small, it was a diverse group, and it was growing:

---

major law firm. Known as the "outside counsel" because he functions from a relatively independent stance outside the client company, this is the lawyer to whom the company looks for guidance on all major legal issues. He in turn frequently assigns specific tasks, depending on the issue, to specialists within his firm. The second group of lawyers are those actually on the client company's staff—the so-called "inside counsel"—the chief of whom at Columbia was Victor Kaufman, a vice president of the corporation. Kaufman worked generally on business issues with legal overtones, e.g., contracts and deals, as distinct from providing strictly legal advice, the province of the outside counsel. The third group of lawyers are those retained temporarily for specific purposes, e.g., Hirschfield's turning to Mickey Rudin for help when the Begelman problem first surfaced. In practice, the three types of lawyers frequently cross into each other's provinces and work together when particular situations necessitate.

Cliff Robertson and his representatives; three Los Angeles-area police departments; at least two people at the Columbia studio in Burbank; and now an increasing number of people in New York. Even assuming an attitude of discretion on everyone's part—which couldn't be counted on—it was impossible to be sure that no one would let a comment slip accidentally to the wrong person over lunch or after a couple of drinks.

It was finally agreed that the SEC had to be told something, but the group postponed a decision on what to say and when. There was also concern about the Beverly Hills police, who had asked for a written statement of whether Columbia wished to prosecute Begelman. Mickey Rudin agreed to act as the company's liaison with the police; anything Columbia might say it should say through Rudin.

Herbert Allen asked if anyone had spoken to Begelman since Fischer's visit the previous week. Todd Lang cautioned that the company was nearly at the point of becoming Begelman's adversary in a legal sense, and thus any conversation other than formal contact by lawyers should be kept to a minimum. Herbert Allen urged nonetheless that someone should telephone Begelman and summon him to New York so that he could be confronted with the allegations against him and given an opportunity to explain himself. Hirschfield heeded Lang's advice and declined the task. But Allen insisted, and went next door to Fischer's office to make the call himself, only to learn that Begelman was at the Cedars Sinai Medical Center in the middle of a physical examination and would not be back in his Burbank office until the next day.

In addition to worrying about leaks, the SEC, and the police, Hirschfield was in a snit about Columbia's annual report to shareholders which was being published that very week. The report featured David Begelman and lavished praise upon him.

"Can't we stop publication?" Hirschfield asked. "It's going to look awful. We're memorializing our stupidity forever. It's got his picture and everything."

Joe Fischer informed him that the report had just left the printer and was in the mail. It was too late.

Mickey Rudin, who had promised to investigate the Peter Choate contract further, reported that he had no new information but expected to hear from his Beverly Hills office later in the afternoon. The remaining question was whether the Peter Choate whom Begelman had claimed was an acoustics consultant working on

Tommy was, in fact, a Beverly Hills architect who had worked on Begelman's house at Columbia Pictures' expense. Rudin was scheduled to return to Los Angeles that evening, at about the same time that the dinner sponsored by Brandeis University in honor of Alan Hirschfield would be getting under way at the Waldorf-Astoria. On his way to the airport, Rudin said, he would stop by the Waldorf and give Hirschfield whatever new information he had obtained.

On the calendar it was the penultimate evening of summer—that Tuesday, September 20—but it felt like the first evening of fall. The temperature had dropped steadily through the day and was in the low fifties by nightfall. Many of the hundreds of dinner guests, still with deep summer tans and wearing light attire, shivered slightly as they made their way into the still-air-conditioned Waldorf and up to the Grand Ballroom on the third floor.

Alan Hirschfield, his wife, Berte, their two oldest children, Laura and Marc, and Alan's parents, Norman and Betty Hirschfield from Oklahoma City, stood outside the ballroom in the large foyer where cocktails were being served and accepted congratulations from the people swirling around them. Behind his smile and happy chatter, Alan was acutely aware of rising to another occasion. However, unlike the *Bobby Deerfield* preview two nights earlier, this was the most important social event of his career. Nothing could be allowed to mar it and, as it turned out, nothing visible did. The pleasure and honor of the moment captured Alan. No one could see his anxiety, even though it was heightened by the knowledge that Mickey Rudin would arrive momentarily, probably with more bad news.

Berte* Hirschfield, a slender woman of understated elegance and beauty, with short black hair, dark eyes, and a spectacular smile, carried off the moment as well as her husband, although she, too, was conscious of Rudin's imminent arrival, and of how very few people, among the hundreds milling about, knew that Columbia Pictures was astride a volcano of scandal that might erupt at any moment. Alan's father, one of his closest confidants, had not been told yet. Their hosts, Chancellor Abram Sachar of Brandeis and the university's president, Marver Bernstein, certainly knew nothing. Nor did any of the Hirschfields' friends, Alan's business associates, the Columbia board of directors, with the exception of Herbert Allen

---

*Pronounced ''Burt.''

and Leo Jaffe, nor the upper echelon executives, except for Joe Fischer. Thank God the Begelmans did not fly in for the event, Berte thought.

No sign of Mickey Rudin. The cocktail hour was ending and the guests were filing into the ornate old chandelier-lit ballroom, the site of hundreds of presidential balls, United Nations galas, Al Smith memorial political dinners, and charity extravaganzas. Then, just as Hirschfield was sitting down at his table, he spotted Rudin at the entrance, dressed in a blazer and polo shirt for his flight to Los Angeles. Hirschfield caught Fischer's eye and the two of them moved back through the crowd and huddled with Rudin in the nearly empty foyer.

Rudin had just spoken with his Beverly Hills office. The message: the Peter Choate in whose name David Begelman had drawn a $35,000 check was not an acoustics consultant for *Tommy* but was the architect Rudin had suspected he was. Rudin's office had determined, by checking building permits at the Beverly Hills City Hall, that Choate had done construction work at Begelman's home. Hirschfield and Fischer knew that Columbia had authorized an expenditure of about $22,000 to outfit a home screening room for Begelman. But that amount had been paid separately. The inescapable conclusion, therefore, was that David Begelman had created a bogus contract and transaction in order to steal an additional $35,000 from Columbia Pictures. That brought his total embezzlements discovered thus far to $45,000.*

In full view of the crowd in the ballroom, Hirschfield and Fischer managed to contain their dismay, and also conceal the awkwardness of the moment. As Rudin stood delivering the bad news in the lowest possible voice, latecomers to the dinner kept approaching and greeting him and Hirschfield. "Congratulations, Alan. Hey, Mickey, where's your suit and tie?" Acting out a previously concocted cover story, Hirschfield escorted Rudin into the dinner so that he could greet some of the people he knew and tell them that he had pressing business in California and had just stopped by to say hello. Joe Fischer, meanwhile, was giving whispered bulletins to Herbert Allen and Todd Lang.

"The second transaction is confirmed. We'll fill you in later."

---

*Peter Choate, who knew nothing of Begelman's use of his name in an embezzlement, was indeed an architect to the stars. He had designed houses for Linda Ronstadt, Ryan O'Neal, Henry Mancini, Carroll O'Connor, Lee Grant, and Mel Brooks and Anne Bancroft, among others.

After a few moments, Hirschfield returned to his table and Rudin left for the airport.

The rest of the evening proceeded pleasantly, although to Hirschfield it evoked a Kafkaesque dream. There were speeches by Columbia board chairman Leo Jaffe; Jack Valenti, the president of the Motion Picture Association of America; Chancellor Sachar and President Bernstein of Brandeis; and Robert Benjamin, the cochairman of United Artists and the newly elected chairman of the Brandeis board of trustees.

Then Hirschfield rose for his speech of thanks. "No remarks about my success," he said, "can be complete without an expression of my deepest thanks to those who are members of our Columbia team, some of whom, like Herbert Allen, are here tonight, and some of whom, like David Begelman, were unable to attend." The talk was relaxed and witty, and people remarked at how effective Alan Hirschfield was in front of an audience.

Hirschfield was presented with a plaque, and then the evening gradually decelerated, as the Mark Towers Orchestra played for dancing, and dozens of people lined up at Hirschfield's table to shake his hand again.

Part II

TEN

When Herbert Allen was divorced in 1971—after nine years of marriage and four children—he moved back to Manhattan from the elegant Westchester County suburb of Irvington and established one of the preeminent bachelor pads in the city on the thirty-first floor of the Carlyle, which vies with the Beverly Hills for the title of finest hotel in America. Herbert's uncle, Charles Allen, lived at the Carlyle, and Herbert grew to savor the life there. The cityscape views were stunning and the hotel's services were the best. Balanced with a sprawling Southampton beach home for weekend variety and space, the Carlyle place was perfect. Jennifer O'Neil, the actress with whom Herbert had a long romance in the early seventies, spent a lot of time there, and Barbara Rucker, the blond model and actress of TV commercial fame (Sheraton, Harvey's Bristol Cream, and Final Net) whom he began seeing later, replaced Jennifer O'Neil on the thirty-first floor. Herbert's children visited frequently.

Because of its convenient midtown location—more convenient in many instances than his Broad Street office—Herbert conducted a good deal of informal business at his apartment. So it was natural for him to invite Alan Hirschfield there on the morning after the Brandeis dinner to discuss the David Begelman crisis with Ray Stark, whom Herbert had called from the pay phone at La Côte Basque Tuesday afternoon and asked to come to New York immediately. The quick summoning of Stark accurately reflected the producer's pivotal role in the affairs of Columbia Pictures and in the lives of Herbert Allen, Alan Hirschfield, and David Begelman.

Hirschfield and Stark arrived at Allen's apartment promptly at 9 A.M., and the three men settled in the den with coffee.

*   *   *

For as long as anyone in Hollywood could remember, Ray Stark had been known to friend and foe alike as "The Rabbit." Although many people assumed that the tag originated as a sexual reference, it actually was a physical description coined by Fanny Brice, who was to become Stark's mother-in-law in the 1940s. When daughter Fran introduced Ray to her mother and later asked what she thought, Fanny answered: "He looks like a rabbit," referring to Ray's prominent teeth, nose, cheeks and brow, and his short stature. Ray was not a homely man, but the term was apt enough to stick, and was used as commonly in the seventies as it had been in the forties and fifties. He had grown rather tired of it over the years, just as he had grown tired of being known principally as Fanny Brice's son-in-law—as if that relationship were wholly responsible for his success. His repeated use of Brice's life story—as the producer of the Broadway musical *Funny Girl*, as well as the movie of the same name and its sequel, *Funny Lady*—had been landmarks in his career, in part because they enabled him to share in the fruits of Barbra Streisand's rise to stardom. But he had made other notable films as well, and by the late seventies had become one of contemporary Hollywood's most successful producers. Although he was far from being what Herbert Allen called him—"the most important producer in Hollywood post-1948" (he had produced little of artistic distinction, and his films had won very few Academy Awards, none as best picture)—Ray Stark had accomplished something that the entertainment industry admires more than anything else because it is so elusive—commercial consistency. Rarely blockbusters and rarely losers, his films generally made substantial amounts of money for him and for the studio that distributed them. More often than not in recent years, that studio had been Columbia Pictures.

Stark's ties to Columbia had been close since the studio distributed *Funny Girl*, which opened in September 1968. Columbia began losing money in 1971, and by 1973 the company's very life was threatened by three expensive box-office failures—*1776*, *Lost Horizon*, and *Young Winston*. Although Stark had produced none of those films, Columbia still owed him millions of dollars in deferred profits from *Funny Girl* and he feared that he might never get the money if the studio were forced into bankruptcy. Stark turned for help to his oldest and closest friends in financial circles—Charles Allen and his nephew, Herbert Allen, Jr.

Ray Stark's relationship with the Allen family began in the 1950s when he was introduced to Charlie Allen by Charlie Feldman, Hollywood's leading talent agent and Stark's boss at the time. When they met, Stark and Allen independently were already well connected in show business—Stark as an agent, and Allen on the more exalted level of financier and adviser to the mighty.

Raymond Otto Stark, after flunking out of Rutgers, went to Hollywood in the late 1930s. He worked as a florist at Forest Lawn, wrote radio scripts for Edgar Bergen, worked in the Warner Bros. publicity department, sold *Red Ryder* radio scripts, and eventually became a literary agent, representing Thomas Costain, J. P. Marquand, James Gould Cozzens, and Ben Hecht. Later as a talent agent he handled Ava Gardner, Lana Turner, Marilyn Monroe, William Holden, and Kirk Douglas.

Charlie Allen was first exposed to the entertainment business through his first wife, Rita, who was a Broadway producer. He later became friendly with a number of important Hollywood people. In addition to Charlie Feldman, Allen was close to Jack Warner, the head of Warner Bros., to Spyros Skouras, the chairman of Twentieth Century-Fox, and to Serge Semenenko, the most active and innovative motion-picture financier in the nation and a top officer of the First National Bank of Boston.

Ray Stark and Charlie Allen found that they had a lot in common and became good friends. The late 1950s and early 1960s were important years for both men as their business activities moved closer and closer together. Both wanted to make substantially more money in show business. Both had innovative ideas for doing it. And both shared a business attitude, common in the hurly-burly world of Hollywood and certain sectors of Wall Street, which accommodates occasional association and conduct of business with people of questionable reputation. There was nothing wrong with dealing with rogues, the philosophy went, so long as one did not dirty one's own hands in the process. Charlie and Ray stayed clean.

• Charlie Allen and banker Serge Semenenko, as Jack Warner's principal financial advisers, joined the board of directors of Warner Bros. in 1956, purchased major blocks of stock in the company, and helped reorganize its troubled finances. Semenenko, in addition to being celebrated for innovations in movie financing, also engaged in unorthodox banking practices which a lot of business people and certain federal agencies found objectionable. He frequently made personal investments in the stock of companies to which he was lending his bank's money. Many banks prohibited their employees from such practices, but Semenenko pooh-poohed the obvious potential for conflict of interest.*

• As part of its effort to raise cash in 1956, Warner Bros. sold its entire library of pre-1948 films to a company called Associated Artists Productions, which was in the business of licensing movies for showing on television. The president of Associated Artists was a man who a decade earlier had pioneered the concept of showing movies on television, Eliot Hyman. The chairman of the board of Associated Artists, and the arranger of the financing for its purchase of the Warner Bros. library, was Louis (Uncle Lou) Chesler, a three-hundred-pound Canadian stock promoter with ties to organized-crime boss Meyer Lansky and various gamblers and bookmakers. One of the vice presidents of Associated Artists was Morris Mac Schwebel, a Chesler associate then engaged in criminal activity for which he later would be indicted and convicted.

• Ray Stark got to know Associated Artists President Eliot Hyman through agent Charlie Feldman, the same man who had introduced Stark to Charlie Allen. In 1957 Stark joined the Associated Artists board of directors alongside Hyman, Lou Chesler, and Mac Schwebel. The next year, Stark and Hyman started a company called Seven Arts which began producing motion pictures and also continued a movie-to-television licensing business similar to that of Associated Artists. Stark left in 1959 to produce his first movie, *The World of Suzie Wong*, with William Holden and Nancy Kwan, but in 1961 rejoined Seven Arts, by then known officially as Seven Arts Productions Ltd. Lou Chesler was board chairman, Eliot Hyman was executive vice president, and Stark was senior vice president in charge of movie production. All three were members of the board of directors. (Mac Schwebel, who was indicted for securities fraud in early 1961, had left his official position with the company but was to become its largest shareholder.)

• At about the same time that Charlie Allen and Serge Semenenko were becoming active in the affairs of Warner Bros. in the mid-1950s, Charlie Allen and some friends were purchasing a 25 percent interest

*In 1967, eleven years after Semenenko and Allen became involved in the affairs of Warner Bros., Semenenko was forced to resign as a vice chairman and a director of the First National Bank of Boston after reporter William M. Carley dissected the banker's activities on page one of *The Wall Street Journal*. Semenenko was sixty-four at the time and the resignation was portrayed as an ''amicable'' retirement. Federal agencies made no formal accusations of wrongdoing against Semenenko.

in a company formed to develop property on Grand Bahama Island, which lay eighty miles off the coast of Florida. The company was called Grand Bahama Port Authority Ltd. When they made the investment, the Allens were well aware that the major partner in the enterprise, with a 50 percent interest, was Wallace Groves, a convicted stock manipulator who had served time in federal prison for mail fraud and conspiracy.

• Subsequent to Charlie Allen's investment in Grand Bahama Port Authority Ltd., Ray Stark, Eliot Hyman, Lou Chesler, Seven Arts, and the Allens all invested in the Port Authority's principal subsidiary, Grand Bahama Development Co. Serge Semenenko was the development company's banker. Seven Arts purchased a 21 percent interest in Grand Bahama Development for $5 million in 1961. At the same time he was chairman of Seven Arts Productions, Lou Chesler became president of Grand Bahama Development, in effect joining forces with ex-convict Groves. Chesler and Groves proceeded to pay hundreds of thousands of dollars to Bahamian government officials for permission to build a gambling casino. Chesler then staffed the casino with associates of Meyer Lansky after meeting with Lansky and other mobsters in Miami Beach. Seven Arts Productions' reports to its stockholders, in addition to reporting on movie projects like Ray Stark's *The World of Suzie Wong* and *The Night of the Iguana*, also reported on Seven Arts' $5 million investment in the Bahamas. The reports did not mention the casino, the payments to the government, or the association with Lansky's henchmen.

It wasn't long, however, before dissension arose over the future course of Seven Arts Productions. Ray Stark and Eliot Hyman wanted the company to concentrate on the entertainment business. In 1964, Stark produced *The Night of the Iguana* with Ava Gardner and Richard Burton and also his first Broadway venture, *Funny Girl*, starring Barbra Streisand. *Funny Girl* had originated as a movie script in 1961, and at that time Stark had wanted Judy Garland for the role of Fanny Brice. To approach Garland, he first had to approach her agent, who turned out to be David Begelman. Begelman and his partner, Freddie Fields, had just started their own talent agency, Creative Management Associates, and their first important client was Judy Garland. She was not interested in *Funny Girl*, but three years later, when Stark decided he wanted Streisand for the Broadway musical, he found himself again dealing with David

Begelman, who in the meantime had added Streisand to CMA's roster of clients. Because of a loophole in Stark's original contract with Streisand, Begelman managed to obtain a substantial increase in her salary for the Broadway run of *Funny Girl,* costing Stark more than half a million dollars beyond what he would have had to pay under the original deal. Although Stark was livid, he and Begelman eventually became good friends. Each recognized that the other was a skilled street fighter, with qualities they mutually admired.

By this time, David Begelman had also encountered Charlie Allen. Judy Garland had met Allen at a cocktail party and asked him to review her financial portfolio. He invited her down to his office at 30 Broad Street, and she asked Begelman to go along. Charlie served tea and the three had a pleasant chat, but Judy Garland decided against putting her funds in the care of Allen & Company.

Judy Garland, indeed, had already put her funds and most other facets of her chaotic life in the care, directly or indirectly, of David Begelman and Freddie Fields, who were well on their way to becoming the hottest talent agents in the country. For both men, their success was the fulfillment of dreams. For Begelman, in particular, the success had been long delayed and the path to it circuitous.

When David Begelman was a Bronx teenager in the 1930s, his first important role model was a talent agent. David frequently visited his father's tailor shop in Manhattan and became acquainted with one of his father's customers, Billy Goodheart, Jr., a co-founder of MCA, whose main business then was booking dance bands and other entertainment acts. Billy Goodheart was the first man David had ever met who sported a limousine and chauffeur. "David," Goodheart would say, "if you ever need a job when you get out of school, just come and see me."* The idea of having a limousine and chauffeur held a strong appeal for David, but by the time he was ready for a job several years later Billy Goodheart had sold his interest in MCA and left show business.

David Begelman spent much of World War II in the Air Force, including a brief period in a technical training program on the campus of Yale University. After the war he attended New York

---

*Sonny Werblin, who gained fame as a leading talent agent and later as a sports impresario, started his career as an office boy for Billy Goodheart, Jr., at MCA.

University briefly and then drifted rather aimlessly into the insurance business. Through an Air Force buddy, Eddie Feldman, David met several people who worked in entertainment. One of them was Eddie Feldman's sister, Esther, who was the secretary to Jack Cohn, a co-founder and the executive vice president of Columbia Pictures. David also met Shep Fields, the band leader. In 1950, David Begelman and Esther Feldman were married, and Shep Fields was the best man at their wedding. David got to know other members of the Fields family, as well, including Shep's younger brother, Freddie, who was an agent at MCA.

A few years later, David finally realized his long-term professional ambition when he left his insurance employer and went to work for MCA as a talent agent. He did well professionally but suffered the personal tragedy of losing his wife to cancer. However, he met and married Lee Reynolds, a television producer and top aide to Jackie Gleason, who was then at the peak of his success on television.

Over the next several years David Begelman became a force to be reckoned with in show business. Bright, charming, and effective as an agent, he loved the rough-and-tumble of the business, and also relished the accoutrements of his position—the limousines, the first-class travel and dining, the expense account, the association with stars. He enjoyed grabbing dinner checks for parties of six or eight at Danny's Hideaway and "21" and the Colony. He gained a reputation as a man who lived high, and also as a man who lived on the edge—the edge of his financial capacity and, occasionally, the edge of truth about himself and his background. In the years since the war, David had allowed his brief Air Force training at Yale to be gradually transformed, in the minds of many people who met him, into the notion that he had attended Yale as a student, that he had graduated from Yale, and even that he had graduated from the Yale Law School. Yale, in one inflated form or another, appeared on his résumés, and he was so urbane and articulate that almost no one questioned his credentials, certainly never overtly. David liked his new image. He liked having people think he had gone to Yale and come from a privileged background. And he hated having people say, as old friends did occasionally upon stepping into his rented limousine, "Well, David, this sure beats the Bronx."*

---

*Begelman's reputation as a man who occasionally stretched the truth later prompted agent Sam Cohn, when he became Begelman's partner, to exact a promise that David would never lie to Sam. "Don't lie to me," Cohn said. "You can lie to anybody you want, but not to me, and everything will be very pleasant."

Begelman was flamboyant. Upon going to work for MCA, he was confronted with its rigid dress code for agents—black suits, white shirts, and plain black neckties. Determined to twit the code, if only in a small way, David commissioned the manufacture of exactly one hundred black ties, each carrying a tiny number from one through a hundred, and displayed them proudly in his closet full of fashionable clothes. As a prank, client Milton Berle once grabbed a handful of the ties from the closet, stuffed them into his jacket, and started to leave the apartment. A meticulous dresser and organizer of clothes, David was dumbstruck.

David Begelman was zealous in the service of his clients. According to Sid Luft, Judy Garland's husband, Begelman gave fresh and literal pungency to the term "starfucker," which usually is applied to representatives—agents, lawyers, and financial managers—who keep constant company with their famous clients. When Garland's multifarious needs required it—and they often did—Begelman spent day and night with her. In a sworn deposition taken in furtherance of a lawsuit against Begelman, Luft alleged that David had an "affair" with Judy, and that Judy "lived with" David at the Sahara Hotel in Las Vegas while she was establishing residence in Nevada so that she could divorce Luft and marry Begelman.

Garland and Luft eventually were divorced, but Judy did not marry Begelman and he denied ever having an affair with her. Their relationship, however, was avidly talked about and speculated upon by friends and acquaintances of David and his wife, Lee Reynolds, who included author Jacqueline Susann. David, Lee, and Judy thus became important models for the characters that Jackie Susann later created in *Valley of the Dolls*. There was some of David in the character of Lyon Burke, the agent; there was a good deal of Lee in the character of Anne Welles, Lyon's wife; there was a lot of Judy Garland in the character of Neely O'Hara, the demanding, pill-addicted singer and actress; and there was a lot of what Jackie Susann imagined to be the relationship between David Begelman and Judy Garland in Lyon Burke and Neely O'Hara's fictional relationship, which included everything from career counseling to sex.*

---

*Judy Garland's demands upon David Begelman at the very least put a strain on David's own marriage to Lee Reynolds. That marriage did not end until several years later. however. when David began seeing Gladyce Rudin. the wife of Lew Rudin. a wealthy New York real-estate man.

David's professional zeal occasionally got him into scrapes. On the night of February 11, 1960—the night Jack Paar walked off the *Tonight* show because NBC had excised a "water closet" joke from his monologue of the previous night—David Begelman, as one of Jack Paar's agents, was standing nearby as a weeping Paar left the NBC studios. After Paar had disappeared into an elevator, an NBC functionary muttered, "That asshole!" Begelman whirled on the NBC man and shouted, "He's not the asshole! You guys are the assholes for bleeping the goddamned silly joke!" Begelman was barred from NBC for a period of time thereafter. A few years later, he was barred from NBC again when a network official accused him of—and David denied—"dealing in bad faith" by arranging a television contract for Barbra Streisand with CBS when negotiations with NBC were faltering.

Begelman was too powerful to be barred from anyplace for long, however. His career flourished. His client list grew to include Paul Newman, Steve McQueen, Robert Redford, and Cliff Robertson, as well as Streisand and Garland. Indeed, he did business regularly with all of the top people in show business, including, with increasing frequency, Ray Stark and Seven Arts Productions.

During the time that Canadian Lou Chesler dominated Seven Arts Productions, its shares were traded only on the small Toronto Stock Exchange. But Ray Stark and Eliot Hyman wanted the company to have the growth opportunities it could only achieve if its securities were listed and traded in a much bigger marketplace—a major stock exchange in the United States. The company decided to apply for listing on the American Stock Exchange, the nation's second largest. In order to obtain access to the American exchange, however, Seven Arts had to pass the inspection of the U.S. Securities and Exchange Commission, enforcing securities laws that were stricter than those in Canada. Thus, Seven Arts had to rid itself of its unsavory elements, personified by Lou Chesler. In a series of maneuvers that Charlie Allen and Serge Semenenko orchestrated, Chesler was removed from Seven Arts and purchased its interest in the tainted Bahama development company. The Seven Arts board of directors was reorganized in 1964. The new directors included Charlie Allen's brother, Herbert Allen, Sr., and a bright, twenty-eight-year-old Allen & Company vice president who had become the firm's entertainment industry expert, Alan J. Hirschfield.

ELEVEN

When Alan Hirschfield joined Allen & Company upon graduating from the Harvard Business School in the spring of 1959, it represented the deepening of a business and personal relationship of Charlie Allen's that was considerably older than—and just as important as—his relationship with Ray Stark, Jack Warner, and most of his other cronies. Charlie Allen and Alan Hirschfield's father, Norman, had been friends since the late 1920s when they began doing business with each other in Wall Street.

Born in 1903 and reared in a cold-water flat on Manhattan's Upper West Side, Charlie quit school when he was fifteen and became a "runner" (messenger) for the brokerage firm of Sartorius & Smith. Four years later, in 1922, he had saved enough money to start his own firm—consisting of a desk, two chairs, and two telephones. Norman, seven years younger than Charlie, grew up on 116th Street in what later became Harlem. When the divorce of his parents depleted the family's finances, Norman, then fourteen, took a summer job as an office boy at the Wall Street firm of A. M. Lamport & Company. For the next few years, until he finished high school, he worked part-time at the firm, learning to be a bond trader, while attending school in the afternoon. Charlie and Norman, whose offices were only two blocks apart, got to know each other in the course of business. Norman would kid Charlie about having his own office but negligible capital—whenever Lamport & Company sold Allen & Company a block of bonds, payment by certified check would be demanded. In 1931, at age twenty-one, Norman became a partner and vice president of Lamport, and Charlie took him out to dinner to celebrate. They dined together over the years at speakeasies from one end of Manhattan to another.

Lamport & Company sent Norman Hirschfield to Oklahoma City

in 1938 to manage a large natural-gas company which it had financed. Finding even more opportunities to prosper in Oklahoma than in Wall Street, Norman, together with his wife, Betty, and Alan, then three years old, became a permanent resident. Norman stayed in close touch with Charlie Allen, however. Through the forties, fifties and sixties, Norman visited New York often, and rarely failed to see Charlie and his brother, Herbert Allen, Sr., who had joined the firm a few years after Charlie founded it.

"It's noon; let's go play golf," Charlie would say, and he, Norman, and Herbert would head for the Deepdale Golf Club on the north shore of Long Island in Herbert's Rolls-Royce convertible.

More than just social and business friends, they actually participated in each other's lives. When one of Charlie's sons was bitten by a dog, Norman and Charlie searched for twelve hours until they found the animal so that it could be checked for rabies. Norman and Charlie, and frequently their wives, spent time together not only in New York but also in the Bahamas, Paris, and Palm Springs, where they were guests in the home of Jack Warner. When Norman and Betty were in New York, Herbert senior sometimes would lend them his apartment if he was traveling or staying at his country place.

Norman participated in some of Allen & Company's business deals, and the Allens invested in some of Norman's ventures in Oklahoma. Norman, in fact, became a sort of informal, untitled Allen & Company representative in the Southwest, always thinking first of the Allens (after himself) if a good business opportunity came along. In the late 1950s and early 1960s, at the request of the Allens, Norman spent a lot of time away from Oklahoma running two Allen-controlled corporations that were in financial trouble. One of them was Teleregister Corporation, which later became Bunker-Ramo Corporation. When Charlie Allen ordered the firing of a top Teleregister executive, he told Norman: "Get rid of him, but be nice to him. Don't hurt his feelings."

Naturally, Alan Hirschfield heard a lot about Charlie Allen and Allen & Company as he was growing up in Oklahoma City in the forties and fifties. Except for a brief flirtation with the idea of becoming a physician, he never seriously considered any career other than working for Allen & Company as an investment banker. Alan attended the University of Oklahoma (where he directed "Sooner Scandals," the annual variety show, and was named one of the ten outstanding senior men) and then went off to Harvard Business

School. His initial assignment at Allen & Company was arranging the first public sale of the stock of Random House, the publishing company, which until then had been wholly owned by Bennett Cerf and his partner, Donald Klopfer. Hirschfield subsequently handled Warner Bros.'s purchase of a major portion of Frank Sinatra's interest in Warner's record company, and in the course of that transaction formed a lasting friendship with Sinatra's lawyer, Mickey Rudin, and with Sinatra himself.

In 1966, while representing Allen & Company on the board of Seven Arts Productions, Hirschfield attempted to promote a merger of Seven Arts and Filmways, a small but growing entertainment conglomerate that was controlled by Martin Ransohoff, the producer of *The Beverly Hillbillies* television show and several movies including *The Americanization of Emily*. In theory, the Seven Arts-Filmways deal made sense to all concerned. But there was one problem: Marty Ransohoff and Ray Stark, who was still a power at Seven Arts, detested each other. Hirschfield, however, convinced them that a merger would be wise and arranged a dinner at "21" where he, Ransohoff, and Stark were to settle the final terms of the deal. Hirschfield, who was savoring the hefty investment banking fee he would earn, urged both men to control their feelings toward each other during the meal and concentrate on the substantial advantages to be derived from the merger. But the three had hardly ordered drinks before Ray Stark launched a withering commentary on Ransohoff's recent picture projects at Filmways. Hirschfield rolled his eyes and sank a bit in his chair. Stark was especially critical of Ransohoff's purchase of the movie rights to the James Clavell novel *Tai-Pan*. Hirschfield sank further in his chair. As the first course was being served, Marty Ransohoff had had enough and said to Stark:

"Ray, you've been producing shit for so long you wouldn't know a real picture if you saw one."

Hirschfield was so low in his chair that he was in danger of slipping beneath the table. The dinner was concluded in tense silence, and the merger of Seven Arts Productions and Filmways never occurred.

Later that year, however, Jack Warner, who had reached his seventies and was thinking of retiring, told Charlie Allen that he wanted to sell his stock in Warner Bros. Pictures. Hirschfield and Allen arranged for Seven Arts to buy Jack Warner's stock for $32 million, and early in 1967, Warner Bros. and Seven Arts merged. Hirschfield took a leave of absence from Allen & Company to serve as vice president for finance of the new corporation, known as Warner Bros.-Seven Arts Ltd., and spearheaded its purchase of Atlantic Records, a rhythm and blues label. Since Warner Bros.-Seven Arts already owned two other record labels, buying Atlantic enabled the corporation to become one of the world's largest record concerns, while maintaining its rank as a major motion-picture maker. But Hirschfield's career as a line officer lasted only a year. He clashed repeatedly with Eliot Hyman, the chairman of the new company, and found himself competing for Hyman's ear with Kenneth Hyman, Eliot's son, who had become head of motion-picture production. (Ray Stark, with a big block of Warner Bros.-Seven Arts stock in his possession, as well as a lucrative consulting agreement with the company, had left to produce the film version of *Funny Girl*.) Kenneth Hyman accused Hirschfield of plotting to overthrow Eliot and take the helm of the company himself. Hirschfield denied the charge but found he could no longer work with the Hymans and left the company.

Only a few months after its debut as a combined enterprise, Warner Bros.-Seven Arts became a target of takeover moves by others. The late sixties was a time of scrambling for corporate power throughout the entertainment industry, and although it was neither the first nor the last such scramble, it was among the most significant because it resulted in the conglomeratization of much of show business in America. United Artists, which was founded in 1919 as an effort to afford filmmakers artistic freedom, and evolved in the early 1950s into a company run by lawyers who still permitted more artistic flexibility than most moguls, was swallowed up by the Transamerica Corporation, a huge and diversified insurance company. Unlike other corporate suitors, Transamerica left United Artists' management in place, and the studio for the time being continued to offer more creative freedom than any other.

Control of MGM was sought by Phil Levin, a real-estate magnate, then by Time Incorporated and Seagram's Edgar Bronfman, and finally was grabbed by Kirk Kerkorian, who was in the airline and gambling businesses and had been the largest stockholder of Transamerica until he sold that interest in order to make his run at MGM.

Columbia Pictures caught the eye of two suitors, a Paris bank and the Lee National Corporation, a diversified U.S. company. Neither bid was successful, and Columbia came under the control of a pharmaceuticals tycoon, Matthew Rosenhaus, who was brought into Columbia by Serge Semenenko. Rosenhaus was friendly to the incumbent Columbia management, which had been in place since the company's cofounder, Harry Cohn, died in 1958.

Herbert Siegel, an ex-agent and would-be movie mogul who headed Chris-Craft Industries, bought a major interest in Paramount Pictures, but only succeeded in driving it into the arms of Charles Bluhdorn's Gulf & Western Industries. Siegel then made a move for Warner-Seven Arts, again unsuccessful. National General Corporation, which owned movie theaters and publishing interests, also tried to buy Warner-Seven, as did Commonwealth United Corporation, a company with interests in movies, juke boxes, vending machines, recording, real estate, and insurance.

The eventual victor in the Warner-Seven contest was Steven J. Ross, the savvy president of Kinney National Service Incorporated, whose varied interests dated back to the nineteenth century and included such prosaic components as funeral parlors, termite and pest control, building maintenance, and parking lots. Warner-Seven's investment banker in the deal with Kinney again was Allen & Company. The combined corporation was called Warner Communications and went on to become one of the largest and most powerful entertainment concerns in the nation. Among those who profited handsomely from the deal or the steps leading to it were the Allens, Alan Hirschfield, Ray Stark, Frank Sinatra, and Mickey Rudin.

The only major motion-picture companies whose structures were untouched by the turmoil of the late sixties were MCA and Twentieth Century-Fox, although each endured painful internal power struggles during the period. Lew Wasserman consolidated his power at MCA, whose form had not changed drastically since it acquired Universal Pictures and a record company and sold off its talent agency business, in a sequence of moves several years earlier. At Fox, the Zanuck era ended when Darryl, and later his son, Richard, left the company after a period of bitter internecine, and even intrafamily, strife. Lehman Brothers, the Wall Street investment banking house that had played a major role in the affairs of Twentieth Century-Fox for decades, installed one of its former partners,

Dennis Stanfill, as Fox's chief executive. (Warburg Pincus, another New York investment concern with a big interest in Fox, also was instrumental in Stanfill's elevation.)

During the fifties and sixties, of course, the seven major motion-picture companies were joined in the Hollywood power elite by the three major television networks. To a large extent, television had replaced "B" movies in the entertainment universe. Instead of making a limited number of "A" pictures and a lot of "B's," as it had done in decades past, Hollywood was making a limited number of "A" pictures and a lot of television shows.

Between 1950 and 1970 the number of American homes with television sets rose from less than 10 percent to more than 95 percent. Movie-theater audiences dropped from sixty million people a week, going to see more than six hundred movies, to fewer than twenty million people weekly leaving their homes to see fewer than four hundred movies. But the shifting statistics tended to obscure the remarkable consistency and durability of the way Americans were entertained. The flickering images of film, whether they emanated from theater or television screens, remained the primary entertainment medium in 1970 just as they had been in 1950. There were only a few excellent movies in 1950—e.g., *All About Eve*, *Sunset Boulevard*, *The Third Man*, *Born Yesterday*, and *The Asphalt Jungle*—and hundreds of less distinguished efforts. There were only a few excellent movies in 1970—e.g., *M*A*S*H*, *Patton*, *Five Easy Pieces*, and *I Never Sang for My Father* in the theaters, *The Price* and *The Andersonville Trial* on television—and hundreds of less distinguished efforts in both media.

The changes over the two decades were undeniable and obvious. But they were hardly revolutionary. The flickering images of 1970 and later were manufactured and sold by a Hollywood that was much like the Hollywood of old. It remained a highly oligarchical institution run by a handful of entrepreneurial businessmen attracted by the glamour and zest, the money and sex, the gamble and gambol of show business.

TWELVE

Well into its second generation, the friendship between the Allen family and the Hirschfield family deepened still further. Herbert Allen, Jr., graduated from Williams College in 1962 and promptly entered the family's investment business. Herbert junior emerged early as the only realistic candidate within the family to inherit the mantle of Allen & Company. Of Charlie's and Herbert senior's five offspring—three boys and two girls—he was the only male who had a strong interest in and aptitude for the business.*

At Williams, Herb was known as a playboy with a sharp and aggressive wit. Having little incentive to study hard, he set as his goal graduating first alphabetically and last academically, and he came very close. His highest college honor was the championship of his fraternity in "wall ball," a handball derivative played with a tennis ball against the wall of the Chi Psi house. Although Herb did not flaunt his wealth at college, he did not conceal it either. Few Williams students had the resources to fly off for holidays as frequently and as far as he did.

Herb was not a stereotypical college playboy, however. He derived negligible pleasure from all-night drinking and carousing. On the contrary, he normally drank sparingly and retired and arose early. There was an almost austere quality about his personal daily habits and regimen. Herb was a young man with more important things on his mind than college, which served for him as little more than an amusing way to spend four years before he assumed the important station that life held for him.

---

*A number of people close to the Allen family considered Charlie's daughter, Terry, to be brighter and tougher than Herbert, Jr., but Terry's gender disqualified her, at least at the time she was reaching maturity in the 1950s, from taking a prominent place in the then-all-male firm. She became a Broadway producer instead.

Immediately upon graduating, Herb married Laura Parrish, a nineteen-year-old Smith College student from Oklahoma City. Laura's father was a prominent physician whose patients included Alan Hirschfield's mother. Alan had dated one of Laura's sisters for a time. Herb and Laura's wedding was held at a Methodist church in the wealthy Nichols Hills section of Oklahoma City, and was followed by a lavish reception at the Oklahoma City Golf and Country Club. The entire Allen clan flew down from New York, and the Hirschfields hosted a round of social events in the days leading up to the wedding.

When Berte Schindelheim, a student at Bennington College, had a blind date in 1959 with Alan Hirschfield, a student at the Harvard Business School, she imagined that Alan was probably one of the few students at the business school willing to take a chance that someone with a name like Berte Schindelheim would turn out to be not only a girl but also an attractive and intelligent girl. Alan and Berte were both very pleased with each other. When they were dating during his last year at Harvard, she would spend weekends in Boston, and he would drive her all the way to Bennington on Sundays and then return—a 350-mile roundtrip. A wedding was planned for June of 1960, right after Berte's graduation, but Alan backed out at the last minute. He was not ready for marriage just yet.

A highlight of his next two years was a brief affair with an exotic young editor at Random House, Maxine Groffsky. Bennett Cerf, whose investment-banking business Alan was handling, introduced them. To Alan Hirschfield, Maxine Groffsky represented the glamour of the New York art and literary worlds. Maxine had had an affair in the middle fifties with Philip Roth, the novelist, and unwittingly had become the model for the character Brenda Patimkin in *Goodbye Columbus*. In the late fifties she had an affair with Larry Rivers, the painter, who also left her an artistic legacy: several portraits he had painted of her. Alan Hirschfield was Maxine's first investment banker. He left her no tangible legacy on the scale of Roth's novel and Rivers's portraits, but he did subsequently acquire a Rivers portrait of Maxine. Though their romance ebbed, they would remain friends, and the portrait would hang in Alan's home permanently.

In the spring of 1962, Maxine Groffsky went off to Paris to edit the *Paris Review*. Late in the year, Alan finally married Berte Schindelheim, who had been working in the interim as an editor at Fawcett Publications and had been quite active socially herself. Through the sixties, Alan and Berte, and Herb and Laura Allen, rented houses for the winter in Palm Springs. Alan was becoming increasingly active in the affairs of Seven Arts and Warner Bros., and there was a lot of socializing with Jack Warner, Ray Stark, and Frank Sinatra. The Hirschfields were frequent guests of Sinatra at his home in Palm Springs as well as in Las Vegas when he was performing. Berte took to calling Sinatra's Palm Springs friends his "local rat pack" to distinguish it from his international "rat pack" (Dean Martin, Sammy Davis, Shirley MacLaine, Joey Bishop, et al.). One member of the local group was Danny Schwartz, a wealthy businessman who had invested in several ventures (including Warner Bros.) with Sinatra and Rudin. At three o'clock one morning at Caesar's Palace, Schwartz asked Alan Hirschfield to stand in for him in a baccarat game. Schwartz was $200,000 in the red at the time, but he was tired and wanted some fresh air. When he returned at sunup, an initially apprehensive Hirschfield had brought him even.

They were heady times. On April 2, 1969, Berte Hirschfield's thirtieth birthday, a party was held for two dozen people in the private dining room of a Palm Springs restaurant. At the appointed moment, Frank Sinatra rose and sang "The Lady Is a Tramp," "Thoroughly Modern Millie," and "But Beautiful," with special lyrics written for the occasion by Sammy Cahn.

> (Tune: *The Lady Is a Tramp*)
> There's no one like her, but no one at all,
> She's got a smile that's a smile to recall,
> The kind of charm that is like wall to wall,
> I mean the lady is a champ.
>
> Back home in Scarsdale they smile and they glow,
> To think that Berte wound up with such dough,
> They thought the guy that she chose was a "schmo"
> Which proves the lady is a champ.
>
> But she chose wisely, as we all know,
> The records show, he is—a whiz—
> Especially when they lower the lamp,
> Which proves the lady is a champ.

The early seventies were relatively quiet for the Hirschfields. They had moved from a Park Avenue apartment to a three-story home on five acres in Scarsdale. Gradually they spent less time in Palm Springs in the winter and more time skiing. After Alan's difficult year at Warner Bros.-Seven Arts, he took a job managing the Allen family's personal assets—a vast array of securities, real estate, and other holdings. He also performed other tasks for the Allens—some of which were quite novel. For example, the Ogden Corporation, in which the Allens owned a controlling interest, once made a deal to buy the "21" Club for Ogden stock worth ten million dollars at the time. Ogden, a decidedly unglamorous conglomerate, included among its diverse holdings a "limited menu" restaurant chain called Doggie Diner. Charlie Allen was not pleased by the prospect of Ogden's owning "21," which had been a vital part of his life for decades, a cherished haven of almost daily sustenance—psychological and otherwise. However, Charlie did not know how to stop the deal. It was not his style to interfere directly in the affairs of companies he controlled. Moreover, his relationship with the head of Ogden had been strained even before the "21" deal arose. Charlie Allen, therefore, sought the counsel of Alan Hirschfield.

Hirschfield thought about the matter and decided that "21" probably was worth more than Ogden was proposing to pay. The many valuable Remington paintings on the restaurant's walls, not to mention its other extraordinary accoutrements, likely made the place worth considerably more than ten million dollars. Hirschfield's analysis made sense to Charlie Allen. The message was conveyed ever so subtly to the management of "21," which valued Charlie's patronage as much as he valued the restaurant. There was discomfort all around. The deal was all but final. Everyone waited, however, and finally, after eighteen months, the deal scotched itself when the market value of the Ogden stock in question fell below the stipulated level. Ogden claimed the purchase was only "suspended," but it was never revived. Charlie Allen was relieved, and although Alan Hirschfield's advice in a sense had been rendered unnecessary by falling stock prices, Charlie knew he could always count on Alan for sage counsel. Furthermore, Charlie never stopped cautioning the owners of "21" against selling the restaurant for too low a price. Twelve years later, in 1982, they still had not sold, despite many opportunities.

* * *

Herbert Allen, Jr., meanwhile, divorced Laura Parrish, settled at the Carlyle, and began an active bachelor life as a man about Manhattan and Southampton. He dated the *most* beautiful actresses and models in New York and, indeed, it seemed to some of his friends that he was a bit compulsive about the physical standards he set for his women. He would mull over fine points of physique with cronies and would shun a woman for such minor failings as exposing what he considered to be too much of her gums when she smiled. A skillful flirt, Herbert employed tools of flirtation not available to every man. He once encountered Amanda Burden (William Paley's stepdaughter) at a party and heard her complaining about a speeding ticket. She had been stopped while driving from Manhattan to eastern Long Island; it was her second offense, and she feared losing her driver's license. Herbert offered to try to help if Amanda could tell him the judge or court with jurisdiction over the case. Amanda produced the summons, and Herbert took it into the next room and made a phone call. (Though he wasn't explicit with Amanda, he knew a man at Allen & Company who claimed to be able to fix traffic tickets.) Reappearing a few moments later, Herbert said everything had been taken care of. Amanda could forget about going to court. She was extremely impressed and thought the gesture very sweet. Some time later Herbert asked her to have dinner with him, and a brief romance ensued. (Unfortunately for Amanda, however, Herbert's fixer proved to be ineffectual. She eventually received a follow-up summons and had to appear in court and pay a fine anyway.)

Some people, including Alan Hirschfield, felt that Herbert was given too much responsibility at Allen & Company too soon, having been made president at age twenty-seven as his uncle and father began to take less active roles. Although Herbert enjoyed some success, the skeptics were proved at least partially correct in the late sixties and early seventies when the firm, under Herbert junior's leadership, became involved in a number of business deals that soured and drew investigations by the Securities and Exchange Commission and allegations of fraud against Allen & Company and others. Some of the problems arose from Herbert's association with a group of men who were to be numbered among the most celebrated stock-market promoters of the period. Most of them were based in Beverly Hills, dabbled in the movie business, and loved the Hollywood high life. There was Burt Kleiner of Kleiner, Bell &

Company, the most flamboyant brokerage firm in the nation for a few years until the SEC and the New York and American Stock Exchanges, in a unique coordinated assault one day in 1970, banished the Kleiner firm from the securities business. There was Gene Klein, the former used-car salesman who controlled the National General Corporation (movie theaters, insurance, publishing, and fried chicken). There was Del Coleman of Parvin-Dohrmann (Vegas casinos) and Commonwealth United (movies, vending machines, juke boxes, real estate, and insurance). There was Allen Manus, a Canadian promoter whose activities were under almost constant scrutiny by law-enforcement authorities. All of these men or their companies sooner or later were enjoined by courts from violating U.S. securities laws.

In one celebrated case, the SEC in 1973 accused the General Host Corporation, a large food concern; its chairman, Harris Ashton; Allen & Company Incorporated; Kleiner, Bell & Company; Allen Manus; the National General Corporation and its chairman, Gene Klein, of participating in an elaborate scheme to gain control of Armour & Company, the big Chicago meat packer, by fraudulent means. As happens in most such cases, the defendants consented to court injunctions against securities law violations without admitting or denying the SEC's charges. Fraud and manipulation charges against Allen & Company Incorporated were dropped, although the firm was enjoined from violating other laws.

Apart from finding the Burt Kleiners of the world amusing, Herbert Allen's association with them clearly was a manifestation of the same family streak of fierce image-be-damned independence which led his Uncle Charlie to go into business with ex-convict Wallace Groves in the Bahamas. Allen & Company's philosophy essentially was: No one tells us how or with whom to do business. As Herbert reportedly would have occasion to say later to *The New York Times*, "We trade every day with hustlers, deal makers, shysters, con men. . . . That's the way businesses get started. That's the way this country was built."*

----

*Although Herbert Allen did not disavow this statement when it was published, he did so four years later when asked specifically about it. In any case, the reader should not infer that the words "hustlers," "shysters," and "con men" necessarily refer to the individuals named in the preceding paragraphs. The degrees of wrongdoing of which they were accused varied considerably from case to case. For example, while Wallace Groves was convicted of crimes, Burt Kleiner's firm was accused of civil violations of federal securities laws.

Some of those who denigrated Herbert's abilities as a businessman noted that he often seemed tense and ill at ease. Usually, however, those were misperceptions. While Herbert's slightly sunken eyes appeared to reveal fatigue and worry, they normally did not. Herbert's eyes were an inherited physical characteristic which rarely revealed anything about his moods. And if he was brusque, if he stood and sat stiffly erect, never slouching, it was not so much because he was tense as because he had a high energy level and a short attention span. Ninety seconds into almost any conversation, Herbert would start to fidget. He was intolerant of interruptions of his daily regimen, which was as ordered as it had been in college. He went to bed early, got up early, and ate his meals early. Through style fad after style fad, year after year, he dressed fashionably but very conservatively in meticulously tailored clothes, and kept his dark-brown hair short. There was a punctiliousness about him, an exactitude, that the women he dated found attractive. They knew where they stood with him. He told them where to be and when. He was not a fussbudget, but was simply consistent and dependable to a fault—a man trying his best to be in control and usually succeeding. Perhaps as a psychological compensation for the risks he took in business, he made it a point to control every other aspect of his life to the extent that he could. He controlled his emotions. He controlled most conversations. He controlled his women. Although his sense of humor was intact and emerged often, he was essentially a serious, pragmatic, and cynical man, who took pride in having few illusions.

Herbert Allen's role in the life of Ray Stark had evolved over two decades from that of the bright young nephew of Ray's friend Charlie Allen, to that of surrogate son after Ray's own son's apparent suicide, to that of Ray's best friend in all the world. The relationship eluded easy explanation. The surrogate-son role seemed natural enough, but it was unclear why it went well beyond that. Ray and Herbert both were cautious men, and were wary about personal relationships. Perhaps they found it easier to trust someone a quarter of a century older or younger than to trust their own peers. Whatever the explanation—and any explanation would be a considerable oversimplification—the relationship was genuine, durable, and as close as a friendship could be. Ray and Herbert saw each other often and spoke by telephone at least once daily, month in and month out, year in and year out, no matter where on the globe they happened to be.

It was natural, therefore, that when Ray Stark became concerned in 1973 about the financial condition of Columbia Pictures, he would turn first to Herbert Allen. Stark first broached the subject early in the year when Columbia's stock was trading at nine dollars; he mentioned the problem again in March when the stock hit seven dollars. In June, after the price had fallen to four dollars, he became insistent. Charlie and Herbert senior opposed any involvement but left the decision to Herbert junior, who was eager at least to explore the possibility of investing in Columbia. Along with Alan Hirschfield, he evaluated the company's problems, and then proceeded to convince the banks, which were considering forcing Columbia into bankruptcy, that new management could save the company. Hirschfield and Allen also gained the confidence of the largest shareholder, Matthew Rosenhaus, the pharmaceuticals tycoon who had bought into the company in the sixties, and of Serge Semenenko, who was on the board of directors as well. Ray Stark arranged a meeting between Herbert Allen and the incumbent Columbia management, and in July, Allen & Company in effect took control of Columbia Pictures.

President Leo Jaffe, who had been at the company since 1930, stayed on as the board chairman, but the power flowed to Herbert Allen, who went on the board of directors, to Alan Hirschfield, who was made president, chief executive officer, and a director, and to Ray Stark, who was acknowledged to be the "master architect" of the takeover, even though he did not become an officer or director. Once inside, the new regime found Columbia's condition even worse than it had appeared from a distance. The company declared a $50 million loss for fiscal 1973.

Less than a month after becoming president, Alan Hirschfield, at the instigation of Ray Stark, and with the full support of Herbert Allen, named David Begelman, then fifty-one years old, to head the motion-picture operations. Later, Hirschfield hired Clive Davis to run Columbia's phonograph-record unit, even though Davis had been fired as head of CBS Records for misappropriation of funds and was under federal indictment for income tax evasion. Despite his legal problems, Davis was an acknowledged talent in the record business, and Hirschfield believed that Davis, like David Begelman, could make money for Columbia Pictures Industries.

"What if Clive goes to jail?" Herbert Allen asked Hirschfield.

"Then he'll run it from Danbury [a federal prison in Connecticut]," Hirschfield replied, only half in jest. Allen again supported Hirschfield's decision. Davis got off with a fine and suspended prison sentence.

The Allen takeover of Columbia gave Ray Stark enormous influence. Although Stark and Herbert Allen spoke daily on the phone, often about business, it was Alan Hirschfield, as the chief executive of the company, who was placed in the position of actually conducting business with Stark. They had known each other well for a decade, of course, and while Hirschfield admired Stark's ability as a producer, he always had been wary of some of Ray's business practices. Stark was extremely aggressive and never failed fully to exploit every situation to the maximum advantage for him personally. While still a full-time salaried officer of Seven Arts, Stark had begun, independently of Seven Arts, to develop various theater and film projects stemming from the life and career of Fanny Brice. The projects included *Funny Girl* and were to make use of Barbra Streisand. Although his contract with Seven Arts permitted this independent activity, some members of the Seven Arts board felt that conflicts of interest were inevitable and that Stark was taking undue advantage of his freedom. There were heated, protracted arguments, and Stark finally decided to leave Seven Arts just before it merged with Warner Bros.

When Hirschfield became president of Columbia Pictures, he knew that Stark's relationship with the company might cause pain as well as pleasure, and decided to assert his authority immediately. Ray had nearly completed *The Way We Were* with Streisand and Redford for release in late 1973 and was preparing to begin *Funny Lady*. Hirschfield examined Stark's deal with Columbia and was not surprised to find that while the terms were very lucrative for Stark, they were not as lucrative as Hirschfield felt they should be for Columbia, particularly in view of its precarious financial status. He also was dismayed to see that the studio had not been enforcing strict controls on production expenses for Stark's films.

On Thursday, September 6, 1973, only six weeks after Hirschfield had been named president and only three weeks after David Begelman had become studio head, Hirschfield dictated a memorandum to Begelman about the "Ray Stark Relationship."

"When you are in New York on your forthcoming trip I believe it important to discuss fully the Ray Stark situation as to specific projects as well as the overall nature of our deal with him. It makes no sense to me whatsoever to be spending the kind of money we are for production and ending up with 35 percent of the profits after substantial gross participations. I also feel that the overheads he is incurring need revising and trimming in accordance with our policy as far as all outside producers are concerned.

"We also have to come to grips with the *Funny Lady* situation as soon as possible." (Hirschfield went on to question the wisdom of keeping the *Funny Lady* project at Columbia, in view of the relatively small amount of money the studio stood to make from what inevitably would be a large expenditure.)

Begelman promised to do his best, but eleven months later, with principal photography completed and the film in the editing room, Hirschfield was still fretting about a lack of effective control over Stark's spending.

"Now that this picture is completed, the most difficult job all of us have is holding down additional expense," he wrote to Begelman in August of 1974. "It appears to me that the cost could rise substantially if the producer is allowed to have free rein of continuing expenditures. At some point someone is going to have to say no to some of the requests or all of the very good efforts that were made to hold down costs during production will be overshadowed by the post-production expenditures. I believe it is important that a very hard line be taken in this regard."

Of course, Stark knew of Hirschfield's memos to Begelman, and occasionally Ray and Alan clashed directly. Prior to the release of *Funny Lady* they fought over the terms of the contract covering that picture as well as others. They sometimes fought over the substantive merit of particular movie projects. (When Hirschfield said he wasn't fond of Stark's concept for filming Neil Simon's *The Sunshine Boys*, Stark took it to MGM, where it became a modest success, starring Walter Matthau and George Burns.) Their most bitter and protracted dispute, however, was over Hirschfield's determination to change and improve Columbia's method of, and attitude toward, the distribution, marketing, and advertising of motion pictures—an attitude that had been prevalent in the industry for decades and had changed relatively little by the 1970s.

To many producers, the process of marketing the average movie (they believed there was such a thing) was very simple: You opened it at Loew's Tower East on the East Side of Manhattan, Loew's Astor Plaza in Times Square, the Bruin in the affluent Westwood area of Los Angeles, and the Chinese on Hollywood Boulevard. You took full-page ads in *The New York Times* and the *Los Angeles Times* beginning a few days before the movie opened and extending a week into its run. If the movie did poorly, you doubled the ad budget. No motion picture was so bad that it could not be sold to the public by an aggressive studio advertising department. Money, since it was the studio's, was no object to the producer.

Alan Hirschfield wanted to change all that. He was determined to bring some of the same modern techniques to the marketing of films that were being used throughout the American economy to market detergents, toiletries, beer, and other products—techniques such as market research, to try to determine just who might want certain products and why; regional analysis, to try to determine what parts of the country might be most receptive to a particular film; and strict controls on ad budgets, to ensure that a full-page ad was not run if a half-page ad would suffice. While not advocating neglect of the crucial New York and Los Angeles markets, Hirschfield wanted to focus more attention on motion-picture audiences in the vast area "between the mountains" as Hollywood put it (the Appalachians in the East and the Rockies and Sierras in the West)—places like Kansas City, Denver, Cleveland, Miami, Dallas, Phoenix, and a hundred other large and medium-sized cities which represented many millions of dollars in potential film revenue but which often had been slighted by the advertising strategists of Hollywood.

Ray Stark did not object to the general principles that Hirschfield espoused, but he found much to criticize about the particular ways in which Columbia marketed his films, and about the people making Columbia's advertising decisions. When *Funny Lady* was being prepared for release, Stark hired two "producer's representatives" to monitor Columbia's advertising and marketing planning. The move incensed Hirschfield; in a memo to Stark on September 13, 1974, he called it a "demeaning gesture to all concerned here at Columbia."

Stark's retort to Hirschfield was typical—long-winded, preachy, patronizing, alternately self-righteous and cynical—the reply of a powerful, sixty-year-old Hollywood impresario to a man he still considered a green and insufficiently deferential Wall Street upstart.

"Friday the 13th would not necessarily seem the likeliest day for you to write me a memo," Stark began. "So, with my usual compassion, I will briefly answer you and then let Gerry Lipsky and Bob Mirisch [Stark's lawyers] leisurely get into the specifics. . . . Does Columbia have anything to hide? Are they afraid someone else may come up with a better or more viable [marketing] suggestion? . . . Yes, I am happy with the [general marketing] decisions you have made and, certainly, I have expressed this not only to you privately but publicly. One day you might find out that this is one of the reasons you are ending up with a lot of the [movie] products you are now getting. My support of Columbia in this town has been a helluva lot more important to helping you acquire product than you may realize. . . . If you would be kind enough to check your facts, Alan, you would find that the term 'producer's representative' is not the manifestation of my troubled mind. For years, top producers (and this is a category that I humbly admit to) have had producer representatives. . . . I believe the success of a picture, Alan, is contingent upon the whole rather than any individual elements. I welcome Columbia's executive advice as to the creative areas of my productions. Your advertising department and I have found a very happy and productive relationship through communications. I know that after you have read this letter you will agree that there is no Frankenstein replacing the lady holding the torch for Columbia Distribution. All we want to do is help make *Funny Lady* the richest lady in the world."

If Hirschfield at times seemed overmatched by Stark, at least Ray was learning that Alan wasn't a pushover. And both men rather enjoyed the parry and thrust. Stark, in particular, had always preferred a stimulating antagonist to a dull friend. He loved to spray incendiary memos around Hollywood and New York: bitchy, gushy, wicked, funny memos. And Hirschfield, still a little unsure of himself but determined to keep up, felt compelled to try to match Stark jab for jab, memo for memo, even joke for joke.

Although the Stark-Hirschfield relationship remained sporadically antagonistic, it had become somewhat more stable and comfortable by 1977. Hirschfield knew better than most how much Stark's ability as a producer had helped Columbia, and Stark knew that Hirschfield's ability as a financial executive not only had helped the company but had helped Stark to enrich himself by keeping the company intact. They still enjoyed each other's company. Ray, with one of his women friends in tow, occasionally visited the Hirschfield home in Scarsdale. The informality of the place and of the Hirschfield family was a welcome relief from the stiff and formal atmosphere of Ray's own home in Bel-Air. He gave Christmas presents to the Hirschfield children, and even gave Alan and Berte his special recipe for charcoal-broiled steak marinated in Jack Daniel's and honey.

Still, the wariness between the two men never stopped infecting their relationship. Stark had grown uncomfortable after he realized that Hirschfield intended to involve himself actively in the affairs of the studio (including Stark's own contract with it) rather than let David Begelman run the studio without interference from New York. And Hirschfield still worried about the degree of Stark's power at Columbia. One of the reasons Alan was glad that the studio had come up with such non-Stark successes as *The Deep*, *Tommy*, *Shampoo*, and *Taxi Driver* was his belief that these films tended to dilute Stark's influence.

Hirschfield, however, was certainly astute enough to know that Stark's role in the company remained important and singular—so much so that it would have been unnatural not to summon Ray Stark to the Carlyle Hotel on the morning of Wednesday, September 21, 1977, for advice on what to do about the revelation that David Begelman had embezzled thousands of dollars from the Columbia studio.

After all, Ray Stark and David Begelman's relationship with each other went back many years, predating either's relationship with Herbert Allen or Alan Hirschfield.

THIRTEEN

Ray Stark stared at his two friends for a long second.

He was shocked, he said, very shocked. Why would David do such a thing? *How* could he do such a thing?

Ray told Alan and Herbert that he knew of no gambling problems or other hidden needs that might have driven Begelman to steal. "It isn't a lot of money—there must be some explanation," he suggested.

"The amount of money isn't the problem, it's the nature of the acts," Hirschfield insisted. "These are premeditated acts of forgery. God knows how many more there might be. How do you have a guy who appears to be a crook running a company? We've got no choice. We've got to get rid of him, or at least suspend him until we investigate and find out the extent of this."

"There's no need to panic, Alan," Stark cautioned. "Surely there's an explanation. Have you talked to David? Is he coming in?"

"We're going to try to get him in tonight or tomorrow," Herbert said. "We weren't able to reach him yesterday."

Stark paused. "Alan, let me make you a proposition," he said. "If you feel you must suspend David and have an investigation, I would be willing, against all my normal instincts, to take over the chores of running the studio, at no salary, for the period of weeks or months the investigation takes. I could turn over power of attorney for my company to someone else, or whatever is necessary, to eliminate any conflict of interest."

Hirschfield smiled. Stark's proposal was perhaps the most ludicrous idea he had heard in his entire business career. The conflicts of interest in Stark's running the studio—real as well as perceived—obviously would be enormous, despite any transfer of power of attorney, or any other technical protective maneuver. The other producers on the Columbia lot would rise up in armed revolution.

But Hirschfield didn't state his feelings. He said: "That's a very generous gesture, Ray, but I'll have to think about it. This is a very confused situation, and there are lots of things we have to consider. It's probably best if I keep my own hand on the tiller out there for the time being. And Danny's pretty well in place by now anyway.* But thanks, it's very generous of you."

Hirschfield got up and went to the bathroom, still shocked by Stark's suggestion. Ray's powerful influence at the studio was worrisome enough as it was. To permit him actually to run the studio, even for a week, would constitute a gross dereliction of duty by Hirschfield and make Columbia the laughingstock of Hollywood. Was anyone naïve enough to believe that Ray under such circumstances would, or even could, in fact relinquish control over his own film projects, while at the same time approve or reject other people's movies? Conflict of interest, indeed! The studio itself would become one huge conflict of interest. What balls the man has even to suggest it with a straight face! Hirschfield mused.

In the den, meanwhile, Herbert was saying: "You running the studio is a great idea. I'd have jumped at it."

"Herbie, we just saw a demonstration of something important—something that shouldn't be missed," Ray said. "This is Alan's way of saying he wants the studio for himself. He wants to make movies."

"Oh, I don't think so. He knows as well as anyone that's the quickest way to destroy yourself in this business—to be in a position where you can get blamed directly for a run of bad pictures. Where he is now, he can't get blamed directly. David has to take the heat. Besides, Alan wouldn't know how to run the studio."

"You're wrong, Herbie. You mark my words. The man wants to make movies. This business has gone to his head. I've seen this coming. You just watch the way he handles the situation."

Hirschfield returned to the den, and he and Stark left the apartment together. Herbert was to try to reach David and summon him to New York. Stark was to talk with David as soon as he arrived and be available for further consultations. Neither Stark nor Hirschfield expressed his true feelings as they parted on Seventy-sixth Street. Ray said he would do anything he could to help, but he was angry

---

*Dan Melnick, who had joined the Columbia studio as head of motion picture production under Begelman just a few months earlier.

that Hirschfeld hadn't accepted his offer to run the studio. Alan thanked Ray again, but he continued to marvel at the brazenness of the suggestion.

Had Hirschfeld known certain other facts that Stark did not reveal that morning, he would have been more amazed and troubled. For Stark's relationship with Begelman was even closer than Hirschfeld imagined.

Herbert Allen telephoned Hirschfeld just before noon. The handwriting expert had reported. "You can never be absolutely sure," the man said, "but it would be a miracle if the endorsement on the Robertson check was anyone's other than Begelman's."

Joe Fischer and Herbert Allen drew the onerous task of taking Matty Rosenhaus to lunch that day and breaking the news about the embezzlements. Sixty-five years old, silver-haired and distinguished-looking, Matthew B. Rosenhaus owned the largest single block of Columbia stock—about 9 percent, slightly more than the Allens owned. There was no contest for control, however. Herbert had cultivated Matty skillfully since the Allens had bought into the company four years earlier. The older man was very fond of Herbert and generally deferred to his judgments. After all, Matty's 700,000-plus shares had risen in value from about $1.5 million to more than $10 million since the new management had taken over.

Rosenhaus had become rich as head of the J.B. Williams Company, the maker of Geritol, whose "tired blood" advertising had been attacked by the Federal Trade Commission for well over a decade as misleading, and finally prompted a record-setting fine against Rosenhaus's company.* Rosenhaus had grown even richer, however, when the company was purchased by Nabisco. He had been induced to buy his Columbia stock in the late sixties by Serge Semenenko of the First National Bank of Boston, a close friend who occupied a neighboring apartment at the Pierre Hotel. Even though Rosenhaus was sixty-five, he had no plans to retire, and continued to serve as president of Williams, vice chairman of Nabisco, and chairman of Columbia Pictures Industries' executive committee. He was an ener-

---

*Although it did not admit any wrongdoing, J.B. Williams had agreed to pay a total of $280,000 in penalties to settle FTC cases which originated in 1962 and covered Geritol and another Williams product. On the occasion of the final payment in 1976, the FTC said the penalty was the largest ever in a false-advertising case.

getic man and a natty dresser, and his life had assumed a new dimension a few years earlier when he married Gila Golan, an actress and former Miss Israel who was much younger than he. Matty had promptly fathered three daughters, Sarita, Hedy, and Loretta. (He had three children from a previous marriage.)

Although Matty's general attitude toward Columbia Pictures' policies was guided by Herbert, he did not shrink from expressing strong opinions about particular management decisions. An emotional, fustian man, his praise was lavish and his criticism harsh. At board meetings it was his style to deliver sermons rather than engage in discussions.

Hearing about Begelman from Fischer and Allen over lunch at Lutèce, Matty began to weep. "My God, this is a tragedy. Does David know what he's done to himself? He must be sick."

"We know very little at this point but we're trying as hard as we can to find out what the facts are, and then do the right thing," Fischer offered.

"That fool! Something must be terribly wrong with him. He must have cracked up. We've got to help him. We've got to save him! This is a terrible tragedy for him, for the company!"

"We're trying to keep it from becoming that," Herbert said. "We'll do everything we can."

"It's a terrible, terrible tragedy," Matty said through his tears.

In his Wilshire Boulevard office that morning after a late-night arrival from New York, Mickey Rudin got a firsthand briefing from Detective Joyce Silvey. Then he telephoned Leonard Wasserstein, the vice president in charge of the twenty Wells Fargo Bank branches on the west side of Los Angeles, including those in Beverly Hills. Wasserstein, whose office was just a block up Camden Drive from Rudin's in the same building where the Cliff Robertson check had been cashed, had had a close business relationship with Rudin for many years. Wasserstein summoned Joe Lipsher, who had approved the Robertson transaction, and instructed him to give Rudin all the pertinent details. Rudin telephoned the information, which essentially confirmed what was already known or suspected, to Joe Fischer, who took the opportunity to tell Rudin that they were summoning Begelman to New York that afternoon. Would Mickey talk to David before he left? Rudin said he would.

*   *   *

Alan Hirschfield, relieved that someone else was confronting Matty Rosenhaus and calling David Begelman, was in his office taking congratulatory calls about his Brandeis award and attending to a variety of other matters.

"The company was great, and the speech was great, but the dinner was lousy, so you owe me a dinner," said William Thompson, the senior vice president of the First National Bank of Boston, the lead bank of the group with whom Columbia had its bank credit. Neither Thompson nor any of the other callers knew of the Begelman problem, and Hirschfield said nothing.

With the Robertson and Choate embezzlements documented and redocumented, it was clear that Columbia had to take decisive action. Hirschfield met again in the afternoon with Fischer and Todd Lang, and none of the three doubted that Begelman would have to be suspended. Perhaps he would have to be fired summarily. Fischer, who tended to favor the latter course, was concerned that Matty Rosenhaus at lunch had seemed more interested in "saving David" than in what might be best for the company overall.

In a projection room on the Burbank lot, David Begelman sat with production chief Dan Melnick and Bill Tennant, a studio vice president, watching a new George Peppard film which Columbia was considering leasing from its producer and distributing. The telephone next to Begelman buzzed softly.

"I'll take it upstairs," he said into the phone.

He rose and said to Melnick and Tennant: "You have my proxy."

Herbert Allen waited on the line while Begelman made his way up the two flights to his office. "There appears to be a serious problem with you, David," Herbert said. "Is it as serious as I'm being told it is?"

Begelman was trembling slightly, his voice quaking. "Yes, I guess it is."

"Could you come in and talk to us about it?"

"I'll come this evening."

"Fine, David, I think it's best if we have a full discussion. That's the only way we can help you."

A moment later Joe Fischer called and asked that Begelman stop at Mickey Rudin's office on his way to the airport.

When the Peppard film ended an hour later, Dan Melnick and Bill

Tennant returned to the executive suite and asked David's secretary where he was.

"He's gone to New York. Herbert Allen called and he went to New York."

Melnick was surprised, but Tennant remembered that Begelman had made enough sudden trips to New York over the years to have been known as "The Phantom" when he was an agent. Melnick and Tennant put the sudden disappearance out of their minds.

Begelman declined Mickey Rudin's offer of coffee or a soft drink. They had known each other for many years, but only casually, and Rudin did not prolong the conversation. He explained that Columbia Pictures had asked him to look into the Cliff Robertson and Peter Choate matters, and that it would be wise if David retained a lawyer. Begelman was so visibly upset that Rudin offered to have his driver take him to the airport. David said he could make it on his own. He caught the 4:30 American flight to JFK.

Alan Hirschfield's parents had come up from Oklahoma City for the Brandeis event the night before, and were staying over in Scarsdale for a few days. After dinner, Alan took Norman into the privacy of the den and told him for the first time about the Begelman problem. Alan felt himself becoming mired in the complexities that seemed to be involved in the proper handling of the matter. To Norman, however, it was all quite clear:

"You're a public corporation, kiddo. I've been an officer of a public corporation for a long time. You can't have a thief around you. It doesn't make any difference how or what he steals. It contaminates all concerned. And you'd better let the SEC know what the hell's going on."

After a few minutes, Todd Lang, whom Alan had asked to drop by (he lived only two minutes away), joined the conversation. Although they did little more than commiserate with each other, Lang underscored the explosive nature of the problem confronting Columbia. The entertainment industry is the most visible industry in the world. Once a scandal becomes known, it will get ten times the publicity, and cause ten times the embarrassment, of a comparable scandal in the steel industry, or the computer industry, or the shoe industry. Columbia had to be absolutely certain that when the Begelman matter became public, as it almost certainly would eventually, the company had observed all laws—the unwritten laws of propriety as well as the written laws of fraud—in the strictest and most conscientious way.

The Allen & Company limousine stopped outside the American Airlines baggage area at half past midnight. Herbert Allen took the escalator to the upper level, passed through the security screen, and headed toward the designated gate. His mood was sour. It was two hours past his usual bedtime, and he was tired. More important, he had wanted Hirschfield to accompany him to meet Begelman as a demonstration that the company was united in its compassion for a valued officer in trouble. But Alan had declined, reminding Herbert that Todd Lang felt it best that contact with Begelman be limited, because of the legal delicacy of the situation, to an official confrontation scheduled for Thursday morning at Herbert's apartment—a meeting at which Todd would preside. Alan had even tried to dissuade Herbert from going to the airport, but Herbert was impatient with Lang's caution and determined to question Begelman himself before the lawyers had at him. The more he pondered what David apparently had done, the less sense it made.

David looked even worse than Herbert had imagined that he might—pale, slightly unkempt, and obviously nervous—a stunning contrast to his usual spiffy, controlled mien. In the limo, Herbert closed the sliding window behind the chauffeur as the vehicle pulled into the Manhattan-bound traffic.

"Well, David, I'm sure you'll agree that the time has come for candor all around. It's time to open up. We're your friends. You've been wonderful to us, and we're prepared to be as good to you as we can be under the circumstances. If we have a problem, let's deal with it together, okay?"

"Okay."

"The first thing we need are the facts—all of them. What about this check? The Cliff Robertson check. Is it your endorsement?"

"I guess it must be, but I have no recollection of writing it."

"Why would you do something like that?"

"I don't know."

"You could have borrowed ten thousand dollars—from me, or anyone."

"I just can't explain it."

"What about this thing with the architect, Choate? That makes no sense to me at all."

"I'm sorry. I know it seems impossible to believe, but I can't come up with a logical, or even an illogical explanation, for any of this."

"Do you remember the Choate thing?"

"Only dimly."

"Are we going to find other things when we look, other checks, other fake contracts?"

"No."

"How can you be sure if you can't remember these?"

"I'm not a thief, Herbert."

"I must tell you, David, that if these two items are all of it, we may be able to help you. But if we find more, you're finished, period. We can't have this sort of thing. No company can condone it, whatever the explanation or lack of one."

"There is no more."

"I hope not."

They passed the rest of the ride in silence, staring out into the New York night. Herbert Allen was deeply worried. Either Begelman was lying or he was mentally unstable. In either case, Herbert suspected that whatever investigation Columbia conducted would turn up more embezzlements, unless they had been concealed in some way. The basic illogic of what they knew so far was staggering. If someone were going to steal from a movie company, he wouldn't go about it in the way that Begelman apparently had, especially if he knew the company inside out—all its nooks and crannies all over the world—like David knew Columbia Pictures. David might have millions of dollars stashed away somewhere that no one would ever find. But if he did, why would he forge a single check, or draw up a single bogus contract?

Herbert also had begun to ponder another problem quite apart from embezzlement—how to replace David if it came to that. The studio presidencies were the most difficult jobs in Hollywood, and one need look no farther than the turnover rate to see how few people embodied the delicate mixture of diverse talents required to perform them successfully. It was relatively easy, Herbert felt, to fill the jobs above and below the studio head. There were enough people around who could run the corporation—essentially a matter of managing and fine tuning a financial structure. There were also a lot of people who could make a particular movie. But it took a very rare combination of abilities to coordinate the making of two or three dozen movies at once: to make judgments about rough cuts of those near completion; to divine whether a picture in mid-production is going well; to decide what to do about it if it is not; to choose just the right producer, director, writer, and cast for a particular project (it was astounding how many people were under the mistaken impression that the studio heads weren't involved in those decisions anymore); to choose the few worthy projects in the first place from the hundreds that come along, anticipating public tastes two years in the future; to maintain cordial and durable relationships in every segment of a community of inflated, distorted, temperamental people; to anticipate the effectiveness of advertising campaigns and release patterns, not only in America, but throughout Europe, Asia, and Latin America as well. Most of these judgments were subjective, and most of the criteria on which they were based were intangible and elusive. Running a studio had always been an arcane business, and when you added television to motion pictures, it became even more so. Begelman had proven that he was one of the very few people who was up to the task. Replacing him with someone as able would be extraordinarily difficult, and Herbert dreaded having to do it.

He dropped Begelman at the Carnegie House, where Columbia Pictures maintained one of its apartments for executives, at 2 A.M.

Thursday, September 22, was Yom Kippur, and although the Columbia offices were open, relatively few people were working. So as not to attract attention, it had been decided to convene the next meeting on the Begelman problem at Herbert Allen's Carlyle apartment at ten o'clock that morning.

Not many of the Columbia executives were particularly devout, but two of them—Joe Fischer and Victor Kaufman, the young inside legal counsel—were religious enough that it was unprecedented for them to work on Yom Kippur and miss attending temple on the holiest of Jewish holy days. Fischer had confided the reason to his wife. Kaufman, who had been told of the Begelman problem only the day before, was acutely conscious of the secrecy that still shrouded the matter and told his wife nothing.

Alan Hirschfield and Todd Lang drove down together from Scarsdale. Begelman arrived with two lawyers, Pete Pryor and

Gideon Cashman, whom he had used in the past mainly for handling entertainment contracts. Neither was a specialist in the law of public corporations. While Lang huddled with Cashman and Pryor in the den, Hirschfield, Fischer, Kaufman, and Begelman sat in the living room. Herbert Allen flitted back and forth between the two groups, frequently making or taking telephone calls. Barbara Rucker was in and out.

Although Allen had briefed Fischer and Hirschfield on his post-midnight conversation with Begelman, Todd Lang cautioned again that morning that no one except the lawyers should discuss the merits of the case with Begelman. The conversation in the living room, therefore, was extremely uncomfortable. These were men who had worked closely together for four years, who were accustomed to an easy, open relationship with each other; who spoke daily on the phone not only about the most confidential business matters but about the state of their personal lives; who had dined and drunk and laughed together in each other's homes; at "21," La Côte Basque, Lutèce, Orsini's, and the boardroom at 711 Fifth; at Chasen's, La Scala, Ma Maison, the Mandarin, La Serre, and the Burbank Studio commissary; in Cannes, Paris, London, Miami, and other cities; as well as in the first-class cabins of countless widebodied aircraft. Now, their talk was stiff, subdued, and bland. They chatted at length about the studio and current film projects, especially the surprising success of *The Deep* over the summer, and the anticipated success of *Close Encounters of the Third Kind*. There were even a few brittle jokes. When lunch was brought in, Begelman said, "I'd be happy to sign for that, but under the circumstances I guess it wouldn't look right."

In the den Begelman's lawyers had tried to convince Todd Lang that while their client's acts were reprehensible, he was deeply contrite, would make restitution, and would seek psychiatric care. Couldn't the matter be concluded simply on that basis, with David remaining in his job? Lang, shocked at such a suggestion, found it necessary to lecture them at length on the responsibilities and imperatives of public corporations, why the SEC must be informed, why Columbia had to launch a full investigation, and why Begelman almost certainly would have to be suspended or terminated. They finally agreed, and after several smaller meetings—Begelman with his lawyers, Lang with the Columbia executives—the full group assembled in the living room.

Lang recited the facts of the Cliff Robertson and Peter Choate embezzlements. Did Begelman have any explanation? Any comment? Begelman elaborated on what he had told Herbert Allen in the limousine.

"I have no logical explanation. I can't give you one. I can't even give myself one. It's like a nightmare. Some people's vice is drinking. Some people gamble. Some people use drugs. Some people have a voracious appetite for women. I wish those were my vices. If they were, I wouldn't be here today. I am here today because I apparently misappropriated funds in a highly improper manner which I cannot explain. I have no pressing need for money. I know that even if I did, I could borrow from any one of several people in this very room. My most painful guilt is that I have caused embarrassment and difficulty to you—some of my closest friends."

Lang explained that the company would have to conduct a full investigation of Begelman's administration of the studio's finances and of his personal finances. "We have to do it, and we have to do it thoroughly, David," Lang said. "If we don't, the SEC will do it for us. I'm sure you can understand that."

"I understand completely," Begelman replied, "and you shall have my complete cooperation. My only option at this point is to plead for your mercy. It may not mean much, but you have my solemn word that you will find nothing else that is improper. You have my word that if you can find it in your hearts to forgive me, you will not regret it. I will do everything in my power to prove to you that your confidence in me and your loyalty to me have not been misplaced."

Although Begelman had managed to inject a bit of poignance into the proceedings, nothing he said changed Hirschfield's and Fischer's conviction that his embezzlements almost certainly exceeded what had been discovered thus far. But they kept their suspicions to themselves as the discussion wore on. There was extended talk of what to tell the SEC, of when the investigation would begin, of investigative procedure, and of a press release. The meeting did not end until the sun was setting behind the mid-Manhattan skyline.

After the meeting at the Carlyle, Begelman took a taxi to the Dorchester on Fifty-seventh Street, where Ray and Fran Stark had maintained an apartment for many years. David and Ray decided to walk. They strolled over to Park, down Park to Fifty-sixth, across

Fifty-sixth to Lexington, up Lexington to Fifty-seventh, back across Fifty-seventh to Park, back down Park to Fifty-sixth, around the block again and again—seven or eight times in all. Though the conversation rambled, most of it boiled down to a repetition of two questions and two answers.

"David, how could you do this?"

"I swear I don't remember doing it."

"There's no other check or anything else is there?"

"On my honor, there is nothing. This is it. Period."

FOURTEEN

In the nine days since Detective Silvey's telephone call, the Begelman problem had been handled informally by a gradually expanding but still small number of key people (primarily Hirschfield, Fischer, Allen, Lang, and Rudin), who acted individually more than they acted as a group. To call them a group, in fact, would imply cohesion that did not exist. Confronted by a problem that none of them had ever encountered before, and guided by little more than instinct and common sense at that early stage, they functioned loosely, without structure, and essentially without leadership. The logical leader, Hirschfield, although he was deeply upset, made little effort to impose a strong unity of purpose on the actions and deliberations of the five. Herbert Allen, a possible alternative leader, took one or two mild initiatives, but did not try to usurp Hirschfield's role as the chief executive.

It is axiomatic that whenever a major problem arises in a large institution and is not solved quickly and informally, the institution eventually finds it necessary to confront the problem in a formal manner. If the institution has a problem-solving apparatus appropriate to the task, it is activated. If it doesn't, one is created. In either case, a large measure of control over the problem-solving process inevitably passes out of the hands of those who discovered the problem and into the hands of the apparatus. More people become involved, and formal procedures are marshaled. Although such steps can be desirable and wise, depending upon the nature of the problem, they invariably are accompanied by certain ancillary effects: Much of the flexibility and freedom of maneuver that existed prior to the activation of the formal process are lost after it is activated. The amount of time that must be devoted to the problem is increased; delay becomes likely. And issues that have little or no relationship to the substance of the problem have an opportunity to enter the process and affect the outcome.

On Friday, September 23, the David Begelman problem was institutionalized by Columbia Pictures Industries. At the time, the move came as a relief to Alan Hirschfield, whose considerable skills as a corporate executive had never included a strong facility for facing down acute crises involving other human beings. Eventually, however, he came to regret that Friday deeply and would continue to regret it for the rest of his life. For it was on that day that his company decided—formally and after lengthy deliberation—that two separate and distinct acts of major embezzlement were insufficient grounds for summarily firing David Begelman.

The nine men who gathered in Hirschfield's office at 11:30 that morning did not leave for six and a half hours, except to use Hirschfield's private bathroom. Lunch was brought in. The nine, comprising a quorum of the board of directors of Columbia Pictures Industries, included four people who previously had not been part of the continuing deliberations on the Begelman problem. They were Matty Rosenhaus, the bombastic Geritol magnate and Columbia's largest shareholder, who had been briefed over lunch two days earlier; Leo Jaffe, the shy Columbia board chairman who had been told nothing since Hirschfield informed him of the problem the previous Friday; Irwin Kramer, who was Charlie Allen's son-in-law, a member of the Columbia board, chairman of its audit committee, and executive vice president of Allen & Company*;

---

*Irwin Kramer was a curious figure at Allen & Company. Behind his gruff, cynical exterior he was a somewhat insecure man who had graduated from modest wealth to great wealth when he married Charlie Allen's daughter, Terry, an assertive woman whom many considered the brightest and in some ways the ablest member of her generation of the Allen family. Although Irwin was given the title of executive vice president at Allen & Company, he wielded less influence than others with the same or lesser titles and occasionally felt the frustration of being surrounded by people whom he perceived to be either smarter or richer than he was.

and Robert Werbel, an amiable and very able thirty-nine-year-old attorney for Allen & Company who had been asked to attend the meeting by Irwin Kramer and Herbert Allen.

Todd Lang, Joe Fischer, and Columbia lawyer Victor Kaufman also attended, as well as Hirschfield and Allen. Not invited were Ray Stark, who was still in town, and Mickey Rudin, who had returned to Los Angeles on Tuesday evening.†

In a thickening cloud of cigar smoke, the group reviewed every aspect of the Begelman matter, knowing that this meeting was different from previous ones. This meeting would not end until the board of directors of Columbia Pictures Industries had adopted a formal course of action—action that would be etched in the archives of the corporation forever and that soon would be subject to second-guessing by law-enforcement authorities, the Wall Street and Hollywood communities, and the public at large.

What should be done with David Begelman?

"We've got to figure out a way to help him," Matty Rosenhaus insisted.

"He ought to be fired and thrown in jail," said Irwin Kramer, a blunt, assertive, paunchy man of fifty-six, who rarely deliberated long before forming and stating opinions.

What would motivate David to steal?

"David has always lived on the financial edge," someone said. "There's no way he can meet Lew Rudin's standard of wealth." (David's wife, Gladyce, formerly had been married to Lewis Rudin—no relation to Mickey—a very rich New York real-estate tycoon.)

The discussion of what action to take against Begelman was protracted, but by the end, much of the spirit had ebbed from the argument that he had to be fired immediately. The majority of the group was persuaded by the notion that they did not yet have

---

†Also absent from the meeting were three other members of Columbia Pictures Industries' eight-man board of directors: David Begelman; Samuel Tedlow, a business associate of Matty Rosenhaus's; and James Wilmot, a friend of Herbert Allen's and, like Herbert, a major fundraiser for Democratic politicians. Wilmot was the chairman of Page Airways Incorporated, a Rochester, N.Y., concern, which was the worldwide sales agent for Gulfstream II jets. Wilmot was then under investigation by the Securities and Exchange Commission for paying millions of dollars in bribes overseas to obtain business for his company. One of the alleged bribes was a Cadillac convertible given to Ugandan dictator Idi Amin.

Generally, the Columbia board was not particularly distinguished, containing not a single independent lawyer, banker, or other voice staunchly independent of the corporation's vested interests as represented by Herbert Allen, Matty Rosenhaus, and the others who tended to be loyal to them.

sufficient information, even about the Cliff Robertson and Peter Choate embezzlements, on which to base definitive action. Thus, they chose to postpone a decision on Begelman's ultimate fate until after the investigation, and instead carve out an interim status for him. He was to resign from the board of directors of the corporation and from his corporate title of senior executive vice president. But he would remain in his most visible position as president of the studio. And he would continue to draw his full $4,500-a-week salary plus benefits.

Implicit in this decision was a judgment that if the Robertson and Choate thefts were the only ones found, Begelman could and should be treated differently from the way he would be treated if more thefts were found. That is, there was nothing inherent in the Robertson and Choate embezzlements themselves that required harsh and irrevocable action.

There was little disagreement about the need for a thorough investigation. The group decided that the inquiry appropriately fell under the aegis of Irwin Kramer as chairman of the board's audit committee, and should be conducted by Todd Lang's law firm, Weil, Gotshal & Manges, with assistance by Price Waterhouse & Co., the big CPA firm which handled Columbia's regular annual audits. Irwin Kramer, feeling very insecure because of his inexperience with such things, insisted that attorney Robert Werbel be permitted to advise him on his responsibilities and monitor the investigation as it proceeded. In effect, that meant Werbel would be second-guessing Todd Lang, a prospect that did not please Lang but about which he said nothing that afternoon.

Lang was to fly to Washington the following Tuesday to brief the SEC privately, and sometime after that a carefully worded press release would be issued.

David Begelman remained in New York to await the results of the board meeting. He sat alone down the hall from Hirschfeld's suite in an office designated for his use when visiting New York. Having been warned repeatedly that the company was about to launch an investigation at the studio, Begelman decided it would be foolish to postpone any longer a ruse he had devised for concealing another embezzlement which the company did not yet know about but which a thorough investigation almost certainly would discover. It was an embezzlement that surely would ruin him for good, even if the

Robertson and Choate thefts did not. Begelman managed to compose his voice to affect nonchalance and dialed the home number in Bel-Air of his close friend, Sy Weintraub. Weintraub had become a multimillionaire in the sixties by developing new Tarzan movies and owning Panavision, the optical process by which most motion pictures are made. In more recent years, Weintraub had lived quietly next door to Ray Stark, speculating in the silver market, buying race horses, and collecting ancient coins. He had accumulated one of the most valuable ancient-coin collections in the world, and had advised Gladyce Begelman on coin investments.

"Sy, I'm in New York. I need a favor," Begelman said.

"Of course, David."

"I wonder if you could accommodate me by letting me have the use of twenty-five thousand dollars."

"Of course. When do you need it? Will Monday morning be soon enough?"

"Monday morning would be fine. I would appreciate it if it could be drawn as a cashier's check, payable to Columbia Pictures."

"I'll take care of it."

"Thank you very much, Sy."

"Not at all. When are you coming back?"

"I'll be back tonight."

Begelman did not say, and Weintraub did not ask, what the money was for.

The only Columbia person Begelman saw after the board meeting was Matty Rosenhaus, who gave him a tearful recital of what had been decided. Begelman was aboard the seven o'clock TWA flight to Los Angeles, and managed to have a pleasant weekend. On Saturday evening, he and Gladyce attended a VIP screening of *Bobby Deerfield* at the Directors Guild. As *Newsweek* would later report, somewhat snidely, Begelman looked that night as if he "owned the town—which, in many ways, he did. He was riding high, universally respected, trim and handsome, a real doer. The man who turned around Columbia Pictures."

On Sunday morning, Joe Fischer flew to Boston, took a taxi to the Ritz-Carlton Hotel, and went to the sedate second-floor lounge where he had arranged to meet William Thompson, the senior vice president of the First National Bank of Boston and Columbia's principal banker.

Aside from Columbia Pictures' top officers and a couple of board members, no one played as crucial a role in the company's affairs in the 1970s as Bill Thompson. It wasn't unprecedented for a banker to be so important. Major banks had been active in the movie business since its beginnings. When the Great Depression hit Hollywood, at the same time as a pressing need for new capital to finance conversion of the studios to sound, Chase Manhattan (then called Chase National) and Morgan Guaranty came to the rescue. In the fifties, Chase was among the backers of Twentieth Century-Fox in developing the Cinemascope process. But banks in general were wary of movies, preferring to deal with industries whose products were more tangible and commercially dependable, and only two banks—the Bank of America and First of Boston—had maintained a strong and consistent presence in Hollywood over many decades. A $100,000 loan from A. P. Giannini of the Bank of America financed the birth of Columbia Pictures in 1920, and the Bank of America was still an important financier of the industry at large more than half a century later.* Columbia Pictures, however, had switched to the First of Boston in the late thirties after Serge Semenenko, who was to become the Boston bank's vice chairman, began making movie loans. Semenenko loved the picture business like no other, and by the seventies, the First of Boston was the principal bank for Warner Communications, Twentieth Century-Fox, Columbia, and several smaller companies in the United States, and for Lord Grade's company in England.

Bill Thompson had assumed responsibility for entertainment lending after Semenenko left the bank, and Thompson's influence was crucial in arranging the Allens' takeover of Columbia Pictures and the installation of Hirschfeld as chief executive officer. Thompson, delighted to see his judgment vindicated by Hirschfeld's success at rejuvenating Columbia, had developed a warm relationship with him and Fischer since the management change. It was for Hirschfeld and Fischer, therefore, that he felt his deepest sympathy when he heard the Begelman news in the Ritz-Carlton lounge. Thompson and Fischer talked for an hour about Columbia's plans for dealing with the Begelman problem, and then Fischer caught the shuttle back to New York.

---

*In 1932, when Frank Capra made *American Madness* for Columbia, he based the lead character, a benevolent banker played by Walter Huston, on A. P. Giannini. "All the other banks thought he was absolutely nuts, lending money on character," Capra recalled years later of Giannini. "He'd take collateral if you had it, but if you didn't and you had character, he'd lend you money anyhow."

*   *   *

Todd Lang, who was to oversee the Begelman investigation, spent several hours at his Scarsdale home that afternoon with the man who actually would go to Los Angeles and conduct the investigation, Peter Gruenberger, a Weil, Gotshal partner who specialized in litigation and the conduct of sensitive inquiries for corporate clients. Forty years old, married with a family in Scarsdale, Gruenberger had been born in Czechoslovakia, reared in the United States, and educated at the Columbia University Law School where he had made the law review. Gruenberger had a strong personality typical in some ways of lawyers who make their reputations as litigators. More comfortable on his feet in a courtroom than in an upholstered chair in a boardroom, more at home interrogating a witness than negotiating a corporate merger, Gruenberger was a spirited man, moody at times, quicker both to laughter and to anger than his more reserved brethren like Todd Lang. With dark hair and eyes, a dusky complexion, and an athletic build, Gruenberger possessed a minor physical quirk that occasionally worked to his professional advantage. His left eye diverged involuntarily to the left from his normal line of vision and his eyelid drooped slightly, giving an effect that some adversaries found distracting if not a bit menacing.

Peter Gruenberger not only had conducted other investigations of comparable sensitivity but also was qualified to confront the unique aspects of the Begelman affair. Having handled Columbia Pictures' litigation for years, he was intimately familiar with the company and, just as important, with the Hollywood community. This was not the ball bearing business in Cleveland, after all. There would probably be publicity and other kinds of problems that only Hollywood seemed to pose. Cor. ucting a discreet investigation of David Begelman, in his own town, surrounded by hundreds of his friends, would require special skills, including but not limited to quick wits, tenacity, and an ability to function in an environment that could occasionally be nonsensical. Todd Lang felt that if Peter Gruenberger could not handle it, no one could. They talked in Lang's living room until nearly sundown.

For Alan Hirschfield, who passed the day at his Scarsdale home just around the corner from Lang's, there was a pleasant little surprise to divert him from his gloom, if only for a moment. The widely read "Suzy" column in the New York *Daily News* on Sunday reported that:

Close Encounters of the Third Kind is Columbia Pictures' long in the making, millions in the spending, blockbuster movie of UFOs. It opens at the Ziegfeld Theater Nov. 15 under the chairmanship of multimillionaires Nathan Cummings, Mary Lasker and Mrs. S. Joseph Tankoos, Jr., as a benefit for the Cancer Research Institute. . . . Alan J. Hirschfield, president of Columbia Pictures and a trustee of the Cancer Research Institute, will be honored at a supper dance after the premiere at the Trianon Ballroom of the New York Hilton. To give you some idea of the prestige of the evening, these are the vice chairmen—Robert L. Bernstein, chairman of Random House; Edgar Bronfman, chairman of Joseph Seagram and Sons; Barry Diller, chairman of Paramount Pictures; Douglas Dillon, chairman of Dillon, Read and Co.; Walter Hoving, chairman of Tiffany and Co.; Donald Kendall, chairman of PepsiCo, Mr. and Mrs. Harding Lawrence (he's the head of Braniff; she's the head of Wells, Rich, Greene); John L. Loeb, Jr., partner in Loeb, Rhoades; Louis Nizer; William S. Paley, chairman of CBS; and Sue Mengers, the top Hollywood agent, a flying object who was identified a long time ago.

FIFTEEN

At home on Linden Drive in Beverly Hills, David Begelman also was preoccupied that Sunday. All of his options had become risky. If he did nothing, the investigators probably would discover the third embezzlement. Then again, they might miss it. If he carried out his concealment plan, it might work. Or the act of concealment itself might arouse suspicions and lead to discovery.

In some ways, the third embezzlement had been the most elaborate of all of Begelman's thefts. A little more than four months earlier—on Thursday, May 19—he had asked one of the studio lawyers, Leon Brachman, to prepare a contract calling for Columbia Pictures to pay $25,000 to a man named Pierre Groleau. The money was for "consulting" work on the marketing of two motion pictures that had been made in France, *Madame Claude* and *The Photographer*. The films were real enough, as was Pierre Groleau. But Groleau was not a marketing consultant and knew nothing of the work he was to do for Columbia because it was entirely bogus—a figment of David Begelman's imagination.

The contract was drafted to Begelman's specifications, a check for $25,000 was drawn to the order of Pierre Groleau, and both documents were delivered to Begelman's office. With the assistance of his friendly banker, Joe Lipsher, Begelman opened an account the next day in Groleau's name at the Wells Fargo Bank in Beverly Hills. The following Tuesday, May 24, Begelman wrote a check for $6,838 to himself on the Groleau account, signing Groleau's name on the front, and his own name on the back as the endorsement, and deposited the check in his own account. That same day, he wrote another check for $8,162 on the Groleau account, signing and endorsing it similarly, and sent it to the Margo Leavin Gallery, a small art gallery on Robertson Boulevard popular among the Beverly Hills elite. The second check was payment for four works of art which Begelman had purchased two weeks earlier—a Jasper Johns silk screen, an Arakawa lithograph, a Jerry McMillen acrylic, and a McMillen coil brass-leaf wall sculpture. Neither Groleau check was challenged by the bank.

David and Gladyce Begelman flew to New York on Wednesday, May 25, in preparation for the wedding of Gladyce's daughter the following Monday. They returned to Los Angeles on Wednesday, June 1, in time for the convention of Columbia's foreign sales executives, during which Begelman learned for the first time that Cliff Robertson's representatives were demanding an explanation of the IRS form indicating a $10,000 payment from Columbia Pictures that Robertson had never received. Two weeks later, having disseminated what he thought was a plausible alibi for the Robertson embezzlement, Begelman cleaned out the Pierre Groleau checking account and deposited the remaining $10,000 in his own account. He was unaware, of course, that on that same day Cliff Robertson was in Winnetka, Illinois, making a series of telephone calls which would promptly result in a report to the police that the Robertson check was a forgery.

Sitting at home on a Sunday three months later, facing an imminent investigation, Begelman decided to proceed with his plan for concealing the Pierre Groleau embezzlement. He drove to the Columbia Pictures building on the Burbank lot. Finding the premises deserted as he had expected, he proceeded to concoct a phony telex message, purportedly from Pierre Groleau in St. Tropez, canceling the consulting contract. He left the message on the desk of Leon Brachman, the same lawyer who had drafted the Groleau contract in May. On Monday morning, after Begelman's friend Sy Weintraub delivered the cashier's check for $25,000 that David had requested by phone from New York on Friday, Begelman sent the check along to Brachman with instructions to prepare a formal release from the Groleau contract.

Later in the day, when the cashier's check and the other documents reached the studio financial office (the last stop before deposit of the check in Columbia's bank account), Lou Phillips, the controller, sensed something peculiar. (Phillips had been extra vigilant, of course, since Joe Fischer's visit ten days earlier and the revelation that Begelman was suspected of embezzlement.) Although there was nothing overtly phony about the Groleau transaction—the original contract in May had not caught Phillips's attention—it seemed odd to him in retrospect that a marketing consultant for two minor French films would be retained by Begelman personally. The same sense of irregular procedure had led Phillips to question the Peter Choate contract. Still, Phillips felt that he probably was being excessively cautious when he took the Groleau material to Jim Johnson, the vice president for administration. It turned out, however, that the Groleau matter had caught Johnson's attention, too. When the original contract had crossed his desk in May, Johnson had thought it sufficiently peculiar to send a note about it to the head of Columbia Pictures' foreign marketing in New York. There had been no response to the note, and Johnson soon forgot about it. But Lou Phillips's independent suspicions, together with their heightened sensitivity to anything unusual in the wake of the other revelations, galvanized Johnson to further inquiry. He sent Phillips for a copy of the canceled $25,000 check that Begelman had requested in May. Though the endorsement "Pierre Groleau" did not look as much like Begelman's handwriting as the Cliff Robertson endorsement had, Johnson and Phillips were devastated to see that there was a distinct resemblance.

Who could Pierre Groleau be? Was it a phony name, or was Groleau a real but misrepresented person, as Peter Choate had turned out to be? Johnson and Phillips were baffled. Neither of them had ever heard the name.

Johnson telephoned Joe Fischer at his home in the New Jersey suburbs at seven o'clock Monday evening, Eastern time. Fischer, too, was unfamiliar with the name Pierre Groleau. He instructed Johnson to say nothing to Begelman and to get the Groleau material to Mickey Rudin's office in Beverly Hills immediately. Then Joe Fischer called Alan Hirschfield: "It looks like we may have another one."

Mickey Rudin hadn't heard of Pierre Groleau either. But Rudin's first move after receiving the Groleau file aroused further suspicions. An assistant whom he sent down the street to the address on the Groleau check—9465 Wilshire Boulevard—could find no trace of a Pierre Groleau. The name was not on the building registry and never had heen. Then Rudin established, through an informal channel, that Sy Weintraub was the purchaser of the cashier's check that Begelman had presented with the cancellation of the Groleau agreement. Although Rudin did not know that Weintraub was a friend of Begelman's, Rudin himself had known Weintraub casually for many years, and it struck him as strange that Sy Weintraub would have bought a cashier's check that David Begelman had used to cancel an obscure Columbia Pictures contract for work in France by a man with a Wilshire Boulevard address that appeared to be phony.

As Rudin sat at his octagonal conference table studying the documents, one of the young lawyers in his firm entered the room and noticed Groleau's name.

"What are you doing with Pierre Groleau?"

"Just who is Pierre Groleau?" Rudin asked.

"He's the maître d' at Ma Maison. I play tennis with him every so often."

The pieces of the Groleau puzzle were telephoned to New York over the course of Tuesday. Although they did not form a complete picture, they strongly suggested another embezzlement. Hirschfield and Fischer knew that Sy Weintraub and Begelman were close friends and also surmised that since Ma Maison was one of Begelman's favorite restaurants, he certainly knew Pierre Groleau. A copy of the

Groleau check was sent to New York on a facsimile transmitter, and Herbert Allen's handwriting contact said that the endorsement appeared to have been written by Begelman.

As in the previous week, appointments and lunches were canceled, secretaries were told to hold all calls, and the high command of Columbia Pictures Industries assembled again at 711 Fifth Avenue. The investigation had not even begun and already they were confronting three separate embezzlements totaling $70,000. The Cliff Robertson forgery was beginning to look trivial when compared to the Peter Choate and Pierre Groleau transactions,* which involved not only forgery but the creation of false contracts and multiple checks, as well as the use of unwitting assistance by high-level studio staff members in their preparation. Even though the Robertson forgery, if viewed charitably and in isolation, might have seemed impulsive, the other two embezzlements clearly were acts of a careful, rational mind.

Furthermore, Columbia had to face the chilling knowledge that if the Cliff Robertson matter had not been *forced* to the attention of the company by Robertson's own persistence—had it not been for a single IRS 1099 form—none of the embezzlements would have been discovered.

And apart from the nature of Begelman's acts and the process of their discovery, still another ominous issue presented itself: the massive dimensions of Begelman's lying. He had lied to Joe Fischer ten days earlier on the Thursday and Friday immediately after Detective Silvey's call. Then he had been summoned to New York and, under threat of summary dismissal, had made an emotional plea for forgiveness, and sworn that they had found everything—that there were no more embezzlements to be found. He had sworn to Herbert Allen in the limousine Wednesday night. He had sworn to the top officers and lawyers of the corporation at the Carlyle on Thursday. Now it appeared that while he was still in New York, swearing and pleading, he had initiated a plan to conceal the third embezzlement through a sequence of additional carefully devised ruses—a check that was not really from Pierre Groleau, a bogus release from a bogus contract, and a bogus telex from France.

Alan Hirschfield, Joe Fischer, Herbert Allen, Todd Lang, and the others deliberated through Tuesday afternoon, adjourned for the

*Like Choate, Groleau knew nothing of Begelman's use of his name to embezzle money.

night, and convened again Wednesday. Joe Fischer in particular found the new developments too egregious to be accommodated by the interim solution that had been devised the previous Friday. Almost from the beginning, Fischer had advocated Begelman's dismissal from his studio job as well as from his corporate post. Lacking strong leadership from Hirschfield, however, he had gone along with the idea of dumping Begelman at the corporate level while retaining him at the studio. The Groleau discovery, however, prompted Fischer to conclude that the company had no choice but to fire Begelman unequivocally and irrevocably.

Agreeing with Fischer was Allen Adler, a thirty-one-year-old senior vice president of the corporation who was invited into the deliberations on Wednesday, September 28, the day after the Groleau embezzlement was confirmed. Adler was a somewhat controversial figure in the Columbia upper echelon. A protégé of Alan Hirschfield's, he was undeniably brilliant and could be charming. But he was also very abrasive on occasion and prone to violent displays of temper. Tall, with curly dark hair, he had agreed to be a "Bachelor of the Month" in *Cosmopolitan* magazine, which quoted him as saying of his Columbia duties, "I function as an energizer. I make things happen!" Some at Columbia considered Adler a hothead, but Hirschfield valued his advice. Hearing about Begelman's crimes for the first time, Adler found himself shocked not only by the substance but by the tone of the discussion. Over lunch around Hirschfield's large glass coffee table, Adler heard talk of nuances, of shadings, of degrees of culpability. He heard talk of resignation versus leave of absence; of precisely what to tell and not tell the SEC; of euphemisms that might be used in the press release to obfuscate Begelman's deeds and blunt their impact while still meeting the company's legal requirements for public disclosure. But Adler heard no talk of what he perceived to be the essence of the situation, and no talk of decisive action. Finally, he pushed back his chair, rose to his feet, and said:

."I want five minutes. I can't believe what I'm hearing. Are you guys crazy? Where have you been for the last few years? Have you never heard of Watergate? I'm not saying Begelman has to be prosecuted, but of course he *does have to leave the company!* It's a shame, but you can't change the fact of what has happened and you've got to suffer some consequences. You can't fog this over. There are people out there, even as we sit here, who know what he's done. What makes you believe the details aren't going to get out? Nixon would still be President if he had revealed the errors at the beginning and fired those responsible. It's the cover-up that makes you look like you're an accomplice.''

Amidst a lot of throat clearing, Adler was assured that there would be no cover-up. But his outburst was counterproductive. Coming from a man whom many in the company considered brash and immature, his thoughts on this occasion were dismissed as brash and immature. This was not Watergate. It was a complex and ambiguous corporate problem that required the application of sophisticated, seasoned corporate minds.

In principle, Alan Hirschfield agreed with Adler and Fischer. Begelman should be fired outright. But Herbert's and Matty's views had to be considered, too. There was a bizarre quality about David's conduct that eluded understanding and seemed to demand further inquiry, despite the rationality and premeditation of the acts themselves.

In the end, the group again found a way to avoid firing Begelman pending the results of the investigation. It was agreed that he should be called back to New York for ''direct discussion.'' ''Absent a suitable explanation'' of the Pierre Groleau matter, the board secretary wrote in the minutes of the meeting, Begelman would take a ''leave of absence'' from the studio in addition to resigning as a director and officer of the parent corporation. The formal action would be taken Friday in New York. So that Begelman would not be lost to the company entirely, however, he would become a ''consultant'' and would continue to draw his full presidential salary.

Of the thousands of journalists who had covered Hollywood over the decades, none had ever garnered the fame that had come to Rona Barrett by the late seventies. Not Hedda. Not Louella. No one. Emerging from Queens into Manhattan in the fifties as Rona Burstein, she first decided that she had to change her name. (''Burstein would never make it in the world of glamour,'' she wrote later in her autobiography. ''Burstein was for the grocery business.'') As Rona Barrett, she got a job as the ''chief coordinator'' of the Eddie Fisher fan clubs. She moved to Hollywood and became a fan magazine columnist. (''There is probably no reporter who knows the Frankie Avalon story better than I do.'') She switched from print to television, first to the ABC affiliate in Los Angeles, then to the Metromedia group of stations, and finally to the full ABC network as the

Hollywood reporter on *Good Morning America*, whose audience (thanks in part to Rona's presence) had come to rival that of *Today* on NBC. In addition to her twice-a-morning broadcasts, Barrett did prime-time specials, published her own fan magazines, made millions in Beverly Hills real estate, and socialized with the mighty and the near-mighty of the entertainment world. She had become a Hollywood institution.

Rona had known David Begelman well for many years and they often saw each other socially. But it was rare if not unprecedented for Rona to go to David's home for breakfast as she did on Thursday, September 29. When she accepted the invitation, Rona thought that David might want to chide her gently for broadcasting so many reports on Columbia Pictures' difficulties in making *Close Encounters of the Third Kind*. The picture's budget had been substantially exceeded. There had been drugs on the set. The studio had found it necessary to banish one of the coproducers from the lot. But David that morning did not mention Rona's reports on *Close Encounters*. He had little to say of substance on any subject. It was just a friendly and very bland chat, and Rona drove away from the house on Linden Drive thinking "What was that all about?"

Alan Hirschfield, Herbert Allen, and Leo Jaffe flew to Washington that morning for an obligatory, long-scheduled meeting of the board of directors of the Motion Picture Association of America. Top officers from each of the major movie companies were there, including Arthur Krim of United Artists, Lew Wasserman of MCA, Dennis Stanfill of Twentieth Century-Fox, Frank Wells of Warner Bros., Barry Diller of Paramount, and several others. (Begelman had canceled earlier in the week.) The film industry showed its flag in Washington every so often and this was an especially auspicious occasion. The group met with President Carter in the Roosevelt Room of the White House early in the afternoon, then went to Capitol Hill for a meeting with the congressional leadership, and then on to Vice President Mondale's mansion for cocktails and dinner. The Columbia people got through the day without letting even a hint slip to their competitors that they were mired in a crisis. (A few weeks later, after the word was out, Frank Wells told Alan Hirschfield that it was the best performance he had ever seen, on screen or off.)

Leo Jaffe, having confirmed with the lawyers in New York that they would be prepared to deal with Begelman by Friday morning, telephoned David from a pay booth in the Capitol building and asked that he fly to New York that evening, be at Todd Lang's office by ten the next morning, and bring a lawyer with him. Begelman agreed to come and did not ask why. He called his financial manager, Jerry Breslauer, and told him that he needed to see him urgently and would be over at two o'clock. He then located his wife, Gladyce, and pal Sy Weintraub, and asked that they meet him at Breslauer's office. There, he told them that he was being summoned to New York to answer for "terrible, terrible financial transgressions" which he had committed against Columbia.

"I am in deep, deep, deep trouble," he said, declining to be specific. David said he would go to New York alone, but Gladyce and Sy insisted on accompanying him. After rushing home for a few overnight traveling items, they caught the 4:30 American flight, the last nonstop of the day before the red-eye. Before leaving Los Angeles, Sy Weintraub managed to track down Herbert Allen by phone on Capitol Hill and made an appointment to see him at his Broad Street office early Friday morning.

Aside from Rona Barrett, the most important journalist in Hollywood was A. D. "Art" Murphy of *Variety*. Instead of having an audience in the millions and international fame, Art Murphy wrote for an audience of only a few thousand and settled for limited local notoriety. For an entertainment writer, however, Murphy's audience was important. It was the Los Angeles-New York entertainment community which read *Variety*, in both its daily and weekly forms, from cover to cover. Among this audience Art Murphy was considered the best-informed writer anywhere on the *business* of Hollywood. A former naval officer and lifelong movie buff, Murphy was not a crusading investigative reporter looking for scandal. He loved Hollywood and its personalities, rogues as well as saints, and derived little pleasure from raking muck; it is muck, after all, that gives Hollywood much of its charm. Instead, Murphy provided authoritative analysis of the corporate side of the movies—studio profits and losses, box office grosses, the commercial outlook for new films, and the shuffles of executives. He was alert not only to numbers but to the machinations of the moguls.

Late that Thursday afternoon, Murphy wrote an innocuous three-paragraph item for publication in the inside pages of *Variety* the next morning, Friday, September 30. Headlined SOMETHING'S COOKING ON HIGH AT COLUMBIA, the item reported that for the second time in two weeks Columbia Pictures had postponed a groundbreaking ceremony marking the beginning of construction of a building at The Burbank Studios. "Col Pictures chief David Begelman late yesterday was called to N.Y. . . ." Murphy wrote. "The groundbreaking ceremony, originally set for Tuesday (Sept. 27), was first shoved back to next Monday (Oct. 3). Late yesterday, it was pushed back to some unspecified date." The item indicated that Murphy did not know the reason for the postponements or for Begelman's trip. He speculated that the developments might be related to Columbia's ongoing search for new financial partners for its films.

Most of the cocktail chatter at the Mondales was about Bert Lance. But when Democratic National Chairman Robert Strauss arrived, Hirschfield, Allen, and Jaffe took him aside and told him quietly about the Begelman problem. Strauss, a close friend of Herbert Allen's, had been a member of the Columbia board of directors prior to becoming party chairman. He was stunned by the news.

The three Columbia executives were back in New York by eleven o'clock that evening. Three hours later, at eleven in California, Jim Johnson stood on the steps of the Columbia building with a studio security man, waiting for the only twenty-four-hour locksmith in Burbank. Earlier in the day—after David Begelman had left for New York—Joe Fischer had told Jim Johnson by phone: "Secure Begelman's office. Change the locks."

Baffled by Johnson's request for a locksmith, the security man said, "Are you kidding me?"

"No," Johnson retorted, "I want you to get somebody and be at the studio at eleven tonight. I'll tell you then what I want you to do. It's fuckin' top secret and it's urgent."

The locksmith arrived and Johnson led the way to Begelman's second-floor quarters, the only suite of offices with a double door. "We've got to change the fuckin' locks—all of 'em," Johnson said. The locksmith went to work on the double outer door and then proceeded to the doors to Begelman's private office and a conference room. The security man remembered a passage from Begelman's office directly into the office of Dan Melnick, the head of production. The two offices shared a bar in the passageway. The lock on that door was changed, too.

For Jim Johnson, who had admired David Begelman even more perhaps than others had, and had then found himself the conduit of an increasing flow of damning information, the changing of the locks brought a wrenching sense of physical finality—like slamming the lid on a steel coffin.

Johnson got home after his wife had gone to sleep. But she awakened at 3 A.M. to find him sitting on the edge of the bed, sobbing uncontrollably.

SIXTEEN

Having arrived at JFK with the Begelmans after midnight, Sy Weintraub struggled out of bed Friday morning in time to be in lower Manhattan at Herbert Allen's office by 8 A.M. Weintraub and Allen had known each other for several years; they had both served on the board of directors of Gene Klein's National General Corporation, the Beverly Hills conglomerate that had bought Weintraub's Tarzan production company.

As one could do with Herbert Allen, Weintraub got right to the point: "I know how deeply concerned you are—and with every justification—about what David has done," Weintraub said. "No company can condone or overlook this sort of thing, and I am not here to suggest that. But David is a very close friend of mine, and I just wanted to let you know what I know about the things he has done. Perhaps it will in some way help your dealing with it."

Begelman, according to Weintraub, had spilled everything on the plane the night before: the Cliff Robertson check, the Peter Choate contract, and the Pierre Groleau contract. David had opened his heart. He had held nothing back. Moreover, he was distraught because he had not revealed the Groleau transaction the previous week when he was in New York. He had not meant to lie. Rather, he had blocked it psychologically. When his colleagues had told him that he would be fired if they found more embezzlements, he had blocked the third one from his mind. Weintraub was convinced, however, after his exhaustive talk with David, that the Groleau transaction was absolutely the last problem they would find. There were only the three. Sy was so firmly convinced of David's truthfulness, in fact, that he was willing to sign a blank check and leave it with Herbert to cover any other defalcations, in the extremely unlikely event that any were found. Sy was willing to guarantee, with his own considerable resources, that Columbia Pictures Industries would not lose a penny from anything David had done. Sy would not do such a thing, of course, if he were not positive that the three transactions already found were the extent of the problem.

In return, Sy asked Herbert, was it not possible for Columbia to find it in its heart to extend forgiveness and mercy to this troubled but fundamentally decent and honorable man, who had given so much of himself to Columbia?

Herbert was impressed. He had rarely seen a human being display such abiding faith in another. He invited Weintraub to accompany him uptown and present his case to the others.

The expanding and prosperous law firm of Weil, Gotshal & Manges occupied the thirty-first and thirty-second floors of the General Motors Building at Fifth Avenue and Fifty-ninth Street, three blocks north of the Columbia Pictures building. Todd Lang's suite was on the northwest corner of the building, facing the Plaza Hotel, the St. Moritz, and the Gulf & Western Building to the west; the Sherry Netherland and Pierre hotels to the north; and in between the expanse of Central Park. That area of Manhattan is sometimes called Hollywood East, and for good reason. Despite the higher visibility of the Los Angeles film colony, a handful of skyscrapers within a half-mile radius of the corner of Fifty-ninth and Fifth house a group of corporations which wield, in the aggregate, considerably more power over the motion-picture, television, and record industries in America than is wielded by their West Coast counterparts. Warner Communications is at Fifty-first and Fifth, four blocks south of Columbia. Paramount is just across the park in the Gulf & Western Building. The headquarters of the ABC, CBS, and NBC television networks, as well as their phonograph-record and tape affiliates, are within five blocks of each other on Sixth Avenue in the forties and fifties, as are the principal pay-TV services, Home Box Office and Showtime. The world headquarters of International Creative Management, the largest of the talent and literary agencies, is on Fifty-seventh, and its principal rival, the William Morris Agency, is just around the corner. Most of the big law firms serving these companies are housed nearby, too, as are dozens of producers, film infanciers, smaller talent agencies, and individual entertainment entrepreneurs of all stripes.

The show-biz ambience of Hollywood East is hard to miss. If New York entertainment executives do not take lunch in their private dining rooms, they frequently can be found at the Russian Tea Room on Fifty-seventh, Orsini's on Fifty-sixth, La Côte Basque on Fifty-fifth, "21" on Fifty-second, or Lutèce on Fiftieth. And if visiting Los Angeles colleagues do not stay in private apartments, such as Columbia's two suites at the Carnegie House and the Drake, they usually stay at the Plaza, or the Sherry (diagonally across from the Plaza), or the Pierre (a few steps north of the Sherry), or the Regency (two blocks over on Park). On a Thursday at the Russian Tea Room, or at the bar of the Sherry Netherland, or in the corridors of Warner Communications, one often sees the same faces and hears the same talk that one encountered on Tuesday at the Beverly Hills Hotel, or Chasen's, or the Fox commissary, or that one ran into on Wednesday in the first-class cabin of American 32, or United 6, or TWA 8. The two Hollywoods, in fact, sometimes seem not so much like separate communities as like a single, homogeneous community which has been divided arbitrarily into two parts and placed at opposite ends of a three-thousand-mile air corridor through which the residents regularly are shuttled.

Such appearances are deceiving, however. The differences between the New York and Los Angeles show-business enclaves are more important than the similarities. One has more perspective in New York. Even though a great deal of power over the entertainment industry is concentrated in a few blocks, one cannot stroll those streets without realizing that Exxon and Mobil and Burlington Industries and Revlon and McGraw-Hill and dozens of other giant corporations in diverse industries make their homes not only in the same city but in the same neighborhood. In Los Angeles, the film studios and television production facilities are physically and psychologically so imposing, and other institutions so lacking in sense of presence, that although the geography is measured in square miles rather than blocks, one can live and work for days, driving considerable distances and experiencing a variety of milieus, without once being reminded that there is any business in the world except show business. The insularity of Los Angeles, after a while, begins to distort the vision and jostle the equilibrium of all but the very strong and the very independent.

Which is where New York comes in. When Hollywood needs an injection of reality, when it needs to be brought up short, it is New York, the true seat of power, that does the job.

New York is the enforcer. New York is where the heads roll.

The command post for the day was Todd Lang's conference room. When Herbert Allen and Sy Weintraub arrived, the others—including Begelman—were already there. Hirschfield, Allen, and Rosenhaus immediately went into the privacy of an adjoining office, where Herbert told of his meeting with Weintraub and asked that he be permitted to speak to the group. Matty Rosenhaus, on the verge of tears, immediately agreed, but Hirschfield was reluctant.

"Look, this has got to be the end," Hirschfield said. "We just can't go any farther. God knows what else is under the rug. Who knows whether he's having emotional blocks or not. There could be hundreds of thousands of dollars out there. The Groleau thing is especially bad. It shows total malice aforethought—a whole, elaborate scheme to write checks against a bank account and defraud the company. I don't know what's going on in David's head, and you can't tell me Weintraub does either. He's no psychiatrist."

"Isn't there some way we can help him," Rosenhaus pleaded. "We can't just throw him out on the street. This is a tragedy. It's terrible. The dumb son of a bitch! How could he have done this to himself!"

"No, Matty, this is the end," Hirschfield declared. "God knows what else is out there. We're dealing with dynamite. We've talked to the SEC. We've gotten down on all fours and said, 'Fellows, this is it. There were only two incidents.' Now we have to call them three days later and say, 'By the way, there's a third incident.' This is a horror show!"

Herbert Allen retorted, "The SEC isn't the point. The point is how we deal with David on the merits. Matty's right. We can't just throw him to the wolves. He's in bad shape, and we've got to give him protection. He probably should be out of the company while we get to the bottom of this, but he's not a common criminal.'' Herbert urged that they stick to the plan developed earlier in the week—Begelman would resign from his corporate positions and take a leave of absence from the studio. ''But first listen to Weintraub,'' Herbert urged. ''I promised him he could say his piece.''

They returned to the conference room and asked Begelman to leave while they spoke with Weintraub, who repeated, in a more elaborate and impassioned way, what he had said to Herbert. ''David has undergone a very pressurized business existence at Columbia for the past several years. The things he has done are very unfortunate, but under the terrible pressure of bringing, or helping bring Columbia out of the desert into the green valleys, he had an emotional breakdown, a temporary one. In other men, it might have manifested itself as a heart attack. With David, it came out in the form of these acts. I have known David for a number of years. I find him a very honorable man, a dedicated and loyal man. He should certainly be made to repay his obligations, and I have offered to guarantee the payment of any other defalcations that may have occurred. But he should be forgiven. Otherwise, he will be destroyed. If you take away his job, it will destroy him. It will disgrace him, his wife, and his family. I can't be sure that he won't take his own life, and I know that no one here wants that, or wants to feel that anything done here contributed to such a result.''

''Of course not, Sy,'' Hirschfield said, ''but we have to deal with the facts before us, and the facts are horrendous. He can't stay in his present position. We're a public company. We'll be excoriated. If the word ever gets out about what's going on here, it's just going to be a horror show for this company. We're going to be taken apart. This is a highly visible industry.''

After an extended discussion, the group took a break and Joe Fischer cornered Hirschfield privately. ''This hairsplitting has got to stop,'' Fischer said. ''David has to go. There's no way around it. He has to be terminated. How can we possibly accept this mental-block theory? It's bullshit! If he was blocked mentally, how did he manage to remember enough about the Groleau thing to call Weintraub, get a cashier's check, and try to cover the whole thing up, while telling us there was nothing more? How did he manage that?''

Hirschfield had no ready answer. He, Herbert Allen, and Matty Rosenhaus left the others and asked Begelman to join them in a private office, where he was told that he would have to resign from his corporate positions and take a leave of absence from his jobs at the studio. Begelman broke down. "I know I've betrayed you, but you just can't take everything away from me now," he said, sobbing and trembling. "I'll be finished as a man, as a husband, as a father. I'll do anything. I'll double my efforts. I'll pay it back. I'll make it up to the company. These are the acts of a desperately sick man. It isn't a question of business. I'm pleading for my life."

Hirschfield stood and embraced Begelman. "David, we're not going to hurt you, we're not going to throw you in the street, we're not going to cut you off, we're not going to judge you without evidence. But we're a public company. We pray that this isn't another Equity Funding, but we've got to take account of the possibility that it could be. We have that responsibility. We have other employees to think about. We can't condone what you've done. Word's going to get out. It's not going to be good for you or for us. We can't whitewash it. We'll have the SEC crawling all over us. It's the most visible industry in the world. So we have to do this. You just cannot stay in place."

Begelman agreed to give up his corporate titles but pleaded to be left in place at the studio.

Herbert Allen said, "Look, David, we just can't do it. You're going to have to take a leave. It's going to take a few weeks to conduct an inquiry and sort this out, and then we'll see what happens. You've got to cooperate. It'll be an ordeal for you and everybody else. But you'll be protected. We'll take care of you."

Begelman finally acquiesced and composed himself. It was suggested that David seek psychiatric counseling. His misdeeds seemed irrational to some. Perhaps they were rooted in a psychological disorder. David agreed to consult a psychiatrist when he returned to Los Angeles.

"Where's Gladyce?" Herbert Allen asked.

"She's at the apartment."

"How much does she know?"

"She only knows that I'm in grave, terrible trouble. Her head is spinning. She can't imagine what this is all about."

"You're in no shape to tell her now, but she's got to be told. Do you mind if I go see her? Just to fill her in?"

"No, I would appreciate that very much."

"Alan, would you rather do it yourself?"

"No, go ahead."

Herbert Allen walked the three blocks to the Carnegie House, went up to the Columbia apartment, and was admitted by the butler. "Gladyce, we have a major problem," Herbert said. "It involves David. He's over in a meeting and can't get away right now, so I came over to tell you about it."

Gladyce Begelman, a handsome woman in her middle years, had been crying but had composed herself. Allen briefed her on the revelations, but chose to be imprecise about David's acts, calling them "offenses" instead of "embezzlements" or "forgeries." Gladyce wept softly, as Herbert outlined the plans for David's resignation and leave of absence. Herbert said he was sorry, wished her well, and left.

Back at the law firm, Herbert took Todd Lang and Peter Gruenberger aside and said: "I don't care how many lawyers you have to use. I don't care what it costs. Just get this investigation done and get it done quickly."

Hirschfield, meanwhile, was conferring privately with Dan Melnick, Columbia's head of motion picture production. As the second-in-command at the studio, Melnick would become acting president while Begelman was away. Forty-three years old, Melnick looked and talked a bit like an erudite Humphrey Bogart. He had sad eyes, heavy dark brows, a persistent five-o'clock shadow, and a smoker's rasp in his baritone speaking voice. Though he had been at Columbia only seven months, he had a long background in show business—at CBS and ABC television in New York for ten years, at David Susskind's company, Talent Associates, for eight years, and at MGM as head of production for four years. While with Talent Associates, he had produced the Sam Peckinpah film, *Straw Dogs*, starring Dustin Hoffman. At MGM, he had supervised the production of *That's Entertainment*, Parts One and Two, and Paddy Chayevsky's *Network*. MGM, however, had chosen to make relatively few films through the 1970s as it committed itself heavily to the gambling and hotel businesses. In early 1977, David Begelman, an old and close friend of Melnick's, had wooed him to Columbia, where he had handled the final editing of *The Deep* prior to its highly successful summer run, and then had gone on to supervise the final stages of production of *Close Encounters of the Third Kind*, which was scheduled for release late in the year, and which Columbia had billed as "unquestionably the most spectacular undertaking in its history.'' By September, Melnick was devoting most of his time to *Close Encounters*.

In New York for a few days the last week of the month, he had felt the tension and noticed the frequent comings and goings of board members at the Columbia executive offices. No one would tell him anything specific. On Wednesday, however, Hirschfield asked him to postpone his return to Los Angeles until Friday, and Melnick suddenly remembered the phone call Begelman had received in the projection room on the Burbank lot and his sudden departure for New York the week before. Although he was stunned when Hirschfield finally broke the news, Melnick was a bit less incredulous than others who did not know Begelman so well. He had never suspected Begelman of being a criminal, but he had always known him to live high—perhaps beyond his means—and with a pronounced sense of abandon. ''Sailing close to the wind'' was the phrase that suggested itself to Melnick, who immediately saw the problem as two issues: how should Columbia treat Begelman the person, and how should it treat Begelman the corporate officer. As a close friend, Melnick urged that Begelman personally be protected in every possible way. ''Alan, the position we must take is that this is aberrational behavior, David is very sick, and we must help him,'' Melnick said. ''Of course,'' Hirschfield replied, mentioning that Begelman planned to see a psychiatrist. Melnick recognized immediately, however, that the circumstances required Begelman to leave the company. He assumed that the leave of absence was nothing more than a polite interim step toward permanent severance. Though Hirschfield confirmed that that would be the likely result, he was vague, and as he talked, it occurred to Melnick that Hirschfield himself could use a couple of sessions with a good psychiatrist. He had never seen Hirschfield so frazzled, so overwhelmed, and without the solid grip one might have hoped for.

''A lot of people will lose because of this,'' Hirschfield declared. ''Nobody will win.'' Even Hirschfield did not know precisely what he meant by that statement, and in the heat of the moment, Melnick did not press him.

At 9:30 that morning at The Burbank Studios, Jim Johnson stood again on the steps of the Columbia building where he had waited for the locksmith the night before. This time he was waiting for Begelman's secretary, Connie Danielson. Someone had to tell her that the president's suite had been sealed and that her boss probably would not be coming to work for a while. As she was parking her car, Johnson intercepted her and they drove to a coffee shop off the lot.

"David is in a lot of trouble," Johnson began. "I've been directed by Joe Fischer, who has been directed by Alan Hirschfield, to keep everybody out of the office, including you. The locks have been changed. I'm sorry, but it's very serious." Danielson tried to pump Johnson. "I can't say any more," he replied, "only that it's very, very serious and there is a distinct possibility that David will no longer work for the company."

Johnson added that he had been ordered to inspect the desks in the office and make sure that no business-related material was removed. Connie could drop by later in the day, he said, and pick up any personal items that might be there. Danielson was especially concerned about a personal diary which she kept in her desk, and also mentioned some tap-dancing paraphernalia. (She taught tap-dancing classes in the evenings.) Johnson assured her that he would set her things aside for her.

Connie Danielson drove home, and a few minutes later Johnson was gingerly searching the desks in Begelman's suite. The diary was precisely where Danielson had said it would be, but it did not look much like Jim Johnson's image of a woman's diary. It was an eight-and-a-half-by-eleven loose-leaf binder filled with entries that were typed rather than handwritten. Flipping through the pages quickly to ensure that the diary was personal, Johnson was shocked to see the word *Mafia* and several references to the Los Angeles Police Department. He closed the diary and froze. The events of the past several days had unnerved and exhausted him. Only hours ago at home he had lost his composure. And now this. He hesitated to read the diary carefully for fear of being accused of invading Connie Danielson's privacy. He hesitated to ignore it because he feared he might be accused of covering up for Begelman.

Johnson called Joe Fischer, whom he found in the boardroom in New York. Fischer asked him to make a photocopy of the diary and return the original to Danielson.

"Wait a fucking minute, Joe. Is that legal? I can't do that."

As Johnson talked, Fischer relayed the news of the diary to Leo Jaffe, who was with him in the boardroom. Finally Fischer said to

Johnson: "I have just been ordered by the chairman of the board of this company to tell you to make a copy of that fucking diary."

Johnson obeyed. So that there would be witnesses, he summoned his secretary and also controller Lou Phillips, and the three of them went into a room where a copying machine was located. They asked another secretary to leave, locked the door, and copied the diary. Johnson sealed the copy in an envelope and instructed Phillips to place it in a safe-deposit box at a nearby bank. Later in the day, Johnson returned the original to Connie Danielson, along with her tap-dancing gear and other personal effects from the office.

The copying of the diary infuriated Danielson, who telephoned several people close to Begelman and complained. Within hours in New York, Herbert Allen and Matty Rosenhaus were accusing Hirschfield and Fischer of using "Gestapo tactics" against Begelman. After a lengthy shouting match in the boardroom, the group agreed that before turning the diary over to the investigators, lawyers would be consulted on the legality of seizing it.

In his office just after five, Hirschfield returned a phone call from William Thompson of the First National Bank of Boston. Thompson wanted him to come to Boston on Saturday. He had very important and very good news which he could not discuss on the telephone. Hirschfield naturally was intrigued. Grasping at a glimmer of hope after the worst two weeks of his business career, he agreed to go. He would fly up in the late morning. Thompson would meet him and they would have lunch.

After Thompson's call, Hirschfield ignored dozens of other phone messages that had accumulated through the week and began making arrangements to fly to Los Angeles on Sunday morning to brief the senior people at the studio on David Begelman's suspension and its ramifications. By telephone and teletype, secretaries passed the word to California that Hirschfield would expect the staff at his Beverly Hills Hotel bungalow on Sunday afternoon.

Hirschfield's office was quiet at last, and he was alone, slumped in his chair. The intensity, the shouting, the tears, the sense of desperation that had filled the day since early morning had ebbed, at least for the moment. All arrangements had been made, all documents signed, all telephone calls completed, all teletypes sent. There was no turning back. By Monday, the world would know that Columbia Pictures had a scandal on its hands.

"A lot of people will lose because of this," he had said to Melnick. "Nobody will win."

Hirschfield shrugged, got up, and packed his briefcase for a week in California. Then he met his children and wife for a long-scheduled evening of *Beatlemania* at the Winter Garden Theater and dinner at "21." As exhausted as he was, especially by the events of that day, he managed to enjoy the evening. The company of his children— Laura, thirteen; Marc, eleven; and Scott, eight—always invigorated Alan, no matter what problems might be plaguing him. The prospect of good news from Bill Thompson was cheering as well.

For the first time in sixteen days, the weight on Hirschfield's shoulders seemed a little lighter.

By early Friday evening in Burbank, the Columbia executive suites were abuzz with rumors that something dramatic was about to happen. It was unprecedented for Alan Hirschfield to fly out on short notice and hold high-level meetings on a weekend. The only person at the studio who knew the full details—Jim Johnson—was sworn to secrecy. Though a few people suspected that the meeting would concern David Begelman, most knew nothing.

Norman Horowitz, a senior vice president of Columbia's television company, flew into Los Angeles Friday evening from Hilton Head, South Carolina, where he had been attending a business conference. He was supposed to be in New York on Monday and would have stayed in the East, but he had promised to attend an *est* seminar that weekend in Los Angeles. Attendance at *est* seminars was all but mandatory, so rather than risk the wrath of his *est* colleagues, Horowitz had decided to endure two cross-country flights in three days.

When he arrived at his hilltop home in Encino about ten, Horowitz's wife immediately told him of the Sunday meeting with Hirschfield. Horowitz was angry; the meeting would keep him from a major part of the *est* seminar. His curiosity grew. Something big must be up. It was too late to call anyone in New York, so he began calling Columbia people in Los Angeles.

"What the fuck is going on?" he asked a studio colleague.

"Nobody seems to know what it is, Norman, but there was one strange thing. David Begelman went to New York very suddenly yesterday, and some time overnight they changed the locks on his office."

"*They what?*"

"They changed the locks on David's office. It's true. Something fishy is going on with David."

"Holy shit!" said Norman Horowitz, thinking that Begelman probably had been hired away by another studio and that Columbia was being awfully heavy-handed in protecting its trade secrets.

SEVENTEEN

On most autumn Saturday mornings, Alan Hirschfield could be found at one of several athletic fields in Scarsdale where he coached not one but two soccer teams. Fortunately they did not play at the same time. His older son, Marc, played for one team; his younger son, Scott, for another. After the games on Saturday, October 1, Hirschfield showered, dressed, drove to the Westchester County Airport and was flown to Boston on a small jet belonging to Time Incorporated. In the course of negotiating a multimillion-dollar investment by Time in Columbia's films, Hirschfield had become friendly with several Time executives and was afforded occasional use of the plane.

Bill Thompson met him at Logan and they went to Jimmy's Harborside, a rustic seafood restaurant on the water across the harbor from the airport. Although Joe Fischer had briefed Thompson the previous Sunday, and Thompson had attended the Brandeis dinner the week before that, Hirschfield and Thompson had had no more than a brief chat in several weeks. The good impression they had made on each other four years earlier, when the Allens were buying control of Columbia Pictures, had grown into warm friendship and admiration. Thompson was a Hirschfield fan and praised him at every opportunity, public as well as private. "We're very proud of the job that Alan Hirschfield has done; he has really put vitality into Columbia," Thompson had told *Film Comment*, the prestigious journal of the Film Society of Lincoln Center, in 1976. "This is a people business, there's no question about it. Alan has brought new blood to a company that was really getting somewhat tired. The record speaks for itself. They were swamping in oceans of red ink, and Alan really did an outstanding job."

Coming from the most influential movie banker in the world, such words were welcome indeed, especially since Hirschfield worked for a board of directors who, he felt, had never given him sufficient credit for his accomplishments, and who were now counseling a cautious response to the flagrant crimes of David Begelman, partly, it seemed to Hirschfield, on the ground that Begelman might be irreplaceable. That was another thing Hirschfield liked about Bill Thompson: he knew that every successful company was run by a team and that no individual was indispensable.

Thompson commiserated about the Begelman problem, and then revealed his news—news that was extraordinary in itself and also accomplished something that Hirschfield was beginning to think was impossible: it placed the Begelman problem in what might prove to be a manageable perspective.

Thompson told Hirschfield that the five top officers of the United Artists Corporation were about to resign because they were dissatisfied with the way UA's corporate parent, Transamerica Corporation, was treating them and their movie company. The five men—Arthur Krim, Robert Benjamin, Eric Pleskow, Mike Medavoy and William Bernstein—were among the ablest and most highly respected people in the entertainment industry. Their resignation meant that they would be free to join another company. Thompson felt that that company might be Columbia Pictures if the correct approach were made. And if Arthur Krim and his associates joined Columbia, the Begelman problem—insofar as his departure might cause a management void—would vanish because Columbia would have no further need for Begelman.

Thompson cautioned Hirschfield that the news must be held in the strictest confidence: Krim and his colleagues would not make their move until around the turn of the year. They had not even told their bosses at Transamerica yet. The prospect, however, seemed to hold much promise. Hirschfield had a warm relationship with the UA group. And Arthur Krim and Herbert Allen knew each other, independently of the movie industry, as fundraisers for the Democratic Party. Hirschfield's mind raced with possibilities. The Krim group's

filmmaking record for the most part was excellent. United Artists
had had the enormous revenues of the James Bond movies and the
considerable prestige of the Woody Allen films. The company also
had distributed some of the most spectacular individual films of
recent years, including *Rocky, One Flew over the Cuckoo's Nest,*
and *Midnight Cowboy.* Equally important, in the new circumstances
at Columbia, the United Artists executives were men of integrity,
whose business and professional reputations were beyond reproach.
David Begelman seemed sleazy by comparison, despite his talent
and any possible extenuating psychological factors that might miti-
gate his criminality.

It was by no means certain, of course, that the United Artists
people could be induced to come to Columbia or, if they could,
under what conditions. And it was too soon to approach them
formally. Thompson suggested that Hirschfield schedule a lunch with
Eric Pleskow, UA's president, whom Hirschfield knew better than
the other four, and tell Pleskow that if he or his colleagues ever
decided to leave United Artists, Columbia would be interested in
discussing their futures with them. Such an approach at least would
put Columbia first in line and might prove helpful later.

Back home in Scarsdale in the late afternoon, Alan gave Berte the
good news and then phoned Herbert, the only other person he had
told about his trip to Boston. He had obtained Thompson's permission to give Herbert the details not only because of Herbert's uniquely
influential position at Columbia but because of his relationship with
Arthur Krim. Even though the UA group's plan remained secret, the
word eventually would leak, and Alan wanted to be the first to tell
Herbert. Still exultant on the telephone, Alan portrayed the news as
the "answer to Columbia's prayers. It would be a world-beater for
us. We'd be the strongest company in the industry if we could land
these people." But to Alan's chagrin, Herbert was not nearly so
enthusiastic. "It sounds interesting—something to think about. Let's
see how things look in a couple of months. It would depend on what
kind of deal we could make."

Alan hung up and said to Berte, "Can you believe that? He was
lukewarm. You'd have thought I was telling him today is the first of
October and winter is just around the corner. 'Ho-hum.' 'Something
to think about.' 'Have to see what develops.' How can anyone be so
blasé about this kind of news?"

What was surprising, however, was not Herbert's reaction but

Alan's failure to anticipate the reaction. It was Herbert's nature—almost a reflex—to be skeptical and blasé in the face of dramatic news, good or bad. Reacting that way made Herbert feel mature, made him feel that he was exercising control, made him feel that he was keeping his head when all about him were losing theirs. Though this trait could be irritating, it was familiar to most people who knew Herbert well, and they had learned to deal with it routinely. But Alan Hirschfield did not handle such behavior adroitly. However, his purblindness was not limited to that particular trait in Herbert, or even to Herbert's personality in general. It was symptomatic, in fact, of a general incapacity in Alan for the rudimentary psychoanalysis that is essential in all close human relationships. Alan could charm strangers, singly or in groups, with almost uncanny skill. But he frequently had difficulty with people close to him. Infected by an unusual mixture of naïveté and laziness, he tended to take friends for granted, not in the sense of forgetting their birthdays, but in the more important sense of failing to discern the nuances of their personalities and the precise nature of his relationship with them. He paid little heed to the shadings of friendship, sometimes treating a close friend as something less, or a casual friend as something more. Naturally, such carelessness occasionally led to awkward moments, miscalculations, and even pain, not only for his friends but for Alan himself. And in 1977 no relationship held more potential for trouble than his relationship with Herbert.

Alan—at least subconsciously—failed to discern that their relationship had never been a dynamic friendship. Although the relationship generally was pleasant—they acted like friends most of the time—they never had been more than close business acquaintances, and the relationship had always contained the seeds of enmity. Indeed, Alan in recent years had come to resent Herbert's role in his life and wanted more independence. But he had never bothered to analyze the ramifications of the conflict between his private feelings and the surface congeniality. And he persisted in conducting the relationship as a close friendship between men of similar inclination and spirit, assuming that whatever excited him would excite Herbert, that whatever horrified him would horrify Herbert.

Thus, when Herbert did not react as Alan anticipated—when he did not exult over the prospect of five prominent United Artists executives joining Columbia Pictures—Alan interpreted the response as an annoying but essentially minor and isolated disagreement between friends. He not only overlooked the reflexive nature of Herbert's skepticism. He also failed to see that Herbert was analyzing the concept not as a friend but as a business associate—an associate, moreover, with interests that did not necessarily coincide with Alan's interests. (Though the presence of the United Artists group might solve the Begelman problem, it might also dilute Herbert Allen's power at Columbia Pictures. It might lessen Ray Stark's role.)

In more than fifteen years of knowing each other—four years of working closely together—Alan's psychoanalytic naïveté rarely had hurt him because he generally had deferred to Herbert's judgment on most matters, or Herbert had chosen not to counter him. It was remarkable, however, that in all that time Alan had never seriously considered the possible consequences of his taking a strong stand against Herbert on a matter of vital importance.

EIGHTEEN

Wyman, Bautzer, Rothman & Kuchel is one of the best-known law firms in Southern California. The late Eugene Wyman was a Democratic Party leader in the state. Gregson Bautzer has been a celebrated Hollywood deal maker and social lion for decades. Thomas Kuchel was a United States Senator from 1953 until 1965. But Frank Rothman, in contrast to his principal partners, has gained prominence entirely through the practice of law. He has represented a wide variety of clients, show business people and others, in criminal matters as well as civil.

Columbia production head Dan Melnick telephoned Frank Rothman on Saturday after returning from New York and asked him to see David Begelman. Melnick had known Rothman through a common association with MGM, Rothman as general counsel, Melnick as head of production before moving to Columbia. But Rothman and

Begelman had never met, though they had dealt occasionally on the telephone for many years. Rothman agreed to confer with Begelman and they rendezvoused Sunday morning at the Bel-Air home of Sy Weintraub, who had loaned Begelman $25,000 a week earlier, pleaded his case in New York, and also was a close friend of Rothman's.

In a quarter century of defending clients accused of wrongdoing, Rothman had encountered many overwrought people. But it struck him that none had been more upset than David Begelman seemed that morning. He was trembling slightly, his voice was unsteady, his pallor suggested physical illness, and he was nursing a large sore on his lower lip. After hearing Begelman's story and being assured that the rest of the stolen money would be repaid, Rothman agreed to represent Begelman in Columbia's investigation and any other inquiry that arose. While Rothman recognized that Begelman theoretically was vulnerable to various law-enforcement actions—by the police, the SEC, and the IRS—he felt that a "psychological problem" defense was workable and could be used to thwart other investigative initiatives, especially since Begelman was about to begin psychotherapy. The Columbia inquiry, therefore, was the first priority, and Frank Rothman promised to begin his work by telephoning Todd Lang and Mickey Rudin on Monday morning.

Begelman drove from Weintraub's home to the residence of Judd Marmor, M.D., less than a mile away, also in Bel-Air. Judd Marmor, sixty-seven years old and a former president of the American Psychiatric Association, had practiced psychiatry in Los Angeles since the late 1940s and had become known as "psychiatrist to the stars." Marmor had counseled Begelman the previous spring about difficulties in his relationship with his daughter from his second marriage. When the Columbia problem arose, friends urged him to see Marmor again. The doctor listened to Begelman's tale and scheduled several sessions with him for the coming week.

As Begelman chatted with Judd Marmor early Sunday afternoon in Bel-Air, Alan Hirschfield was two miles east checking into Bungalow 8 of the Beverly Hills Hotel, having come out with Joe Fischer on the morning American flight from New York.

Of the twenty-one bungalows on the grounds of the Beverly Hills Hotel, Bungalows 6, 8, and 9—for reasons long forgotten—carry the highest status. They face Crescent Drive, the quiet street that borders the hotel on the east, away from the noise of Sunset Boulevard and the traffic at the hotel entrance. Like the rest of the hotel, they are salmon pink with white trim and ocher tile roofs. Shaded by maple, spruce, and fruit trees, as well as by coconut and date palms, the bungalows are bordered by privet hedges and flowering shrubs. Bungalow 8 seems to be preferred by moguls and executives more than by stars. Steve Ross of Warner Communications and Ahmet Ertegun of Atlantic Records like it, as does Alan Hirschfield, although he is less particular than some people. Bungalow 8 is the only bungalow with a small Spanish-style walled patio in front. Inside, the thirty-foot living room is light, with white walls, beige carpeting, and at one end, a walnut fireplace with gas logs. An Oriental tapestry hangs on the wall above a yellow sofa and a large rectangular mahogany coffee table. The occasional chairs are orange, yellow, and green, the same colors as in the three floral prints on the walls and two fresh floral bouquets. The cheery dining room, with windows on three sides, is off the northeast corner of the living room.

The top executives of the Columbia studio gathered in Bungalow 8 around 1:30 as they had been instructed to do. Dan Melnick, the head of worldwide production; Norman Levy, the executive vice president for marketing; John Veitch, the senior vice president in charge of physical production; Eli Horowitz, the senior vice president for business affairs (no relation to Norman Horowitz of television); Robert Cort, the young vice president for advertising; Jim Johnson, the vice president for administration; and several others.

There was negligible small talk. "I'm sorry to have interrupted your weekends," Hirschfield began, "but I had to ask you here today to hear some bad news. David Begelman is leaving the company. It may be temporary; we don't know yet. Some of you undoubtedly have heard a certain amount about this problem, and others may know little or nothing. In order that everybody is working with the same information, I'm going to read you a press release which we will be distributing this afternoon and tomorrow.

"NEW YORK, October 3, 1977—Columbia Pictures Industries Inc. announced today that the Audit Committee of the Board of Directors has commenced an inquiry into certain unauthorized financial transactions between David Begelman and the Company. The amounts involved in these transactions, of which the Company recently became aware, are in the aggregate not material to the Company. Mr. Begelman has resigned as a Director and Senior Executive Vice President of the Company and is taking a leave of absence from his operating responsibilities with the Company.

"Alan J. Hirschfield, President and Chief Executive Officer of the Company, expressed both confidence in, and enthusiasm for, the executive teams of the motion picture and television divisions. The Company's plans for a substantial increase in motion picture production and expansion of its televsion activities will proceed unabated. The motion picture division will continue to operate under Dan Melnick, who is in charge of feature production, Norman Levy, who is in charge of marketing, and Pat Williamson, who is in charge of international operations. The television division will continue to operate under the direction of Larry White, who is in charge of television production, and Norman Horowitz, who is in charge of worldwide syndication.

"Mr. Hirschfield stated that the Company is in a strong financial position and he expects the Company's progress to continue."

Hirschfield gave a copy of the release to each person in the room, and before anyone could break the stunned silence, went on to say that the company lawyers had ordered him and Joe Fischer not to elaborate on the press release, even to other officers of the company. "Please don't pump us," he said. "We just can't say any more right now." He asked the group to cooperate with the team of investigators who would be at the studio for the next few weeks, and to refrain from discussing the Begelman matter with anyone outside the company.

"As serious as this is, it's not the end of the world. We're a strong company, we have *Close Encounters* coming out, and we're going to have another good year. So just keep doing your jobs, and we'll get this behind us as soon as possible."

The shock in the living room was the shock of amazement, sadness, and anger, but it was not the shock of disbelief. No one said, "I don't believe it. It can't be true." On the contrary, someone had the tactlessness to say, with a grim chuckle, "I always knew David was a crook."

The remark enraged Dan Melnick.

"That is totally uncalled for and out of line," Melnick declared. "A lot of you people in this room have seen your careers prosper under David. Whatever your personal feelings may be, you have no right to prejudge him. The one crucial thing that this press release does not say, because it's too sensitive and personal—and should not leave this room—is that David is a sick man. He has emotional problems that may take a while to sort out, and the thing he needs and deserves most from all of us is compassion. *Rachmones.* Compassion in the deepest sense. He needs our understanding. He does not need any fucking sneering, cheap prejudgments."

Hirschfield seconded Melnick's sentiment, and the meeting broke up, some people going home, others to the Polo Lounge for a drink.

The executives of the television division assembled at three for a similar session. As it was adjourning, Norman Horowitz, an excitable, assertive man who had learned by phone Friday evening about the changing of the locks but knew nothing more until Sunday, took Hirschfield aside and pressed for more insight, if not detail.

"Whatever this bullshit is, isn't there some way he can make restitution and clean it up?" Horowitz asked.

Hirschfield rolled his eyes toward the ceiling, sighed and shook his head. "Norman, it isn't that simple. We can't maintain any level of morality in the company if someone is allowed to steal, and then be forgiven, and then have the opportunity to steal again."

"This isn't a Clive Davis bar mitzvah then?"

"No, it's more serious than that."

"Holy shit!"

Rona Barrett had been getting cryptic calls from sources all weekend.

"Something really big is brewing at Columbia."

"In what area is something brewing?" Barrett asked.

"How about right at the top?"

"The top of what? The corporation? Herbie Allen?"

"The top of the studio."

"Begelman?"

"Yes. This is so bizarre that nobody knows what to do. Nobody knows what to say. It's just awful."

"Nobody knows what to say about *what? What* is happening?"

"You'd never believe it anyway. You're just never gonna believe it."

"Believe what? Has someone murdered someone, and there's a cover-up?"

"Try financial irregularities."

By Sunday evening, Barrett had gathered enough information to prepare a report for her Monday morning ABC network broadcast, introduced as usual at 7:40 A.M. by David Hartman.

Good morning, David, and good morning, America.

The post-Watergate insistence on full disclosure for public corporations has caught up with Hollywood. This afternoon, Columbia Pictures Industries will issue a release stating that Columbia Pictures President David Begelman has resigned from the board of directors and has been temporarily relieved of his duties, pending an investigation into the manner in which Begelman dispersed funds authorized for his personal use. Current production chief Dan Melnick will assume some of Begelman's duties. The official release stresses that the money in question is not of a substantial amount and would not affect the financial stability of the company. When reached for comment, David Begelman said he concurs with the release and emphasized that he and Columbia are "not adversaries." He said the investigation centered around a difference in judgment as to how money allocated for his personal use was dispersed. Begelman emphasized his judgment in dealing with motion-picture projects was not in question, and added that he is confident he can stand on his record. While the official release says the leave of absence is temporary, sources at the studio say the dismissal may be permanent, depending on the outcome of the inquiry. Those same sources further allege that while the money in question does not exceed one hundred thousand dollars over a four-year period, the way in which the money was used is reportedly illegal and could spark an investigation by various state and federal authorities. Both Begelman and the studio concur that as a public corporation, all executives are answerable to this sort of scrutiny. The release comes on the heels of reports that indicate the studio is currently enjoying its strongest financial showing in more than a decade, with Wall Street sources claiming the stock will soar even higher with the release of *Close Encounters of the Third Kind* next month. Furthermore, under Begelman's administration, the Columbia debt was reduced from a staggering one hundred sixty million-plus to under sixty million. David Begelman is also considered one of the most benevolent executives in the motion picture industry, having, without fanfare, supported many worthwhile ventures. We will certainly be following the ramifications of this story over the next few weeks.

Rona Barrett finally understood why David Begelman had had her to breakfast the previous Thursday.

The Begelman story was the talk of the entertainment world on Monday and Tuesday, not only in Los Angeles but in New York and London as well. *The New York Times, The Wall Street Journal,* the *Los Angeles Times, The Washington Post,* and other major newspapers carried lengthy stories, as did the AP and the UPI. Under a banner page-one headline in *Variety,* Art Murphy called the affair "a development believed to be without parallel in the film business."

Neither Art Murphy nor Rona Barrett nor any other journalist was able to learn the nature of the "unauthorized financial transactions." However, Murphy wrote, "It is understood that the matters are gray areas of personal judgment," echoing Begelman's statement to Barrett that the problem concerned "a difference in judgment" in dispersal of funds.

Some Columbia Pictures insiders felt that that was an awfully gentle way to refer to forgery. However, Columbia made no effort to correct any of the press reports.

Alan Hirschfield spent most of the week attempting to reassure important people around Hollywood that the studio would continue to function well without Begelman. In addition to briefing Columbia's own executives, he decided to see several independent producers and other major outsiders, e.g., David Gerber, producer of Columbia's most successful television series, *Police Story* and *Police Woman;* Leonard Goldberg of Spelling-Goldberg Productions and one of David Begelman's closest friends; Dino De Laurentiis; Lee Rich of Lorimar Productions; Michael Phillips, coproducer of *Close Encounters of the Third Kind;* J. William "Bill" Hayes, attorney and financial manager for several television producers; Marty Ransohoff; and, of course, Ray Stark.

Hirschfield's most taxing encounter was with David Begelman

himself, who had agreed to brief Hirschfield and Fischer on a long list of pending studio business matters—movie deals, television deals, the release plans for *Close Encounters*, and a host of other items. The three men met for lunch on Monday at La Serre, one of the most exclusive French restaurants in Los Angeles and the only elite restaurant of any kind near The Burbank Studios. They were seated off the green-and-white trellised main dining room in a small, semiprivate room with Belgian tapestries on the walls and fresh red roses on the table.

Begelman immediately began musing about the exaggerated importance of friends, enemies, and gossip in a community as small and self-conscious as Hollywood. His troubles, he said, were certain to be exploited by his enemies in the form of gossip. "I'm concerned about the effect on Gladyce."

"Don't worry about what people say," Hirschfield advised. "Everybody has enemies, and you've got plenty of friends."

"I know who my worst enemy is," Begelman said, and his eyes suddenly filled with tears.

Hirschfield and Fischer exchanged confused looks, momentarily missing the point.

"My worst enemy is sitting right here at this table," he went on. "It's me."

Now crying openly, he said, "I'm the only one I really have to fear. I can't accept success. Right on the brink of success, something within me says that I don't deserve it, and I snatch it away from myself by committing crimes."

Hirschfield and Fischer were speechless, and for a few seconds the only sounds were Begelman's sobs and the hubbub of the restaurant just a few feet away.

"I have a compulsion to destroy myself," Begelman said. "I have no self-respect. That's why I committed these acts. I was trying to punish, defeat, and destroy myself."

Finally, Hirschfield said, "I'm sure your doctor will be able to help you understand why all this happened. It won't look so bleak once it's out on the table. It'll be easier to understand and control."

Begelman composed himself and they proceeded through the checklist, with Hirschfield and Fischer unaware that they had just heard, through Begelman's tears, a competent distillation of the psychiatric analysis that was to become his principal defense.

NINETEEN

Perhaps the most acute reaction to the public announcement of Begelman's suspension was the relief that Cliff Robertson felt when Dina telephoned him Monday in London. It had been seven months since Robertson had discovered the 1099 form, three and a half months since he had discovered Begelman's forgery, three weeks since he had briefed the FBI in Washington, and two weeks since he had begun skulking around London like a fugitive, covering himself with a blanket in the back of his limousine and feeling vaguely silly. In all that time he had received no indication—formal or informal— that his initiatives had produced any result. Paranoia had become part of his daily life. Therefore, the news that Begelman had left Columbia pending an investigation of "unauthorized financial transactions" came as a great relief, primarily because it indicated that enough people now knew of Begelman's crime or crimes to render any attempt to silence Robertson himself futile and superfluous. He hungered for details of Columbia's internal investigation and wondered what role, if any, the law-enforcement authorities had played in spurring the company to action. Since his own name had not surfaced in the public reports, he resisted the temptation to blurt out his story to colleagues at the London studio where he was filming. Still, it was nice to ride to work Tuesday morning sitting upright, without the cover of a blanket. And it was with eagerness instead of trepidation that he looked forward to meeting Dina in Monaco that weekend for the Merv Griffin celebrity tennis tournament.

At the Begelman home on Linden Drive, the telephone rang constantly from the moment the news broke. Most of the calls were from friends in Beverly Hills expressing sympathy, support, and, in a few instances, suspicion. Was the vagueness of Columbia's announcement a hint that the investigation might be a camouflage for something not evident—a political fight within the company perhaps? Could Alan Hirschfield be seizing upon some trivial indiscretion by Begelman to run him out of the company? Such notions were inchoate at first, but they began circulating in limited Hollywood circles as early as Monday—the predictable reactions of an insular and insecure community. It is almost axiomatic that when a prominent and respected citizen of a small island nation is vilified by a powerful outsider, the defendant's fellow citizens will rally to his side first and examine the outsider's charges later.

Telegrams of sympathy arrived, too, and one of them was signed "Jo and Gunther Schiff." How ironic, Begelman thought, that Gunther Schiff, a lawyer who for years had represented Cliff Robertson, the man who started all this, would send a telegram of sympathy. Begelman was not bitter, just amused. He and Schiff had been friends for a long time and he assumed that Gunther had had nothing to do with Robertson's report to the police.* Begelman telephoned Schiff and arranged to see him on Tuesday at his Wilshire Boulevard office. After giving Gunther the details leading up to the investigation, David said he wanted Cliff Robertson to know that Columbia was "handling the matter in the most appropriate manner possible." It would serve no purpose for Cliff to take any further action, e.g., speaking publicly. The matter was in good hands.

Gunther offered to fly to London to confer with Cliff but first, he told David, it seemed appropriate to get confirmation of David's story from a top officer of Columbia Pictures Industries. David telephoned Leo Jaffe and asked him to call Gunther. Leo confirmed to Gunther everything that David had said, and extended an invitation through Gunther to Robertson to visit Columbia's offices in New York when he returned from Europe and receive a full briefing on the investigation from Hirschfield or Jaffe. Jaffe also urged that Robertson refrain from any public statements. Schiff got to Robertson on the phone in London that evening and relayed Columbia's concern. Cliff said there was no need for Gunther to fly over. He was perfectly willing to leave the issue in Columbia's hands for the time being and assured Gunther that he did not intend to air it in the media or on the cocktail circuit.

---

*See explanation on pages 34–35

*   *   *

Another of Alan Hirschfield's delicate tasks that week in Los Angeles was a meeting Tuesday with a group of visiting executives from
IBM, which was developing the laser-based video disc system for
which Columbia wanted to supply the programming. IBM's work on
the system remained such a closely held secret that there was a
signed secrecy agreement between the two companies. Hirschfield
even withheld the visitors' identity from the Columbia studio staff
people who were presenting programming ideas to them. In view of
the fresh Begelman news, and knowing what a straitlaced company
IBM was, Hirschfield invited the group to breakfast at his bungalow
that morning and did his best to convince them that the Begelman
problem was isolated and did not reflect high-level immorality at
Columbia Pictures. A dinner for the IBM people, which had been
scheduled for that evening at Begelman's house, was shifted to Ray
Stark's home. Stark screened his new film, *Casey's Shadow*, which
had not yet been released publicly, and everyone seemed to have a
good time. Hirschfield felt that Columbia's incipient alliance with
IBM had been advanced another step.

Late Wednesday afternoon at the Todd-AO building, a shabby
two-story structure in a decrepit stretch of central Hollywood, the
top ten executives of Columbia Pictures Industries, in strictest privacy
and for the first time, saw a complete rough cut of *Close Encounters
of the Third Kind*. Hirschfield, Melnick, Fischer, and the others had
never been more nervous. The studio already had proclaimed to the
world that *Close Encounters* would be "the most beautiful, frightening,
and significant motion-picture adventure of all time," and none of
the executives had ever before been associated with so expensive a
film—a film in which they had invested not only an unprecedented
amount of money but an extraordinary amount of emotional energy
as well.

Their discomfort was compounded by the presence in the projection room of David Begelman, who had been invited to the screening at Dan Melnick's insistence and over Alan Hirschfield's objections.
Under the circumstances—Peter Gruenberger's team of lawyers and
CPAs that very afternoon was establishing an investigative command
center in Begelman's own office—his appearing at the *Close
Encounters* screening made it seem to many of those present as if
they had been joined in the projection room by a large elephant

which no one could acknowledge was in fact an elephant. Hirschfield, in particular, felt it was wrong for a man who had embezzled thousands of dollars from the company to be present at such an occasion. But Melnick, who was less concerned about appearances than about Begelman's mental state, had overcome Hirschfield's remonstrations. And no one, after all, could discount David Begelman's crucial role in bringing *Close Encounters* along a tortuous path to the brink of completion.

When David Begelman joined Columbia Pictures in the summer of 1973, the first deal he made was for two pictures to be produced by Michael and Julia Phillips, who had just produced *The Sting,* the highly successful suspense comedy with Robert Redford and Paul Newman which went on to win the Academy Award for "best picture" of that year. The first film the Phillipses arranged to make for Columbia was *Taxi Driver,* which was to be directed by Martin Scorsese and written by Paul Schrader. The second film, also to be written by Schrader, was then titled *Watch the Skies,* a story about unidentified flying objects. The story had been suggested to Schrader by Steven Spielberg, a young director whose first major film, *The Sugarland Express,* was about to be released.

Begelman had been Spielberg's agent before becoming head of the Columbia studio and, in conjunction with the Phillipses, named Spielberg to direct *Watch the Skies,* whose budget was set at $2.8 million. Before beginning *Watch the Skies,* however, Spielberg was loaned by Columbia to Universal Pictures to direct a film about a great white shark terrorizing a beach community. The result, *Jaws,* came out in 1975 and became the biggest box-office hit of all time (until it was eclipsed two years later by *Star Wars*). During the latter stages of the *Jaws* project, Spielberg rewrote Paul Schrader's script of *Watch the Skies* and retitled it *Close Encounters of the Third Kind.* (The new title was a reference, in UFO parlance, to actual contact with extraterrestrial beings. The "first and second kinds of encounter" were the sighting of the beings and physical evidence of their presence.)

The rewritten version was much more elaborate than the original and required the use of grandiose visual effects. The budget climbed to $9 million, then to $12 million, and grew still further after shooting began. Having vowed when they took over the company that Columbia would shun big-budget blockbusters, Alan Hirschfield and Herbert Allen grew very concerned about the cost of *Close*

Encounters. They seriously considered inviting another studio to become a partner in the venture, bearing half the cost and cutting both the risk and potential profit. But David Begelman was convinced that *Close Encounters* would be a big hit and fought protracted battles with his colleagues in top management against seeking a partner. On one occasion, in front of several directors in the boardroom in New York, he sketched on a blackboard an analysis of the film's cost and likely revenues, concluding with the prediction that it would gross $80 million. Everyone laughed skeptically, especially Irwin Kramer, Herbert Allen's cousin-in-law. Eventually, however, Begelman talked Hirschfield and the board out of soliciting a full partner, in part because Joe Fischer had become convinced that Columbia could cover much of the production cost with advance guarantees from theaters.

(In the end, Columbia took investments in the film from three outsiders—Time Incorporated; EMI Ltd., the British entertainment conglomerate; and a group of German tax-shelter investors. But the investments totaled only $7 million out of what became a production cost of $19 million, and Columbia was to spend upwards of $10 million more on advertising.)

Close Encounters initially was scheduled to open at Easter of 1977, then was postponed to June, and then to the fall. After Dan Melnick became head of production and saw parts of the film, he persuaded Begelman and Hirschfield to commit an additional $4 million to permit Spielberg to shoot a new beginning for the movie.*

The intensity of the top executives' anxiety over money was matched at the production level where, by the late summer of 1977, bitter disputes were raging between Spielberg and coproducer Julia Phillips over every major aspect of the film from its content and editing to its marketing and advertising. Phillips, who was carrying much of the producer's responsibility at that stage while her husband, Michael, was occupied elsewhere, wanted total control of the *Close Encounters* project. Her demands were seriously disrupting Spielberg's efforts to complete the editing of the film and also were disrupting the studio advertising staff's efforts to formulate its advertising and marketing plans, which were the most expensive and elaborate ever

---

*The scene is a desert sandstorm. The time is the present. Scientists discover several military aircraft missing since World War II. Although there is no sign of the pilots, the planes are in perfect working order and show no evidence of aging. It is as if they had been in a time capsule somewhere, perhaps in outer space, and then suddenly were redeposited on earth.

mounted by Columbia. Finally, David Begelman felt compelled to assert the studio's ultimate legal authority to control the project. He barred Julia Phillips from the premises, sending her into a rage that reverberated through Hollywood's gossip networks for days.

The Phillips brouhaha erupted in August, a few weeks before Begelman and the corporation were engulfed by the embezzlement crisis. After the revelations about Begelman, Hirschfield and Fischer necessarily had ignored *Close Encounters,* trusting the people directly responsible for it to rise to the occasion. As they were gathering in the Todd-AO screening room, however, the great importance of the film came flooding back. If it became the commercial success that they all hoped for, *Close Encounters of the Third Kind* held the possibility of garnering enormous profits and of turning Columbia Pictures Industries into something quite rare in corporate America—a debt-free, cash-rich company with virtually complete freedom to expand in any direction it wanted, unfettered by obligations to banks and other creditors.

If, on the other hand, the film fell short, Columbia stood to lose millions of dollars. While Joe Fischer's prediction of substantial advance guarantees by theaters had been correct, the guarantees still did not cover nearly all that the company would spend on the movie. Commercial failure, therefore, would curb severely Columbia's flexibility and capacity for growth.

As the projection room darkened and the film began, Director Spielberg and Douglas Trumbull, who had created the special effects, were feeling their own anxieties. Having been hunched over editing equipment day and night for months, they were emotionally and physically exhausted and had lost much of their perspective on the film. They felt it was wonderful, of course, but could hardly judge it objectively.

The least worried people at the screening—and even they were anxious—were Melnick and Begelman, who had followed the project closely enough and had seen enough of the movie to be convinced of its high quality and commercial potential.

An hour into the film, anxiety was ebbing and excitement was growing. After two hours, as the space ships began descending around Devil's Tower, the people in the projection room knew they were seeing something very special. By the time the mother ship loomed over the mountain and settled to earth, they knew they were seeing one of the most spectacular motion pictures ever made. When the film ended, the first audible reaction was from Robert Cort, the young vice president for advertising, who leaped in the air like a giddy child, whooping and giggling and pounding Spielberg and Trumbull like players who had just won the seventh game of the World Series. The others were enthusiastic, too. The joy and relief were palpable. A few people rather awkwardly paid respects to Begelman. Others confined their congratulations to Spielberg, Trumbull, and Melnick.

Maybe, just maybe, Hirschfield thought as he left the building, this picture will attract enough attention to make the Begelman scandal seem insignificant.

Chief Investigator Peter Gruenberger had flown out from New York on Sunday evening and had been joined on Tuesday by two other lawyers from Weil, Gotshal & Manges and by Michael Passarella, a senior partner from the New York headquarters of Price Waterhouse & Company. Those four, who would stay in Los Angeles for the duration of the investigation, except for brief trips to New York, were supplemented by four CPAs from Price Waterhouse's Century City office. The investigation would comprise what Price Waterhouse called a "fraud audit," in which normal auditing procedures were expanded to include correlation of all of Begelman's corporate financial records—such things as his salary and his travel and entertainment expenses—with all of his and his wife's personal financial records, including income tax returns and bank deposits and withdrawals.

Peter Gruenberger's immediate concern, as he was setting up his headquarters in David Begelman's locked and deserted office, was the diary of Begelman's secretary, Connie Danielson. The seizure of the diary by Jim Johnson the previous Friday had quickly been labeled "the pantie raid." Columbia had sought an opinion of the legality of the seizure under California law from a Los Angeles law firm. The firm's opinion was that if the diary was read only by Peter Gruenberger, and if Connie Danielson was interrogated only on entries which concerned the business of the company, its seizure was legal. The diary had been left on company premises, after all, and certain entries did mention business matters as distinct from Danielson's personal life.

Gruenberger determined from Danielson, and eventually confirmed with other sources, that the references in the diary to the Mafia and the Los Angeles Police Department related to a plan at the studio to develop a motion picture based on the so-called ''Skid Row Slasher'' killings—a series of random murders in Los Angeles in the mid-seventies in which the killer slashed the throats of his victims from ear to ear and occasionally drank their blood. The killer had struck several times in slum neighborhoods of downtown Los Angeles and again in the Hollywood area before being caught. A would-be producer had approached the studio early in 1977 claiming he had exclusive access to the police department's confidential investigative file on the slasher case. The project appealed to Begelman but he had made no final decision to proceed. Then Begelman began getting telephone calls from a man who urged him to buy the slasher project. The man, identifying himself as the producer's uncle, claimed his name was Carlo Gambino. David Begelman doubted that the man was *the* Carlo Gambino, who was an East Coast Mafia boss and very elderly. Further checking revealed that the would-be producer might have obtained the slasher file by bribing a Los Angeles police officer or former officer.

Connie Danielson had recorded several musings about these events in her diary, and when Gruenberger arrived to begin his investigation of Begelman, the slasher matter remained unresolved. Gruenberger's greatest concern was not the slasher project. His greatest concern was the possibility that David Begelman might have had contacts with Mafia boss Gambino. Gruenberger located on Begelman's telephone log the calls from the man claiming to be Gambino, and found the name Carlo Gambino and a telephone number in Begelman's office Rolodex. However, Gruenberger's efforts to trace the phone number to anyone named Gambino, or anyone familiar with the slasher project, proved fruitless. And Begelman assured Gruenberger that he had never known anyone named Carlo Gambino before the recent spate of calls. The Los Angeles police, meanwhile, revealed to Columbia investigators that someone indeed had obtained the slasher file through improper means and had been trying to peddle it at just about every studio in town. The police were embarrassed and were attempting to identify the person or persons responsible.

In the end, Columbia Pictures dropped the slasher movie project and Peter Gruenberger dropped his line of inquiry, satisfied that David Begelman had no connection to Mafia boss Carlo Gambino. It would not be Peter Gruenberger's last blind alley.

Later in the week, one of Gruenberger's investigators turned up

something much more germane to the inquiry into Begelman's
finances—a letter to Begelman from his financial manager warning
David that his personal monthly cash flow was in the red. On its
face the letter proved nothing. But it could help establish a motive
for embezzlement.

Centering the investigation in David Begelman's office suite, instead
of at a less conspicuous site at the studio or away from the studio
altogether, posed a visible daily distraction for studio executives and
staff members already stunned by the dramatic circumstances of
Begelman's departure, and by the absence of Begelman himself.
David Begelman was a popular president, very active in the day-to-
day activities of the studio, a calming influence in an anxious
business. Under the most benign of circumstances his absence would
have been felt. Under the existing circumstances, it caused dislocations.
Very little work got done at the studio on Monday and Tuesday, as
people clustered, gossiped, exchanged what few fragments of information were available outside of the press reports, and took a deluge
of inquisitory telephone calls from their friends at other studios. By
the end of the week a sense of siege had set in. The obtrusive group
of strangers who had commandeered their leader's office would be
there indefinitely. Every phone call to anyone at the studio still
began with a question about the Begelman crisis. Moreover, it was
clear that the leadership void at the studio had not been filled
effectively. Danny Melnick, for all his filmmaking talent, had no
interest in studio administration. And Alan Hirschfield would be in
New York most of the time and knew little about running the studio
anyway.
    Perhaps the calmest of the studio executives that week was Eli
Horowitz, the fifty-eight-year-old senior vice president for business
affairs, the man who negotiated the details of all motion-picture
contracts, once the studio heads had structured the deals' outlines.
The oldest of the top studio officers, Eli Horowitz was never confused with the garrulous Norman Horowitz of Columbia television
by people who knew them. Eli Horowitz was a quiet, perceptive
man, a product of working-class New York City in the Depression.
He had been with Columbia Pictures since 1946 when he was laid
off as a garment-industry bookkeeper and joined the film company
as an accounting clerk. Horowitz had seen a lot of studio presidents
come and go. As he was glancing through *Newsweek* on Wednesday,

he spotted an essay on the "My Turn" page which, he felt, coincidentally enunciated an important lesson on the Begelman episode. Entitled "Replaceable You," the article had been written by an ABC newsman out of a job. It began:

> There is an immutable law of the universe that most of us are destined to learn, forget and relearn over and over again during our lifetimes: no one is irreplaceable.
>
> There is a corollary also: everyone is expendable. I suspect that these laws are better known than the Ten Commandments and certainly are observed with religious fervor by those who have the power to enforce them. It is ironic, but fortunate, that those holding power do so only temporarily, for the rule is never broken. Those who decide who is expendable themselves become expendable someday and are replaced by other expendables. . . .

Eli Horowitz was so struck by the article that he distributed copies to several of his colleagues. But even Horowitz did not realize just how prescient the article would turn out to be.

The week exhausted Alan Hirschfield. From breakfast through nightcaps, he had reassured everybody in town that the Begelman problem was under control while fearing privately that it might never be. He had seen Begelman weep at La Serre. He had soothed the group from IBM. He had thrilled to *Close Encounters of the Third Kind*. He had sat through a less-than-thrilling presentation of the marketing and advertising plans for *Close Encounters*. After a long argument, he had convinced Michael Phillips, the film's coproducer, that the sound-track album from the movie should go to Arista, Columbia's own label, instead of being put out for bids.

Hirschfield thought his performance through the week had been pretty good, and it had been. He had made only one serious mistake, though he did not realize it at the time. He had failed to spend enough time in private with Ray Stark. They had been in the same groups at dinner twice during the week but had been alone together for only about an hour. Stark was still miffed at Hirschfield's refusal, two weeks earlier at Herbert Allen's apartment, to appoint him as interim head of the studio.

He remained skeptical of Hirschfield's motives. It would take much more than an hour to repair the relationship. But, in much the way that Herbert Allen's signals too often eluded Hirschfield, he failed to discern the depth and complexity of Ray Stark's concerns.

After nearly a full day of meetings on Friday, Hirschfield boarded a late-afternoon flight for New York. It was past 2:30 A.M. when he turned off his light in Scarsdale. He was up Saturday morning, however, in time to coach two soccer games.

On Sunday afternoon, Hirschfield made his way through heavy rain to Todd Lang's nearby home where he spent a couple of hours with Lang and Peter Gruenberger, who had flown in for the weekend. Aside from the inevitable tension of the investigation itself, another problem had arisen: tension between Gruenberger and the chairman of the board's audit committee, Allen in-law Irwin Kramer. Lang and Gruenberger felt that Kramer should confine himself to a general overview of the investigation. Instead, Gruenberger claimed, Kramer and his own lawyer, Robert Werbel, were on the verge of becoming a nuisance. It was almost as if Kramer did not trust Gruenberger—as if they were adversaries rather than allies.

TWENTY

David Begelman gave an interview to Martin Kasindorf of *Newsweek* about the "unauthorized financial transactions."

"It involves things that I had relatively unlimited authority over— and I may have abused that authority," Begelman said. "I want to say that any judgments I made I stand by. I like to think of myself as a doer, and if you are a doer you are going to make mistakes. I am prepared to say I was wrong."

Published Monday, October 10, the article reported that Begelman "hopes to be back in a matter of weeks, and one source close to Columbia agreed he has a good chance—if the investigation finds no further blot on the record."

Hirschfield's week was even busier than usual—shortened by the Columbus Day holiday and glutted with tasks that had accumulated while he was in Los Angeles. He conferred with Sam Cohn of International Creative Management, one of the top talent agents in the world, about the film rights to the Broadway musical *Annie* and about a possible investment by Columbia Pictures in a new Bob Fosse stage musical to be called *Dancin'*. He talked with Peter Guber, the producer of *The Deep* and *Midnight Express*, about a new production deal for Guber; with Richard Munro, a group vice president of Time Incorporated, about Time's investment in Columbia's film program; with Fred Pierce, the president of ABC television, about possible candidates to head Columbia's television arm; with Ira Harris, an investment banker at Salomon Brothers in Chicago, about two companies that Columbia might want to buy; with John Vogelstein, a New York investment banker and the chairman of the executive committee of Twentieth Century-Fox, about Columbia's possibly purchasing a big block of stock in Mattel Incorporated, the toy company; with Joe Fischer and Victor Kaufman about a plan for the General Cinema Corporation, operator of the nation's largest movie theater chain, to make a multimillion-dollar investment in Columbia's film projects; with Robert Stone, who had been fired seven months earlier as chief executive of the Hertz Corporation, about joining Columbia in some executive capacity; and with *Rolling Stone* publisher Jann Wenner, who wanted Hirschfield to become a director of the *Rolling Stone* company.

All of these people, and dozens of others with whom Hirschfield spoke, asked about the Begelman problem, and all of them, with only slight variations, got the same answer: We're still looking into it and we expect to have it clarified in a few weeks.

Over lunch on Tuesday with Herbert Allen and Matty Rosenhaus, Hirschfield suggested that it might be wise if he began at least an exploratory survey of potential candidates for the studio jobs that Begelman had vacated. (The motion-picture and television presidencies historically had been held by two people.) Herbert Allen, recalling that Hirschfield had refused to accept Ray Stark's offer to run the studio, asserted that the management gap did not appear to be an emergency and recommended that they await the investigators' report on Begelman.

The three men then joined other Columbia directors and top executives to hear a report from Peter Gruenberger on the initial stages of the inquiry and his plans for carrying it on. Since it appeared impractical to peruse all of the hundreds of thousands of checks that the studio had dispensed during Begelman's tenure, Gruenberger proposed to examine each check for $10,000 and over, which had been drawn in round thousands of dollars, i.e. $11,000, $17,000, or $50,000, as distinct from, say, $12,217 or $37,142.89. The search, which would be aided by computers, could be expanded later, but it appeared from the three embezzlements discovered to date—$10,000, $35,000, and $25,000—that Begelman did not bother with odd amounts.

In addition to surveying Begelman's personal and corporate financial records, the investigators planned to check the leases covering his house and automobiles. In only a few days on the job they already had turned up indications that there might have been abuses in those areas, as well as in his use of limousines. And a major issue looming over the entire inquiry was gambling. Did Begelman gamble? If so, did he have large gambling debts? There were persistent rumors that he did.

Alan Hirschfield left his office at noon Thursday and took a taxi to a small Italian restaurant called San Stefano in a disheveled block on East Fourteenth Street. San Stefano was one of the finest Italian bistros in Manhattan, but it had not been in business long and was virtually deserted at lunch. Hirschfield found it useful when he did not want to be recognized by friends and business acquaintances as he was at La Côte Basque and the other restaurants around the Columbia building. Thus, San Stefano was perfect for his meeting with Eric Pleskow of United Artists.

It had been thirteen days since banker Bill Thompson had told Hirschfield that the five top officers of United Artists were planning to resign from their posts because of differences with their corporate parent, the Transamerica Corporation. But since he had been in California the previous week, Hirschfield had not had an earlier opportunity to schedule a lunch with Pleskow as Thompson had suggested.

Instead of grilling Pleskow, Hirschfield began by pouring out his own problems stemming from the Begelman affair. Implying that Begelman would not be returning to Columbia, he said, "I'm not soliciting; I'm just saying that I have an obvious hole in my organization. I don't know what you're up to, or what you're thinking, or where you hope to be in a year or five years. If you're going to stay at Transamerica, power to you. But if the event should take place that you're available, or you together with your associates, I think there could be a lot of magic in putting your talents together with our talents. We could build the kind of company that we would both be proud of. At Columbia you wouldn't be dealing with the kind of people you are at Transamerica, who are watching every penny and have no appreciation of what you do or how you do it."

Pleskow was more candid and receptive than Hirschfield had anticipated. He confirmed that he and his colleagues were unhappy at Transamerica and that they were going to take some sort of action soon. He wasn't able to say much more just yet, but he wanted Hirschfield to know that he respected him and appreciated his interest. They would stay in touch.

Herb Allen, hearing about the meeting from Hirschfield the next day, remained as cautious as he had been the first time Hirschfield had broached the possibility that the United Artists group might want to join Columbia.

Herbert Allen's weekend retreat in Southampton originated as a modest cottage, reportedly in 1720, and grew gradually upward and outward over the next two and a half centuries into a sprawling, two-story-plus-attic, Colonial mansion. The house contained little art and few books but many photographs: Herbert with Ray Stark; Herbert with Fritz and Joan Mondale; Herbert with Bob Strauss, with John Tunney, with Hugh Carey, with Tom Brokaw, with Candy Bergen, and of course with his children and girl friends (film actress Jennifer O'Neil in the early seventies, and model-actress Barbara Rucker in the middle seventies). Like many other large beach houses in the Hamptons, the Allen place was not literally a beach house as the term is used in Malibu, where spacious homes are situated just a few steps from the surf and sometimes wash away in the winter storms. Herbert's house was a hundred yards or so from the water line at high tide. But so that one could experience the immediacy of the Atlantic without really roughing it, the main house had its own small satellite beach house, down the path just beyond the tennis court, right above the sand—a one-room structure with a deck and sauna overlooking the ocean. Herbert Allen had had some of his most intimate conversations in that sauna. On Saturday, October 15, his guest was Marty Ransohoff, and their subject was David Begelman.

Allen had met Ransohoff through Hirschfield a decade earlier when Ransohoff was still doubling as a movie producer and chief executive officer of the Filmways Corporation, a medium-sized television and film production company which Ransohoff had founded in 1952 with a capital investment of $200. A blunt, profane man of medium height with receding brown hair, a persistent paunch, and a baritone bark for a voice, Ransohoff in years past had been called "the messiah of the New Hollywood" by Budd Schulberg and "L. B. Mayer without overhead" by Joyce Haber. His record, however, was never spectacular or consistent enough by Hollywood standards to qualify him for either label. He produced some of the most successful television series of the early 1960s, including *The Beverly Hillbillies* and *Petticoat Junction*. Yet the moviegoing public did not know quite what to make of his films. Whether they were intelligent and pungent (*The Americanization of Emily*) or pretentious and boring (*The Sandpiper*), they rarely were in the mainstream of commercial Hollywood blandness and rarely were commercial hits, although most earned modest amounts of money.

In 1966, Alan Hirschfield had attempted to arrange a merger between Filmways and Seven Arts, and probably would have succeeded had it not been for the enmity that existed between Marty Ransohoff and Ray Stark. In 1972, Ransohoff left Filmways, whose growth and diversity demanded more time t..an he was willing to give it, and began producing movies full-time. But he stayed in touch with the corporate side of the business, and his friendships with Hirschfield and Allen deepened after they took over Columbia. Herbert Allen's close relationship with Ray Stark, and the continuing animosity between Stark and Ransohoff, never kept Herbert from liking Marty and finding him amusing.

In May 1977 (just ten days, in fact, before David Begelman embezzled $25,000 through the phony Pierre Groleau transaction), Ransohoff had signed a contract to make four pictures for Columbia.

When Begelman was suspended at the end of September, one of the first people briefed prior to the press announcement was Marty Ransohoff. When Ransohoff came to New York the second week of October, he and Hirschfield had breakfast at the Sherry Netherland. "The situation looks intolerable," Hirschfield told him. "David has lied to us repeatedly, and everywhere I turn another shoe drops."

The issue seemed simple to Ransohoff, who knew from his years as chief executive of Filmways how much outside scrutiny is directed at publicly owned companies—from the SEC, from the stock exchanges that regulate trading in the company's stock, and from hypercritical shareholders and their lawyers, some of whom will sue without much provocation. He assumed, therefore, that Begelman unquestionably would be fired and that Columbia's investigation was a formality—a polite way of easing David out. Although Hirschfield had mentioned that Herbert felt differently, Ransohoff still was surprised in the Southampton sauna the next day by the extent of Herbert's naïveté. Marty did not leaven his opinion.

"I believe David's a genuinely sick man," Herbert said.

"You don't buy that psychological shit, do you? Nobody on the coast does."

"If you had seen David's condition in the last couple of weeks, you might think differently."

"No matter how you slice it he was taking the fucking money. He's a felon. If this thing turns around and bites you, you'll get the shit kicked out of you in the press."

"The press is overrated. Ray feels that even if the details get out, it'll blow away in three weeks."

"My ass, it'll blow away. It'll blow away like Dorothy and Toto. If this were the steel-flange business or the ball-bearing business, who knows whether anybody would give a shit. But we're living in a fishbowl. This is the glamour biz. You can't tell me there aren't six twenty-eight-year-old reporters who'll blow this thing sky high. You're walking into the fire barefooted."

"What should we do then?"

"Give David an independent deal and get him out of the studio."

"Who'll we get to replace him? I can't think of anybody who can do that job like he's done it."

"There are plenty of people. You can find somebody. Alan thinks it's feasible."

"Ray thinks Alan wants to run the studio."

"Ray's been smoking something. That's ridiculous. Alan's got the best of both worlds now. He can go to Beverly Hills and play for a week a month, and he's got final approval of everything the studio does anyway. It's bullshit to think he'd ever want to leave the point of real control—New York. But that's beside the point. The point is how do you justify in a public company keeping a felon in office? The SEC will never sit still for it."

"They have so far."

"They obviously think you're going to get rid of him."

"The SEC has no right to run Columbia Pictures."

"Maybe not, but you watch what they do if you let Begelman stay. And what about your liability as a director? You'll give the shareholders twenty-twenty hindsight. What if you keep David and then the company's fortunes go bad? You'll give the shareholders a twenty-twenty hindsight shot at you. Who the fuck needs it? Are you willing to set your ass up? Is it worth it? Forget yourself. Is it worth dragging your uncle and your family through this? You're in a position now to treat David very well and get the monkey off your back at the same time. This monkey has big claws. If I were on the board I'd throw his ass out in a minute."

"You're not on the board."

"Hey, baby, you asked my opinion! Don't walk on me with your 'Fuck you' shoes! If you hadn't asked, I wouldn't have volunteered. You're a big boy, you're twenty-one, and it's your show."

Herbert and Marty had had enough of the sauna and enough of Begelman. They adjourned up the path to the tennis court.

At the Hirschfield home in Scarsdale that evening, the dinner guest was one of Alan's newer friends, David Geffen. Geffen had been the most spectacular impresario in the record business until he had grown weary of the grind and sold his company to Warner Communications. A small, skinny man of thirty-four with a slight resemblance to Lenny Bruce, Geffen had grown up in Brooklyn, the son of a brassiere maker. He had lied about his college record in order to get his first important job, at the William Morris Agency, but had achieved quick success as an agent and later as a record executive. He had guided the careers of Bob Dylan, Joni Mitchell, and other top stars, and emerged as a multimillionaire before he was thirty, with a Rolls-Royce, several homes, a large art collection, and an ego, as one friend put it, "as large as all outdoors and the energy of a hyperkinetic child on a sugar binge."

David Geffen and Alan Hirschfield had met at Ray Stark's home and had quickly grown fond of each other. Hirschfield loved the record business even more than the movie business. He had enjoyed music since he was a child, and from the time he was a teenager he had liked staying abreast of current trends in popular music. As president of Columbia Pictures Industries, he secretly preferred listening to advance pressing of new Arista releases in Clive Davis's office to watching rough cuts of new films at the studio. David Geffen, on the other hand, was still tired of the record business and was considering producing movies.

Apart from their common interests, Hirschfield enjoyed Geffen's personality. Geffen was something of a *kochleffl* in the Hollywood community—a pot-stirrer, an energizer. Wired snugly to the important power grids and grapevines, which tended to intertwine with each other, causing frequent sparks and smoke, Geffen usually knew the difference between truth and idle rumor. Thus, he was well positioned to appraise the significance of the Begelman affair as a phenomenon in the subculture of Hollywood—how it was being received, what effect full disclosure, or total concealment, of the facts might have, who stood to gain or lose the most from David Begelman's troubles or from his restoration.

It was ironic that Geffen had met Hirschfield at Ray Stark's, because on this October Saturday evening in Scarsdale, Geffen was warning Hirschfield to be careful of Stark. He claimed that Stark was beginning to work against Hirschfield on the Begelman issue. Though David Geffen and Ray Stark were very friendly, they had become engaged in a running argument over the Begelman affair and Hirschfield's role in it. According to Geffen, Stark was impugning Hirschfield's "moral" stance and claiming that Alan in fact was being disloyal to Begelman and trying to inflate his own power at the studio by exploiting Begelman's problems. Geffen had defended Hirschfield but he was now cautioning Alan that Ray could be a powerful foe if his ire was aroused.

Hirschfield thanked Geffen and told him to keep his ears open. But he failed to see how Ray Stark's comments to friends on the Hollywood social circuit—particularly an opinion as bizarre as

Hirschfield considered that which Geffen attributed to Stark—could affect the resolution of the Begelman issue.

After dinner, everyone went downstairs to the Hirschfields' projection room to see *Julia,* one of the major fall releases from Twentieth Century-Fox.

TWENTY-ONE

Hirschfield took his brash young senior vice president Allen Adler, the *Cosmopolitan* Bachelor of the Month, to lunch on Monday to discuss a meeting they were to have in the afternoon with an IBM executive about the laser video system that IBM was secretly developing. Hirschfield was confident that Columbia still stood an excellent chance of landing the software contract, despite the embarrassment of the Begelman affair. He felt he had sufficiently reassured the IBM people who had visited the studio two weeks earlier, the second day of Begelman's suspension, and he looked forward to continuing the discussion of the video system.

Adler and Hirschfield had not been together since a meeting in Hirschfield's office nearly three weeks earlier when Adler had tried, without success, to persuade Columbia's top executives to act more decisively against Begelman than they were disposed to act. Adler was surprised, therefore, to hear Hirschfield confide at their table at La Côte Basque: "I've got news for you. Begelman's not coming back."

"What do you mean he's not coming back? I thought you weren't going to decide until after the investigation."

"I won't, officially," Hirschfield said. "But it's already clear he's guilty as charged, so as far as I'm concerned he's finished. We'll make him a producer and that will be that. It's not the end of the world. This should make it easier to make some of those changes we were talking about months ago."

Adler was skeptical. As his longtime mentor, Hirschfield typically displayed toughness and decisiveness when he was alone with Adler, as an older brother might to a younger brother, but he showed less fortitude with the more powerful people at the company, Herbert Allen in particular. The "changes" to which Hirschfield referred had been suggested to him by Adler the previous January. Hirschfield had asked Adler to organize his thoughts about the current problems and future directions of the corporation. On January 5, the Wednesday after New Year's, they had walked over to the company apartment in the Carnegie House and talked for three hours. The meeting was kept secret; Adler marked his summary memorandum to Hirschfield "for your eyes only."

Adler spared few major people in the company, but he was especially critical in the memorandum of David Begelman's performance as president of the studio. "It is clear that none of the recently discussed plans for reorganization would work because they do not deal with the real problem, and involve hiring around the real problem, which is DB," Adler wrote. While acknowledging the value of Begelman's deal-making ability and his excellent contacts with actors, directors, and agents—the so-called "creative community" —Adler charged that Begelman's management of the studio and the film-production program was erratic and lax. He had hired a number of people at the studio who were incompetent and overpaid, and had neglected important administrative issues, Adler claimed. The result was an insufficient number of films at too high an overall cost.

On a deeper level, Adler was convinced that Begelman, at fifty-six, was too old to be counted on for the vision and acuity needed to lead the studio into the new era of multifarious video forms such as cassettes, discs, and satellite television, and to adapt to the uncertain demands the new forms would make on the studios as the conventional suppliers of motion pictures and television programs.

As a solution, Adler proposed that Begelman's job be redefined and renamed—perhaps elevated in status and called "chairman" of the studio—enabling Begelman to concentrate solely on assembling the major motion-picture deals. A new president—a younger man— could be hired to manage the studio, run the production program, hire and fire, plan for the future, and take on the other tasks which Begelman, in Adler's opinion, was failing to accomplish.

Hirschfield had agreed with most of the suggestions but, to Adler's chagrin, had never acted on them. Adler felt that was because

Hirschfield dreaded the inevitable confrontation with Herbert Allen and other board members who felt that Begelman's performance was outstanding in every way. Adler suspected that Hirschfield would be even more reluctant to face such a confrontation now because it surely would become entangled with the deliberations on Begelman's embezzlements.

"I think you're kidding yourself," Adler said at the luncheon table in response to Hirschfield's tough talk about Begelman. "I think you've blown it."

"How so?"

"You had a chance to fire Begelman three weeks ago, and you've had a chance to bring up these other issues for months. Since you didn't do either one, you're now obligated to go through with this investigation, not just pay lip service to it, but actually go through with it and judge the results on the merits. If nothing more is found, and the board isn't any more outraged about these thefts than it is now, you may have trouble getting rid of him."

"We'll find other things, and we will get rid of him. He's not coming back. You can bank on it. Then we'll have total flexibility to reorganize out there." (Hirschfield did not feel free to mention the possibility that some top United Artists officers might join Columbia.)

Though Adler remained doubtful, the conversation turned to lasers and the coming revolution in home video.

Close Encounters of the Third Kind was shown to selected public audiences for the first time at the Medallion Theater in Dallas, Texas, on the evenings of Wednesday and Thursday, October 19 and 20. Alan Hirschfield flew down from New York Wednesday afternoon, the studio executives having arrived from Los Angeles the previous day. Two weeks earlier Hirschfield had instructed Dan Melnick to keep limousines and other standard accoutrements of movie-studio junkets to a minimum in Dallas; ostentation did not seem appropriate while the company was investigating its studio president for stealing.

The temperature was in the nineties when Hirschfield stepped off the plane. Instinctively, as he did when he arrived at an airport anywhere in the world, he looked around for someone in a chauffeur's uniform there to meet him. Seeing no one, and irritated at Melnick who was supposed to have made the arrangements, he trudged to the baggage claim area. There, he was approached by an attractive young woman in jeans.

"Mr. Hirschfield?"

"Yes."

"I'm here to take you to the hotel."

"Oh, fine."

The woman insisted on carrying Hirschfield's overnight bag out to the curb where he saw a decrepit Volkswagen and behind it a gleaming white limousine. A uniformed chauffeur took the bag and put it in the limo. The woman, however, insisted that Hirschfield climb into the back seat of the Volkswagen. "Mr. Melnick's orders," she said. In the Volkswagen was a warm bottle of pink New York State champagne. The woman poured some into a plastic cup and handed it to Hirschfield. "Compliments of Mr. Melnick," she said. With the white limousine following, Hirschfield rode the thirty miles to his hotel in the back seat of the Volkswagen, where it was even hotter than outside.

"I've learned my lesson. You'll hear no more from me about limos," he told a convulsed Dan Melnick at the hotel.

Hirschfield went immediately to the Medallion Theater, situated in a large shopping center, to see Director Steven Spielberg. One decision yet to be made about *Close Encounters* concerned the music for a scene near the end of the movie in which the Richard Dreyfuss character boards the spaceship. The music was "When You Wish Upon a Star" from *Pinocchio*. The decision was whether to use an orchestral arrangement of "When You Wish Upon a Star," written specifically for *Close Encounters,* or an excerpt from the original *Pinocchio* soundtrack on which Cliff Edwards sings the song, supplying the voice of Jiminy Cricket. A third option was to use different music entirely. Alan Hirschfield had fallen in love with the Jiminy Cricket version and insisted that Spielberg use it in one of the screenings in order to gauge the audience's reaction. Spielberg agreed, and if he felt it improper for the president of the parent corporation to involve himself in artistic judgments, he showed no disapproval. The musical choice in question was one of several points in the film where Spielberg badly needed the help of a fresh, detached viewpoint in making final editing decisions.

The dozen Columbia executives present were as nervous as they had been two weeks earlier at the private screening in Hollywood. As much as they loved the movie, they all were intimately and painfully acquainted with the unpredictability of audiences. The reaction of the two Dallas groups, however, was overwhelmingly favorable. The enthusiasm on the second evening was even greater than on the first. (The Jiminy Cricket version of "When You Wish Upon a Star" drew a number of titters and was not used in the final cut of the film.)

David Begelman attended the Dallas screenings, and his presence caused no less "elephant-in-the-room" discomfort than it had in the Todd-AO projection room. Wanting to go to Dallas very badly, Begelman had sought Melnick's approval. Melnick had called Hirschfield, and they railed at each other over the phone, Melnick claiming, quite seriously, that Begelman might commit suicide if he were not included, and Hirschfield contending that it was outrageous for a suspended thief to participate in critical company events as if nothing had happened. But Hirschfield finally relented. Begelman not only sat with the Columbia group in the theater but also insisted on conferring alone with Spielberg after each screening and sitting in on marketing discussions with Melnick and Hirschfield at the hotel pool.

All in all, however, Hirschfield was elated with the Dallas results and looked forward to the next crucial tests of *Close Encounters*—screenings for reviewers and the rest of the press beginning November 1, and the world premiere in New York on Tuesday, November 15.

On Friday—the day after the second Dallas screening—Peter Gruenberger telephoned a progress report from Burbank to Robert Werbel, the Allen & Company lawyer who was acting during the Begelman inquiry as counsel to the audit committee of the Columbia board of directors. In more than two weeks, the investigators had not turned up any instance of embezzlement comparable to those already discovered. They were, however, beginning to find expense-account abuses totaling thousands of dollars. For example, it appeared that Begelman, while in Florida overseeing location-filming on *The Greatest*, starring Muhammad Ali, had used limousines for personal purposes having nothing to do with business, and had charged their $6,000 cost to the budget of the film

Gruenberger told Werbel that by the end of the investigation the team would have examined roughly twenty thousand checks issued by Columbia Pictures during Begelman's tenure. The minimum size of round-thousand-dollar checks to be examined had been lowered from $10,000 to $5,000 and Gruenberger had decided to examine all checks of any amount issued to a so-called "hot list" of about fifty people who had close personal or business ties to Begelman, e.g., Ray Stark and Sy Weintraub. Moreover, Gruenberger said he expected to have interviewed at least fifty or sixty people before concluding the inquiry. The work would take another two or three weeks, he felt, and then Begelman would be interrogated on the findings.

In addition to perusing, analyzing, and marshaling thousands of facts—data which were verifiable and often documented—the Gruenberger team found itself confronted with another category of information: rumor, gossip, scuttlebutt, every form of whisper about David Begelman. Gossip in Hollywood is not just idle back-fence chatter. It is an energizer of the town's central nervous system, a stimulant essential to the stability of an insecure community gripped by chronic self-doubt. Rumor and gossip tend to assuage one of the chief psychological dilemmas of Hollywood, the nagging confusion between illusion and reality. By occupying space between illusion and reality, rumor and gossip make the need to differentiate seem less important. Thus, by focusing on what transgressions David Begelman *might* have committed, Hollywood was able to amuse itself until it could learn what transgressions he had *in fact* committed.

The Begelman affair permeated the community like a thick, piquant mist. As the weeks wore on there were few conversations anywhere—at morning tennis games in Beverly Hills, over lunch at the Russian Tea Room on Fifty-seventh Street, during breaks in filming at the Pinewood Studios in London, in the upstairs lounges of New York-Los Angeles 747s—that did not contain at least a passing reference to David Begelman. Were the gambling stories true? Had he really charged his European honeymoon to Columbia Pictures as a business expense? Did he really forge a check? What would Columbia do? What was Alan Hirschfield up to? There were rumors about Begelman's recent past, distant past—even his future—and most of the rumors eventually made their way to Peter Gruenberger.

Although the Columbia board of directors had decreed that the investigation be limited to Begelman's time at Columbia, it was impossible to ignore some of the reports from his past, particularly if they overlapped the 1973–77 period. The most persistent of these reports was that Begelman was and always had been a gambler—a heavy gambler, a losing gambler, a gambler who, even as he was being investigated in the fall of 1977, owed hundreds of thousands of dollars to a multitude of interests, some of them unsavory, in Las Vegas, Monte Carlo, and London. (The gambling rumors had been heard when Columbia hired Begelman in 1973, and he assured Hirschfield and others at the time that though he had gambled in the past he had stopped and had no plans to resume.)

While multiple themes and variations ran through Begelman's "gambling profile," the figure $400,000 and the name of his producer friend Leonard Goldberg of Spelling-Goldberg cropped up often. *Theme:* Once in the 1960s Goldberg personally had carried $400,000 in cash to Las Vegas in a suitcase to bail Begelman out of a gambling debt. *Variation:* Goldberg had sent the $400,000 to Vegas via a shady messenger. *Theme:* The payment had cleared Begelman's accounts and he had not gambled since. *Variation:* The payment had cleared his accounts for the time being, but he had run up another $400,000 in debts since then, and the mob was pressing him. *Theme:* During his Columbia years—probably while in France for the Cannes Film Festival in May 1976—he had lost a bundle in Monte Carlo. *Variation:* He had won a bundle in Monte Carlo.

Begelman and Goldberg flatly denied all versions of the Las Vegas loan story. Gruenberger exhausted his investigative resources and could not confirm it. Alan Hirschfield finally asked Mickey Rudin to look into the matter, particularly the question of whether Begelman owed any current debts or had owed any that he might have settled with stolen money. Rudin ran a credit check on Begelman in Las Vegas and found nothing. The issue was dropped. Another blind alley.

Eventually, it was determined that Begelman had in fact gambled in Monte Carlo in 1976, but only very modestly.

Peter Gruenberger's efforts to sift fact from rumor, and innocent fact from guilty fact, would have been difficult even in isolation. Since he did not represent a law-enforcement body, he did not have subpoena power and could not compel anyone to help him, much less tell him the truth. And since Columbia was preoccupied with keeping secret the nature of Begelman's misdeeds and the details of the investigation, Gruenberger was forced to proceed in total privacy. He could not, as the Los Angeles district attorney would a few months later, publicize a special telephone number which everyone with information about corruption in Hollywood was invited to call.

The difficulties posed by these limitations were complicated, moreover, by the peculiar climate within which the investigation was being conducted—the climate of a small, insular one-industry town under attack from the outside, a climate which by late October was becoming hostile and political. Columbia's decision not to fire David Begelman a month earlier, but instead to suspend him and embark upon an investigation, had given Begelman's partisans time to appraise the situation and mobilize support for the notion that he should be reinstated as president of the studio. Their campaign had barely begun to form and was almost as private as the investigation. (The press had carried very little on the Begelman affair since the burst of publicity during the first week of October.) Nevertheless, the campaign was real, and as it gained momentum, the hostility facing Peter Gruenberger increased. Fewer and fewer people were willing to give him more than grudging cooperation. Some of those who were interrogated leaked selectively the information which they gleaned or inferred from his line of questioning, if they felt leaks would inhibit his efforts. Indeed, one of the pro-Begelman forces' most potent weapons was information—essentially the same agglomeration of fact, rumor, and gossip with which the investigators were grappling. As in any propaganda campaign, the Begelman partisans were interested not in establishing the truth but in formulating a plausible story that could aid their cause. The story which they concocted employed a few facts, a few half-truths, a few rumors, and a few lies. It also involved—in a crucial and fundamental way—the attempted confinement of certain facts, i.e., the true nature of Begelman's wrongdoing, to a small circle of people, and the assumption that those facts would never become known outside of that circle.

The gist of the pro-Begelman story, as it was evolving in late October, was that his problems lay in his expense accounts and executive perquisites. According to this story, a routine audit by Columbia's accountants had turned up a few questionable transactions in Begelman's expense account—transactions through which he may, in effect, have made personal use of company funds by including in his business-travel and entertainment accounts certain expenses that, strictly defined, were personal. While this sort of thing theoretically was not condoned, it could not be denied that a lot of people did it, sometimes inadvertently. A careful audit would find questionable items in the expense accounts of most top executives in America, Begelman's partisans contended. In Hollywood, especially, business and personal lives are melded most of the time. The business of Hollywood is the life of Hollywood. A great deal of business— ostensible and occasionally more than ostensible—is conducted on tennis courts, in or around swimming pools, on sailboats, in home screening rooms, and of course, over breakfast, lunch, cocktails, dinner, and midnight suppers, not only in restaurants but in homes as well. Nearly all such expenses, which would seem personal to many outsiders, are charged in Hollywood to the studio, or to the production company, or to the record company, or to the budget of the picture or television series. "Who do you know who isn't a write-off" was the expression that covered the subject when it came up.

In the area of perquisites, many executives' contracts permit them to take their wives on business trips at the studio's expense. And the studios frequently pay, directly or indirectly, part or all of their executives' housing and automobile expenses. Many executives drive Mercedeses or Cadillacs or Jaguars or Rollses that are leased for them by the studio, and live in homes that are leased for them by the studio, or that the studio has enabled them to purchase at reduced prices.

The Hollywood financial climate, in short, is permissive. It always has been permissive. Everybody takes advantage of it. Was David Begelman any worse than anyone else? Decidedly not. Why, then, was he being singled out? He was being singled out, the story went, because Alan Hirschfield wanted to get rid of Begelman and have more power himself. Thus, he seized upon Begelman's indiscretions (if they could even be called indiscretions) and was applying an ultrastrict post-Watergate standard in an effort to portray Begelman as a crook.

By the third week of October, this story was taking root among growing numbers of people in Hollywood. The same gossip networks that were carrying Begelman rumors were being used to spread pro-Begelman propaganda. And quite apart from inhibiting the work of Peter Gruenberger, the propaganda was tarnishing the image of Alan Hirschfield. The story made sense, and people were getting angry. David Begelman, their friend, a popular leader of the community, seemed clearly to be the victim. Hirschfield, the outsider from Wall Street, was the heavy. It appeared that Hirschfield might turn out to be the latest of a breed of interloper that had plagued Hollywood throughout its history—the eastern banker who knows nothing about making pictures but is swept up in the glamour of it, and believes that his financial stake gives him the right to control the destinies, and even the day-to-day work, of the true creative geniuses of film, people like David Begelman. Hollywood had developed a number of ways of dealing with such intruders. If they had a weakness for attractive women, it was sometimes possible to preoccupy them with extraordinary sex in the Beverly Hills Hotel for the length of their stay on the coast. If they insisted on doing business, it was sometimes possible to dazzle them with introductions to a few film stars and visits to sound stages. Some intruders, however, came to town with grander notions of exercising genuine, long-term power. They had to be dealt with more carefully, more subtly, and on an individual basis.

In addition to anger, Hirschfield's apparent stance against Begelman generated a degree of pragmatic discomfort in the Hollywood community—discomfort crystallized in a widely read interpretive article by Art Murphy in *Daily Variety*. As Murphy saw it, Columbia's investigation of Begelman served to focus new and critical scrutiny on Hollywood executive perquisites in general. "The ultimate specifics of the Begelman-Columbia matter are really of minor importance," Murphy wrote. "It's the entire environment that is now under focus and fire. . . . The gravy train hasn't stopped, but it's going to slow down." In other words, if Hirschfield could get tough with Begelman, then every studio might be forced to get tough with everybody. The entire perk-laden financial structure within which thousands of people lived, and on which they depended, could be threatened, according to this reasoning. A discomfiting thought, to say the least.

The story and underlying rationale of Begelman's plight depended for its plausibility, of course, on suppression of the truth about Begelman's actual misdeeds. A lot of people who were prepared to condemn Hirschfield for investigating Begelman, and for whom expense-account chiseling was a daily practice, would have been horrified, and would have applauded the investigation, if they had known that its target was not perks and expense accounts but the quite different issues of check forgery and embezzlement.

As of late October, the secrecy was holding pretty well. It was naïve, of course, to think that it could be preserved forever. But naïveté is as much a part of the Hollywood way of life as the permissive financial climate. David Begelman, for one, was secure in the belief that the euphemism "unauthorized financial transactions" would endure and that the details would never be widely known. He was devastated, therefore, when a close friend said one day: "You're kidding yourself. Everybody knows you forged Cliff Robertson's name on a check." Although the friend was wrong—relatively few people outside of Columbia knew of the Robertson forgery at that time—the friend at least alerted Begelman to the likelihood that the word would spread. But how soon would it spread? Would it spread widely enough to undermine the cover story of the expense account and the perks?

The answers to those questions lay in part with the people in possession of the truth, and as of the third week of October, their motives and inclinations varied considerably. Barring revelation of major new embezzlements, Ray Stark wanted Begelman reinstated and was preparing to accelerate his efforts toward that end. Marty Ransohoff felt that Begelman should be fired but was unwilling to become an active lobbyist, aside from venting his views privately to Alan Hirschfield and Herbert Allen. David Geffen, who sided with Hirschfield on principle, found himself being used as a conduit between Hirschfield and Stark.

The small number of people who knew about the embezzlements, however, was no longer limited to people with close relationships to the top echelon of Columbia. It had gradually expanded by that time to include a handful of top executives at other film studios. After recovering from the initial shock, some of these people quickly became concerned that Alan Hirschfield was being too lenient with Begelman. The top executives of MCA-Universal, for example, thought it odd that Columbia was taking so long to dismiss Begelman in view of the seriousness of his reported crime. They whispered to each other over lunch that if a forger-embezzler had been caught in their company, he would have been fired immediately. What could be delaying Columbia?

Ironically, therefore, Hirschfield was gradually losing support—for opposite reasons—in two important constituencies: *le tout* Hollywood, who felt angered and threatened by his apparent persecution of Begelman for what they believed were minor indiscretions; and his fellow chief executives, who feared that he perhaps was being lenient and indecisive in a situation that required prompt, tough action.

Hirschfield, however, was all but oblivious to such considerations.

Aside from David Geffen, whose warning had been specifically about Ray Stark and had not left a strong impression, no one had seen fit to warn Hirschfield about possible reactions in Hollywood to his handling of the Begelman affair. And he had not figured it out for himself. He had taken account of the SEC, the police, the banks, Wall Street, the business and financial community, the stockholders, and "the public." And yet, through more than a decade in and out of show business, he had never grasped that the Hollywood community is a constituency, too, and must be catered to if one proposes to flourish there.

It was not too late, though. Hirschfield still had time. Hollywood was not yet ready to step forward and confront him. Except for cocktail-party whispers, its plotting was proceeding in private. Outwardly, the town was keeping its own counsel, watching and waiting

Despite Herbert Allen's suggestion that no replacement for Begelman be sought actively until the investigation was completed, Hirschfield began a preliminary survey of candidates for the jobs in question. On the morning of Wednesday, October 19, just before leaving for the Dallas preview of *Close Encounters*, he had breakfast at the Dorset Hotel with Fred Pierce, the president of ABC television. Though Pierce was not a candidate for Columbia himself—he saw his future at ABC—he suggested some other people as possibilities. One of them was his own colleague, Fred Silverman, ABC's programming head, whose contract would expire in a year and who was getting a little restless. Silverman had guided ABC into first place in television ratings among the three networks, duplicating his success at CBS a few years earlier. Hirschfield took Silverman to lunch on Friday at "21" and, in a general way, posed the notion that Silverman might be an appropriate replacement for Begelman as head of motion-picture and television operations at Columbia. As it turned out, Silverman was not yet prepared to decide whether to stay at ABC. He confirmed that he was restless, however, and even asked Hirschfield to recommend a lawyer skilled at negotiating executive employment contracts. Hirschfield referred him to Mickey Rudin.

Conversations like those with Pierce and Silverman were difficult for Hirschfield because they invariably began with questions about Begelman: "Is he coming back? What exactly did he do? We hear the problem is in the perk area." Hirschfield did not feel free to answer any of these questions candidly. He made clear that he would not be surveying possible replacements if there were not a strong possibility that Begelman would not return. Without detailing Begelman's crimes, Hirschfield did confide to a few people that they were more serious than "perk or expense account problems."

Hirschfield finally got to have a relaxed and open conversation with close friends on Saturday evening when he and Berte dined with the Clive Davises and went to Trax on Seventy-second Street to hear Dwight Twilley, a rock singer who recorded for Arista. Though there was no new information on the Begelman crisis to be exchanged, commiseration with Clive always soothed Alan.

TWENTY-TWO

Among Alan Hirschfield's most important achievements in 1976 and 1977 was the establishment of new business relationships between Columbia Pictures Industries and prestigious corporations outside the movie production industry. As well as opening new financial opportunities for Columbia, these relationships helped to build its reputation as a company that no longer was just a second-echelon film studio but was moving toward the front ranks of respected, multinational entertainment conglomerates like Warner Communications and MCA. One of Columbia's new relationships was with Time Incorporated, the world's preeminent magazine publisher, which had agreed to invest several million dollars in Columbia's motion pictures. Another relationship was with IBM, which was considering making Columbia its partner in the development of a laser video system. Still another was with the General Cinema Corporation, a large Boston-based concern which made half its money from soft-drink bottling and the other half from its original business—the nation's largest chain of movie theaters. In financial terms, the General

Cinema relationship was the most important. The two companies had been negotiating a plan by which General Cinema would invest upwards of $26 million in Columbia's motion-picture production program over a period of years.

When the Begelman problem developed, one of Hirschfeld's most acute fears was that it might jeopardize Columbia's carefully cultivated relationships with Time, IBM, and General Cinema. None of them, he felt, would want to be associated with a company whose top management included an embezzler and check forger. Hirschfeld made special efforts, therefore, to reassure each of the three corporations that the Begelman problem was isolated, under control, and did not reflect a lax ethical climate at Columbia.

On Monday morning, October 24, Hirschfeld and Dan Melnick flew to Boston for a visit with the chief executive officer of General Cinema, Richard A. Smith. Dick Smith's unpretentious manner and appearance belied his prominence in the business and cultural affairs of New England. The son of General Cinema's founder, he had graduated from Harvard and had remained active in the university's affairs, as well as serving on the boards of the First National Bank of Boston and the Boston Symphony Orchestra.

Hirschfeld wanted to show off Melnick, one of the brightest and most articulate people in Hollywood, as a way of assuring Smith that Columbia's film program, with Melnick as head of production, was in good hands no matter who was president of the studio. Before introducing Melnick, however, Hirschfeld spent a few minutes alone with Smith. Hirschfeld was ready with his usual carefully worded explanation of how Columbia was handling the Begelman problem, why it was investigating carefully, and why it had suspended Begelman rather than dismissing him. But he did not have to deliver the speech. Dick Smith, it turned out, already knew the pertinent facts and had formed strong opinions about them.

"I don't understand what all the confusion is about," Smith declared in his mild New England brogue. "Why don't you just fire the man and be done with it. It seems clear from what I know that he's a crook."

"I appreciate your sentiments, Dick; they're my sentiments, too," Hirschfeld said. "But I've got a board to contend with, and not everybody on the board sees the issue that clearly. The prevailing view is to wait and see what the investigation reveals before doing anything."

"Let me make one thing very clear to you," Smith replied. "We have no interest in investing in Columbia if Mr. Begelman has anything to do with the company. We just don't run our business that way. As far as I'm concerned, we're investing in Alan Hirschfield and his management team. We want to meet Melnick and make sure he has his head screwed on straight, but basically we're looking to a relationship with Columbia as represented by you. If Begelman comes back into the company, there will be no deal with General Cinema. We can't afford those kinds of relationships. That's not the way we run our business. I assume your board will come to the same conclusion. I don't know what's taking so long."

"I'll certainly see that your feelings are conveyed to the board," Hirschfield said. "I appreciate your candor, and I know your feelings will carry a lot of weight."

Dan Melnick then gave Smith an informal briefing on Columbia's motion-picture production plans for the next two years. Smith was very impressed, and Hirschfield and Melnick left for the airport and a flight to Los Angeles with General Cinema's $26 million investment plan still intact. Hirschfield was elated. He was gratified by Smith's support of his desire to get rid of Begelman. And he was confident that Smith's threat to withdraw from the deal if Begelman returned surely would help nullify any attempt to resurrect Begelman.

Having been warned by Herbert Allen to make amends to Ray Stark, whom he had slighted inadvertently while in Los Angeles three weeks earlier, Hirschfield scheduled a long lunch with Stark for Tuesday. They ate at Ray's favorite restaurant in the immediate vicinity of The Burbank Studios, Chow's Kosherama Delicatessen, the only spot for miles around that featured tongue on rye and chicken with walnuts on the same menu.

Hirschfield was more surprised than he should have been that Stark was lobbying for Begelman's reinstatement as president of the studio. He knew that the investigative team was finding evidence that Stark and Begelman had a closer relationship than he had thought. And David Geffen had warned him that Stark's comments were tilted for Begelman and against Hirschfield. But he had not grasped the ramifications of these signals and thus was unprepared for a sophisticated encounter with Stark, who not only sketched a rationale for Begelman's restoration but also hinted that the continuation of the Rastar multipicture contract with Columbia might depend on Begelman's return. The Stark contract, which Columbia valued very highly, was in the midst of renegotiation.

"I really can't sign any deal until I know who's going to be running the studio," Stark told Hirschfield. "Maybe you'll bring in somebody I don't like or who doesn't like me." Hirschfield pooh-poohed that notion. Stark then said he understood that Begelman was making excellent progress in his psychotherapy with Dr. Judd Marmor. Hirschfield pooh-poohed that as well (and concealed his shock that Stark was so well informed on something so intimate as another person's psychotherapy).

"At best," Hirschfield said, "David has severe psychological problems that will take a lot of time to treat. At worst, he's nothing but a crook. In any event, he has lied up and down. There's nothing he can say to me ever again where I could rely on what he says or trust his motives."

"Alan, you've got to have a more flexible attitude," Stark replied. "He's coming along well. Besides, he's the best in the business at what he does, and you two have been a great team. It would be a tragedy to break it up."

"My God, have you forgotten what he's done—the horrendous nature of the acts! The man has forged checks, he's stolen money, he's falsified documents!"

"But it isn't that much money. I would have given it to him. You would have given it to him. I'm sure he's learned his lesson."

"Ray, what do you do the day you catch some vice president in your company stealing? Do you say everybody gets one chance? And who knows what else we're going to find in this investigation?"

"I'm convinced you've found all you're going to find. You're at least obliged to wait for the results before making up your mind."

That evening Hirschfield took Leonard and Wendy Goldberg to dinner at La Scala. Although he was friendly with the Goldbergs, the occasion was not an idle, relaxed retreat from the cares of the day. It was a "relationship dinner"—a genre of event which is common in more than one industrial subculture but which nowhere rises to the level of vital social ritual quite the way it does in Hollywood. Relationship dinners (the label is never used openly) are big in Hollywood because many important relationships depend for their perpetuation on a degree of contrived, artificial stimulus. The town is so small that one does not have the luxury of dealing only with people that one genuinely likes and respects. Sooner or later, one must do business with just about all the important people, whether one likes them or not. Hollywood is still one of the most oligarchical societies in the world. There are only seven major studios, three television networks, two or three important talent agencies, a handful of truly important motion picture producers, and another handful of truly important television producers. A hostile relationship with even one or two of these entities or people can be very harmful, so one tries to be everyone's friend. However, disputes, quarrels, and general hostility are so common in Hollywood that efforts toward harmony are defensive more often than they are offensive. One spends more energy attempting to isolate and limit the harmful effects of wounded relationships than one spends maintaining healthy relationships. If, for example, an important relationship deteriorates, and an important friend becomes an enemy, one must try to ingratiate oneself with the important friends of the new enemy in hopes that the ill feeling will not spread from the individual to an entire circle of people.

Alan Hirschfield, therefore, arranged a relationship dinner with the Goldbergs for two reasons. First, Leonard Goldberg, along with his partner, Aaron Spelling, was one of the most important television producers in the industry. Four of the top ten TV shows—*Charlie's Angels, Love Boat, Fantasy Island,* and *Starsky and Hutch*—were Spelling-Goldberg programs. Goldberg wanted to produce movies, too, and had been in the process of negotiating a production deal with Columbia when David Begelman was sidelined. The second reason for the dinner was that Leonard and Wendy Goldberg, individually and as a couple, were among David and Gladyce Begelman's closest friends. (Wendy and Leonard accompanied David and Gladyce on their European honeymoon in the late summer of 1975.)

Hirschfield thus hoped that he could maintain Leonard Goldberg's good will, even in the face of Columbia's suspension of Begelman and even if it became necessary to dismiss David permanently. The dinner was pleasant and cordial, as most relationship dinners are. They sat in one of the red-leather banquettes in La Scala's brightly lit main dining room just to the right of the bar. They were seen by a number of mutual acquaintances (a helpful occurrence at a relationship dinner). Talk of David's misdeeds was kept brief and confined to generalities. Assuming that the Goldbergs knew the details of the thefts—but not knowing for sure that they did—Hirschfield refrained from invoking the words "forgery" and "embezzlement." He merely offered sympathy when Leonard and Wendy expressed sadness at David's plight and surprise that he might have strayed from his usual pattern of honorable conduct.

The talk of Leonard's movie-production plans, however, was more specific. Alan said he was confident that the conversations which Leonard had been having with David could be consummated satisfactorily. Columbia very much wanted Leonard to produce pictures for it. Alan even confided that Columbia was seriously considering purchasing the motion-picture rights to *Annie*, the Broadway musical which had become a major hit since opening the previous April. If Columbia were to buy *Annie*, Alan asked, would Leonard be interested in producing it? Leonard was enthusiastic. Although he had been skeptical about *Annie* before it opened, he said, he had been pleasantly surprised—even astounded—by how well it worked on the stage and how much the audience obviously loved it the night he and Wendy saw it. Yes, he would be very interested in producing *Annie*. (Neither Alan nor Leonard bothered to mention an obvious fact: *Annie* would be a big-budget film, and the producer's fee would be very large.)

The evening ended with visions of *Annie* dancing in Leonard Goldberg's head, and with Alan Hirschfield hopeful that the Goldberg relationship was intact.

Hirschfield faced two awkward encounters on Wednesday with men he knew well—breakfast with Frank Wells, the president of Warner Bros., and lunch with Lew Wasserman and Sidney Sheinberg, the chairman and president of MCA-Universal. Hollywood labor problems were the subject of both meetings, but David Begelman loomed over the conversations, almost as if he were present in Frank Wells's home for breakfast and in the MCA executive dining room for lunch. Frank Wells had not seen Hirschfield since they were at the White House together four weeks earlier, the day before Begelman was suspended. "That was the greatest performance I have ever seen, on screen or off," Wells said, recalling that Hirschfield's demeanor had been typically affable and droll, and had revealed nothing of his inner tumult.

Wells, Wasserman, and Sheinberg had all learned by late October that check forgery was at the heart of the Begelman problem. They were having difficulty understanding why Hirschfield seemed to be having such a tough time handling the matter. But they hesitated to broach it. The head of one movie company does not tell the head of another movie company how to manage his business. The other executives thought perhaps there were extenuating circumstances which, if known to them, would make Hirschfield's behavior fathomable. Hirschfield, for his part, was beginning to feel an acute need for moral support and wanted to confide in Lew Wasserman and seek his advice. He admired Wasserman more than anyone in Hollywood. But Hirschfield was not sure that Wasserman knew the salient facts of the Begelman affair and did not feel free to volunteer them. Therefore, instead of the candid discussion that all four men would have preferred, they confined themselves to generalities; Wells, Wasserman, and Sheinberg expressed sympathy for both Hirschfield and Begelman, and Hirschfield acknowledged that it was a difficult situation but said it would be resolved satisfactorily in the near future.

By the end of the week, Hirschfield was more eager than ever to find a replacement for Begelman. In addition to the discomfort of straddling a secret scandal and the public obligations of a continuing business, Hirschfield was feeling the extra pressure of his responsibility for direct supervision of Columbia's movie and television operations in Begelman's absence. The week had been littered with meetings on details of studio operations that normally would have been handled by the president of the studio. It appeared that Hirschfield would have to spend two weeks a month in Los Angeles instead of one. The prospect depressed him as he flew home Friday afternoon.

The sense of siege felt by the officers and staff of the Columbia studio during the Begelman investigation also was felt by the investigators. For Peter Gruenberger and his team, the days were long and lonely. Gruenberger fell into a routine of getting up early in the morning, driving from the Beverly Hills Hotel over Coldwater Canyon to The Burbank Studios, having breakfast at the commissary, and arriving at his command post in Begelman's office by around eight. He rarely left before eight in the evening. The World Series— the first Yankee-Dodger series since 1963—had given him something to look forward to for a week in the middle of October. With games starting at 5 P.M. Pacific time, Gruenberger and his group would turn on the big color TV set in Begelman's office and monitor the games as they continued with their work. The work itself was tedious and grew more so as the days and weeks passed. Except for an occasional enlightening interrogation, it consisted of examining documents—thousands and thousands of documents—upwards of twenty thousand checks alone, front and back. It was not work a computer could do. Someone actually had to peruse each check—payee, signers, endorsers, dates, and other information. Some checks were parts of complex and often twisting documentary trails through particular transactions—film deals and the like. Other checks stood alone—single payments for thousands of individual services that had been rendered to the studio.

Nearing the end of the fourth week of October, the lawyers and accountants had compiled a list, still lengthening, of expense account abuses totaling thousands of dollars. They had determined that Begelman had misrepresented the terms of the lease of his two automobiles for which the studio paid. They had determined that he had not been forthright about the terms under which he leased his house, payments for which were also made largely by the studio.

In nearly four weeks of searching, however, the investigators had found no other forgeries or embezzlements comparable to the Cliff Robertson, Peter Choate, and Pierre Groleau thefts which had come to light even before the investigation began. Could incriminating documents have been removed before the start of the inquiry? Anything was possible, but there was no indication that files had been tampered with.

Late in the afternoon of Friday, October 28, Nancy Barton, a young Weil, Gotshal lawyer and the junior member of the investigative group, sat in Begelman's office staring at a Columbia Pictures check for $5,000 that had been drawn in 1975 to the order of Martin Ritt, a film director best known for *Hud*, *The Spy Who Came In from the Cold*, and *The Long Hot Summer*. Barton turned the check over. There were two endorsements. The first was "Martin Ritt." The second was "David Begelman." The handwriting looked familiar. Nancy Barton had become the team's expert on Begelman's handwriting. She knew his nuances. She knew that he wrote differently with a felt-tip pen than with a ball-point, and that his signature differed from other forms of his writing. The endorsements on the Martin Ritt check appeared to be in Begelman's handwriting. Moreover, the check had been cashed at the Wells Fargo Bank in

Beverly Hills and approved by Joe Lipsher, just like the Robertson and Groleau checks.

Barton passed the check around the room. The studio's file on Martin Ritt was summoned and revealed that Ritt's handwriting was different from that on the check. Further research revealed that at the time the check was drawn, Marty Ritt had begun work for Columbia Pictures on *The Front*, a film about the blacklist, starring Woody Allen. It was logical that the studio would have been making various payments to Ritt at that time—payments that could easily have helped camouflage a single forged check.

Peter Gruenberger telephoned Ritt and asked him to come in for questioning. Ritt agreed, and after hanging up, immediately called Ray Stark. Stark immediately called Begelman. Begelman immediately called Gruenberger and, in a very agitated state, expressed his profound apology and regret. He had simply forgotten about the Ritt check. He had totally blocked it from his mind.*

Gruenberger said he would be in touch.

TWENTY-THREE

Andrew Tobias, the author and *Esquire* columnist, was one of the wittiest and most insightful writers on money and business in the country, and was always alert for intriguing stories. But he hardly expected to hear such a story in the East Harlem pizzeria where he dined on Sunday evening, October 30. Tobias's initial concern that evening was East Harlem itself. It seemed a needlessly remote and dangerous place to go just for pizza. Perfectly good pizza was available in safer districts of Manhattan. East Harlem, however, was where Tobias's friend, The Unimpeachable Source from Hollywood, wanted to go. And so it was in East Harlem that Andrew Tobias

---

*Like Robertson, Choate, and Groleau, Ritt had no knowledge of Begelman's use of his name.

became the first journalist anywhere to learn the inside story of the David Begelman scandal.

The Unimpeachable Source from Hollywood did not get around to the subject of Begelman and Columbia Pictures immediately, but the details eventually poured forth. Aside from his enjoyment of the intrigue, the Unimpeachable Source had grown concerned that the secrecy cloaking Begelman's crimes—secrecy that had been imposed for reasons that had seemed valid a few weeks earlier—was now being manipulated in Hollywood to the detriment of the source's friend Alan Hirschfield. The false but plausible story that Hirschfield was using minor indiscretions as weapons in a power play against Begelman was hurting Hirschfield. And the source had concluded that the only effective way of countering the false story was somehow to get the true story—the facts of Begelman's forgery and embezzlement—into the public domain. He had urged Hirschfield to talk directly to Andrew Tobias, but Hirschfield had refused. The Unimpeachable Source felt compelled, therefore, to take the first step himself. He had to be careful. If it became known that he had leaked the story, or even that he was a Hirschfield partisan at heart, it would damage his relationships in Hollywood, where his circle of friends included Ray Stark and indeed David Begelman himself. So it was with the understanding that Tobias could never disclose the identity of his source that his friend revealed the essence of what he knew: Columbia Pictures' investigation of Begelman for "unauthorized financial transactions" was much more serious than outsiders generally realized; the "transactions" were hardly "gray areas of personal judgment," as *Variety* had speculated; Begelman had embezzled thousands of dollars from Columbia Pictures; he had forged Cliff Robertson's name on a check.

Andrew Tobias was riveted. It clearly was a major and sensational story. The Unimpeachable Source hinted that if Tobias could ferret out the details from other sources, Alan Hirschfield might be persuaded to confirm them privately and perhaps even furnish additional information. Tobias vowed to look into the Begelman affair as soon as he could, but there were two potential problems: he was preoccupied with other projects and could not begin work on Begelman immediately. And he worked for a magazine, *Esquire,* whose cumbersome editing and production processes, like those of most monthly publications, consumed two or three months. Even if he researched and wrote a Begelman article within a few weeks, it probably could not be in the hands of readers until February. Suppose someone else broke the story in the meantime?

At *Esquire*'s request Tobias decided to take the chance and not publish the story elsewhere. But his fears of being scooped were well grounded. His friend was not the only person who had considered leaking the Begelman story. Another was a man who had hated David Begelman for many years—Sid Luft. Luft had been in the last stages of his tumultuous marriage to Judy Garland when David Begelman had become Garland's agent in 1960. The two men had clashed repeatedly. Luft had become convinced that Begelman was mismanaging Garland's career, that Begelman was sleeping with Garland, that Begelman was stealing Garland's money. Eventually, Luft began a lawsuit against Begelman, who denied all the allegations. Luft did not pursue the suit aggressively, but even after Garland's death in 1969, the suit technically remained alive. It was mentioned in a widely read biography of Garland by Gerold Frank, published in 1975. The suit, however, had never received the public attention that Sid Luft believed it deserved. In the fall of 1977, nearly a decade and a half after the activities covered by the suit, Luft felt that perhaps the time was finally right. Though Sid Luft did not know the nature of Begelman's misdeeds at Columbia, he decided that he might be able to interest the press in the proposition that the Columbia affair was not the first time that David Begelman had been accused of financial chicanery. In late October, at about the time that Andrew Tobias's friend was arranging the pizza rendezvous in East Harlem, Sid Luft telephoned the *Los Angeles Times*. His calls were not returned. He called *Rolling Stone*. It was not interested. He called *New West* magazine, the Los Angeles-based sister publication of *New York*. *New West*, it seemed, had already assigned a reporter, Jeanie Kasindorf, to look into the Begelman affair, and she took Luft's call. They agreed to meet on Friday, November 4.

An unexpected magazine article ruined Monday, October 31, for Alan Hirschfield and a lot of other people at 711 Fifth Avenue and The Burbank Studios. The article did not involve Andrew Tobias or Jeanie Kasindorf and was not a Begelman exposé, which Hirschfield secretly would have welcomed. Instead, the article purported to be an exposé of *Close Encounters of the Third Kind* and predicted that the movie would be a commercial failure. *New York* magazine had sent one of its columnists, William Flanagan, who normally wrote about personal finance, to Dallas on October 19 to try to sneak into one of the invitation-only *Close Encounters* screenings. The task proved easy. Flanagan's article, published twelve days later, was entitled "An Encounter With 'Close Encounters.' "

"I can understand all the apprehension," Flanagan wrote. "In my humble opinion, the picture will be a colossal flop. It lacks the dazzle, charm, wit, imagination and broad audience appeal of *Star Wars*—the film Wall Street insists it measure up to. . . ." A six-panel drawing showed a space ship landing atop Devil's Tower in Wyoming and, with a roar of flatulence, laying an egg.

The article sent Hirschfield into a frenzy. His normally soft, friendly speaking voice became a hard, desperate whine as the day spun out of control into a random sequence of frantic meetings and telephone calls exploring the possibility of legal action against *New York* magazine and various ways in which the damage might be repaired. Columbia's stock, which had closed on Friday in trading on the New York Stock Exchange at $18.375, its high for the year, began to deteriorate soon after the appearance of the Flanagan article on Monday morning. The stock had risen over the past several months from around $7, in part because of anticipation that *Close Encounters* would be a big and profitable hit.

Characteristically, the only person who remained outwardly calm that Monday was Herbert Allen, who had always taken pride in his ability to maintain equanimity in the face of dramatic news, good or bad. "This is a test, Herbert," Hirschfield insisted into the telephone. "We're going to get that magazine for this, and you people are going to have to choose between Columbia Pictures and *New York* magazine." He referred to an investment banking relationship between the owner of *New York*, Australian publishing tycoon Rupert Murdoch, and Allen & Company, which had aided Murdoch's seizure of control of the New York Magazine Company from its founder, Clay Felker, less than a year earlier.

Herbert ridiculed Hirschfield's concern. "It's only a movie review, Alan. It doesn't mean anything."

"How can you say that? The stock's sinking beneath the waves!"

"It'll balance out," Herbert said.

"We're going to sue that fucking Murdoch!"

"You can't sue, Alan. Haven't you ever heard of freedom of the press?"

"They have no right to do this. This isn't freedom of the press. it's abuse of the press. We'll pull our advertising."

"Alan, that's like Jack Kennedy canceling his subscription to the *Herald Tribune*. Those guys don't care. It doesn't make any difference. You'll do more damage by going after Murdoch than by just letting it lie. They'll be writing long after we've been complaining. They can write anything they feel like writing about this movie, and so can anyone else."

Despite Herbert's nonchalance, the stock continued to fall and a number of stockbrokers and securities analysts telephoned their concern to Hirschfield, whose rage was shared by Director Steven Spielberg, Producer Michael Phillips, and all of the studio marketing and advertising executives.

Suddenly, on Monday afternoon, the new issue of *Time* magazine appeared with a lengthy review of *Close Encounters* by Frank Rich, *Time*'s chief film critic. Rich's opinion of the movie was precisely the opposite of William Flanagan's. It turned out that Rich, too, had sneaked into one of the Dallas screenings, and his article, accompanied by color photographs and cover billing, pronounced *Close Encounters* a dazzling movie. Rich pointed out that one reason for the intense interest in *Close Encounters* was that it was the first movie directed by Steven Spielberg after *Jaws*, one of the most successful motion pictures ever.

"*Close Encounters*," Rich said, is "richer and more ambitious than *Jaws* and it reaches the viewer at a far more profound level than *Star Wars*. . . . Although the movie isn't a sure blockbuster . . . it will certainly be a big enough hit to keep Columbia's stockholders happy."

Though Columbia was relieved at the appearance of the *Time* article, the company knew that relatively few people saw *Time* magazine on Monday, and feared that since the stock market was skittish anyway the damage caused by the *New York* article might be difficult to repair. The stock closed Monday at $17, down $1.375, on a volume of nearly 170,000 shares, and the New York Stock Exchange refused to permit trading to open on Tuesday morning because the influx of sell orders was too heavy to handle in an orderly fashion. It was a typical display of the mob psychology that afflicts the stock market—particularly the market in stocks of corporations that make products whose value is as difficult to anticipate as the value of movies. Stocks of movie companies frequently rise sharply in anticipation of a hit film—anticipation based on little more than intuition. The steeper the stock's rise the more vulnerable it is to a sharp drop on receipt of information that is just as flimsy as that which caused it to rise. Investors in Columbia Pictures, having seen their stock soar from $7 to $18 in just a few months, grew anxious as the opening of *Close Encounters* approached, and many of them panicked when the *New York* magazine article appeared.

Columbia shares resumed trading at noon Tuesday, opening at $15.50, off $1.50 from Monday, and $2.875 from Friday. But the stock rose slowly through the afternoon and closed at $16 on a volume of nearly 185,000 shares.

Alan Hirschfield met Herbert Allen for lunch Tuesday at the same La Côte Basque table where he had given Herbert the news about Begelman precisely six weeks earlier. As they had several times since then, the two men discussed the Begelman issue without total candor: Hirschfield recited the arguments against reinstating Begelman—it will look as if we're condoning thievery; the SEC will object; and the press will crucify us. But he stopped short of asserting unequivocal opposition. Allen recited the arguments for reinstatement—Begelman is responding well to psychotherapy; he is owed another chance because of his contributions to the company; and replacing him with someone as talented will be very difficult. But he stopped short of unequivocal support for reinstatement. Herbert stressed, in fact, that Hirschfield, as the chief executive officer, would be expected to make the final decision and that the board of directors would support whatever he decided.

Hirschfield outlined his conversation with Richard Smith of the General Cinema Corporation in Boston the previous week. Again, however, Alan miscalculated Herbert's reaction to a crucial development—this time the prospect of losing General Cinema's proposed investment in Columbia if Begelman were reinstated in his job.

"Baloney," Herbert Allen said. "He's just bluffing. He'll be with us with or without Begelman. He needs us more than we need him. And even if he isn't, there are other General Cinemas in the world. That's no problem."

"Herbert, you don't understand this guy. You're dealing with a real straight shooter who is very sensitive to public image. You mark my words, there will be no General Cinema. In addition to which, there will be no IBM. I've met with them, too. They think this

Begelman thing's been put to bed. Potentially, these are two of the most important deals this company will ever do. General Cinema is a bird in the hand—twenty-six million bucks and more than that every year for the rest of our lives if we're smart."

"I know Dick Smith. I've met him. It's just baloney. But we shouldn't be deciding this issue based on what some other company thinks. It's none of their business."

"We're living in the world, Herbert, not in a vacuum. We've got to think about how this looks."

At Hirschfield's insistence, Herbert Allen arranged a meeting with Rupert Murdoch, the owner of *New York* magazine, so that Hirschfield could vent his rage over the article on *Close Encounters*. Hirschfield, Murdoch, and Allen had breakfast at the Carlyle Wednesday morning. Hirschfield assailed the magazine's failure to observe a generally accepted rule of movie reviewing: films shall not be reviewed before they open to the public. He claimed that the article had severely damaged Columbia Pictures and its shareholders. The company was considering legal action and the withdrawal of its advertising from all of Murdoch's publications, Hirschfield said. Murdoch, a droll, disarming man, listened patiently and then expressed sorrow about any damage that Columbia may have suffered. But he pointed out that he had to give his writers the freedom to write what they felt; otherwise, no writers would work for him. Surely, he added, the *Time* review, which also had appeared prior to the public opening of the film, had righted the balance and the film could look forward to other good reviews.

With just a hint of condescending smirk, Herbert Allen listened to the conversation and said little. Instead of backing Hirschfield, he belittled the significance of the article. Hirschfield could do nothing but seethe.

There was little time for plotting grand strategy at 711 Fifth Avenue that week. Most of Hirschfield's time was consumed by the details of the moment. He discussed with an intermediary the possibility that Michel Bergerac, the chairman of Revlon, might like to become a member of the Columbia board of directors. He conferred with a delegation from the Cancer Research Institute about the program for the evening of the *Close Encounters* world premiere. He received a report from Mickey Rudin in Las Vegas that there was no evidence of gambling by David Begelman. He questioned Joe Fischer and Allen Adler on the advisability of Columbia's buying *Book Digest* magazine. He promised to bring his personal tax and investment adviser's services to the attention of Barbra Streisand and Jon Peters, who would be his guests in Scarsdale on Saturday. He took hundreds of phone calls. Ray Stark. Dan Melnick. Herbert Allen. Michael Phillips. Peter Gruenberger. Lew Wasserman. Melnick again. Stark again. Terry Allen Kramer. Dino De Laurentiis. Jack Valenti. Melnick again, from Paris this time. Todd Lang. Nathan Cummings. Dick Munro of Time Inc. Herb Ross. Alan King. Ray Stark again. Michael Phillips again. Jann Wenner. Herbert Allen again. Mike Nichols. Jack Valenti again. Leonard Goldberg. John Tunney. Matty Rosenhaus. David Geffen. Gerald Levin of Time Inc. Terry Allen Kramer again. Jack Valenti again . . .

More than Hirschfeld let on, he had been upset by his talk with Herbert Allen on Tuesday and by a discussion with Matty Rosenhaus later in the week. It appeared that the board of directors actually was preparing to support the restoration of David Begelman to the presidency of the studio. They seemed unimpressed by Hirschfeld's arguments against it. And their own rationale was beginning to take on a rehearsed tone; undoubtedly they were discussing the question among themselves and then repeating the most compelling arguments to him at every opportunity. Even if they honored their pledge to leave the final decision to him, they were eminently capable of rendering the decision-making process highly uncomfortable. If it were just another close call on a routine business matter, Hirschfeld would not have been so concerned. But he failed to understand how anyone could seriously advocate Begelman's reinstatement, particularly in the light of the newly discovered Marty Ritt forgery. The arguments in favor of Begelman were naïve, and it was unlike Herbert and Matty to be naïve. Maybe David Geffen was right. Maybe Ray Stark was casting a spell right into the Columbia boardroom. Maybe people did see things differently in Hollywood.

Hirschfeld hoped the board would come to its senses without any angry confrontation. Peter Gruenberger would not complete his inquiry for another week or two. Maybe he would find still other forgeries. How many would it take to convince Herbert? Hirschfeld wondered.

In the meantime, Hirschfeld felt the need for independent counsel, verification that his stance against Begelman was logical and correct, assurance that he was not blind to some crucial insight that validated the board's position. On Friday, November 4, a mild, dank day in Manhattan, he walked the block and a half to International Creative Management on Fifty-seventh Street to have lunch with Sam Cohn, perhaps the most influential talent agent in the world. Though Cohn worked for ICM, the world's largest agency, he functioned with a great deal of independence, essentially as an agency within an agency. Cohn's power stemmed in part from the diversity of his clients—directors, producers, screenwriters, and authors, as well as stars. Woody Allen. Mike Nichols. Sidney Lumet. Meryl Streep. Roy Scheider. Arthur Penn. E. L. Doctorow. Jay Presson Allen. Bob Fosse. Robert Benton. Robert Altman. Lily Tomlin. Liza Minnelli. Peter Yates.

A small, middle-aged, sandy-haired, chain-smoking man given to sweaters, chinos, and loafers, Sam Cohn dealt with Hollywood not as a single place (he hated Los Angeles) but as a global state of mind enveloping Beverly Hills, Manhattan, London, Paris, and any number of other locales which easily could be reached from the constantly blinking telephone console in his office eighteen floors above Fifty-seventh Street. Sam Cohn had an overview that many people on the coast lacked, and it was this overview that Alan Hirschfield sought. Cohn also knew David Begelman well as a friend and professional associate, having worked closely with him in the same talent agency for years. But Sam Cohn also was fond of Alan Hirschfield and the way he had run Columbia Pictures. And Hirschfield was gratified to learn that on the issue of David's embezzlements he had Cohn's support.

"As badly as I feel for David as a friend," Cohn said, "it's morally and socially unacceptable for him to get off. He should not stay in the company and he should not be given a lush production deal."

"Social and moral considerations are not paramount with my board," Hirschfield replied.

"Well, you have to deal with the issue of the poor black guy who robs a gas station versus the white-collar criminal. There's no way around it."

"The board thinks David is irreplaceable."

"That's ridiculous," Cohn said. "He's not irreplaceable. No one is irreplaceable. There are lots of good people. Melnick is sensational. Whether for the interim or permanently, he's very good.''

Hirschfield left Cohn's office feeling much better.

Jeanie Kasindorf of *New West* magazine spent four hours at Sid Luft's apartment on Wilshire Boulevard that afternoon and left convinced that she was on to a major exposé. Although Luft rambled and was emotional and nervous, he seemed to be able to show in elaborate detail how David Begelman had mishandled Judy Garland's money in the early sixties. The documentation was voluminous and Kasindorf would have to examine it meticulously. Fortunately, there did not seem to be much competition on the Begelman story. The press had been silent for a month.

A limousine pulled into the driveway of the Hirschfield home in Scarsdale Saturday afternoon and deposited Barbra Streisand, Jon Peters, and Streisand's son, Jason Gould. It was a ''relationship'' visit, somewhat similar to Hirschfield's dinner with Leonard and Wendy Goldberg in Beverly Hills the previous week. Hirschfield, on the one hand, and Streisand and Peters, on the other, were circling each other, neither knowing quite how the absence of David Begelman might affect the Streisand-Peters relationship with Columbia Pictures. David Begelman and Barbra Streisand had been close for more than a decade. David had helped to guide the formative years of her career in the sixties, and while at Columbia had presided over the making of some of her most popular pictures including *Funny Lady* and *For Pete's Sake*. Streisand was close to Ray Stark, as well. Separately, in 1977, Jon Peters had agreed to produce a film for Columbia. Tentatively entitled *Eyes*, it would star Faye Dunaway and would be Peters's first film production not involving Streisand.

It had been rumored in Hollywood that if Columbia did not reinstate Begelman the studio would lose Peters and Streisand. Hirschfield did not take the rumor seriously, but since the Begelman issue remained unresolved, he chose not to confront them with it. Instead, Alan strove simply to provide a few hours of easy conversation through which they might at least get to know him better and see what a bright, capable, engaging fellow he was. As it turned out, Peters and Streisand had no interest in talking about David Begelman or motion pictures. Their main concern was money. Jon Peters wanted to meet Hirschfield's investment and tax advisers. And

Barbra Streisand said, not for the first time or the last, that she had never made any money from investments and had never had a satisfactory investment adviser. Hirschfield suggested that they consider placing at least part of their fortune under the care of his people or others in New York who he felt were generally more reliable than Hollywood money managers.

Streisand and Peters left at dusk, having enjoyed the relaxed afternoon in the woodsy autumn of Westchester County.

Hirschfield took his children, Laura, Marc, and Scott, to see the Giants lose to the Dallas Cowboys at Giants Stadium Sunday afternoon. Then they met Berte at the Ziegfeld Theater on Fifty-fourth Street in Manhattan for the first of two private screenings of *Close Encounters of the Third Kind* which Columbia was holding that evening for several hundred members of the press from around the country. Herbert Allen brought his children as well. Because of the tension between their fathers, Laura Hirschfield felt uncomfortable around Christie Allen, Herbert's daughter, whom Laura had not seen recently. They had been friends at one time. The children all loved *Close Encounters,* however, which was more than could be said for Herbert, who expressed little enthusiasm.

A frustrated Alan Hirschfield asked himself how Herbert could be so blasé.

TWENTY-FOUR

Promptly at 9:30 Monday morning, November 7, David Begelman reported to Bungalow 14 of the Beverly Hills Hotel to begin two days of interrogation by Peter Gruenberger.

Gruenberger had reserved the bungalow just for the interrogation. He wanted to question Begelman on neutral ground, and the Beverly Hills Hotel was as neutral as anyplace in Hollywood. Gruenberger also wanted to keep the proceedings as calm as possible. To have conducted the interrogation in Begelman's own office at the studio, which symbolically had become Gruenberger's office, would have heightened the psychological tension of the encounter. Privacy was a consideration, too, but there was no way to guarantee privacy absolutely at any location that was convenient. So Bungalow 14 was deemed satisfactory. It was away from the main part of the hotel, away from the street, on the second row of bungalows, backing on the hotel employees' parking lot.

David Begelman was as drained as the investigators. Except for the two days in Dallas for the *Close Encounters* screenings, Begelman had stayed in Los Angeles, rarely venturing more than a few blocks from his home on Linden Drive, emerging for little other than his thrice weekly sessions with Dr. Marmor and occasional dinners with very close friends like Sy Weintraub and the Leonard Goldbergs. Mostly, he had waited, brooded, and wondered what Gruenberger was finding and what Peter would do with his findings. Dan Melnick telephoned Begelman frequently, as did Herbert Allen, ostensibly to talk business but really to cheer him up. They and others were genuinely concerned about David's emotional stability—afraid that he might "put a gun in his mouth." "Hollywood is a funny community," Herbert would say later; ". . . it's a community full of poseurs and out there it's not a negative. And David always had a tremendous facade of respectability and I thought that this might cause him enough damage—I just didn't know what he'd do with himself. . . ." The suicide speculation was even given literary impetus around Allen & Company by Herbert's lawyer, Robert Werbel, for whom Begelman and his plight were reminiscent of the poem "Richard Cory" by Edwin Arlington Robinson.

> *Whenever Richard Cory went down town,*
> *We people on the pavement looked at him:*
> *He was a gentleman from sole to crown,*
> *Clean favored, and imperially slim.*

> *And he was always quietly arrayed,*
> *And he was always human when he talked;*
> *But still he fluttered pulses when he said,*
> *"Good morning," and he glittered when he walked.*

And he was rich—yes, richer than a king—
And admirably schooled in every grace:
In fine, we thought that he was everything
To make us wish that we were in his place.

So on we worked, and waited for the light,
And went without the meat, and cursed the bread;
And Richard Cory, one calm summer night,
Went home and put a bullet through his head.

Occasionally someone would call Begelman with a fragmentary report on what Gruenberger was up to, whom he had questioned, what he had asked. There had been a flurry of phone calls ten days earlier when the Martin Ritt check was discovered. Begelman had effectively camouflaged his exhaustion and worry, however, by the time he arrived at the bungalow on Monday morning. He was impeccably coiffed, groomed, and dressed in a suit and tie, and was cordial to everyone present.

Except for the setting, a dining-room table in a hotel bungalow instead of a conference table in a law office, the interrogation was similar to a formal deposition. Gruenberger sat at one end of the table, flanked by his two colleagues from Weil, Gotshal & Manges, Joel Harris and Nancy Barton. Begelman sat at the other end of the table with his lawyer Frank Rothman on one side and Marianna Pfaelzer, another partner from the firm of Wyman, Bautzer, Rothman & Kuchel, on the other. Stationed nearby was Michael Passarella, a senior partner from the New York headquarters of Price Waterhouse & Company. Peter Gruenberger's secretary from New York sat in the next room behind a closed door typing copious notes of the proceedings as the notes were made and passed to her by Nancy Barton. (Gruenberger had decided that a standard courtroom stenographer was not necessary and might be intimidating.)

Gruenberger began by taking Begelman through the four documented acts of embezzlement—Cliff Robertson, Peter Choate, Pierre Groleau, and Martin Ritt. Begelman admitted everything.

Gruenberger then recited a list of major expense account abuses:
• Begelman had charged $6,000 worth of personal use of limousines in Miami, Florida, to the budget of the film *The Greatest* starring Muhammad Ali.
• He had drawn a total of $4,372 in cash from several European

hotels, put the withdrawals on his hotel bills, and charged the total bills to Columbia Pictures. It was unclear how much of the money had been used for business. Gruenberger calculated that about $2,000 had not been properly accounted for.

• He had charged Columbia $4,145 for a trip to the French Riviera in September 1975, shortly after his wedding to Gladyce Rudin. The Leonard Goldbergs had accompanied the Begelmans on the trip, which appeared to Peter Gruenberger to constitute a honeymoon, not a business trip.

Begelman acknowledged the limousine allegation and put up only mild resistance to Gruenberger's conclusions on the travel expenses.

Gruenberger then questioned Begelman about his automobiles. Under Columbia's contract with Begelman, the company was obligated to furnish him with and pay all expenses on two cars, which he was free to select. At the time the contract was negotiated, Begelman was driving a Mercedes and a Jensen. Later he sold the Mercedes and obtained a Rolls-Royce. Despite Begelman's contractual freedom to choose whatever car he wanted, Alan Hirschfield let it be known that he did not want Begelman driving a Rolls-Royce. So Begelman asked the man who was leasing him the Jensen to raise the amount that Columbia was being charged for the Jensen to an amount equivalent to what it would pay if the Rolls were included. Peter Gruenberger contended that Begelman should have settled the issue with Hirschfield openly instead of, in effect, creating a false charge to pay for a car that Hirschfield did not want him to have. The important issue to Gruenberger was Begelman's lack of honesty, not his technical rights under the contract. Begelman contended that Columbia should simply have paid him the cost of leasing two cars and left the allocation to him. He agreed, however, in the interest of harmony, to reimburse Columbia for the cost of the Rolls.

Gruenberger raised similar issues of forthrightness and honesty in discussing the arrangements under which Columbia Pictures paid a major share of Begelman's housing costs. As far as Columbia knew, Begelman had a three-year lease on a house in Beverly Hills owned by an entity called Burton Way Management Company. What Columbia did not know was that Burton Way Management Company was wholly owned by a lawyer named Gerald Lipsky, one of whose principal clients was Ray Stark, the most important producer on the Columbia lot. Columbia furthermore did not know that Gerald Lipsky had bought the house and leased it to Begelman specifically at

Begelman's request, that the master lease in fact ran for thirty years, and that Begelman and Lipsky had an informal understanding that Begelman might purchase the house if and when he could obtain sufficient financing.

Gruenberger posed the questions about the house in the context of David Begelman's extensive overall relationship with Gerald Lipsky and Ray Stark, with whom Begelman did a great deal of motion-picture business on behalf of Columbia. Gruenberger had no evidence that the overall relationship affected the terms of the house deal. But would it not have been more forthright of Begelman, Gruenberger asked, to have let his employer know that Gerald Lipsky, a man with whom Begelman was engaged in frequent and vitally important negotiations over Ray Stark's pictures, was also Begelman's landlord, and that the landlord-tenant arrangements, in fact, were more extensive than Columbia had been led to believe?

Begelman saw nothing improper about any aspect of the housing arrangements or the degree to which he had informed Columbia of them.

Gruenberger went on to explore Begelman's direct financial relationships with Ray Stark. Begelman confirmed that he had borrowed $15,000 from Stark in 1964 or 1965 and another $27,500 in 1976. He had kept the $27,500 in cash in his desk and used it for various purposes as the need arose. Stark also apparently had guaranteed a $185,000 loan to Begelman from the City National Bank of Beverly Hills in 1972. All the loans had been repaid. Gruenberger implied nothing improper about any of the loans. But the loans did show that Begelman's relationship to Ray Stark had been closer than Alan Hirschfield or Columbia Pictures had known it was.

Begelman was asked about a long list of rumors which the investigators had been unable to verify—stories of gambling and the like. He denied them all. He was asked about a report that in the early 1950s, when he was working in the insurance business, he had left a job with an insurance concern under some sort of financial cloud. Something about premiums or loans being handled improperly? Begelman acknowledged that there had been a misunderstanding but denied there was anything improper and said that he had been intending to leave the job anyway. Frank Rothman suggested to Peter Gruenberger than whatever might have happened twenty-five years earlier was irrelevant and that it was improper to raise such questions. Gruenberger found Begelman's answer to the question about the insurance matter unsatisfactory, but since there was no hard evidence of misconduct, Gruenberger let the matter drop.

And there it was—a tedious, exhaustive two-day interrogation following a hurried five weeks of investigation. David Begelman stood revealed as a man who had committed four separate acts of embezzlement totaling $75,000; who had stolen thousands more by the more genteel method of cheating on his expense account; who had been less than forthright about the terms under which Columbia Pictures paid for his home and automobiles.

Although the interrogation did not necessarily mean that the investigation was at an end, Gruenberger doubted that he would find anything else. Alan Hirschfield and the board probably would have to decide Begelman's fate on the basis of what was already known.

During Begelman's suspension, Alan Hirschfield found himself nagged by numerous small responsibilities that normally would have fallen to the president of the studio. The burden was even worse in early November because Dan Melnick, the acting studio head, was in Europe. On Monday, as Peter Gruenberger was grilling Begelman at the Beverly Hills Hotel, Hirschfield sat in his office in Manhattan trying to persuade a recalcitrant Al Pacino to cooperate with *People* magazine, which wanted to do a cover story on him and his companion, actress Marthe Keller. Pacino claimed that the story in fact was about Marthe only, and that his photograph on the cover would imply that it was about both of them. The studio was urging Pacino to permit the use of the photograph as a means of promoting his current film, *Bobby Deerfield*, whose box-office receipts were lagging. Robert Cort, the studio's advertising vice president, had tried to induce Pacino to cooperate with *People*, as had Sydney Pollack, the director of the picture. The actor was still balking, so Bob Cort asked Hirschfield to see Pacino. After half an hour of cajoling, Pacino relented.

The Pacino meeting was followed immediately by a somewhat similar session with Steven Spielberg, the director of *Close Encounters of the Third Kind*. Spielberg was reluctant to provide *Newsweek* with photographs of the most dramatic scenes in *Close Encounters;* he was determined that audiences would experience the scenes for the first time on the screen, not in a magazine. *Newsweek* wanted to do a cover story on the movie but had told Columbia it would do the story only if it had the photographs. Bob Cort and producer

Michael Phillips had been unable to sway Spielberg. Again, Cort appealed to Hirschfield, who told Spielberg: "We desperately need the cover story to validate the importance of the movie. It's critical." Spielberg finally agreed, and at four Monday afternoon, Bob Cort trudged five blocks with the photographs, through the heaviest rain of the year, to the Newsweek building on Madison Avenue.

Hirschfield dined that evening with David Geffen, whose warnings about malevolence in Hollywood were finally beginning to sink in. From the mists of the Bel-Air cocktail circuit were emerging the outlines of an organized effort to discredit Hirschfield's motives and portray the Begelman problem as something different from what it was. And on the East Coast, each time Herbert Allen and Matty Rosenhaus stated the case for Begelman, as they did at every opportunity, it was another version of the same campaign. These people all had a common goal: to apply pressure to Alan Hirschfield. And though Hirschfield saw and felt it, he still did not fathom it. *He* hadn't forged the checks; Begelman had. *He* hadn't embezzled thousands of dollars from Columbia Pictures; Begelman had. *He* wasn't a criminal; Begelman was. And yet the focus of attention seemed to be shifting from Begelman to Hirschfield. No one seemed to care what Begelman had done. They only seemed intent on impugning Hirschfield's motives.

Hirschfield felt disoriented. The following week Columbia Pictures would experience the most spectacular event in its history—the world premiere of *Close Encounters of the Third Kind*. During the same week the company would experience what seemed to be developing into the most traumatic event in its history—the climax of the Begelman drama. The premiere would quite literally be bathed in the brightest of light, one of the biggest entertainment occasions of the year, or of any year. The Begelman denouement, by contrast, would unfold in strictest secrecy. If the company had its way, only the result would become known. Either Begelman's suspension would be made permanent, or he would be reinstated as president of the studio. Outside of a small group of people, no one would ever know what he had done, or be privy to the trauma that his crimes had caused the company.

Thus, the most gratifying event and the most dismaying event of Alan Hirschfield's business career marched inexorably toward him, almost in lockstep.

*   *   *

"I have something I want to tell you this morning," Rona Barrett confided to her millions of viewers early Wednesday. "Yesterday I saw a movie which was both an experience and a revelation. The film is Steven Spielberg's *Close Encounters of the Third Kind*, and although I'll review the film this Friday, there are a few thoughts I'd like to share with you now. Since the film was put into production a few years ago, we've reported on its escalating budget that propelled the final cost of *Close Encounters* to almost twenty million dollars. Because we were, of course, not privy to the film's dailies, we questioned Columbia's rationale for okaying the cost. Now, however, having seen the film, it is clear those dollars were well spent. But the sad truth is that Columbia executives did not approve the additional money because they had faith in Spielberg's genius, but because they felt they were already in way over their corporate heads. I know that over the next few weeks those same studio executives that damned the picture in production will be saying they believed all along that *Close Encounters* was a winner. However, the truth is that even after its first sneak in Dallas just last week, Alan Hirschfield, president of Columbia Pictures Industries Inc., told associates that *Close Encounters* was no *Jaws* or *Star Wars*. Well, I say to Mr. Hirschfield that any executive who cannot recognize the power and excellence of a film like *Close Encounters* has no business making movies.

"Furthermore, it's ironic that David Begelman, the one executive at Columbia who did believe in *Close Encounters* from day one, is now under a cloud of mistrust because of reported financial irregularities. While I do not condone whatever alleged misdeeds Begelman may have done, the fact is that an executive with the vision to nurture *Close Encounters* should be guaranteed a place in our industry. . . ."

On Thursday, Hirschfield found it necessary to rise to another public occasion—the annual meeting of Columbia Pictures Industries' stockholders. He was particularly eager in the circumstances to give a good performance. "Do your best, boy," Matty Rosenhaus had implored. The meeting, which was attended by more than two hundred people was held in a large auditorium on the second floor of the new Manufacturers Hanover Trust Company skyscraper in lower Manhattan. Hirschfield, Leo Jaffe, Joe Fischer, and Victor Kaufman sat on the stage, while the rest of the officers and directors, except for Herbert Allen and Irwin Kramer, sat in the first few rows of the audience. Allen and Kramer sat together in the last row.

Board Chairman Jaffe opened the meeting and then turned it over to Hirschfield, whom he characterized as "the helmsman and driving force" of Columbia Pictures Industries.

"When I took this job four years ago," Hirschfield said when the applause faded, "I didn't think either Columbia or I would still be around at this point. I didn't know which of us would falter first. But we're still here and we have a lot of good news to report." He then sketched the company's bright financial picture.

• Operating earnings for the first quarter of the current fiscal year had risen 400 percent to new record levels from the same period of the previous year.

• The company hoped to resume the payment of cash dividends within several months. (It had not paid dividends since 1970.)

• *Close Encounters of the Third Kind* had the potential to equal or surpass the performance of *Star Wars* at the box office and thereby achieve the highest gross revenues in the history of motion pictures.

• The Gottlieb pinball machine company was manufacturing a *Close Encounters* pinball game.

• Arista Records had the biggest month in its history in October and would be releasing the *Close Encounters* soundtrack album.

• Columbia hoped to establish ongoing financial relationships with Time Incorporated and the General Cinema Corporation.

In their back-row seats, Herbert Allen and Irwin Kramer whispered to each other frequently during the meeting and smiled at private jokes.

Most of the questions from the shareholders were soft and most comments complimentary. Hirschfield and Jaffe had cautioned at the beginning of the meeting that it would be inappropriate for them to comment on the David Begelman affair since it remained under investigation. "Mr. Begelman has made a most significant contribution," Hirschfield said. "He is a friend and remains a friend. On the other hand, no one person constitutes an entire business. I would be derelict if I ran Columbia in that fashion. And I can assure all of you that there is capable management in all divisions of the company, including motion pictures and television."

A vociferous female stockholder suggested that Columbia might want to base a motion picture on the Begelman affair. "It would be greater than *The Last Tycoon*," she said.

Hirschfield was asked why *The Greatest*, starring Muhammad Ali, had not done better at the box office. "It wasn't the greatest," he said. "We lost some money on *The Greatest*. You couldn't call it a flop. You couldn't call it a hit. It was just a mistake in terms of what we thought was a market. People are willing to pay to see Muhammad Ali fight. They aren't willing to pay to see Muhammad Ali make love or whatever he does on screen. . . . We thought the picture would work well foreign. It didn't. We thought it would work well domestically. It didn't. We thought it would work well in black and white neighborhoods. It didn't work well in either."

Hirschfield ticked off future production plans. "We have pictures like *California Suite*, which is the Neil Simon play. . . . We have the new movie of Bob Fosse, who is, in my opinion, one of the most talented directors in America. It is called *All That Jazz*. It will be a semimusical adventure. We have a movie that will, hopefully, at least on some levels, compete with sharks. This one is about bats. It's called *Nightwing*. We have a wonderful book that we bought, which is called *Kramer vs. Kramer,* which is a dramatic portrayal of a family confronted by divorce. We think it is going to be a terrific movie for the company. We have the new Paddy Chayevsky book. I believe it is going to be called *The Experiment*.* As you know, Paddy Chayevsky is one of the most talented play and screen writers. His last work was *Network*. This one will give Paddy the opportunity for an all-out commercial adventure, special-effects and fantasy film. It is just a spectacular project. It will be, hopefully, our major release for the summer of '79. It will become a very controversial show."

"It has been rumored," a stockholder said, "that Columbia is a candidate to be taken over by ITT, rumored at a price of twenty-two dollars a share."

"I wouldn't want to do anything to dispel the rumor," Hirschfield said.

"In other words, you haven't heard anything."

"No, but it's always been a dream of mine to be caught between the countries of Kuwait and Saudi Arabia in a proxy fight," Hirschfield added, to prolonged laughter.

---

*The eventual title was *Altered States*.

*   *   *

Hirschfield knew he had performed well and was pleased after the meeting when several stockholders approached and congratulated him on his leadership of the company. The board of directors then convened its own meeting and Hirschfield grew quietly furious when not one of the board complimented him on his good job before the shareholders. He returned to 711 Fifth Avenue alone.

The board decided to assemble the following Wednesday, November 16, the morning after the premiere of *Close Encounters,* to hear Peter Gruenberger's report on his investigation. They would then decide what to do about David Begelman.

TWENTY-FIVE

"They're gonna shove him up your ass."

Sipping a cocktail at the Hirschfields' in Scarsdale on Sunday evening, Marty Ransohoff was appraising the Columbia board of directors' attitude toward the Begelman issue. Ransohoff had discussed the problem with both Alan Hirschfield and Herbert Allen several times since Begelman had been suspended, and had been particularly attentive since his argument with Herbert in the Southampton sauna in October. Ransohoff continued to believe that Columbia Pictures had little to gain and much to lose by restoring Begelman to his studio position. He verified many of the things David Geffen had told Hirschfield about the growing criticism in Hollywood of Hirschfield's handling of the matter. And he told Hirschfield something that Alan had not heard elsewhere and that he had not figured out for himself: Herbert Allen appeared to have committed himself on an emotional level—something he rarely did in any business situation—to the reinstatement of David Begelman to the presidency of the studio. He seemed to have invested his ego on the side of those who felt that Begelman should be forgiven. And

Herbert was angry at Hirschfield for what he viewed as a failure of nerve—an inclination to base the decision on "what people will say" (the SEC, the press, the banks, et al.) instead of on "what is right" (showing compassion for a talented man whose crimes resulted from a mental illness which was being cured).

"Herbie's steamed up and he doesn't usually get this steamed up," Ransohoff warned. "He's got his 'fuck you' shoes on. He's got the board primed. And they're gonna shove Begelman up your ass."

"But they've promised to support my decision, whatever it is."

"You just wait and see how they support your decision. That kind of support you don't need."

"Good morning, Rona."

"Good morning, David, and good morning, America.

"From the big business front . . . this Wednesday the board of directors of Columbia Pictures Industries Incorporated will meet in New York City to decide the corporate fate of David Begelman, former president of the studio, who admitted several weeks ago to financial wrongdoing. We understand that meeting will be particularly volatile due to the fact that half the board is reportedly in favor of reinstating Begelman, while the other half is determined to keep him out. It's interesting to note that Begelman's fate will be decided three days before the first box-office returns on his pet project, *Close Encounters of the Third Kind,* can be known."

Delivered by special certified messengers, the letter was on the official letterhead of the law firm of Weil, Gotshal & Manges and carried the heading:

Privileged and Confidential. Attorney's Work Product.

To the Board of Directors of
Columbia Pictures Industries Inc.

At the request of Irwin Kramer, chairman of the audit committee, I hand to you for your confidential information a legal memorandum which we prepared. . . . Irwin felt that this might be of interest to you in preparation for the meeting this Wednesday. . . .

Sincerely yours,
Robert Todd Lang

In addition to depending on Weil, Gotshal & Manges to investigate David Begelman's crimes, Columbia Pictures Industries looked to the firm to outline and analyze the corporation's legal options for resolving the Begelman problem. Thus, while Peter Gruenberger and his team were poring over canceled checks at The Burbank Studios, other lawyers in New York, under the direction of Todd Lang, were preparing memoranda to aid the deliberations of the board of directors. Was the company legally required to fire Begelman? To sue him? To prosecute him? Could it reinstate him to his position in the company? If so, under what circumstances? What were the corporation's and the individual directors' potential liabilities under the various courses of action open to them? How much information had to be disclosed to the Securities and Exchange Commission and to the public?

In two confidential memoranda—a forty-eight-page document laden with legal citations and an eleven-page tract that was less formal and more candid and pointed—Weil, Gotshal & Manges told the Columbia board that its actions in the Begelman matter were governed by the so-called "business-judgment rule"—a principle that has evolved in American corporate law and jurisprudence over many years. Under the rule, a corporate board of directors has considerable freedom in deciding any issue before it as long as the decision represents the board's genuine "business judgment" of what is best for the corporation. Courts ordinarily will not challenge such a judgment unless the board's ability to make the judgment is somehow impaired, or the judgment is tainted by bad faith, breach of trust or fraud, or the judgment can be shown to be "grossly unsound." To the extent that a judgment is flawed in any of these ways, the directors who made the judgment risk suits by shareholders, law-enforcement actions, and other assertions of legal liability.

The threshold decision of whether to sue or prosecute David Begelman was within the ambit of the business-judgment rule, Weil, Gotshal said, and since Begelman was in the process of repaying the money he had stolen from Columbia, the company was not legally obligated to sue or prosecute him. (Left unstated was the company's obvious right to sue or prosecute if it chose to do so.)

Beyond that, in the lawyers' opinion, Columbia had three options, each of which could be deemed a legitimate exercise of business judgment under certain conditions. The company could terminate Begelman's employment unequivocally. It could terminate his employment and retain him instead as an independent film producer, without an employer-employee relationship. Or it could reinstate him as head of the studio. (The lawyers based their analysis on the assumption that Begelman would not be reinstated as a director or officer of the parent corporation under any circumstances.)

Since reinstating Begelman in his studio post obviously would raise the most questions about the company's business judgment, the lawyers devoted most of their analysis to that issue. Reinstatement was within Columbia's rights, the lawyers advised, if the company decided that Begelman was "in large measure" responsible for its success and that losing him therefore would harm the company. If it reinstated him, however, the company would have to take account of several potentially negative ramifications of that decision. It would be obliged to impose restraints on Begelman sufficient to prevent recurrence of his misdeeds—perhaps restricting his authority to sign checks and commit large sums of money. And in imposing such restrictions, it would be obliged to consider whether the restrictions would impair his ability to run the studio.

Apart from Begelman himself, the lawyers noted, certain negative effects on the company at large would be more likely if he were reinstated than if he were not reinstated. The SEC would be more likely to insist on public disclosure of the details of Begelman's embezzlements. The SEC also would be more likely to launch its own investigation of the company's handling of the Begelman affair, as well as a broader inquiry into Columbia's executive perquisites. And the financial community, i.e., Columbia's lenders and underwriters, would be more likely to react adversely, possibly impairing Columbia's ability to obtain financing and underwriting services.

Todd Lang disseminated the legal material on Monday afternoon, November 14.

Since legal advice is not rendered in a vacuum, but instead is often given to people under the severe pressure of difficult decisions, the advice can have unpredictable, unexpected, and unintended results. Clients sometimes expect more from lawyers than can reasonably be expected. Clients sometimes want lawyers to make decisions that the clients must make themselves. In Columbia Pictures' case, Todd Lang's memoranda had the effect of further inflaming the already highly contentious atmosphere.

By the middle of November, of course, Alan Hirschfield had discussed the Begelman case with Todd Lang many times in many settings—their homes in Scarsdale, their automobiles, their offices.

Lang, in several unguarded moments, when he was speaking person-ally rather than as the corporation's lawyer, had made clear that he felt that it would be unwise to reinstate Begelman. Hirschfield, eager for support, had tended to blur the distinction between Todd Lang, the person, and Todd Lang, the lawyer, and had come to expect that Lang, at the appropriate time, would take a formal stance against Begelman in advising the board of directors. Hirschfield depended on Lang's advice as a last resort if Alan's own sway with Herbert Allen proved insufficient, and indeed Alan had already begun pre-dicting to Herbert that Lang would advise against reinstating Begelman for legal reasons.

When Lang's formal advice finally was committed to writing and disseminated, therefore, Hirschfield was surprised and deeply disap-pointed that the memoranda contained no clear recommendation that Begelman be fired. And Herbert Allen was delighted to see that the reinstatement of Begelman was after all a genuine legal alternative. He accused Hirschfield of having misled him for weeks on the legal issues involved. The memoranda, of course, contained no recommen-dation of what the board ultimately should decide. That would have exceeded the appropriate role of the legal advice under the circumstances. Alan and Herbert, however, proceeded to seize upon those portions of the memoranda that tended to support their respec-tive points of view. And in the process their opposed positions hardened.

Newsweek appeared Monday with an elaborate and lavishly illus-trated seven-page cover story on *Close Encounters of the Third Kind*. Proclaiming that the film would command a "historic place in movie entertainment," critic Jack Kroll wrote that "*Close Encounters* is the friendliest, warmest science fiction epic you've ever seen. It brings the heavens down to earth. . . . Never has a movie produced such an overwhelming, ever-changing rhapsody of light." There were separate articles on director Steven Spielberg, special-effects wizard Douglas Trumbull, and astronomer J. Allen Hynek, a UFO expert and the movie's technical adviser.

It was the sort of send-off that picture people constantly pray for and rarely get.

Upset by the lawyers' memoranda and by the board's reaction to it, Alan Hirschfield also was angered to learn that the directors, without consulting him, had invited David Begelman to appear at the Wednesday board meeting and present his "side of the story." Begelman had had two days to answer the charges when Peter Gruenberger had interrogated him at the Beverly Hills Hotel the previous week. Inviting him to the board meeting, in Hirschfield's view, represented an effort by Herbert Allen and Matty Rosenhaus to inject emotion and sympathy for Begelman into a meeting that was supposed to be a dispassionate discussion of the investigators' report. Hirschfield stated his feelings to Allen and Rosenhaus late Tuesday afternoon. They were unmoved, but reassured Hirschfield that they would support whatever decision he made on the fate of Begelman.

"Have you made up your mind yet, Alan?" Herbert asked.

"No."

"If you had to decide right this minute, what would your decision be? I think we have a right to know."

"I don't have to decide right this minute."

"Just hypothetically."

"I wouldn't take him back."

"Will you still feel that way tomorrow, or next week."

"I don't know."

In this atmosphere of rancor, Hirschfield, Rosenhaus, and Allen parted and prepared for the events of the evening, the world premiere of *Close Encounters of the Third Kind*, the most important evening in the fifty-seven-year history of Columbia Pictures.

TWENTY-SIX

The jarring juxtaposition of pleasure and pain on Tuesday night reminded Alan Hirschfield of the dinner at the Waldorf in September when he had received public acclaim from Brandeis University and private bad news from Mickey Rudin. It was much worse this time, however.

Tuesday night was a night of wonder. It was a night when a new motion picture transformed a black-tie audience of seen-it-all celebrities and tycoons into a gaggle of wide-eyed children. It was a night when Alan Hirschfield, standing before that audience, was honored for his work as a trustee of the esteemed Cancer Research Institute and witnessed the establishment of an institute scholarship in his name. It was a night when Alan Hirschfield, sitting in that audience watching the film, finally sensed with absolute certainty that the corporation which he had led from the brink of bankruptcy to respectable but still modest prosperity would shortly become very rich and take its place as a truly important purveyor of entertainment to the world.

Tuesday night also was a night of menace. It was a night when Alan Hirschfield received a signal that the smoldering dispute over David Begelman—a dispute over one man's misdeeds, a dispute that had grown so gradually from the chance discovery of a single forged check—was about to explode into something much more ominous and much more consuming than a dispute over one man. Though the full dimensions of the confrontation were not yet evident that evening, it appeared that the dispute was on the verge of degenerating into a bitter, ugly, personal clash of wills between Alan Hirschfield and the Allen family. The circumstances momentarily were baffling. But the signal could hardly have been more sinister: It seemed that the board of directors of Columbia Pictures Industries was about to launch a serious attack on Alan Hirschfield's personal integrity, and on the personal integrity of his wife, Berte.

Having made their way past television lights and popping flash bulbs, the gowns, furs, and tuxedos jammed the garish lobby of the Ziegfeld Theater on Fifty-fourth Street, one of the largest and technically best-equipped movie theaters in New York. Alan and Berte Hirschfield and other Columbia personages mixed with the crowd, appearing casual and relaxed but knowing that this was their biggest premiere. They had been through *Funny Lady*, *Shampoo*, *Taxi Driver*, and *The Deep*—big films all—but *Close Encounters* was the biggest and they were excited.

Just before 7:30, the scheduled starting time, Todd Lang sought out Hirschfield and took him aside. Lang had talked to Peter Gruenberger, who had gotten a phone call from Irwin Kramer, the Allen in-law who was chairman of the Columbia audit committee and was the board's overseer of the investigation of David Begelman. It seemed that the audit committee was going to broaden the investigation. In addition to investigating Begelman, it was going to investigate Alan and Berte Hirschfield. More precisely, it was going to investigate a possible conflict of interest in the employment of Berte Hirschfield by a company that conducted market research for Columbia Pictures.

Alan was stunned. "That's absurd," he said to Lang. "We cleared that with the board two years ago. It was clean as a whistle. You said so yourself."

"I know," Lang replied, "but they're determined to bring it up again. They claim they never got to the bottom of it."

"This is blackmail," Hirschfield asserted. "This is nothing but a lever to get me to cave on Begelman. It's out-and-out blackmail!"

The conversation was interrupted. Hirschfield was due inside the theater where the festivities were about to begin. He quickly whispered Lang's news to Berte, and then took his place in front of the auditorium for the ceremonies in which he was to be honored by the Cancer Research Institute.

Berte was even more shocked than Alan because she remembered the details more vividly. She *had* worked for a market-research company and Columbia Pictures *was* one of the company's clients. There was no question about any of that. Market research was Berte Hirschfield's professional career, to the extent that she had a career. It was difficult for the wife of the chief executive of a major corporation to have an independent career. The husband's activities made frequent demands on the wife. Berte, however, had decided in 1974—a year after Alan became president of Columbia—that she could accommodate his needs and still pursue her own career. She had sought the advice of her sister's husband, Andrew Fogelson, who at the time headed Columbia Pictures' advertising and did business with several market-research firms—firms that measured public response to new products by means of psychological testing. One of the companies Fogelson recommended to Berte was E. J. Wolf & Associates Incorporated, a respected New York firm which conducted research for a range of clients including Warner-Lambert, Monsanto, Burlington Industries, and Pepsi-Cola, as well as Columbia Pictures. Berte took a job with the Wolf company, whose proprietor, Ed Wolf, had a background similar to hers in psychology and counseling. She did some work on movies, including a few Ray Stark films. Most of her time, however, was devoted to clients in the fashion and toy industries, where she had independent expertise and contacts. She was responsible for bringing substantial new nonmovie business to the Wolf firm, and in late 1975 Wolf offered Berte a 5 percent participation in the firm's profits as a way of rewarding her contribution and spurring her incentive. (Her annual salary had never exceeded $20,500 and she received negligible bonuses.) After conferring with Alan, and with two Columbia lawyers, she decided to turn down the profit participation because it might give the appearance of being related to the volume of work Wolf did for Columbia Pictures. His Columbia business was increasing in direct proportion to Columbia's commitment to extensive market research. Alan Hirschfield discussed Berte's employment with the Columbia board of directors, who in turn consulted Todd Lang. The consensus was that so long as Berte did not have an equity position or profit participation in the Wolf firm there clearly was no conflict of interest because Alan Hirschfield would have no significant stake in the amount of business Columbia did with Wolf. It was agreed, however, that if Berte should ever decide to accept Wolf's offer, she and Alan should review the matter again with Columbia's legal counsel. The Hirschfields, of course, fully appreciated the possible appearance of a conflict of interest and eventually concluded that Berte could never realize her financial potential at the Wolf firm without having it look as if her advancement was related to her position as the wife of the president of one of the firm's client companies. Therefore, she left the Wolf firm and began seeking opportunities elsewhere.

Irwin Kramer, as chairman of the Columbia audit committee, which ruled on possible conflicts of interest, had been informed of Berte's employment at the time and had raised no objection. Now, nearly a year after her employment had ended, and two years after the conflict-of-interest question had been resolved in her favor, it was being raised again by Irwin Kramer on behalf of the board of directors in the heat of a dispute on a wholly unrelated issue on which the board was trying to bend Alan Hirschfield to its will. The odor of blackmail seemed unmistakable to Berte, who could not believe that Irwin and Herbert would stoop to that level. She had known that Alan was feeling a lot of pressure to reinstate Begelman but she had not realized that the dispute had gotten out of control. The Hirschfields had nothing to hide, of course. Berte's employment had been perfectly legitimate. But suppose a twisted version of it were leaked to the press. She could picture the headline: HIRSCHFIELD, TRYING TO CENSURE BEGELMAN, HAS SKELETON IN OWN CLOSET. The facts never quite catch up with such headlines.

The cancer institute ceremonies ended, Alan took his seat, and the movie began. But the pleasure of the evening had been punctured, and the rest of it became a blur. There was a gala supper dance after the premiere, across the street in the Trianon Ballroom of the New York Hilton. Berte ran into Herbert Allen and Ray Stark on her way into the ballroom. When Stark leaned forward to kiss Berte, she shrank back, saying softly, "I'm not kissing you, Ray," then glared at Herbert and moved on through the crowd. Herbert and Ray lingered only for a few minutes; it was past Herbert's bedtime. But nearly everyone else stayed.

The guests at the Hirschfields' table included Andrew Heiskell of Time Incorporated, Richard Bloch of the Filmways Corporation, Judd Weinberg of Columbia's pinball-machine company, and their wives. Berte was a bit subdued during the meal, imperceptibly so to anyone who did not know her well, but subdued nonetheless. Alan, however, was at his gregarious and expansive best, working the room avidly, greeting and chatting with Barry Manilow, Clive Davis, Michael Phillips, David Bowie, Buck Henry, Louis Nizer, Mary Lasker, Edgar Bronfman, Monique Van Vooren, Nathan Cummings, Sam Lefrak, and others until well past midnight.

"I was impressed," Earl Wilson wrote in his syndicated column the next day, "by the beautiful party at the Hilton where Alan Hirschfield and Michael Phillips, the bosses and creators, were confident about a booming box office."

Almost everyone loved the evening, and almost no one knew that their host was a man in agony.

TWENTY-SEVEN

The Columbia Pictures Industries board of directors room on the eleventh floor of 711 Fifth Avenue was bland in comparison to other movie company boardrooms. Unlike, say, the MGM boardroom in Los Angeles, which contained an immense antique conference table that had been in the Lincoln White House, the mostly beige Columbia Pictures chamber boasted little finery. It was distinguished only by the 109 golden Oscars that peered from glass cases at both ends of the forty-foot room. *From Here to Eternity. Lawrence of Arabia. All the King's Men. Bridge on the River Kwai. On the Waterfront. It Happened One Night. A Man for All Seasons.*

The meeting on the Begelman issue was called for ten o'clock Wednesday morning. Everyone was on time except Alan Hirschfield, who was in his office across the hall, suddenly entrapped by telephone in an emergency board meeting of another company, an oil concern called Diamond M Drilling. Hirschfield had helped form Diamond M a few years earlier, and it was a major asset of the Allen family. Assuming that Herbert Allen, who knew about the Diamond M meeting and had a stake in its outcome, would cover for him, Hirschfield did not bother to inform the Columbia board of his whereabouts. Unbeknownst to Hirschfield, however, Herbert told the Columbia directors only that Alan had an important call and offered no further explanation. The directors became predictably angry as the time passed. 10:15. 10:30. 10:45. The angriest was James Wilmot of Page Airways, who had flown down from Rochester especially for the meeting and had narrowly escaped death that morning when his small private jet just missed hitting an airport service vehicle which had suddenly appeared out of the fog on a runway at La Guardia. Wilmot, a close friend of Herbert's, was attending his first Columbia board meeting since before the Begelman problem had arisen.

Hirschfield finally ambled into the boardroom at 11:15, an hour and a quarter late, as casually as if he were returning from the men's room.

"Well, one down, one to go," he muttered.

"You have treated this board with contempt and disdain," Jim Wilmot growled.

The mood of the meeting deteriorated from there. Leo Jaffe gaveled it to order and called on Todd Lang, who reiterated the "business-judgment rule" and the main points of the two legal memoranda the board had been given.

Peter Gruenberger, joined by Michael Passarella of Price Waterhouse, outlined the methods and techniques they had used in investigating David Begelman. "I know David Begelman's personal finances better than I know my own," Passarella said. Gruenberger then began a detailed recitation, lasting more than an hour, of the facts his group had developed.

The pro-Begelman directors frequently interrupted Gruenberger with hostile comments or questions. When he explained how Begelman had embezzled $35,000 to supplement what the company had appropriated for his home projection room, someone said: "That's not very important. If he'd asked, we'd have allowed him the extra money."

Hirschfield spoke up: "The point is, he didn't ask, and instead stole thirty-five thousand dollars."

When Gruenberger described the misleading automobile lease, someone said: "So what. He was entitled to two cars. What difference does it make how he accounted for it?"

"He lied about it," Hirschfield said.

When the Martin Ritt forgery was outlined, Matty Rosenhaus said: "That's nothing new. It's just like all the others. If you don't have anything new, why are we wasting our time?"

Gruenberger then mentioned Begelman's employment in the insurance business. "While we haven't been able to establish the details, we have heard reports that when Mr. Begelman was associated with an insurance concern in New York in the early 1950s, he left that employment under questionable circumstances."

The boardroom erupted in angry shouts. Herbert Allen accused Gruenberger of character assassination. Jim Wilmot said: "What may have happened thirty years ago is none of our business. This is supposed to be confined to his time at Columbia. You're doing a hatchet job!''

"I'm not going to sit here and be accused of doing a hatchet job!'' Gruenberger shouted back. "I won't stand for it! I have nothing personal against David Begelman. In fact, I like him. But I've had a dirty job to do, which someone had to do, and I will not have my motives or my abilities as a lawyer impugned!''

Hirschfield interrupted: "Look, one of the claims that has been made on David's behalf is that his behavior is aberrational, that these are things he has never done before and will never do again. If there is evidence to suggest that he did something in the fifties that is even remotely similar to what he's been doing over the last few years, it may indicate that this is not aberrational behavior. We may be looking at a life pattern.''

Todd Lang came to Gruenberger's defense. "Peter has done a meticulous and outstanding job of carrying out a very unpleasant and sensitive assignment. He has done it efficiently and without interfering with the operations of this company. He has been on the coast for several weeks away from his home and family. It has been an exhausting and an exhaustive effort. His report is as detailed as it is because the chairman of the audit committee gave specific instructions that nothing be left out. So nobody on this board has any right to accuse Peter of doing a hatchet job.''

"Let him continue,'' Irwin Kramer said.

Gruenberger went on: "All we really have heard is that when Begelman was at this insurance concern, there were some questions raised about premiums and questions raised about loans. He was given the option of resigning or being dismissed. He resigned. When we questioned him about it, he flatly denied any wrongdoing and said the whole thing had been a misunderstanding.''

After several more questions, David Begelman was invited into the meeting. He had flown in from Los Angeles early Tuesday evening and had passed the hours alone in Columbia's suite at the Drake, as the world premiere of the biggest picture of his career was unfolding just three blocks away. On Wednesday morning he had walked to Columbia and waited in Leo Jaffe's office for the board to receive him. Dressed in a conservative dark suit and carrying a large manila folder, he shook hands around the table and was greeted like a returning hero by those favoring his restoration. He sat down and opened the folder, his voice quavering slightly as he began to speak.

"When I came to this company, it was a shambles. You took a gamble that I could help rescue it. Along with others, I worked long and hard to make it work, and we succeeded. There were days when we didn't know whether we'd have enough money to make the next picture. But we found the money, we made the pictures, and we succeeded. I for one am very proud of these successes, especially of our crowning achievement—*Close Encounters*. But somehow, just when I was at my peak, I began somehow to self-destruct. I committed grievous transgressions, vile acts, against Columbia and against you, my friends. I must face the fact that I did these things, even though, emotionally, it is still impossible for me to believe that I did them. But over the past six weeks, with the help of one of the finest doctors in the country, and indeed the world, I have learned a great deal about the roots of my misdeeds. The roots go deep, all the way back to my childhood and my relationship with my parents and with my siblings. In sum, the problem amounts to an unnaturally low self-esteem, a feeling of unworthiness, and an inability to accommodate success. Subconsciously I didn't like myself. I felt undeserving. I was not consciously aware of these forces at work within me. But the tangible results were a series of highly neurotic acts by which I tried to punish and injure myself. There is no logical, rational excuse for what I did, no justification. But in the therapy which I sought immediately upon the revelation of these acts six weeks ago, it became quickly clear to me that there were valid—not justifiable, but understandable in retrospect—reasons for these highly neurotic acts, which were not directed against Columbia or against any individual, but against myself. I was trying to punish and injure myself. In the very truest sense I was trying to destroy myself, and I very nearly succeeded. Perhaps I did succeed.

"But now I appear before you with the acts revealed, with the investigation completed, with restitution made, or in the process of being made, and with my psychological health well on the way toward restoration. I am a man who was sick and is very nearly cured. I am engaged in active, dynamic psychotherapy which is helping me enormously. Because I now understand the roots of my transgressions, it is inconceivable that I could ever repeat them. Thus, I appear before you to ask for mercy, to ask for a second chance. If you feel you cannot grant me that second chance, I will certainly understand. But if you can summon up the mercy to grant me another chance, you will find that I will work day and night and do everything humanly possible to justify your faith in me. I will rededicate my life to the success of Columbia Pictures."

Tears streamed down the face of Matty Rosenhaus as Begelman spoke, and other eyes in the room were moist as well. The only people not visibly moved by Begelman's words were Alan Hirschfield, Herbert Allen, and the lawyers.

With hands trembling slightly, Begelman picked up a stack of letters and telegrams from his folder and held them aloft.

"In case any of you are concerned about my standing in the Hollywood community as a result of my difficulties—and I well understand how you might have such concerns—I want to share with you a number of expressions which I have received in recent weeks." He proceeded to read messages from Paul Newman, Mel Brooks, Sue Mengers, George Segal, Barbra Streisand, and many other big names in Hollywood. Although few if any of these people knew what Begelman had done to cause his suspension from the company, they all declared him to be an outstanding executive whom they would be delighted to work with in the future.

Then Begelman shifted in his chair slightly and looked straight at Alan Hirschfield. "Now, Alan, I'd like to talk directly to you. You have been a friend to me, you took a chance with me by hiring me, and you have stood by me through some very difficult times. I've betrayed you. I've lied to you. I've given you every reason not to trust me. I know that the only way in which you will ever trust me again is if I actively win back your trust, win back your faith, win back your admiration. I want you to know that I will work with every breath of my body to accomplish this if you will just give me a chance. If you find that you can't do it, I'll understand. But if you do, it will be the best decision you ever make in your life. You will have no more loyal servant than me. I beg of you to give it to me."

With that, Begelman rose, picked up his folder, and again circled the table shaking hands. Jim Wilmot said: "It took a lot of courage for you to come here today and go through all of this." Matty Rosenhaus, still dabbing at his eyes with a handkerchief, escorted Begelman from the room.

As Rosenhaus was returning to his seat, Hirschfield said: "That was quite an act, trembling hands and all."

Rosenhaus shouted, "I deeply resent that comment! What kind of man are you, anyway, to say something like that. For God's sake, the man bares his heart and soul, and you say something like that. It's despicable and unforgivable!''

''I didn't forge the checks, Matty,'' Hirschfield retorted.

Everyone in the room not a member of the board of directors, including the lawyers, was asked to leave so that the board could deliberate in private. Each of the seven men expressed himself in turn. Herbert Allen, Irwin Kramer, and James Wilmot repeated the familar arguments in favor of reinstating Begelman: He is not a criminal but an emotionally disturbed man who is nearly cured. He has stolen less than one hundred thousand dollars, not a large amount. He is an extraordinarily valuable asset to the company, and indeed is irreplaceable. Reaction from outside the company to reinstatement is irrelevant: Under the ''business-judgment'' concept, as outlined by the lawyers, we have the right to reinstate him. Neither the SEC nor anyone else has the right to tell us how to run our business. Even if there's some unfavorable publicity, it will fade quickly.

Matty Rosenhaus was never content simply to register assent in such a situation. He liked to deliver sermons.

''I don't know when I've ever been more moved than I was by David here this morning. This clearly is a reformed man. He's seen the light. Can you imagine the suffering he's been through, and not only privately, but his wife, his family, his loss of face, his loss of standing in the community. It must have been pure hell. Alan, you *have* to be a big enough man to forgive him. If we can forgive, you can forgive. It's in your lap. The man is telling you that you'll have a friend for life, who'll be more loyal to you than anyone. Loyalty is the most important thing there is in life, Alan. Nothing is more important than loyalty. Here you have a person who will be loyal to you for life—to Alan Hirschfield. Not only does David deserve another chance, he *needs* another chance. He needs our approval in order to recover. God knows what will happen to him if we don't give it to him. He was in such a state. Couldn't you see the way his hands were shaking? He could hardly speak. We have to trust him. Every famous name in the business wrote him, saying they believe in him. We have to believe in him, too. It's up to you, Alan. You have to look into your heart, and then open your heart to David.''

It was Leo Jaffe's turn.

''I understand the pleas you're making. I, too, was touched by

David's talk. I know the people who wrote to him. They all meant what they said. In his heart, David wants to do as well as he can. But there are certain things you can forgive a man for doing as a human being, but that have no place in a publicly owned company. We are a public company. We have to think about the public, the shareholders, and our employees. What do we say to the next person who steals? Do we give him a second chance? Do we have a double standard? Executives can steal, but employees at a lower level can't? Besides, how do we know we can trust David? How do we know this isn't a lifelong habit? Six weeks is an awfully short period of time in which to judge how well he is. Maybe we should wait six months or a year and then consider taking him back. I don't want to see David have to suffer any financial loss, or be deprived, or be thrown out on the street. He's made an enormous contribution to the company. No one here is taking anything away from that. Wouldn't we all be better off trying to make a production deal with him, giving him some financial security, and then reconsidering his situation vis-à-vis the company a year or two down the line?''

Finally the floor was Hirschfeld's. After seven difficult weeks, during which he had decided he had to oppose Begelman's return to the company, but had managed to avoid most confrontations with the other board members on the subject, the time for confrontation was at hand.

"First of all," Hirschfeld began, "the question of David's qualifications was never an issue. The fact that he brought in all these recommendations from people in the industry only affirms a self-evident truth. David is a very able, very qualified man. His value to the corporation has never been an issue and has never been doubted by me. This has nothing to do with his competence. I also agree that it is unlikely that he would commit the kind of acts in the future that he has in the past. But I don't think it's cut and dried, and I can't assure anybody that we won't continue to find evidence of other things from his past. I just don't want to be around the day somebody walks in and says we found another twenty-five-thousand-dollar item for David Begelman. We would get sued from here to tomorrow. I just don't want to be a part of it.

"I also think it's highly questionable that we're dealing with temporary aberrational behavior. I'm convinced from Peter's presentation and from talking to other people that we're dealing with a lifelong habit. And you just don't change lifelong habits in six weeks. Whatever deep-seated emotional problems have come to the fore, there is no doubt that he has lived on the financial edge all his life. We have indications that there may have been a problem as far back as the fifties.*

"The issue of the double standard worries me. If we bring him back, we're in effect condoning this kind of behavior for other employees. We can't have a double standard.

"As to outside appearances, I think they're vital in this day and age. I challenge any person sitting in this room to tell me one, just one, company in the *Fortune* 500, or even the *Fortune* 1,000, that, faced with this same problem, would take a person like this back."

Herbert Allen spoke up. "Northrup Aviation reinstated Jones, Thomas Jones, last year after their scandal."

"That was an entirely different kind of issue," Hirschfield said. "It was political and foreign payoffs. Those people didn't steal from the company and put it in their own pockets. However illegal it might have been, they were using the company's money to get business for the company."

"Well, it doesn't make any difference what the rest of the *Fortune* 500 do," Herbert replied. "We can be the exception."

"There should be no exceptions," Hirschfield insisted. "Matty, what would happen in your company, Nabisco, if you caught somebody stealing? How long would Nabisco put up with this kind of behavior? Would they give him a second chance?"

"It would be handled on a case-by-case basis," Rosenhaus said.

"I doubt that very much. In my opinion, he'd be bounced out on his nose and prosecuted in all probability. If we bring David back, we're going to stick out like a sore thumb. We're going to destroy the credibility we spent four and a half years regaining after being on the bottom of the heap. Our standing in the investment community, the financial community, and the entertainment community would be totally destroyed by taking him back. In addition to which, our ability to do acquisitions, our standing with our banks . . . we're going to look like utter fools. And in my opinion, there's going to be a holocaust in the newspapers. There's going to be a firestorm of

---

*The questions raised about Begelman's employment in the insurance business were never resolved, and no evidence of wrongdoing by Begelman was presented. Begelman later said that if there had been any misunderstanding when he left the insurance business—and he did not recall any misunderstanding—it resulted from the abruptness of his departure to join MCA, a move he had wanted to make for many years.

publicity. It's not going to go away in twenty-four hours. It's going to last us a lifetime if we keep him here. And every time he says a word, or does a deal, it's going to be there, sticking out like a sore thumb.

"I can tell you for sure," Hirschfield continued, "that the minute we take him back we'll have no deal with General Cinema. We'll blow a financing and a relationship that is worth tens of millions of dollars to this company. And I can also tell you for sure that we will not do business again with Time Inc. if David Begelman is running our production program. Also, I think you people are underestimating the response of the SEC. This company has to do business in Washington. We have a continuing need to have good relationships with the SEC for getting financings approved, mergers, acquisitions. We're kidding ourselves if we think this isn't going to hurt us. They're on a kick about white-collar crime and aren't about to stand back and watch us reward somebody who has done these things by putting him back in his position.

"There has been a myth created that David Begelman is indispensable. Yes, he's done a brilliant job and has played an important role in the success of the company. But we aren't the company we were four and a half years ago. We're a highly visible, highly successful enterprise, and we aren't depending on the motion-picture division to live or die anymore. TV is doing all right. We have Arista. We have Gottlieb. We have a strong balance sheet. We have credibility in the community. We have the best marketing of any company in the industry. In fact, it's an insult to the people at this company to say that any one person, including myself, is indispensable to the success of this company. Begelman is not irreplaceable, nor is anybody else. Other picture companies have done fine when they lost the heads of their studios.

"On a personal moral basis, taking him back goes against everything I stand for. I have great sympathy for David. I have great anguish in my heart. This is a man I've lived and died with for four years trying to make this company work. We've shared a lot of agony together and we've shared a lot of success together. I don't want to see him hurt financially in any way, shape, or form. I don't want to see him prosecuted. I'm happy to consider giving him a production deal if the lawyers say that won't cause us trouble. But we cannot have a forger and embezzler in this company, whatever the extenuating circumstances.''

After a few seconds of silence, Matty Rosenhaus spoke: "Alan, we have committed ourselves to support whatever decision you make as the chief executive officer, and we are prepared to honor that commitment. But I implore you, I beg you, I ask you as strongly as I possibly can, to reconsider your position and try to find a way to work with David. The decision doesn't have to be made today. We still have to get a report directly from David's doctor, and Peter still has to clear up a few loose ends of the investigation. So I would ask you to think it over for a few days before making a final decision."

"I'm 90 percent sure," Hirschfield said.

"With 10 percent, there's always hope," Rosenhaus replied.

Hirschfield reluctantly agreed. He promised to render a tentative decision by Friday and, depending on what was learned from Begelman's psychiatrist and the other remaining steps of the investigation, to give a final decision the following week.

The board meeting was adjourned at three o'clock. Hirschfield returned to his office and summoned Joe Fischer, Allen Adler, and Victor Kaufman to brief them on the board's private deliberations. Hirschfield was devastated. He had known that the board meeting would be difficult, but it had been much worse than he had anticipated. Despite David Geffen's warnings about Ray Stark, despite the warnings of Marty Ransohoff ("They're gonna shove him up your ass!"), despite the extraordinary revelation that Berte's employment might be made an issue in the Begelman case, Alan had clung to the hope that when the directors actually sat down behind the closed doors of the boardroom—with the full array of Begelman's crimes, lies, and manipulations spread before them—their minds would be open, they would be able to engage in genuine collaborative reasoning, and in the end, they would agree with his conclusion that reinstating Begelman was not only unwise as a practical matter but flatly wrong in every respect. It seemed to Hirschfield, however, that every mind in the boardroom had been made up before the meeting began. David Geffen had been right about Ray Stark all along. He obviously had swayed Herbert and everybody else. The entire event appeared to have been staged so as to put the most pressure on Hirschfield: Begelman's tear-jerking *mea culpa;* the rude treatment of Peter Gruenberger; the refusal to accept Alan's decision and the insistence that he reconsider.

Alan had not expected them to raise the "Berte" issue in the boardroom and they had not. They would wait a few days and see whether he changed his mind on Begelman. He knew, however, that he could not and would not reconsider.

Begelman had to go.

At dusk, Hirschfield strolled alone over to the Ziegfeld and was thrilled to see that the lines of people waiting to see *Close Encounters* stretched all the way to Sixth Avenue. The movie had received rave reviews in the New York papers that day and, having been open to the public only since noon, was playing to record crowds at each showing.

Someone had suggested after the board meeting that Hirschfield and Begelman meet privately before David returned to Los Angeles. They agreed, and Hirschfield went to the Columbia suite at the Drake for breakfast on Thursday morning. It was the first time that he and David had been alone together for more than two months—since before the revelation of the first embezzlement. Both men were somewhat uncomfortable and guarded. David did not repeat his emotional plea for mercy. Alan did not flatly reject the idea of reinstatement.

"When I went on leave of absence," David said, "you indicated or implied that if this was not another Equity Funding situation, you might have a different view of it than you would have if it were an Equity Funding. Without in any way minimizing the seriousness or importance of my transgressions, I think you can agree that they do not add up to another Equity Funding."

"Of course not, David, but it's still a very difficult situation for us. We live in an age when corporations are under close scrutiny from all sides and have to be above reproach. This case is a tough call. I have to consider how I would be perceived if I took you back. I have to consider how I will look to the banks, to the Street, to the public. I know it doesn't matter in Hollywood. I know they love you out there and you're already forgiven. So I'm not concerned about your effectiveness in the community if you came back. That's not an issue. But I do have to consider carefully how the company as a whole will look."

"I understand that," David replied, "and I'm sure that whatever decision you reach will take those issues into account, as well it should.''

The meeting ended on a cordial note. ''Things will work out,'' Alan said.

On his way to JFK in the limousine, Begelman felt more hopeful than he had felt in some time.

Hirschfield had had Joe Fischer searching urgently, before and after the Wednesday board meeting, for the file documenting Berte's employment with the Wolf market-research firm. When Alan returned from seeing Begelman Thursday morning, he was relieved to learn that Fischer had finally found the file. There were two letters, both dated February 26, 1976, both signed by Leo Jaffe, and both marked ''personal and confidential.'' The first letter was to Hirschfield, who had voluntarily made Berte's employment known to Columbia and its lawyers in order to obtain an objective appraisal of whether her job represented a potential conflict. The second letter was to Irwin Kramer, the chairman of the board's subcommittee that periodically examined the outside business interests of employees to determine whether there was any conflict with Columbia's interests and whether anyone was using his position at Columbia for improper personal gain. Both letters had cleared Berte of any conflict.

''Our examination, which was made thoroughly in this instance, indicates there is no conflict of interest,'' Jaffe had written to Kramer. Todd Lang had concurred.

It was Irwin Kramer, of course, who was now asking Peter Gruenberger to reopen the matter. Hirschfield sent Gruenberger copies of Jaffe's letters, hoping they would squelch any effort by the board to make an issue of Berte's employment. Hirschfield realized, however, that if the board was determined to inflame the issue, it was capable of doing so, even in the face of the letters.

Herbert Allen called at noon on Friday.

''What's your decision, Alan? You said you'd have a tentative decision on Begelman by Friday.''

''I haven't made it yet. You'll get a final decision by Tuesday.''

''But you promised you would have a tentative decision by today. You gave your word.''

''I have the right to change my mind about my word.''

''That's a very bizarre statement, Alan. You gave your word to the board that you would decide by Friday, pending the final questioning of the doctor.''

"This is a ridiculous conversation, about as ridiculous as you people trying to make something corrupt out of Berte's employment with Ed Wolf.''

"Nobody's above reproach, Alan.''

"Well, Berte certainly is, and I certainly am on that issue, and I have letters to prove it.''

"I don't recall that we ever got to the bottom of that.''

"You know goddamn well that we got to the bottom of it. I disclosed it to the board, I disclosed it to the lawyers, and everybody agreed that it was clean. She hasn't even worked there for nearly a year.''

"Well, Irwin feels it needs another look. We don't recall that we ever got all the details.''

"Irwin can go fuck himself! This is blackmail! If you think you can bludgeon me into taking David back by raising a phony issue about Berte, you've got another think coming!''

"Oh, Alan, don't be ridiculous. Why are you so excited if you've got nothing to hide?''

"I have a right to be excited! You can't convince me to take Begelman back on the merits, so you come up with some phony bullshit about my wife that has nothing to do with Begelman or anything else. It's the lowest kind of tactic!''

"You're overreacting, Alan. The audit committee has a responsibility to examine any situation where there might be a question.''

"There is no question here and you know it, and you've pushed me as far as you're going to push me.''

Hirschfield slammed the receiver into the cradle.

TWENTY-EIGHT

As Alan and Berte Hirschfield and their children flew west on Saturday afternoon for an annual Thanksgiving reunion with West Coast relatives, Judd Marmor, Begelman's psychiatrist, flew east for a Sunday rendezvous in Manhattan with Irwin Kramer and Peter Gruenberger.

Many people were skeptical about David Begelman's psychotherapy. Wags had labeled it the "six-week Beverly Hills miracle cure," in part because Matty Rosenhaus, with fustian solemnity, had been quick to proclaim David "cured" and his treatment a "miracle." Alan Hirschfield considered it a "joke." Anyone familiar with psychotherapy knew that serious emotional problems generally could not be "cured" in so short a time.

As much as they yearned to, however, the skeptics could not ignore Begelman's therapy. He had, after all, sought out a renowned doctor and had placed emotional illness at the center of his defense. Judd Marmor had his detractors in the Los Angeles psychoanalytic community, as any psychiatrist does, but since no one had insisted that Begelman get a second opinion, Marmor's diagnosis was the only professional opinion that counted. David had waived the doctor-patient privilege of confidentiality and urged that Marmor be questioned directly and independently. Peter Gruenberger had spoken informally with Marmor in his Wilshire Boulevard office several days earlier, but the meeting on Sunday morning at Irwin Kramer's apartment on Park Avenue was to be the official interrogation, wherein Marmor presumably would confirm everything that Begelman himself had told the board on Wednesday about his mental problems and treatment.

Judd Marmor, a slight, bald man of sixty-seven, with a deep tan, arrived at the Kramer apartment promptly at 10:30, only to find that he had been preempted temporarily by televised history-in-the-making. The Kramer family and the Columbia contingent were gathered around a television set in the den watching Egyptian President Sadat address the Israeli parliament in Jerusalem. It was a momentous day in the history of Egyptian-Israeli relations, and millions of people in America and abroad were riveted to the live television coverage that morning. Judd Marmor's time was limited, however, so after about half an hour, he and the Columbia group adjourned to the library. In addition to Irwin Kramer and Peter Gruenberger, the meeting was attended by Robert Werbel, the Allen & Company lawyer, and Nancy Barton, the Weil, Gotshal lawyer who had discovered the Martin Ritt check.

Marmor was asked to give a précis of David Begelman's condition and treatment.

"David's problem fundamentally is a neurotic disorder rather than a flaw of character," the doctor began. "That means that he can function at a high level professionally and personally, but at the same time occasionally display neurotic symptoms. Although the roots of his neurosis go quite deep, the neurosis itself constitutes a subconscious feeling of self-loathing, low self-esteem, a feeling of lack of worth, which makes it difficult for him to accommodate great success and acclaim. This conflict sets off a self-destructive mechanism, which manifests itself in the acts he committed. They in turn represent a need to be caught and punished.

"All of this is different from a psychopath, who has no guilt and, if caught, only regrets being caught. David knew he was doing something wrong. He knew he was guilty then and thereafter. As a result, he now feels enormous guilt and self-condemnation and is willing and anxious to pay any price to make up to the people whom he has hurt."

Peter Gruenberger began to question Marmor:

"As you may know, David swore to us in September after we found two defalcations that there were no more. We found a third. He swore to us he had blocked that and was sure there were no more beyond the third. A month later we found another forged check, the Martin Ritt check. He says he blocked that, too. Is all of this plausible?"

"Yes, absolutely. I believe he totally repressed the Ritt episode. It is possible for an event itself to be repressed, but for the guilt over having committed the event to be manifest."

"How can we be sure that there are no other events?"

"I told him at the outset that he had to tell me everything, and I believe he has. I've pressed him very hard."

"How can we be sure that he acted alone?"

"I believe it to be absolutely true that nobody helped him commit any of these acts. This was a secret neurosis."

"Is there any possibility that he needed this money because he was gambling?"

"No."

"Is it possible that he was blackmailed?"

"I don't think so."

"Then what was the conscious motivation?"

"He had to maintain a dignified front, and while one ordinarily would think of blackmail or gambling, the simplest explanation—so simple that one tends to reject it—is that this was a man living beyond his means and unable to admit it. But that's neurotic, not realistic, behavior."

"Could you describe the type of treatment?"

"It is intensive psychoanalytically oriented psychotherapy. There are no drugs or hypnosis. We meet three times a week and may do so for several years, although we may winnow down after a while to twice a week. I'm getting a high level of sincerity and cooperation from David. The prognosis for correction of the condition is excellent. He has a definite capacity for correctability. I expect the changes to be fundamental and not veneer. I feel confident in saying that he won't do these things again, not just because of what I have done in treating him, but also because the bubble has burst. I think the prospect of recurrence is absolutely minimal, and I think David will try hard to vindicate himself."

"How well will he be able to function with his peers, with subordinates, and with outsiders?"

"I think he has the capacity to adapt and I certainly think that he will maintain dignity and poise. He has no resentment toward the investigation. He understands the necessity for it. In fact, he feels he caused it to happen. He says 'I want to pay any bill to clear my slate.' "

"Do you feel it is necessary to impose any special controls or protections on or around David to guard against a recurrence?"

"If you do that, it would be a good idea to make it a company rule for everybody."

After about two hours in the Kramer apartment, Judd Marmor left and flew back to Los Angeles.

*   *   *

Perhaps the most enthusiastic movie review in the history of movies appeared in Sunday's *Los Angeles Times*—an article about *Close Encounters* by science-fiction author Ray Bradbury.

> *Close Encounters* calls. We feel ourselves being born, truly for the first time. . . . *Close Encounters* is, in all probability, the most important film of our time. . . . For this is a religious film, in all the great good senses, the right senses, of that much-battered word. . . . Spielberg has made a film that can open in New Delhi, Tokyo, Berlin, Moscow, Johannesburg, Paris, London, New York and Rio de Janeiro on the same day to mobs and throngs and crowds that will never stop coming because for the first time someone has treated all of us as if we really did belong to one race. . . . I dare to predict that in every way, aesthetically or commercially, it will be the most success-ful film ever produced, released, or seen. It will be the first film in history to gross $1 billion, all by itself. . . . Every priest, minister, rabbi in the world should preach this film, show this film to their congregations. Every Moslem, every Buddhist—Zen or otherwise—in the world can sit down at this moveable feast and leave well fed. That's how big this film is. That's why it will be around the rest of our lives making us want to live more fully, packing us with its hope and energy. . . .

Ray Stark staged the premier of his new film *The Goodbye Girl* in Manhattan that Sunday evening. Among the guests at the party following the movie were Herbert Allen, the Leo Jaffes, and Cliff Robertson and Dina Merrill. Robertson had recently completed his own film in London and returned to New York. Although Cliff had ignored Columbia Pictures' offer, issued through his lawyer, to brief him privately on the Begelman investigation, he and Leo Jaffe, who had known Cliff for many years, found a private spot amidst the hubbub of the party.

"I'm sorry for whatever grief this matter has caused Columbia," Cliff said. "I know you understand that I had to do what I did, being faced with a possible tax investigation."

"Of course," Leo replied, "and I want you to know that we have the situation fully under control. We've had the most complete inves-tigation imaginable, and we appreciate your discretion in the matter."

"Well, as far as I'm concerned, it's closed. I was only concerned about the tax issue, and that's been clarified."

For the third time in seven weeks, Alan Hirschfield settled into Bungalow 8 of the Beverly Hills Hotel—this time for a two-week stay that would include the traditional California Thanksgiving reunion of the Hirschfield family. The occasion was spearheaded by Berte and her sister, Susan Fogelson, whose husband, Andrew, was in charge of advertising at Warner Bros. (Earlier he had a similar post at Columbia.) Alan's parents would come from their winter home in Palm Springs. Berte and Susan's brother would come down from Seattle.

As his family began a week of recreation, Alan stepped back into the Begelman fray like a battlefield commander returning to a war after a weekend pass. He found the Columbia studio so preoccupied with the controversy that the conduct of business was being impeded. Staff members spent much of each day speculating among themselves: Will David be reinstated? What did the investigation find? How many checks did he forge? How can he be reinstated if he stole money? Is he in hock to the Mafia? Will he be prosecuted? Will he go to jail? Is he emotionally disturbed?

One of the few people who had resolved not to be engulfed by the affair was Columbia's newest production vice president, Sherry Lansing, whose first day on the job was Monday, November 21. Lured by the prospect of increased responsibility, Lansing had moved to Columbia from MGM. She had been urged to take the job by a number of people, including Columbia's production chief Dan Melnick, who had come from MGM several months earlier. Melnick had been Lansing's mentor at MGM, and before that at David Susskind's company, Talent Associates. Another friend who had encouraged her to come to Columbia was Allen Adler, the corporation's young senior vice president. Over a drink at the Polo Lounge several weeks earlier, just before the Begelman problem arose, Adler had told Lansing, "Columbia is the hottest company in town. We've got great people in place at the studio and in New York. Sherry, it's almost Camelot."

"Camelot, indeed," Lansing mused at Columbia on Monday, November 21. The lances and maces were certainly there, and the jealousy and intrigue. But it was obvious that she would have to wait a while for the shining moments and wisps of glory. Trying to ignore the crossfire in the Begelman fight, she concentrated that day on script conferences with director James Bridges and producer Michael Douglas, who were developing a picture tentatively entitled *The China Syndrome.*

At five Monday afternoon, Hirschfield drove to Mickey Rudin's office on Wilshire Boulevard. He and Rudin had spoken frequently by phone but had not seen each other since the night of the Brandeis University dinner at the Waldorf in September when Rudin had whispered his confirmation of the Peter Choate embezzlement.

Although he had never used Rudin for routine corporate legal work—that was not Rudin's specialty—Hirschfield over the years had sought Rudin's counsel in solving sensitive, ambiguous problems that occasionally confront every corporate chief executive but for which there is no pat legal solution—problems that demand wisdom and judgment, as well as a knowledge of the law.

Alan brought Mickey up to date: While the Columbia directors ostensibly had promised to support his decision not to reinstate Begelman, they strongly favored reinstatement and were applying enormous pressure to try to force Hirschfield to reverse his decision. They even were threatening to "blackmail" him by making an issue out of his wife's previous employment, twisting something which had been entirely legitimate into something corrupt. The inescapable inference was that if Alan did not yield on Begelman, the "corrupt" version of Berte's employment record might wind up in the newspapers. Once the lie was public, the truth might never catch up, and the Hirschfields might be tainted unjustly for life.

Alan was committed to announce his final decision on Begelman to the board the next day. Did he have any options left? Could anything be done to avoid what promised to be an extremely ugly and volatile confrontation?

Mickey Rudin fully supported Hirschfield's basic position on Begelman. While Rudin grasped the pro-Begelman line, he felt that reinstatement was unwise in every respect. It would invite publicity. It would invite closer scrutiny by the police and the SEC. It would invite stockholder lawsuits. And it was unnecessary. There were other talented people who could do Begelman's job. It seemed to Rudin that even from Begelman's point of view the wisest and least painful course would be to take an independent production deal that Columbia was prepared to offer.

With Hirschfield still in the office, Rudin telephoned Frank Rothman, Begelman's lawyer, with whom he had last spoken during the first week of October. Rothman had called then to announce that he had been retained to represent Begelman and to ask Rudin's assessment of the inclination of the Beverly Hills Police Department in the Cliff Robertson matter. (Rudin had told Rothman that the police, in the person of Detective Joyce Silvey, did not seem to regard the forgery as a "major crime" and seemed content for the moment to leave the matter in the hands of Columbia's lawyers and the Securities and Exchange Commission. But, Rudin cautioned, the case had "bounced around" the police bureaucracy a good bit, and he advised that if Rothman wanted to make sure the case went no farther, he should "touch base" with Detective Silvey.)

Now, at dusk on the Monday before Thanksgiving, these two elite members of the Beverly Hills legal fraternity, professional friends for many years, were discussing a more complex subject than the mood of the Beverly Hills police. Rothman was learning for the first time that Alan Hirschfield had, in effect, retained Mickey Rudin as his personal counselor in the Begelman matter—an indication to Rothman that Hirschfield was having considerable difficulty wrestling with the decision of whether to reinstate Begelman.

"Frank, I want to talk to you as a friend," Rudin began. "I wouldn't presume to tell you how to practice law, but it seems to me you're trying to accomplish too much by trying to have your client reinstated as president of the Columbia studio. It's too arrogant to expect that you or he will get away with it. If he steps back, resigns, takes an independent production contract, there's a good chance that things will quiet down and nobody will get hurt. But if he stays in office, I think you may end up with him being prosecuted. It's sort of spitting in everybody's eye just to keep a guy in office and hope to get by with it, where there's evidence that he stole money. The SEC will get up in arms, the police may get up in arms, and I think you're making your task too tough. The sooner it's quieted down, the less chance there is that somebody will come along and jump all over you. Alan doesn't want to see David hurt and is trying to base his decision on what is best for all concerned. And yet there are people like Ray Stark, who may have their own interest in keeping David in office, pressuring Alan to reinstate him, when it's not in David's own best interest to stay as president. Maybe David isn't aware of all these issues. My recommendation to you is that you talk to your client and try to convince him to step back."

"I disagree, Mickey," Rothman said. "I see things from an entirely different perspective. David is under the care of a very reputable psychiatrist who has assured us that his acts stemmed from emotional problems which are being successfully treated. This is not a criminal matter, it is not an SEC matter, it is a medical and psychiatric matter. The doctor has given assurances that David is well on the way to recovery, and is eminently able and ready to resume his duties. It is important for his continued psychological health that he be reinstated, and in fact it would be a severe psychological blow to him if he were not. So, contrary to what you say, it is very much in David's interest that this suspension be lifted."

"I still think you're making a mistake, Frank. Whatever the merits of David's psychiatric treatment, the SEC, the police, the press, and whoever takes a look at this situation may not put all the stock in his treatment that you do. They may put no stock in it at all. Alan has to take all of this into account in making his decision. He has to consider how all of this will be perceived by skeptical outsiders who may take a look at it. And beyond all of that, it's very unfair for Alan, the chief executive who has to make the decision, to be subjected to the kind of pressure he's getting from his board."

"Alan's relationship with his board is none of my business," Rothman said.

"I think it becomes your business if your client knows about the kinds of things that are being done in his behalf."

"I have no idea what you are talking about."

"For example, a few years ago, Alan Hirschfield's wife was involved in a business venture, a company that did some business with Columbia. The situation was examined by the board at the time and declared clean and proper. Now the board is suggesting that there might have been a conflict of interest, and it has been reported to Hirschfield through an intermediary that if he insists on holding David Begelman to a strict standard and insists on his leaving the company, he had better be prepared for full disclosure of his wife's relationship to Columbia, which the board is now claiming may have been corrupt. Alan is very angry about this and considers it blackmail."

"I can only repeat that I have no idea what you are talking about," Rothman said. "This comes as a total surprise to me. It's the first I've heard of it."

"I'm not implying that you do know anything about it. I'm only saying that this is the kind of tactic that your client's friends and associates are using to force Alan to keep him in the company. It is highly improper and it also will be counterproductive, because Alan feels very strongly, and I agree with him, that David runs the risk of being hurt badly in the long run if he returns to his job. I still believe you should talk to him and make sure that he recognizes the dangers."

"I will talk to him because I'm certain that he is not a party to any of the kind of pressure tactic that you are suggesting is being used. But none of this changes my feeling that he belongs back in his job."

Rothman's staunchness did not surprise Hirschfield or Rudin, but at least the message had been delivered. If there was even the slightest chance of Begelman's backing down, it was worth a try.

The board meeting was scheduled for four o'clock on Tuesday afternoon, New York time. Herbert Allen, Irwin Kramer, Joe Fischer, Todd Lang, and Victor Kaufman gathered around a speaker-telephone in Leo Jaffe's office. Matty Rosenhaus was on a telephone in his office three blocks up Fifth Avenue. James Wilmot was listening in from Rochester.

Hirschfield sat alone at a large desk in the visiting-executives' suite in Burbank. Spread before him were five sheets of yellow legal-size paper on which he had made notes with a black felt-tipped pen. He had gone over the notes twice, underlining certain points first in black and later in red.

"Is everybody there?" Hirschfield asked.

"Yes, we're all listening, Alan. Go ahead."

"I stated my basic position on this matter last Wednesday. But I have reconsidered it from every angle. I don't think my past reputation, or your experience with me, has been that I've been stubborn or uncompromising. On Wednesday I listened carefully to the lawyers' report and all the members of the board. I accept your decision that in the end I have to decide what's best for the company and I have to live with and believe in that decision. I am also mindful of the board's promise to support my decision. So, for all of the reasons I stated last Wednesday, I have decided not to reinstate David in any kind of management position."

There was hostile muttering at the New York end of the line.

"I think you've made a terrible mistake," Rosenhaus said.

"Let him go on," Jaffe said.

"There is now a more important issue I have to discuss," Hirschfield continued, "and that is my relationship with the board. I feel I've been treated shabbily. I feel the board is ungrateful. I feel that after four and a half years of a good record, good decisions, and having given everything I've got, after four and a half years where every man on this board has benefited—that when push came to shove and when I asked for support—even begged—the board walked away, made me the villain, allowed an adversary relationship to develop, acted behind my back, and is now attempting to blackmail me and my family. I won't stand for it.

"Instead of supporting me, it's obvious that the board has let Ray Stark become the final word and authority where Columbia is concerned. Somehow, he in effect is calling the shots. He's the one you listen to in terms of what's best for Columbia, not the man who led the company out of the wilderness. Suddenly, after four and a half years of a performance and life-style which speaks for itself, I became a power-hungry megalomaniac who would 'Go Hollywood' at the first opportunity. There's not a shred of evidence in this accusation. You can ask anyone in the community here. You can ask anyone in the investment community in New York. One of the reasons Columbia has sold at a higher multiple than any stock in the entertainment industry is that I was perceived as a *financial-managerial* person who had been able to restructure the company, not because I wanted to 'Go Hollywood' at the first chance. I have been able to assemble a bunch of highly visible, creative people, all of whom have egos substantially greater than mine. One of my abilities has been to live with that, and give wide range to their egos, and subordinate mine. In the end, that makes me look terrific along with them. But now, all the confidence and friendship I have engendered for Columbia has suddenly become Alan Hirschfield versus David Begelman. What I am now asking for is support and confidence, at least the same support and confidence given to David Begelman. This does not mean that I want blind faith and no right to disagree. I never have wanted that. But it does mean that until the record proves otherwise, the board, after reasonable consideration, will support me in personnel decisions, in deals, in the direction of the company and so forth.

"If the board isn't willing to do this, it will have a fight on its hands. I haven't spent four and a half years building Columbia to throw it away because Ray Stark is unhappy that he's not calling the shots.

"There is a further issue in the future of this relationship with Ray. He is a valued producer whom I want to keep. But under no conditions will I accept or tolerate his interference or involvement in any business of this company other than that which relates to his own movies. Ray has benefited from this relationship. So has Columbia. Neither owes the other anything.

"I have heard threats that Ray will bury me. If he does, then Columbia will be buried by him, too. Ray is in no position to threaten or blackmail. I assure every one of you that with two phone calls—to the SEC and IRS—Ray will be busy for the rest of his life. I will not hesitate to make those calls.*

"I've brought the company a long way in four and a half years. I hope to bring it just as far in the next four and a half years, and I would like to do it with your support and approval. If not, I still intend to fight for what I believe is best for the company. It has been said that David Begelman is irreplaceable. Well, we've got plenty of good people, most of them recruited by me, and I'll recruit more. The company can make progress without David Begelman and without Alan Hirschfield. The only difference is that I'm here and I intend to stay here. Thank you for your attention."

Hirschfield's diatribe stunned the board. It was uncharacteristic of him to be so intemperate and blunt. Herbert Allen spoke: "Ninety percent of what you've said, Alan, is incorrect, offensive to this board, and irrelevant to the issue."

"I think what I've said is right on target."

"Well, at least you've finally made a decision, even if it's a bad one, and even if it's from behind a telephone three thousand miles away."

"What difference does it make? The decision is made. It was you who asked me to reconsider."

Rosenhaus trembled with anger. "This is a terrible day for this company. It's a shocking and terribly disappointing decision that you've made, Alan. You've got to learn how to forgive people, give them another chance. I'm very disappointed, very upset."

"This has nothing to do with forgiveness, Matty. It's the best

---

*This was a threat, made in the passion of a heated meeting, which turned out to be empty. Hirschfield had no evidence of any wrongdoing by Stark that would have been of interest to the SEC or IRS. Having many future opportunities to make accusations against Stark, including during sworn testimony before the SEC, Hirschfield accused him only of having unduly strong influence on the Columbia board of directors.

thing for David and for the company. He'll be better off in the long run. I'm willing to give him a production deal, a generous deal within the limits of the law. I don't want to see him hurt."

"Who's going to tell David?" Herbert asked. "You've made yourself conveniently unavailable, Alan, unless you want to call him. He's here in town at the apartment waiting."

"I can't help the fact that I'm in California, Herbert. I come out here for Thanksgiving every year."

"There are some of us who feel you owed the board the courtesy of delivering this decision in person."

"It's irrelevant where the decision is delivered. It's made and that's it. And I resent being accused of being discourteous. The board hasn't exactly showered me with courtesy."

Leo Jaffe spoke up: "Whether we like this decision or not, and I for one am in favor of it, we as a board are committed to support the decision, and we will."

It was decided that Herbert and Matty would go to the Columbia apartment and inform Begelman of Hirschfield's decision, and that the company would issue a press release by the next day.

Hirschfield hung up the phone elated.

He actually had fired David Begelman.

He finally had accomplished what he had yearned to do since September.

And he had done something else that he had been longing to do for months. He had vented his rage at the board of directors, and at Ray Stark. He had really let them have it. They had expected him to cave in and take David back, and he had surprised them.

So what if they were upset! Let them be upset. They had no choice now. They had promised to support his decision and they had to do it. What alternative did they have? They couldn't fire *him* under the circumstances.

And that nonsense about Berte apparently had all been a bluff. They hadn't mentioned it. Maybe Rudin's message to Rothman had gotten back to them.

In any case, it was over. The press release would be out tomorrow and that would be that. It had been a war of nerves, and he had won.

Alan was proud of himself. He felt strong. He felt like celebrating.

The Hirschfields dined that evening at Ma Maison with Berte's sister and brother-in-law, Susan and Andrew Fogelson. How ironic and appropriate, Alan felt, that they were celebrating at Ma Maison—the scene, at least implicitly, of one of Begelman's crimes. So far as Hirschfield knew, no one had informed Pierre Groleau that Begelman had used his name to steal $25,000 from Columbia Pictures. Groleau probably would never know. He was not at the restaurant that evening, but the owner, Patrick Terrail, who also was oblivious to Begelman's crimes, sent a nice bottle of wine to the Hirschfield table, a gesture he frequently made to visiting dignitaries from New York.

Alan had told Berte about the board meeting but withheld the news from the Fogelsons until the wine arrived.

"I have some news," he said. "It's a secret until tomorrow, but I fired David Begelman today. It's all over."

"Congratulations," Andy Fogelson said. "That's terrific."

They toasted the firing of David Begelman. They toasted the irony of dining at Ma Maison.

Andy Fogelson, as a close relative and an executive in Hollywood, had become familiar with the details of Begelman's misdeeds and had grown concerned that Alan somehow might mishandle the situation. Fogelson was reassured.

"You have done something, Alan, that a lot of people in this industry probably wouldn't have done," Fogelson said. "You should be proud of yourself."

The glasses were lifted again.

TWENTY-NINE

With the national press still silent on the Begelman affair, *Variety*'s Art Murphy published an article the day before Thanksgiving:

> L'AFFAIRE BEGELMAN: IT COULD BE A NO-WIN SITUATION FOR COLUMBIA.
> . . . Within the filmmaking community, Begelman is consid-

ered a crucial element in Columbia's financial recovery via the film program he shaped over four years. Within the financial community, where Begelman's departure might be treated as one-of-those-things, the same people will shortly begin wondering about the effects of a production management change: Will there be a production lull? Wall Street doesn't like either surprises or uncertainties.

On the other hand, if a consensus evolves in favor of Begelman's reinstatement, he'll return in triumph from exile, leading both Hollywood and Wall Street to begin wondering what all the ruckus was about in the first place. This, too, is not the most favorable reflection on parent company management since (rightly or wrongly) one assumes that a company does not blow the public whistle on a key executive without being reasonably assured of no later embarrassment.

A real dilemma, this one.

Still aglow from the events of the previous day, Alan Hirschfield took his family on the Universal tour that Wednesday morning and then to the commissary for lunch. While Berte and the children were finishing their meal, Alan stepped outside to a coin booth and called the Columbia studio for messages. There was only one: "Joe Fischer in New York needs to speak with you urgently." He dialed Fischer from the booth.

"We have two problems," Fischer said. "One, we had to cancel the press release. Two, Irwin Kramer is still up in arms about the Berte Hirschfield-Ed Wolf thing and is demanding a full investigation."

"I can't believe any of this!" Hirschfield exclaimed.

"Well, I'm afraid it's true. First, you should know that all hell broke loose at the board meeting yesterday after you hung up. I've never seen Matty, or Herbert, or Irwin so crazy. They were climbing the fucking walls."

"What did they say?"

"Nothing specific. It wasn't what they said, it was the way they said it. They're just outraged at your decision."

"Well, they promised to support it. What choice do they have?"

"None, I guess. But it's going to take a long time for them to cool down. They're really on the warpath."

"What's the problem with the press release?"

"Begelman vehemently objected to the way it was worded. It said he wasn't coming back to the company but it said nothing about what he'll be doing as an alternative. He claims the details of his new production deal should be included. I didn't know who had agreed to what, so I recalled the release. It had already been sent out, but I got it back. David said he'd talk to you about it when he gets to LA. He's going back this weekend."

"That release should go out today. It's a major piece of news that should be disclosed."

"Todd and Victor feel it can wait till Monday, since we're going into a long weekend."

"What about the Ed Wolf thing?"

"Irwin wants all the details. He says the board never got a complete picture and he's determined to examine it from top to bottom."

"I won't stand for this! That matter is as clean as a hound's tooth and they know it! It's none of their fucking business!"

"I don't know that you'll have much choice. They're really steamed."

"We'll see about that."

"Nothing much can happen now until next week in any event. Happy Thanksgiving."

"Yeah, sure."

Alan returned to the commissary and told Berte the news.

"This is the latest form of death by torture," he said. "One day you're on the hook, then you're off, then the next day you're back on."

"I still can't see how they can make anything out of my job," Berte said. "There's nothing there to make anything out of."

"They'll find something," Alan replied, "even if they have to twist it or create it out of whole cloth."

"I can't believe this is happening to us, to you, or to me," Berte said.

"I can't either, but it is, and it looks like it'll get worse before it gets better."

Alan went to the studio and Berte and the children returned to the hotel.

How naïve we all were, Berte felt, to have celebrated last night.

Alan Hirschfield's heart wasn't in Thanksgiving. There was the obligatory watching of the football game on television with the children at the hotel in the morning, the obligatory touch-football game on the Fogelsons' lawn in Hidden Hills in the afternoon, the obligatory carving of the turkey, the obligatory toasts, the obligatory socializing with relatives he had not seen for months. But even though he tried to put up a jovial front, it was evident to everyone that Alan was preoccupied. He talked on the telephone from the Fogelsons' more than one normally would during a Thanksgiving gathering. He held whispered conferences with his father, the only person other than Berte who was fully informed on the latest developments at Columbia. He tried, with difficulty, to explain to his children why "you and Mr. Allen are mad at each other."

Norman Hirschfield deeply resented the way the board, and Herbert Allen in particular, were treating his son, and hoped that Charlie Allen eventually would step into the fray and restrain his nephew as well as his son-in-law, Irwin Kramer. Norman was counting on it.

"Thanksgiving Day table talk yesterday in Hollywood," wrote Art Murphy in Friday's *Daily Variety*, "was focused on the widespread report that David Begelman's return to full-time status at Columbia Pictures Industries has been nixed by CPI Prez Alan Hirschfield, whose prez-chief exec officer management prerogatives include specific okay of key company exex. As a result, some sort of indie production deal for Begelman is now said to be in the offing."

Jim Johnson, the vice president for administration, found Hirschfield alone in the visiting-executives' suite late Friday morning.

"Alan, I know you and Joe have taken a lot of shit for the way Phillips and I let some of David's dealings slip past us. I just wanted you to know that if it would be any easier if I left the company, I'd be willing to go. I don't want to see you suffer for something that I fucked up on."

"Don't be ridiculous, Jim. Nobody's leaving the company. Nobody except David. What happened to you could have happened to anybody. There's nothing wrong with our controls. Begelman just circumvented them."

"You have no idea how relieved I am to hear you say that. I've lost a lot of sleep over this."

"I know what you mean. We all have. But with a little luck, it'll all be behind us soon."

"I gather David definitely isn't coming back. You hear all sorts of things around this fuckin' place."

"It's confidential until we get out a press release, but you can rest assured that there is no fucking way that David Begelman is coming back to this company."

The Hirschfields spent much of Saturday at David Geffen's home in Malibu. The low two-story house, one of four residences owned by Geffen on both coasts, was separated from the Pacific Coast Highway by a walled garden and from the ocean by thirty yards of sand. The glare from the sea and sky was permitted full access to the house and blurred the subtle features of the art on the walls—Stella, Hockney, Johns. Santa Ana winds that weekend had swept most of the smog and mist out to sea and warmed the air to the low eighties. It was a day for sun, swimsuits, the Jacuzzi, the surf, chilled wine, a leisurely buffet lunch and, to no one's surprise, extensive talk of the David Begelman crisis.

"I'm such a babe in the woods," Hirschfield whined, readily admitting that he had been wrong to belittle Geffen's warnings about the Hollywood juggernaut that had arisen in support of Begelman. Although Hirschfield's direct and immediate struggle was with the Columbia board of directors in New York, he now knew that the board's thinking reflected in large part the thinking of Ray Stark and others in Hollywood. Both parts of the pro-Begelman rationale—one, that Begelman was a filmmaking genius with forgivable problems and irreplaceable skills, and two, that Hirschfield was a power-hungry megalomaniac without the talent to succeed as the mogul he wanted to become if he could banish Begelman—had been nurtured and refined not in New York but in Hollywood.

Although Wall Street and the corporate boardrooms of New York were proficient generators and users of rumor, they were novices compared to Hollywood. The Columbia board on its own was incapable of concocting the elaborate fictions that had become an important part of Begelman's defense. It needed the help of a community where elaborate fiction was a way of life—a community which successfully had imposed fantasy upon reality and melded lies with truth for so long that it no longer had any interest in distinguishing between the two, and had devised an arsenal of sophisticated defenses against any outsider who suggested that it should.

"It's as if Watergate never happened out here," Berte Hirschfield was saying to David Geffen over the roar of the Pacific. "It's as if this town were an island that doesn't have to live by the rules of civilized society. I just can't accept that David Begelman doesn't have to conform to the rules, and that Alan Hirschfield can't impose those rules without being beaten up like this.''

"It isn't an island, but it is a very seductive community which changes the perceptions of many people who live here,'' Geffen replied.

"Nobody is seduced who doesn't want to be seduced, who doesn't aspire to be seduced,'' Berte insisted. "I refuse to accept the idea that if Alan and I were to move out here we couldn't live our lives, and that Alan couldn't function successfully in business, without being seduced and having our perceptions changed.''

It was a conversation David Geffen and Berte Hirschfield had had before. Geffen was sympathetic to the Hirschfields' anguish but could do little except reiterate both his support for Alan's position and his warning that Alan had enraged Ray Stark, who could be a dangerous enemy.

The conversation was interrupted by a succession of visitors from the beach. Malibu on weekends is very informal and very social and everybody strolls up and down the beach and drops in on everyone else. Freddie Fields stopped by. Then Barry Diller and Diane von Furstenberg. Then Jack Nicholson and Warren Beatty. Then Polly Bergen, who used to be married to Freddie Fields, and whom Alan Hirschfield had always found very attractive. As Polly Bergen was approaching Geffen's deck, Hirschfield tripped on the edge of the Jacuzzi and wrenched his left big toe.

Although the visitors were eager for the latest Begelman gossip, they were polite enough not to ask pointed questions, and instead exchanged generalities with Hirschfield. "We think we're almost through it,'' he said. "The result will be satisfactory for everybody, and we'll go on about our business.''

The pain in his toe increased through the afternoon, through dinner that evening at Chasen's with the Fogelsons, and through the night. He had the toe X-rayed on Sunday and found that it was broken. A doctor bandaged it and gave Alan a cane.

Berte and the children returned to New York on Sunday, and Alan began his week's business that very afternoon with the most sensitive meeting of all, a session with David Begelman and Joe Fischer to discuss Begelman's new arrangements with Columbia Pictures as a producer and consultant. Begelman, who had flown back Saturday from a Thanksgiving holiday in New York, arrived at Bungalow 8 at four o'clock, and Fischer, who had come out Sunday, joined them an hour later.

Hirschfield dreaded the meeting. He hated giving people bad news or dealing with people who had just received bad news for which he was responsible. On Tuesday afternoon in New York, after perhaps the angriest board meeting in the modern history of Columbia Pictures, Herbert Allen and Matty Rosenhaus had walked to the Columbia apartment and told Begelman that Hirschfield did not want to take him back into the company. Hirschfield was sure that Rosenhaus and Allen had made clear to Begelman that the majority of the board favored his reinstatement, and that although they had felt compelled to back Hirschfield as the chief executive officer, they felt deep sympathy for Begelman and anger at Hirschfield, and were prepared to protect Begelman financially. The next day it had turned out that Begelman still wielded enough power in the corporation to block a press release announcing Hirschfield's decision. It had also turned out that the board was still so angry at Hirschfield that it was proceeding with a plan to investigate his wife's entirely proper employment record.

Hirschfield, therefore, had been forced to assume a very uncomfortable negotiating posture. On the one hand, Matty and Herbert had ordered that David be "made whole" financially. On the other hand, they were taking no responsibility for the actual terms of the deal, but were insisting that Hirschfield do the negotiating, thereby forcing him not only to obey their orders but also to shoulder the potentially contradictory problem of having the deal scrutinized by the SEC, the press, and other outsiders. The deal had to be rich, but not too rich. It had to be lucrative enough to satisfy the board but not so lucrative that it would appear that Columbia Pictures was rewarding Begelman for criminal behavior.

Begelman looked wan and discouraged when he arrived at the bungalow, and Hirschfield tried to couch the conversation in positive terms. He was terribly sorry, he said, that he had had to decide against reinstating David. Nothing personal, of course. But he knew that David would be pleased with the "terrific" production deal he was going to get. To Hirschfield's chagrin, David's fatigue and depression had not dulled his negotiating skills. David had been negotiating motion-picture and television production deals for more than two decades and was among the best negotiators in the business.

While Hirschfield and Fischer were not strangers to the process, they had never negotiated deals as a primary occupation and were not in Begelman's class. David was far from pleased with the general terms Hirschfield outlined. Alan kept saying that the deal had to be "reasonable and fair." David kept saying that he had to be "made whole." The terms that Hirschfield proposed were vague and were too low for Begelman. The terms with which Begelman countered were specific and were too high for Hirschfield. They weren't even close.

Then Hirschfield surprised Begelman. Recalling that Columbia was considering acquiring the motion-picture rights to *Annie*, Alan asked if David would be interested in producing the film version?

It was another display of carelessness by Hirschfield. Just a month earlier, at dinner with Leonard and Wendy Goldberg at La Scala, he had asked Leonard Goldberg if *he* would be interested in producing *Annie*. Leonard had said yes. Hirschfield had not considered the overture formal, but Goldberg had taken it at the very least to be an informal offer. Naturally, in the intervening weeks, Leonard had told David, one of his closest friends, that Alan had offered *Annie* to him. Now, sitting in the living room of Bungalow 8 with his bandaged left foot propped on an ottoman, Hirschfield seemed to be making the same pitch to Begelman. Obviously Alan had not forgotten that he had discussed *Annie* with Goldberg. Was he naïve enough to think that Leonard would not have relayed this major piece of news to his friend David?

"Well, Alan," David said, "it's going to be a little crowded on the set of *Annie* when I arrive to produce it and Len Goldberg is standing there."

"I didn't offer it to Len."

"He says you did."

"Well, it came up in conversation. I certainly didn't offer it to him."

"Leonard is under the distinct impression that you made at least an informal offer of the *Annie* project to him."

"Well, he's mistaken," Hirschfield replied. "But maybe you and Len could produce it together."

Begelman looked skeptical. "Well, that's a different issue. That's possible. That might work."

The conversation withered. Instead of attracting Begelman, Hirschfield's raising of the *Annie* issue had heightened the awkwardness that they had felt at the beginning of the meeting. Obviously they remained far apart. Begelman agreed to meet again in a few days, and obtained Hirschfield's assurance that no press release about his leaving the Columbia studio presidency would be issued until the terms of his future were settled.

Joe Fischer had never seen Hirschfield so upset as he was during the hours after Begelman left the bungalow.

Not on September 14 when Detective Silvey called. Not on September 26 when they discovered the third embezzlement. Not on November 16 when the board of directors made clear it wanted Begelman reinstated. Not on November 23 when the board renewed its threat to investigate Berte.

As unnerving as those episodes and others had been, they seemed to have fused by the Thanksgiving weekend into something more sinister and more difficult to control than any of the events had appeared in isolation. The dispute over David Begelman had grown into a broad crisis of corporate governance at Columbia Pictures Industries. Though the schism had a philosophical core, it had been inflamed by strong egos and emotions into something much more ominous and volatile than a philosophical confrontation. The high command of the corporation seemed to be on the verge of a very ugly war, with the combatants' specific goals unclear and the result uncertain.

Hirschfield was thoroughly discombobulated. He did not understand how the problem had grown into a crisis. He did not know what to do next. Puffing nervously on a cigar and sipping a glass of wine, he ranted about Herbert, Matty, Irwin, and Ray. He had always thought he understood them, but now, individually and together, they bewildered and infuriated him. And it was Herbert, whom Alan had thought he knew best, who baffled him the most. In the past, he and Herbert had usually found themselves in agreement on most major issues. In this instance, Herbert seemed inexplicably to have taken the wrong side of the Begelman issue at the beginning, and then somehow become strongly committed to it emotionally. It was unprecedented in the nearly two decades they had known each other for Herbert to invest the amount of ego and emotion in anything that he had invested in the Begelman problem.

Fischer sat smoking, listening and commiserating as Hirschfield alternately slumped in his chair with his injured foot propped up, hobbled slowly about the living room, and stared out at the hotel's east lawn, which was strewn on this warm night with palm fronds torn loose by the Santa Anas.

They ordered dinner from room service. Fischer, his body still on Eastern time, excused himself at 10:30.

Hirschfield was awake for hours.

He was beside himself.

THIRTY

The last time the studio executives had gathered in Bungalow 8 was the first Sunday in October, when Hirschfield had broken the news that David Begelman was to be suspended pending an investigation of financial irregularities. On Monday morning, November 28, they assembled there again for the regular quarterly review of motion-picture projects.

Hirschfield preferred to hold the quarterly meetings in his hotel bungalow; it was less formal than the studio offices across the hills in Burbank and there were fewer interruptions. Even though the meetings were long—typically 9:30 until about 7:00 with lunch brought in—the studio people generally did not mind them. They were a break in routine. And many of the motion-picture executives rather enjoyed watching Hirschfield and Fischer conduct a meeting. It was faintly reminiscent of a good cop-bad cop routine. Hirschfield, the droll, playful chief executive, often would appear to be paying only minimal attention to the proceedings. Though he missed nothing important, he would flip through *Playboy*, or doodle on his agenda sheet, or crack jokes, while Fischer, his tough, solemn deputy, would actually conduct much of the meeting, asking pointed questions, insisting on specific answers, and challenging deviations from film budgets. It required an agile sensiblity to banter with

Hirschfield and fence with Fischer at the same time, and seeing who could do it best had become almost a game.

November 28 was different, however. The lingering Begelman problem infected everyone in the room. Only Hirschfield and Fischer knew the gravity of the crisis, but it was obvious to the studio people that the issue remained contentious and that Alan and Joe were preoccupied.

As Fischer listlessly ran down the agenda of film projects in various stages of production or development, Hirschfield's concentration wavered and he was interrupted frequently by telephone calls from New York.

"*Hardcore.*"

"On schedule, on budget."

"*California Suite.*"

"Ray has it well in hand."

"*Nightwing.*"

"Those fuckin' bats look so real you wouldn't believe they're special-effects bats."

"*Altered States.*"

"Paddy's heart attack has slowed us up a bit," Dan Melnick said, "but we have effective control of the release of both the hardcover and paperback."

"*All That Jazz.*"

"Delayed to allow Fosse to do his Broadway thing, which is tentatively entitled *Dancin'*. We'll have a piece of the show."

The telephone rang and the secretary came in from the next room and put a note in front of Hirschfield: Todd Lang, NY. He took the call in the master bedroom. "They're really gearing up to go after Berte. We'll have to sit down with her and go over the Ed Wolf thing from scratch."

"*Kramer vs. Kramer.*"

"The script's been revised again. It's terrific."

"*Ice Castles.*"

"We're considering three people. Tatum, Jodie Foster, and Marie Osmond."

"Marie Osmond?"

"Yes, and there are two potential problems with Marie. First, can she act? Second, she's a very, very serious Mormon. There's a sexual encounter in the film, and we don't know how she'll take to it.

If she turns out to be our choice, considering everything else, we'll have to play with that scene to see how important it is to the picture.''

The telephone again, and the secretary with a note: Leo Jaffe, NY. Hirschfield took the call in the bedroom. "It's chaos back here. Herbie and Matty are still livid. They're on the warpath. How was your talk with David yesterday?''

"Not good. He wants more than we can possibly give him.''

"It's got to be wrapped up soon and a press release issued, or we may be back to square one.''

"The board has me coming and going, and I refuse to be placed in this position," Hirschfield said. "I'm handling this in the best way I know how. What about all the support I was promised?''

"It just isn't there.''

"Keep me posted.''

"*1941.*''

"Christmas, 1979.''

"*Justice for All.*''

"We've got Pacino.''

"*The Ravagers.*''

"It's a junk-food picture.''

"What about the Joan Rivers deal?''

"We feel that Joan Rivers can be for us what Mel Brooks and Gene Wilder are for Fox," Melnick said. "She's mad, she's gifted, and she knows where the jokes are. The problem is money. She makes incredible money in Vegas, and looks to us to replace those earnings.''

The secretary with a note; Herbert Allen Jr., NY. Hirschfield hobbled into the bedroom again. "You still have a chance to change your mind, Alan.''

"My mind is made up. I have no intention of changing it.''

The talk in the living room turned to the subject of contractual clauses under which filmmakers can be penalized financially for permitting costs to exceed a film's budget. Melnick urged everyone to be "realistic.''

"It's difficult to control certain people, and there are certain directors I won't work with for that reason. But I'm enough of a whore that if it's a sensational project, I'll take a deep breath and jump in anyway. You can't penalize a filmmaker for getting a new idea. It increases his appetite. And you've got to be pragmatic about other problems. We've got an overage on *Eyes*. You have to be realistic when you hire certain artists. Faye's entourage costs a hundred thousand dollars. The hair-dresser and makeup people we wanted to give her, she didn't want. But we wanted her, so we had to go along."*

"There will be two singles from the *Close Encounters* music," Hirschfield reported. "Clive is reworking it. The basic symphonic, and then a disco."

"That poker game with *Newsweek* over the cover story was ridiculous," Melnick asserted. "They had to bluff us into giving up the photos. Jack Kroll had to ask! Our press manipulation isn't up to snuff We don't have people sufficiently schooled in that sleazy world."

The secretary with a note: Allen Adler, NY. "You better watch your ass," he said. "They're really hammering away back here."

"So I hear," Hirschfield replied.

"What about delaying the foreign opening of *Close Encounters* till the fall?" somebody asked. "Doing a really proper job of dubbing is going to take a lot of time. We'll really have to rush to get it out in the spring."

"It'll lose its momentum by the fall. It won't be the event that it will be in the spring."

"It has to be dubbed in French, Italian, Japanese, German, and Spanish, with subtitles for Scandinavia."

"Let's forge ahead for the spring," Hirschfield finally interjected. "I don't care if they have to work around the clock, seven days a week. The longer we wait, the greater the chance that we'll lose the sense of a cosmic event that we've built up now." He ordered that Columbia's top dozen foreign executives be flown to New York to see the film the following weekend. "Show it to them at the Ziegfeld and then bring them up to my house and I'll give them a pep talk."

The phone calls from New York tapered off toward evening and the meeting in the bungalow broke up around seven. Hirschfield, Fischer,

---

*The film's final title was *The Eyes of Laura Mars*.

and Melnick had dinner at the Mandarin and talked about various ways of replacing Begelman. Was Melnick a realistic candidate for permanent president of the studio? No, he did not want the administrative burdens. He only wanted to "make pictures." Could Fischer move to California as co-head of the studio, handling the business and administrative functions while Melnick confined himself to the substance of pictures? No, Fischer did not want to move to California.

"Let's face it," Hirschfield said. "The board would consider that a jerry-built solution anyway. The only way to get the board off my back is to come up with somebody from outside, somebody demonstrably sensational, a known quantity. It's going to be tough."

"Good morning, Rona."

"Good morning, David, and good morning, America. Industry speculation as to the fate of Columbia Pictures' president David Begelman, who took a temporary leave of absence from the studio several weeks ago due to reported financial irregularities, has now been settled. After a series of highly charged, closed-door meetings, the board of directors of Columbia Pictures Industries is expected to announce that they will offer Begelman the opportunity to serve out the remaining two years of his Columbia contract as both an independent producer with the studio as well as a studio adviser. . . . It is expected that Begelman will accept the Columbia offer, although we understand that he has been approached by three top studios to be an independent producer for them. The decision to remove Begelman from the presidency reportedly came at the insistence of Alan Hirschfield and was allegedly contested by other board members. The board is also expected to publicly exonerate Begelman from any financial wrongdoing, noting that the former president returned to Columbia some thirty-seven thousand dollars which was in dispute. . . . This removal of Begelman leaves the studio without any strong hand at the helm, and industry insiders say confidence in Columbia is low. Therefore, while winning the battle, the forces opposing Begelman may have lost the war."

Hirschfield found the press coverage exasperating, but he supposed his reaction was another reflection of his naïveté. The only voices being heard consistently were those of Rona Barrett and Art Murphy, whose coverage seemed to Hirschfield to be unduly harsh on him and unduly sympathetic to Begelman. It was the standard Hollywood line—David's misdeeds were matters of "judgment"; Hirschfield stood alone against the board in ousting him; it was David who was mainly responsible for Columbia's financial recovery; removing him would leave the studio leaderless and shake confidence in the company. Rona had said the board was expected to "exonerate Begelman from any financial wrongdoing"—an extraordinary concept in view of what he had done. Alan wondered if Rona knew that David had forged checks and embezzled thousands of dollars. He found it difficult to believe that Rona, as the best-informed reporter in town, didn't have at least some of the facts. Why wasn't she putting them on the air? Alan assumed that Rona was getting many of her "insights" from Ray Stark and, secondarily, from Sue Mengers. (Rona and Sue were called the "Starkettes" in some quarters.)

And where was the national press? A sensational story was unfolding and nobody seemed to be covering it. Hirschfield, for one, had kept the vow of secrecy toward the press taken by everyone inside Columbia who was privy to the details. Still, one would have anticipated leaks by now. It had been more than two months since the company had known of Begelman's embezzlements. Hirschfield's task would be so much easier if the world knew the nature of David's crimes. The board couldn't possibly take the stand it had if the public knew Begelman was an admitted forger.

Unbeknownst to Hirschfield, a few nonentertainment reporters were beginning to work on the Begelman story. *The Wall Street Journal* was interested. And Andrew Tobias, who had been briefed by a friend a month earlier, had finally found the time to investigate. In only a few hours of telephoning from his New York apartment in late November, Tobias had confirmed the salient facts of the Cliff Robertson, Martin Ritt, and Pierre Groleau embezzlements. Unfortunately for Tobias, he had promised the story to *Esquire* which could not publish it until February.

Jeanie Kasindorf of *New West*, meanwhile, had nearly completed her examination of Sid Luft's files on David Begelman's handling of Judy Garland's funds in the early 1960s. Indeed, while the studio executives were conferring at Hirschfield's bungalow on Monday, Kasindorf had spent nearly all day at Luft's Wilshire Boulevard apartment, sifting through old manila folders spread across his dining-room table. But Kasindorf still had not had time to investigate Begelman's more recent difficulties at Columbia. And she could not expose what he was alleged to have done in 1962 without placing it in the current context.

The phone calls into Bungalow 8 from New York became a barrage on Tuesday. The big rumor of the day was that Ray Stark had informed Columbia Pictures that he would not continue negotiations toward a new contract until he knew who would replace David Begelman as president of the studio. The inference was that if Stark did not approve of the replacement, he might not renew his contract. There were rumors that other producers, as well, might leave. And apart from the rumors, it appeared that the board's anger at Hirschfield was deepening. Irwin Kramer wanted studio vice president Jim Johnson and controller Lou Phillips removed from their jobs. Hirschfield had promised Johnson just the previous Friday that no one except Begelman would be fired.

In the middle of the afternoon, Joe Fischer said privately to Hirschfield: "Listen, this is crazy. You're obviously totally distracted. You're not listening to people here. You're not asking the right questions. You're running to the phone every fifteen minutes. I think you'd better call this off, go back to New York, and try to get a handle on what's happening there."

Hirschfield agreed. Meetings scheduled for the next two days with executives of the television division were canceled, and he returned to New York on Wednesday, leaving 80-degree sunshine and arriving at Kennedy late in the evening in a cold, 40-degree drizzle.

THIRTY-ONE

Ray Stark indeed had been busy on Begelman's behalf. As Stark later told an investigator for the Securities and Exchange Commission, "I called everyone I knew and said I thought the guy was sick, and if there was anything you can do to retain his services, because he has been a fabulous asset to the company during the period he was there . . .''

"Let me ask you this," the SEC investigator said. "You said you were calling everybody. Do you mean the creative community, or within Columbia Pictures, exactly what do you mean?"

"Just within the people I knew at Columbia," Stark answered.

Since the people Stark knew at Columbia were the ones making the decision, he hardly needed to call anyone else. Apart from the influence implicit in his close friendship with Herbert Allen, Stark's pictures had generated in excess of $200 million for the corporation— far more than any other producer—and on that basis alone the board of directors was prone to listen to him. Thus, while Ray Stark concentrated on the Columbia board, others in Hollywood had been lobbying indirectly through the "creative community." Sue Mengers, Begelman's longtime close friend who had become one of the two most powerful agents on the coast after starting as his protégée, urged her clients, friends, and acquaintances to send telegrams to Alan Hirschfeld and the board. Barbra Streisand, Mel Brooks, and many others agreed. Mengers dispatched telegrams for some of them from her office at ICM, even sending a wire on behalf of an actor whom she had not consulted, Jack Nicholson. He was not pleased.

Another lobbyist operating secretly from inside the Columbia studio was William Tennant, a production vice president, who closely coordinated his efforts with Mengers and Stark. A former agent representing Mike Nichols, Bo Goldman, John Schlesinger, Roman Polanski,* and others, Tennant had been hired by David Begelman in 1976 and had become very friendly not only with Ray Stark and David but also with Gladyce Begelman, with whom he frequently lunched at La Serre. Tennant fed information to Stark about the supposed deteriorating state of the studio in the absence of Begelman's leadership—information that Stark could then relay directly to Herbert Allen and other board members. Billy Tennant also generated a sizable number of letters and telegrams supporting Begelman's restoration. (Few if any of the people who wrote or wired the board of directors knew what David Begelman had done to warrant suspension. They merely expressed general admiration for his ability as an executive. And not every person who was asked to send an

---

*When Roman Polanski's wife, Sharon Tate, and her friends were slaughtered by the Charles Manson gang in Benedict Canyon above Beverly Hills in August 1969, Bill Tennant was one of the first people summoned to the scene and identified the bodies.

expression of support did so. Richard Dreyfuss waffled. Mike Nichols flatly refused.)

Alan Hirschfield had told no one except his secretary and Joe Fischer that he was returning two days early, so he was able to spend a few hours Thursday, December 1, in his office, quietly appraising the crisis before stepping back into it. Although some problems seemed less threatening at close range than from afar, this one was worse. He was astonished at the change from only a week earlier when the board of directors, albeit angrily and grudgingly, had seemed to acquiesce in his refusal to reinstate Begelman. Now, it was as if his decision, and the board's promise, had never been made. Somehow Begelman's crimes had been forgotten, and the focus of the dispute had shifted to him, the intransigent Hirschfield. The crisis of authority in the corporation which he had sensed in recent days seemed less and less abstract. It was clear that Herbert Allen had increased the scope and intensity of his pressure.

To Hirschfield's horror, he began getting signals on Thursday that his own job might be in jeopardy. The first indication came in a telephone conversation with William Thompson of the First National Bank of Boston, with whom Herbert had spoken within the past twenty-four hours. According to Thompson, Herbert had said of Hirschfield:

"We're going to get him for the way he's handled this situation."

"How can you get rid of Hirschfield at the same time you get rid of Begelman?" Thompson claimed to have asked Allen.

"If we don't get him now, we'll get him in six months. He can be replaced in three days," Herbert reportedly replied.*

No sooner had Hirschfield spoken with Thompson than Irwin Kramer called. "Look, I just thought you ought to know that you're in trouble," Kramer said. "Herbert and Matty are really pissed. It won't go away. If you don't come around, there are going to be problems, big problems."

"I can't believe this! What kind of people are you! A week ago, and the week before that, you committed yourselves to support my decision, like it or not. Now it's like those promises were never made. You're not only going back on your word, you're using the

---

*Recalling this conversation later, Herbert Allen said that his remarks did not constitute an explicit threat to fire Hirschfield, but rather were part of an attempt to convince Thompson that Hirschfield had behaved badly and was naïve if he thought he could win a fight with the board of directors.

dirtiest kind of blackmail tactics. How dare you drag my wife into this thing!''

"We have every right and responsibility to examine the outside business connections of key executives," Kramer said.

"Bullshit! You know fucking well that's bullshit, that Berte is above reproach, that I'm above reproach, and that this is nothing more than the slimiest kind of blackmail!''

"I know no such thing. All I'm telling you is that if you don't change your mind, you're in big trouble.''

Hirschfield hung up, incredulous.

He spent the rest of the day conferring by phone with some of his principal allies—David Geffen in Malibu, Clive Davis at the Beverly Hills Hotel, and Dan Melnick at The Burbank Studios.

Clive Davis took it upon himself to speak directly to Herbert Allen and telephoned him from Beverly Hills.

"From what I know," Davis said, "I suspect that you may be laboring under a misapprehension, not only of Alan's motives in this immediate situation centering on David, but of Alan's overall abilities and the major role he has played in the success of this company."

"Tell me about it," Herbert said.

"The impression is abroad that Alan wants to 'Go Hollywood,' that he wants to run the studio himself, and is seizing on David's problems to banish David and inject himself directly into the creative area that has been David's province. Nothing could be further from the truth. Of course Alan is mesmerized by show business. Everybody is. Of course he likes to give advice on films. He frequently offers his opinion to me on recordings. But none of that means that he wants to impose his judgment on us. He knows that he must ultimately defer to my judgments, just as he knows that he must defer to David or whoever is in charge of the studio. But his interest in the creative side of the business, far from being a detriment, is in fact a major reason for our success. It's very advantageous to have someone at the head of the company who knows how to create a viable and healthy creative atmosphere. To the extent that you don't have that, the corporation can be in serious trouble. Alan has been very farseeing in this sense. He is very good at getting creative executives together and establishing rapport and closeness. In no way was he gleeful when the Begelman problem arose. On the contrary, it was a bombshell to Alan. It was traumatic. I remember how he was at the time of the Brandeis dinner. It was like he was hit by a bombshell.''

Their discussion lasted for a full hour, but Herbert rejected Clive's reasoning, and Clive reported back to Alan that Herbert seemed uncharacteristically unable or unwilling to discuss the subject rationally.

Thursday's final blow came in the evening when Norman Hirschfield, who was in Manhattan on business, telephoned Alan at home to report that Herbert had called and asked Norman to "talk sense" to Alan. "Can't you get Alan to see it our way?" he quoted Herbert as saying. The deteriorating relationship between Alan and Herbert had deeply distressed Norman, who had always been very proud of his son's success in business, and had been particularly gratified that it had been achieved in conjunction with the Allen family, whose role in Norman's own business and personal life had been so crucial for so many years. His own son's well-being was one of the few things, in fact, that mattered more to Norman Hirschfield than his relationship with the Allens. He had been a close friend of Charlie and Herbert senior for half a century and had known, liked, and befriended their children, Herbert junior in particular, since they were infants. The Hirschfields and the Allens had had too many good times together—and had made too much money together—for the implications of a serious breach between Alan and Herbert to be anything less than staggering to Norman.

Herbert's attempt to enlist Norman's influence infuriated Alan, who considered it another illicit pressure tactic. A family relationship, Alan felt, no matter how deep and enduring, was irrelevant to a decision of whether a thief should be running the two largest divisions of Columbia Pictures Industries. In lengthy conversations on the phone that evening and in Alan's office the next morning, Norman tried to act as a peacemaker and mediator. While he backed Alan's position on the Begelman issue, he urged him to consider carefully the ramifications of his decision and to try to shape a solution that would not damage irreparably his relationship with Herbert.

"These are tough people, rough people, and you're making a difficult bed for yourself if you get on a collision course with them," Norman said on Friday morning. "Herbert wouldn't admit it in so many words, but he feels you owe him your allegiance. He feels that he *made* you, that everything you have, you made through Allen & Company. 'By God, I put him here, and his allegiance ought to be to me!' That's the way he feels.''

"Bullshit," said Alan.

After leaving his son, Norman had a talk with Charlie Allen. A frail, balding man of medium height, with delicate features, white hair, and the same slightly sunken eyes of his brother and nephew, the seventy-four-year-old patriarch of Allen & Company listened patiently to his old friend.

"Charlie, you've got to make your voice heard here," Norman pleaded. "There's a lot between us. It's my son and your nephew, not a couple of outsiders."

"It'll all work itself out somehow," Charlie said quietly. "You can't rush these things."

"Well, you and I have to help," Norman insisted. "No matter how bad it is, we ought to close ranks. It's in the family. We've done too much together to let this come between us."

"Let's give it time," Charlie said. "They'll work it out."

Herbert Allen strode into Hirschfield's office and closed the door.

"Have you reconsidered your decision, Alan?"

"No, my decision stands."

"I feel compelled to restate," Herbert said, "that I think you're making a very serious mistake which is threatening severe damage to this company. From what I hear, the studio is on the verge of collapse."

"The studio is on the verge of collapse? That's certainly news to me. I just came from there, and as of the day before yesterday, it wasn't on the verge of collapse."

"Melnick appears to be a horror as a stand-in for Begelman. Danny can't run the studio. The most important producers on the lot are threatening to leave."

"Who's threatening to leave?" Hirschfield asked.

"Peter Guber. Jon Peters. Ray might even leave if this thing isn't cleared up."

"Well, that's all ridiculous, and you should know enough to recognize that it's ridiculous. It's nothing more than another dose of Ray's efforts to get his friend back in office."

"You couldn't be more wrong," Herbert said. "There is a leadership vacuum and a real threat to the viability of the studio as a result of your position on this thing."

"Bullshit! First of all, Melnick is not a horror, to use your word. He's been running the studio on a de facto basis for several months now, since long before the Begelman problem developed. You know that was the plan. As Begelman got more involved with television, Danny—who you'll recall was David's handpicked choice for the job—would assume more of the burden of the studio. He's done that and has been functioning well. Ray has been doing business with him. Guber has been doing business with him. Peters has been doing business with him. And so has everybody else. The Guber deal is not in jeopardy. I've been in touch with Peter, as has Danny. The Jon Peters deal is for one picture—*Eyes*—which is proceeding. The deal may or may not be extended, but Peters is working well with Melnick. As for Stark, I can't speak for him because he's obviously the man behind your scenario that the studio is on the verge of collapse.''

Like jousters about to charge, Hirschfield and Allen stood facing each other from opposite ends of the thirty-foot office.

"You're wrong! You're absolutely wrong!" Allen declared, in a voice higher, louder, and more agitated than Hirschfield had ever heard from him. "The studio *is* going to collapse! It *is* a horror show. The studio can't make deals with anybody. There's no one there who can make deals. Melnick can't do it. The only one who can do it is Begelman and we've got to bring him back!"

"If you and the board would only give me your support," Hirschfield shouted, "there are plenty of people who we can get! No matter what you say or think you know, the studio is not the problem! I plan to get someone to oversee both pictures and TV like Begelman has done. And it won't be hard if I have the board's support. What happened to all the support I was going to get, that you pledged to give me? What happened to that scenario?''

"That was then, and now is now, and you've got to bring David back.''

"No way.''

Neither man spoke for several seconds.

"Look, Alan," Herbert said, his voice quieter, "do it for me. I've never put anything on a personal basis before, but we do have a long personal relationship that means a lot to me. Leaving aside everything else, how about doing it for me, because of who I am, because of who you are, because of who *we* are. I am making a personal request to you that you reinstate David.''

"This is not a personal matter, Herbert.''

"I'm making it a personal matter. I want you to do it for me.''

"Well, I won't do it for you.''

It was time to join Matty Rosenhaus, Irwin Kramer, and Leo Jaffe in the boardroom for an informal meeting of the principal directors. Rosenhaus had demanded the meeting once he learned that Hirschfield had returned early from Los Angeles.

Old arguments were repeated, and Herbert stated his new argument that "the studio is on the verge of collapse."

"First of all," said Hirschfield, "the studio is not collapsing. Second of all, I can and will find someone just as good or better to replace David. But to do it, I need the support of the board. True support. Without that support I'll get nowhere. There's nothing wrong with the company—Melnick's doing well, as is everybody else in management. The only impediment is the board."

"Can you guarantee that we won't lose Guber?" Herbert parried. "Can you guarantee that we'll make a new deal with Jon Peters?"

"Obviously I can't absolutely guarantee anything, but I have every reason to believe that these will be ongoing relationships."

"We may lose Ray," Matty said.

"If we lose Ray Stark, we lose Ray Stark," Hirschfield replied. "The whole studio doesn't depend on Ray Stark. We can't run our whole business on Ray Stark's whim. We've been trying to negotiate a new deal with Ray for a year. Supposedly everything was fine. Now he's holding out, supposedly because he doesn't know who'll be running the studio. It's a phony argument. Melnick will be running the studio just as he has been for the last six months, and somebody else who is just as qualified as Begelman will be overseeing both pictures and television."

"Ray's the most important asset this company has," Herbert said.*

"This company has a lot of important assets," Alan retorted. "Ray is one, but there are others. Furthermore, I must reemphasize

---

*The question of Stark's possibly leaving the studio if Begelman was not reinstated prompted the following later exchange between Stark and an SEC investigator:

"Did you ever imply to anyone at Columbia Pictures Industries, Inc. that your services would be conditioned in the future upon the return of Mr. Begelman to some position at Columbia Pictures?" the investigator asked.

"No, sir," Stark replied. "I did say that I had been a true independent producer all my life, which means that I have to know who I am reporting to, if anyone, and that if Begelman were not the head of the company, I would just sit out the rest of my contract—well, not sit it out, but I would work out whatever there was left, but I would not make any other deal until I knew who it was that I was reporting to. This was finally settled by my willingness to report to Leo Jaffe. However, if they wanted to bring somebody in that I would have to report to, and that I did not like, I wouldn't make the pictures. . . ."

that if David Begelman comes back into this company, there will be no deal with General Cinema, there will be no deal with IBM, and there will be no relationship with Time, Inc. Nobody respectable will have anything to do with us.''

Leo Jaffe said: ''If Begelman is brought back—I'm not saying Alan should change his mind, but if he should decide to bring David back—the board must show its support for Alan with a new contract, so that people will know that Alan is running the company—not David, not the board, but Alan.''

''Absolutely,'' Rosenhaus said. ''Alan should have the best deal in the industry.''

''I feel,'' said Hirschfield, ''that it is somewhat inappropriate to be discussing my contract in connection with whether I bring Begelman back. In less polite circles, it might be called a payoff.''

''Alan, please don't be unreasonable,'' Rosenhaus replied. ''It would be the most appropriate thing in the world for us to show the world and you how much we value you by giving you a new contract.''

''I really don't think we should be discussing something like that at a time like this,'' Hirschfield said.

''Well, be that as it may,'' Rosenhaus said, ''we're asking you, on behalf of the entire board, to once again reconsider your decision, to look at this thing with a fresh eye. You and David have done so much together. You're a winning team. I remain convinced that it would be a tragedy for the company if the team were to break up.''

Hirschfield sighed. ''All right. I'll do this: In an effort not to appear to be just a totally stubborn human being, I'll think the whole thing through again this weekend. I'll reconsider in good faith. And I'll let you know Monday.''

The meeting broke up and Hirschfield limped back to his office.

Later in the afternoon, following his father's lead, Alan Hirschfield had his own audience with Charlie Allen.

''Look, Charlie, I have no animus toward you, or the family, or anyone else,'' Alan said. ''This thing has to do with being responsible for running a company. The man is a crook, an admitted crook. I feel badly for him, and maybe he is sick. But there's not a company in the United States that would take him back under the circumstances, and I'm not about to be the one that does it. If I did, there would be a holocaust of publicity.''

"They can't hurt you with what they write," Charlie Allen said. "It would blow over."

"It wouldn't blow over. It would be embarrassing to everyone, not the least of whom would be Allen & Company."

"Well, please try to reconsider whether there isn't some way around it."

"I am reconsidering, Charlie, but I don't think you're seeing the whole picture. You're only listening to one side—from Herbert, Irwin, and Ray. You're just not hearing the whole story, and I think you're being misled and misguided. If you wanted to put an end to this thing, you could put an end to it."

"I can't interfere, Alan. This is Herbie's deal. There are too many problems if I interfere. You understand that."

"I think in this case you should. Everybody's going to be the loser if somebody with leadership and authority and intelligence doesn't interfere."

"I just can't."

Hirschfield had tried being tough and tenacious, and it had not worked. During the telephone board meeting the previous week, he had thrown the knockout punch and gone to his corner, savoring his victory, hearing distinctly the count of ten, only to turn around and find his opponent standing—clear-eyed, uninjured, and demanding that the fight continue. Angry and bewildered, Alan had swung again and again with no effect. His opponent, with a flurry of low blows, had regained the offensive.

The decision to banish David Begelman hung suspended over the company, unimplemented, unannounced, and—it was now evident—flatly and forever unacceptable to the board. Hirschfield's contractual right to hire and fire the officers of the corporation seemed to have been rendered moot. While the directors technically were required to accept his decision, they had shown that they would spare no tactic to induce him to change it.

Moreover, the threat to investigate Berte, the attempt to mobilize Norman Hirschfield against his son, the statement to Bill Thompson that "if we don't get him now, we'll get him in six months," all represented to Alan something more sinister than illicit tactics over a single issue. The tactics appeared to signal a broad assault on Hirschfield's authority to run the company—not just his right to rule on Begelman but his overall contractual right to function as the chief executive officer without undue interference from the board.

They could not fire him—at least not immediately. But they could undermine his authority. It was clear that the merits of the Begelman case were no longer the issue. The issue was who was the boss of the corporation, and Herbert Allen seemed intent on proving at all costs that he was.

Alan considered resigning. It would be a dramatic gesture, but what would it accomplish? It would amount to a betrayal of the people in management, people like Joe Fischer, Allen Adler, and Clive Davis, whom he had brought into the company and who had supported him not only on the Begelman issue but on other issues as well. He couldn't expect them all to resign with him. By resigning, he also would forfeit the opportunity to enjoy the results of the company's success—success that he had orchestrated.

He decided not to resign.

He thought back to the board meeting of November 16, barely over two weeks earlier. It seemed like months. He had been prepared to render his decision that day, but at the board's request he had agreed to reconsider. In fact, he had only pretended to reconsider, and had announced his decision the following week. The decision had not adhered, and now the board was demanding that he reconsider again. He had agreed again.

Was he weak? Should he truly reconsider this time? Could he? Were there any conceivable circumstances under which he could justify changing his mind and reinstating David Begelman?

Before leaving the office for the weekend, Hirschfield telephoned Todd Lang and asked that he and Peter Gruenberger come to the Hirschfield home on Saturday morning.

THIRTY-TWO

"What would the consequences be if I decided to bring him back?"

Hirschfield and the two lawyers sipped coffee and munched pastry in the Hirschfields' sunny, art-adorned living room. The double doors were closed but the voices of children at play occasionally penetrated the room.

Hirschfield's question was not a total surprise to Lang and Gruenberger, who had sensed that the pressure on Hirschfield was growing torturous. They had been among the targets of the board's vehement anger two and a half weeks earlier when Gruenberger had reported the results of his investigation of Begelman. They also were privy to the pressure tactics being applied to Hirschfield, including the bitter clash over Berte's employment. Although their legal work for the corporation was scrupulously objective, Lang and Gruenberger personally were sympathetic to Hirschfield's plight. The resolution of the Begelman problem, as it had evolved, turned less on strictly legal issues than on issues of morality, philosophy, public relations, and business judgment. The core of Lang's advice, in fact, had been that *legally* the corporation could either reinstate Begelman or fire him, as long as it could show that its decision was rooted in "prudent business judgment." Aside from citing guidelines by which business judgment could be measured, Lang had offered no formal opinion to the board on whether Begelman *should* be reinstated, and the board had not sought such an opinion. Alan Hirschfield had sought Lang's opinion, however, and by early December Lang as well as Gruenberger had often expressed privately their general agreement with Hirschfield's point of view. They could do little more than commiserate, therefore, as Hirschfield told of the difficult Friday meetings with Herbert and the other directors.

"Essentially, I have my choice of disasters," Hirschfield told the lawyers. "If I fire him, the board will be so down on me that my own days at the company are numbered. They won't let me accomplish anything. If I bring him back, all the bad things we've talked about will probably happen—the publicity, the image, and so on and so forth. So let's suppose hypothetically for the moment that I brought him back. How can we minimize the bad things?"

Lang began by reiterating the ramifications of the "business-judgment rule," which he had analyzed in two confidential memoranda distributed to the board three weeks earlier. To protect itself against allegations of imprudence if it reinstated Begelman, Columbia should impose restrictions sufficient to prevent him from stealing again. Generally, he would have to be denied direct access to corporate funds. The company, for instance, should prohibit him from drawing checks on his own authority.

In addition to sealing the cash drawer, the company should withhold, at least for the time being, the new contract it had promised Begelman just a few weeks prior to the discovery of the embezzlements. He would have to return to the studio under his existing contract. Otherwise, it would appear that he was being rewarded.

If Columbia was willing to take such steps, Lang said, there was a chance that it could reinstate Begelman without inordinate risk of acute public embarrassment and other problems. Just a few days earlier, the lawyers had briefed staff members of the SEC on the status of the case—the results of Gruenberger's investigation and the decision not to reinstate Begelman. The SEC people had seemed impressed with the quality of the investigation and somewhat less concerned about Begelman's fate than the lawyers had anticipated they might be. So it was possible that reinstatement would pass the SEC's "smell test." There could be no guarantee, however—no guarantee that the SEC would not launch its own investigation, and no guarantee that the SEC would not require public disclosure of the details of Begelman's misdeeds, which remained a closely held secret within the company and a relatively small number of outsiders.

Hirschfield told Lang and Gruenberger that he had to give the board his final decision by Monday and would let them know if there was any change in his stated anti-Begelman position.

It was noon. Lang went home. Gruenberger stayed to go over with Berte the details of her employment with the Wolf market-research company. And Hirschfield went upstairs to the privacy of his study and telephoned Herbert Allen at the Carlyle.

"I've just had a meeting with Todd and Peter, and I'm seriously considering taking David back into the company."

"That's great news, Alan."

"I really feel it may be the only way to bind up the wounds we've all suffered, and get on with the business of the company. We can't go on like we have been."

"That's certainly true. It's been a difficult period."

Hirschfield explained the restrictions that would be placed on Begelman if he was reinstated. Herbert endorsed them.

"I haven't yet made up my mind for sure," Hirschfield said, "but I wanted you to know that I'm reconsidering it in good faith and will let you know my final decision on Monday."

"Fine, I'm sure you can work it out. We'll all feel better once this is behind us."

At home on Linden Drive in Beverly Hills, Begelman took a call from David Geffen.

"Are you happy?" Geffen asked.

"Happy about what?"

"Alan's going to reinstate you. Haven't you heard?"

"I've heard no such thing."

"It's not definite, but he's leaning heavily in that direction. The board essentially has given him no choice. It's been at a fever pitch the last couple of days. Alan feels that if he doesn't do it, they'll fire *him* eventually and make it impossible for him to run the company in the interim. They've got him by the throat."

"In other words, or rather using your word, I'm being stuffed down Alan's throat."

"That's one way of putting it."

"I thought everything was final," Begelman said. "I was just getting used to the idea of being an independent producer."

"Well, you can think again. Everything is far from final, and you're probably going to be offered your job back. I suppose I should congratulate you and say that I'm pleased for you, and I am in a way, but in reality, David, I must tell you that I think it would be very unwise for you to return to this job. If you go back, you'll only succeed in drawing a great deal of attention to this situation that thus far it hasn't attracted. You'll cause a spotlight to rest on you which will be very hot and could cause you tremendous trouble. Besides, if Alan does this only under extreme duress, and really doesn't want you, the job may not be worth having. The situation could get even worse than it is now.''

''I wish Alan would discuss this with me directly,'' Begelman said.

''Also,'' Geffen continued, ''you'd be much better off as a producer in the long run. You'd make far more money. And who needs all the aggravation of the bureaucratic life anyway?''

When Begelman dialed the Hirschfield home, Alan was in the basement playing table tennis and pinball with his children. The Houston-Texas A&M game was on television.

''Hello, Alan, it's David.''

''Hello, David, how are you?''

''Fine, how are you?''

''Well, it's been difficult.''

''I know what you mean, believe me.''

''I'm sure you do.''

''Alan, the reason I'm calling—I just got a call from David Geffen, who tells me that he understands that you are seriously considering reinstating me, that you've been under unbearable pressure from the board, and that in effect I'm being shoved down your throat. I just wanted you to know, first, that I've had nothing to do with any pressure on you—I've literally just found out about it within the last few minutes—and second, that I've come to terms with my immediate future in terms of the production deal we've discussed and am fully prepared to make a production arrangement. I'm emotionally ready to do it, and I feel it's probably the best thing for me, for you, and for everybody else under the circumstances. As much as I'd like to come back, to have an opportunity to make up to you all the grief I've caused you, I certainly don't want to be stuffed down your throat. If that's the only way it can happen, then I think it best that it not happen, and that we proceed along the lines we discussed last Sunday. I've accepted the idea, I feel it's the best way for me to go, and I just wanted you to know that I'm committed to it and that I feel badly about any pressure that has been brought to bear on you. I assure you that I had nothing to do with it.''

''Well, David, I'm glad to hear you say these things. It makes it much easier for me. The fact is, I am reconsidering, and I don't know where I'm going to come out. It's a tough decision. It's become impossible for me to run the company the way things have been, and

I'm really down to groping for a way to salvage the company itself at this point. But you've made it much easier by what you've said, and I appreciate it.''

Hirschfield was flabbergasted. Was Begelman suddenly giving up? Could it be that after more than two months of fighting tenaciously for his job he was giving up? No, it couldn't be. It was inconceivable. After the discovery of the embezzlements, Begelman had sobbed and pleaded not to be suspended. After the investigation, he had mesmerized most members of the Columbia board of directors with his impassioned plea for reinstatement. As recently as last Sunday at the Beverly Hills Hotel, Hirschfield had interpreted Begelman's impractical contract demands as an attempt to induce reinstatement. Moreover, Hirschfield had assumed that Begelman, while he had not been an active participant, had certainly known of the building pressure on Hirschfield, and approved it at least passively. Could Alan have been wrong? Why would David pick this moment, when Alan actually was considering reinstatement, to change his mind?

The phone rang again. It was Herbert. Begelman had called him, too, related his conversations with Geffen and Hirschfield, and told Herbert that he wanted to proceed with his independent production arrangement. David was tired of the battle, Herbert said, and could not endure any more uncertainty.

"I just wanted you to know, Alan, that if this is what David wants, then it's what I'll support."

"I'm still in shock from David's call. It's hard to believe he has his wits about him."

"He seems to have adjusted himself to being a producer and consultant. All I've ever wanted was what was good for David, and to make sure that he was treated fairly. If he's happy, then I'm happy."

"Wait a minute, Herbert. Too much has gone on here for this just to be sloughed off this easily. I think you should call David back and go over it with him again, and make sure that he's thought it through and is sure of his position. As I said to you earlier, I've been seriously considering bringing him back. It appears to be the only way the company's going to function."

"David says he doesn't want it. All I want is to make sure David's happy and being treated fairly."

"Please call him back and go over it with him again. I just want us all to be sure of ourselves and not live to regret this."

Herbert called back in the late afternoon. David had assured him that he meant what he said.

"Look, Alan," Herbert said, "I know I've put pressure on you. I don't question I've put pressure on you, but as far as I'm concerned it's all off if David wants to be an independent producer. All I want is to help him get what he wants, after all he's done for us."

"I can't believe this is happening, Herbert. What about Matty and Ray? I've seen how hysterical Matty is. You've told me my relationship with him is irreparable. You've told me Ray isn't going to sign his new contract."

"I'll call Matty and Ray. They'll be all right, once they know the circumstances."

"Would you mind calling Leo, too. I think he should hear this and I think it would be appropriate if he heard it from you."

Leo Jaffe, who was as astounded as Hirschfield, called Alan late that evening and related a conversation with Herbert that was nearly identical to Hirschfield's. "If I hadn't heard him say it with his own voice, I would not have believed it," Jaffe said.

Hirschfield then telephoned Joe Fischer, who was at home in New Jersey playing bridge with his wife and close friends.

"A miracle has just happened! We won!" Alan said, explaining the latest developments to his bewildered aide. "It looks like it's finally over. I can't believe it, but it looks like we can get back to running the company."

Fischer returned to his bridge game elated and immediately downed two stiff shots of Scotch.

THIRTY-THREE

It was inevitable, Hirschfield supposed, that gatherings of Columbia's foreign executives would forever remind him of the Begelman crisis.

Precisely six months earlier, on a balmy evening in Los Angeles, Hirschfield had been presiding over a festive party at Chasen's for his foreign staff when David Begelman had told him quietly that he needn't worry about a "problem with a check made out to Cliff Robertson."

On the cold, clear first Sunday in December—the morning after the Begelman fever had broken—Hirschfield, in his own home in Scarsdale this time, was entertaining the same group from abroad and at the same time celebrating his victory over the Columbia board of directors. The entertaining was gregarious but the celebrating was silent and almost conspiratorial; the only people in the house who had lived through the ordeal and knew the latest developments, in addition to Alan and Berte, were Dan Melnick, who had flown in from Los Angeles on Saturday, and Leo Jaffe and Allen Adler. The foreigners knew little of the Begelman problem. They had come to New York, as Hirschfield had instructed the previous week, to see *Close Encounters of the Third Kind* and begin preparations for its foreign opening in the spring. Most of them had never been so excited about a film and hardly needed Hirschfield's pep talk.

"This is the greatest opportunity of your professional lives," Hirschfield told the group when it had assembled in the living room. "You have an opportunity to release this picture in a way never done before. You have a chance to use your imagination in spending advertising dollars like you never have before."

The Hirschfields served a buffet brunch of lobster, Nova Scotia salmon, roast beef, turkey, and assorted salads and desserts, which they had purchased themselves on Saturday at their local delicatessen.

(Alan disdained the Hollywood tendency to have even the smallest parties professionally catered, usually by Chasen's.) Several of the visitors brought gifts. Erich Mueller, the studio's man in Germany, gave Berte a bottle of her favorite German wine and Alan a box of his beloved Monte Cristo No. 1 Cuban cigars.

When the guests had left, Hirschfield asked Melnick, Adler, and Jaffe to stay. The events of Saturday had mystified them all, and they speculated about David Begelman's and Herbert Allen's motivations. "I think it might be very simple," Melnick suggested. "I think it's entirely possible that David just doesn't have the stomach for any more fighting. He's emotionally exhausted and would do just about anything to end it."

"There must be more to it than that," Adler said. "Something must have happened to scare them off. Maybe some awful new revelation about David is about to come out."

Hirschfield said, "I keep hearing rumors that the FBI is getting involved. Cliff Robertson is supposed to have gone to the FBI. Maybe they've turned up something new, and David feels a low profile is the best policy. We may never know."

"Before you count your blessings," Adler cautioned, "you'd better wait and see what kind of production deal David wants to make. If he's as unreasonable as he was last Sunday, you may still have problems."

"He sounded awfully meek and reasonable on the phone yesterday," Hirschfield said.

"It's not in his nature to be meek," Adler said. "I'd wait to pour the champagne till the deal is done."

On Monday morning, Hirschfield, Fischer, and Melnick were seated around the coffee table in Hirschfield's office discussing candidates for the presidency of the studio when Leo Jaffe walked in. Jaffe looked stunned.

"Matty just called. He wants to know when the meeting is."

Hirschfield looked at Jaffe incredulously.

"What's he talking about? Didn't he hear from Herbert?"

"No. No one's contacted him."

"But the meeting's off. There is no meeting."

"That's what I told him—that you had spoken to me, that Herbert had spoken to me, that everything is settled, and there is no meeting to discuss it. He didn't know what I was talking about. He wants a meeting.''

Hirschfield called Herbert Allen.

"We just heard from Matty. He wants to know when the meeting is. Didn't you speak to him?''

"No, I didn't speak to him.''

"You said you were going to call him and tell him the meeting is off.''

"Well, what's your decision?''

"What do you mean, what's my decision?''

"What's your decision on Begelman?''

"Herbert, you told me on Saturday after David called and after you spoke to him that as far as you were concerned everything was settled and there was no need for a meeting. You were going to call Matty and take care of him, and you were going to call Ray and square him away, and there would be nothing to meet about.''

"Well, maybe we misunderstood each other. We do have to get your decision.''

"Herbert, I told you on Saturday that I was reconsidering, but after we talked to David you said there was nothing to decide anymore, and there was no need to have a meeting, and that you'd take care of Matty and Ray, and that all was well and right with the world.''

"Well, I don't remember saying all that. If Matty wants to have a meeting, then there should be a meeting, and you really have to give your decision.''

"Herbert, this isn't what we discussed! If you're changing your mind, tell me you're changing your mind. Or if something else has happened, tell me! Has Begelman had a change of heart?''

"I haven't spoken to him.''

"Well, you said there was no need to have a meeting, because if David was happy not being reinstated, you were happy, and it was at an end.''

"Well, people hear words in different ways, and if Matty wants to have a meeting, then we better have a meeting.''

Furious and dumbfounded, Hirschfield slammed down the phone.

"Am I going crazy? That is the most bizarre conversation I've ever had on the telephone with any human being. These people are determined to hold my feet to the fire. They're determined to make this thing as horrendous as they possibly can. Leo, thank God

Herbert called you on Saturday so I've got a witness. Otherwise, it would be like I dreamed the whole weekend.''

They were silent for a few moments. Then Melnick said, ''You know what probably happened? Somebody must have gotten to David and Herbie and turned them around. Either Matty or Ray must have said something like, 'We've been fighting to get you back in. We've got Hirschfield on the ropes. He's reconsidering. And now you say you don't have the stomach for it. Well, fuck you.' They won't let him stop at this point. And David is probably saying 'Hey, I'm the one who may go to jail for all this.' ''*

Hirschfield finally telephoned both Allen and Rosenhaus and told them that his original decision stood. Begelman would not be returning as president of the studio. To Rosenhaus he said, ''David fully understands this, Matty. He knows he can never again have my trust and confidence. He doesn't want to be shoved down my throat.''

''This is a tragedy for the company,'' Rosenhaus declared. ''You're making a very serious mistake.''

After he hung up, Hirschfield said to Fischer and Melnick, ''These people will stop at nothing.''

That afternoon, Hirschfield returned a phone call from Ira Harris, the investment banker from the Chicago office of Salomon Brothers who had fostered Columbia's $50 million purchase of the Gottlieb pinball-machine company a year earlier. They made a date to meet Wednesday when Harris would be in New York.

On Tuesday morning at the Beverly Hills Hotel, Todd Lang had breakfast with Frank Rothman, David Begelman's lawyer, to discuss the terms of Begelman's new production relationship with Columbia Pictures. Since the deal would have to pass a ''smell test'' at the SEC and otherwise would be scrutinized publicly, Lang urged Rothman to urge his client to be ''reasonable.'' Although Columbia wanted to make use of Begelman's talents, the company could not ''reward'' him for his misdeeds and did not want to appear to be doing so.

As Lang and Rothman were leaving the Polo Lounge, Hirschfield was sitting down to lunch at La Côte Basque with Allen Adler. Although Adler and Hirschfield had been together occasionally in groups through the autumn—on the previous Sunday in Scarsdale,

---

*Ray Stark later denied that he pressured Begelman as Melnick speculated.

for instance—they had rarely talked privately, and Adler had not participated in the Begelman battle to nearly the extent that others had. His last lengthy conversation with Hirschfield on the subject had been in the middle of October, at the same table in the same restaurant, two weeks after Begelman had been suspended. With a touch of quiet bravado, Hirschfield had assured Adler then that Begelman would not be returning to the company and that they probably would be able, therefore, to fashion a more efficient structure for the movie and televison operations as Adler had been recommending. Adler, though pleased by the news, doubted that solving the Begelman issue or reorganizing the studio would be as simple as Hirschfield indicated. Over several years of working for Hirschfield, Adler had learned to allow for the extra degree of boldness that Hirschfield, as his primary mentor, often displayed when they were alone together. By December, however, Hirschfield showed little boldness with anyone, even Adler. He was emotionally exhausted by the protracted struggle with Herbert Allen and deeply depressed by his inability to make his decision on Begelman adhere.

"Goddammit, what do I have to do to prevail here," Hirschfield said to Adler. "I'm a seasoned adult. I'm forty-two years old. I've been running this company damned well for four years, and I'm still treated like an employee of the Allens. Herbert can't see the merits of this thing anymore. He's only interested in proving to the world that he owns me as well as this company, and he won't stand for any challenges to his authority."

"Look, Alan, I know you've worked for these people since 1959, and your father's been associated with them all his life," Adler said. "But at this point you've got to face the fact that there really is only one answer: There is no longer any possibility that this is going to get solved. You're never again going to be able to live with these people. You'll never be anything but their employee as long as you're in the same company together. And there's only one solution: Finding someone to buy them out and take over this company, or at least buy enough of it to dilute their influence."

"That wouldn't be easy."

"No, it wouldn't but it's the only way. These people are acting crazy. They're rewriting history. They're crediting Begelman with things he never did. They're discrediting us for things we never did. The real solution is for them to be taken out. Almost anybody else would be better."

"Who could it be?"

"Who knows?" Adler said. "It would have to be somebody big—somebody willing and able to spend two hundred fifty million or three hundred million, which is what this company is worth on the open market. It would have to be somebody outside the business; the Justice Department won't let anybody in the business buy us. It would have to be somebody willing to be in business with a bunch of Jews; that eliminates a lot of Waspy companies. It would take somebody with the nerve and sophistication and stomach to fight the Allens. A big pocketbook and a strong stomach, that's what it would take. There aren't that many candidates around."

"What about our friends over at Time, Inc.?" Hirschfield asked.

"Well, they're very white-shoe and wouldn't want to get their skirts dirty. They think the picture business is a dirty business."

Neither man spoke for a few moments.

"Let's think about it," Hirschfield said.

The conversation with Adler, of course, was not Hirschfield's first thought of independence from the Allens. Even before the Begelman problem had arisen, he had resented Herbert Allen's dominion over his life. Hirschfield considered himself a smarter, abler businessman than Herbert, who occupied his station in the business world, Hirschfield felt, in large part because he had been born to it, not because he had earned it. Particularly over the past year or so, with Columbia's recovery nearly complete, Hirschfield had pondered how he might assert his independence of Herbert. Until their relationship had ruptured in the wake of the Begelman revelations, Hirschfield's thoughts had been inchoate musings. In the last month, however, he had begun to think specifically not only about how he might win the battle over Begelman, but about how he could win what seemed to have become a battle for control of the company itself and a direct, bitter, and very personal contest of egos. The intensity of Alan's fury clouded his ability to think clearly. Moreover, he had been so preoccupied with the day-to-day twists of the Begelman controversy that he had been unable effectively to consider possible long-range solutions.

The conversation with Adler helped him focus his thoughts. Adler was right, of course. The only way he could win was to enlist the aid of an outsider willing and able to help him win. Hirschfield resolved to try to find such help. He knew the search would be risky and would have to be conducted in the strictest secrecy. If Herbert learned of his intentions before he was ready to implement them, not only would he fail, but his defeat almost certainly would be swift and painful, and he might never recover. In all probability, Herbert had the power to destroy Hirschfield's business career if he chose to. Still, Hirschfield had to try.

THIRTY-FOUR

Ira Harris had become one of the half dozen or so leading investment bankers in America in the eight years since Salomon Brothers, the large and prestigious New York-based securities house, sent him to Chicago to head its corporate-financing activities there. He had conceived and fostered many major mergers and acquisitions, including the purchase of the Avis rental-car company by Norton Simon Incorporated, and Columbia Pictures Industries' purchase of the Gottlieb pinball-machine company.

A forty-year-old native New Yorker, Harris was an imposing man: Aggressive and self-assured to the point of occasional abrasiveness, he was tall and portly, chain-smoked cigars, and liked to ride around in telephone-equipped limousines. As a deal maker, he was both creative and tenacious and had brought a number of deals to fruition where others had failed.

Harris and Hirschfield met for cocktails Wednesday evening in the bar of the Regency Hotel. They had been fond of each other since becoming acquainted at the time of the Gottlieb acquisition, and though they had not discussed the Begelman problem, Harris had gleaned the general impression from other sources that the top echelon of Columbia had divided into two contending camps over the issue.

"You simply would not believe it," Hirschfield said. "I can't believe what's going on. I'm in a battle over whether to take him back or not."

"How can there be any argument?"

"There shouldn't be, but there is. It's become a test of wills, and I'm in an untenable, no-win position. If I bring him back, the company will look terrible. It will look like I'm coddling a criminal. If I don't bring him back, the board has made it plain that it will crucify me in every way they know how. They have no confidence in me and feel the company can't run without Begelman."

"Amazing," Harris said.

"I'm totally exhausted. The only thing I have to look forward to is going to London next week for the opening of *The Deep*. Sort of a forced vacation. But I have no idea how this situation is going to be resolved. I think there's a real chance that this company is just going to tear itself apart. Begelman is no longer the issue. The issue is control of the company."

"That's really tragic," Harris said. "Is there any chance the Allens might want to get out?"

"I doubt it."

"Or that the whole company could be bought?"

"I don't know. Actually, maybe there is. They're so down on me, and they feel the company's going to collapse without Begelman, maybe there is a chance they would be receptive to the right approach."

"Since you're going to be in England," Harris said, "there's someone there I think you should meet. He might be interested in this situation."

"I'll talk to anybody. I'm really at my wits' end."

"It's Jimmy Goldsmith, Sir James Goldsmith," Harris said.

Though he had heard of Jimmy Goldsmith, Hirschfield had never done business with the flamboyant multimillionaire tycoon, who controlled major European food companies and the United States-based Grand Union supermarket chain and had recently purchased *L'Express*, the French weekly news magazine, and a sizable interest in the Beaverbrook Newspapers, publisher of the *The Daily Express* in London. A citizen of both Britain and France, Goldsmith also led an openly double personal life. He had a wife and two children in Paris, and in London lived with Lady Annabel Birley, by whom he had two children.

"Jimmy's been looking for an opportunity in the entertainment business," Ira Harris was saying. "He and the Allens know each other. If he thought there was an opportunity at Columbia, he just might be willing to buy them out. He'd be a good kind of partner to have. He'd let you run the company without interference. I think you ought to meet him."

"If you can arrange it, I'd be delighted."

The board of directors of Columbia Pictures Industries assembled at 711 Fifth Avenue for their regular monthly meeting at one o'clock on Thursday, December 8. Although the most important directors, Hirschfield, Rosenhaus, Allen, and Kramer, had conferred several times informally, the entire board had not been together in one room since November 16, when David Begelman had made his dramatic plea for mercy, the majority of the board had endorsed his reinstatement, and Hirschfield had stated his opposition. Since then, in a succession of ugly clashes, Hirschfield had tried to make his decision adhere, but the board's increasingly severe pressure had broadened the dispute into an acute crisis of authority within the corporation. Even though it had appeared briefly over the previous weekend that Hirschfield had won, Herbert's position had hardened again by Monday, and by Thursday it was clear not only that the Begelman issue remained unresolved but that the authority crisis had deepened still further. The hatred and loathing in the boardroom were palpable.

The meeting began with a brief report from Todd Lang on the conclusions of the investigation of Begelman. He had misappropriated a total of $61,008.* With interest, the amount came to $67,225. The investigators also considered him responsible for an additional $23,200, representing travel, entertainment, and other personal expenses which the company had paid but which had been improperly documented. In all, he owed $90,425, a portion of which he had already repaid.

The board then discussed Columbia's future relationship with Begelman. Matty Rosenhaus, in a typically impassioned speech, proclaimed that if Begelman was not to return to the presidency of the studio, he must have producing and consulting arrangements that would "make him whole and happy" financially. "He has saved

---

*Even though Begelman had embezzled $75,000 in the Robertson, Choate, Groleau, and Ritt episodes, it was determined that a portion of the $35,000 stolen by means of the bogus Choate-*Tommy* contract and used for Begelman's home projection room would have been allowed by Columbia if Begelman had asked for it properly, and that in any event Columbia benefited by Begelman's having a nice projection room. Thus, it was determined that he should not have to repay the full Choate embezzlement.

this company, and it's not his fault that he's not coming back," Rosenhaus declared.

Alan Hirschfield said: "I have an obligation to this board to tell you that it makes no sense to get into more trouble for giving away the store to Begelman than we would get into for bringing him back into the company. This entire deal will be subject to public scrutiny. It's going to have to pass the smell test at the SEC. There are people out in the woods who would love to get their hands on this, and if it appears that we are rewarding him for his transgressions, we're all going to look like a bunch of fools, we'll have no integrity left, and we're going to be subject to legal action."

"You're making too much out of this," Herbert Allen asserted. "Just go ahead and make a deal with him."

"It's not just another production deal, Herbert," Hirschfield responded. "I've got to negotiate with him at arm's length, and I've got to have the board's backing in order to do that."

"What do you mean 'production deal'?" Rosenhaus shouted. "It's a production *and consulting* deal! Are you trying to make just a production deal?"

"No Matty, I misspoke," Hirschfield retorted contemptuously. "It's obviously a production and consulting deal."

Rosenhaus proposed that Columbia Pictures purchase full-page advertisements in the industry trade publications "thanking David Begelman for his enormous contributions to the company." Leo Jaffe suggested that if that were done, ads also should be run thanking "Alan Hirschfield for his leadership and contributions to the company." Herbert Allen responded: "Alan's still here. We don't need to take any ads for Alan right now." No ads were taken for either man.

Later in the meeting, Leo Jaffe presented for board approval a television production arrangement between Columbia's television company and two Hollywood producers. The deal had been approved by the top officers of the television company, as well as by Hirschfield, Joe Fischer, and Jaffe, but it was standard procedure to clear such deals with the full board.

Matty Rosenhaus insisted that David Begelman's approval be sought before the board voted.

"But Matty," Hirschfield said, "this already has been approved by all the appropriate people."

"Are you afraid to let David express his opinion?" Rosenhaus asked.

"Matty, David's no longer with the company."

"Well, he's a consultant, isn't he?" Rosenhaus said. "We just authorized him to be a consultant. In his capacity as a consultant, he should approve deals like this."

"Matty, David has nothing to do with this deal," Hirschfield said. "You're not going to be able to run to David every time you want to approve a movie or television project."

"But that's what consultants are for," Rosenhaus insisted. "He's supposed to approve these projects."

"Matty's right," Herbert said. "That's a great suggestion. That's what we've got David as a consultant for. We'll really get our money's worth."

Leo Jaffe was instructed to go to his office and telephone Begelman in Los Angeles. Begelman blessed the TV deal.

Toward the end of the board meeting Herbert Allen reiterated his opinion, expressed the previous week, that Dan Melnick was not capable of running the studio, and that several important producers might leave if Begelman were not reinstated: Peter Guber, Jon Peters, even Ray Stark. Hirschfield repeated his confidence in Melnick and his belief that the producers would stay.

"You'd better get the next Streisand movie," Herbert said to Hirschfield.

"What do you mean, 'I'd better get it'? Is that some sort of threat?"

"Never mind," Herbert said. "Just be sure you get it."

The meeting ended after the board ordered Hirschfield to summon David Begelman to New York immediately and conclude a production and consultation deal with him by the beginning of the following week.

In his office with Fischer and Adler, Hirschfield felt like a battered soccer player in a locker room after a losing game. He slumped speechless at his desk.

"That was the worst board meeting I've ever attended," Fischer said. "I have never in my life seen anything like that."

Adler looked at Hirschfield and said, "I assume you see from what went on in there that even if Begelman isn't reinstated, he's going to be running the company from his consulting position.''

"I see very clearly," Hirschfield replied. "They're systematically emasculating me, my ability to run this company. This isn't the end. It's just the beginning.''

Ira Harris, who had returned to Chicago that morning, had left a telephone message for Hirschfield. "Important! Pls call when alone.'' When Adler and Fischer left, Hirschfield phoned Harris. The investment banker had spoken to Jimmy Goldsmith, and Goldsmith was indeed interested in discussing Columbia Pictures when Hirschfield was in London.

In Los Angeles that evening, David Begelman was relaxed and charming—and still looked very much like a mogul—when he and Gladyce turned out for the black-tie West Coast premiere of Ray Stark's *The Goodbye Girl* and the supper party at the Century Plaza following the film.

THIRTY-FIVE

For at least two decades, David Begelman had been known as one of the most skilled negotiators of deals in the entertainment business—perhaps the most skilled without exception. His mind was agile and creative. He could marshal broad concepts and tiny details with equal ease. He could charm. He could bludgeon. Quite conceivably, therefore, he could have negotiated his production-consultation contract with Columbia, and the settlement of his old contract, without assistance. But he chose to supplement his own skills with those of his lawyer, Frank Rothman, who flew to New York on Begelman's behalf Thursday afternoon.

Hirschfield, by contrast, felt ill equipped for the negotiation. Aside from lacking anyone with Begelman's special mixture of skills to represent the company, Hirschfield believed that the board, by

insisting that Begelman be made "whole and happy," had undermined the company's ability to conduct a strong negotiation. The
board, in effect, had thrown its power to Begelman, and Hirschfield
assumed that Begelman and Rothman knew that.

To handle the negotiation, Hirschfield appointed Joe Fischer,
Victor Kaufman, Todd Lang, and Peter Gruenberger, and also summoned Eli Horowitz, the chief contract negotiator at the studio.
Horowitz flew in late Thursday, and the negotiators began their
work Friday morning in Todd Lang's suite at Weil, Gotshal &
Manges. Begelman, after conferring twice with Rothman by phone
on Friday, came east that evening, and joined the group on Saturday.

The temperature was in the twenties and a strong wind off Central
Park buffeted the General Motors Building, chilling the underheated
and otherwise deserted law offices, and forcing the negotiators to
face each other in sweaters and overcoats. Lunch was brought in. By
the middle of the afternoon, it began to appear unlikely that an
agreement could be reached without personal intervention by
Hirschfield. Begelman was demanding that his production deal include provisions that Columbia had never given any producer. The
company negotiators were refusing. Begelman and Rothman were
threatening to leave and return to Los Angeles with the deal unresolved.
Finally Todd Lang advised Hirschfield by telephone that "only two
people can conclude this—Alan Hirschfield and David Begelman.
You'll have to see him yourself." Hirschfield reluctantly agreed and
asked that Begelman be told to come to Scarsdale on Sunday morning.

Begelman balked. His last conversation with Hirschfield had been
unsatisfactory. Peter Gruenberger insisted, however, that David go
to Scarsdale. After conducting a difficult six-week investigation and
then waiting through another three weeks of uncertainty, Gruenberger
had little patience left. "David, I won't stand for a scene over this,"
he said. "Do it as a favor to me. I think I've treated you fairly
during this whole ordeal. I could have hurt you. Now, do me the
favor of going to see Alan."

David agreed. He would see Hirschfield alone. Frank Rothman
had to return to Los Angeles to prepare for a Monday court appearance on another matter.

Berte and Alan Hirschfield rarely dined alone, even when Alan was
not traveling. When they were home, one or more of their children
usually was present. When they went out, they normally were with

other people. Alan occasionally remained in Manhattan on weeknights, and in Scarsdale on the weekends there frequently were guests. While not dissimilar to the habits of many busy affluent couples, the Hirschfields' daily routines signaled an additional factor: their fifteen-year marriage was under strain. As in many troubled marriages, however, each remained the other's closest confidant, particularly in a crisis. So it was that on the evening of Saturday, December 10, a bitterly cold evening, the coldest since the previous winter, Alan Hirschfield sought the private solace of his wife. They drove up Interstate 684 into northern Westchester, across Bedford Road, and up the Old Post Road to the hamlet of Bedford and a cozy, informal restaurant called Nino's. Situated in a converted barn, Nino's was the antithesis of the high-profile Manhattan and Beverly Hills restaurants where the Hirschfields usually dined, and they had gone there in the past when they wanted privacy. Anonymous, and free of interruption, they talked quietly for hours about Alan's plight and his pain. And Berte became the first to know that Alan had tentatively decided to succumb to the pressure and reinstate David Begelman to the presidency of the Columbia studio.

"There no longer is a right answer and a wrong answer," Alan said. "There are only wrong answers. There are only bad decisions. As compelling as the arguments are against reinstating him, they lose a lot of their compelling quality when I see that if those arguments are followed, it will be impossible for me to run the company. It's not being run now. The company is convulsed by civil war. If Begelman is not reinstated, the war will go on and get worse. The board made it abundantly clear on Thursday that it is willing to systematically undermine my ability to run the company, and that it is going to treat Begelman as the de facto president of the studio whether his title is president or only consultant. That's entirely unacceptable to me. So what options do I have left? I can't and won't resign. That would be a betrayal of the people I've brought into the company. It would be total surrender, and I'm not going to leave without a lot more of a fight than I've put up so far. I'm primarily responsible for this company's return from the abyss. I orchestrated one of the most spectacular corporate recoveries on record—from the brink of bankruptcy to full prosperity and an almost unlimited future. This is my company in a very real way."

"Right," Berte said. "You're one with the company. You're a big part of it, and it's a big part of you."

"So it's quite possible that the only thing to do under the circumstances is to take him back. It's a short-term solution. It's not a cure. It's like a shot of morphine to relieve the pain overnight, but if I don't take it I may be dead by next week. I'll just have to go from day to day and see what happens. If I bring him back, it will at least establish a truce with the board, even if only temporarily. Meanwhile, maybe somebody like Jimmy Goldsmith will come along and make the Allens an offer they can't refuse. If something like that could be encouraged or arranged, I could always get rid of Begelman later."

"The most important thing now is to do what is best for you personally," Berte said. "If this is what you have to do, then this is what you have to do. You've tried to do what you think is right, and it doesn't seem to work. What you see, no one else seems to see. Your friends have betrayed you. If they hadn't been your friends all your life, it would be easier. But in any event you're not compromising your principles. You're just opting for a short-term solution. If the short-term problem isn't solved, the long-term won't mean much."

"Maybe I'm deceiving myself. Maybe this will only make things worse. Maybe all the bad things that I've predicted if he's reinstated will in fact happen."

"You'll just have to improvise. It can't get any worse than it is now."

"I know one thing. I'm never again going to subject myself to a board meeting like that one on Thursday."

"Nor should you have to."

"I haven't definitely decided yet, but it can't go beyond tomorrow."

With large windows on three sides, the Hirschfields' living room was one of the brightest rooms in their ninety-year-old, three-story home. The living room was on the east side of the house, off a large foyer-gallery and the main staircase. The dining room was on the opposite side of the foyer, and beyond the dining room was a large, sunny den. The kitchen, pantry, and another staircase were behind the dining room at the back of the house. Most of the family traffic was through the den, dining room, and kitchen, as well as on the upper floors via the back stairs. So the living room, somewhat isolated by the foyer, was the best place in the house for private business meetings, and it was there that Hirschfield's negotiating team—Fischer, Lang, Gruenberger, Kaufman, and the studio's Eli Horowitz— assembled at ten Sunday morning.

Since it had fallen to Hirschfield himself to conclude Begelman's production arrangement and contract settlement, it was necessary that he be briefed on the lengthy and complex negotiations that had taken place on Friday and Saturday. There was a general consensus that unless either he or Begelman was prepared to make major concessions, it would be difficult to strike a deal.

Begelman arrived at noon and was surprised to find six people from the opposition camp instead of one; he had thought he was going to a genuine summit meeting. Soon, it turned out that he was. Hirschfield and Fischer stayed. The others repaired to Todd Lang's home just around the corner to await recall if needed. Fischer settled in the Hirschfields' den with the Sunday *New York Times* and football on television. And Hirschfield and Begelman shut themselves in the living room, Hirschfield having told everyone that he and David would require no more than an hour or so.

Except for a bathroom break, they did not leave the living room for six hours.

Hirschfield explained why he could not give Begelman as "rich" a deal as David wanted. It would embarrass the company publicly and would be scorned by the SEC. Begelman explained why he could take no less; he couldn't worry about what the SEC would say. He was getting on in years and had his own security and that of his family to consider.

They talked about the consulting Begelman would do, apart from producing films.

"If it was up to the board," Hirschfield said, "you're the de facto president of the company, so I guess you'll be a full-time consultant."

"Well, in my opinion, I have a large contribution to make. I can be very helpful."

"I'm sure that's the case. There's never been any question about your talents. Except that no one can have two bosses. Danny Melnick can't report to two bosses. Norman Levy can't report to two bosses. We can't run a company where someone is the president in title and someone else is the president in fact. We can't have the board running to you to second-guess every deal that the president of the studio or the president of TV wants to make."

Hirschfield recounted the board meeting of the previous Thursday. "There have been all kinds of threats and mandates laid down by the board," Hirschfield continued, "about how the company is to be run—the role you have to play, the role I have to play. I am in deep trouble with the board, and quite frankly, David, you are really no longer the issue here. I'm in a spot where I can't win. If I bring you back I've compromised my position and I'm letting the company in for a lot of grief from the various communities and people with whom we have relationships. If I don't bring you back, I've alienated the board. I think my tenure here is certainly going to be limited, and my ability to be effective is highly limited. I assume you've heard about Herbert's threats, and I assume you've heard about Ray's threats, and I assume you know about the telegrams and phone calls, and I assume you know about Berte and the threats that have been made against her.''

Begelman professed ignorance of the details of the pressure on Hirschfield.

"Well, all of that has been a way of life here for the past couple of months," Hirschfield said. "I've been put in a position where it's me versus the board. You are no longer the issue. Whether you come back or you don't come back, this is a contest of wills between me and Herbert Allen, and me and Matty Rosenhaus, but essentially Herbert, who feels that he has the right to call the shots as to who's going to run this company. Herbert and I are really on the outs, and it looks like irreparable damage has been done there. Matty and I are on the outs, and it looks like irreparable damage has been done there. Irwin Kramer, who was for your conviction and hanging at the beginning, saw the light of day and became the loyal son-in-law, your strong advocate, and Berte's prosecutor.''

"Alan, perhaps I could be of help in repairing that damage. I'd be happy to do anything I can.''

"I don't think there's anything you can do. Quite frankly, the issue is not you. You're simply a pawn at this point in time. But I must say that faced with the prospect of having you become a consultant and in effect run the company in that capacity without my direction, it might be better if you came back into the company and we tried to use that as a mechanism whereby perhaps we could put this whole thing to rest and get on with the remainder of our lives. As far as I'm concerned, just sitting here and talking to you, I'm probably better off bringing you back simply because it's the only chance that I see for any kind of rapprochement with the board, and any kind of peace and quiet, and any kind of settling down of the problems, so that I can go back to running the company. David, I cannot run the company! It's clear that I no longer have the backing to run it!''

"Look, I'll do anything you want me to do. Obviously, more than anything else in the world, I would like to come back. I'll give up everything I've asked for in terms of the independent arrangement. I know I can't have a new contract. I know I'll have to abide by my old contract. But all that aside, I can't help but recall that a week ago, you said I was being stuffed down your throat. In spite of everything you've said, I still don't believe it would be good for either of us for me to come back if you feel that way about me.''

"Well, I've had to think about this in broader terms. You're really looking at a man who is beaten down. I've tried to do what is right. I've been accused of 'Going Hollywood.' I've been accused of being out to get you. I just don't have any good answers anymore. But I do know that the company's coming apart at the seams. This fight is just splitting it apart, and everything we worked for for the last four and half years is just being torn asunder by what's going on, and I see no prospect of any improvement. One way or the other, the board is going to have you back. You're either going to be called a consultant, or you're going to be called president, but as far as they're concerned, they want you back.''

"Look, I'll do whatever you say. I'll never forget this opportunity if you give it to me. I'll spare no effort not only to do my job, but to justify your confidence, and I'll also spare no effort to try to square things between you and Matty and Herbert and the rest of the board for being big enough to give me this chance. But in order to succeed I must have bona fide support from you. We can't be working against each other. You would have to be willing to give me a chance. There would have to be at least a measure of true willingness by you to have me back.''

"Really, David, at this point, it doesn't make any difference to me, quite frankly, whether you come back or you don't come back. Except that if you do come back, maybe there's a chance to pull it together. If you don't come back, I see no chance.''

"Alan, I can make it work. I'll double my efforts to build these businesses. I know it will work. I know I can do it if I have your support and your confidence. We can make things right with the world. You just name the terms and I'll sign the piece of paper.''

"Well, I want to think about it a little more. But it seems to me as I sit here and talk to you and listen to myself, that I'm going to be wrong either way, and I may as well be wrong in the direction of giving the company a chance to survive. Because it ain't going to survive the way we're going. That's clear.''

*   *   *

Six o'clock. Hirschfield and Begelman sat in chilly shadows. It was dark outside and the temperature had dropped below 20 degrees. Only one lamp was on in the big living room.

Hirschfield went across to the den and asked a bewildered Joe Fischer to summon Lang and Gruenberger. With the five men assembled in the living room, Hirschfield asked the lawyers to reiterate the likely consequences of Begelman's return. They listed the well-known risks. If Hirschfield wanted to change his mind, they would inform the staff of the Securities and Exchange Commission the next day.

"I want to think about it some more," Hirschfield said.

"Alan, please," Begelman said, "I'll do whatever you want, but I must know for sure before I leave here. The uncertainty is tearing me apart."

Hirschfield stood by a window staring up into the cold, star-lit sky. His attention was momentarily diverted by what appeared to be a meteor. "There's a shooting star or something," he said. "There wasn't a space shot tonight, was there?"

"Don't think so," someone answered.

Hirschfield paused, still gazing out the window. Then he turned back to the group.

"Okay, I'll take him back."

David Begelman's eyes glistened with tears. He stood and embraced Hirschfield. "I won't let you down," he said.

The limousine dropped Begelman at the Drake at 7:30.

His first call was to Gladyce, who was dumbstruck. "Are you sure this is right?"

"No, I'm not sure of anything, but that's where I'm at."

His second call was to Herbert Allen, who laughed. It was not a laugh of merriment or glee, but a laugh of cynical surprise and bemusement.

"What did Alan say?"

"He said to me that I'm not just the best man for the job. I'm the only man for the job."

"Well, what do you want to do?"

"I'd like a chance to make up for all the horrible things I've done to you and to all the other directors and to the company."

"Well, whatever you two fellows want is fine with me," Herbert said.

Begelman's third call was to Frank Rothman, who was at home in Beverly Hills preparing for his court appearance the next morning. Rothman chuckled.

* * *

In Scarsdale, Alan said to Berte, "It's a shot. It's an expedient for the moment. It may buy enough time for things to calm down so that I can find a suitor to come along and buy these people out. Then I can walk in the next day and fire Begelman. That's my fantasy."

Alan telephoned Herbert later in the evening, "You've made him the de facto president of the company, anyway. He might as well have the title. This is what you've always wanted. Maybe it'll give us an opportunity to repair some of the damage. Maybe we can move forward. It's certainly a disaster where we're at. So he's coming back, unless I have a change of heart in the next couple of days."

Without responding to Alan's anger, Herbert said simply and gently:

"I think that's terrific. That's the right decision. You two will work it out."

"It may not work out so well, Herbert. There's going to be a firestorm of publicity."

"It'll all blow over in a week."

"I hope so. I'm gonna call Matty."

"You should call Matty," Herbert said.

To Hirschfield's horror, Rosenhaus was angry.

"How could you do this? I thought you were going to negotiate a deal."

"Matty, we couldn't negotiate a deal. It was the wrong deal. It was an outrageous deal."

"There's nothing wrong with the deal. We can give him whatever we want. If you don't want him, you shouldn't bring him back."

"Matty, it's not a question of what I want anymore. It's the only way I see to try to preserve this company and bring it back together instead of tearing it apart and ruining everything we've done for the last four and a half years."

"Well, you shouldn't do it unless you really want him. He was willing to become a consultant."

"He wasn't a consultant, Matty. He was going to be the de facto president of the studio."

"Well, consultants can get into everything."

"Look, Matty, this is what you want and you've got it. For better or worse, you've got it, Matty! This is what all the fighting has been about for the past three months! He's back! I'm going to bring him back!"

Part III

THIRTY-SIX

A euphoric David Begelman flew back to Los Angeles on Monday in time to accompany his wife to a party whose timing could not have been better. Given by producer Allan Carr at his home in Benedict Canyon, the party honored the publication of a book that Gladyce Begelman had coauthored—a book which had become an embarrassment both to the Begelmans and to Columbia Pictures because of its coincidental juxtaposition with the investigation of David for "unauthorized financial transactions." Entitled *New York on $500 a Day (Before Lunch)*, the book was a tongue-in-cheek but quite comprehensive guide for wealthy freespenders.

The Begelmans' embarrassment (if not Columbia's) had been instantly nullified, however, by Hirschfield's decision to reinstate David to the presidency of the studio. Despite all of Todd Lang's warnings, David had convinced himself that when he returned to his job it could be made to appear that he was being exonerated on the "matters of judgment" that had been in question, and that no one except the inner circle ever would know what he had really done.

Since David's restoration was to remain confidential for a few days, he and Gladyce could not give free rein to their joy while at Allan Carr's party. But it was with light hearts indeed that they mingled with the two hundred or so guests, many of whom were close friends—Ray Stark, Sue Mengers, Dan Melnick, David Geffen, Candice Bergen, Marty Ransohoff, Ed McMahon, and many others. Allan Carr, producer of the soon-to-be-released *Grease*, had a reputation for giving some of the more flamboyant parties in a town long noted for flamboyant parties. Carr's invitations were imitation "Master Charge" cards in Gladyce Begelman's name. Six colorfully costumed carolers roamed through the crowd singing Christmas songs. And red and white poinsettias were everywhere.

Ray Stark, as it happened, already knew David's news but resisted the temptation to spread it around the party. However, the glaring irony of Gladyce's book and David's predicament, whatever the outcome, was a source of amusement rather than discomfort for the guests in general. Hollywood is a town that takes delight in spitting in the face of irony.

For Alan Hirschfield, the next several days amounted to a brief period of pretending—pretending that the Begelman crisis had been contained, pretending that a week in London and Paris would ease his problems in New York and Los Angeles, and pretending that he could meet secretly with Sir James Goldsmith, one of the world's most rambunctious business tycoons, without anyone's finding out. In part, the pretending reflected a natural yearning for rest and recreation after three months of intense, seven-day-a-week pressure. But in a more fundamental sense, it reflected the somewhat homespun naïveté that was a deeply ingrained part of Alan's character— "the Oklahoma in him" as Berte saw it—a quality that endeared him to many people but also occasionally left him vulnerable.

Alan and Berte flew to London on Tuesday to head the Columbia Pictures delegation at the British premiere of *The Deep*. The premiere, which Prince Charles and Lord Mountbatten would attend, was to be held on Thursday evening at the Odeon Theater in Leicester Square as a benefit for the English National Opera and Sadler's Wells Benevolent Fund, and the Variety Clubs of Great Britain.

The most important event of the week, however, was not the premiere. It was the rendezvous with Jimmy Goldsmith. In two phone conversations with Ira Harris on Monday in New York, Hirschfield had agreed to a meeting Friday afternoon at Goldsmith's estate outside London. The plans for the meeting were highly confidential; Berte, for one, was acutely conscious of the secrecy and made a point of reminding herself not to mention it, even to close friends they were to see in London.

It was Alan Hirschfield's first royal premiere and he savored all of it—walking up the red carpet, being announced to the prince, and being a center of attention at the gala dinner dance after the movie in the ballroom of the Savoy. Director Peter Yates, producer Peter Guber, and the author of *The Deep*, Peter Benchley, flew in for the event. Most of the leading figures in the London film world were present, as well, and most of them paid their respects to Hirschfield, the man who had saved Columbia Pictures. Aside from a few whispered exchanges through the evening, nothing was said about the Begelman affair. So far as the guests knew, it was still under investigation, and Hirschfield said nothing to the contrary.

In New York, Cliff Robertson and Dina Merrill had begun hearing rumors that Columbia was going to reinstate David Begelman to the presidency of the studio. Incredulous, they pondered what to do. Cliff decided it would be inappropriate for him directly to contact Leo Jaffe or anyone else at Columbia. Dina, however, had an idea. As one of the wealthiest women in the nation and the daughter of the late E. F. Hutton, she knew people in Wall Street and had met Charlie Allen on occasion. It occurred to her that Charlie might not know the nature of David Begelman's misdeeds and that if he were informed, he might prevail upon Columbia Pictures not to reinstate Begelman. Dina tried to contact Charlie but was unable to reach him. She was telling her troubles to a friend over lunch at "21" when the friend pointed out that Charlie Allen's daughter, Terry Allen Kramer, was seated just across the room. Dina, who had never met Terry, went over and introduced herself, and explained that she had been trying to reach Terry's father to discuss David Begelman. She had heard a rumor that Columbia was about to reinstate Begelman and was sure there must have been a misunderstanding of what Begelman had done. Terry assured her that Columbia and the Allens were fully informed and that Dina should not worry about it.

"But you don't understand," Dina said. "David Begelman forged my husband's name on a check. He's a crook."

Terry Kramer assured Dina that she *did* understand and the situation was under control. She repeated her suggestion that Dina not worry about it.

Dina turned and walked away, nonplussed. "You'll never believe what just happened to me," she said to Cliff a few minutes later at the UN Plaza.

From his suite at Claridge's, just before leaving to see Jimmy Goldsmith, Alan Hirschfield participated by telephone in a meeting of the Columbia board of directors, which was called to ratify the reinstatement of Begelman. It was agreed that his return to the studio would be announced the following Monday.

*   *   *

Hirschfield's limousine required the better part of an hour to make its way through the late Friday afternoon traffic to the estate in the London suburbs. Jimmy Goldsmith turned out to be an engaging man—strapping and energetic—whose baldness made him look older than his forty-five years. Tea was served in the study in front of an open fire. Children were about, and it occurred to Hirschfield that Christmas was only nine days away.

Someone—presumably Ira Harris—had sent Goldsmith two of Columbia Pictures Industries' annual financial reports, but it appeared that he had only glanced at them. As an astute businessman, he knew that an annual report contained only a minor portion of the information that one needed before making an investment. Hirschfield spoke for more than an hour about the American entertainment business, about Columbia and its financial recovery, about the Begelman problem, and about the festering enmity at the top of the company. Goldsmith was very interested and made it clear that if he were to invest he would want to purchase all the stock owned or controlled by the Allens and by Matty Rosenhaus—a total of just under 1.5 million shares, or about 18 percent of the company. On the open market the block was worth $30 million, but a single purchaser buying directly from the owners would be expected to pay a premium. The amount of the investment did not faze Goldsmith. He told Hirschfield that he would speak to the Allens, whom he had known for a number of years, on his next trip to New York.

Hirschfield had not had such a cordial and hopeful meeting with anyone in weeks, and he was optimistic when he returned to Claridge's. His mood at dinner with close friends that evening, and in Paris over the weekend, was brighter than it had been in weeks—perhaps since the Tuesday before Thanksgiving in Los Angeles when he and Berte had dined at Ma Maison and toasted the firing of David Begelman.

In his suite at the Plaza Athénée late Sunday morning, Hirschfield met with one of his closest European business acquaintances, David Karr. A shadowy, controversial figure, David Karr had made a fortune in recent years acting as the broker in business deals between the Soviet Union and various corporations in the United States, Europe, and Japan. The fifty-eight-year-old Brooklyn native had worked in the United States as a newspaperman, theatrical producer, public relations man, and hotel manager before moving to Paris in the early sixties. When Allen & Company posted Alan Hirschfield to Paris to establish an office there, he got acquainted with Karr, who then owned both the Plaza Athénée and Georges V hotels. At one time the two men considered going into business together.

David Karr was friendly with a number of leading Democratic politicians in the United States—Edward Kennedy, John Tunney, Alan Cranston, Sargent Shriver, Henry Jackson, and Jerry Brown, among others—and occasionally acted as an informal and secret liaison between the Soviet and U.S. governments on issues such as arms limitation and the emigration of Soviet Jews.

Karr also did business occasionally with Jimmy Goldsmith. He knew of Goldsmith's interest in the motion-picture business, and coincidentally, just before Ira Harris had placed Hirschfield in touch with Goldsmith, David Karr had telephoned former Senator John Tunney to ask about investment opportunities in Hollywood. Having lost his 1976 bid for reelection to the Senate, Tunney had been practicing law and doing business in Los Angeles, and had excellent contacts in the film community. Among the people John Tunney contacted on Karr's behalf was Herbert Allen, with whom Tunney had been very friendly since Allen had contributed to his 1970 Senate campaign. Tunney was generally familiar with the Begelman trouble at Columbia Pictures and thought perhaps the Allens' interest, or even the whole company, might be for sale. Herbert assured him that it was not, and after making a few more inquiries, Tunney reported back to David Karr that there did not appear to be any current opportunities for Jimmy Goldsmith in the motion-picture business in America.

Karr was quite surprised, therefore, when he learned on Sunday, December 18, in Alan Hirschfield's Paris hotel suite of Hirschfield's meeting with Jimmy Goldsmith less than forty-eight hours earlier. Actually, Karr had heard a rumor about the meeting before seeing Hirschfield.

On Monday, David Karr again telephoned John Tunney in Los Angeles.

"Did you know," he asked Tunney, "that Alan Hirschfield is over here talking to Jimmy Goldsmith about buying Columbia Pictures?"

"You must be kidding," Tunney replied.

"No, he met with Jimmy on Friday in London, and I talked to Alan here over the weekend."

"I can't believe it."

"This must be kept confidential."

"Of course," Tunney said, "but I do feel obliged to tell Herbie Allen because of our previous inquiry."

Tunney called Allen in New York. "Herbie, you won't believe what I just found out!"

"What?"

"Alan Hirschfield is in Europe trying to sell Columbia Pictures to Jimmy Goldsmith!"

As information on Hirschfield's secret negotiations with Goldsmith was being flashed quietly from Paris to Los Angeles and back to New York that Monday, Columbia was disseminating a press release about the return of David Begelman.

FOR IMMEDIATE RELEASE

NEW YORK (December 19, 1977)—Columbia Pictures Industries Inc. announced today that David Begelman has been reinstated as President of its Motion Picture and Television Divisions. Mr. Begelman has been on a leave of absence since September 30, 1977, pending completion of an investigation by the Audit Committee of the Board of Directors into a number of unauthorized transactions involving Mr. Begelman and the Company. The investigation established that in a number of separate and unrelated transactions from January 1975 to May 1977, Mr. Begelman obtained through improper means corporate funds in the amount of $61,008 for his personal benefit, and that the emotional problems which prompted these acts, coupled with ongoing therapy, will not impair his continuing effectiveness as an executive.

The release stated that Begelman had repaid the money with interest, together with an additional $23,200, "representing adjustments of travel, entertainment and other expenses." It then quoted Alan Hirschfield:

The Board of Directors and I are pleased that we are able to reach the conclusion that David Begelman shall continue as the President of the Motion Picture and Television Divisions even though he will not serve as a director or officer of the Company.

Our record over the last four years to which David contributed greatly speaks for itself and we all look forward to continued progress.

At Columbia's Paris offices on the rue Troyon Monday morning, Hirschfield encountered Norman Horowitz of the TV division, who was in Paris on business separate from Hirschfield's. They had not spoken privately since the first Sunday in October when Horowitz had been forced to miss an *est* seminar in order to attend Hirschfield's briefing at his hotel bungalow on the imminent suspension of David Begelman. Norman Horowitz, who was in charge of both domestic and international distribution for Columbia Pictures Television, traveled a lot and had been unable to follow closely the unfolding of the Begelman drama. But he felt considerable affection for both Hirschfield and Begelman, and had grown concerned about both men, especially during the past two weeks as the studio rumors of Begelman's fate changed almost daily. Seizing the opportunity in Paris, Norman Horowitz took Hirschfield into a vacant office and closed the door.

"Alan, what the fuck is going on?"

"He's coming back."

"He's coming back? Is it definite? We can't run our businesses with all this uncertainty! He is, he isn't, he might be, they are, they aren't!"

"Well, it won't be uncertain much longer. The release goes out today, as a matter of fact." Hirschfield sank into a chair and looked at Horowitz. "Norman, they're killing me," he said. "The board won't let me make a fucking decision. Those cocksuckers go to David. They review everything with David. I've got him in my life whether he's officially in the company or not. So I might just as well have him in the company where I can handle him better. I had no choice. They wouldn't let me run the company without Begelman."

"Holy shit!" said Norman Horowitz.

Oblivious to the compromise of the secrecy of his negotiations with Jimmy Goldsmith, Alan and Berte enjoyed another festive evening. Alan was feted at a large cocktail party at Ledoyen attended by many celebrities of the French film community, including François Truffaut, who had an important role in *Close Encounters of the Third Kind*. As flashbulbs popped, the Hirschfields shook upwards

of two hundred hands. Later in the evening Alan hosted a dinner for
fifty in a private room at Lasserre. He and Berte flew back to New
York the next day.

> In an unprecedented event in motion picture business history,
> wrote Art Murphy in Tuesday's *Variety*, David Begelman has
> been reinstated as president of Columbia Pictures and Columbia
> Television, though he'll not return as an exec or director of the
> parent, Columbia Pictures Industries.
>
> Emotional problems and current psych-therapy are indicated
> in the formal announcement of his reinstatement. . . . When
> Begelman was first suspended on full pay, his chances of
> reinstatement were deemed virtually non-existent. Although he
> had a long-term contract, he certainly was not in a position of
> strength as to negotiating a settlement. But a combination of
> factors—including widespread support of many board members
> and much industry support, . . . in time worked to Begelman's
> advantage. . . .
>
> Begelman quite early in the affair freely conceded that some
> of his actions might be debatable as to their judiciousness and
> propriety, and Hollywood has raged with assorted rumors as to
> what the facts were. . . .

Murphy's article specified neither the rumors nor the facts, but
The Wall Street Journal, in a lengthy article that day, reported that
Begelman's "improper means" of obtaining money to which the
press release referred actually involved the forgery of checks and the
use of the names of Cliff Robertson and Martin Ritt. Coming eleven
weeks after the announcement of Begelman's suspension, the *Journal*
article was the first public disclosure that what Columbia Pictures
first had called "unauthorized financial transactions," and then labeled "improper means," were in fact outright embezzlements and
forgeries. The *Journal* also described the fight within the board of
directors, named Ray Stark as Begelman's principal supporter outside the company, disclosed the involvement of the police and the
Securities and Exchange Commission, and identified Begelman's
psychiatrist, Dr. Judd Marmor.

Cliff Robertson and Dina Merrill sat in their UN Plaza apartment
thirty floors above the East River with *The Wall Street Journal*

article spread before them. To Cliff Robertson, Columbia's reinstatement of Begelman not only was a brazen flaunting of justice, but also a deep insult to Cliff personally. Although it had been foreshadowed by Dina's encounter with Terry Allen Kramer at "21" and although Cliff had doubted that Columbia's internal investigation was sufficiently thorough or independent, he still found it difficult to believe that a major U.S. corporation, in the wake of Watergate and widespread corporate bribery scandals, would knowingly employ an embezzler as one of its highest officers, whatever the extenuating circumstances. Cliff, moreover, was embittered and demoralized by his own apparent impotence in galvanizing law enforcement authorities to action. The Los Angeles police. The Burbank police. The Beverly Hills police. The FBI. After he had lost faith in the Los Angeles authorities, the FBI had seemed genuinely concerned. What had it been doing for three months?

Cliff felt like a fool. He had exposed a criminal. He had put the criminal's employer on notice, as well as four law enforcement agencies. Nothing had been done. No, that wasn't quite correct. Something had been done. The criminal's company had placed him on "leave of absence," and "investigated." Not only had the inquiry confirmed Cliff's original allegation. It had found other embezzlements as well—"a number of separate and unrelated transactions," the press release called them. Then, in an extraordinary display of brazenness, the company had simply restored the criminal to his job, one of the most important in show business.

Begelman and the rest of the Columbia people must really be chortling at me, Cliff thought. He was enraged.

Should he just drop the whole thing? Did he have any other recourse?

Cliff had thought about the press, but he had promised Leo Jaffe and others that he would not discuss the matter publicly. He had kept his promise. But then his name, along with an account of Begelman's crimes, suddenly appears in *The Wall Street Journal*. The secrecy which Columbia had managed to preserve for three months was broken. It seemed to Cliff that his promise of silence therefore was moot.

Cliff thought about Watergate and *The Washington Post*. *Washington: Behind Closed Doors* had just been on television. Cliff had liked the film and was proud to have been a part of it.

In complete agreement with all of his thoughts and feelings, Dina picked up the telephone and called her long-time friend Katharine Graham, the chairman of the board and publisher of *The Washington Post*.

"Cliff has a story to tell your newspaper, Kay."

THIRTY-SEVEN

When Hirschfield arrived at his office Wednesday morning, having returned the night before from Paris, he was confronted immediately by Leo Jaffe. "Herbert is looking for you," Jaffe said. "He's on the warpath about some meeting you supposedly had with Jimmy Goldsmith." Hirschfield looked surprised, then recovered to a neutral stare. "Thanks, I'll call him," he said.

Can't anybody keep a confidence in this world? Hirschfield thought. He considered phoning Ira Harris, or David Karr, or Jimmy Goldsmith, but he knew it was too late. Herbert Allen, indeed, was furious.

"If you want to sell the company, don't you think you have an obligation to talk to me first?" Herbert said. "We came in together, and if we're going to go out, we should go out together."

"I'm not trying to sell the company."

"You talked to Jimmy Goldsmith last Friday and you talked to David Karr over the weekend about selling the company."

"If you'll calm down for five minutes, I'll be happy to tell you what happened. Goldsmith wanted to see me. I had drinks with Ira a couple of weeks ago and told him how unhappy things were in the company. He already knew things were a mess. He suggested that Goldsmith might have an interest in the company. Would I meet with him? I said fine. I met with him. I knew he knew your uncle well. I left it that I would report back to you, and if Goldsmith had any interest and you had any interest, he'd be in touch with you."

"Why did you do it behind my back?"

"I didn't do it behind your back. I was going to brief you. This is my first day back in the office."

"You *did* do it behind my back! You set all these wheels in motion without a word to me. It doesn't make any sense. First of all, it's personally insulting to me. We came in together, and at this stage for you to be trying to sell it out without me is wrong. Just plain wrong! Second of all, it's stupid of you to think you could get by with it. It's a very small world out there."

"I didn't intend to keep it from you. If I'd been trying to pull something like that, I certainly wouldn't have gone to somebody who knows your uncle and your firm. This isn't some Arab mystery man. It's a man who knows your uncle and who certainly would be in touch with him and with you if he had any interest."

"It was underhanded, and it was wrong, and I won't stand for it! And the board won't either. This hasn't done you any good with the board. I've told them about it. It's not a way to repair relationships." Herbert Allen strode from the room.

The Columbia Pictures bureaucracy in Burbank and New York, which had been jolted by the suspension of David Begelman in October, and then enervated by the protracted investigation, was stupefied by Begelman's restoration.

Studio executives and staff members knew by December that his acts were much more serious than questionable expense claims, and many knew, or at least had heard, that he had forged checks and embezzled funds. While many of these people felt affection and sympathy for David, they tended to be somewhat cynical about the psychiatric rationale for his crimes, and they believed, all things considered, that his suspension should be made permanent. "You can rest assured that there is no fucking way that David Begelman is coming back to this company," Alan Hirschfield had told Jim Johnson, the vice president for administration, on the day after Thanksgiving.

When word of Begelman's likely return began spreading the morning after his long Sunday meeting with Hirschfield in Scarsdale, the studio people at first thought it was just another rumor. When the decision was ratified by the board four days later, and announced publicly on Monday, December 19, they were benumbed and, in varying degrees, disoriented. Dan Melnick, John Veitch, Jim Johnson, Eli Horowitz,* Norman Levy, and the others had adjusted to life without David Begelman. Not all of them were morally outraged at Begelman. Not all of them felt that Hirschfield's motives were entirely pure. But they had accepted Begelman's departure as unavoidable, and they looked forward to the naming of a replacement and a return to normalcy at the studio.

Since Hirschfield had gone to Europe for a week, the task of briefing the principal studio people fell to Joe Fischer, who was deeply dismayed himself by Hirschfield's sudden reversal but was resigned to it. Although Fischer was kept from total candor by the secrecy of the boardroom and the extreme sensitivity of certain issues—the controversy over Berte Hirschfield's employment, for instance—he tried, in many lengthy conversations in his New York office and over the phone to California, to convey a sense of the extraordinary pressure on Hirschfield and to convince the staff that reinstatement, in the end, was the only way to end the war. Fischer asked that personal feelings be put aside and that both Hirschfield and Begelman be supported, as they tried to resume normal management of the company. Fischer's entreaties were only partly successful, and by the middle of the week before Christmas, a mood of dispirited resignation cloaked the studio.

The gloom deepened when *The Wall Street Journal* published the details of Begelman's crimes. Outsiders who had fallen for the expense-account rumors began calling their friends at Columbia to apologize and express horror that the studio would reinstate a forger and embezzler. There was further concern when it became known that *The Washington Post* had begun an investigation.

"This is the beginning of a scandal that will never die," Dan Melnick told production vice president Bill Tennant, who secretly had lobbied for Begelman's reinstatement and was one of the few studio people openly pleased by the result.

"Don't be silly," Tennant replied. "It's all over. Nothing can unseat David, because nothing can stop the Rabbit. The Rabbit controls the company. You'd better realize that. None of these New

---

*Eli Horowitz, the senior vice president for business affairs, had left the negotiations in New York on the weekend of December 10–11 believing not only that Begelman would not return as president but also that he probably would not even join the studio as a producer because of the negotiators' inability to reach agreement on his production and consulting arrangements.

York people has ever wrestled with Ray Stark before. They thought he was just this little old man.''

"You wait," Melnick cautioned. "This will never go away."

Begelman's reinstatement angered Allen Adler more than perhaps anyone else in the company. Hirschfield had assured Adler privately in October that Begelman would not return. Though Hirschfield had seemed less sure of himself when they talked in early December about ways of diluting or eliminating Herbert's role in the company, he had given no clue that he was considering reversing his basic decision against Begelman. On the day after the long meeting with Begelman in Scarsdale—the day before Hirschfield flew to London— Adler had urged him to reconsider, and had heard nothing more until the reinstatement was announced a week later. On Wednesday, December 21, Hirschfield's first day back in the office, Adler tried repeatedly through the day to obtain an audience with him. He did not succeed until 6 P.M.

"I just want to ask you a few questions," Adler began. "The first is: how could you do it?"

"In the end, I decided it was the only way to have any chance of healing the wounds and getting on with the running of the company. You saw how they were at the board meeting. Begelman is the president of the studio whether he's called president or consultant."

"Did you do it to save your job?"

"In a sense, yes. The situation isn't going to be helped if I lose my job."

"So what you're saying to me is that you've taken back a man who is a confessed thief, after one meeting at your house, in order to save your job."

"Yes, within the confines of this room, that is the answer."

"Fine, I want you to know that when the dust settles, when it's over, I'm leaving. I cannot work for you any longer. I have no respect for what you've done, and I think inevitably it will blow up in your face."

"I can understand what you're saying, but I can't believe you're saying it. What about all your tough talk about finding an outsider to take over the company. We can't do that if I'm not here."

"Of course, we can. You could lead an effort from outside."

"That would be very difficult. We'd *really* have a war on our hands then. It's more effective if I'm here."

"I can't believe you did this just to save your job."

"Look, I brought this company through one of the more spectacular recoveries on record. You and others helped, but I orchestrated it, and I'm not about to leave just as we reach the peak of our prosperity. I have no interest in being right but out. I plan to stay."

"You've weakened yourself and the company by taking him back. You should have hung in there and fought. You never really went nose to nose with them. If you had, they wouldn't have had a choice. They would have had to back down, and they couldn't have fired you. They wouldn't have dared."

"They would have gotten me eventually, and still might."

"By then you would have had a chance to find outside help. Now you've weakened yourself. It'll be much harder."

"I'm sorry you feel that way. I wish it were different, but it isn't."

The week dwindled toward Christmas. Hirschfield went shopping, took relatively few calls, held relatively few meetings, and tried to avoid the subject of David Begelman. The only substantive business he conducted was concluding arrangements with agent Sam Cohn, who represented the producers of *Annie*, for Columbia Pictures to purchase the motion-picture rights to the show for $9.5 million. It was the highest price ever paid for movie musical rights,* but Alan Hirschfield loved *Annie* and was determined that Columbia would buy it.† He and Cohn also agreed that week on the final details of Columbia's investment in *Dancin'*, the Broadway musical review to be mounted by Bob Fosse, who would delay preparations of *All That Jazz* in order to stage *Dancin'*.

By early Friday afternoon, Christmas parties had begun in each corporate department at 711 Fifth Avenue: business affairs, creative affairs, foreign distribution, accounting, payroll, public relations, and the rest. At Christmas of 1973—Alan Hirschfield's first at the company—he had discovered that the party in the eleventh-floor

---

*If the $5.5 million which Warner Bros. paid for *My Fair Lady* in 1962 were adjusted for inflation to 1977 value, that price would have been higher.

†Had David Begelman been president of the studio through the autumn when the *Annie* deal was negotiated, he would have opposed the purchase and conceivably might have talked Hirschfield out of it. Begelman had seen a preview performance of *Annie* in New York a week before its official Broadway opening. Over a drink at Gallagher's after the show, Begelman told Sam Cohn and producer Lewis Allen that he did not feel *Annie* would convert well to film.

executive suite was substantially more lavish than those held on the other floors. He asked that in subsequent years the other departments be permitted the same food, beverages, and other trappings that the executive suite had. The gesture had endeared Hirschfield to every Columbia employee in the building, and it had become customary for him to visit each of the parties, shaking hands and wishing seasons greetings. Everyone looked forward to those visits. But as he and Joe Fischer made the rounds on Friday, December 23, 1977, the atmosphere was more poignant than celebratory. The idle chatter was a bit awkward, the meeting of eyes a little tentative. Columbia's New York employees generally felt considerable affection for Alan Hirschfield, and still did. But they knew that something bad had happened to their company. Apparently David Begelman had been caught stealing, and Hirschfield, for reasons that remained mysterious, was not going to do anything about it. There had been a lot of angry, cynical talk about the episode in the ranks of the company in recent days. However, the only emotion evident during the Christmas parties, behind the smiles and obligatory conversation, was a wistful sadness.

An even more awkward Christmas party was held that afternoon in the luxuriantly landscaped atrium of the Columbia building at the Burbank Studios. Instead of separate gatherings, the studio threw a single large party to which all employees were invited. There was a live band, lots of food and liquor, and a special guest, added at the last minute, David Begelman. Friday was Begelman's second day back as president. After returning briefly to Los Angeles from New York the previous week, he and Gladyce had flown to Colorado for a vacation and had not come home until Wednesday, December twenty-first.

A few of the senior studio executives gathered in Begelman's office just after noon, in effect to escort him to the party and make him feel as welcome as possible. Sitting around the office before going downstairs, they tried hard to talk and act as if nothing had happened, as if there had been no forgery investigation, as if David had just returned from a routine business trip, as if it were just another relaxed, preholiday Friday afternoon.

Then someone decided it would be better to break the tension with a David Begelman "joke." Hollywood contains more amateur comedians *per capita* than any other community in the world, and the

Begelman affair had spawned a number of jokes, none particularly witty but each good for a chuckle.

"Hey, David, I hear they're going to make a movie about your life."

"Oh, really?"

"Yeah, Cliff Robertson is playing the lead."

The laughter was brittle. To the group's surprise, however, it turned out that Begelman, who had not lost his sense of humor and had a particularly fine sense of black humor, had somehow heard all of the David Begelman jokes and immediately joined the fun.

"How would the Polish government have handled the David Begelman problem?" he asked.

"Just like Columbia Pictures," someone answered.

The laughter was less brittle.

"Free the Beverly Hills One," somebody said.

Louder laughter.

"Well, it looks from now on like Columbia Pictures will be *forging ahead* with David Begelman," somebody else said.

Roaring with laughter, Begelman and the others proceeded down the stairs to the party.

THIRTY-EIGHT

Cliff Robertson told his story to Jack Egan and John Berry of *The Washington Post*, and the *Post* published their article on Sunday, Christmas Day. With a Beverly Hills dateline, the story began:

> From the banquettes of the Polo Lounge bar to the elegant tables at Chasen's restaurant, wherever movie industry people meet this Christmas season, the No. 1 topic of conversation is the surprise reinstatement of David Begelman as head of Columbia Pictures

studio and speculation about what drove him allegedly to embezzle from the company in the first place.

It is a measure of Begelman's renewed power that the subject invariably is discussed in hushed tones, after a quick glance to make sure that nobody will overhear. It is also, says one director, "typical of the fear that permeates this industry."

"One who has been willing to speak out is actor Cliff Robertson . . ." The article contained a lengthy account by Robertson of how he had received the IRS form, communicated with the studio, discovered that Begelman had forged his signature, reported the matter to the police and FBI, and then grown frustrated at the lack of law enforcement action.

"I'm not going to race to the witness stand," Robertson was quoted as saying, "but I don't see how I can avoid it. It'll probably be pretty lonely up there." And he added: "There is a spreading cancer of corruption in Hollywood, of which the Begelman incident is but one example."

The article was sprinkled with other general allegations about Hollywood, mostly anonymous. From a "Hollywood insider": "The producers want David Begelman back. They don't want the boat rocked. A little thing like theft doesn't mean anything in the movie business, because in the movie business, people have been stealing for years." From a "Hollywood director": "Wrong has become right. These powerful guys are just like Nixon was—they simply are not accustomed to being questioned."

Neither the *Washington Post* article nor the *Wall Street Journal* article the previous Tuesday captured much immediate public attention. The articles appeared on inside pages, and newspapers are read with less attention on Christmas, when the *Post* piece came out, than on any other day of the year. The officers and directors of Columbia Pictures and the entertainment community at large, however, were acutely aware of both articles. Having hoped in vain that the *Journal* article would spark no further coverage, Columbia awaited the *Post* story with apprehension. A Columbia employee was assigned to buy the *Post* in Manhattan on Christmas morning and read the article by telephone to Joe Fischer at his New Jersey home. Fischer in turn briefed Hirschfield. The article or gists of it were read that day over dozens of long-distance telephone links to Los Angeles, and between the coasts and several Rocky Mountain ski resorts.

Early the following morning, the telephone rang in a suite in Vail, Colorado, where Cliff Robertson and his daughter, Heather, were staying for several days. It was Ray Stark, calling from his house in Sun Valley, Idaho. Stark assailed Robertson for talking to the *Post* and implored him not to speak further on the matter publicly.

"The SEC was perfectly happy with Columbia's investigation," Stark said. "What's the point of bringing it all out? You don't want to be responsible for a man [Begelman] putting a pistol in his mouth, do you?"

Cliff scoffed at the notion that Begelman might kill himself. After a lengthy conversation, during which Stark did most of the talking, Robertson said he intended to conduct himself precisely "in line with what a citizen should do in this situation. And now I'm going to ring off and go skiing with my daughter." There was a long pause at the other end of the line.

"All right, Cliff. Happy New Year."

During the four-day, quasi-holiday week between Christmas and New Year's, Alan Hirschfield had only three important meetings.

On Tuesday, he submitted to a long interview with Andrew Tobias of *Esquire*. Still sensitive about talking to the press, Hirschfield insisted on talking at Tobias's Central Park West apartment instead of the Columbia offices.

On Wednesday, over lunch at the Harmonie Club, Hirschfield explained the latest Columbia developments to Eric Pleskow, the president of United Artists, and assured Pleskow that Columbia remained interested in affiliating with him and the other top officers who were about to leave UA. Pleskow said that he and his colleagues were hesitant to join a company whose atmosphere was as fractious and lines of authority as murky as Columbia's.

On Thursday, Hirschfield conferred with Herbert Allen—their first meeting in weeks at which neither man yelled at the other. Herbert said that if Alan wanted to repair his relationships with the directors he would have to approach them individually. He could no longer use Herbert as his emissary to the others. Herbert suggested that he start with Matty Rosenhaus, whose anger, Herbert said, was the deepest of that felt by the several alienated directors. Hirschfield said he would think about it. He dreaded meeting privately with Matty Rosenhaus, whom he loathed. At his best, Rosenhaus was a self-righteous buffoon, Hirschfield felt, and he was usually not at his best. But Hirschfield's aides unanimously advised him to see Rosenhaus.

"Look, Alan, you're a charming fellow," Allen Adler said. "Go see Matty. Don't call him in to see you. Go see *him*. Sit on his back lawn. Talk to the man. Hear him out. Let him vent his spleen. It's your only chance."

Joe Fischer said, "So he's an asshole. What else is new? What you have to do is stop treating him like an asshole. You've eaten a lot of shit already. It won't hurt you to eat a little more. It might help put the lid on."

Clive Davis said, "You've got to be able to get your point across to these people individually. From every discussion I've had with them, the board doesn't know you as you really are. Their picture of you is erroneous. It's very clear that the way they see you is not the way you are. You've got to make every effort, not just at board meetings when they're massed and you're there with your colleagues, to meet with them individually, to try to see whether there are any chinks in their armor, to see whether there's any opportunity."

Hirschfield telephoned Rosenhaus at his winter home in Florida on Tuesday afternoon, January 3, and arranged to visit him there the following Monday.

From his call to Rosenhaus he went immediately into a meeting with financial columnist Dan Dorfman, whose calls he had been avoiding. Dorfman was preparing an article on the Begelman affair for the coming week's *New York* magazine and had obtained statements from Rosenhaus, Allen, and other directors that were highly critical of Hirschfield. He wanted Hirschfield's side of the story.

"There was an honest disagreement over the propriety of bringing Begelman back," Hirschfield said. "I think I've done a good job. This company's record speaks for itself. If what you say is true, I'm sorry to hear it, I'm sorry they're airing it in public."

Rona Barrett had been on vacation during the holiday period and thus had not reported on David Begelman's reinstatement or the revelation of his forgeries.* Her last broadcast on Begelman had been in late November when she predicted that Columbia would

---

*Asked later why she did not break the story of the forgeries, Barrett said she had learned of the Cliff Robertson forgery around December 1 but had been unable to "get proof" and therefore was prohibited by ABC's lawyers from using the story.

make Begelman a producer, "exonerate" him of wrongdoing, but by not reinstating him, leave the studio "without any strong hand at the helm." Her next comments came on Tuesday, January 3.

> A comic scenario is currently being played out in the corporate corridors of Columbia Pictures that would make a dandy little film farce, should any producer like to do to movies what *Network* did to television. The situation in question centers around the return of David Begelman to the presidency of Columbia Pictures. His recent reinstatement has caused executives who abandoned support of Begelman during the controversy to quickly learn some new routines now that all has been forgiven. The name of the game at Columbia now is: tell David we love him—and the refrain reads: and we always did. Just how many can fool some of the people enough of the time remains to be seen. What is for certain is that over the next few weeks and months, no less than seven major periodicals are planning in-depth reports on Begelman, the man and his machinations. Therefore, don't look for the heat to be out of this kitchen yet.

Having been scooped by *The Wall Street Journal* and *The Washington Post*, *The New York Times* was groping for an original approach to the Begelman story. The financial editors, national editors, and editors of the Sunday magazine all were mulling over the Columbia developments. Then one of the editors of the magazine, Lynda Obst, got an idea. Obst, twenty-seven years old, was one of several new editors the *Times* had hired a year earlier to rejuvenate its tired, staid magazine. A doctoral candidate in psychology at Columbia University, Obst had edited the *Rolling Stone* history of the sixties and contributed the text for the Broadway musical show *Beatlemania* before joining the *Times*. Hollywood was one of her beats on the magazine, and having edited a cover story in the summer of 1977 called "The New Tycoons of Hollywood," she had taken a special interest in the Begelman case. Just after Christmas, while at a party at the home of literary lawyer and agent Morton Janklow, Obst overheard a conversation about the strife within the board of directors of Columbia Pictures over the Begelman affair. From the conversation she inferred that the most important aspect of the story was what had happened in New York, not what had happened in Hollywood, and it was the "New York angle" that the *Times* magazine chose to pursue.

To research and write the article under Obst's supervision, the *Times* retained Lucian K. Truscott, IV, a young free-lance journalist best known for his extensive writing (much of it in *The Village Voice*) about West Point and the problems he had had as a cadet there. Like many of the so-called (and inaptly labeled) "new journalists," Lucian Truscott liked his audiences to feel that he was revealing himself completely.

On his Army career:

"I fell apart as a leader and as a man. I began drinking heavily and eating huge quantities of mescaline and methamphetamine. I guess I had problems with authority figures all my life, and in the Army, the problems got worse, not better."

On the Ali-Frazier fight:

"I hate fight fans. They are liars and cheats and thieves and murderers and chickenshitted, lowlife, contemptible sons of bitches. Worst of all, they are just plain dishonest, which is probably the most revealing comment you can make about their despicable souls. I am one of them. . . ."

On journalism:

"I have a reputation in the journalism business for moving fast and loose. . . . Everything I write I filter through my own pock-marked psyche. You have a right to read me as well as my words."

In early January of 1978, after completing a novel about West Point, Lucian Truscott turned his "pockmarked psyche" to the Columbia Pictures scandal on behalf of *The New York Times*. It was an assignment that the *Times* would come to regret.

Had Columbia Pictures not restored David Begelman to the presidency of the studio, and had the press not exposed Begelman's acts as forgery and embezzlement rather than questionable expense-account claims, it is likely that the interest of law-enforcement agencies in the Begelman case would have waned and eventually disappeared. Columbia—informally, at least—had declined to prosecute; it did not want to call any more attention to the matter than was absolutely necessary. And Begelman had repaid the money. Therefore, without a complaining victim, Detectives Joyce Silvey in Beverly Hills and Robert Elias in Burbank were content to defer action for the time being and let the Securities and Exchange Commission monitor the case. The SEC, in turn, was content to let Columbia's outside lawyers and accountants conduct their own investigation without interference. The SEC and the two police departments (like law-enforcement agencies generally) were swamped with fraud cases involving seriously aggrieved victims and massive amounts of money, and felt compelled to allocate their meager investigative resources accordingly. Moreover, there was a tacit assumption among the few law officers familiar with the Begelman case that Columbia Pictures, knowing what it knew, would not reinstate Begelman.

However, when the company did reinstate him, and when the first press accounts indicated that law-enforcement agencies might have been negligent, the case for the first time attracted the attention of high officials of the Los Angeles County District Attorney's office, who in turn queried the police. Like everyone else, law enforcement people hate bad publicity. Detectives Silvey and Elias determined that the Burbank Police had primary jurisdiction, and on Tuesday, January 3, Elias telephoned Columbia Pictures in New York and asked for a formal letter stating whether it wanted to prosecute. Elias also called Begelman's lawyer, Frank Rothman, who drove to Burbank that same day and promised Elias that Begelman would cooperate with any police investigation.

The SEC's interest was heightened, as well. The agency's director of enforcement, Stanley Sporkin, previously had not intervened in the case personally. Columbia's lawyers had dealt with Sporkin's aides. But the reinstatement and accompanying publicity caught Sporkin's eye, and he asked for a private, informal meeting with Alan Hirschfield. On Wednesday, the day after Rothman and Elias met in Burbank, Hirschfield flew to Washington with Todd Lang and Peter Gruenberger and spent three hours briefing Sporkin, who was interested primarily in the pressures that had induced Hirschfield to return Begelman to his job. Hirschfield explained the circumstances. Sporkin said that the SEC might have to launch its own investigation.

On Friday, Leo Jaffe dispatched a letter to Detective Elias in California. "Columbia Pictures Industries Inc. has no intention of filing charges against or in any way seeking prosecution of David Begelman. . . ."

Hirschfield, at lunch with Clive Davis at the Palm Court of the Plaza, ruminated about how he might induce an outsider to make a bid for the Allens' share of Columbia Pictures. "I know I can't deal with this situation over the long haul,'' Hirschfield said. "It's a makeshift arrangement. I know in my heart that I can't live with these people permanently.''

"When the emotion dies down it might be livable," Davis advised. "You can't tell at this point. It's too soon. It's too fresh."

"You don't have to put up with what I do on a daily basis," Hirschfield said.

Back in his office, Hirschfield met with Jeanie Kasindorf of *New West*. He had been avoiding her calls from Los Angeles, but she had flown to New York and had interviewed Herbert Allen, among others. Knowing that the board members had given interviews to Dan Dorfman, Hirschfield decided to see Kasindorf. She also had talked with Ray Stark, who had told friends that he had "charmed her out of her pants." Hirschfield found it difficult to believe that the directors and Stark would renew their war with him, and surely not in public print, but he felt a growing need to protect himself.

THIRTY-NINE

Alan Hirschfield buckled himself into his seat on the Monday morning National Airlines flight to Miami and immediately opened *New York* magazine.

INSIDE THE SCANDAL AT COLUMBIA PICTURES: HIRSCHFIELD IN TROUBLE said the headline on Dan Dorfman's article.

The whole movie industry and probably half of Wall Street continue to talk about one man—David Begelman. In an astonishing move, the board of Columbia Pictures Industries recently reinstated the flamboyant 56-year-old Begelman as president of the [studio] after he stole more than $60,000 from the company. But by focusing solely on Begelman, everybody is overlooking an amazing twist to the Columbia story: Begelman's boss, Alan

J. Hirschfield, the president and chief executive officer of the parent company, may himself be bounced out of Columbia long before the final script is written on the bizarre Begelman affair.

The article appalled Hirschfield. The directors' comments vilified him even more than Dorfman had indicated they would. Worse, the article seemed to indicate that the Columbia board—far from trying to close the rift with Hirschfield—was determined to inflame the fight to a new level of intensity, by airing its grievances against him at length in public.

Hirschfield is reported to have fed the board half-truths and innuendos in an effort to exaggerate the extent of Begelman's guilt [and] is reported to have leaked information to people in the entertainment field about Begelman's problems even before they had been disclosed publicly. . . .

Hirschfield's motivations? Sources close to the board say that "Hirschfield wanted to bury Begelman because he also wanted to run the studio; it's that simple." It may well be, of course, that Hirschfield acted out of strong moral convictions in pushing for Begelman's ouster. After all, there's no denying that Begelman's acts were clearly criminal offenses. . . . If Hirschfield did act out of moral conviction, however, Matthew (Matty) Rosenhaus, for one, doesn't believe it. "If you want my frank opinion," said Rosenhaus, "the answer is no. The reasons Hirschfield gave for his decision didn't cut ice with me. But don't ask me to psychoanalyze Hirschfield's motivations. If I thought Begelman was a thief, I wouldn't have him around Columbia. But we're not defending a thief, but a sick man who did some stupid things . . . who had psychological problems that have now been corrected . . . [Hirschfield] no longer enjoys the full confidence of the board, myself included, and he knows it."

Dorfman quoted an unnamed board member as saying: "If Hirschfield's contract were up for renewal today, there's no way he would be rehired as chief executive, because too many people here don't trust him."

Though he lacks the confidence of the board, Hirschfield is not without support in the business community in his opposition to Begelman's reinstatement. For example, the chief executive of one of the classiest companies in the country told me that had he been on the Columbia board he would have moved to fire Hirschfield if he had tried to bring back Begelman. "What Columbia did was to give every corporation a black eye, to make a mockery out of ethical standards for business."

And from a source very close to Hirschfield: "Alan's problem is that he refuses to be Herbie Allen's puppet anymore. Alan's grown up, but the people at Allen & Company want him to act like he's still in the crib. He rolled over and played dead by taking back Begelman . . ."

Although it included only two innocuous quotes attributed to Herbert Allen, the article obviously reflected his views as well as Rosenhaus's. Hirschfield telephoned Allen from the Miami airport and assailed him for talking to Dorfman. Allen claimed that Dorfman had "misquoted" some people he had talked to, and had taken other statements "out of context."

"Sure, Herbert, tell me about it," Hirschfield said. "And furthermore, what's the point of going to see Matty after he's said these things about me publicly."

"There's no question that Matty is steamed at you. That's why you're there—to talk to him directly and settle your differences."

"This is a helluva way to greet somebody you want to make peace with," Hirschfield replied.

At the Rosenhaus estate on Biscayne Bay, Matty greeted Alan cordially. Lunch was served, and then the two men settled on a terrace overlooking the bay. The blue water and a dozen white sails reflected a bright sun, which tempered a cool breeze.

Instead of mentioning the Dan Dorfman article, Hirschfield proceeded to the substance of his differences with the board of directors.

"Well, Matty, this has been a very unpleasant situation for all concerned. I think your feelings have been clearly expressed. You seem to have no confidence in me or my management. I felt that if I could come down, and we could at least make an attempt to clear the air, it would be in everybody's best interest to do so. I make no apologies for what's been done. I was very forthright in my feelings about what to do with David, and you were very forthright in your feelings. I object to some of the tactics that were used; I don't think I was dealt with fairly. But I really can't blame you for a lot of that, and if I've gone astray, or done something that lost your confidence, I'd like to know it. I feel that from the time we first met four and a half years ago I have fulfilled every commitment that I've made to you in terms of what would be done with this company, and I think we've all succeeded beyond our greatest expectations. You have been the primary beneficiary of all this because you, as the largest stockholder, had a stock that was nearly worthless, and today is worth many millions of dollars. And it will be worth many millions of dollars more if we can be left to continue the job of building this company. The main reason that I decided to bring David back was that there was no other way that I saw that I could manage the company. It was an effort to bind up the wounds and see if we couldn't get the company going again. I want to do whatever is necessary to try to regain your confidence. If there is something that is troubling you, I'd like to know it so that we can deal with it.''

"I appreciate your coming down," Rosenhaus said. "I know it took a lot on your part to get on the plane and come down, and I do appreciate it. But I want you to know that the basic problem is that I simply don't trust you. I've never trusted you. You're a smooth talker, and you're a good salesman. God knows, you're one of the best salesmen I've ever seen. You can sell anything when you want to, when you put your mind to it. But I don't trust salesmen. You remind me of a man who worked for me several years ago. He was a publicity guy. He once doublecrossed me, and I caught him. I never forgot it. And you remind me of him. And the main reason I don't trust you is that you are a disloyal person. You've been disloyal to your best friend.''

"Who's that?"

"You've been disloyal to Herbert."

"Well, Matty, let me set the record straight. Herbert's been a friend, but not a particularly close one, and certainly never a best friend.''

"Well, he brought you into this company when you needed a job.''

"What do you mean, needed a job?"

"You didn't know anything about the entertainment business, but Herbert brought you in because you needed a job. Herbert's a good boy, a fine boy, and I didn't argue very much because I figured

Herbert would do most of the work, and at least you'd have a job. And after he does all that for you, you turn around in this situation and are disloyal to him.''

Hirschfield was shocked. ''Matty, this may come as a surprise to you, but I was gainfully employed at that time. I certainly didn't need a job. In addition to which I had a background in the entertainment business, and had a contribution to make at Columbia. And if you think Herbert's been running the company for the last four and a half years you're very much under the wrong impression of what's been going on here.''

''No, I recognize what you've done. You've brought in some good people. I like Clive. He's a good man.''

''Matty, I also brought in David Begelman if you'll recall.''

''No, that was Ray Stark. Ray Stark is the best friend this company has. He's responsible for Begelman, and he's responsible for most of our success. But you've been disloyal, not only to Herbert, but to Ray and to David. I don't like disloyal people, Alan. Loyalty is the most important thing in life. This country was founded on loyalty. It's what makes the country work, it's what makes business work, it's what makes life work. And you've been disloyal to your friends.''

''Well, Matty, what about loyalty to the shareholders of the company. That's where I feel my responsibilities lie. They're the people to whom we're all ultimately responsible. What about them?''

''I don't worry about them. The first thing is to be loyal to your friends. The company will do fine. Begelman was your friend, and you were disloyal to him. You didn't back him up when he needed it. When the man was down, when he was lying in the gutter, you kicked him. The first thing you wanted to do was to get rid of him.''

''The first thing I did, Matty, was *not* get rid of him. That's probably what I should have done. But because of my feelings for the man, my sympathies, I chose not to fire him the first day. We all tried to give David a chance. But in my wildest dreams, I didn't think the board would want to bring him back. We're just beginning to feel the consequences of bringing him back. Look what the press is doing.''

''No, if you support him everything will be fine. It will be great. And if you had supported him from the first day, there wouldn't have been any problem.''

''Well, that's wishful thinking.''

"It's the truth."

Hirschfield felt disoriented. He was gazing out at a scene of tranquility and surpassing beauty—blue water and sky, white sails, and lush green tropical foliage—and at the same time listening to the incoherent ramblings of a misinformed man who didn't trust him and was capable of destroying him.

"I'm very distressed that you don't trust me, Matty. I don't think I've done anything to engender your mistrust." Hirschfield then reviewed Columbia's remarkable recovery and reiterated his reasons for opposing the reinstatement of Begelman. "Loyalty to individuals can go only so far. In the end, in a situation like this, you have to be loyal to the company at large, its shareholders, and loyal to your own principles of right and wrong."

"Well, Alan, you're a great salesman. If I sat here and listened to you all day, you could probably convince me. You've always been able to turn my head. You're a smoothy. But you've got a lot to learn about the world, you've got a lot to learn about loyalty, you've got a lot to learn about dealing with people. As far as I'm concerned you're on trial. I'm willing to keep an open mind. People will have confidence in you if you're out there leading the company the way you're capable of leading."

"I can't lead without your support and the support of the board."

"You'll have to earn our support."

The necessity for Hirschfield to catch an early evening flight to Los Angeles mercifully enabled him to end the conversation. Although he tried on the plane to concentrate on his briefcase full of work, he could not rid his mind of the picture of sitting in the sun on the spectacular seaside veranda and hearing a flushed, angry Matty Rosenhaus accuse him of being dishonest, untrustworthy, disloyal, and even unemployable except through the charity of his "best friend," Herbert Allen. Having begun the day reading in *New York* magazine that he was a liar and a character assassin who wanted to "bury Begelman" so he himself could "go Hollywood," Hirschfield found it all too much to absorb and analyze rationally. The board members, it seemed to Hirschfield, had proven to be the worst kind of bullies. He kept trying to appease them. They kept reaffirming, in progressively more dramatic fashion, that they were bullies. They had proven it again that Monday. But he was determined not to give up. He had to buy more time.

His solitude was broken by another passenger in the first-class cabin, Dino De Laurentiis, whom Alan knew casually but had not seen for a couple of months.

"I read that David is-a back with-a you," De Laurentiis said. "That's a-nice. I didn't understand the whole hullabaloo, but it's a-good that he's back. He's a good man."

"Yes, Dino, we're very happy that everything worked out," Alan said.

In Los Angeles, where Hirschfeld last had been on a bright, warm day in late November, winter had begun in earnest. His Miami flight landed at LAX in a chilly rain, which persisted through Tuesday. Joe Fischer had flown out from New York, and the meetings they held at the studio that week were notable less for substance than for mood.

The studio twitched with tension.

David Begelman had been back in his office less than three weeks, two of which were slowed by holidays. While retaining his sleek, controlled demeanor, he propelled himself through a packed schedule of meetings and other activities, determined to appear worthy of what had come to be perceived as an extraordinary if not bizarre gesture of support by his employer. His underlings mustered a kind of brittle ebullience in his presence. Privately and among themselves, however, they fretted about how his unexpected return, and the tangle of circumstances that lay behind it, would affect their relationships with him and with each other. There was unspoken tension, for example, between Begelman and Dan Melnick, who had quietly supported Begelman's ouster; and between Melnick and production vice president Bill Tennant, who had schemed ardently for Begelman's reinstatement.

The arrival of Hirschfeld naturally heightened the tension. The reversal of his decision on Begelman had bewildered the studio people, and now they had been bewildered again by the Columbia board of directors' public pillorying of Hirschfeld in *New York* magazine. Though he continued to benefit from a considerable reservoir of affection among the staff, no one knew what to say to him or how to react to him. His authority was in doubt. No one knew whether he was truly in command.

Hirschfeld had lunch on Wednesday with Ray Stark. Like his mission to Miami to see Rosenhaus, the meeting with Stark was a peace overture made at the suggestion of Herbert Allen, who had told Hirschfield that it would be necessary for him to repair his relationships with each of the board members individually. Since Stark wielded at least as much power over the company as most board members, he was in the same category. Hirschfield, of course, had grown to hate these men—Stark, in particular—and it was difficult for him to feign even a modicum of good will. He held Stark personally responsible for much of the pressure to reinstate Begelman and had assailed Stark many times in conversations with others. He and Stark had talked occasionally by phone but had not met privately since late October. In the same setting as that meeting, Chow's Kosherama Deli, just off the Burbank lot, Stark was being both magnanimous and nonchalant.

Hirschfield certainly had made a wise decision, Stark said, in bringing Begelman back into the company. What Alan should do now is forget the past, give David his full support, make peace with the board of directors, and get on with the important business of the company.

"How do you expect me to forget the despicable things that were done to me?" Hirschfield asked.

"Put it in perspective, Alan. It was nothing personal. It was like a war. All's fair in war. But once it's over, it's over. You'll drive yourself crazy by dwelling on it. We all have to get on with our lives. A year from now, or sooner, we'll all be laughing about this."

"What about the board's responsibility for making peace? What am I supposed to do when the board calls me a liar in print, and says I'm untrustworthy and am on probation?"

"Just let it roll off your back. It's only a magazine article. We all have things written about us that we don't like."

"There's more coming."

"Forget it. It'll all blow over in two weeks. It'll be like yesterday's newspaper. Doesn't mean a thing."

"We'll see."

Hirschfield, Begelman, and Fischer talked through that afternoon and into the evening at the studio about *California Suite*, which Neil Simon had adapted from his play, and which Ray Stark was producing for Columbia. Despite the potential appeal of the film's cast—Jane Fonda, Alan Alda, Walter Matthau, Richard Pryor, Michael Caine, and Maggie Smith—Hirschfield questioned whether the film stood much chance of making a profit and posed the idea of selling a half interest in *California Suite* to another studio. But Begelman, who had considerable faith in the project, staunchly opposed dividing it. They argued until nearly eight o'clock and decided to continue over dinner.

Hirschfield wanted to avoid the main-line Beverly Hills restaurants where they inevitably would be seen and interrupted by acquaintances in the industry. Everyone in town was gossiping about whether Begelman and Hirschfield truly were reconciled. Hoping to attract a minimum of attention, they went to the Beverly Hills Hotel's main dining room, recently redecorated and renamed The Coterie. The Coterie served some of the finest food in Los Angeles, but unlike its sister establishment across the lobby, the Polo Lounge, where anonymity was impossible, The Coterie had never acquired the cachet of an official movie industry hangout. The odds of dining undisturbed, therefore, were greater.

Bored with *California Suite*, Hirschfield began complaining about his fight with the board and Matty Rosenhaus in particular.

"Matty says he doesn't trust me. He said to me, 'I never trusted you, Alan, from the day you came to this company. I never trusted you.' How could Matty say a thing like that to me?"

"Well," said Begelman, "attribute a lot of it to emotion and to overheating."

"It's more than that," Hirschfield said. "He's had a chance to cool off. Instead he's turning up the heat, saying those things in *New York* magazine."

"Alan, I don't know what passed between you and Matty," Begelman said, "but I know what must pass between you in order for this to be resolved. You've got to make a speech to Matty that goes something like this: 'This has been a time for which no textbook has ever been written. Perhaps no one has acted as well as one would have liked, given all the circumstances, but we must forget the events of the recent past. We must wipe the slate clean. We must start anew, refreshed, and renew our labors for the company with the same amount of trust and resolution that we had when we all came together in the late summer of 1973, and continue to do our good work for this company!' If you make that speech, I can't imagine a reasonable man in the world who won't say, 'Amen, okay, done!' "

"Matty's not a reasonable man."

"He's not so unreasonable that he wouldn't respond to a plea such as that," David said. "I can almost guarantee it. In fact, I'll set it up. When I'm in New York next week, I'll make it a point to meet with Matty and create the environment in which that speech can be made."

"You're underestimating the depths of their feelings," Alan said.

"No, I know their feelings are deep. They feel you misled them all the way through the investigation, and you did. People had reason to believe by the things you said or implied that you were going to be open-minded. If you were going to be open-minded, then they felt that, as a reasonable man, you were available for persuasion. But it turned out that your mind was made up all along. And yet you never let on that it was made up."

"It wasn't made up until all the evidence was in," Hirschfield said.

Warming to his subject, Begelman continued with his own speech that he had been waiting for months to make.

"The one thing you were never able to say to me, Alan, man to man, was 'David, I don't want you back. Period.' Nicer than that, but clearly, in words that were unmistakable. They might have been sympathetic or commiserating words, but unequivocal. And you never said that to me. You never said that to me on the day I was placed on leave of absence. You never said that after the board meeting in November when you apparently indicated to the board that you were leaning against me. We had breakfast the next morning, and you gave me reason to hope there was a chance. If you had said, on the advent of my leave of absence, 'We're going to go through this investigation because we have an obligation to our shareholders and to the Securities and Exchange Commission. I pray it isn't Equity Funding, and I pray we know most of what there is to know. If it's this and no more, then, in consideration of your seeking psychiatric assistance, in consideration of your past service to this company, which has been extraordinary, in consideration of your ability to render further service to this company, we will make an arrangement which will see you self-employed as an independent producer making pictures for Columbia so that your talents and abilities will not be lost to Columbia. But under no circumstances are you coming back to Columbia.' If you had said that, it would have been a *clear signal* to everyone, to me, but more important, to your associates, to Herbert, and to Matty. And none of this brouhaha would have gotten started. But you never said that.''

"Yeah, that was our original mistake," Fischer agreed.

"You never said that," Begelman continued, "and therefore, everybody else assumed the option of reinstatement was open, and they're thinking, okay, we'll go through this investigation, and when we come out of it, we'll see everything laid on the table, and if we find nothing of any substance that is new, we'll talk it through, with the distinct possibility that David can come back to the company. You allowed them to believe that you were part of that approach to the problem."

"I was," Alan said.

"Well, it didn't appear so in the end. The only new thing that was found was Ritt, which was not of such a different character as to make it a new ball game. It was the same ball game, a ball game you had a fix on. And yet you then surprised everybody by turning out to be adamant, which would have been fine had you made your position clear at the outset. But since you did not make your position clear, the board, in the end, felt you had led them on a merry chase. They felt betrayed."

Hirschfield shrugged, sighed, and rolled his eyes. He did not have the energy to respond. Chief executive officers had fired line officers for comments far less blunt and critical than Begelman had just uttered. But both men knew that much of Hirschfield's authority as chief executive officer had been eroded by the events of recent weeks. As a practical matter, Hirschfield had been stripped of a number of the prerogatives he once had had, including the prerogative of firing David Begelman.

Depressed, Hirschfield flew back to New York Thursday and did not go to the office until Monday.

FORTY

In order for any event, public or private, to become a major news story, a story that dominates the media for weeks or months, the event and the coverage of the event must acquire a key ingredient. Without that ingredient, the story drifts and eventually withers. The ingredient is reaction—broad public reaction. Until there is reaction, either in the form of growing attention in the press, or visible public attention of other kinds, the event is like an airplane moving along an endless runway, unable to get up enough speed to take off. Some events are sufficiently momentous to compel substantial and varied reaction from the time they occur until far into the future. Just as often, though, reaction develops gradually, and then is sharply accelerated by some form of catalyst—a particular news article or a subsequent event.

For months after *The Washington Post* began reporting the Watergate scandal, reaction was tentative and grew gradually. Then there were two catalysts: the attention devoted to the story by the CBS evening news with Walter Cronkite, which introduced it to a substantially larger audience than was reached by *The Washington Post*, and the attitude of Judge John J. Sirica, which induced a number of people to tell more of the truth than they previously had been disposed to tell.

In the case of the Columbia Pictures scandal—a less cosmic event than Watergate to be sure, but still the focus of a major media onslaught—one of the most important catalysts was an article by syndicated gossip columnist Liz Smith, published in the New York *Daily News* and about sixty other newspapers on the morning of Thursday, January 12, 1978.

Most reactions to developments in the Begelman affair until that time had reverberated inside the entertainment and business communities. *The Wall Street Journal*'s revelation on December 20 that Begelman had forged checks and embezzled funds had shocked many in Hollywood and on Wall Street but attracted little attention elsewhere. *The Washington Post*'s long interview with Cliff Robertson, published on Christmas, took several days to circulate because of the *Post*'s negligible distribution in Los Angeles and New York, and low newspaper readership in general over the holiday period. The *Journal* and *Post* pieces, moreover, were published on inside pages, reflecting the editors' judgments that the Begelman story was not front-page news.* The *Los Angeles Times*, which had the resources to cover Hollywood better than any other publication but never had done so, waited until Friday, December 30, and then ran, deep inside the paper, a severely truncated reprint of the previous Sunday's *Washington Post* story. Even fewer people saw the *Times* reprint than had seen the *Post* original.

Rona Barrett, with all of her fame, and *Variety*'s Art Murphy, with all of his prominence as a trade journalist inside the industry, were not well positioned to be catalysts because they were so closely identified with Hollywood that whatever they said or wrote tended to be perceived only as Hollywood reacting to itself.

As the new year began, therefore, the Columbia Pictures story was still on the runway and still not moving fast enough to take off. Dan Dorfman's article in *New York* magazine January 9 gave the story a push. Because of the nature of its readers, *New York*, the first and flashiest of the new breed of city and regional magazines, exerts an influence substantially greater than its modest circulation would indicate. *New York* is seen by just about everyone who runs the international communications and media institutions headquartered in New York City. Whether they admitted it or not, the editors of *The New York Times*, *Time*, *Newsweek*, the Associated Press and United Press International, as well as executives of the television networks, motion-picture companies, talent agencies, book publishers, and the advertising community, used *New York* magazine (among other things) as a tip sheet, a loose guide to what's hot and trendy. *New York*, therefore, was automatically influential because, week in and week out, it touched the perceptions of this potent group of people.

Washington Post publisher Katharine Graham, who had initiated the *Post* story after Dina-Merrill's call, was surprised on Christmas morning to find that her editors had not played the story on page 1.

But though the Dorfman article on Monday added momentum to the Columbia story, it was Liz Smith on Thursday who lifted it off the ground. After her syndicated column was begun in 1976, Liz Smith quickly had become the leading newspaper gossip columnist in America and a prime practitioner of the new form of gossip journalism that burgeoned in the seventies and effectively eclipsed the Hedda Hopper-Walter Winchell school of gossip that had flourished in past decades and lived on in publications less respectable and powerful than the New York *Daily News*. Unlike the old columnists, Liz Smith wrote with a droll sense of humor and a lack of malice. She did not take herself or her work more seriously than the subject merited, but she did strive for accuracy, and on the few occasions when she erred, she corrected herself openly. A skilled reporter by any standard, Smith consistently broke major news stories—not only show-business stories but also stories from other fields such as politics and publishing. Thus, she had helped to redefine gossip, elevate it to a new level of respectability, and broaden the audience for it. And even though she wrote mostly about entertainment and personalities, she was based in New York and did not suffer from the close identification with Hollywood that sometimes worked to the disadvantage of Rona Barrett. By the late seventies, Liz Smith's column was very influential and, in a way, essential. In much the way that a change in U.S. foreign policy was not certified as major news until it had appeared in *The New York Times*, and the bankruptcy of Penn Central was not certified as major news until it had appeared in *The Wall Street Journal*, the scandal at Columbia Pictures was not certified as major news until it was addressed at length by Liz Smith.*

AND NOW FOLKS, "HOLLYWOODGATE" was the headline on her January 12 column.

The saga of tycoon David Begelman and his improper behavior concerning finances while running Columbia Pictures is not over yet, even though the company has forgiven and reinstated him, he has repaid the money, almost everyone in the film community has rallied around and closed ranks, and the devout wish is that it will all be quickly forgotten. *It won't be.*

*Ironically. Liz Smith would have written sooner about Columbia and Begelman if agent Sue Mengers had not convinced her for a time that the story was unworthy. Mengers also had succeeded in influencing Rona Barrett's reporting.

Even as I write this, *The Washington Post*—that scourge of Watergate—has deployed top reporters to California to dig further into the Begelman-Columbia story. The name that these behind-the-scenes diggers have for the situation is "Hollywoodgate." They say that what has been published so far, pro and con, is merely the tip of the old iceberg . . .

Even though she had only one piece of marginal new information— that the *Post* was still working on the story—Liz Smith, merely by devoting the bulk of her column to the subject, drew more attention to it than the combined enterprise of *The Wall Street Journal*, *The Washington Post*, and *New York* magazine had drawn by that time. She certified it as a story of broad interest to the general public and helped make up the minds of important editors all over New York and all over the country, who had been only vaguely aware of the story and were wondering whether they should cover it. Liz Smith thus played an integral part in launching one of the most intense, frantic, and chaotic media pursuits of a story of less than life-and-death importance that America had seen in many years. The resulting climate would serve to heighten the impact of the major magazine articles then in preparation by Andrew Tobias for *Esquire*, Jeanie Kasindorf for *New West*, and Lucian K. Truscott, IV, for *The New York Times*.

That Thursday afternoon, the *New York Post* appeared with a prominently displayed story under the headline HOLLYWOODGATE COVERUP: CLIFF ROBERTSON BLASTS TREATMENT OF FILM MOGUL.

"Actor Cliff Robertson has charged an 'incredible coverup' of the Columbia Pictures president's forgery of a $10,000 check made out to him. . . . 'It is as though Begelman is above normal law enforcement. This scandal has to do with Hollywood and I think it involves an enormous amount of money, an incredible coverup and I believe it is the tip of the iceberg,' " Robertson told the *Post*.

The New York Times published an article on the front page of its business section Friday morning. Written by the *Times*'s Los Angeles bureau chief, Robert Lindsey, the story began: "Three months after David Begelman was ousted as chief of Columbia Pictures and one month after his reinstatement in one of Hollywood's most powerful jobs, controversy and mystery continue to surround the flamboyant film mogul." The article reviewed information previously published elsewhere but contained little new information.

In the *Los Angeles Herald Examiner* on Friday, entertainment columnist James Bacon wrote: "*The Washington Post* apparently is incensed because the Hollywood trade press never used the word 'embezzlement.' There's a reason for that. Embezzlement is not a sin in Hollywood. It's a way of life. I once asked a well-known Hollywood producer, who has never made a picture for less than $10 million, if he wouldn't be happier if he were making $1 million pictures. Less headaches and all that. His answer: 'You can't steal $1 million from a $1 million picture.' Hollywood, for all its prestigious industry awards, which one segment of the industry gives to another and vice versa, is really the greatest concentration of con artists in the world."

Cliff Robertson, after months of silence, and then a soul baring to *The Washington Post* after his name was published in *The Wall Street Journal*, now was talking to just about anyone who called. Having been interviewed by the *New York Post* on Thursday, he talked on Friday to the Associated Press, which circulated a story on its major wires around the world. "Actor Cliff Robertson says the case of Columbia Pictures President David Begelman—still on the job despite his admission that he embezzled $60,000 from the studio—raised 'disturbing kind of remembrances of Watergate.' . . . Robertson said that the lack of legal action in the case 'leads one to think that there are two levels of justice' in Hollywood. 'Wealth and power create a kind of atmosphere of fear. I think they begin to believe that they are above the law.' "

That was enough for the Los Angeles District Attorney, John Van de Kamp, who announced Friday that his office would examine police investigations of the case to date. "One of the problems for police agencies involved in this case," Van de Kamp said, "is that neither Columbia Pictures nor Robertson has wanted to file a criminal complaint."

Van de Kamp's announcement fueled another series of news stories across the country.

DA WILL REVIEW SCENARIO WITH MOGUL AS HEAVY (New York *Daily News*)

DA STEPS INTO PROBE OF COLUMBIA STUDIOS CHIEF (*Los Angeles Times*)

BEGELMAN CASE . . . BETTER THAN A MOVIE (*Los Angeles Herald Examiner*)

Columbia Pictures top brass will be holding an emergency meeting here to "re-examine" the David Begelman case. There may be another explosion shaking the upper echelons. (Earl Wilson's syndicated column)

FILMDOM AGONIZES OVER HIGH-LEVEL JUGGLING OF COMPANY FUNDS *(The Washington Post)*

QUESTIONABLE ENCOUNTERS: STRANGER-THAN-FICTION HAPPEN-ING AT COLUMBIA PICTURES *(Time)*

BEGELMAN'S ENCOUNTERS *(Newsweek)*

BEGELMAN CASE AND ISSUES OF FILM ETHICS *(The New York Times)*

The story had become a fixture on the wire services. The AP and the UPI kept their thousands of clients supplied with updated dispatches every twelve hours. Television and radio newscasts carried stories as well.

As it gained strong national momentum, the press's handling of the Columbia scandal began to display traits typical of heavy, rapidly mobilized coverage of major news events. Many stories contained small errors. There were reports that Burbank Detective Elias had gone to New York and personally informed Alan Hirschfield and the Columbia board of directors about the Cliff Robertson forgery as early as June or July. In fact, Elias had gone only to The Burbank Studios and informed senior vice president John Veitch, who told David Begelman, who convinced Elias that the case was being handled internally. There were reports that the "third forgery" had involved the name of Patrick Terrail, owner of Ma Maison. The correct name was that of Pierre Groleau, Terrail's aide. There was a report that Columbia had discovered the Ritt check early in its investigation. In fact, the Ritt check wasn't found until the inquiry was nearly complete.

On a more important level, unable to establish significant new facts not contained in the original *Wall Street Journal* and *Washington Post* stories, the press hurriedly searched for fresh themes—generalizations which could justify repeating the now-familiar facts. The generalization that was dominating most stories by the middle of January was represented by the words "tip of the iceberg," i.e., David Begelman's crimes were indicative of a broad pattern of corruption pervading Hollywood.

The "tip of the iceberg" theme had begun to emerge in the

Washington Post article on Christmas when Cliff Robertson said: "There is a spreading cancer of corruption in Hollywood, of which the Begelman incident is but one example." Robertson repeated the theme, in progressively more elaborate form, to other reporters. None of them pressed Robertson for additional examples of corruption, however, and no specific instances were identified and reported. But by mid-January the tip-of-the-iceberg theme had become an accepted premise of many articles.

According to knowledgeable people in the film industry [*The New York Times* said on Monday, January 16], bribes, payoffs, and other financial improprieties almost certainly run into millions of dollars annually. The dealings are said to take a variety of forms, and include the following:

Bribes paid by independent motion-picture and television producers to studio executives who are in a position to approve a project. . . . Bribes paid by independent television producers—after a network pilot is made—to members of network programming departments whose influence is important in winning approval of a proposed television series. . . . Loans made to studio executives . . . by independent producers or agents who, because of the debt, can virtually call the shots in negotiating deals with the studio. . . . The practice of studio executives about to be dismissed by a film company of negotiating a high-cost deal with themselves before departing. The deal contains extra money that, in effect, is stolen from the company. . . . Bribes to film company executives from theater owners who want favorable treatment or play time on a new film. . . . Besides these practices, industry sources say, there are other forms of corruption [ranging from] payoffs by production companies to union officials for favorable arrangements on a movie project to expenditures of large amounts of company funds to underwrite personal living expenses.

The *Times* article appeared in many papers across the country.
Amid the daily barrage of national press coverage, there appeared a prominent journalist to defend David Begelman and essentially

ignore the larger issues. In the *Los Angeles Times* of Monday, January 16, Charles Champlin, the paper's arts editor and principal film reviewer, wrote:

> Hollywood in its time has lived out as well as acted out on the screen murders, rapes, abductions, extortions, assaults, defalcations, treacheries, coups, tragedy, comedy, and a good deal of farce. The curious case of David Begelman has followed no previously familiar scenario either public (fictional) or private (real). At this point in the drama, there are some resemblances to much earlier works which might carry titles like *The Fallen Saved* or *The Prodigal Son Returned*. But it is a long while since Hollywood has lived or filmed those stories. And, in its obscurities, its psychological overtones and its avoidance of traditional plot formulations, the Begelman situation is more the stuff of a European film. It is closer to Georges Simenon than to Ed McBain's 87th Precinct, although the older, wearier Lew Archer might understand.
>
> The victimless crime has become a term in common use. On the present evidence, and in the absence of any complainants or criminal prosecutions, what we seem to have here is a crimeless crime which is not, however, without a victim. What we have here, it might be said poetically, is a culprit who doubles as a victim. It is a paradoxical and confusing situation which Hollywood and the media, including this newspaper, have been uncertain how to handle. . . .

After a laudatory recitation of Begelman's career, Champlin then quoted an anonymous source as saying: "This ain't no Equity Funding, or anything like it. He had a problem. It's too bad it wasn't a drinking problem—society understands that better. I'm not sure I understand why a man does self-destructive things to cope with pressure, but there it is."

Champlin closed by writing, ". . . while humiliation is not punishment that is likely to earn much sympathy from someone behind bars, it is a real enough punishment for a man who legitimately earns upwards from $300,000 a year."

FORTY-ONE

The Columbia Pictures executive suites at 711 Fifth Avenue and The Burbank Studios were like bunkers under accelerating fire. Along with new bursts of press coverage, each day brought a new spate of press telephone calls. Reporters sought Alan Hirschfield at his office, at home in Scarsdale, and at the Beverly Hills Hotel. They called Herbert Allen at Allen & Company and the Carlyle, Matty Rosenhaus at his Pierre apartment and in Florida, and David Begelman at the studio and his house on Linden Drive. Few of the calls were accepted or returned, but they were distracting and somewhat unnerving. Although each of the executives had been well known for years in his own sphere, widespread public notoriety and the accompanying intense press pursuit were new experiences which they found very unpleasant.

The atmosphere inside the company remained foul. Hirschfield, more than ever, was emotionally committed to inducing an outsider to purchase the company or at least a sizable enough interest in it to dilute Herbert Allen's power. Alan hoped that Herbert still might grow frustrated enough to accept a bid from Jimmy Goldsmith, despite his anger at Hirschfield's having approached Goldsmith secretly. Alan also hoped for some interest from Time Incorporated, or from Mattel, the big toy company in which Columbia had made a major investment in the fall.

Hirschfield and Adler lunched at La Côte Basque on Monday, January 16, and continued their private talks on how Herbert might be overthrown. Having retreated from his angry threat to resign in December following the restoration of Begelman, Adler had some new ideas. He would be in Los Angeles later in the week, and would be talking to friends who had told him of two major corporations that conceivably might be interested in buying Columbia Pictures.

The two companies were Philip Morris, the cigarette and beer maker (Marlboro, Miller High Life), and Penn Central, which had risen from the ashes of its railroad bankruptcy and had built a profitable company around real estate and energy holdings. Adler would know more about both possibilities in a week or so, he said, and would get back to Hirschfield.

That night, David Begelman caught the TWA red-eye out of rainy Los Angeles, landing in New York early Tuesday morning in snow and sleet. After freshening up in his suite at the Drake, he made his way to an eight o'clock appointment with Matty Rosenhaus at the Pierre. Begelman was keeping his promise to Alan Hirschfield, made over dinner in Beverly Hills the previous Wednesday, to attempt to act as an intermediary in laying a foundation of reason and peace upon which Hirschfield could base further efforts to assuage Rosenhaus's anger and disaffection.

Rosenhaus, however, had nothing good to say about Hirschfield and was irrational on the subject: "He's Iago, he's Iago, he's Iago," Matty muttered, not looking at Begelman.

"But Matty," David interjected, "this simply is not good for the company. There is not only a rift, but the rift is now publicly perceived. Until it is closed, the company will continue to suffer. Everybody tells me I'm no longer the issue between you people, so in a sense it's none of my business. But certainly it was my behavior which was the springboard for all this. Therefore, I feel a double obligation, an extra obligation, to help make things right. So please, let's try to put it to rest."

Matty brightened. "Of course, of course, you're right, David. I just got carried away, but you're absolutely right. Let's get on with it."

Half an hour later at Allen & Company, Begelman made the same speech to Herbert Allen. Considerably more pragmatic and less emotional than Rosenhaus, Herbert agreed immediately with David's suggestion that the company must establish and project a strong united front. As their conversation was ending, Herbert said, "You know, David, it's odd. I keep hearing, and learning, and reading through all of this that Alan Hirschfield was my best friend. He was never my best friend. When we came together to Columbia, we came with the reputation of being best friends. Alan was never my best friend. We were supposed to be like twins, and we were never twins. I've let it go, I haven't said anything, or challenged it, but we were never the best of friends.''

David Begelman had overestimated his peacemaking prowess. Not long after he left Allen's office, Herbert went upstairs and walked in on Hirschfield unannounced.

''Look, Alan, I know the company's at a standstill and something has to be done,'' Herbert said. ''I've got a plan to make everyone happy.''

''What's that?''

''What would you think of you and Lufkin* being co-chief executive officers?''

''Co-chief executive officers? What the hell does that mean?''

''You'll divide up your responsibilities. You and Dan have good chemistry together. You'd get along well. He could help you a lot. And it would take care of a lot of Matty's concern.''

''Herbert, that's the most harebrained scheme I've ever heard. I've never heard of co-chief executive officers. It's a new concept in American business. What would Lufkin do, based on his long experience in the entertainment business, which he doesn't have?''

''He's a smart guy, a fast learner; it would work well. You'd work it out between yourselves.''

''It's ridiculous, the most ridiculous idea I've ever heard.''

''Well, then, what about Dan becoming chairman, and Leo moving over to chairman of the executive committee. Matty would resign as chairman of the executive committee.''

''That makes no sense. Lufkin has no experience in this industry, or even with this company. He's only been to one board meeting. He would clearly be perceived as my successor. There would be speculation. It would confuse the employees. It would confuse our business relationships. It would cause more, not less turmoil, particularly at a time when the whole credibility of the company is being questioned. The next step would be that Lufkin would be positioned to take my job. I'm not that stupid.''

''No, it wouldn't be that way at all. Dan doesn't want to work full time. But he could help us a lot in doing deals.''

''I'm unalterably opposed.''

---

*Dan Lufkin, a close friend of Herbert's and an occasional participant in politics, had gone on the Columbia board of directors at Herbert's instigation just before the first of the year and had not participated actively in the fight over Begelman. Lufkin had become wealthy in the sixties as a founding partner of Donaldson, Lufkin & Jenrette, a Wall Street investment house.

"Well, think it over. Meanwhile, I think we should get together on a public statement of unity. We—Matty and I—would endorse you, express support for you. You would express your support for Begelman. We would make clear that you are to get a new long-term contract. We've got to have a united front to get all this behind us."

"That I agree with," Hirschfield said.* "But what if David's indicted? As far as I'm concerned, he'd have to go."

"If he's indicted and pleads guilty, he'd have to go, but I doubt if it'll go that far. I doubt it'll be a problem. They'll settle it in some way."

"Well, in any event," Hirschfield said, "it is critical that my situation vis-à-vis the board be clarified if we're to have any chance of landing the United Artists group. I've been in touch with Pleskow and I'm seeing him again this week. It's one of the most important deals we could ever do. It would be a bonanza for this company. But we've got to move on it. They're talking to other companies, so we've got to make a positive move now."

Herbert promised to call UA's top officer, Arthur Krim, whom he had known for years as a fellow fund raiser for Democratic Party candidates, as soon as Hirschfield and Pleskow had met.

"But the important thing now," Herbert said, "is an announcement to clear the air between all of us here."

"I agree," Hirschfield said, "but I think we've still got some tough sledding ahead in the press."

"I think it'll soon be over. The worst is behind us."

At half past noon, the regular monthly meeting of the Columbia board of directors was convened in the boardroom across the hall. The meeting was not an "emergency session," as Earl Wilson's column had said, but was extraordinary nonetheless. Although David Begelman was no longer a director or officer of the parent corporation, he was the unchallenged star of the meeting, displaying a degree of power and influence surpassing that of most board members and officers. There was no reference to his crimes or the disgrace he had caused the company. On the contrary, he was

---

*A month having passed since Begelman's restoration, Hirschfield was less concerned that his own potential new contract would be perceived as a payoff, and more concerned that he was being perceived as a lame-duck chief executive. He felt that the stronger he appeared to be—an offer of a new contract would be evidence of his own strength—the better would be his chances of attracting an outsider to wrest control from the Allens.

greeted and hailed as an almost heroic figure who had been absent for a time and had been sorely missed. While letting it be known that he had flown in on the red-eye, as if to imply that he hadn't wanted to waste a minute, he looked well and, as always, was meticulously dressed, groomed, and coiffed. He was his old self again, or so it seemed.

With typical lucidity, and an extra touch of briskness, Begelman briefed the board on eight new motion-picture and television deals, including new production arrangements with Peter Guber, the producer of *The Deep* and *Midnight Express*, and with Leonard Goldberg, Begelman's close friend and a principal of Spelling-Goldberg.

Hirschfield and Fischer exchanged chagrined looks. It was company policy for all movie and TV transactions to be discussed thoroughly with, and be approved by, Hirschfield and Fischer before being presented to the board. Normally, memoranda on pending transactions were sent to New York several days before board meetings. In this instance, however, most of the deals had not been cleared in advance. Begelman had shown them to Hirschfield and Fischer only a few minutes before the meeting. There had been little time for discussion, and Hirschfield had serious questions about several of the deals, especially those with Peter Guber and Leonard Goldberg. The Guber deal was unduly lucrative for Guber, Hirschfield felt. The board had issued a harsh warning to Hirschfield to maintain certain restrictions in the Guber contract. That was in December, before Begelman's reinstatement, when it appeared that Hirschfield would handle the Guber negotiations himself. Begelman, however, had subsequently negotiated the more lucrative deal that Hirschfield had been warned against, and now no one was objecting.

As Begelman was finishing his presentation, Fischer expected Hirschfield to object, to call for a recess, to indicate somehow that the top management of the corporation disapproved of, or at least had reservations about, most of the transactions that Begelman had brought to the meeting. But Hirschfield said nothing. He simply stared glumly straight ahead.

Matty Rosenhaus spoke up: "Isn't that great! David is only back three weeks, and he's accomplished all these things which nobody else has been able to do." The board passed all eight deals with only brief discussion. Fischer and Adler, who had no authority to say anything, looked at each other in dismay. They knew they had just witnessed a reaffirmation of the power of Begelman and the emasculation of Hirschfield.

After Begelman left the room, the board authorized Leo Jaffe to conclude contractual arrangements with Ray Stark. With Begelman again running the 'studio, Stark had signaled his willingness to resume negotiations toward a new production deal. It was indicated that Begelman would not participate directly in the negotiations with Stark.

The board's discussion then turned to the necessity for drafting and disseminating a public statement of unity. Rosenhaus and Allen agreed that the statement should include expressions of the board's support for Hirschfield—including its intention to give him a new long-term contract—as well as stating Hirschfield's support for Begelman. Hirschfield asked what the company's position would be if Begelman were prosecuted. Several board members said that Columbia should, as a matter of policy, fight any indictment. The company already had declined to prosecute. Begelman had repaid the money and was under psychiatric care. Criminal action against him would be unwarranted and unfair.

Hirschfield got angry. "Don't expect me to be David Begelman's defender. I agreed to bring him back in order to try to bind up the wounds in the company, but I'm not going to be his defender, in the sense of leading his defense if he's indicted."

"Let's not worry about an indictment now," Herbert suggested. "It'll probably never happen. It's just newspaper talk, essentially a PR problem."

"It will be a lot more than a PR problem if Mr. Van de Kamp decides to indict Mr. Begelman," Hirschfield retorted. "He'll have to plead guilty, and then we'll be the only company in the United States with a convicted, admitted crook running our biggest divisions."

"Let's wait and see," Herbert said, and the meeting broke up. It was clear, however, the price of the board's support of Hirschfield was Hirschfield's support of Begelman, even in the event of an indictment.

MORE RUMORS THAN CLARITY MARK BEGELMAN CASE said Wednesday's *Variety*. And Earl Wilson wrote: "David Begelman, Columbia Pictures' controversial executive, emerged smiling and with seeming confidence from a meeting of Columbia's board of directors. Leo Jaffe said nothing drastic was done but said he 'couldn't answer' whether the Begelman case was taken up."

*   *   *

Hirschfield had lunch at Le Cirque Wednesday with his friend Herbert Siegel, the chairman of Chris-Craft Industries. Siegel, an ex-agent and would-be mogul who had bought and sold a number of substantial investments in movie companies over the years, had just purchased a major block of stock in Twentieth Century-Fox.

"For the money," Hirschfield said, "you could have Columbia easier than you can have Fox." Siegel replied that he felt that Fox's balance sheet and asset values were superior to Columbia's. Hirschfield tried unsuccessfully to persuade him otherwise.

Herbert Allen called Hirschfield that afternoon. "I hear you had lunch with Herb Siegel. Are you trying to sell him the company?"

"I'd love to sell him the company," Hirschfield said, "but he's got one more movie company than he can handle already."

On Thursday, the New York *Daily News*, the *Los Angeles Herald Examiner*, and dozens of other papers published a lengthy Liz Smith interview with Cliff Robertson. "In an exclusive, two-hour interview," Smith wrote, "Oscar-winning actor Cliff Robertson told me that during the first months of 1977, after discovering that someone had forged and cashed a $10,000 Columbia Pictures official check in his name, he came to fear for his life. And to worry about the safety of his wife, actress Dina Merrill, and their young daughter.

"Under advice from his Los Angeles attorney, Robertson, at one point when passing through Hollywood, did not stay as usual at the Bel-Air Hotel but went anonymously to the home of a friend. Then, during the making of a film in London last fall, the actor was constantly checked on by the FBI, which advised him to be wary, to watch his step, and to report anything mysterious immediately.

" 'It was all like a dime novel,' says the actor, who blew the lid off the puzzle that is Hollywood's own miniature Watergate . . ."

The interview contained little that Robertson had not said to *The Washington Post* on Christmas. Liz Smith felt, however, that it bore repeating since so few people had actually read the *Post* story. And she did add a few new details, asking, for example, about rumors that Robertson was conducting a "vendetta over a past falling-out when Begelman was acting as his agent. Cliff said: 'I knew they'd find something to cloud the issue here. Listen, my conscience is clear. It is true we were involved in a contractual thing where he represented me. I shot some aviation footage in Ireland for a company that went out of business. Later they said I had an obligation to continue the project. I had first rights to it, but no obligation. But when depositions were taken, David waffled and did not tell the truth. He did not want to be my witness in the deal. It disillusioned me but it was just one of those things. We never quarreled over it. . . . It was just an ugly, unfortunate incident.* But I would not take a reprisal on David Begelman and I am just amazed, that's all, amazed that he refers now "to the unfortunate use of my name," which is—after all—a new way to refer to forgery. David's public statements and those of others in Hollywood depict him as a victim. He is Joan of Arc at the gates of Paris, or the tragic Irving Thalberg.' "

Smith dropped Robertson a note late that day: "Response to the column today has been tremendous. . . . Everyone is saying to me what balls you have. And I just want to tell you I think so too. I was told today that Ned Tanen of Universal says he would hire you anytime . . . in answer to Sue Mengers' assertion that you will never work again. (All of this is off the record. Michael Black will tell it to you himself.) Sue called Michael this morning and told him he also was ruined for being quoted. I told Michael to tell her, 'I am Cliff's agent and I would still be his agent if he had been in an accident, and I am still his agent and still telling the truth even though he has been involved in something not his own fault.' Thank you, Cliff, for giving me a great story and for your integrity."†

At 711 Fifth Avenue, various executives and public-relations aides were sitting in their offices with yellow legal pads, attempting to draft a statement of unity that would be satisfactory to Hirschfeld on the one hand and the board of directors on the other. Since there was no genuine unity, the task naturally was difficult. Words praising Alan Hirschfeld were written for Herbert Allen and Matty Rosenhaus to utter. Words praising the board were written for Hirschfeld to utter. Words stressing the "good faith" of both sides were written for Leo Jaffe to utter. Handwritten drafts were circulated, edited, typed, reedited, rewritten, discarded, and begun anew.

Someone felt it would be appropriate for the statement to begin: "Leo Jaffe, chairman of the board of Columbia Pictures Industries Inc., announced today that the board of directors of the Company has authorized him to negotiate a new long-term employment agreement with Alan J. Hirschfield. . . ."

Someone felt it would be appropriate for Matty Rosenhaus to say:

"While Mr. Hirschfield and I, as well as other board members, had an honest difference of opinion concerning David Begelman's ongoing role in the company, this did not in any way change my belief that Alan has masterminded a brilliant turnaround in the company during his tenure and that, by far, Mr. Hirschfield is the best individual to guide us into the future. . . ."

Someone felt it would be appropriate for Herbert Allen to say:

"I have been associated with Alan Hirschfield for many years and hold him in the highest regard. I consider that Columbia Pictures is fortunate to have Mr. Hirschfield as its chief executive officer. . . ."

Someone felt it would be appropriate for Alan Hirschfield to say:

"I appreciate the board's expression of confidence and assert my strong commitment to the company, its board, and its employees. I look forward to continuing an association that has been amicable and successful. . . ."

The effort continued for days and eventually waned. As tough and sophisticated as Hirschfield, Rosenhaus, and Allen were, they ultimately found it impossible to mouth words which so fundamentally misrepresented their true feelings.

FORTY-TWO

Aside from Lew Wasserman of MCA-Universal, whom he considered the most skilled executive in show business, Alan Hirschfield admired no one in the industry more than the top officers of the United Artists Corporation—Arthur Krim, Robert Benjamin, and Eric Pleskow. Since taking control of United Artists more than a quarter-century earlier—in February 1951—Krim and Benjamin (and later Pleskow when he joined them in the top ranks) consistently displayed an unusual combination of ingenuity, taste, and business acumen, and had come closer than most in the modern era to mastering the still-mysterious process of making movies. There were many reasons for UA's success, but perhaps the most important was the company's sense of how to strike the right balance between the filmmaker's creative independence—essential for artistic integrity—and the studio's financial control—essential for corporate health and stability. Striking that balance had been at the heart of successful filmmaking since the industry's birth and always would be, as indeed it underpins all art forms that depend upon mass commerce for their survival. Achieving the proper balance between freedom and control is a perpetual struggle. Nothing in the entertainment business is more difficult. Nothing is more rewarding than consistent success at it. Nothing is more destructive than failure to achieve it. And nothing has fostered more feuds than differing opinions of how to achieve it.

Although Krim and Benjamin were never able to reduce their success to a formula, they undoubtedly were aided by the fresh, pragmatic, myth-free outlook that they brought to the movie business in the early fifties. And it was appropriate that the company they took over was atypical in the industry, having been born of an idea for giving film artists an unusual degree of freedom.

Mary Pickford, Douglas Fairbanks, Charlie Chaplin, and D.W. Griffith founded United Artists in 1919 in an effort to preserve the near-total artistic control, and the extraordinarily lucrative financial remuneration, which they had won in recent years but which the increasingly monopolistic film industry was reluctant to keep giving.* By starting their own company, they hoped not only to continue producing their own films but to distribute them as well and keep all the profits. It was not long before they encountered problems. They had to invest a lot of their own money to build and maintain a nationwide distribution organization. Their own films were insufficient in number to generate revenues needed to maintain the distribution company. They needed the help of businessmen and other artists. Joseph Schenck, a skilled executive and the brother of Nick

*Contrary to a popular notion, Barbra Streisand and other top actors and directors of the seventies and eighties were not the first to wrest a large measure of control over their films from the studios and reap huge rewards in the process. The four founders of United Artists possessed the same degree of control and made more money, adjusted for inflation, than the top stars and directors of today.

Schenck of Loews-MGM, was hired to run United Artists. Sam Goldwyn subsequently joined the company. Through the late twenties, thirties, and early forties, Howard Hughes, Walt Disney, David O. Selznick, Darryl Zanuck, and other independent producers distributed films through United Artists. The careers of the founders declined, however, and the company never functioned entirely as they had intended for more than a few years.

Instead of becoming a durable base for independent filmmakers, UA more often was a stop on the way to other destinations. Its management was erratic and contentious. Joe Schenck left and was followed as chief executive in rapid succession by vice president Al Lichtman, founder Mary Pickford, A. P. Giannini of the Bank of America, and foreign-sales chief Murray Silverstone, none of whom could get along with the dominant force in the company, Sam Goldwyn. After a bitter fight with Pickford, Fairbanks, and Chaplin (D. W. Griffith had sold out in the early thirties), Sam Goldwyn left UA in 1941. Amid continued feuding by the owners and executives, the company gradually declined through the forties until it was taken over by Arthur Krim and Robert Benjamin of the prominent New York law firm of Phillips, Nizer, Benjamin & Krim, whose best known partner was trial attorney Louis Nizer.

Krim and Benjamin had done a lot of legal work for film companies and knew the business well. By altering the United Artists founders' concept slightly, the new owners made the company a consistent success. Instead of attempting to function essentially as a nonprofit distribution company, with all profit going to the film producers, United Artists became a financial partner of the producers, putting all or part of the money up to finance their pictures and sharing the profits with them. The idea still appealed to many producers because they continued to be given more creative independence than the other studios would give. It was by no means total independence: United Artists would sponsor no film on which it had not first agreed with the producer on the story, cast, director, and budget. But the rising number of talented producers who found the degree of autonomy attractive made some of the most successful movies of the fifties. Instead of panicking in the face of competition from television, United Artists observed Nick Schenck's old adage— "There's nothing wrong with this industry that good pictures cannot cure"—and drew audiences away from their TV sets to see such pictures as *Around the World in Eighty Days, Twelve Angry Men,*

Some Like It Hot, *The Moon Is Blue*, and *The Man with the Golden Arm*. Through the sixties and seventies, it released many noted films including *In the Heat of the Night*, *Midnight Cowboy*, *West Side Story*, *Elmer Gantry*, *Judgment at Nuremberg*, *Tom Jones*, *Sunday Bloody Sunday*, *Last Tango in Paris*, *Lenny* and *One Flew over the Cuckoo's Nest*. The studio also distributed all of the James Bond and Woody Allen movies. In 1976, three of the five films nominated for the Academy Award as "Best Picture" were distributed by United Artists—*Rocky, Network*, and *Bound for Glory*. (*Rocky* won.)

United Artists constantly adjusted the degree of control it exerted over film projects. In 1977 it decreed that if a film's cost exceeded its budget, the producer, not the studio, must pay the difference. But Krim, Benjamin, Pleskow, and their colleagues at the same time were straining under the restrictions placed upon them by their corporate parent, the Transamerica Corporation, which had acquired UA in 1967. The top UA officers finally decided to resign as a group and start a new company in affiliation with a major studio.

Alan Hirschfield had first heard of their plans in strictest secrecy from banker William Thompson at Jimmy's Harborside in Boston on the first Saturday in October. With the Begelman crisis just engulfing Columbia, Thompson had felt that the availability of the UA group might help solve any management problem posed by the departure of Begelman. During the fall, Hirschfield clung to the hope that he could woo the UA people. The prospect had helped sustain him through the darkest moments of the Begelman fight, even though he knew that Herbert Allen did not share his enthusiasm for bringing the group to Columbia. Even after Begelman's reinstatement, he continued to hope. By mid-January, with the UA defections having been announced and the group already negotiating with several film companies, Hirschfield knew he had to act quickly.

On Friday, January 20—with Manhattan quiet and nearly immobile under a fresh foot of snow—he had lunch with Arthur Krim and Eric Pleskow at the Harmonie Club. It was Hirschfield's fourth meeting with Pleskow on the subject, but his first with Krim. Hirschfield proposed that their new company be launched from a minimum base of $75 million—$25 million from Columbia as an advance against distribution fees, and a $50 million line of bank credit, which Hirschfield had tentatively arranged through Bill Thompson. Columbia would have the exclusive right to distribute their films. The profits would be divided evenly between Columbia and the new company.

Krim and Pleskow liked the terms, and expressed confidence in Hirschfield personally. But they identified two general concerns about affiliating with Columbia—"the Begelman mess" and the "Ray Stark problem."

Arthur Krim felt that reinstating Begelman had been a "terrible mistake" and that the clash over the issue had clouded Columbia's internal authority structure and placed in doubt Hirschfield's authority in particular. Hirschfield revealed that the board, informally at least, had offered him a new contract and he said he hoped the board "would soon publicly clarify my role and endorse my position in the company."

As for Ray Stark, the Krim group had never particularly liked Stark and were concerned about the extent of his authority at Columbia. Would they have to listen to Stark's opinion of each of their film deals and in effect clear deals with him?

"Ray has nothing to do with running Columbia. Ray runs Ray. I run Columbia," Hirschfield said, without total conviction.

Krim and Pleskow said they would consider Hirschfield's proposal seriously but remained concerned about "the Begelman mess" and "the Stark problem."

Arthur Krim later talked with Herbert Allen, who said, "Quite frankly, Arthur, we have a contentious atmosphere here."

After a weekend slowed by snow, Hirschfield on Monday went to see Andrew Heiskell, the chairman of the board and chief executive officer of Time Incorporated, in his office high in the Time-Life Building. Hirschfield had valued Columbia's relationship with Time very highly since its inception eighteen months earlier when the publishing giant had agreed to invest several million dollars in Columbia's movie productions. Andrew Heiskell had said at the time: "We have been impressed by the record of Columbia Pictures . . . in its selection of properties and in the aggressive marketing approaches it has pursued in distributing its films theatrically."

Spurred by Allen Adler, who had negotiated the deal with Time, Hirschfield had courted Heiskell, hoping that the film investment might lead to a broader and closer relationship. Heiskell and his wife, Marian Sulzberger Heiskell, had been among Alan and Berte Hirschfield's guests at the party after the premiere of *Close Encoun-*

ters of the Third Kind. Hirschfield worried that the Begelman scandal might damage the relationship, but at the same time he wondered whether Time might be of help. When he began pondering how to change the power balance at Columbia by inducing an outsider to invest in the company, he and Adler had thought of Time. But there had been no pursuit, and on this cold January afternoon Hirschfield made no explicit overtures and tried to put the best face on the situation as it stood: he expected to get a new contract, and he expected the Columbia board to endorse him publicly.

While Heiskell sensed that Hirschfield needed help, he was uncertain what to do. Heiskell was totally bewildered by Columbia's handling of the Begelman affair. It was entirely foreign to his experience and, he suspected, to the experience of most major corporations. If an embezzler had been caught in the upper reaches of Time Inc., there would have been no controversy. The offending party simply would have been removed from the company. The law-enforcement authorities might or might not have been called. A psychiatrist might or might not have been consulted. There surely would have been a thorough investigation. But whatever the circumstances, the embezzler would have been removed. There was simply no other way to approach such a situation, Heiskell felt. Except that Columbia Pictures seemed to have found another way; thus Heiskell's bewilderment. He was too well-mannered to press Hirschfield for private details, however, so he merely wished him well.

"You have friends at Time," Heiskell said.

Hirschfield left, feeling defensive and a bit silly.

Hirschfield had lunch on Tuesday with Samuel Lefrak, the New York real-estate magnate. Lefrak had a lot of spare cash and wanted to invest in the movies. What did Hirschfield think of remaking *It Happened One Night* with Barbra Streisand and Robert Redford? Alan thought it was a pretty good idea and promised to look into it.

After lunch, he conferred with Herbert Allen, Leo Jaffe, and Irwin Kramer in the Allen & Company offices.

Not for the first time, Hirschfield said, "There's a serious morale problem at the studio. People are embarrassed to be working for David. And there are lots of rumors that now that he's back I'm going to get bounced."

"I'm sick and tired of hearing about morale problems," said Irwin

Kramer, in one of his more belligerent moods. "Those people are getting paid lots of money. If they're gonna complain, they should be terminated. The hell with 'em."

"The problem at the moment," Hirschfield said, "is the definition of my own role. Still, at this date, more than two weeks after the publication of Dan Dorfman's piece in *New York* magazine, that article remains the board's only public statement about me—that they have no confidence, that they mistrust me. That has caused substantial upset and a decline in the morale of the employees, and it's also causing outsiders to question the direction of the company. What about that wonderful public statement of support that was going to go out?"

"The whole problem, Alan, is caused by your failure to publicly support David," said Herbert. "It's critical for you to go to LA and make clear to the employees and everyone else that you are embracing David, that he has your confidence and support."

"I was just out there week before last and it didn't do any good. I'll consider going back, but the real problem is clarifying my own position in the company."

Irwin Kramer spoke up again. "I'm sick and tired of hearing you complain about problems, and the West Coast people complain about problems. Everybody ought to go back to work. I don't give a damn if you or anyone else walks out of this company. You're all replaceable."

"That's a rotten thing to say, and it's a destructive attitude for the company and its shareholders," Hirschfield protested.

"I don't give a damn," Kramer declared. "I'm sick of hearing all this. I don't care if the stock goes to two dollars. It doesn't make any difference to me. I can live without the money."*

"That's an outrageous attitude for a director and the head of the audit committee to take," Hirschfield shouted. "If that's your attitude, there's no sense continuing this discussion." Hirschfield got up and started toward the door.

"Don't go, Alan," Herbert said.

---

*Irwin Kramer later denied that he ever said he didn't care if the stock fell to two dollars and could live without the money. The statement as it appears in this conversation was attributed to Kramer by a person who attended the meeting and later made notes of it, and by a second person who claimed to have heard Kramer make the same statement during a discussion separate from the meeting reported here.

"I don't have to take this kind of abuse!" Hirschfield retorted, and left the room.

Just about all the trust that Alan and Herbert had ever felt had been destroyed. They spoke privately less and less, and began communicating mainly in writing and through intermediaries. On Wednesday, January 25, Hirschfield wrote Allen a letter about the executives leaving United Artists. "Needless to say, I feel that if we could make a deal with this group it would be a bonanza for Columbia; it would materially enhance the product availability in our domestic distribution organization and put us in a position in foreign markets which this company has never previously enjoyed." The sole purpose of the letter was to establish a written record of Hirschfield's views. If Columbia failed to land the Krim group, Hirschfield was determined not to share the blame.

Allen Adler had been busy in his role as Hirschfield's secret emissary to outsiders who might be induced to buy Columbia Pictures and overthrow the Allens. Adler had just conferred in Los Angeles with two men who were in touch with Philip Morris Incorporated and the Penn Central Corporation. Each wanted to meet Hirschfield and explore the possibility of making a run at Columbia. Appointments would be arranged soon.

"Hollywood is waiting for a Jeanie Kasindorf article in *New West* next week on the David Begelman forgery embezzlement affair," Liz Smith wrote in her column on Thursday morning. "Those who have read it say it is very strong, very thorough, very hard on the reinstated head of Columbia Pictures. The magazine's publisher, Joe Armstrong, feels he'll now be 'about as welcome as a pork chop at a kosher wedding in LA.' Then there is the big Hollywood producer pal of Begelman's who is going around telling one and all that there is nothing to fear from the projected Andrew Tobias dissection of the scandal set for *Esquire*. The producer says the piece is being killed because of his friendship with publisher Clay Felker. Said producer is probably in for a rude shock. The piece will run and now it may run stronger than ever."

Hollywood, indeed, was waiting anxiously for the *New West* and *Esquire* articles. The word was getting around that the *New West* piece contained explosive material on Begelman's relationship to

Judy Garland. A nervous Herbert Allen telephoned Jeanie Kasindorf at home early Thursday morning demanding to know whether and in what manner he was being quoted in the article. Ironically, the Kasindorf piece itself was being buffeted by another storm unrelated to the article's substance. Its preparation during January coincided with the firing of the two top editors of *New West* magazine. As a result, several political factions at the magazine had a hand in editing the article—a process that senior editor Jonathan Kirsch promptly labeled "the gangbang edit."

Hirschfield, Fischer, and Adler met Friday afternoon to plan a presentation the company was scheduled to make to the New York Society of Security Analysts on Tuesday, February 14. The New York Society, an organization of brokerage-firm members who analyze corporations as a basis for investment recommendations to their firms' clients, was the largest group of its kind in the nation and provided a daily Wall Street forum in which companies could tell their stories and be questioned by the analysts. Most major U.S. corporations appeared before the New York analysts annually, and the press covered each meeting.

Hirschfield had decided to proceed with the appearance after receiving a memorandum from Jean Vagnini, Columbia's public-relations director: "This meeting will most likely draw a crowd of very anxious analysts. Because of their basic insecurities with the company, only a well-thought-out and 'sincere' presentation will be acceptable. Under the current circumstances, a cancellation would not be unexpected. However, if we don't show, the 'instability' of the company will be accentuated. If conducted properly, it could be a good *first* step of re-establishing support."

It would be another occasion to which Hirschfield would have to rise.

The man on the phone to *The Wall Street Journal* reporter would not give his name. He wondered, however, if the reporter knew that Alan Hirschfield, who had taken such a moral stance on David Begelman, wasn't so clean himself. It seemed that Hirschfield had his wife working for a market-research firm on Columbia Pictures' payroll, a firm called Wolf Associates or something similar. It sounded like a potential conflict of interest to the man on the phone. Hirschfield might stand to gain a lot personally by diverting Columbia business to the Wolf firm. And yet here he was playing "Mr. Clean" against the crook, Begelman.

The reporter investigated the allegations carefully and determined that there was no conflict of interest. First, Berte Hirschfield had not worked for Wolf for more than a year. Second, she had been proscribed while there from benefiting financially from whatever business Wolf did with Columbia. The restrictions on her, which had been designed by Columbia explicitly to prevent any conflict or even the appearance of one, were so onerous, in fact, that it was impossible for her to receive compensation commensurate with the value of her work.

The reporter wondered whether other publications which the anonymous tipster might call would check the allegation so carefully before printing it.

After many days of dodging Lucian Truscott, the writer retained by *The New York Times Magazine*, Hirschfield finally took a call from Truscott at home Saturday evening. He patiently reviewed the entire Begelman affair and its aftermath under Truscott's questioning. They agreed to talk again the following morning.

After the interview, a weary Hirschfield screened Mel Brooks's *High Anxiety* for his family in the basement projection room.

The "tip of the iceberg" theme which the news media had been pursuing so avidly was given new impetus by a major front-page article in Sunday's *New York Times*. The article was prepared by a team of three excellent reporters*—Robert Lindsey, Jeff Gerth, and Aljean Harmetz—and carried the headline: "Critics of the Movie Business Find Pattern of Financial Irregularities."

LOS ANGELES, Jan. 28—Disclosure of financial improprieties by a senior executive of Columbia Pictures have drawn attention to what some industry critics say is a pattern of questionable financial practices throughout the motion picture industry. According to Columbia and law enforcement sources, the film business is permeated by financial irregularities that extend

---

*In addition to Lucian Truscott's work for the magazine, the main news department of the *Times* newspaper had reporters working on the story as well.

from the executive suite to the movie backlot to the local theater box office. . . .

"Nobody can skim as well as Las Vegas because they invented it," said Richard Brooks, the Academy Award-winning writer and director. "But Hollywood is second. It's a time of corruption."

The article failed, however, to document all the allegations in its provocative lead paragraphs with specific examples. It cited a lawsuit filed by actors Sean Connery and Michael Caine against Allied Artists Pictures, alleging that the studio had cheated the actors out of profits due them from *The Man Who Would Be King*. Only deep in the article was it acknowledged that the Connery-Caine suit was not unusual. Rather, it was the latest example of a long-standing complaint by actors, directors, and others that the studios routinely manipulated financial records so as to minimize or eliminate money due the artists. The article implied that the artists' complaints were valid but cited no proof. Reciting at length the familiar facts of the Columbia Pictures case, the story quoted "critics of the industry" as saying that the Begelman episode "illustrates the kind of loose financial controls that characterize the industry and that permit such abuses." No other examples of embezzlement were cited, however, and though the article indicated that bribery, kickbacks, and other abuses were widespread, it failed to identify any specific instances of such conduct. Having failed properly to document its central assertions, the *Times* then went on to discuss allegations by theater owners that the studios were guilty of a number of antitrust and monopolistic practices. But the paper did not acknowledge that—reprehensible as such practices are—controversies over alleged monopolies are as old as the movie industry itself.

The *Times* article exemplified the extraordinary momentum of the Columbia scandal as a media event. The "tip of the iceberg" theme, first enunciated by Cliff Robertson in *The Washington Post* on Christmas, implied that corruption was rampant in the executive suites of Hollywood. It implied that check forgery and other forms of embezzlement were commonplace. Even though the allegation was not substantiated by Robertson or anyone else, it had gained widespread credence in the press by mid-January, and was gradually expanded to embrace allegations of bribery, kickbacks, and all manner of corruption, none of which was documented. But by the end of the month, *The New York Times*, one of the most responsible newspapers in the world, chose not only to perpetuate the ''iceberg'' theory in a big front-page story but to expand the dimensions of the ''iceberg'' still further by appending to it allegations of other types of illegality whose relevance to embezzlement was highly questionable. If one man's check forgeries were indicative of widespread check forgery and other forms of embezzlement (and they might have been); and if the embezzlement was indicative of general corruption, including bribery, kickbacks, and other felony crimes (and it might have been); and if all that corruption could legitimately be said to encompass decades-old courtroom wrangling over film-profit percentages and antitrust questions (one could argue that it did), *The New York Times* failed, at each juncture of its article on Sunday, January 29, to make the case. But no matter. It was on the front page of *The New York Times*. There was no stopping the snowball now. The *Times* story was mild compared with what was to come.

The *Los Angeles Times*, the *Los Angeles Herald Examiner*, the London *Observer*, and many other papers carried more modest stories on the Columbia scandal that Sunday. On Monday, *The Wall Street Journal* ran a lengthy page-one analysis of the power sturggle inside the company.

FORTY-THREE

Alan Hirschfeld and Joe Fischer read the *Journal* article aboard the nine o'clock American flight to Los Angeles Monday morning. Though he was still furious with Herbert Allen, Hirschfeld again was doing Herbert's bidding. He was returning to the studio, expressly this time to show support for David Begelman. ''If you want us to back you, you're going to have to back David,'' Herbert had said. Hirschfeld thus would meet with the motion-picture executives Monday afternoon and the television executives Tuesday, and he would try to rally them from the stupor that had numbed them since Begelman's reinstatement. "Despite what you might have read or heard," Hirschfield would say, "David has my full support and I, in turn, have the full support of the board of directors. David and I both are at Columbia to stay. It's time for the company, its executives, its staff, and all its employees to forget the past and work hard for the future." Hirschfield wondered how he and his listeners would get through the speech without bursting into either laughter or tears. For unlike Herbert Allen, Hirschfield was convinced that the Begelman problem could not be talked out of existence. From daily telephone conversations and from his own observations at the studio earlier in the month, it was clear to Hirschfield that the "elephant in the room" phenomenon, which had been so evident during the fall when Begelman had attended studio functions while on suspension, was worse than ever. Now, the check forger not only was in the room. He was president of the studio again.

But Hirschfield had to carry on. He had to maintain an appearance of order and harmony. He had to keep buying time—until it became clear whether he would succeed in inducing a strong outsider to bid for control of the company. And that meant supporting Begelman for the time being, no matter how false the sentiment.

For the first time in years, Hirschfield did not stay at the Beverly Hills Hotel. Hoping to avoid the press, which had been pursuing him day and night on both coasts, he chose the equally elegant but newer, smaller, less pretentious, and less known L'Ermitage, which was situated on Burton Way in Beverly Hills and had become a favorite hotel of wealthy Europeans who wanted to avoid the charged, show-business atmosphere of the Beverly Hills and the Beverly Wilshire.

After checking into the hotel, Hirschfield went immediately to the studio, and in the visiting-executives suite found a very pale Joe Fischer.

"Have you seen this?" Fischer asked, handing Hirschfield a copy of the new issue of *New West* magazine, which had just come out that day. The magazine's cover story, entitled "The Incredible Past of David Begelman," was Jeanie Kasindorf's exposé of Begelman's disputed handling of Judy Garland's funds in the early sixties when he was her agent. Spread over seven pages, the article reported the details of Sid Luft's decade-old allegations that Begelman had embezzled hundreds of thousands of dollars from Garland in part by manipulating her checking accounts. Checks—the same method he had employed in stealing from Columbia Pictures.

"Sid Luft's files go back to 1961," the article said. "He is sure they show that David Begelman's check-cashing problem is more than 'aberrational.' "

Alan Hirschfield was nearly incoherent. "Jesus Christ, I cannot believe what I am seeing," he said, scanning the article, whose most dramatic illustration was a photocopy of the front and back of a check for $6,000 which Begelman allegedly had written on Judy Garland's New York checking account and cashed in Las Vegas. There was Begelman's sweeping signature—the same handwriting that had been found on the Cliff Robertson check, the Martin Ritt check, and the Pierre Groleau checks.

"Does that signature look familiar?" Fischer asked.

Questions about the checks had been raised in a report prepared by a Beverly Hills accountant, Oscar Steinberg, who had audited Judy Garland's financial records in 1963 at Luft's request. According to Kasindorf, Garland was in rehearsal for a CBS television series when she saw Steinberg's report and did not want to be bothered. Kasindorf quoted Luft as saying, " 'When Judy got a copy of the report, she said, "Look, suppose he did steal $200,000 to $300,000; sweep it under the rug now. I'm going to make $20 million on these television shows. What is $300,000?" ' "

"That sentiment would be echoed on the Columbia Pictures lot fourteen years later," Kasindorf wrote, and again quoted Luft: "Columbia has covered up for David just like Freddie Fields once did fifteen years ago. There's a list a mile long of people who've covered up for David Begelman."

In addition to reporting Luft's allegations, Kasindorf's article reviewed the current brouhaha at Columbia, giving particular attention to Ray Stark's ties to Begelman and to Allen & Company. And she revealed that even though Begelman often had indicated to people that he was a graduate of Yale and its law school, the university had no record of awarding him a degree.

As Hirschfield was reading the article, Dan Melnick walked in. "You've seen it," he said. "Stark really charmed Kasindorf out of her pants, didn't he?"

"I knew she was too smart," Hirschfield said.

There were calls from New York on every phone line into the

suite. It turned out that the Kasindorf article had appeared that day, as well, in *New York* magazine under the title, BEGELMAN BABYLON. Hirschfield spoke with Jaffe, Adler, Lang, Kaufman, Gruenberger, and others. No one knew what to do next. Everyone was shocked. And everyone was responding, of course, not so much to what the article said in a literal sense, as to what it suggested and implied: that David Begelman had been a crook all his adult life, that his embezzlements from Columbia were, indeed, the "tip of the iceberg"—an iceberg not of corruption in Hollywood (a subject the article did not address) but of corruption in David Begelman's past, an iceberg which Columbia's supposedly careful and thorough investigation of Begelman had missed entirely.*

"If this is true," Hirschfield told the others, "the jig is up. There's nothing that can be done for him now. It's the same pattern. God knows what else we're going to hear about. It's like the breaking of a logjam. This stuff is going to be coming from everywhere."

A meeting of the top officials of the studio, including Begelman, had been scheduled previously for early afternoon. Begelman arrived, looking ill and exhausted.

"I guess you've seen it," he said to Hirschfield. "I've authorized my lawyers to sue. Freddie and I have legal documents, signed by Judy, releasing us from any financial obligation to her. Sid Luft has been walking around with this stuff for fifteen years. He's a publicity hound. We went through it all years ago. It's dead and settled. I'm going to sue him."

"Maybe you'll want to talk to your lawyers this afternoon instead of meeting," Hirschfield suggested.

"No, let's go ahead and meet."

Feeling foolish, Hirschfield proceeded with the remarks he had prepared. "Look, these are tough times," he told the studio executives, more than perfunctorily but less than enthusiastically. "We've got to

---

*A close reading of the article would have revealed that it actually documented and stated far less than it suggested and implied. While the accountant's report in 1963 raised legitimate questions about Begelman's handling of Garland's money, it neither answered the questions nor proved wrongdoing. While Garland and Sid Luft had brought suit against Begelman and Fields in 1967, Garland had dropped the suit the next year, formally released them from any financial obligation to her, and subsequently become their client again. While Luft had continued the suit on his own, he had not pursued it for ten years. While failure to pursue a lawsuit is not necessarily evidence of lack of substance, it surely raises the question of whether the suit has merit. In most jurisdictions, failure to pursue a suit automatically results in its dismissal by the court. However, there is no such procedure in New York, where the Luft suit was filed, so technically the suit was still alive.

pull together. Regardless of anything you read or hear, David has my backing. I wouldn't have brought him back if I didn't know he could do the job. We've got to pull together here.''

The group went on to an agenda of regular studio business. Begelman was called out of the room every few minutes to take phone calls. During his absences, there was whispering about the *New West* article. The agenda finally was covered and the meeting was adjourned.

Early that evening Hirschfield kept an appointment with a man who wanted to discuss the possibility that Columbia Pictures Industries might purchase the Howard Johnson hotel and restaurant chain. Hirschfield had difficulty concentrating; he kept seeing the photostat of Begelman's signature.

Joe Fischer, too, couldn't get his mind off the article. Dining with Jim Johnson at The Saloon in Beverly Hills, he studied the piece line by line. Fischer was seared by a sentence that Begelman had uttered in 1963 in rebuttal to a charge by Sid Luft. "I swear on the life of my child," Begelman had said.

Looking incredulously at Jim Johnson, Fischer said: "That's what he told us in September when he was claiming we had found everything! Then we found more!"

DAVID HARTMAN: Good morning, Rona.

RONA BARRETT: Good morning, David, and good morning, America. The media investigation of Columbia Pictures president David Begelman, who admitted to financial wrongdoing before being reinstated to his executive post, has started an investigative juggernaut that has Hollywood in an uproar. Regardless of how industry executives view the Begelman situation, the consensus is that whether he now resigns under pressure or not, his conduct has already opened up Hollywood to such strong scrutiny that the industry may not withstand the pressure of so many prying eyes. Currently, *The New York Times* and *The Wall Street Journal* are conducting full-scale, across-the-board investigations of industry activities, and executives are worried that before the spotlight is off Hollywood, its already precarious reputation as an upstanding industry will be demolished. Ironically, this scrutiny comes at a time when industry profits have never been higher. However, with the billions of dollars Hollywood earns, it must be accountable to the same standards of behavior ethical people apply to all businesses. Therefore, while I deplore the headline-grabbing stories that are long on accusations and short on insights that have been published in regard to Begelman, I am confident that a reasonable look at our industry, by well-informed analysts who know the territory, can only do Hollywood a world of good in the long run.

Hirschfield's meetings at the studio on Tuesday with the television staff were as awkward as the session with the motion-picture executives had been. Begelman again was called out of the conference room frequently, and during his absences staff members nervously whispered jokes back and forth about the *New West* article.

"Maybe we can get the rights from *New West*."

"It would make a great movie, but no one would believe it."

On the other side of Burbank that morning—several miles up Olive Avenue, away from the Burbank Studios, the Disney Studios and NBC, past the Masonic Temple, the municipal power plant, Ben's Body Shop, and the Golden State Freeway—Detective Bob Elias sat at his desk on the second floor of police headquarters questioning Cliff Robertson. Robertson was on the telephone in his apartment in New York. Also on the line were Deputy District Attorney Walter Lewis and Robertson's lawyer, Seth Hufstedler. The interview was a formality; no new information was elicited. But Robertson did allude to what he viewed as the most serious problem confronting him as a result of reporting Begelman's crimes.

"Do you expect to lose any money as a result of this forgery?" Elias asked.

"Well, that's a conjecture, I would say that there is a strong possibility that because I've taken a forthright stand there is always the possibility that certainly in some areas of the industry there is the possibility that I might find that I won't work as much."

Hirschfield had breakfast Thursday with Lew Wasserman of MCA to discuss Hollywood labor issues. The subject of Begelman naturally came up. Wasserman made clear that he felt the affair was a "disaster for the entire industry."

Hirschfield then had a secret meeting with Richard Smith, the chief executive of General Cinema, the nation's largest movie-theater chain, in Smith's suite at the Beverly Hills Hotel. They had not had a candid, face-to-face discussion since late October when Smith had told Hirschfield in Boston that if David Begelman was reinstated as president of the studio, General Cinema would drop its tentative plan to make a major investment in Columbia's motion-picture production program. Smith had monitored subsequent events closely and, despite the reinstatement, sympathized with Hirschfield's plight. It seemed clear to both men, particularly in the light of the Judy Garland disclosures, that Begelman could not last. He would have to be removed again—permanently this time. To Smith, the principal question was not whether Begelman would remain at Columbia but whether Hirschfield would.

"I don't know," said Hirschfield. "I hope so." He brought Smith up to date on the seemingly irreparable rift with the board, and told him that the only solution seemed to be intervention by a strong outsider who might buy Columbia and install a new board of directors, or at least purchase a sufficient block of stock to have an influence over Allen and Rosenhaus. They discussed the possibility that General Cinema might be such an outsider or that Smith might be able to help Hirschfield find one. Smith was mildly encouraging.

Hirschfield caught the noon United flight to Kennedy, feeling better than he had in some time. Although he had embarrassed himself in endorsing Begelman, he felt that most of the studio people understood the circumstances. In any case, all his predictions about a holocaust in the press were coming true. Begelman surely would have to be banished now. More important, the list of potential outside allies in Hirschfield's struggle to prevail over Herbert Allen had grown to include General Cinema.

The media storm grew even worse after the Judy Garland revelations. There were stories on the CBS evening news with Walter Cronkite and on other network programs. And the press forged ahead.

HOLLYWOODGATE ROLLS ON! (Liz Smith)
CRITICISM OF COLUMBIA PICTURES GROWS (*The Washington Post*)
DAVID BEGELMAN SAYS HE IS "ABSOLUTELY NOT" GOING TO RESIGN (The AP)

Even the telephone talk shows on radio entered the fray.
"This is Bob Grant, you're live on WOR. Hello."

"Bob, I'm calling in regards to the David Begelman affair out in California. You know, I don't understand. Some people are just never satisfied. Here's a guy who was making three hundred thousand dollars a year and Columbia Pictures was just about to give him a million-dollar bonus because he helped them build their industry back up, and he still had to embezzle ten thousand dollars, and that's not the worst of it. The thing that got me was that they made Cliff Robertson out to be the skunk. His friends—Begelman's friends out there—are on Cliff Robertson's back because he wanted to prosecute Begelman."

Robertson's concern about being blackballed was well-founded, more even than he realized. The previous August, Cliff had agreed to direct and star in a picture based on James Kirkwood's novel *Good Times, Bad Times*, about a sequence of tragedies involving the headmaster and students of a New England preparatory school. The producer employing Cliff was James Bradley, an associate of Merv Griffin. Bradley, who had produced and directed several television programs but no theatrical films, was attempting to raise money to make *Good Times, Bad Times* and had developed a number of promising leads, including an informal commitment for a little more than half of the picture's $1.9-million budget. The project had been announced in the Hollywood trade press.

In late January, after the Begelman-Robertson controversy had erupted, Jim Bradley began getting anonymous telephone calls in the middle of the night. The voice on the phone—the same mature male voice each time—said in essence: Get rid of Cliff Robertson or you'll never get your picture made, and you'll lose everything you have. The calls came every night between midnight and three, including weekends, for two and a half weeks, and then stopped.

Bradley told a few close friends about the calls but did not tell Cliff Robertson or report the calls to the authorities. (The caller had not threatened physical harm to Bradley or Robertson.) Although Bradley was shaken, he kept Robertson as the centerpiece of the film project and continued his efforts to raise money. But the leads he had developed gradually ebbed and eventually disappeared.

FORTY-FOUR

Ignoring calls on Friday from Barbara Walters, *Time* magazine, *The Washington Post*, *The New York Times*, Ray Stark, *The Hollywood Reporter*, *Business Week*, and Sam Cohn, among others, Alan Hirschfield took the elevator down two floors to Allen & Company.* The last time he had been in the Allen offices—Tuesday of the previous week—he had left shouting, "I don't have to take this abuse." His trip to California had calmed him, however, and he found Herbert, as well, to be more subdued than Alan had seen him in weeks. Though neither man was happy, they both knew what had to be done.

"Morale, despite my efforts, is at an all-time low," Hirschfield reported. "The *New West* article and the daily press coverage has everybody upset. *New West* was just devastating. David's effectiveness is really at an end. He can't focus on business. He's so busy defending himself that he can't concentrate. No human being could. The barrage is just unrelenting. He's like a fighter in the ring getting hit not only by his opponent but by the referee and his manager as well. It's like seeing an animal taunted. While I feel great sympathy, I also have a responsibility to run the company."

"Should he resign?" Herbert asked.

"For the good of the company, he should."

"I agree. I'll call Sy Weintraub and discuss it. I think it can be worked out. Can we give him a production deal?"

"We probably can if we do it quickly. The more time passes, the more attention and scrutiny it will get. We can't revert to the December situation of a big contract settlement, plus a rich produc-

---

*In early December, Allen & Company moved its offices from Broad Street in lower Manhattan to the ninth floor of 711 Fifth Avenue, two floors below the executive suite of Columbia Pictures Industries.

tion deal, unless we're prepared to accept a lot of criticism and potential liability.''

"I'll talk to Sy," Herbert said.

Telling no one their destination, and with a figurative look back over their shoulders, Hirschfield and Adler made their way to 100 Park Avenue, just south of Grand Central, and the world headquarters of Philip Morris Incorporated. Adler had established contact with Philip Morris through a business consultant friend in Los Angeles, Robert Fell, who had performed a number of services for Columbia and had been made aware by Adler that Alan Hirschfield was looking for a savior. Fell suggested Philip Morris.

Philip Morris Incorporated was no longer just a cigarette maker. Although its principal brand—Marlboro—remained the world's best seller, and Benson & Hedges, Merit, and Virginia Slims were leaders, too, Philip Morris also had acquired the Miller Brewing Company and transformed it into the second-largest brewer in the United States, selling countless bottles, cans and barrels of Miller High Life, Miller Lite, and Löwenbräu. With revenues exceeding $4 billion annually, Philip Morris was the fifty-second largest industrial corporation in America (twenty-eighth in terms of profits) and wanted to establish a strong "third leg" by acquiring a major company in a business outside of cigarettes and beer—probably in the consumer-products or leisure-time fields where its potent marketing skills could be fully utilized.

Among the industries it had considered was entertainment. Philip Morris's vice chairman and soon-to-be-chairman, George Weissman, had started his business career as a publicist for Sam Goldwyn. He still liked the picture business and was intrigued by the notion of acquiring Columbia Pictures. Weissman received Hirschfield and Adler in his office, and they were joined by Philip Morris's acquisitions specialist, Robert Critchell. As a statue of Johnny, Philip Morris's old symbol and mascot, looked on, the four men had a promising chat, and the Columbia people left a packet of financial information on Columbia Pictures Industries. It was agreed that Adler and Critchell would continue the talks on a more detailed level within a few days.

Back at 711 Fifth, Hirschfield returned a call from David Karr, his old friend in Paris, who in December had told John Tunney about the secret talks with Jimmy Goldsmith. Karr wanted Hirschfield to know that, despite any misunderstanding over confidentiality, Goldsmith was still interested in Columbia. He would be in New York in a couple of weeks and planned to approach the Allens. Perhaps there was hope on that front yet.

Herbert Allen telephoned Hirschfield at home that evening and told him that Begelman was prepared to resign immediately. Begelman and Sy Weintraub wanted to fly to New York on Saturday and spend Sunday negotiating with Hirschfield. Alan, who dreaded another personal confrontation with Begelman, suggested instead that David submit his resignation in Los Angeles and that Leo Jaffe be dispatched to the coast on Monday to work out the details. Hirschfield felt it was important, tactically and psychologically, for the resignation to precede the negotiation, rather than have the resignation itself become a bargaining chip, i.e., risk that Begelman would refuse to resign unless he got the terms he wanted. But Herbert insisted that David be permitted to come to New York and see Hirschfield and Alan finally relented.

Grasping for new angles, the press made more and more mistakes. MOVIE DEAL STARTLES HOLLYWOOD said a headline in the Friday *Los Angeles Times*. A more apt headline would have been MOVIE DEAL STARTLES THOSE IN HOLLYWOOD WHO ARE POORLY INFORMED. The story concerned Columbia Pictures' ownership of Rastar Productions, one of the several corporate entities through which Ray Stark did business. In purchasing Rastar Productions in 1974, Columbia had simply acquired Stark's interest in certain of his movies such as *Funny Girl* and *The Way We Were*. The transaction had been motivated primarily by tax considerations and was legal in every respect. Since the deal lacked broad significance, Columbia did not announce it publicly but merely included it in periodic public reports to the Securities and Exchange Commission. *Variety* had reported the purchase at that time. However, when the *Los Angeles Times* stumbled across the deal three years later, while scrambling to rebut charges that it had neglected the Begelman-Columbia scandal, the paper presented the Rastar Productions purchase as a startling revelation of the true extent of Stark's influence at Columbia Pictures and of his motivations for becoming involved in the Begelman fight. The *Times* also hinted that Columbia's failure to announce the purchase when it occurred might have been illegal.

The New York Times, in an article on Ray Stark the following day, repeated the essence of the *Los Angeles Times* story, and the *Los Angeles Herald Examiner* then reprinted the *New York Times* story.

Ray Stark, through his attorney, demanded and got published clarifications from all three papers.

Sunday, February 5, was one of the coldest and bleakest days of the winter in New York. Seven-eleven Fifth Avenue was uncomfortably chilly, even the windowless boardroom where a sullen group of Columbia officers and directors gathered at noon to confront David Begelman and Sy Weintraub. Hirschfield was flanked by Joe Fischer, Victor Kaufman, Peter Gruenberger, and Leo Jaffe.* There to ensure that David Begelman got what they felt Columbia owed him were Herbert Allen, Irwin Kramer, and Dan Lufkin.

Though Hirschfield held to his view that Begelman should submit his resignation before negotiations began, the board members insisted that the two men meet privately to hear each other's positions before the larger group became involved. Alan and David went into Hirschfield's office, which was even colder than the boardroom.

Alan implored David to "be reasonable. I'm conscious of your problems. I know this is a low ebb in your life. But for God's sake don't create more problems for yourself and the company by making demands that aren't reasonable. There are limits today. It's not December. This is a national story. This deal is going to be scrutinized, no matter what we do, and it's going to be the subject of lawsuits in my opinion. So if you truly want this thing to die down, to damp the fires and go away, you have to be reasonable. Now is a chance to at least begin to put this thing to rest. Don't do it for me. Forget my position. I feel my days are numbered here, too. But serve yourself by being reasonable."

Begelman was even more haggard than he had been a few days earlier in Los Angeles, and Hirschfield found himself again deeply saddened just by the sight of him—so different from the dapper, enthusiastic, self-assured man he had grown fond of over the past four and a half years.

"I hear what you're saying, Alan, but I just can't accept anything less than a full settlement of my contract plus an independent

---

*Todd Lang was vacationing in the Caribbean.

production deal that is competitive with my position and record in the industry. Look, Alan, I'm broke. The only thing standing between my sanity and putting a gun in my mouth is the prospect of a financial arrangement that will leave me whole and give me security for the future. If I can't get it here, I have assurances that Warner's, Fox, and Paramount stand ready to make an appropriate deal with me. But if I can't even get a sufficient settlement of my contract here, there's no sense in resigning. I truly am at the end of my rope.''

As he listened to Begelman, who was near tears, Hirschfield was touched and depressed. In contrast to his cynical reaction to David's plea for mercy at the board meeting in November ("That was quite an act, trembling hands and all"), Alan now felt compassion. To hear the proud and normally controlled David Begelman say that he was "broke" and that he might "put a gun in my mouth" was wrenching for Hirschfield. Yet it was confusing as well, and even disorienting. Could this be just another act? Another skilled performance? Alan's emotions told him it wasn't, but how could he be sure? As he had at other moments since Detective Silvey's call in September, Hirschfield thought of Herman Melville's story of illusion and reality, "Benito Cereno," in which the main character comes to accept a particular version of events, only to find that it is entirely false.

Shivering from the cold, their differences unresolved, Hirschfield and Begelman returned to the boardroom.

"I've basically come here to resign," Begelman told the group, "and I need to know what Columbia has in mind for me following my resignation. It seems to me there are three possibilities: I don't resign, and Columbia stands foursquare behind me, and we fight this through. I resign, my contract is settled, and I make an independent production arrangement with Columbia. Or, I resign, my contract is settled, and I go elsewhere."

"The only realistic option," Hirschfield said, "is a reasonable settlement that includes a reasonable production deal at Columbia."

Dan Lufkin, who had had little to say since joining the Columbia board two months earlier, suddenly turned on Hirschfield. "Alan, you're at a crossroads here. It is my opinion that if you threw your full support behind David, together with the board's support, we could fight the present situation through, even including an indictment. Your failure to support David has helped create the present set of circumstances. If you're not prepared to support David, then we should do one of two things: give him a fair settlement and let him go elsewhere, or keep him at Columbia by giving him a fair settlement of his contract and an independent production deal that is competitive in the industry. . . .''

Hirschfield interrupted: "I think it's outrageous that you choose to blame me for this public outcry, to say that this has become a national story because of my failure to support Begelman! The real problem was the failure of the board to support me! You haven't been around long and maybe you don't know all the facts, but it's outrageous for you to be rewriting history like this. I will be happy to spend the rest of the day with you, updating you on the fact that I warned the board and every right-thinking person who would listen that all of this would happen. What this board has done—the way this board has behaved—has never happened before in the history of American business!''

"Either you support him or you don't," Lufkin asserted. "If you don't have the guts to support him, at least have the guts to make the right kind of deal with him. Either get rid of him with the proper settlement, or make a fair deal to keep him.''

Herbert Allen endorsed the notion of making Begelman a producer at Columbia. It was suggested that Hirschfield, Jaffe, and Fischer, on behalf of Columbia, and Sy Weintraub, on behalf of Begelman, begin negotiating. The talks lasted far into the evening and were very acrimonious. Weintraub occasionally left the boardroom to confer with Begelman. Herbert Allen and Irwin Kramer stayed to monitor the negotiations. Slowly, point by point, the Columbia negotiators agreed to give David Begelman much of what he wanted—a deal from which he stood an excellent chance of making more money than he had made as president of the studio.

Although Hirschfield knew that his authority had been eroded still further, this latest acquiescence to Herbert Allen's wishes did not depress him as much as the events of December had. The second compromise always is easier than the first. Furthermore, David Begelman at least was out of the company. To that extent, Hirschfield had won a minor victory. And he had bought still more time for his secret efforts to overthrow Herbert.

A public-relations consultant was brought in to draft a press release. After a long, loud argument over phrasing, the release was completed and prepared for dissemination Monday morning.

The weary negotiators shuffled out onto Fifth Avenue late in the evening, just as the snow was beginning to fall.

FORTY-FIVE

The phone rang in Rona Barrett's Beverly Hills home at 10:30 that evening, California time. It was Begelman. "I have just left the boardroom of Columbia Pictures Industries," he told her. "I wanted you to know before anyone else that I have resigned."

"I'm sorry," Barrett said.

"I will become an independent producer doing motion pictures and television for Columbia," Begelman added, choking back tears.

They talked for about twenty minutes, after which Barrett decided that the story was big enough to justify rewriting and retaping her Monday morning broadcast. Normally, she taped her reports in the evening at the Los Angeles ABC studios for use the following morning on *Good Morning America*. Earlier that evening she had taped a story saying that David Begelman was expected to resign within forty-eight hours—a story that Begelman's phone call had made obsolete. At 11 P.M., Barrett aroused her entire television crew and asked them to meet her back at the studios. At 3 A.M. she fed a new report to New York:

> Good morning, David, and good morning, America.
>
> From New York City, David Begelman has confirmed to me that late last night he resigned from the presidency of Columbia Pictures, and that a public announcement from Columbia is expected momentarily. Begelman's resignation thereby ends a personal ordeal that began last October when he admitted to financial misdeeds and temporarily removed himself from his executive post before being reinstated to the presidency two months later. His resignation today has been speculated about these last few days, despite adamant denials of any such impending intention by Begelman himself, and assurance from

Columbia's board of directors that he enjoyed their total support. David Begelman also confirmed that he will now become an independent producer associated with Columbia, the position many thought he should have assumed immediately after admitting to his financial misconduct. Begelman, sounding emotionally drained, said his decision to resign stemmed from his inability to stand by and watch innocent men and women, many of them friends, be torn apart by headline-grabbing accusations and innuendos. What effect Begelman's resignation will have on the community remains to be seen, since what might be termed a civil war has been in effect between pro-Begelman supporters and anti-Begelman agitants. Whether that emotional split can now be healed and goodwill restored will be a formidable task for industry leaders to face. Adding to the chaos is the massive media attention now focused on the industry, a direct result of the Pandora's box the Begelman affair opened. . . .

It snowed in New York from late Sunday until Tuesday afternoon— eighteen inches officially by the time it stopped, blown into high drifts by strong north winds. The storm was the most severe for several years, but it did not prevent the Columbia principals from conducting business. Many of those who did not live in Manhattan stayed in the city overnight.

A dour Herbert Allen dispatched a blunt, perfunctory note on Monday to Hirschfield, Fischer, and Jaffe.

"I am asking all the people I know to come up with recommendations [of candidates to head the studio]. These are some of the names I've heard so far today. I don't know if they're available or qualified, but it's a beginning." He listed Dan Melnick; Bob Evans, the producer and former head of production at Paramount; David Picker, a producer who had presided over both Paramount and United Artists; Stan Kamen, the William Morris agent; Freddie Fields; Sue Mengers; David Geffen; Marty Ransohoff; Ned Tanen, the president of Universal Pictures; and several other people.

In contrast to Herbert's feeling of urgency, Hirschfield preferred to conduct the search more deliberately and perhaps use it as an opportunity for reorganizing the studio to solve some of the management lapses he and Adler had discussed months earlier. Moving slowly would also give him more time to search for a buyer for the corporation at large.

By special messenger on Monday, Hirschfield received a package of documents and pamphlets on Philip Morris assembled by its acquisitions man, Robert Critchell. The package was marked "Personal and Confidential—Eyes Only," and bore no return address or other Philip Morris marking. The contact between the two companies was especially sensitive for Bob Critchell. He had been a fraternity brother of Herbert Allen's at Williams College.

The Begelman resignation story appeared on virtually every network television and radio news program and in just about every newspaper in the country. And though *Time* and *Newsweek* had gone to press before Begelman's resignation became known, both magazines appeared Monday with major "Hollywoodgate" articles. *Newsweek* did a splashily illustrated seven-page cover story (INSIDE HOLLYWOOD: HIGH STAKES! FAST BUCKS! SHADY DEALS!). *Time* published a more modest piece which concluded: "The Begelman affair reawakens old suspicions about Hollywood—that it is dominated by a handful of imperious men who can benefit from a double scale of justice and a one-sided set of books." Liz Smith concluded her Monday column with an ominous little item: "The further story on this sordid matter, now being prepared by *The New York Times*, will pop Hollywood open because it will go all the way back to the days of Meyer Lansky, and the names involved will not find it funny when they read about themselves." Though Smith was not specific, she was referring to the exposé being written by Lucian Truscott, IV, for the *Times* magazine under the supervision of editor Lynda Obst.

To Alan Hirschfield, Monday's biggest and most depressing news was the announcement that Arthur Krim and his fellow defectors from United Artists had decided to affiliate with Warner Bros. instead of Columbia. The deal with Warner was very much like that which Hirschfield had devised and offered. Having begun his wooing of the Krim group three months before anyone else had even known they were leaving United Artists, Hirschfield was certain that they would have come to Columbia, were it not for the way the board had handled the Begelman affair. It was a major loss to Columbia both in money and prestige, and Hirschfield feared that other important relationships—such as those with IBM and Time—might suffer as well. His bitterness toward Herbert Allen found new depths.

Mired in Manhattan by the snow, Hirschfield dined Monday

evening with Jean Vagnini, Columbia's attractive young public relations director. After a good deal of wine, they slipped into the Ziegfeld Theater and saw part of *Close Encounters*. By ten o'clock, they were on Fifty-fourth Street, giggling and throwing snowballs at each other.

The full Columbia board of directors met on Thursday, February 9, for the first time since mid-January. After weeks of inconclusive argument, the issue of Alan Hirschfield's status with the company was discussed formally. Leo Jaffe stated that he felt it was time to begin negotiating a "new and extended employment agreement" with Hirschfield.

Herbert Allen angrily objected and waved a *Wall Street Journal* article whose headline indicated that Begelman's resignation represented a victory for Hirschfield. "This is a disgrace and a slur," Allen said. "We can't live with this."

James Wilmot said, "How can we consider giving him a new contract when he keeps embarrassing the board in public? He plays the white knight. We're still the black hats."

Hirschfield said, "I can't be responsible for the way people perceive things."

It was suggested that Hirschfield would have an opportunity the following week to begin repairing his relationships with the board: his appearance before the New York Society of Security Analysts. If he could make a clear and unequivocal statement in that public forum that it had been *his* decision to reinstate Begelman in December, the board would consider the admission evidence of good faith.

"We can't keep having these divisive stories," Dan Lufkin said.

Hirschfield replied, "That's fine with me. We agreed weeks ago that no one would talk to the press, and somehow some of you made a mistake and talked to Dan Dorfman, and that story in *New York* magazine, as far as the record is concerned, is still the last definitive statement the board has made about me—you don't trust me, I'm on my way out, and if I didn't have a contract I'd be out tomorrow."

Hirschfield agreed to make the statement the board wanted at the analysts meeting, and the discussion returned to his new contract. Jaffe argued that the endorsement of Hirschfield implied by a new contract would put the company "in a better position to attract a new head of the motion-picture and television divisions and enhance the employees' feeling of solidarity." Herbert Allen asked if Hirschfield wanted to begin negotiations. Hirschfield replied that he was prepared to do so for the reasons stated by Jaffe. The board formally authorized Jaffe and Allen to negotiate with Hirschfield.

With the city still in the grip of the blizzard, it was a week of few meetings and lots of phone calls. Ray Stark, William Thompson, David Geffen, Mickey Rudin, Sam Cohn, Clive Davis, Lord Delfont of EMI, Detective Elias of the Burbank police, Barbara Walters, Peter Guber, David Begelman, Marty Ransohoff, Sam Cohn again, William Thompson again, Jack Valenti, Geffen again, Sid Sheinberg of MCA-Universal, David Gerber, Dennis Stanfill of Fox, Leonard and Wendy Goldberg (separately), Ray Stark again, Geffen again, Barbara Walters again, Robert Daly of CBS, *Time, The Washington Post,* the *New York Post, The Hollywood Reporter,* the *Los Angeles Times, Variety* . . .

Adler had a stealthy lunch with Bob Critchell of Philip Morris on Friday at La Caravelle. Even though it was only half a block from Columbia, few Columbia people went there, preferring La Côte Basque right downstairs in the Columbia building. Still, the two men worried about being seen together, especially by Herbert Allen, Critchell's old fraternity brother. They continued to exchange information and talk about how Philip Morris might get in on the coming video revolution by buying Columbia Pictures.

David Begelman flew into New York that evening, conferred early Saturday morning with his New York lawyer, Gideon Cashman, and then the two of them proceeded to the Fifth Avenue apartment of Rupert Murdoch, the Australian tycoon who owned *New York* and *New West* magazines. Murdoch's lawyer, Howard Squadron, and the magazines' publisher, Joe Armstrong, were present as well. Aided by a number of documents, Begelman and Cashman attempted to refute Sid Luft's allegations, as presented in Jeanie Kasindorf's article on January 30, that Begelman had embezzled funds from Judy Garland.

When Gideon Cashman had announced Begelman's intention to sue, he had disseminated copies of a written statement, signed by Garland and notarized, releasing Begelman, as well as Freddie Fields, from any financial obligation to her. The statement had been signed in 1968, and Cashman had noted that Garland subsequently resumed her client relationship with Begelman and Fields.

In Rupert Murdoch's apartment, in addition to the Garland statement, Begelman and Cashman gave Murdoch and his aides copies of three other letters purportedly signed by Garland. Two of the letters, dated in late 1962 and sent to Charles Renthal, her New York business manager, stated that thirteen checks, which the letters listed by number and amount, were drawn by David Begelman with Garland's "consent and knowledge and distributed in accordance with my instructions." The checks were among those later questioned by the Beverly Hills accountant, Oscar Steinberg, whose report was quoted by Jeanie Kasindorf in her article.

The other Garland letter, addressed to Fields and Begelman, was dated July 23, 1963, about a month after the date of the Steinberg report, and set forth a paragraph-by-paragraph acceptance of Fields and Begelman's explanation to her of each of Steinberg's questions. The letter also stated that Garland had no financial claim against Fields and Begelman and released them from obligation for any such claim.

The 1963 letter bore the signature of a purported witness to Garland's signature. The 1962 letters did not indicate that her signatures were witnessed. None of the letters was notarized.

Based on the letters and other material presented to the Murdoch group, Begelman and Cashman demanded a retraction of those portions of the Kasindorf article dealing with Begelman's handling of Judy Garland's funds. Murdoch's lawyer, Squadron, suggested that Begelman and Cashman put their request in writing and also write a letter of refutation to the editors of the magazines, which they would consider publishing. Begelman and Cashman held out for retraction.

Finally, it was agreed that the lawyers would discuss the matter further after Murdoch's people had examined the new material in detail.*

Begelman flew back to Los Angeles that evening.

*   *   *

---

*In 1964, a year after the Garland letters to Fields and Begelman accepting their explanations and releasing them from any claims, Garland seemingly contradicted herself by testifying in a divorce deposition that she had not given Begelman permission to draw cash from her account during part of the period covered by the Kasindorf article. Whatever the truth—and it was impossible fifteen years later to establish the truth beyond doubt—it is important to recall that Judy Garland was unstable mentally and physically, and was under the influence of sleeping pills, liquor, and other substances so much of the time that the validity of anything she wrote, signed, said, or testified to is open to question in retrospect on that basis alone.

Hirschfield fretted through Monday and into Tuesday morning over his appearance before the New York security analysts, which was scheduled for noon Tuesday at the Banker's Club on lower Broadway near Wall Street. He dreaded answering the embarrassing questions that might be asked. He dreaded keeping his commitment to the board to take public responsibility for reinstating Begelman in December. He dreaded the necessity of portraying the management of Columbia Pictures Industries as stable and peaceful when, in fact, it was unstable and in turmoil.

He interrupted his preparations to participate in a meeting at 10:30 Tuesday morning with Herbert Allen, Leo Jaffe, Irwin Kramer, and Matty Rosenhaus who wanted to be briefed on his plans for replacing Begelman.

"I have various people in mind," Hirschfield said. "One option is to put a good administrative man in the slot but not replace David as such in a creative sense. If we go that route, it's possible that Joe Fischer might go out."

Matty Rosenhaus, who was in Florida listening on a speakerphone, shouted, "You told us you were going to replace David!"

"Matty, I never said I was going to replace David, as such," Hirschfield replied, "I said I was going to get somebody or somebodies to in effect administer what David was doing. It's possible that a different structure may be better than what we've had. But if I can get someone who is a strong overall executive in both administration and creative, I'll consider him."

"You said you were going to replace *David*!" Matty shouted.

More than at any other time since the crisis began five months earlier, Alan Hirschfield lost his temper. "Matty, if you think you can do this job better, then you can come up and run the fucking company!" Hirschfield shouted into the phone. "You don't understand this business and you never have! If this is the kind of cooperation I'm going to get from you, I'm not going to take it any longer! I'm supposed to be making a presentation before the security analysts in an hour, and I'm not going to take any more of this shit. If you think I'm going to go downtown and talk to a bunch of people and feed them a lot of shit that I don't want to give them to begin with, then you've got another think coming! I've had it!"

Hirschfield slammed down the phone, cutting Rosenhaus's connection to everyone in the room, and strode out the door. The others were stunned. After a moment, Joe Fischer went after Hirschfield and finally found him sitting alone in the projection room on the other side of the building. Allen and Kramer came in after a few seconds.

"So why didn't the two of you open your mouths?" Hirschfield shouted at the two board members. "You were sitting there enjoying every minute of that. If you're such geniuses, why don't the two of you go down and make the fucking presentation at the analysts. Or why don't you fly Matty up here to do it. I'm sure the analysts would love to hear his view of the company and the movie industry."

Hirschfield walked out again and went back to his office. Fischer followed and said: "Don't pay any attention to these people. They're fucking fools. Don't let it get to you. You gotta make the presentation. It'll be good for you to do it."

"Let them make the fucking presentation!" Hirschfield said.

Joe managed to calm Alan, and the two of them, together with the other Columbia officers attending the analysts luncheon, got in the limousine at 11:30. Hirschfield finished the notes for his speech on the way downtown. Snow was falling but they managed to arrive on time.

Before everyone finished eating and he was to begin his speech, Hirschfield worked the tables, shaking hands and bantering with several of the Wall Street people whom he knew. It seemed miraculous to Fischer that Hirschfield had recovered from his near hysteria barely more than an hour earlier. With his speech to the analysts, however, Hirschfield again demonstrated his remarkable ability to mask his private feelings and get the most out of a public occasion. He had done it at the Brandeis dinner in September, with the first secret details of Begelman's embezzlements still fresh and frightening in his mind. He had done it at the *Close Encounters* premiere, immediately after being confronted with the board's threat to investigate his wife's employment record. And he was doing it again now, with the enormity of his alienation from the board having just been confirmed by Matty Rosenhaus's long-distance shouts and the ugly scene at the office.

"Before I start our presentation," Hirschfield said from the podium, "I'd like to say a few words about our recent problems. All in all, they constitute a tragedy for a man I still consider a friend—David Begelman. Hopefully, it's behind us. The nature of his acts and the enormous media attention have implied that there was more wrong than we found, and that's not the case. But my decision to bring him back proved to be wrong, and we had to move ahead.''

Hirschfield then described the various business activities of Columbia Pictures Industries and reported that operating earnings for the second quarter and first half of the June 30 fiscal year had risen more than 300 percent from like periods a year earlier. The results included only three weeks of revenues from *Close Encounters* which, said Hirschfield, ''as of today, has achieved a box-office gross of approximately $72 million. The retention to Columbia has been approximately $51 million. As of next week, it will be the seventh-largest-grossing picture in the history of motion pictures in the United States. Our foreign prospects on the movie look extraordinarily promising. We expect by the time we're through *Close Encounters* at the very least will be the third- or fourth-highest-grossing picture in the history of motion pictures.''

There were many questions from the audience.

''Can you run down your new films and where you might see a blockbuster within those—what names in particular?''

''*Eyes,* scheduled for release this summer, stars Faye Dunaway and is produced by Jon Peters. It's a thriller that has really good upside. We've got a sleeper called *Midnight Express,* which I hear is absolutely sensational. It's in the genre of *Taxi Driver,* which has grossed $20 million for us. Our current biggest-budget picture is *California Suite* from the Neil Simon play. This should be a knock-out of a movie. It's produced by Ray Stark and has one of the biggest casts ever assembled, for a picture: Walter Matthau, Jane Fonda, Alan Alda, Michael Caine, Richard Pryor, Bill Cosby, and Maggie Smith. We just started a picture tentatively called *Eyewitness* with Jane Fonda, Michael Douglas, and Jack Lemmon, which deals with a nuclear-power-plant cover-up story.* *Nightwing,* which is about vampire bats, is directed by Arthur Hiller, with Marty Ransohoff producing. It has an enormous shot at being a breakaway thriller movie. We also have a new Norman Jewison picture called *And Justice for All,* which is a people-against-the-system kind of movie with great potential. We have *Sinbad Goes to Mars* in production. You can laugh, but the last Sinbad movie did $15 million and it's still going strong.

''The three especially big movies that we have on the boards are

---

*Eventually entitled *The China Syndrome.*

Electric Horseman, which is the new Redford-Pollack picture in partnership with Universal. The next Steven Spielberg movie is tentatively titled *1941.* John Milius is writing and producing. It's a broad farce, special-effects comedy in the genre of *Mad, Mad World* and could be an enormous picture. It's a big-budget movie and likely will be partnered with Universal. We have the new Paddy Chayevsky book, the movie of which will go into production late in the year or the beginning of 1979. It portends to be a big breakaway movie. It's a cross between reality and science fiction with a very commercial theme, one that's never been done on the screen before."

With the aid of charts and graphs projected on a large screen, Hirschfield explained in detail the financing of *Close Encounters,* as well as the projected financing of *Annie* and other aspects of Columbia's financial structure. He convinced just about everyone in the room that the corporation was in robust financial health and had a very bright future. "We believe we understand more about our basic business and its nuances than any company in our industry," he asserted.

Surprisingly, and to his great relief, there were no difficult questions about the Begelman scandal or the rift within the company. He sat down to warm applause.

David and Gladyce Begelman flew to the Far East Wednesday. They would vacation in Hong Kong and Japan, and on Friday, February 25, David would represent Columbia Pictures at the Tokyo premiere of *Close Encounters.*

Late on the Sunday evening he resigned, David's last request had been that he be permitted to attend the two principal foreign premieres of *Close Encounters*—in London and Tokyo—even though he would no longer be president of the studio. Joe Fischer had been shocked by the request, but Hirschfield, who was exhausted and apathetic by that point, gave his assent.

Since the Queen was expected at the London premiere, all guests had to be cleared by Buckingham Palace. The palace rejected David Begelman; it seemed inappropriate for the Queen to receive an admitted check forger who was at the center of a major American business scandal.

Begelman, therefore, had to settle for Tokyo only.

*　　*　　*

Still angry at the press, Ray Stark dispatched a lengthy telegram to Liz Smith accusing her of being "curt" and assailing her for not seeking his comment on an item in her column.

> . . . Of course, Liz, you could call me and even reverse the charges. . . . I'm surprised and shocked at your lack of professionalism and friendship in not calling me. . . . You are a nice lady, a good reporter and I hope you are not letting yourself get caught up in the vicious, irresponsible media circus. Again, please feel free to call me anytime, whenever you wish. My home number is in the phone book.

Smith replied with a letter.

> Dearest Ray,
> . . . I could not wait any longer to take a tougher stance on the Begelman affair.
> I did let Sue [Mengers] talk me out of a tough line for many weeks. And I am aware of your pro-Begelman interest. . . . I don't even know him, I have no personal animus, and I understand he is a very nice guy.
> But this was an important story. When we talked when you were off skiing, I knew you were trying to be helpful and you did not make any secret of your feelings. I kept all that off the record. In fact, Ray, I guess you simply have no idea of how much I have kept out of my column and off the record. I have omitted you from story after story on Begelman.
> I know I can call you and would have called you more on all of this, but I did NOT WANT TO PUT YOU ON THE SPOT. So Ray, I feel if anything, I have been protective of you in this matter. As much as I could be. I like you very much. I admire your work. I think of us as friends, and I appreciate your kind words. . . .
> . . . Anyway, Ray, I wasn't asking you for gossip nor meaning to be curt. I was trying to explain why I had to come down harder on the Begelman affair than you might want me to, considering your friendship. All these items on my desk saying he owes you $600,000 and you had a deal with him to take all

your worthless as well as good projects for Columbia, and on and on. All that has been kept out of my column. I consider that friendship, Ray. . . .*

Hirschfield coasted through the rest of the week and flew with his family to Vail, Colorado, on Friday evening for a week of skiing. The first day on the slopes, trying to avoid colliding with his son, Hirschfield fell and broke his right thumb. It was set, and his entire hand and forearm were put in a cast so that he could continue to ski. While dining in Vail, he and his party spotted Cliff Robertson with a group of people across the restaurant. Someone suggested that Alan should get Cliff to autograph his cast. Cliff cordially agreed, and while he was signing his name, Hirschfield said, "I don't know why I'm having you do this, Cliff. I should get David to sign it."

FORTY-SIX

Sir James Goldsmith and investment banker Ira Harris sat with Herbert Allen in Allen's office and talked about the possibility of Goldsmith's buying control of Columbia Pictures.

Goldsmith assured Allen that he did not intend to "act aggressively"; he came as a friend and was interested in buying only if the Allens and Matty Rosenhaus were genuinely interested in selling. There was no pressure.

Herbert was tempted. Over the past month, the stock had dropped from around twenty dollars a share to around fifteen. He knew Goldsmith could be induced to pay well in excess of twenty dollars a

---

*Smith handled Stark skillfully—by flattering him and making him feel powerful, the only way one realistically could handle Stark if one needed his goodwill. Of course, the "items" about a $600,000 debt and Begelman's buying Stark's "worthless" projects for Columbia were omitted from Smith's column not because of friendship but because she could not verify them as anything more than unfounded rumors.

share—six or seven times what the Allens had paid for the stock in 1973. Apart from the financial incentive, Herbert had to admit to himself that he was sick of the long fight with Hirschfield, sick of the frustrating search for a solution, and pessimistic about ever finding one. (Actually, Jimmy Goldsmith was not the only potential buyer who had approached Herbert. Other opportunists, seeing the dissension in the company, had made less explicit overtures. They included Kirk Kerkorian, the controlling shareholder of MGM, who less than a year later would purchase a major interest in Columbia.)

Though he acknowledged to Jimmy Goldsmith that there had been tension between Hirschfield and the rest of the board, Herbert did not mention that Hirschfield's approach to Goldsmith in December had been made without Herbert's knowledge, and that it had made him very angry at both Hirschfield and at Ira Harris. There was no need to get into that. Since no one but Hirschfield, Harris, and perhaps David Karr and John Tunney, knew that Hirschfield had initiated the contact behind Herbert's back, it easily could be made to appear to everyone else that the investment by Goldsmith had been Herbert's idea, either as an initiator or as the recipient of a proposal directly from Goldsmith. Alan Hirschfield need not be perceived as having had anything to do with it. It could be portrayed as a victorious exit from the company by the Allens and Matty Rosenhaus with an enormous profit in their stock, having nothing to do with the strife in the company, nothing to do with Hirschfield, nothing to do with anything except an economic opportunity that was too good to pass up.

Herbert told Jimmy Goldsmith that he would think seriously about it, and be in touch Wednesday or Thursday.

Ira Harris telephoned Hirschfield in Vail Wednesday morning to tell him that Goldsmith was in New York and that his talks with Herbert looked promising. A few minutes later Goldsmith himself called Hirschfield essentially to confirm what Harris had said, and to add that he hoped Hirschfield and his management team would remain at Columbia if Goldsmith, indeed, did take control of the company. Hirschfield was joyous.

In accord with the board of directors' decision, Herbert Allen also began talking early in the week with Alan Hirschfield's lawyer, Robert Haines, about a new long-term contract for Hirschfield. They made some progress, although Herbert made no promises.

*   *   *

With the press coverage hurtling onward—each major article seeming more sensational than the last—the principals in the Columbia drama anticipated with trepidation the impending article in *The New York Times* Sunday magazine by Lucian Truscott, IV. Truscott had interviewed Alan Hirschfield, Herbert Allen, and many others. Liz Smith had reported in early February that the Truscott piece would "pop Hollywood open because it would go all the way back to Meyer Lansky. . . ." On Wednesday, February 23, Smith ran a longer item about the *Times* article and said that it would appear that Sunday.

Through his cousin, theatrical producer Terry Allen Kramer, who knew a Broadway press agent with contacts at the *Times,* Herbert Allen obtained a copy of the article on Wednesday. He was devastated by what he saw. Reduced to its essence, the article, entitled "Hollywood's Wall Street Connection," suggested that the Allens' controlling interest in Columbia Pictures had been secretly for sale for some time, that Herbert Allen and others had tried to "hush up" the Begelman scandal in order to keep the market value of the stock from declining, and that Allen's actions were consistent with a history of dealing with disreputable people, including criminals. Charles Allen was labeled "The Godfather of the New Hollywood." He was said to have been a "mystery power behind the Hollywood set ever since" the early fifties and to have business links to a number of criminals, the most prominent of whom was Meyer Lansky, the boss of organized crime in America. The article was accompanied by photographs of Meyer Lansky and other shady characters, and also by a large candid shot of Charlie Allen, taken ambush-style as he was dining at the Carlyle Hotel.

Even if the article had been entirely accurate, Herbert Allen naturally would have been dismayed to see it published. But he was more than dismayed—he was deeply angry and even desperate— because the article was not accurate. It was strewn with falsehoods, large and small. And where Truscott had come close to the truth, he revealed information that Herbert did not want revealed. The article quoted Alan Hirschfield extensively, reflecting his version of the Begelman fight, a version highly critical of the Allens, and disclosed the direct link between Hirschfield and Jimmy Goldsmith.

Herbert suspected that Hirschfield was behind the entire article. But since he couldn't prove that, he confined his immediate efforts to *The New York Times*. He quickly summoned his lawyer, Robert Werbel, who informed a *Times* lawyer by phone that Allen & Company would sue the *Times* if the article was distributed. On Friday morning, Charlie Allen, Herbert Allen, Robert Werbel, and two other attorneys visited James Goodale, a *Times* executive vice president and publishing lawyer. They presented Goodale with a four-page letter outlining the Allens' objections to Lucian Truscott's piece and demanding that it be withdrawn from circulation. Goodale said it was too late; the magazine already had been distributed to thousands of news dealers for insertion in the Sunday *Times*.

Word on the article was beginning to circulate, the price of Columbia's stock was plummeting, and at noon on Friday, the New York Stock Exchange stopped trading in the stock because an influx of sell orders had made orderly trading impossible.

That afternoon, Allen & Company announced publicly that it would sue *The New York Times* for $150 million for publishing false and defamatory statements.

Privately, Herbert Allen told Jimmy Goldsmith that he was no longer willing to consider selling the Allens' interest in Columbia Pictures. And he told Alan Hirschfield's lawyer that there would be no further talk for the time being of a new contract for Hirschfield.

Herbert Allen was mystified by *The New York Times*. Just a little more than a year earlier the *Times* had published a lengthy and flattering feature article on Charlie Allen. And now this. It seemed inexplicable. Reports quickly began filtering into Herbert's office about Lucian Truscott's past (the drugs and the trouble with the Army) and about the background of the editor of the article, Lynda Obst. Herbert had never met Lynda Obst, but he objected to everything about Truscott: his manner, his assertive personality, his dress and hair style, not to mention his writing and research. Herbert sensed that he might be the victim of something quite rare in the upper echelon of American journalism: a prominent investigative article which would be widely believed because of the good reputation of the newspaper in which it appeared, but which had been prepared so carelessly that it obviously was an aberration when measured by the standards of *The New York Times*. The article somehow had slipped through the editing process and into print with its major as well as its minor flaws intact. Instead of being savaged by an established, credentialed investigative reporter, Herbert appeared to have been the victim of a fluke—a hatchet job perpetrated by an eccentric, long-haired polemicist from *The Village Voice* and a young female editor from *Rolling Stone* and *Beatlemania*. Where were the *Times* editors? Where was Abe Rosenthal?

Herbert knew that he could and would refute the article, but he also knew that the process would take months. Having published the piece, the *Times* would feel obliged to defend it vigorously. He was right. Three months later, after elaborate negotiations between lawyers for the two sides, *The New York Times* found it necessary to publish perhaps the most elaborate retraction, correction, and apology in the history of major American newspapers up to that time.*

The article was not entirely false, of course. Lucian Truscott and Lynda Obst were on to something. They had sensed correctly that somewhere in the morass of the Begelman scandal there lurked a good story that had not yet been told. But even after weeks of groping, Truscott had not grasped correctly what the story was. He wrote it as he saw it, however, and he wrote it sloppily.

Truscott's central thesis—that Columbia Pictures was for sale—was true on its face. But it was true only in a very narrow sense, which Truscott did not emphasize. The Allens had not put their interest in Columbia up for sale. The sole initiative to sell the company or any part of it had come from Alan Hirschfield, who was trying to wrest power from Herbert Allen by enlisting an outsider willing to acquire enough stock to neutralize or eliminate the Allens' influence and anoint Hirschfield the chief executive in fact as well as in title. (Outsiders indeed had expressed interest in the company, and the extraordinary irony was that, had Truscott's article not appeared when it did, Hirschfield might have succeeded: Herbert Allen, for reasons quite different from those set forth in the article, might have accepted an offer from Sir James Goldsmith that very week.)

---

*A. M. Rosenthal, the *Times'* executive editor, was away when the Truscott article was published. It is unlikely, however, that the article would have been stopped even if Rosenthal had been on duty. Several editors below Rosenthal had more direct responsibility for the Sunday magazine than Rosenthal did, and those editors all approved the article. Two clear mistakes were made: First, because of a zealous commitment to speed, mainly by Lynda Obst, normal fact-checking procedures were not observed as carefully as they normally are. Second, the higher editors failed to supervise Obst sufficiently closely to compensate for her relative inexperience with this type of article. In a broader sense, too, some *Times* people naturally questioned in retrospect whether Lucian Truscott should have been hired in the first place. A careful review of his previous work might have cast doubt on his suitability for such a sensitive assignment, despite some creditable investigative stories in the *Voice* and an obvious talent for other types of writing. The *Times* naturally tried to avoid another such debacle. Truscott was not asked to do any more complex business investigative articles. Several months later he published a successful novel about West Point. And the Columbia Pictures article led directly to Lynda Obst's departure from the magazine. Subsequently she became a Hollywood producer.

Truscott's portrait of Charlie Allen also embraced some truth. Charlie *had* been active in the motion-picture business, but it was hardly his "career" and he had made most of his money elsewhere. To call him the "Godfather of the New Hollywood" grossly inflated his true role. And Charlie *had* had business dealings with unsavory men in the Bahamas. But to link him by innuendo to Meyer Lansky, and to portray Allen & Company as a firm that habitually dealt with mobsters was a reckless and irresponsible overstatement of the facts.

With those major errors of theme and substance, it hardly seemed worth worrying about Truscott's many smaller mistakes. He misstated several crucial aspects of Columbia Pictures' financial condition. And he couldn't even spell "Carlyle," as in "hotel."

The events of the week exhausted Alan Hirschfield emotionally and left him more depressed and pessimistic than ever. He had known Goldsmith was coming to New York. He had been exultant to the point of disbelief when Ira Harris and Jimmy Goldsmith both had told him on Wednesday that it appeared Herbert might accept an offer and turn the company over to Goldsmith. The *New York Times* article, however, seemed to have scuttled not only the Goldsmith deal but all other possibilities that the company might be sold. Even though the article was far off the mark, Herbert was not about to give it even a modicum of credence by selling now under any circumstances. Moreover, Herbert's conviction that Alan had aided and abetted the Truscott piece, and the suspension of negotiation toward Alan's new contract, left the relationship between the two men as incendiary as ever.

On Friday, with his hand still in a cast, Hirschfield met *Rolling Stone* publisher Jann Wenner, who had been skiing at Aspen, and together they flew in a private jet to Los Angeles to appear on the dais at a black-tie charity dinner honoring Clive Davis. Hirschfield returned to Vail early Saturday to spend the balance of the weekend with his family. He flew back to Los Angeles late Sunday for a week of budget reviews and, more important, the beginning of the search for a new studio president.

Hirschfield knew that the search would be difficult, complicated, and perhaps ultimately futile. Who would want to work for a company whose atmosphere was contentious and whose lines of authority were clouded? Everyone in Hollywood knew or suspected that he and Herbert remained at odds, and thus no one knew who really was running the company, or who would be running it in six months or a year. Would the civil war end or worsen? Would Hirschfield be fired or kept on? What was the true extent of Ray Stark's influence in Columbia's affairs? Hirschfield suspected that even if he and Herbert gave solemn assurances of peace and stability they probably would not be taken seriously. Even with a long-term contract and a lot of money, it seemed doubtful that any qualified person would want to work in an environment where his own authority was in doubt and he might be distracted frequently by fights in upper management.

FORTY-SEVEN

The Securities and Exchange Commission had watched patiently as Columbia Pictures suspended David Begelman in September, conducted an internal investigation, decided tentatively in November to make the suspension permanent, reversed itself and reinstated Begelman in December, and then finally accepted his resignation from the company in February after the media attention made his position untenable. The SEC is affected by the news media like everyone else. As one senior enforcement official said to another in late February, "All the times I've been in California and didn't notice before: the Mercedeses, the Lincolns, the Cadillacs. There's got to be fraud." On Tuesday, February 28—two days after the publication of the Truscott article—the commission authorized the enforcement staff to launch its own formal investigation of the Begelman affair, Columbia's handling of it, and any evidence the investigators might find of fraud elsewhere in Hollywood. ·

Although the SEC's decision did not surprise many people at Columbia, Herbert Allen was incensed. He telephoned SEC enforcement chief Stanley Sporkin and angrily protested. But Sporkin would not be deterred. He wanted to see for himself whether there was any substance in what he had been hearing and reading.

*   *   *

Though Cliff Robertson had submitted to many press interviews by late February, he had refrained from appearing on television. But the networks were persistent, appealing to his sense of "fair play," and he finally decided to grant their requests in the most efficient manner possible—all in one day—all in one trip around midtown Manhattan. On Wednesday morning he was driven to NBC for *Today*, then to ABC for *Good Morning America*, and then to CBS where he taped an interview for use on the evening news. No new information was elicited from Robertson, but the unusual concentration of appearances was itself considered news. Stories appeared in newspapers across the nation. The people at Columbia Pictures again were furious at Robertson.

While Alan Hirschfield sought an experienced show-business executive for the Columbia studio post, the most promising candidate he saw that week was not an executive. He was a lawyer, Deane Johnson, the managing partner of O'Melveny & Myers, the largest and most prestigious law firm in Los Angeles and one of the few West Coast firms with a major national reputation. O'Melveny & Myers employed more than two hundred lawyers in Washington and Paris as well as Los Angeles and served a diverse array of clients. Deane Johnson's specialty, however, had always been entertainment. His clients included stars (Burt Reynolds and Ryan O'Neal), producers (Norman Lear and Marty Ransohoff), and corporations (several major studios). Johnson also had been Ray and Fran Stark's personal lawyer for more than two decades, and it was Ray who had recommended that Hirschfield see Johnson about the Columbia job. Johnson as well had long been friendly with Charlie Allen, and with Herbert, who had endorsed Stark's suggestion that Johnson might be right for Columbia.

Since two of Hirschfield's main enemies had initiated the contact with Johnson, Alan might naturally have been leery. But he knew that Deane Johnson was exceptional. As close as Johnson was to Stark and the Allens, he was also close to a multitude of other people, and yet was beholden to no one. Indeed, it was his independence that made him attractive. At the age of fifty-nine, Johnson's stature in the Hollywood community, his reputation for integrity, his international social connections (Mrs. Johnson was the former Anne

McDonnell Ford), his interests outside of show business, and his wealth all were too substantial for him to be in anyone's pocket.

Deane Johnson received Alan Hirschfield in the late afternoon of Thursday, March 2. Instead of commuting to O'Melveny's large quarters in downtown Los Angeles, Johnson occupied a comfortable corner office in the firm's smaller Century City suite, overlooking the Los Angeles Country Club, adjacent to Beverly Hills, close to his home in Bel-Air. Unlike many of his gold-chained, open-necked brethren in the Hollywood legal community, Johnson preferred conservative suits and ties. He had a tanned, lined face, open and friendly, with heavy brows and prominent features.

Hirschfield explained the problems at Columbia and the job Johnson would have if he could be persuaded to take it. He would preside over both motion pictures and television on a high, policy-making level, and would become a senior officer of the parent corporation and a member of the board of directors. To Hirschfield's surprise, Johnson was intrigued. He had been offered similar posts in the past by other motion-picture companies and had turned them down. But the Columbia situation sounded challenging, and although he and Hirschfield did not know each other especially well, Johnson had grown to like and respect Alan over the course of a number of business contacts. Johnson had not followed Columbia's recent problems closely as they had unfolded, but he agreed with Hirschfield's retrospective judgment that Begelman should have been fired immediately upon Columbia's learning of his embezzlements. Johnson accepted at face value Hirschfield's assurance that the disagreements within Columbia's management were healing. Hirschfield encouraged him, however, to speak directly with Ray and Herbert, and Johnson agreed to do so.

Deane and Anne Johnson chatted through most of that evening at home about the Hirschfield overture. Anne was even more captured by the idea than Deane and urged him to consider it seriously.

Alan Hirschfield, meanwhile, was dining nearby at the Bel-Air home of television producer David Gerber and discussing the Columbia studio post with Gerber and his other guest, Fred Pierce, the president of the ABC television network. Hirschfield admired Pierce as much as any executive in show business of his generation (people still under fifty). He had sought Pierce's counsel occasionally through the fall and winter and Pierce was among his top choices to replace

Begelman. Pierce, however, had assurances that he would move to higher levels at ABC and preferred to stay there.

In addition to establishing Philip Morris as a candidate to acquire Columbia Pictures, Allen Adler put Hirschfield in touch with a Los Angeles management consultant, Victor H. Palmieri, who had done extensive work for the Penn Central Corporation. Penn Central, whose assets were built upon the profitable remains of the bankrupt railroad company, was looking for another company to acquire. Having experienced huge losses in the past, Penn Central possessed substantial ''tax-loss carryforwards,'' meaning it could earn substantial profits for years into the future without paying any taxes. It owned some amusement parks and was interested generally in entertainment, among other industries. Adler's link to Victor Palmieri was a mutual acquaintance, Jerry Perenchio, the chairman of Norman Lear's company, Tandem Productions. Adler had told Perenchio of Hirschfield's desire to find a buyer for Columbia Pictures, and Perenchio sent Adler to Palmieri, who agreed to see Hirschfield. Hirschfield and Palmieri had dinner in Los Angeles and discussed Columbia Pictures at length, but Penn Central eventually decided that it was not interested.

Andrew Tobias, the first journalist to know the details of David Begelman's crimes, wrote by far the best of the major articles published on the subject. Unfortunately, the impact of the Tobias article was limited since it came out so late. Because of the unwieldy production schedules at *Esquire,* the piece did not appear until around March 1, four months after Tobias's source briefed him over a pizza in East Harlem on a Sunday night in the fall. Tobias wrote about Begelman's forgeries and their impact on the subcultures of Wall Street and Hollywood with his usual wit, common sense, and accuracy—qualities which so many other articles had lacked. After discussing the entire affair and adding some theretofore unknown details, he concluded with what he called a ''sermonette.''

> . . . when the board of directors of this public company actually moved to reinstate him (having paid him all the while he was on leave), they truly made a practical and, I think, an ethical blunder.
> *The man forged checks.* Not once, in a drunken stupor, but at

least three times. You can argue that a bar mitzvah attended by all your industry colleagues is good for business—and hence deductible. You may not win the argument, but you can make it. You can argue that illegal wiretapping, if done in the belief that it would save the country, has some supralegal moral justification. You may not win the argument, but at least you can make it. You can argue about marijuana, you can argue about draft resistance, you can probably even argue about the millionaire with a compulsion to shoplift at the five-and-dime. You may have to make these arguments from behind bars, and you may lose them—but you can make them.

How can you possibly argue about forgery?

A board of directors in today's corporate America cannot describe a series of forgeries as "certain unauthorized financial transactions" and then reinstate the perpetrator, hoping that no one will notice or make a stink.

The best that can be said is that in doing so, out of compassion for a friend and in hopes that he could make their company yet another $100 million, the board of Columbia Pictures made an honest mistake.

It is a mistake few other boards of public companies would have made, I think, and one that—after this—fewer still will be inclined to make.

Robert Critchell, the acquisitions specialist from Philip Morris, had his fifth secret meeting with Columbia's Allen Adler on Saturday at Adler's apartment on East Sixty-fourth Street. They had nearly completed their exchange of information on their respective companies and discussion of Columbia's plans for participating in the rapidly expanding home-video market. Critchell shortly would prepare a report for the high command of Philip Morris which it would use in deciding whether to make a move toward acquiring Columbia Pictures.

Back in slushy Manhattan on Monday, after the rainiest week of the winter in Los Angeles, Alan Hirschfield had lunch with Herbert Allen at "21." It was an entirely cynical and quite awkward gesture, like two weary fighters pausing after the seventh round to have tea in the center of the ring. Both men laughed about the lunch before, during, and after. "Why don't we have a public lunch so everybody can see that we're still talking to each other," Herbert had said on the phone late the previous week. "Fine," Alan replied, "let's go to '21.' I can't think of a more public place, although with our luck, no one will show up at '21' that day. No one will see us." He was right. No one of consequence did see them, and not a single gossip columnist reported the meeting. Alan talked about Deane Johnson. Herbert talked about his planned suit against *The New York Times*. They tried hard to appear relaxed and informal.

Herbert had convinced himself that appearances were important. Having calculated incorrectly around the first of the year that the press coverage would (as Ray Stark had put it) "blow over in two weeks," Herbert and most of the other Columbia directors eventually had seized upon a new and equally superficial appraisal of their dilemma: We have a PR problem. The solution? Obvious. Hire a public relations firm. Columbia already employed a capable public relations director, Jean Vagnini, whose work was considered excellent by objective observers outside the company, as well as many inside. The board of directors, however, had lost confidence in Vagnini's ability to handle the continuing media onslaught alone. They also suspected that Vagnini's loyalty, in the continuing animosity between Hirschfield and the board, was to Hirschfield. Since she was young, relatively inexperienced, and female, she was a convenient target for a group of men who did not want to confront the true source of the "PR" problem—themselves and their own actions. So they instructed Alan Hirschfield to retain an outside firm—not a show-biz publicity outfit but a firm experienced in dealing with the public-relations problems of major corporations. Recognizing the futility of the gesture but reluctant to spark still another fight with the board, Hirschfield acquiesced. He interviewed some of the best known public-relations firms in the country—Hill and Knowlton, Rubenstein Wolfson, Burson Marsteller, and Adams & Rineheart— but for the time being deferred a decision on which to hire.

FORTY-EIGHT

Alan Hirschfield's secret effort to overthrow Herbert Allen was not a tightly controlled, meticulously organized, all-or-nothing-at-all plot. It was an improvisational and occasionally haphazard scheme whose intensity varied from week to week depending upon Hirschfield's mood and the degree of Allen Adler's success in finding a potential savior.

In the wake of the Jimmy Goldsmith debacle, Hirschfield had grown pessimistic, despite Adler's ongoing contacts with Philip Morris. Even if Philip Morris were to acquire Columbia Pictures Industries and get rid of the Allens, there was no guarantee of bliss and contentment. After the flush of victory had faded, Hirschfield would have to face the fact that he still did not control his own destiny. Instead of being the Allens' employee, he would become Philip Morris's employee. He could not imagine anything worse than working for the Allens, but how much better working for Philip Morris would be was unclear.

Meanwhile, as he continued his search for someone to seize control of the company, he also was scheming more modestly for help simply in *reducing* Herbert's power, even if only slightly. If another company—say Time Inc. or General Cinema—bought a sufficiently large block of Columbia Pictures stock, it could legitimately demand a seat or two on the Columbia board of directors and presumably would fill those seats with allies of Hirschfield. A second approach was for Columbia to acquire another company whose management, while publicly neutral, would side with Hirschfield once it was a part of Columbia and held a substantial enough financial stake in the combined enterprise to demand a voice in the company's affairs. As Hirschfield saw it, the Mattel toy company was a candidate for such an arrangement. He had talked intermittently with Mattel since Columbia Pictures had purchased a block of the toy company's stock the previous fall.

Another such candidate was Filmways Incorporated, whose chief executive, Richard Bloch, had been a friend of Hirschfeld's for many years and had been very sympathetic to his position on the Begelman issue. Merger talks between Columbia and Filmways had come to naught a year earlier, but Hirschfeld decided to try to revive them and broached the possibility to Bloch over breakfast at the Regency Hotel on Thursday, March 9. Hirschfeld believed that Filmways could help in three ways: First, it would give Columbia a stake in the publishing industry; Filmways owned Grosset & Dunlap. Second, it would fill the management gap at the Columbia studio; Bloch, a skilled executive of stature, could replace Begelman as president of both motion pictures and television. Third, and most important to Hirschfeld personally, Bloch would be a natural ally on the board of directors of the combined company. Dick Bloch was interested in Hirschfeld's new overture. But he had been appalled by Columbia's handling of the Begelman problem and was leery of, in effect, enlisting in a war for control of the corporation, no matter how subtly it was waged. He promised Alan he would think it over.

Late Friday afternoon, Columbia Pictures Industries formally reported to the Securities and Exchange Commission, and simultaneously made available to the press upon request, the terms of its settlement with David Begelman. With some arithmetic it could be determined that Columbia had agreed to pay Begelman substantially more money as a film and television producer over the next three years than it had been paying him as an officer of the company. Depending on the fulfillment of certain formulas in the contract, Begelman could earn at least $500,000 annually. And there were a number of additional outlays not included in the public report: Columbia would furnish Begelman with office space at The Burbank Studios and a staff consisting of two secretaries, an assistant, a story editor, and when needed, a projectionist. It would provide a car; $25,000 annually for medical, auto, life, and other insurance premiums; $26,000 annually for entertainment expenses; first-class travel plus $1,500 a week in expenses while on trips; and legal fees associated with the pictures he would make. And he would get on-screen credit reading "A David Begelman Production" above the titles of his films in letters 75 percent of the size of the title.

*   *   *

Alan Hirschfield was not available to answer news-media questions about Begelman's new deal. He and Berte flew to London Friday for the European premiere of *Close Encounters of the Third Kind*. As in December, surrounding the opening of *The Deep*, there was a tightly scheduled sequence of social events, which the Hirschfields had to work at enjoying, and several business meetings, at which Alan's mind wandered.

The Queen and Prince Philip attended the premiere on Monday evening at the Odeon Leicester Square. Hirschfield's right hand was still in a bandage as a result of his skiing accident in February, and in the receiving line the Queen asked what had happened.

"I broke it skiing," Hirschfield said. "I'm better at making space movies than I am at navigating on earth."

"You'd better stick to dry land," the Queen said, with a little chuckle.

Richard Dreyfuss, Steven Spielberg, and François Truffaut were present, as was most of the British motion-picture community. The last person through the receiving line was five-year-old Cary Guffey, who played the child in the movie. He presented the Queen with a bouquet of roses. Then, as the bugles blew a fanfare, the Queen led the dignitaries into the Royal Enclosure and the movie began.

The evening concluded with a gala supper party in the ballroom of Claridge's. In their suite upstairs later, Alan and Berte Hirschfield agreed that they had probably just attended their last royal premiere—at least as representatives of Columbia Pictures.

They returned to New York the next day on Pan Am 1.

Having purchased the motion-picture rights to *Annie* for $9.5 million, Columbia Pictures was obliged to appoint a producer for the film. Hirschfield had suggested to Leonard Goldberg that he might produce *Annie* and Goldberg had liked the idea. Hirschfield had suggested to David Begelman that *he* might produce *Annie* and Begelman had mentioned that that might conflict with Goldberg's expectations. Hirschfield had retreated and posed the possibility that David and Len might produce it together.

When Begelman was reinstated as president of the studio, thus eliminating any chance that he would produce individual films personally, Len Goldberg's star had risen. But when Begelman left the presidency again and became a producer after all, he emerged as the leading contender to produce *Annie*. The Columbia board of directors wanted to give it to him. The studio would spend more money on *Annie* than on any film since *Close Encounters*, and the producer's fee would be huge, probably well over a million dollars. The board felt that it was only right, in view of David's tragic experience, that he should be awarded this prize.

The likelihood that David Begelman would produce the film version of *Annie* shocked and dismayed the people who had created *Annie* on the Broadway stage—producers Mike Nichols and Lewis Allen, composer Charles Strouse, lyricist and director Martin Charnin, and the writer of the book, Thomas Meehan. Although they had no legal right to participate in the choice of producer, which was solely within Columbia Pictures' discretion, the Broadway group protested to agent Sam Cohn, who on their behalf had sold Columbia the movie rights. The creators were horrified at the notion of having the biggest and most visible children's movie in years produced by a confessed check forger and embezzler. In addition, they complained that David Begelman, despite his many accomplishments as an agent and studio head, had never in his life actually produced a motion picture. Perhaps, the creators suggested, he could get his on-the-job training on someone else's movie.

Sam Cohn, as agent and friend of the Broadway group, and also as a friend of Begelman's, tried to act as a mediator. Suppose Mike Nichols and Lewis Allen produced the film and Begelman was the executive producer, Cohn asked. Nichols and Allen rejected that idea; they wanted nothing to do with Begelman.

On Thursday, March 16, Sam Cohn conferred with Alan Hirschfield, who told Cohn that he agreed with his clients' complaints but had no power to override the wishes of the Columbia board of directors.

The decision stood. David Begelman would produce *Annie*.

Aside from David Begelman and Herbert Allen, who each had announced that they would file multimillion-dollar libel suits, no one was more outraged by the press coverage of the Columbia scandal than Ray Stark. By mid-March he had demanded and gotten a total of six published corrections of erroneous or misleading statements about him that had appeared in *The New York Times*, the *Los Angeles Times*, and the *Los Angeles Herald Examiner*. He took issue with an implication in the *Herald Examiner* that there might be something sinister about his lawyer's ownership of the Beverly Hills house which David Begelman occupied. He took issue with an implication in all three papers that there might be something improper about Columbia's ownership of one of his production companies. He took issue with a story in *The New York Times* which attributed to him a statement that actually had been made by Robert Evans, the former head of production at Paramount. Stark had every right to demand these corrections, of course, and rightly believed that the coverage of the Begelman scandal at large had encompassed the sloppiest media treatment of a major news story in America in many years. But Stark was too angry, and too combative by nature, to be satisfied with mere published corrections. He decided to write an open letter to the film community about the press coverage and publish it as an advertisement in the two principal Hollywood trade papers, *Daily Variety* and *The Hollywood Reporter*. Ray worked hard over the letter. He thought about starting it with the biblical quotation "And ye shall know the truth and the truth shall make you free." He thought about employing the question "Remember Joe McCarthy?" But he discarded both of those notions and finally began the letter:

> INNUENDO IS BELLOWED FROM THE ROOFTOP.
> Corrections are whispered from the cellar.
> The film industry, because of its high visibility, often finds itself in a particularly vulnerable position where the press is concerned. . . . Some "investigative" reporters have been so busy creating headlines and meeting deadlines that either they failed to check their facts, made accusations by omission, or butchered the truth by innuendo—all for a more provocative story. Freedom of the press brings with it its own responsibility. . . .

Stark purchased double-page ads in both papers, placing his letter on the left page and reprints of five of the corrections on the right page. Just about everybody in Hollywood (West and East) saw the ads. Some applauded. Some were startled. Some just laughed. Liz Smith, for one, thought it was all a giant hoot. She sent a copy of the ad to Cliff Robertson with a note: "Ray Stark on the attack!"

*   *   *

Allen Adler had not given up the notion that Time Incorporated might come to the rescue of Columbia Pictures. Although Hirschfield's meeting with Andrew Heiskell in January had been inconclusive, there was still a lot of warmth between them and between the companies. Adler had spoken several times with his own principal contacts at Time, Gerald Levin, the president of Time's rapidly growing Home Box Office subsidiary, and J. Richard Munro, the group vice president of all Time's video operations and the man who would succeed Andrew Heiskell as the chief executive officer of the corporation.

On Tuesday, March 21, Adler sought out Gerald Levin. Adler had a bad back and could not sit; he could only stand or lie. So he met Levin during the noon hour in front of the St. Regis Hotel at Fifth Avenue and Fifty-fifth Street and they went for a stroll. They walked down Fifth for several blocks, over to Madison, up Madison, back to Fifth, and down Fifth again.

"Jerry, you've got to help us," Adler said. "You've got to come in and buy us."

"You know how sympathetic we are," Levin replied, "but you also know that it raises a whole host of difficult questions."

"Let me try and deal with your main concerns," Adler began. "First, you think our business is a dirty business. Well, there are a few dirty people, but it's not a dirty business. It's filled with a lot of nice people, very warm and friendly. You'd enjoy them. Second, you think the business is mercurial, that it's way up one year and way down the next. We've run our company to avoid that. We have the outside financing for pictures so we spread the risk, we have the potential for more and more sales of ancillary rights, we have diversification with Gottlieb, and we'll have more diversification. Third, you think the business is inherently unmanageable, that you wouldn't know how to deal with Hollywood guys, guys like Begelman, guys who have a different value system from yours, who take a limo for two blocks, who don't write everything down, who don't impose strict rational controls on the way they manage things. Well, we're changing all that. We do impose strict rational controls more and more, and you would have us there to manage it for you in the first place. You wouldn't have to do it yourselves."

Jerry Levin remained sympathetic but gave Adler little reason for hope.

The next day Adler repeated his walking sales pitch to Levin's boss, Dick Munro. Munro was no more optimistic.

The last half of March was a dull blur for Alan Hirschfield. On one level it was relatively peaceful. Herbert, who was preoccupied with preparations for his lawsuit against *The New York Times*, called far less often. And Matty Rosenhaus had hardly spoken to Hirschfield since their angry clash on the telephone the day of the security-analysts presentation. So Alan was almost able to pretend that it was business as usual and concentrate on issues less cosmic than the control and governance of Columbia Pictures Industries—issues even less important than who would produce *Annie*. One such issue was choosing a title for the Jane Fonda-Jack Lemmon film about a nuclear accident and the reporter who covers it. Although the movie only then was going into production and would not be released for a year, there was already a sharp debate within the company about the title. Should it be *The China Syndrome* (the working title), or *Eyewitness*, or *Power*, or something else? How about *Newsbreak* or *Alert* or *Ready Alert?* While acknowledging that the title *The China Syndrome* was the most "interesting," several Columbia people feared that potential audiences would not know what the phrase "China syndrome" meant. Somebody said it sounded like an ailment you came down with after eating in a Chinese restaurant. Somebody was afraid that moviegoers hostile toward Jane Fonda's political activities would surmise that it was a "message" picture about Communist China. The studio finally decided, after many lengthy and heated debates, to launch a market research effort to try to determine which title would "play best."

Late in the month, Hirschfield received two pieces of very bad news.

Philip Morris Incorporated, after considering the report prepared by its acquisitions specialist, had decided against trying to acquire or otherwise seek control of Columbia Pictures Industries. Columbia was attractive to Philip Morris in many ways. Unfortunately, however, the talks between the two companies' representatives had coincided with the most intense period of bad publicity about Columbia, and in the end Philip Morris decided that it was unwise to acquire any company still under the cloud of a major scandal. All of the secret meetings between Bob Critchell and Allen Adler, and all of their work individually, thus went for naught. Privately, Bob Critchell was relieved, and hoped that Herbert Allen would never know that his old fraternity brother had been a party to Alan Hirschfield's attempted putsch.

From Los Angeles, Hirschfield got a call from Deane Johnson, the lawyer to whom he had offered David Begelman's old job. Johnson said he deeply appreciated the offer but had chosen not to accept it. He had discussed it at length with his wife, as well as with Ray Stark, Herbert Allen, Marty Ransohoff, and others. Stark had spent several hours on a Saturday at the Johnson home in Bel-Air discussing the Columbia job with Deane and Anne and urging Deane to take it. As Johnson told Hirschfield, however, his loyalty to his partners at O'Melveny & Myers, and to his clients, was too deep for him to leave after so many years with the firm. Besides, he valued the "independence" of his law practice too much to give it up.

Although he had suspected from the beginning that Deane Johnson would turn the job down, Hirschfield was deeply disappointed. He considered Johnson a strong and exceptional man—a man who not only could run Columbia's West Coast operations but would also bring considerable prestige to the company and might even be able to help calm the animosity.* It had become clear to Hirschfield, however, that most good candidates for the job would want to see the animosity erased *before* they joined the company so as not to risk becoming part of it. And the Columbia board of directors had done nothing toward that end. There had been no further negotiations on a new contract for Alan. And there had been no proclamation of support for him. The promises of late January seemed far away. And despite their "happy" lunch at "21" in early March, Alan knew that Herbert's bitterness was as intense as ever.

---

*In late 1981, Warner Communications announced that Deane Johnson would move to New York and join its four-man Office of the President under Chairman and Chief Executive Steve Ross.

Part IV

FORTY-NINE

The woman had dark eyes, full and sensuous lips, a Mediterranean complexion, and long black hair, which she often wore tucked under a short, curly, black wig. She was about five and a half feet tall, and a bit chunky, especially in the legs. A divorcée, forty years old, she lived with her two teenage daughters in a small brick and frame house in a working-class section of North Hollywood.

From a distance the house appeared ordinary, but it was not. It was the only house in the vicinity with marble floors and custom-designed stained-glass windows. The windows were covered by bars and secured with locks, and there were heavy, imposing locks as well on every door into the house, on the front and back gates to the small lot where the house stood, and on the door to the woman's second-floor bedroom. Only a few people had ever seen the inside of the house and knew that the tight security was a residue of a time, years earlier, when the woman had been placed under official protection after she testified against her ex-husband, a small-time mobster, and thus helped federal authorities convict him of violating gambling laws. Though the protection gradually had been reduced, the woman had stayed in close touch with one of the men hired to provide it, a private detective. She had also kept the locks in place, and had the stained-glass windows installed so that no one could see into the house.

The woman spent most of her free time at home. She did not own or drive a car—very unusual in Los Angeles—and took taxis to and from her office a few miles east in Burbank where she worked as an accountant. On weekends she occasionally would take a bus, as she phrased it, "to the Boulevard," by which she meant Ventura Boulevard, the main east-west commercial artery along the south edge of the San Fernando Valley. Alone, she would stroll and shop and then catch a bus home, where she would occupy herself with the offerings of the Doubleday Book Club, the Literary Guild, the Movie Book Club, and the Columbia Record Club. She loved Rubinstein and the other great pianists and purchased a lot of their recordings.

The woman did not have many close friends, partly by choice, and partly because of her personality. She was aggressive, severe, and even bossy around the people at the office, with the exception of the man for whom she worked. In his presence she was prim, and insisted to his bemusement on calling him Mr. Kerns, never Dick, even though he was informal and accessible and had employed her for more than a decade. His bemusement was lost on her, however. She was a serious person who believed in observing the formalities. To some at the office she was known as "Marian the Librarian."

Sometime in 1976 or early 1977 people began to notice that the woman had money. She started wearing fine jewelry. Expensive clothing appeared in her formerly drab wardrobe, and she mentioned to a few colleagues that she was having dresses made at Profils du Monde, an exclusive shop on Wilshire Boulevard in Beverly Hills.

Then there were the dogs. She purchased several show dogs of the breed called Bouvier des Flandres. She hired a dog handler, traveled to France and Belgium where the dogs were bred, and began flying off to dog shows on weekends.

The few people who knew about these things—mainly other women at the office—assumed that the money was coming from the private detective who had been her bodyguard at one time and with whom she obviously was very friendly. The detective frequently dropped by the office to see her. He looked prosperous and carried a gun inside his jacket. There was an air of mystery about him. The office people assumed he was her lover and the fount of her new prosperity.

It never occurred to them that they might have guessed wrong. The detective was not her lover. And it was not until the auditors suddenly arrived one day in the spring of 1978 and sealed the woman's office that her colleagues realized that she had been financing her dogs, jewelry, custom-made dresses, and trips to Europe by embezzling hundreds of thousands of dollars from the company for which they all worked, Columbia Pictures Industries.

*　　*　　*

The woman's name was Audrey Bride Lisner. She had grown up in a small town in Illinois, the daughter of a farmer who was sixty-five years old when she was born and a mother who was twenty-five. (Her mother died young; her father lived to be one hundred and five.) After moving to California around 1960, Audrey met and married Jerry Lisner, a minor-league hoodlum who had been arrested numerous times in Las Vegas and Los Angeles on a myriad of charges including robbery, illegal bookmaking, assault with intent to commit rape, simple assault and battery, drunkenness, and contributing to the delinquency of a minor. His only convictions were for bookmaking. In the mid-sixties, Audrey and Jerry were divorced and Audrey, through her court testimony, helped the IRS and the Justice Department convict Jerry of tax violations associated with gambling.

While still involved with the trial and its aftermath, Audrey Lisner took a job in the accounting department of Columbia Pictures, which was still occupying its original quarters on Gower Street in Hollywood. She quickly gained a reputation as a conscientious, loyal, and capable employee, and eventually was given full responsibility for all of the accounting and bookkeeping for a division of Columbia known as EUE-Screen Gems, which was the nation's leading producer of television commercials. Screen Gems was housed about a mile from the main Burbank lot in a small building at the so-called "ranch," a site where many western movies had been filmed in the thirties and forties. Along with geographical isolation, Screen Gems also had considerable financial autonomy. It used a different data-processing service from that of the Columbia studio and was rarely audited thoroughly.

Audrey Lisner began embezzling money from Screen Gems in 1974. She stole small amounts at first, but the thefts grew in 1975 and 1976, and by early 1978, she had taken more than $300,000. Although the head of Screen Gems' West Coast arm, Richard Kerns, was Lisner's supervisor, the chain of command over routine financial transactions ran from Lisner directly to Lou Phillips, the controller of all of Columbia's Burbank operations.

Lisner's work load had grown over the years, and in 1977 Lou Phillips assigned a young member of his staff, Kirk Borcherding, to become her assistant. It was not long before Borcherding began noticing irregularities in Screen Gems' traveler's check accounts. Although he first became suspicious in the fall of 1977 (about the time David Begelman was suspended from the studio), he was unsure of himself and procrastinated until the following March when he secretly went to Lou Phillips and said he believed that someone, perhaps Audrey Lisner, was stealing. Phillips asked Borcherding to go back to Screen Gems and, without revealing his suspicions to Lisner, prepare an analysis of how much might be missing. Borcherding returned a few days later with an estimate: $250,000. Phillips pondered the matter over the weekend, and on Monday, March 27, he placed a call to Joe Fischer in New York. Fischer did not return the call.

At about seven Wednesday evening, after most employees had left for the day, Lou Phillips walked down the long second-floor hallway of the main Columbia building to the office of Jim Johnson, the vice president for administration. It had been just under ten months since Phillips had traversed the same hallway bearing the Cliff Robertson problem. Even though no one else was in the executive suite to overhear the conversation, Phillips closed Johnson's door before sitting down. It took him most of an hour to outline Kirk Borcherding's suspicions.

Jim Johnson immediately grasped the ramifications of the discovery. Seen in isolation, it appeared to be a serious embezzlement but it could be handled. Seen in the wake of the Begelman scandal, it was like a huge time bomb, dropped suddenly into the midst of a battlefield of contending armies already bloody and weary from protracted combat. Although Jim Johnson personally had not experienced all the pain that had been suffered by Joe Fischer and Alan Hirschfield, he had seen and felt very vividly the damage to the company and its people that had flowed from the Begelman scandal—a scandal set in motion by a single, questionable financial transaction, revealed to him by Lou Phillips in a quiet conversation just like this one.

Johnson dismissed Phillips and telephoned Joe Fischer at home in New Jersey. Fischer was at a hockey game in Manhattan, but his wife, Edie, answered the phone. Johnson asked that Joe call either him or Lou Phillips. "It's urgent," Johnson said. "I think we may have another irregularity, and I'm not talking about a bowel movement."

When Fischer got home he couldn't reach Johnson so he phoned Phillips. True to his cautious nature, which he had displayed previously when the Cliff Robertson check was discovered, Phillips did not use the word "embezzlement" or accuse Audrey Lisner in his conversation with Fischer. He merely noted that the use of traveler's checks at Screen Gems had been inexplicably heavy and might suggest some sort of irregularity.

Fischer said he would get back to Phillips within a few days.

FIFTY

Alan Hirschfield and the Columbia board of directors spoke less to each other directly and more through Leo Jaffe. Thus, when Hirschfield wanted to brief the board on his search for a successor to David Begelman, he wrote Jaffe a "confidential" memorandum:

"While it may sound self-serving, it does bear repeating that one of the problems I have had in surfacing good people, and in eliciting even initial interest among others, has been the uncertainty regarding the management situation here at Columbia. In virtually every case, the first question from potential candidates concerns the status of my own position. While I have attempted to be glib in terms of an answer, most of the people are smart enough to realize that there is no present resolution. This certainly has not helped in terms of attracting and/or negotiating with potential candidates. While there may be people who would be happy to take the job, irrespective of my own situation, there are very few that all of us would agree upon as being qualified. Nevertheless, I have continued to make every possible effort to find qualified personnel and will continue to do so."

Once the media coverage of the Columbia scandal gained momentum, much of it implying that the attitude of Los Angeles law-enforcement authorities had been lax, the likelihood of formal criminal proceedings against David Begelman increased. Two deputy district attorneys spent much of February and March studying the case with

Burbank Detective Bob Elias. Although Cliff Robertson and Columbia Pictures still refused to sign complaints, the press and the public at large clearly believed that crimes had been committed. It was obvious that Begelman had repaid the stolen money only after he was caught.

On Friday morning, March 31, the Los Angeles District Attorney's office charged Begelman with four felony crimes—one count of grand theft and three counts of forgery. Bail of $2,500 was asked. The grand-theft charge carried a penalty of one to ten years in prison, and each forgery count carried a penalty of one to fourteen years. It was arranged for Begelman to surrender to the Burbank police the following week and enter a plea in municipal court.

Alan and Berte Hirschfeld flew to Los Angeles on Monday to head the Columbia Pictures delegation at the fiftieth annual Academy Awards. Dan Melnick and Leo Jaffe also attended. *Close Encounters of the Third Kind* had been nominated for nine awards, including best director but notably not including best picture. No other Columbia films had received any major nominations. By contrast, Twentieth Century-Fox had garnered nearly three-dozen nominations. *Star Wars, Julia,* and *The Turning Point* each was nominated for eleven awards, including best picture. Some people wondered whether the Begelman scandal had hurt Columbia in the voting.

Outside the Dorothy Chandler Pavilion, the Jewish Defense League demonstrated against Vanessa Redgrave's best supporting actress nomination for her performance in *Julia,* continuing a campaign which the JDL had been waging for weeks because of Redgrave's association with the cause of the Palestine Liberation Organization. When it turned out that she had won the Oscar, Redgrave ascended to the stage and said, "My dear colleagues, . . . you should be very proud that in the last few weeks you have stood firm and you have refused to be intimidated by the threats of a small bunch of Zionist hoodlums whose behavior is an insult to Jews all over the world. . . ." Dan Melnick and others in the audience booed loudly. ". . . I salute all of you," Redgrave continued, "for having stood firm and dealt a final blow against that period when Nixon and McCarthy launched a worldwide witch-hunt against those who tried to express with their lives and their work the truth that they believed in . . ." Redgrave sat down to more boos, mixed with applause and a reprise of the music from *Julia.* Knowing that Paddy Chayevsky was scheduled to present the screen-writing Oscars, Dan Melnick cornered him in the men's room and insisted that he reply to Redgrave's remarks. When Chayevsky took the podium more than an hour later, he began, "Before I get on to the writing awards, there's a little matter I'd like to tidy up. . . . I'm sick and tired of people exploiting the occasion of the Academy Awards for the propagation of their own personal political propaganda. I would like to suggest to Miss Redgrave that her winning an Academy Award is not a pivotal moment in history and does not require a proclamation. A simple thank you would have sufficed."

Close Encounters won only two awards—for cinematography and sound-effects editing. *Star Wars* seven, and *Julia* three. *Annie Hall* was named best picture.

David Begelman did not attend the ceremony, but Cliff Robertson did, having been invited, as a past winner, to participate in the opening ceremony. Asked about the Begelman case, Robertson told *Daily Variety* columnist Army Archerd: "When and if I'm called, I'll tell the truth."

Early the next morning, David Begelman surrendered for booking at the Burbank Police Headquarters, then crossed the street to the municipal court and entered pleas of not guilty to the four felony counts against him.

B.O. Clicks. Image Nix: Scandals Rock Hollywood in Its Best Year Ever. and Jack Valenti Is the Man in the Middle. The headline was on a *People* magazine interview with Valenti, the former aide to Lyndon Johnson and president of the Motion Picture Association of America.

> "How could something like the Begelman affair happen?"
>
> "Frankly, this whole thing would have died down if Begelman had not been reinstated. . . ."
>
> "What would you have done?"
>
> "My advice was not sought. If it had been, I would *never* have reinstated Begelman. He committed a crime, and he has no right to be the head of a publicly traded corporation."
>
> "In your opinion, did Cliff Robertson do right by pressing to have Begelman investigated?
>
> "Robertson did what I or any other person in that position

would have done. If there are wrongdoers, I encourage and applaud their exposure. I would stand up and cheer.''

''Are bribes, payoffs, and financial improprieties rampant in Hollywood?''

''I'm not suggesting for one minute that there aren't plenty of crooks, cheats, and charlatans in Hollywood. I am saying that the vast majority are well-intentioned people of probity and integrity who care very much about their public reputations.''

''Is it worse than in other businesses?''

''I don't know. Of course, it's not *like* any other business. It's really a crapshoot. . . .''

''Which is more corrupt, Washington or Hollywood?''

''There are rascals, double-dealers, and scoundrels in both places, but nine out of ten people in politics and the movies are solid. I don't want to be put in the position of a public defender for Hollywood. Frankly, I don't know if somebody is going to be accused, indicted, and convicted next week. But the vast majority in the film business want to do one thing: make the best goddamned movie they can.''

Over cocktails at the Beverly Wilshire Tuesday evening, Hirschfield offered Begelman's old job to Stan Kamen, the senior West Coast officer of the William Morris Agency and, along with Sam Cohn of ICM, one of the most important talent agents in the world. Kamen, with whom there had been exploratory discussions of the Columbia job through intermediaries such as Marty Ransohoff, politely declined the offer.

Hirschfield flew back to New York the next afternoon after attending a board meeting of the Motion Picture Association of America.

Joe Fischer reported to the audit committee of the Columbia board of directors on Thursday that as a result of the Begelman embezzlements Columbia's insurance carrier had increased the deductible on its fidelity bond from $5,000 to $100,000. Fischer pointed out that the fidelity bond would not cover the company at all against anything Begelman might do in his capacity as a producer.

The full board then convened and approved several motion picture and television transactions, including *California Suite* at a revised budget of $9.4 million; a fee of $2 million to Dustin Hoffman for *Kramer vs. Kramer*, which was scheduled to begin filming in

September; Marty Ransohoff's *Nightwing* at a revised budget of $6.6 million; and a new contract for TV producer David Gerber covering *Police Story, Police Woman*, and other shows.

It was reported that Columbia Pictures probably would make "significant profits" from its 50 percent interest in *Dancin'*, the new Bob Fosse musical review which had just opened to critical acclaim and a healthy box office on Broadway. There were mutterings of approval from the board but not congratulations for Hirschfield, who had championed the investment in *Dancin'* against strong resistance from the directors several months earlier. It had become bad form to admit that Alan Hirschfield might have sound artistic judgment.

Although Hirschfield and Herbert Allen had hardly spoken since early March, Herbert had been thinking a lot about Hirschfield and the overall management of the corporation. He was as angry at Hirschfield as ever—for all the same reasons. He would never forgive him for what he considered Alan's duplicity in the Jimmy Goldsmith episode. And as the spring wore on, Herbert's list of grievances lengthened. He believed that Alan's seeming inability to attract a replacement for David Begelman demonstrated one of two things: Either Alan's search for a new studio head was not genuine because Alan secretly wanted to run the studio himself, or the search was inept and evinced a general lack of ability as an executive. (Herbert ignored the argument that Alan's efforts were being undermined by the board's failure to certify its support for him with a new long-term contract.) Herbert also was frustrated by what he felt was a failure by Alan to keep another commitment he had made—to strengthen the management at the top of the corporation by appointing a chief operating officer, someone whose principal function would be the tightening and monitoring of *administrative* controls of the corporation, which Herbert felt were loose.

Pursuing the second goal in early April, Herbert asked Hirschfield to interview a man who had recently contacted Herbert in search of a job—a former RCA and NBC executive named Robert Stone. Balding, fifty-six years old, and stiff in his demeanor, Stone had been unemployed since early the previous year when he left abruptly as head of the Hertz Corporation, an RCA subsidiary, after a tiff with RCA Chairman Edgar Griffiths. It turned out that Alan Hirschfield already had met Stone. An executive recruiter had introduced them not long after Stone had left Hertz, and Hirschfield had concluded then that

Stone was not suitable for Columbia Pictures Industries. Although it was clear that Stone had talent—Hertz's profits had quadrupled in his four and a half years at the helm—he had a reputation as an abrupt, exacting manager-by-fear-and-edict, a style which Hirschfield felt was inappropriate in a company like Columbia whose principal businesses depended upon careful nurturing of a creative environment. While at Hertz, Stone had fired a sizable number of vice presidents and even threatened the jobs of secretaries for overusing copying machines. "Captain Queeg" they called him. Hirschfield's view of Stone had not changed since their interview, but at Herbert's insistence, Alan spoke with Stone again on Friday morning, April 7. Hirschfield did not take the opportunity to reject Stone flatly. Instead he said that Columbia would not be hiring a chief operating officer until it had finished staffing the studio. Perhaps they could talk again then.

Unfortunately for Hirschfield, he failed to sense that Robert Stone over the next three months gradually would become an inflammatory symbol of Hirschfield's "intransigence" and the focus of bitter new animosity in the struggle with Herbert Allen for control of the corporation.

FIFTY-ONE

In the days following his late-night phone conversation with Lou Phillips, Joe Fischer groped for a prudent approach to the possible financial irregularity at Columbia's television commercials company in Burbank.

Jim Johnson urged Fischer to take quick action. Not reticent like Phillips, Johnson told Fischer that the "irregularity" almost certainly amounted to a sizable embezzlement and that the likely culprit was Audrey Lisner, implausible as that might have seemed in view of her flawless employment record. Johnson wanted an immediate investigation and was prepared to launch it himself. Fischer, however, had to consider the broader ramifications of the problem. If an embezzlement was confirmed, it inevitably would ignite another ugly controversy within the high command of Columbia Pictures Industries. Thus, it was imperative that the Screen Gems matter be handled delicately. It was the *handling* that was crucial. If the Begelman affair had been *handled* differently in the beginning, Fischer had always felt, it might not have gotten out of control.

Fischer decided not to tell Hirschfield or anyone else about the Screen Gems problem just yet. He decided that the least disruptive course was to keep the problem within the financial-control systems of the company to the extent possible.

Let it be handled by the systems that were designed to handle such things. It was the "system," after all, in the person of Audrey Lisner's assistant, Kirk Borcherding, that brought the matter to light, not some zealous outsider like Cliff Robertson. It seemed to Fischer that if the system already in place was permitted to deal with Lisner, it could prove just as effective as, perhaps more effective than, the Burbank police or Price Waterhouse. And the political damage to Hirschfield (and to Fischer himself) might have a better chance of being contained.

An important part of the control system within Columbia Pictures, as in most big companies, was its department of internal audit, a sort of interior Price Waterhouse which specialized in policing the corporation's financial control systems, identifying abuses, and thereby filling whatever enforcement gap might exist between the annual audit by the outside accountants and the day-to-day self-policing of the system itself. Columbia's director of internal audit was a young CPA whom Fischer had hired away from Price Waterhouse, Ilana Cytto. An intense, dark-haired woman in her early thirties, Cytto had come to the United States from Israel, having served for a time in the Israeli Army. Because of the unique manner in which the Begelman embezzlements had surfaced, she had not participated in that investigation.

Joe Fischer checked Cytto's travel schedule and found that she was planning to be in Los Angeles during the second week of April for routine auditing work at the studio. It seemed to Fischer that the best approach to the Screen Gems matter would be for Cytto to "discover" the problem at that time. He summoned her and told her of Kirk Borcherding's findings.

Ilana Cytto knew that if she arrived at Screen Gems unannounced,

Audrey Lisner would surmise immediately that she was under suspicion. Therefore, Cytto telephoned Lisner on Monday, April 10, to say that she would be at the studio later in the week and would be dropping by Screen Gems. Sounding very anxious, Lisner said it would be inconvenient for her to accommodate an audit that week. Cytto thereupon flew to Los Angeles that evening and drove to Screen Gems in Burbank the next morning. She first saw Richard Kerns, the head of the West Coast office, but did not reveal that she suspected Audrey Lisner of anything improper. Then Cytto confronted Lisner, who became even more upset than she had been on the telephone the day before. Lisner told Cytto that she had to leave shortly for Europe and it would be impossible to audit her books for the time being.

Ilana Cytto returned to Dick Kerns's office. "Did you know Audrey is leaving the country?" Cytto asked.

"No, I didn't know that."

"She says she's going to Belgium. Something about her dogs. She says it's an emergency. I must go ahead with this audit."

Kerns summoned Lisner and told her that Cytto would proceed with her work and that if Ilana had any questions about the Screen Gems books, Audrey could answer them when she returned from her trip.

Lisner left immediately for home and Cytto prepared to begin her examination of the traveler's check accounts. From home, Lisner telephoned Joe Fischer in New York and asked that he order Cytto to delay the audit. Fischer called Dick Kerns and asked, "What the hell is going on out there?"

"I don't know," Kerns replied. "Ilana wants to audit Audrey's books and Audrey doesn't want her to."

"It gets very suspicious if the accountant wants to leave when the auditor arrives," Fischer observed, instructing Kerns to let the audit proceed forthwith.

Well past midnight, Audrey Lisner telephoned two friends and implored them to come to her home immediately. When they arrived they found her nearly hysterical and incoherent. She claimed she had embezzled several thousand dollars from Screen Gems and was about to be found out. The amounts she had taken, she claimed, were small compared to what others had taken, and she was not going to be a scapegoat for them. She would "blow the whistle" on them, but she was afraid they might try to kill her. She was also thinking of killing herself.

The friends stayed with her and toward dawn she calmed down. One of the friends suggested that Audrey would arouse more suspicion by staying in town than by going ahead with her trip to Europe.

Within the next couple of days—by the time Lisner was scheduled to leave—it was clear to Ilana Cytto that there indeed were irregularities in the traveler's check accounts. She recommended to Dick Kerns that Lisner be detained. It was too late; her flight had left.

Suspecting that Lisner might try to destroy records, Cytto flipped through Lisner's Rolodex and found a listing for her travel agent. She phoned the agent and learned that Lisner was scheduled to return from Europe via San Francisco. The Bank of America depository where the Screen Gems traveler's checks were stored was in San Francisco. Ilana Cytto caught a PSA shuttle, went to the bank depository, and examined the traveler's checks. As she had suspicioned, all of the checks in question bore the signature of Audrey Lisner.

Taking photocopies of all necessary documents, Cytto flew back to Los Angeles and sealed Lisner's office, having the locks changed and posting security guards. Then she reported by telephone to Joe Fischer.

Fischer felt as if he had been distraught—not too strong a word— for at least half of the two hundred or so long days and nights since Detective Joyce Silvey's telephone call in September. The rest of the time he had felt merely anxious. He had experienced the convulsion of a major corporation. He had seen and heard things that even to him—a tough, seasoned veteran of corporate show business— were shocking. He had witnessed behavior among adult men that had seemed inconceivable to him prior to its occurrence. Repeatedly, he had grown depressed, then allowed his hopes to rise ever so slightly, and then seen them obliterated by some fresh event more horrible than the last—another forgery, another ugly row in the boardroom, another magazine article.

And now Audrey Lisner.

Although Alan Hirschfield had agreed to tighten certain money-control procedures at the studio after the Begelman embezzlements were discovered, he had defended the integrity of the control systems themselves, and he and Fischer had refused to fire or transfer those directly in charge of enforcing the controls. Jim Johnson and

Lou Phillips, as had been suggested by Audit Committee Chairman Irwin Kramer. With the new embezzlements, it would be difficult to protect Johnson and Phillips.

In a much broader sense, it seemed obvious to Fischer that Herbert, Irwin, Matty, and the rest of the board would seize upon Audrey Lisner as further "evidence" that Alan Hirschfield was inept and unfit. Not only did Hirschfield mishandle the Begelman affair, Fischer imagined the board saying, but after two months he still hasn't replaced Begelman, and now we find that he can't even keep employees from looting the company. Ultimately, Fischer knew, the Lisner episode would explode into a political issue between Alan and the board just as everything else had.

Immediately after Ilana Cytto's call, Fischer summoned Dick Kerns to New York and demanded that Kerns disclose anything he might know about the embezzlements. Kerns denied knowing anything about them. Fischer said it had been rumored that Kerns and Lisner were having an affair. Kerns was incredulous. "Give me a break, Joe," he said. "You've seen Audrey. You know what she's like and what she looks like. She's not the type I would go after."

Audrey Lisner returned to Los Angeles the following Wednesday, April 19, and the next morning was called to Dick Kerns's office where she found Ilana Cytto with Kerns. Following instructions given by Joe Fischer, Cytto and Kerns told Lisner she had a right to have a lawyer present. She declined. Cytto then confronted her with the evidence against her and Lisner confessed to stealing the money. She promised to do everything she could to make restitution.

Joe Fischer flew to Los Angeles that evening, checked into L'Ermitage, and interrogated Lisner and Kerns in his suite the next morning. Lisner again waived her right to an attorney and again confessed.

"Audrey, we're going to have to do a thorough job of investigating all this," Fischer said. "We can't do anything to protect you. The best thing you can do is cooperate and tell the truth. We'll get this done as quickly and painlessly as possible, but I cannot promise you that Columbia won't prosecute."

Fischer flew back to New York and on Monday told Alan Hirschfield for the first time about the Lisner embezzlements.

"Is Kerns implicated?" Hirschfield asked.

"We don't think so."

"The board will be thrilled," Hirschfield said. "They'll be able to blame me for this."

"No," Fischer replied, "the only person they should blame is me."

"It's not your fault."

"I was supposed to be watching the people who were supposed to be watching Audrey."

"Nonsense," said Hirschfield. "It's nobody's fault except Audrey's. But to the extent that anybody gets blamed, it'll be me. Kramer will have a field day. And Audrey won't have a chance. Everything they did to try to protect Begelman they'll do in reverse to her. We're going to see American justice at its best. You'll hear no talk of mercy, or second chances, or psychiatrists, or tragedy, or anything. They'll flatten her. We're going to see a real double standard go into action."

FIFTY-TWO

Alan Hirschfield stayed as far from the Lisner investigation as he could. He knew there was nothing he personally could do, and he knew that Joe Fischer would do everything possible to contain the problem while handling it with full propriety.

Moreover, Hirschfield felt compelled to give his full attention to the broader and more urgent problems that he sensed were beginning to encircle him. It had been too quiet. Except for a few brief conversations, and a perfunctory board meeting in early April, he had had no contact with Herbert Allen or Matty Rosenhaus for several weeks. All talk of a new contract for Hirschfield, and all talk of a mutually laudatory public statement of unity, had ceased. It seemed to Hirschfield that the war for control of the corporation had not abated but rather had moved into a new phase. Instead of constantly pressuring him, as they had while Begelman was still in the company, the board members now, by withholding their support, were quietly rendering him unable to accomplish his most important task—replacing Begelman and reorganizing the studio. Columbia's main businesses—motion pictures and television—had been drifting without strong, day-to-day leadership since September. Having made his task impossible, the board would let an appropriate amount of time pass, declare him incompetent for failing to accomplish the task, and fire him. Or so Hirschfeld suspected in the rare moments when the clouds of emotion and frustration lifted and he thought he saw the future clearly.

But even though he was depressed, even though his more dramatic efforts to seize control of the company—Jimmy Goldsmith and Philip Morris—had failed, and even though the odds remained with Herbert, Hirschfeld was not finished. He had invested too much of himself in Columbia Pictures to quit now. By any legitimate standard, he felt, it was his company as much as anybody's. He had not run out of stamina and he had not run out of ideas.

After weeks of looking elsewhere, Hirschfeld decided that the only realistic choice for the presidency of the studio was its acting president, Dan Melnick. No one was enthusiastic about the idea. Hirschfeld would have preferred someone with more experience and a more consistent record. And Melnick hated the kind of administrative work that was part of the president's job. He had even balked at becoming head of production until he was assured that his administrative duties would be negligible. But Melnick finally had made known to Hirschfeld, over the course of a number of meetings in New York and Los Angeles, that he would take the job under certain conditions: He would have to be paid a great deal of money. And he would have to be free contractually to leave the president's job and become a producer, retaining substantial remuneration, if Hirschfeld were to leave Columbia, or if other circumstances arose that were unacceptable to Melnick.

Hirschfeld accepted Melnick's terms, and then Melnick enhanced his attractiveness as a presidential candidate by locating a qualified person to succeed him as second-in-command at the studio in charge of motion-picture production. The new prospect was Frank Price, the president of the highly successful television arm of Universal and a nineteen-year veteran of the MCA-Universal organization. Price had been recommended to Melnick by Sherry Lansing, a Columbia vice president and friend of both men. Frank Price, after many years in television. longed to get into movies. There were no immediate opportunities for him at Universal, so at Lansing's suggestion, Dan Melnick discussed the Columbia production post with Price. He was interested, and on April 26, he flew to New York and conferred with Alan Hirschfield. They liked each other immediately, and although no final agreement was reached, Hirschfield believed that the studio would be in good hands with Melnick and Frank Price at its helm.

Hirschfield continued to nurture the idea with the board of directors that Columbia should acquire or merge with another company. Even if a merger did not substantially diminish Herbert Allen's control, Hirschfield felt, at least it would introduce one or more new voices to the Columbia inner circle. Hirschfield hoped that the new voices would side with his. At least they might help to diffuse the tension. Herbert Allen, of course, was not naîve about Hirschfield's motives. But Herbert was too pragmatic to ignore the possibility that a merger might make economic sense, whatever its other ramifications. At least he was willing to listen. By late April, Hirschfield was negotiating seriously with two companies—Filmways, the small entertainment and publishing conglomerate controlled by his friend Richard Bloch, and the Mattel toy company (Barbie dolls, Ringling Bros. circus). As it turned out, one of Herbert Allen's allies on the Columbia board of directors, Dan Lufkin, favored the talks with Mattel, having had a close relationship for a number of years with Mattel's chief executive, Arthur Spear.

Hirschfield was right about one thing. It had been too quiet. The calm of March and April had been unnatural. While Alan imputed the worst of motives to the board of directors, however, he still welcomed the relief from the almost daily winter confrontations. As a man who lived for the moment perhaps more successfully than most who try, Hirschfield managed to savor the quiet, knowing all the while that it was superficial, and it would end.

When the end of the interlude came, Alan supposed it was appropriate that it came in a quarrel with Irwin Kramer, the Columbia board member whom he despised even more than Herbert Allen and Matty Rosenhaus. As much as he loathed Herbert and Matty, it was a less focused, more general loathing, set against the background of their power which Alan held in a degree of grudging awe. In no sense did

Alan hold Irwin Kramer in awe. Irwin's power was largely in-law power, and at Columbia Pictures he wielded it mainly as Herbert's blunt instrument as chairman of the board's audit committee. What had particularly incensed Hirschfield since the beginning of the Begelman investigation in the autumn was the belligerence Irwin displayed, and the obvious relish with which he carried out his part of the campaign of pressure on Hirschfield. Alan would never forget that it was Irwin who had handled the dirtiest job of all—threatening to investigate Berte Hirschfield's employment on the excuse that David Begelman might not be the only tainted officer in the company. And it was Irwin who had countered Alan's legitimate concern about employee morale by shouting that he was "sick and tired" of hearing about morale and, allegedly, that he didn't care if Columbia's stock fell to two dollars a share.*

In late April and early May, Irwin Kramer, again in his capacity as head of the audit committee, made two moves that angered Alan Hirschfield as much as anything he had done earlier. First, Kramer expressed doubts about the personal integrity of Joe Fischer, whom Hirschfield respected and valued as much as any other corporate officer. Second, Kramer again dragged up the issue of Berte's employment record, which Alan thought had been resolved months ago by Todd Lang and Peter Gruenberger (after having been previously addressed two years earlier).

Kramer attacked Joe Fischer because Fischer had not informed him of the Audrey Lisner embezzlements immediately upon learning of them. Fischer had chosen to wait until he and Ilana Cytto had completed their initial inquiry and established the pertinent facts. He had given Kramer a full briefing the same day he told Hirschfield, Monday, April 24. Kramer, however, had been secretly tipped about the Lisner problem days earlier by someone at Screen Gems in Burbank. Instead of confronting Fischer, Kramer had waited, growing progressively angrier and more suspicious, until Fischer told him. After the April 24 meeting, Kramer wrote a memorandum to Hirschfield criticizing Fischer.

The memo infuriated Hirschfield not only because of its attack on Fischer but also because it appeared to constitute another challenge to Hirschfield's authority to run the corporation—the opening of a new front in his war with the board. As chairman of the audit

---

*Kramer later denied making the remark about the stock.

committee, Kramer insisted that in the future he be informed at the first indication of a possible malfeasance anywhere in the company, instead of after the appropriate executives had investigated and determined the extent of the problem. To Hirschfield, Kramer's stance constituted an attempt to harass him and Fischer by usurping their functions, and on Tuesday, May 2, he dispatched an angry letter to Kramer rejecting all his charges and demands.

Enraged, as well, by the reinvocation of Berte's employment with the Wolf market-research firm, Hirschfield attempted to counterattack by alleging possible conflicts of interest in Irwin Kramer's own business affairs. He sent memos to Leo Jaffe, pointing out that Kramer was on the board of Teleprompter, the cable-television company, and had a business relationship with Seeburg, a competitor of Columbia's pinball-machine company. Both of those relationships, Hirschfield charged, constituted possible conflicts with the interests of Columbia Pictures.

On Thursday afternoon, May 4, Hirschfield talked with Todd Lang about Irwin Kramer's new aggressiveness. Lang was upset, especially about the issue of Berte's employment. Weil, Gotshal & Manges had assured Kramer in December that there had been nothing improper about her employment with the Wolf firm. It seemed that Kramer implicitly was questioning the law firm's integrity, as reflected in its handling of that matter, as well as questioning Joe Fischer's integrity, as reflected in his handling of the Lisner affair.

"What do you think Herbert wants in this whole thing?" Lang asked Hirschfield.

"He wants my head, that's what. And he won't be satisfied until he gets it."

FIFTY-THREE

Herbert Allen telephoned Alan Hirschfield on Friday morning to announce that he had tentatively decided to sell 250,000 shares of the Allens' stock in Columbia Pictures—about a third of their holdings and a sixth of the combined Allen-Rosenhaus block—to David Begelman's close friend Sy Weintraub. Herbert just wanted to let Hirschfield know.

"What you do with your stock is your business," Hirschfield said, "but it surprises me, in view of Weintraub's extensive relationship with Begelman."

"That's irrelevant," Herbert replied. "The point is, Sy's very smart, a great guy, and he could help us a lot. He knows everybody in Hollywood."

"I still think it looks peculiar," Hirschfield said.

"Think about it over the weekend," Herbert asked.

Over lunch in the office, Hirschfield and Richard Bloch, the chief executive of Filmways, had still another discussion of Columbia's buying Filmways, and of Bloch's heading the two companies' combined motion-picture and television operations on the coast. Both men felt the deal made sense economically and Hirschfield felt that Bloch would be an excellent choice to replace Begelman.* Herbert Allen dropped in on the meeting for a while, and though he said nothing definite, Hirschfield inferred from his comments that he might favor the merger with Filmways.

After Herbert left, Bloch asked Hirschfield, "What do you *really* feel?"

---

*Hirschfield did not feel that naming Bloch to Begelman's old job would be inconsistent with naming Dan Melnick president of the movie division. Melnick was not sensitive about titles, and Bloch could assume many of the administrative burdens that otherwise would fall on Melnick.

"I feel it would be a sensational deal, but in the end, even though Herbert is mouthing these words, I don't believe he really means it. I view the chances as slim. The board won't look at the merits of the deal, only whether it makes me stronger or weaker."

Friday's mail brought Joe Fischer a six-page handwritten letter from Audrey Lisner.

> Dear Joe:
>   . . . Although I feel [that] all involved in this matter understand my sorrow, shame, and embarrassment, I feel it necessary to express these feelings to you personally at this time. There *are* no reasonable excuses for unreasonable acts. I know this. After much soul searching I can offer you only the truth *as I see it*. It was the desperate act of an extremely ill woman to try and secure the future of her children, the catalyst, perhaps, being the shock of learning that the thousands of dollars in back child support due me were now totally inaccessible and out of the question. . . . The situation was totally overwhelming, and my decision, as irrational and inexcusable as it was, seemed the only alternative open to me. . . . I expect no sympathy from you. However, I must ask you to remember that this insane chain of events began with my children and now ends with them. This is not easy for me, but for the sake of my children, I *beg* you not to destroy the one thing that is left to insure their future—my earning potential.
>   Very simply, Joe, I am all the children have—If I am unable to work, my girls will have nothing. . . .

The more Hirschfield thought about the prospect of a quarter of a million shares of Columbia Pictures being owned by Sy Weintraub, David Begelman's close friend, the uneasier he became. Could it be that Herbert would try to make Weintraub a member of the board of directors? "Sy could help us a lot," Herbert had said.

Alan telephoned Herbert Monday morning. "While it's none of my business whom you sell your stock to, I would have severe reservations if you have any thought of putting Weintraub on the board."

"Anybody who owns a lot of stock deserves to be on the board," Herbert replied casually, as if the point were self-evident.

"I think that would be a terrible error," Hirschfield said. "I have nothing personal against Sy. I hardly know him. But putting him on the board is like putting David back on the board. Sy would be seen as David's surrogate. The public reaction, the SEC reaction, the employee reaction would be that it is an outrage. This is the man who loaned Begelman the money he used to cover up his crimes."

"I disagree," Herbert said. "His relationship with Begelman is irrelevant. I don't believe in guilt by association."

A meeting of the board of directors was scheduled for Thursday, and Herbert let it be known during the week that he planned to propose Sy Weintraub for membership.

Although he doubted that Herbert ever would approve Columbia's buying Filmways, Hirschfield had higher hopes for a merger with Mattel, principally because Dan Lufkin seemed to favor the deal. Dan was an ally of Herbert's but he also had a close business relationship with the chief executive officer of Mattel, Arthur Spear, and had encouraged Herbert and Matty to consider the merger seriously. Hirschfield and Spear liked each other and felt they could work well together. Spear, although he had lived for many years in Southern California, was a New England native and retained, at age fifty-seven, the accent and mien of a New England gentleman. He and Hirschfield not only had discussed the structure of a combined company, but also had talked of possible future acquisitions of other companies, e.g., EMI, the British entertainment conglomerate.

Art Spear and other top Mattel executives came to New York for a formal meeting with Columbia on Wednesday, May 10. Prior to the meeting, Hirschfield, Allen, Rosenhaus, and Lufkin conferred privately. Rosenhaus was opposed to Columbia's buying Mattel. He referred repeatedly to Nabisco's having had a bad experience in the toy business through the ownership of Aurora, another toy company.

"It was terrible," Rosenhaus said.

"But Matty, that's like saying Allied Artists is in the movie business," Hirschfield said. "Mattel is the biggest company in the toy business, and to compare it to Aurora, a small and troubled company with enormous problems, is ridiculous."

Though Rosenhaus remained doubtful, the Columbia people proceeded on down to Mattel's New York quarters in an office tower above Penn Station, where the Mattel executives staged a compelling presentation of their company's various lines of business, how they would fit into Columbia Pictures Industries, and how the combined entity would be even stronger than the separate companies. Everyone was impressed, including Rosenhaus and Allen. Though there were no commitments, the Columbia group agreed to think it over seriously.

In a taxi on the way back to Columbia, Leo Jaffe remarked that it appeared that Sy Weintraub would become a member of the board of directors at the meeting the next day. Allen Adler lost his temper.

"This is ridiculous!" Adler said. "When are you people going to learn to say no?"

"Don't yell at me!" Jaffe retorted, but Adler went on.

"When do you people learn to say 'This is just wrong, and we will not support it.' I never heard of a situation in a big publicly owned company where a guy who owns seven percent of the stock just says 'This is what I want,' and even if it's wrong, you guys agree."

"We don't agree," Hirschfield said, "and we're going to try to stop it."

Three hours later, at 7 P.M., Art Spear, Alan Hirschfield, and Dan Lufkin were seated at a corner table at Quo Vadis. They talked about how impressive the Mattel presentation had been and how much they wanted to make the deal. Then Lufkin said, "Look, I think I can get Herbert and even Matty to do this deal. It's a deal that should be done for the sake of both companies, especially Columbia. Aside from all the obvious benefits, it's a chance for us at Columbia to get our minds on some big important issues and off of the divisive things we've been going through. So I think I can convince Herbert and Matty, but on one condition: that I would become chairman and chief executive officer of the combined company. Art, you would be president, and Alan, you would be executive vice president."

Hirschfield and Spear were nonplussed. They looked at each other and at Lufkin. No one spoke for a few moments. Then Art Spear said, "Dan, let me make it easy for you. I like you very much. You're a very capable person. But let me make it very clear that the only way this deal is going to get done is if I'm chairman and chief executive officer and Alan is president and chief operating officer. We've worked that out ourselves. Alan is willing to defer to me because I'm several years older but am not yet at the point in my life where I'm ready to step down. If you want to be chairman of the executive committee, or vice chairman, or something along those lines, maybe it could be worked out. I'm not hung up on titles, and neither is Alan, but he and I would have to have the executive and operating authority for running the company. That's the only way it will work.''

For the remainder of the meal the three men groped unsuccessfully for a compromise. Spear pointed out that Lufkin had had virtually no experience in running a large corporation. Lufkin finally left, and Hirschfield walked Spear the four blocks to the Plaza Hotel where Spear was staying.

Spear said, ''That was really one of the most extraordinary propositions I've ever heard in my business life.''

''Look, Art,'' said Hirschfield, ''this is a demonstration of the kind of people we're dealing with. I'm sure they mean what they say.''

''Well, it's a great deal for Columbia and it's a great deal for Mattel, but you know and I know that it would never work that way.''

''You're right.''

Hirschfield met Joe Fischer for breakfast at the Sherry Netherland at eight the next morning. Fischer was a furious and desperate man. He reported that Irwin Kramer was ''running rampant'' over him and his staff in an effort to ferret out possible embezzlements in the company.

''I can't live with this!'' Fischer said. ''They're killing me. They're killing my department. How can we know something's suspicious until we investigate. In the ordinary course of a week, there could be ten things. A check doesn't come in or go out. An account doesn't jibe in some foreign country. We make inquiries. Ninety-nine percent of the time it's a bookkeeping error. But Kramer demands that he know everything the moment I do, before I know whether it's serious or not. It's impossible. They're running roughshod over us.''

''Just tell them to go to hell,'' Hirschfield said. ''We're not going to stand for it. If you have any problems, just go to the lawyers.''

Hirschfield and Fischer walked down Fifth to the Columbia building to keep an appointment with Irwin Kramer, and the meeting immediately deteriorated into invective.

''This is an absolute outrage,'' Hirschfield shouted. ''I'm backing

Joe. If you don't like it, let's have it out right now. If you want to get rid of Joe, then you'll have to get rid of me at the same time. It's an outrage for you to accuse us of covering up and not cooperating. You've created a circumstance which is a totally bizarre, Catch-22 kind of situation, where you say we have to let you know whether a situation is a problem before we know whether it's a problem. We're willing to cooperate with any reasonable request. You knew about Audrey Lisner before I knew about Audrey Lisner. We're bending over backwards to do a proper job, and I regard this as just baiting Joe, and baiting me, in an effort to discredit everybody.''

Kramer staunchly defended his right to challenge Fischer and vehemently denied doing anything improper. Nothing was settled and the meeting had to be adjourned. It was time for the regular monthly meeting of the Columbia board of directors.

Herbert Allen informed the board of Sy Weintraub's purchase of 250,000 shares of stock and suggested that it might be "appropriate" if Weintraub were made a director of the corporation. Allen gave a brief campaign speech, which was enthusiastically seconded by Matty Rosenhaus, who said he had "met Sy a couple of times and he's a great guy."

So as not to inflame the meeting any sooner than necessary, Hirschfeld did not respond immediately but deferred to Leo Jaffe.

"Sy is a fine person," Jaffe said, "but putting him on the board now would be a disaster for the company. He would be viewed as David Begelman's surrogate in the eyes of the public and the SEC. Perhaps in the future we could reconsider, but there's no worse time than now."

Todd Lang was asked to explain the "potential legal ramifications" of Weintraub's election to the board. "It would be the worst possible thing the company could do at the present time," Lang said. "It would only exacerbate the SEC situation and the company's posture with regard to pending lawsuits. The company has the *right* to do it, of course, but in terms of legal posture, it would be a terrible mistake.''*

Hirschfeld then added his opposition, whereupon Herbert Allen suggested that the matter be dropped until a future board meeting.

*The SEC's investigation of Columbia was proceeding apace. And several stockholders had begun lawsuits against the company alleging various violations of federal securities laws in connection with the Begelman affair and other matters.

However, Allen asked that Weintraub, who was waiting in the Allen & Company offices for the board's decision, at least be invited to join the board for lunch.

Of all of the awkward moments in the Columbia boardroom, none was more awkward than when Herbert Allen, who was having difficulty hiding his anger and embarrassment, ushered in Sy Weintraub, who was having difficulty hiding his anger and disappointment, and introduced him around the table. The directors' reactions varied from jarring warmth and cordiality on the part of Matty Rosenhaus, to politeness on the part of Leo Jaffe, to neutral civility on the part of most others. Weintraub's stock purchase and potential board membership were not mentioned and the conversation was strained.

When the meal was cleared away and the meeting resumed, Weintraub surprised a number of those present by remaining in the boardroom. Though corporate board meetings generally are confidential, Herbert Allen permitted Weintraub to listen to the board's discussion of motion pictures, television, Arista, Gottlieb, pay TV, and other matters. After Weintraub left, Herbert again suggested that Sy be elected to the board. "If we're going to do it eventually, why not now?" Jaffe and Hirschfield again expressed vehement opposition, and Allen angrily retreated without trying to force a vote.

At one point during the afternoon, Dan Lufkin scrawled something on a yellow legal pad and slid it in front of Herbert, who nodded his agreement. The words on the pad were "This company is out of control."

Even though Hirschfield had known the resumption of hostilities was inevitable, and even though he had been hardened by the traumas of the previous autumn and winter, he was bewildered and shaken by the spasmodic nature and sequence of the new events that suddenly had buffeted the company in recent weeks, some of them in just the last couple of days. Audrey Lisner, the very model of the conscientious, trusted employee, is revealed as the embezzler of a quarter of a million dollars. A distressing event, to be sure, but certainly manageable by the corporation's existing control systems which indeed had caught her. And yet Irwin Kramer, the belligerent chairman of the audit committee, leaps on the case as if it were a Brink's job and maligns the integrity of Joe Fischer, one of the most capable financial executives in the entertainment industry. For good measure, Irwin also reignites the Berte Hirschfield controversy—an entirely unrelated issue which had been settled not once but twice previously. Herbert Allen, meanwhile, in surely the most irrational of all his irrational acts, tries to put one of David Begelman's most intimate friends—the man from whom Begelman borrowed to repay the money he stole—on the Columbia board of directors. The Filmways and Mattel deals, which Hirschfield had seen as his last realistic chances to dilute Herbert's control and adjust the balance of power in the corporation, appear to have collapsed. Although Herbert would cite other reasons for opposing both acquisitions, Alan was convinced that the real reason was Herbert's mistrust of his motives.

Hirschfield was growing desperate again, but as he said to Adler, who was urging tough initiatives against the board, "I've got to live to fight another day. I've got to survive as long as I can. Our ambitions will be meaningless if we're not here."

Audrey Lisner had had long-standing arrangements to spend the last half of May in Mexico City at a major international dog show. However, because of the investigation of her embezzlements, she had agreed not to leave Los Angeles. She had been cooperating with Ilana Cytto's audit of Screen Gems' records, and had promised to cooperate, too, with Peter Gruenberger, who was scheduled to go to Los Angeles and take command of the investigation the third week of May. The Los Angeles District Attorney's office was on the case as well, having been called by an anonymous tipster, but had agreed to await the results of Columbia's internal probe before taking any action.

Peter Gruenberger flew to Los Angeles the evening of Sunday, May 14, intending to confer with Ilana Cytto the next day and see Lisner later in the week. However, earlier that Sunday, Mother's Day, without telling any of the investigators, Audrey Lisner flew to Mexico City with her dogs and dog handler, Ric Chashoudian.

When it became clear early in the week that Lisner was missing, Richard Kerns obtained from her travel agent the name of the hotel where she had been scheduled to stay, and was surprised when she answered his call.

"Audrey, this is Dick."

"Oh, hello, Mr. Kerns."

"What the fuck are you doing? You know you were supposed to meet with Peter Gruenberger! You agreed to the date!"

"My dogs wouldn't act properly if I wasn't with them."

"But you weren't supposed to go in the first place."

"Why can't he interview me by phone?"

"He needs to see you in person. That's what you agreed to."

"Well, I'll be back in a few days. He can see me then."

In New York, Todd Lang sent Irwin Kramer a five-page, single-spaced letter, marked "Confidential/Attorney-Client Privilege," setting forth in elaborate detail the history of Berte Hirschfield's employment with the market-research firm of E. J. Wolf & Associates.

> At your request, in order to support our initial view, we recently have conducted an investigation of the circumstances of Berte Hirschfield's employment by Wolf and of Wolf's contractual relationship with Columbia. We have interviewed Berte Hirschfield, Ed Wolf, and certain present and former employees of Columbia with knowledge of the facts.

The letter concluded:

> No facts developed in the course of this investigation suggested that there was anything improper about the business relationship between Columbia and Wolf or with respect to Berte Hirschfield's employment by Wolf. Nor have any facts come to our attention suggesting that Columbia did not receive the services from Wolf which were expected under the contracts from Wolf.
>
> Accordingly, based upon the scope of the investigation and the facts revealed by that investigation, as detailed above, we confirm our view previously expressed to you that Columbia has not been required under the federal securities laws to disclose publicly Berte Hirschfield's employment with Wolf.

On Tuesday, May 16, and again the following Sunday, *The New York Times* published one of the most sweeping retractions ever to appear in a major American newspaper. Still under threat of a libel suit by Allen & Company, the *Times* retracted major portions of the February article by Lucian Truscott, IV, which had suggested that the Allens had tried to "hush up" the Begelman scandal so as not to interfere with an alleged plan to sell the Allen interest in Columbia, that the Allens had dealt with organized crime figures, and that Charles Allen had been a "mystery power behind the Hollywood set ever since" the early fifties.

"The phrases 'Godfather' and 'hush up' and the use of the photograph of an organized crime figure may have created the incorrect impression that Charles Allen was connected with the Mafia or had engaged in illegal activities," the *Times* said. "The article did not intend to suggest that [the Allens] were connected with organized crime or involved in illegal activities. The *Times* regrets any such unwarranted implication."

The breadth of the retraction in effect covered every indication of "illegal activities" in the article, including an attempt to conceal the Begelman scandal in order not to interfere with a sale of stock.

"The statement used as a basis for the article's assertion that [Charles] Allen had been a power behind Hollywood for 25 years was incorrect," the *Times* said. The paper also corrected the false statement that Columbia Pictures had been unprofitable for a number of years until *Close Encounters* put it in the black.

The retraction was notable not only for its scope but also for the prominence of its publication. Unlike most corrections, it was highlighted by a note on the front page and another note in the news summary and index. The notes referred to an article *about* the correction under a two-column headline on page one of the business and financial section. That article reported the gist of the correction, whose text then appeared in a headlined box on the letters page of the Sunday magazine, and was flagged by a note in the magazine's table of contents.

Having achieved their essential goal, the Allens agreed to drop the lawsuit.*

David Begelman made an unexpected appearance in Burbank Superior Court on Wednesday, May 17, and entered a plea of "no contest" to the charge of felony grand theft. Sentencing was sched-

---

*Despite the magnitude of the Truscott retraction, it came to look relatively modest in 1982 when the *Times* found it necessary to retract an entire article its magazine had published on Cambodia. Large portions if not all of the article apparently had been fabricated. A year earlier, *The Washington Post* admitted that one of its major articles, which had won a Pulitzer Prize, was a hoax.

Meanwhile, David Begelman's threatened suit against *New West* and *New York* magazines for suggesting that he had mishandled Judy Garland's funds was never begun. Lawyers for the two sides discussed possible forms of rebuttal Begelman might make, but nothing was published and, as Begelman later put it, the matter "dwindled away."

uled for June 28. Begelman did not change his not-guilty pleas to
the forgery counts, but it was generally assumed that those charges
eventually would be dismissed. *Variety* noted that the judge who
would pass sentence had a reputation for being a "very lenient trial
judge." Looking dapper in a double-breasted blazer, Begelman told
a throng of reporters and cameramen, "I feel this was the right and
appropriate thing to do at this time." Everyone assumed that David
would get off with probation and perhaps a fine. The change of plea
made headlines across the country. (A no-contest plea stands as a
conviction of the crime and is legally tantamount to a guilty plea
except for one technical difference: a no-contest plea cannot be used
as evidence against the defendant in a civil lawsuit, while a guilty
plea can.)

After a session with his psychiatrist the next morning, David
Begelman, along with Gladyce, caught the noon United flight to
New York and attended the opening of a new Columbia film, *Thank
God It's Friday,* and a party afterward at Studio 54.

Alan Hirschfield and Joe Fischer flew to Dallas that day for the
world premiere of *The Buddy Holly Story* followed by a party at a
barbecue joint whose reputation for rowdiness prompted the local
Columbia office to provide Hirschfield with a bodyguard.

Hirschfield spent the next two weeks concluding arrangements for
Dan Melnick to become the permanent president of the studio and
trying again to interest the board of directors in acquiring Filmways
or Mattel. Both efforts increased the acrimony in the company.

Though the board members grudgingly approved the Melnick
appointment, they ridiculed Hirschfield for taking nearly four months
to choose the person who was already occupying the studio presidency in an acting capacity. Hirschfield angrily retorted that if the
board had kept its promise to support him and to certify his own
position in the corporation he could have filled the studio position
much sooner, perhaps with someone even more qualified than Melnick.

As for Mattel and Filmways, Hirschfield finally realized that there
was no hope, and that his persistence was only alienating Herbert
Allen further. A tentative offer by the investment banker for Filmways
to purchase the Allens' interest in Columbia Pictures was, of course,
rejected.

FIFTY-FOUR

Audrey Lisner and her dog handler, Ric Chashoudian, took a taxi to the Mexico City airport for their flight back to Los Angeles. It was Tuesday, May 30. They had been in Mexico just over two weeks.

As they were walking through the airport after checking their luggage, Audrey suddenly told Ric that she had forgotten something at the hotel and had to go back. Since it was too late to recover their luggage she insisted that he go on ahead and she would catch a later flight. Before he could stop her, she hurried away.

Chashoudian took the flight as planned and at LAX gathered their luggage and took it to Lisner's home where his wife, Sandra, had been looking after Audrey's two daughters. (The dogs were transported directly to their kennel.) Audrey did not arrive on any subsequent flight that day, and by late evening the Chashoudians became concerned. They opened Audrey's luggage and found a large envelope addressed to Ric. Inside were four documents which shocked the Chashoudians. The first was a handwritten letter from Audrey to Ric dated that day:

Dear Ric,
Unfortunately, I will not be joining you on the flight home. . . . When you read this you will wonder why and what has happened. I can only say that you have become a dear friend and I feel I can rely on you to take care of that which is most dear to me. I don't know at this moment what I will do or where I will go. I have no future. May I thank you for all you have done and most of all for what must be done now. I cannot face the problems that are about to happen to me. Soon you will be aware of what they are. I can offer no explanation at this point because there is

none. . . . My friends have always been my family. I love them dearly, second only to my children; therefore I must spare them any embarrassment.

I remain as always,
Audrey

Also in the envelope were a general power of attorney, notarized at the U.S. Embassy in Mexico City five days earlier, giving the Chashoudians full power to act for Audrey Lisner in all types of business and legal affairs; a handwritten note giving custody of Audrey's sixteen-year-old daughter to the Chashoudians; and a second handwritten note giving custody of her fourteen-year-old daughter to another friend.

Totally bewildered, and unsure of what to do next, the Chashoudians spent the next few days conferring with their lawyer, police detectives, Columbia Pictures' investigators, and Audrey's friends. There was no further word from Audrey.

(Actually, Lisner had reappeared at the Mexico City airport the same day she left Ric Chashoudian and had taken a Texas International flight to Houston. No one found that out until weeks later, however, when U.S. Customs in Texas turned up Lisner's reentry form in response to a request by the Los Angeles Police. By that time, Lisner had disappeared.)

Robert Stone, the former Hertz and NBC executive whom Alan Hirschfield had considered, and then privately rejected, for employment at Columbia Pictures Industries, very much wanted to work for Columbia. Although Hirschfield had not definitely said no to Stone when they met in April at Herbert Allen's request, Hirschfield had not contacted Stone again and Stone held little hope that Hirschfield would hire him. However, Stone made it a point to stay in touch with Herbert, and the more Herbert saw of Stone, the more impressed he became. After the revelation of the Lisner embezzlements, Herbert grew more convinced than ever that Columbia's financial control procedures were deficient. He recalled Dan Lufkin's note to him during the May board meeting: "This company is out of control." In late May, Herbert introduced Bob Stone to Matty Rosenhaus, who also was impressed. They convinced themselves that Stone, with his reputation as a tough administrator, was just the kind of executive Columbia needed.

Having been unemployed for more than fourteen months, Stone naturally was looking elsewhere as well, and on June 1 he was offered a high executive post with a Dallas company controlled by Bunker and Herbert Hunt, the oil and silver magnates. Stone promised the Hunts that he would give them an answer by Tuesday, June 6.

Stone still wanted to work for Columbia, however, and he told Herbert Allen of his dilemma: He had had no call from Hirschfield but had an offer from the Hunts which he had to accept or reject within a few days. Herbert asked Stone to come to his office early Monday morning, June 5. "I'm very anxious," Herbert said, "that you meet with Alan Hirschfield and somehow get something worked out where you can become executive vice president and chief operating officer of Columbia." Stone was delighted and said he was available to see Hirschfield immediately. Herbert promised Stone he would get a call by noon. Stone left, and Herbert went to the eleventh floor, found Hirschfield in the hall, and the two of them went into the boardroom.

"I have a plan which will help the company and also solve all your problems with the board," Herbert said.

"Really," Alan replied skeptically. "What is it?"

"Hire Bob Stone as executive vice president and chief operating officer."

Hirschfield sighed and rolled his eyes. "If you'll recall, Herbert, I met with Stone about a year ago, and I met with him again in April, and I decided he's the wrong person for us. He's the wrong kind of personality for this business."

"On the contrary," Herbert said, "I think he's perfect. You ought to reconsider. He's just the man to get this company under control. He's had a job offer from the Hunts in Dallas and he has to let them know by noon tomorrow. But if something can be worked out here, I think he'd prefer to be here. If you make a deal with him today, it would really clear the air between you and the board. You'll get your new contract and we can get back to business around here."

"I must say, Herbert, that this is just about the most bizarre suggestion I've ever heard. Not only do I hire a guy I don't want, but I hire him today."

"I've gotten to know the guy, Alan, and he's perfect for what we need. This company is out of control, and the Lisner thing proves it.

Matty, Irwin, Dan, and I all feel that the company is out of control, and Stone has the perfect kind of strong operating background to deal with it."

"Saying the company is out of control is an outrageous statement!" Hirschfield declared. "Is that the 'big lie' you're now going to promulgate—that the company is out of control? There's not one shred of evidence to support it. It's just another excuse to harass me. The fact that one man and one lady out of thousands of employees have superseded the control system doesn't mean the company's out of control! Our controls are very good. We've got the lowest operating costs of any company in the industry. It's a ludicrous statement to make today, at the peak of the company's success. Nobody was saying it was out of control five years ago when it was on the verge of bankruptcy! I have no objection to hiring a qualified person, but it's just plain crazy to hire a man for a job in the space of an afternoon, especially when he isn't qualified. Everyone I've talked to about Stone says the same thing—he's very competent, a good operating man, but totally inflexible, abrasive, tied to budgets and numbers, and operates by fear and by the book. That's totally inimical to the kind of company and the kind of people we have."

"I've heard the same things," Herbert said, "and that's exactly why I'm for him. He won't be involved in the creative process. He'll handle budgets and control the flow of money. We need somebody like that around here. We say yes to everybody on everything. How about somebody who can say no. An operations officer shouldn't be loved by everybody in the company. We have enough love to go around, but we don't have enough efficiency."

"That's an insult—this is an efficient company," Hirschfield asserted. "Maybe Stone's right for U.S. Steel or Hertz, but not for the creative environment of an entertainment company. None of my people—Fischer, Adler, Melnick—would report to him."

"That's ridiculous. It depends on how you handle it. You can set the guy up to be destroyed or you can support him and set him up to succeed."

"There's no way Bob Stone can succeed in this company under any circumstances. And to hire him in one day is absolute madness."

"You could work it out if you wanted to. It would cure this company's problems, and it would get you a new contract. At least see him before you decide."

With great reluctance, Hirschfield agreed to interview Stone again that afternoon. He told Stone that the management environment at Columbia remained "unsettled" and that he was very hesitant to hire him, particularly on less than a day's notice. But he agreed to consider it further and let him know later in the day or Tuesday morning.

After Stone left, Hirschfield summoned Fischer and Adler, whom he had already briefed on his meeting with Herbert.

"I'm not going to hire him in one day," Hirschfield said. "This is crazed. It makes no sense. It's a bunch of crap that once I hire him they're suddenly going to give me a contract. Once I hire him, they don't have to give me a contract. They would have a logical successor for me in place. They'd say, 'We're letting Alan Hirschfield go, but at least we have a chief operating officer.' They must think I'm completely stupid."

Bob Stone, meanwhile, telephoned Herbert Allen and said it appeared doubtful that Hirschfield would offer him the job. Allen asked Stone to be at the Allen & Company offices first thing Tuesday morning. When Stone appeared, he found Matty Rosenhaus there with Herbert. "We want you to join Columbia Pictures Industries as executive vice president and chief operating officer," Herbert said.

Stone was discreet enough not to press for details of how Allen and Rosenhaus intended to install him over Hirschfield's objections. Instead he said, "Look, I'm very interested in the Columbia thing, very enthusiastic about it. I feel I could make a major contribution. But I just want to be very certain that things will in fact work out for me here."

"We feel it will work out," Allen replied.

"Can you give me any kind of time frame?" Stone asked.

"Two or three weeks at most."

A delighted Bob Stone returned to his apartment, telephoned the Hunts, and turned down their offer.

Hirschfield, who was at home in bed with a bad back, called Herbert to say that he had decided against Stone. "You're making a big mistake, Alan," Herbert said, "but we'll talk about it when you're back in the office." Hirschfield then called Stone and told him he had decided not to hire him. Stone thanked Hirschfield for his consideration. He did not reveal that he had just been promised the job by the men who controlled the corporation.

*   *   *

Todd Lang's lengthy letter to Irwin Kramer in the middle of May, reiterating that there had been nothing improper about Berte Hirschfield's employment with the Wolf market-research firm, did not satisfy Kramer. He raised further questions and called a meeting of the audit committee for the morning of Wednesday, June 7. Hirschfield, having found previously that displays of sheer fury did no good, took further steps this time. He prepared notes for the meeting and asked his personal lawyer Robert Haines, to attend. Hirschfield had been quietly consulting Haines for weeks on what legal recourse he might have against the board of directors for its conduct toward him.

His back still hurting after a day in bed, Hirschfield arrived at his office and asked the audit committee to come to him so that he could keep his back as still as possible. Irwin Kramer refused and insisted that the meeting be held in his office. They argued and railed at each other, partly through secretaries and intermediaries, for more than an hour before Hirschfield finally agreed to go down to Allen & Company

"What occasioned the renewed interest and investigation concerning Berte and Ed Wolf?" Hirschfield asked, referring occasionally to his notes. "Why did it take over two years for Irwin Kramer as chairman of the audit committee to conclude there could be potential problems? If you're not satisfied with Weil, Gotshal & Manges's report, why has the audit committee failed to hire independent counsel? I view this as a deliberate effort to discredit the integrity of Weil, Gotshal & Manges. . . . a deliberate effort to place on the record innuendo, suspicion, and cynicism—two years after the fact and in the face of full voluntary disclosure to the board of Berte's employment. There is an unusual double standard being applied where I am concerned that does not seem to apply in similar situations where [other] board members are concerned, and where favoritism might be alleged or suspected."

Hirschfield noted that Irwin Kramer was a member of the board of directors of the Teleprompter Corporation, the nation's largest cable-television system, and had a business relationship with Seeburg Corporation, which manufactured pinball machines in competition with Columbia's Gottlieb unit. He also noted that Columbia Pictures had invested in a Broadway musical, *I Love My Wife*, which had been produced by Kramer's wife, Terry Allen Kramer. In each instance, Hirschfield alleged, there was at least as much if not more potential for conflict with interests of Columbia Pictures as there had been in Berte Hirschfield's employment, and yet none of Kramer's relationships had been investigated.

Kramer essentially ignored Hirschfield's points, but Hirschfield demanded that the issue of Berte's employment be resolved formally and immediately. Peter Gruenberger, who had emerged from the Audrey Lisner investigation long enough to again address the Berte Hirschfield situation, proceeded to answer Kramer's latest questions forthwith. The committee then voted unanimously that the matter was closed.*

That afternoon, Dan Lufkin called and asked if he could see Hirschfield late in the day. "It's very important," Lufkin said. He arrived at Alan's office at six o'clock. Since Dan Lufkin had joined the board of directors several months earlier at the height of the Begelman crisis, a modicum of warmth had developed between him and Hirschfield. Even though Lufkin was a partisan of Herbert's, he at least had acted toward Hirschfield in a more congenial fashion than Herbert, Matty, and Irwin had. It was possible for Alan and Dan to have a civil conversation—something Alan had not had with the others in months.

"Look, no one knows I'm here, I haven't been sent by anyone," Lufkin began. "But I wanted to discuss your situation with the board, particularly Herbert. I believe time is running out and that if you don't take some quick action, it's my best opinion that you will be out of the company. The situation is close to being out of hand, and you're the only person who can cure it."

"I'm shocked," Hirschfield replied. "What's going on?"

"The board is very upset, specifically Herbert, Matty, and Irwin, and I believe they're prepared to get rid of you."

"How much time do I have?"

"Something needs to be done in the next twenty-four hours or it's my best guess—I'm almost sure—that you'll be out."

"That's somewhat awkward, in that I'm scheduled to go to Los Angeles over the weekend for the yearly budget reviews, and the following week I have all our other divisional budget reviews in New York."

"You may have five or six days, but that's it. What needs to be

---

*Hirschfield offered no evidence to support his suggestion of possible conflicts of interest in Kramer's business relationships and did not press the issue. Kramer denied any conflicts.

done is for you to meet with Herbert, tell him it's been a difficult period for everyone, but that you're prepared to work with him to make the company succeed and get all the crap behind us. And the key to it is for you to take Bob Stone as chief operating officer if that's what Herbert wants—do that as a gesture to Herbert.''

Hirschfield, surprised to hear that Robert Stone was still available in light of the Dallas job offer, explained to Lufkin his reasons for opposing the hiring of Stone at Columbia.

"It's bullshit that the company's out of control," Hirschfield said. "Herbert and Matty have invented a myth and then come up with a solution to the myth. It's the 'big lie' technique.''

"Alan, like it or not, Herbert and Matty are the controlling shareholders and believe that this entitles them to call the shots as they see fit—even if you disagree and even if everyone in management thinks it's wrong for the company. But if you'll take Stone, the problem will be solved and your contract will be renewed.''

"Have you met this man Stone?''

"No, but it doesn't make any difference. That is what Herbert and Matty want.''

"I'm not prepared to commit an act which I sincerely believe to be against the best interest of the company and the shareholders. I'm in a better position to judge the kind of people needed to operate the company than the board is, certainly Matty and Herbert. My record over five years speaks for itself, both in performance and in attracting the best people available for the job. I'm more than willing to find a chief operating officer, if the board and I can agree that there is such a need, and I'll proceed to do so immediately. But to hire Stone on twenty-four hours notice would give credence to the board's ridiculous view that the company's out of control. It would destroy the management staff's confidence in me and themselves, and it's just plain crazy.''

Lufkin reiterated his warning. "I'm trying to come as a friend. I'm trying to come as somebody who wants to see the thing stay together rather than be torn apart. You should talk to Herbert as soon as possible.''

Hirschfield knew he would not be fired in the next twenty-four hours, and he doubted he would be fired in the next five or six days. But Lufkin's visit still shook him. The war was intensifying. Though it was unclear whether Dan had been carrying a message from Herbert or truly had come on his own, Herbert's words at the height of the December furor resonated in Alan's memory as if they had been spoken yesterday: "If we don't get him now, we'll get him in six months."

Alan had considered it an empty threat then. But six months had passed. And he knew that Dan Lufkin's warning—delivered softly, on this cool, rainy evening in early June—was serious.

FIFTY-FIVE

The regular monthly meeting of the board of directors the next day was acrimonious from beginning to end. However, it was no *more* acrimonious than the May or April meetings, and for that at least Hirschfield was grateful.

One of the few peaceful interludes in the meeting was a report on the studio's motion-picture production plans from Dan Melnick, whose appointment as president of the studio had been announced a week earlier. Having flown in from the coast for the board meeting, Melnick lived up to his reputation as one of Hollywood's most articulate executives, and the board—Herbert and Matty in particular—ladled praise upon Melnick as if he were a reincarnated Irving Thalberg. Alan Hirschfield, who had been assailed by the directors only a few days earlier for failing to hire someone superior to Melnick—and for taking four months to hire him—found their comments somewhat hypocritical. Herbert and Matty were so warm that a cynic might have suspected they were trying to establish an independent relationship with Melnick—a Hirschfield partisan—that could be employed in the event Hirschfield left the company. Hirschfield, however, did not say anything. Who could worry about a little hypocrisy in the middle of a war? As for Melnick, who possessed the most cynical spirit and acute sense of irony in the boardroom that day, he too kept his thoughts to himself but rather enjoyed the moment.

The board discussed and approved several new motion picture projects: *Somebody Killed Her Husband*, which would be the movie debut of Farrah Fawcett-Majors; *The First Deadly Sin*, on which Columbia Pictures had spent more than a million dollars developing a script since it acquired the rights in 1973; and *By Reason of Insanity*, a new Shane Stevens novel whose screen rights would cost Columbia $350,000. It was disclosed that David Begelman had expressed an interest in producing the film of *By Reason of Insanity* before he tackled *Annie*. There was a pause in the boardroom, and then someone suggested that perhaps David's very first effort as a producer after leaving Columbia should be something with a different title.

Alan arrived at Herbert's office at 8:30 Friday morning.

"I just want you to know that I'm terribly disturbed about Lufkin's visit. If you have messages to send, you know me well enough to send them in person."

"I didn't know anything about it until afterwards. I'm sure Dan did it on his own."

"Whether you knew about it or not, it clearly reflects the attitude of the board toward me, which at the very least was distressing to hear."

Herbert said nothing.

"Well," Alan went on, "if I'm going to be gone in three or four days, or I have only a week to cure all of our ills, I'd like to know about it now, because I'm getting ready to go into all the budget reviews for next year for all the divisions. I'll be in California all next week, and I have another big meeting in Chicago in a couple of weeks. It's going to be a very strenuous period, and I'm not going to go through some sham act. At this point every executive in the company wants to know whether I'm still going to be with the company in the foreseeable future. It's an intolerable position to be in. I don't want to waste my time. It's just not worth the effort on my part."

"If you would hire Bob Stone, you would solve a lot of problems. It would solve Matty's and Irwin's anger with you. I can't control them. I can influence Matty, but I can't control him. I don't know if anybody can control him at this point."

"I've spoken with the key executives in the company, and those who know Stone regard bringing him in as a disaster for the company.

I just can't break faith with these people by bringing in someone not qualified for the job. This so-called paragon of American management hasn't even been able to get a job for over a year. I owe a great sense of loyalty to our executives, and I'm not going to prostitute myself doing something that is just to save my own skin, if that's what this is really about. I'll be happy to seek someone else who is qualified, but not Stone.''

"I still think Stone is the man," Herbert said. "Your problem isn't with me. Rosenhaus and Irwin are after your scalp. Stone will help solve that problem."

"Lufkin seems to think you're the one who needs to be satisfied. Herbert is my major nemesis here, he says. I better do something to give Herbert a victory or I'm going to be out on my ass."

"That has absolutely nothing to do with anything. I can't control the board. But hiring Stone would certainly help. If you hire him, your contract will be agreed upon. I suggest you go on to the coast, think it over, and let me know about Stone."

"I've already let you know, but for what it's worth, I'll think it over some more over the weekend."

Alan and Berte flew to Oklahoma City that afternoon for the twenty-fifth reunion of Alan's high school class—the class of 1953 of Classen High. "We propose a toast," the program said, "to all those giggly, gangly gals and linky, lanky guys of the Class of 1953 who have matured into beautiful people in 1978." Alan was the master of ceremonies at the Saturday evening banquet and dance.

By three o'clock Sunday afternoon, the Hirschfields were ensconced again in Bungalow 8 of the Beverly Hills Hotel. By four, Joe Fischer, Dan Melnick, and Clive Davis had wandered in. Gradually, a lethargic, rambling conversation among depressed people evolved into a council of war. It was clear to all that Alan's efforts to overthrow Herbert had failed and that in view of the fresh threat to fire Alan another plan had to be devised. Melnick, Fischer, and Berte had no new ideas, but Clive Davis did. Davis, who had not been so close to the daily fray as had the others, had always believed in the possibility of resolving Alan's and Herbert's differences through negotiation—without a putsch organized by Alan against Herbert, and without Herbert's firing Alan. Davis believed that the board's case against Hirschfield was based almost entirely upon premises that were false—demonstrably false. Hirschfield hadn't "gone Hollywood" in a destructive way; his active participation in the affairs of the studio was one of the keys to its creative vitality. The Begelman and Lisner embezzlements did not constitute evidence that the company was out of control; no controls were perfect, and Columbia's were among the best in the industry. Hirschfield did not object to hiring a chief operating officer; he objected to Robert Stone because he felt Stone was the wrong man for the job.

Clive Davis, a quiet, astute, and articulate man, had made a number of attempts over the months to reason with Herbert Allen, always to no avail. The emotional flames were too high. Davis also had failed to persuade Hirschfield to use caution and avoid extreme measures. But Clive Davis had not given up, and in the bungalow that afternoon he suggested a new idea: The top two officers of each of Columbia's divisions—motion pictures, television, phonograph records, pinball machines, and so forth—should assemble in New York and, as a group, confront the Columbia board of directors. They should demand an audience. And they should present the case for Alan Hirschfield—the case that had been obscured in the angry war for control—the logical, rational, compelling reasons why they felt that Hirschfield was an excellent chief executive officer. There should be no haranguing, no stated threats. The mere assembly of the group would be dramatic enough (and an implied threat that they would all resign if Hirschfield was fired). They should be calm, reasonable, and unemotional. Clive Davis believed that such a gesture might bring the board to its senses.

Although Hirschfield was touched by the suggestion, he doubted it would have the desired effect. He also was deeply ambivalent.

"I'm sick of fighting, and I have serious doubts that I even want to be associated with these people anymore. What do I need this for? Maybe I should just let 'em fire me, pay me off, leave me alone, and I'll go do something else."

"It's worth a try, Alan," Clive said. "You've invested too much of yourself to quit now, or let them run over you. This is your company as much as anyone else's. A lot of people are depending on you."

Alan sighed and shrugged.

Since Columbia Pictures Industries' fiscal year extended from July 1 through June 30, the most important of the quarterly budget reviews were those held in June, when the budgets for the fiscal year about to begin were examined, refined, and approved. In contrast to the procedure at some companies, where top officers merely give *pro forma* approval to budgets developed by underlings, Alan Hirschfield and Joe Fischer actively managed the Columbia budget process. The quarterly sessions were arduous, as Hirschfield and Fischer questioned, challenged, and prodded the motion-picture and television executives through three and sometimes four long days in Hirschfield's bungalow. Hirschfield normally displayed a light heart and a sense of humor through the tedious meetings, knowing that Fischer would supply the sober, relentless attention to each detail that both men felt was required when hundreds of millions of dollars were being spent on things as ephemeral as movies and TV shows.

A year earlier, in 1977, the motion-picture and television meetings had been held during the week of Monday, June 6. The company had looked forward to the release of *The Deep* and *Close Encounters of the Third Kind*. Everybody had been in a good mood, and Fischer and Hirschfield had nearly forgotten that they had learned the previous Friday that Cliff Robertson had raised questions about an odd check for $10,000.

On Monday, June 12, 1978, however, it was very difficult for Hirschfield, Fischer, and their top movie and TV aides to concentrate on budgets. Everyone knew the company was still at war, and the questions enshrouding the meeting were: Will Hirschfield be fired? and Can anything be done to prevent it? There was some loose talk of cabals against the board, but most of those present felt there was little they could do to influence events.

During a break on Monday, Hirschfield telephoned Herbert Allen and said that he had decided definitely not to hire Robert Stone.

There were a few moments of humor during the budget meetings, despite the gloom. With everyone assembled, Dan Melnick, having assumed the studio presidency only the previous week, strode into the conference room attired in riding breeches, boots, tunic, and helmet, carrying a riding crop, and looking very much like General Patton.

Slamming the crop onto the conference table, he bellowed: "All right! This company has been accused of being out of control! We're going to shape up and get some discipline into the organization! And furthermore, I'll countenance no more talk around here about inflated egos!"

After a moment of startled silence the group was convulsed by laughter.

Hours later, torpor again cloaking the meeting, studio marketing czar Norman Levy was estimating that an upcoming film called *The Fifth Musketeer* would attract about $3 million in box office admissions domestically. Alan Hirschfield, depressed and preoccupied, snapped:

"Just what do you base *that* figure on?"

There was an awkward pause, during which David Chasman, a senior production vice president, whispered to Dan Melnick, "Norman's totaled the grosses of *The Three Musketeers* and *The Four Musketeers,* and it averaged out to three million per musketeer."

Melnick repeated Chasman's line aloud. Amid the laughter, Hirschfield said, "That's as good a basis for an estimate of the gross of a picture as I've ever heard."

Having failed to induce Jimmy Goldsmith, Philip Morris, Time Incorporated, or Penn Central to make a bid for Columbia, and having failed also to dilute Herbert's power by merging with Mattel or Filmways, Alan Hirschfield by June had begun to consider the more drastic alternative of himself leading a public fight for control of Columbia Pictures Industries. The fight would take the form of a so-called proxy contest in which one who aspires to take control of a corporation nominates his own slate of directors and officers, and the shareholders then elect either the dissidents or the incumbents.* Proxy fights are very costly in money, time, and emotional energy, but sometimes they are the only way. A number of people had urged Hirschfield to wage a proxy fight; Mickey Rudin had suggested that he consider it as far back as the fall when it became clear that the board of directors was going to oppose his decision to fire Begelman.

Hirschfield always had felt that Herbert Allen's and Matty Rosenhaus's control of Columbia Pictures—represented by their ownership of 18 percent of the stock—was thin. Although it was widely assumed that they could influence enough additional shares to comprise a majority, Hirschfield had come to believe that if he could mount a strong and compelling challenge, he would stand a good

---

*Like many procedures in large public corporations, contests for control are waged almost entirely by mail and newspaper advertisement, with the shareholders sending ballots, or "proxies," to the representatives of the side they favor. Hence the label "proxy fight."

chance of attracting a sufficient portion of the 82 percent *not* owned by Allen and Rosenhaus to give his side a majority and thus victory in a proxy contest.

Hirschfield had discussed a proxy fight with his lawyer, Robert Haines, and with Allen Adler but with no one else. Secrecy was crucial. Hirschfield was sure that if Herbert Allen learned that such plans were afoot he would fire Hirschfield immediately, thus rendering the battle much more difficult to wage. Hirschfield, however, did authorize Robert Haines to take the necessary preliminary steps, and Haines began on Wednesday, June 14, by retaining a top attorney who specialized in proxy fights to manage Hirschfield's effort. The attorney was Sidney J. Silberman, a senior partner of the renowned Park Avenue firm of Kaye, Scholer, Fierman, Hays & Handler. Kaye, Scholer was not a show-biz firm. It offered a full range of corporate legal services, and its clients included Bankers Trust Company, Texaco, General Foods, and New York Life. It had a reputation as a tough litigator of antitrust and other intricate corporate legal issues. When Bob Haines called, Sid Silberman had just spent several months representing the Curtiss-Wright Corporation in a struggle to take over Kennecott Copper. Silberman told Haines (they had been students together at Columbia Law in the forties and both made the law review) that he would be available whenever Alan Hirschfield wanted to begin.

On Thursday morning, Hirschfield had breakfast with Ray Stark at the producer's antique-brick home on Mapleton Drive in Bel-Air. They ate in the dining room and then settled with coffee outside in the sun in Stark's sculpture garden.

"Look," said Stark, "whether you believe it or not, I'm really your friend and I want these problems to get settled. Why is it that you don't want to hire Bob Stone?"

Hirschfield sighed, and recited the reasons.

"Well, I don't know the man," Stark said, "but he sounds like he would be good for the company. If it will solve your problems with the board, it seems like a small thing to do. You're crazy if you don't. You're throwing away a promising career. You've built a wonderful company, along with David and Herbert. I don't know why you're being so stubborn. It would make Herbert happy, it would make Matty happy, it would make Irwin happy. It would prove to people that the company's not out of control and that you're doing something.''

"Ray, if I hire Stone, it will not be a signal that the company's in control. It will be a signal to everyone in the company that I, in effect, have lost control of the company, and that I am simply the board of directors' errand boy. The issue really isn't whether I get a new contract. The issue is whether I keep faith with people who have broken their asses for five years to make this company work. It would be an absolutely corrupt act on my part to hire someone I know is wrong.''

Stark tried to sway him, but Hirschfield said: "I don't see the logic of how hiring one man would suddenly erase the last eight months of turmoil and blatant hatred showed by the board toward me. These things don't disappear overnight. I view this purely as a test of wills. I've always tried to accommodate the wishes of the board over the years, and I've probably been too flexible. But this is a question of right and wrong.''

In addition to plotting cabals, putsches, and proxy fights, as well as pondering more modest means of curbing Herbert Allen's power, Hirschfield by the middle of June also had conferred at length with attorney Haines on ways in which Hirschfield's rights under his Columbia contract might be asserted to combat the board of directors' conduct toward him. Bob Haines felt it would be wise for Hirschfield formally and explicitly to identify his grievances as a basis for possible future legal proceedings against the board. Thus, Hirschfield and Haines drafted a formal letter to Leo Jaffe, in his capacity as chairman of the board, claiming that several of the board's actions constituted breaches of Hirschfield's contract, which gave him the "authority" to run the company and prohibited actions which "detract from such authority . . . or render it difficult or impossible . . . to carry on his duties.''

One of the latest breaches, the letter charged, was Irwin Kramer's action ". . . deliberately, in my judgment, seeking to embarrass or harass me by raising again questions regarding my wife's employment . . . which ended over eighteen months ago, which was voluntarily disclosed by me about three years ago, which was reviewed by the Conflicts of Interest Committee (of which Mr. Kramer was chairman) over two years ago . . . , which has been cleared by our inside and outside counsel, and which has been and is still being pursued. . . .

The only real purpose of the expenditure of time and money involved in this is to detract from my authority and render it difficult for me to perform my duties.''

The letter also cited a provision in Hirschfield's contract giving him the ''right to approve the appointment of any officer of Columbia. . . .

''In this connection is the present attempt by Herbert Allen and other board members to force me to hire as chief operating officer of the corporation a man I rejected for any position in the company several months ago. They have implied that any new contract for me would be contingent on this hiring. Such efforts have continued despite my conclusion and those of my associates that his employment would severely disrupt the operations of the company and that I believe him to be the wrong man for the job. This move has caused severe consternation and unrest among the key executives of the company, further undermined my authority, and severely jeopardized my own effectiveness as chief executive officer.''

Only Hirschfield and Haines knew about the letter, and Hirschfield had not definitely decided whether to send it. He took the draft with him to California to refine it and, while there, showed it to Allen Adler. Adler, who normally counseled an aggressive posture, advised caution. ''This letter forces them to respond, and you might not like the response you get,'' Adler warned. Nevertheless, Hirschfield dispatched the letter to Jaffe, who was very distressed.

''I feel it will cause an open breach with Herbert and Irwin and all of them,'' Jaffe said. ''They'll take it very badly.''

''Leo, the open breach already exists,'' Hirschfield said. ''If they want to go to war, as they have threatened, fine. I'm not going to sit back like some shrinking violet and just let them walk all over me as they have for months.''

Jaffe decided to keep the letter to himself and not distribute it to the rest of the board for the time being.

FIFTY-SIX

The Audrey Lisner embezzlements, which quickly had become the catalyst for new tension between Hirschfield and the Columbia board of directors, culminating in the declaration that the company was "out of control" and Herbert Allen's insistence upon hiring Robert Stone, still were known to only a small number of people within the corporation and the Los Angeles District Attorney's office. Although Columbia had had little choice but to cooperate with the district attorney's investigation, once the DA had been tipped to the crimes by an anonymous informant, the company naturally hoped that the Lisner episode would remain private. On Tuesday, June 20, however, the DA's office announced publicly that it had charged Audrey Lisner with grand theft and obtained a warrant for her arrest. To Columbia's dismay, the announcement made headlines across the nation and the media naturally stressed that the embezzlement was the second at Columbia Pictures within months. UPI's story, which was published in hundreds of papers, was typical: "Columbia Pictures, barely recovering from one alleged money-stealing scandal, was rocked Tuesday with another—the chief accountant of its television-commercial division has been charged with embezzling more than $250,000."

Robert Stone met with Herbert Allen to discuss the general conditions of his prospective employment at Columbia Pictures Industries. They talked about such things as his salary level, and while no binding commitments were made, they encountered no obstacles. The meeting further bolstered the indication given Stone on the morning of June 6 that Allen and Rosenhaus wanted Stone to take the post of executive vice president and chief operating officer of the corporation.

Hirschfield had set aside much of the week for budget reviews of Arista records, Gottlieb pinball machines, and the Screen Gems television-commercial company. But his schedule was interrupted when Matty Rosenhaus called Leo Jaffe and said that several members of the board wanted to meet on Thursday to discuss two subjects: Alan Hirschfield's contract and Columbia's internal financial controls. Rosenhaus refused to be more specific. Jaffe immediately informed Hirschfield, who became suspicious. It was unusual for a board meeting to be called on short notice. Perhaps they were going to fire him. They knew that he was scheduled to preside at a meeting of the presidents of all of Columbia's divisions in Chicago beginning on Sunday. Perhaps the board feared that he was organizing some sort of cabal, or dramatic public gesture to further his own cause against the board. He had no choice, however, but to attend the board meeting and face whatever the directors presented.

Herbert Allen began the meeting by stating that it was "appropriate" that negotiation of a new contract for Hirschfield be "commenced." (The board was contractually obligated to begin negotiations by July 1, eight days away.) Leo Jaffe pointed out that the board had already authorized such negotiations the previous February but had not proceeded beyond a few preliminary conversations. Those facts notwithstanding, Herbert suggested that negotiations should begin and the board agreed.

Herbert then introduced a second resolution, which he read from a draft he had prepared. "It is incumbent upon this board of directors that we act in swift, diligent, and thorough manner to review the structure and function of the operations of Columbia Pictures Industries." Herbert spoke as if he were delivering a formal speech in a large hall, his voice revealing uncharacteristic amounts of anger and passion. "We have been the target of more than two defalcations and major thefts—one, after the audit committee recommended remedial steps, which were ignored by Columbia management.* We are the trustees of a great and prospering enterprise which is encountering correctable operating difficulties. In order to regain a fine

---

*The "remedial steps" to which Allen referred were Irwin Kramer's recommendations after the Begelman investigation that Lou Phillips, the West Coast controller, and Jim Johnson, the studio's vice president for administration, be removed from their jobs. The weekend after the board meeting of Thursday, July 22, 1978, Lou Phillips was fired by order of Hirschfield and Fischer. While no one accused Phillips of complicity in any of the embezzlements, it was felt that he might have been more vigilant in monitoring Audrey Lisner. Jim Johnson remained in place, having had no responsibility for supervising Lisner, even indirectly.

reputation and repair operating deficiencies, I move that we immediately engage an independent management expert to report to the board so that the board may recommend . . . immediate policy to correct our course. The charge to the management expert is to review all procedures and operations of Columbia Pictures, both structural and operational, and to report the findings to the board as soon as possible. Present management shall be directed to cooperate completely with the board in order to facilitate this study. . . .''

James Wilmot, whose attendance at board meetings was erratic, said, ''The resolution is on the table. Let's vote on it.''

''Wait a minute,'' said Hirschfield. ''The last time I checked the rules under which the company operates, we have an opportunity to discuss resolutions before we vote on them.''

''If you've got something to say, say it in a hurry,'' Wilmot retorted.

''I view that remark as insulting, and as uncalled for as this resolution,'' Hirschfield said. ''This resolution is a fancy version of the accusation that the company is out of control, which has been floating around for the past several weeks. The company is *not* out of control and the claim that it is is an absolutely untrue and unwarranted attack on the management of the company. We are regarded in the industry as one of the best managed and best controlled companies. I'd like to know from the board just one instance where the company is out of control.''

Irwin Kramer said, ''Audrey Lisner stole three hundred thousand dollars. Are you in control of that? David Begelman stole all that money repeatedly over a period of years. Were you in control of that?''

''Price Waterhouse has fully analyzed our controls,'' Hirschfield said, ''and found that the controls in place were not materially deficient, and that the problem was a human failure to follow established procedures. Nevertheless, we have tightened the procedures. This board knows full well that I have never been opposed to the strengthening of controls. When I came to the company, controls and systems and procedures were virtually nonexistent, but the board knows that I brought in outside experts and there have been a lot of improvements. So this 'out of control' business is nonsense. Who would conduct such a study if it were conducted?''

''That's a separate issue and has nothing to do with the basic issue of having a review of operations,'' Allen said.

"We have a right to know who would conduct the review."

"We'll get to that as soon as we've voted on this resolution," Herbert said. "Let's vote."

Everyone voted for the study except Hirschfield, who abstained.

Herbert Allen then moved that the review of controls be conducted by Robert Stone.

Hirschfield was enraged. "As far as I'm concerned, the board has now thrown down the gauntlet! This is a deliberate effort to inflame an already difficult situation! To pick someone to conduct a study who has just been turned down by management for a job with the company is like asking the fox to go out and investigate why the chickens, in the board's judgment, aren't performing adequately. He'll obviously inflame everyone in the company. No one wants anything to do with him. This is infantile behavior. It smacks of being a punitive kind of investigation, rather than an investigation to get the facts. If you want the facts, our auditors are available. They've already reported. If you want them to do another study, fine. If you want to bring in McKinsey, or Arthur D. Little, fine. But to bring in Bob Stone is nothing more than an effort to harass the management of the company, and me in particular, and I find it outrageous."

Herbert Allen defended Stone as fully qualified to conduct the study, and then asked for a vote. Everyone voted for Stone except Hirschfield, who voted no, and Leo Jaffe, who abstained.

The meeting was adjourned.

Hirschfield, Fischer, and Adler were demoralized. Fischer expected Hirschfield to be fired within days or, at most, weeks. But he had seen so many dramatic shifts in the company's course that he knew nothing could be counted upon. "If you tried to explain to an outsider what is going on in this company," Fischer said, "you couldn't do it and have it make any sense. They wouldn't believe it. It makes no sense."

The board had authorized the negotiation of a new contract for Hirschfield as the chief executive officer, thus implying approval of his performance. Then the board had contradicted that implication by declaring Hirschfield's control of the company deficient and commissioning a review of that control by the man whom Hirschfield had rejected for a management post and who had become the symbol of Herbert Allen's furious determination to impose his will on Hirschfield. The illogic and cynicism seemed blatant but not surprising, in Hirschfield's view. Logic, rationality, and sincerity had not been present in the Columbia board room for months. Why should they play any part on June 22?

Adler, nevertheless, thought it important that the moment not go unrecorded. He wrote a memorandum for his file and sent a copy to Hirschfield:

> The sudden shift in attitude resulting in the desire to immediately negotiate with Alan Hirschfield seems suspicious to me. There has certainly been no general goodwill expressed toward him and lots of negative comments on both a personal and business level. My feeling is that they feel that he is in an awkward position at this time due to the Audrey Lisner matter (which cannot really be specifically blamed on him in any way). . . . Chances are that there will be a disagreement over certain items of Hirschfield's contract regarding his authority and under what conditions they can dismiss him. My feeling is that they will clearly seek to erode his position and then say they were unable to reach agreement with him.

As for the prospective review of the company's controls, Adler wrote that it would serve "no real purpose other than to harass present management and to support the uninformed and outrageous claims of [those] who presently control the board."

Herbert Allen and Matty Rosenhaus had recruited Bob Stone for the control study a day or two before the board meeting. Herbert's basic pitch to Stone was: "If you do the study, it will give you an insight into the company. It will give you an opportunity to meet people. It will give you a familiarity with the business. And should something work out on a permanent basis, it will certainly give you a great leg up in getting into the job in an operating capacity."

On Friday, Hirschfield and Adler had the first of several private conferences with Sidney Silberman, the lawyer who would manage Hirschfield's proxy fight if Hirschfield chose to launch it. Silberman stressed the difficulties of waging a proxy contest: Secrecy is essential but difficult to maintain. Before announcing his intentions, the potential aggressor must quietly recruit an alternative board of directors, test the sentiment of a cross-section of stockholders, and line up as much financial support as possible, all without having the enemy learn his secret. The more people aware of the aggressor's plan, the greater the risk of compromise. Silberman also informed Hirschfield and Adler that the costs of waging a proxy battle, including the legal fees, full-page newspaper advertisements and other expenses, could range from half a million to a million dollars, particularly if the antagonists become embroiled in litigation, which often happens.

Although he had not yet made up his mind, Hirschfield said he saw no obstacles that were inherently insurmountable. He was willing to bear the expense himself and felt he would have widespread support among Columbia stockholders and other people who controlled large amounts of money—Richard Smith, the chief executive of General Cinema, for one.

Sid Silberman pointed out that the Allens wielded considerable influence in Wall Street and, in the event of a fight, could be expected to call in whatever chits they might have outstanding.

Later in the day Hirschfield met with Todd Lang, who had been unable to attend the Thursday board meeting but was deeply worried by what he had heard and by recent developments in general.

"The only way this is going to be resolved," Lang said, "is for you and Herbert to talk it out." (Lang, who knew nothing of Hirschfield's plans for a proxy fight, had said the same thing to Herbert Allen.)

"Those conversations always turn out to be one-way conversations," Hirschfield replied. "I talk and rant and rave and Herbert just sits there staring at me. And then he says 'It'll all work out' or my real problem is with Matty and Irwin, or something equally evasive."

"You've got to do something to try to break through that, because only you two can settle it. It's worth one more try."

"I'll attempt to do something when I get back from Chicago."

FIFTY-SEVEN

The Chicago meeting exemplified Alan Hirschfield's fondness for assembling groups of people to promote camaraderie in the corporation. Apart from the substantive necessity of quarterly budget reviews, which he conducted with the top executives of each company individually, he felt it was beneficial occasionally to convene all the executives and have each company make a presentation to the group. In that way, Hirschfield believed, each executive would know what was going on in other parts of the corporation: The motion-picture people would appreciate the problems of the pinball-machine people, the television-programming people would better understand the television-commercial makers, and so forth. Even though the business presentations generally turned out to be tedious, the overall idea worked. As Norman Horowitz of Columbia Pictures Television had put it, "You go through the numbers and nobody gives a shit. But the real purpose is to be together and go away joyously, and that we do." The food always was excellent, the drinks abundant, the tennis games intense, the poker games boisterous, and the cigar smoke thick. There also were screenings of the latest Columbia films and appearances by Arista artists.

The first problem at the 1978 meeting—as the participants began arriving in Chicago on the rainy evening of Sunday, June 25—was the hotel. Hirschfield had intended to hold the event at the Hyatt Regency O'Hare, which he knew from experience had excellent facilities. When he gave instructions to his assistant weeks earlier, however, he confused the Hyatt Regency with the Marriott O'Hare, a less illustrious hotel. Because of the size of the group it was too late that Sunday evening to change hotels without notice. And since the Columbia executives were accustomed to only the best accommodations, they ribbed Hirschfield mercilessly for the next two days.

As it turned out, the facilities were the only source of humor at the meeting, which should have been canceled. None of the business presentations, none of the cocktail parties, not even the poker games, all of which proceeded as planned, could compete for the attention of the participants with the corporate management crisis. No one could concentrate on anything but the plight of Alan Hirschfield.

Hirschfield, Fischer, and Adler, sometimes joined by one or two others, spent much of their time huddled in the hallway outside the main conference room discussing what to do next in New York. The other executives held impromptu meetings of various sizes proclaiming their support for Hirschfield but uncertain how to marshal it.

Despite many interruptions, the conference proceeded on schedule through Monday night. Late Tuesday morning, however, there was a rash of telephone calls from New York and Los Angeles. *Variety*'s Art Murphy had published an article disclosing the Columbia board's intention to have Robert Stone review internal financial controls. And Jack Egan had written in *The Washington Post* that Hirschfield's job might be in jeopardy. "Among a litany of charges board members privately are hurling at Hirschfield," Egan wrote, "are that 'he has difficulty making decisions,' 'he tends to blame others when something goes wrong,' 'it is tough for him to have strong people around him,' and he does not really deserve much credit for Columbia's financial turnaround in the last five years."

Hirschfield's first impulse was to issue a press release from Chicago refuting both articles. As Clive Davis spoke from the podium about Arista's latest recording plans, punctuating his talk with loud excerpts from the latest Barry Manilow album, Hirschfield and his public-relations aide, Jean Vagnini, tried to draft a statement. It soon became obvious, however, that it would be futile to carry on a public argument with the Columbia board of directors by issuing a press release from Chicago. Hirschfield decided he had to return to New York and confront Herbert Allen. As soon as Clive Davis had finished speaking and lunch was served, Hirschfield announced that he was adjourning the conference "to go back and deal with this intolerable situation."

"Go get the bastards!" somebody said, and that remark set off a round of emotional exhortations and expressions of support from the assembled executives. There were misty eyes in the room as Hirschfield, Fischer, and Adler left to catch their flight.

Airborne from O'Hare, Hirschfield began scribbling notes on a yellow legal pad for his meeting with Herbert Allen.

"Cut out bullshit. I've had it. Both know what's going on. Thursday board meeting an outrage . . . devious . , . unnecessary . . . lied . . . bad faith . . . sandbagged . . . company not out of control. Simply an attack on me.

"Been attacked for last time without fighting back.

"What I want—call off dogs.

"No sense being called chief executive officer. That's not what I've been. If want war, up to you. I'll defend myself. I'm going to do what I have to do to be chief executive officer of this company no matter what.

"Getting board off back of AH & management.

"HA fucking AH . . . killing AH publicly . . . denying my role in success of company . . . saying Begelman responsible for profits.

"Not going to get sandbagged in board meeting.

"No Bob Stone . . . outside firm ok.

"No one hired except by me.

"Not going to live with hostile board. Add independent people to board.

"Not going to have board take shots at me.

"Got to call off dogs.

"Tired of seeing management and me beat up.

"Shareholders getting killed. I'm getting killed. Management is getting killed. *I've had it*."

Alan and Herbert met in Herbert's office the next morning. The fury reflected in Alan's notes had subsided to controlled anger and the meeting was surprisingly calm. Alan's remarks, however, elicited little more than Herbert's usual stare of preoccupation and the body language of boredom.

"Herbert, this is it. It's the last chance. If you want to try and square things, if you want to have a meeting of the minds, if you want to try and put this thing back together, I'm prepared to do it. But I can't do it with you leading the charge against me. Whether you admit it or not, if you want it to work, it'll work. If you don't want it to work, it won't work. I'm saying here and now I'm prepared to try and make whatever accommodation we can come to.

If you're not, then say so. Stop hiding behind everyone else's skirts and just say so. Stop deferring to Matty and Irwin. You're the key to this.''

"I don't think we have anything more to discuss at this point," Herbert replied. "I've already given you my opinion on everything you've brought up here."

Hirschfield got up and walked out of the office.

The letter to the board of directors which Hirschfield and his lawyer had drafted and presented to Leo Jaffe two weeks earlier, but which Jaffe had not disseminated, had been revised to include the events of recent days. Hirschfield still had shown the letter to no one but Adler, who had cautioned him not to send it in its original form. On Wednesday afternoon, Hirschfield edited the letter again and had it retyped.

David Begelman, dressed in a gray suit and dark polka-dot tie, stood before Judge Thomas C. Murphy in the Burbank Municipal Court House.

The probation officer's report had been completed and the time had come for sentencing. The probation officer did not recommend jail. He had received twenty highly complimentary letters about Begelman from a variety of people including Sidney Poitier, Matty Rosenhaus, Dino De Laurentiis, Herbert Allen, Mel Brooks, Sy Weintraub, Aaron Spelling, Gunther Schiff (Cliff Robertson's lawyer and Begelman's friend), John Tunney, Ray Stark, Frank Wells of Warner Bros., Sam Cohn of ICM, Art Murphy of *Daily Variety*, and Aaron Stern, a psychiatrist-turned-movie-producer who was one of Begelman's closest friends.

Aaron Stern in his letter portrayed Begelman as a man whose psychological problems stemmed in part from his own decency.

David Begelman is, in my judgment, a man who suffers from very decent feelings in essentially a very indecent business. The narcissistic supplies provided within the film industry revolve around power, excessive material rewards, and the glamour of being a media celebrity. These contribute to eroding the capacity for caring among those who work in the business. The stakes are so high that feelings for other human beings serve to undermine one's capacity to ruthlessly compete. In this regard, the motion-picture industry has been aptly compared to "thousands of people fighting each other in the open sea to get to a lifeboat that seats only ten to fifteen." Each film studio represents a lifeboat that might produce ten to fifteen pictures a year. Thousands of energetic, creative people compete with one another to be chosen as one of the few whose efforts will be rewarded by a studio's commitment to produce his or her project. Heavy lies the head that wears the crown! As president of Columbia Pictures, David had to make such choices. He had to disappoint close friends and reject countless numbers of business acquaintances in making his decisions. If he permits himself to feel for those that he must turn away, then David Begelman would be plagued by a constant stream of guilt. But feel he does, and consequently plagued by guilt he is!

Begelman's lawyers argued for leniency. Deputy DA Sheldon Brown argued for punishment, noting that Begelman had moved to repay the money he stole only after Cliff Robertson's inquiry attracted police attention and caused Columbia to investigate. "He did not make restitution . . . or seek psychiatric care . . . until after he could see the consequences coming," Brown declared.

Judge Murphy called the case "bizarre." "It almost looks like a death-wish," the judge said to Begelman. "You are neither violence-prone nor case-hardened." Judge Murphy sentenced Begelman to a $5,000 fine and three years probation, and instructed him to continue his psychiatric care and perform community service as ordered by the probation department. The community service consisted of producing a film on the drug PCP, or "angel dust."

Outside the courthouse, Begelman told a crowd of reporters, "I have been subjected to the judicial system and I found it fair."

Alan Hirschfield took his younger son, Scott, to La Guardia Airport early Thursday morning and put him on a plane for Maine, where he was to spend several weeks at camp. After arriving at the office, Hirschfield sent his revised letter, accusing the board of breaching his contract, to Leo Jaffe with specific instructions that copies be forwarded to each member of the board of directors. The existence of the letter still was known only to attorney Haines, and to Allen Adler, who had seen it only in a previous version. Hirschfield had not shown any version of the letter to Joe Fischer, Todd Lang, Clive Davis, or any of the other people whose advice he normally sought.

In the letter, Hirschfield accused the board of a "deliberate, reckless effort to take yet another step in a campaign to discredit me as chief executive officer of this company."

> To authorize negotiation of a contract with me and follow that with prearranged resolutions, which can only be based on a claim that I am an incompetent executive, is so inconsistent as to defy rational explanation, except if it is based on the premise that I should be continued as chief executive officer for appearance's sake, but that I should not be allowed to function as chief executive officer.

This has been true ever since I committed the unforgivable sin of being right on the impossibility of retaining David Begelman after the story of his embezzlement broke. You and I know under what enormous pressure I finally and reluctantly agreed to his reinstatement, loyally, as I thought, putting the best public face on it I could. You and I know that the board rejected our advice, the admonitions of our counsel, and ignored public or SEC reactions, only to precipitate the worst possible publicity for Columbia, with adverse consequences not yet fully felt.

. . . There has been a studied program of harassment by Mr. Kramer and a pattern of interference with my functioning as chief executive officer, and of usurpation of my authority. It is not the company but the board which is "out of control."

. . . All my efforts have been devoted to maintaining some stability in the company and preserving its public image, despite the vexatious and obstruent actions of the directors. I hope that the attacks on me will cease, but I will not be alone in respecting the contract between Columbia and me. If they do not, and if good-faith negotiations are not undertaken, I shall take such action as may seem advisable to preserve my position as chief executive officer of this company and to meet my responsibilities in this regard to our management, our stockholders, and the public.

After taking a few calls on Friday, Hirschfield went home, picked up Berte and their daughter, Laura (Marc was at camp in Wyoming), and drove to East Hampton where they were to spend the long Fourth of July weekend at the summer home of their close friends, bank president Mark Maged* and his wife, Marion, a fashion designer.

FIFTY-EIGHT

Behind all his neutral stares, indifferent shrugs, and cocksure remarks, Herbert Allen was struggling. His decision to fire Hirschfield did not come easily. Apart from anger, Herbert felt deep sadness at the collapse of their relationship. Rosenhaus and Kramer and Wilmot would have dumped Hirschfield weeks earlier, but they deferred to Herbert, and Herbert hesitated.

Although he and Alan had never been "best" friends, as Herbert kept telling everyone who would listen, they had been *friends*— genuine, warm friends—through all their adult lives. Herbert enjoyed Alan. Alan could make him laugh. In their early days at Columbia Pictures, with the company still fragile financially, Herbert had referred to himself and Alan as "the Hardy boys"—breezing through difficult situations and laughing all the way. He could not think of Alan's eleventh-floor office without thinking of the laughter they had shared there, usually with their feet up in the early evening after others had left for the day. There had been good times, too, in Palm Springs and Beverly Hills and Southampton and Scarsdale. And the families. Charlie and Norman back to 1925. Since Herbert's childhood, he had always liked and respected Norman Hirschfield, and Herbert's children had developed the same kind of affection for Norman. Herbert mourned the potential destruction of that relationship, and rued the estrangement between him and Norman, and between

---

*Rhymes with *ragged*.

Norman and Charlie, who had rejected repeated pleas by Norman over the past few months to intervene in the dispute between Alan and Herbert.

In his office, in his apartment, on his deck in Southampton staring out to sea, Herbert brooded about Alan. Alan had betrayed him. He had betrayed him not just once but several times, Herbert felt. How could a guy this smart, Herbert asked himself, be so *disloyal* to the people who *made him* and so *stupid* as to go up against the people who *own this company*? Herbert had no answer, but Alan most definitely had committed those sins.

He had been disloyal.

He had been stupid.

He had been wrong on both the merits and the handling of the Begelman affair.

He had tried to sell control of Columbia Pictures behind Herbert's back.

He had taken four months to staff the studio.

He had pooh-poohed the significance of the Audrey Lisner embezzlements.

He had sabotaged Sy Weintraub.

He had been stubborn about Bob Stone.

And again the main theme—the ultimate sin—kept repeating itself: *He has been disloyal to the people who made him and gone up against the people who own this company.*

Despite all that, Alan still might have found a way to retreat and survive, Herbert felt. Instead, he now has the astounding effrontery to write a formal letter accusing the board of directors of breaching his contract in a "deliberate, reckless" effort to discredit him.

Even before making a firm decision to fire Hirschfield, Herbert had pondered who might replace Alan. He thought of people in the industry. He explored the possibility of offering the job to Jack Valenti, the president of the Motion Picture Association of America, but Valenti was not available. Then Herbert settled on a different approach. He decided that he wanted someone brand new—brand new to the board and management of Columbia Pictures Industries, and brand new to Hollywood, someone without a past in show business, someone who would not come laden with alliances, with friends and enemies in the industry, or with preconceived notions of what had happened at Columbia. Experience in the entertainment business was not important and might even be a detriment, Herbert decided. The most important task of the new chief executive would not be making pictures. Others could handle that. The most important task would be cleansing the corporation of all the venom, ugliness, and tension that had accumulated over the nearly ten months since the discovery of David Begelman's forgeries. Everyone had lost perspective. Everyone was exhausted. They badly needed someone entirely fresh.

Herbert telephoned his lawyer, Robert Werbel. "What would you think of Fay Vincent as president of Columbia Pictures?" Herbert asked.

"I don't know," Werbel said. "I'd like to think about it. You know how highly I regard him."

Francis T. "Fay" Vincent, Jr., had been two years ahead of Herbert at Williams College. A serious student, Vincent was a devout Roman Catholic who as a young man considered taking Jesuit training. He played tackle and center in football at Williams before severely injuring his back and legs in a four-story fall from an icy ledge outside his dormitory window to the snow-covered ground below. (His roommates had locked him in his room as a prank.) The accident left Vincent with a severe limp and, among other things, disqualified him for the rigors of Jesuit training. He did well at the Yale Law School, however, and practiced law in New York for a few years before settling at the well-regarded Washington firm of Caplin & Drysdale, whose senior partner, Mortimer Caplin, was the Commissioner of Internal Revenue in the Kennedy Administration. In March 1978, Vincent had left Caplin & Drysdale to become Associate Director of the Division of Corporate Finance of the Securities and Exchange Commission, a typical mid-career step for a securities lawyer. A bland, quiet man, Vincent planned to return to private law practice after a period at the SEC.

Although never intimate friends, Fay Vincent and Herbert Allen had stayed in touch over the years, and Vincent also knew Werbel, who pointed out to Herbert in the office that Friday, June 30, that "Fay obviously doesn't know anything about the movie business."

"That's his great strength," Allen said. "Nobody knows him. Nobody can lay a glove on him. We need a healer in this situation. We need a Judge Landis. We can put people around him who can help him learn the business."

Having determined that Vincent was not involved in the SEC's ongoing investigation of Columbia Pictures—he was in a different division from that conducting the investigation—Allen arranged to meet Vincent early Friday afternoon in the coffee shop of the Hyatt Regency Hotel on Capitol Hill near the SEC. They stated the obvious to each other. "I don't know anything about the film business," Vincent said. "That's okay—none of us did either until we got into it," Allen said. Then Herbert sketched Columbia's need, and Vincent said he might be interested but wanted to talk first to his wife and a few friends, including Bob Werbel.

Thus began an intense sequence of secret weekend deliberations, mostly by telephone, that produced a tentative plan of quick action. A special meeting of the Columbia board of directors would be called for the following Wednesday, July 5, the first full business day after the four-day holiday period. Alan Hirschfield would be fired at the board meeting, and Fay Vincent probably would be installed as president and chief executive officer. Bob Werbel would draft a "script" for the meeting, consisting of the resolutions that the board would have to pass in order formally to execute the firing. Fay Vincent would fly to New York sometime during the weekend to meet and presumably gain the approval of Matty Rosenhaus. Hirschfield would be given only short notice of the board meeting, and would be told only that it was being called to discuss his letter to the board, which most of the directors had received on Friday. Unless Hirschfield were prescient, he would not know that he was to be fired until it happened.

FIFTY-NINE

Saturday and Sunday were spectacular in the Hamptons—sunny, warm, dry days and crisp, cool nights. The Hirschfields' hosts, Mark and Marion Maged, had a house on Crossways, a narrow lane between Georgica Road and Ocean Avenue in East Hampton. Far from the cheap summer rentals, it was a neighborhood of great lawns, stately homes, and huge maple, poplar, and cedar trees. The Mageds' house was one of the least formal in the area—a two-story converted barn with a gambrel-style roof, surrounded by acres of grass, trees, and shrubbery, a quarter of a mile from the beach. The Clive Davises occupied a large, three-story home nearby on Georgica. Allen Adler and his girl friend, actress Donna Mills, were a mile away.

Surrounded by friends and family, with tennis, jogging, bicycling, and ocean swimming to amuse him, Alan Hirschfield felt more relaxed than he had in weeks. Although he expected a strong response from the board of directors to the letter he had sent, the act of sending it was a modest catharsis, and he felt there was a chance, however slight, that the board might come to its senses and give in.

Both the mood and the weather changed almost simultaneously Monday morning when the humidity returned to Eastern Long Island, rain began to fall, and Leo Jaffe telephoned Alan Hirschfield.

"They're calling a special board meeting for Wednesday," Jaffe said. "Matty is crazed about your letter. Herbert says, 'This is it.' That's a direct quote. They say the purpose of the meeting is to discuss your letter, but I think it's all over. I think they're going to get rid of you."

Hirschfield hung up the phone rather nonchalantly and gave the news to Berte and Mark Maged. Maged was familiar only with the broad outlines of the Columbia Pictures drama. Although he knew several people at Allen & Company, having once represented the firm as a lawyer, and also had been a law-school classmate of Clive Davis's, he did not have a sense of the depth and immediacy of the crisis until the July Fourth weekend. Maged was shocked by the prospect of Hirschfield's being fired, and he and Berte both were upset by Alan's attitude.

"What are you going to do?" Maged asked. "You've got to do something."

"What can I do?" Hirschfield said. "I've been yelling and screaming for months and it does no good. They've got me outvoted."

"You can't just let this happen," Berte said. "You've got to respond with strength. What about Clive's idea of having the executives come in and confront the board?"

"That's futile," Alan contended. "This board is beyond any rational appeal by anybody."

"Who's talking about rational appeals?" Berte said. "The only thing these people understand is power. You've got to show them some. You can't back down.''

Berte explained to Mark Maged the plan espoused by Clive Davis a few weeks earlier to assemble the top two executives of each of Columbia's divisions for a confrontation on Hirschfield's behalf with the board of directors. Maged endorsed the idea.

"It's too late to get everybody together,'' Alan said. "The meeting's day after tomorrow and this is the Fourth of July weekend. Everybody's out of touch. Danny's on his way to Europe.''

Maged said, "Alan, you must do this. You can't just let these people walk over you.''

"I don't want to ask people to interrupt their weekends and come to New York on a wild-goose chase.''

Berte said, "Alan, for God's sake, this is more important than the July Fourth weekend! This is your job, your career, your company! You've got to fight! If you don't do it, nobody else will!''

Mark agreed, and he and Berte finally persuaded Alan to call Clive Davis, who insisted that they try to reach as many of the executives as possible and have them fly to New York the next day. Adler was summoned, Hirschfield was finally persuaded to go along with the plan, and the telephone calls began to go out from the Mageds' bedroom, from Adler's house, and from a small alcove off Clive Davis's kitchen.

It was mid-afternoon of the third day of the four-day weekend. The rain appeared to have settled in for the evening.

Dan Melnick had missed the Chicago conference the previous week because of a kidney infection. He felt better toward the weekend, however, and tentatively decided to proceed with plans to spend a few days in St. Tropez with a woman friend who lived in Paris. Though Melnick did not know of Hirschfield's letter to the board of directors, he did know that the crisis had grown so intense that a provocative action was inevitable—probably a move by the board to fire Hirschfield. Melnick had phoned Hirschfield late in the week.

"Are you sure the shit isn't going to hit the fan while I'm away?'' he asked.

"No, no, it's a holiday weekend and a three-day week next week,'' Alan said, urging Melnick to go ahead with his trip.

Melnick also checked with Joe Fischer (who also was ignorant of

Hirschfield's letter to the board). "What can they do?" Fischer said. "It's a holiday weekend."

Melnick left Los Angeles on Sunday afternoon. He stopped in London, flew on to Paris, met his friend, Marie-France, and together they flew to Nice. After renting a Mercedes, they drove to the villa of some friends near St. Tropez, arriving late Monday evening. Melnick was exhausted by both his illness and the long trip. He and Marie-France had a cold snack from some food their friends had left in the refrigerator and then went to bed, only to be tormented by mosquitoes. After an hour of switching the light on and off and swatting at mosquitoes, they finally fell asleep.

The phone rang at midnight. It was Melnick's secretary, Elizabeth Nathan, calling from Los Angeles and apologizing profusely. Within the last forty-five minutes she had had calls from Alan Hirschfield, Clive Davis, and Allen Adler. She had made polite excuses—Melnick had instructed her to give his number to no one—but she thought he should know that his colleagues were trying anxiously to reach him.

"I can't deal with this," Melnick told her. "Call them back and tell them the phones are out all over St. Tropez and you can't get through."

Back in bed, Melnick was nagged by doubts and curiosity. Something serious must have happened. He got up again, called his secretary back, and told her to give his number to Hirschfield, Davis, or Adler, whomever she could reach first. A few minutes later Allen Adler called.

"They've scheduled a board meeting for Wednesday morning. It looks like they're going to fire Alan. There's a movement afoot to have the division heads come in and confront the board."

"Should I come in?"

"Alan says we shouldn't impose on you. It's your vacation."

"What do you think?"

"I think you should come. Your voice would carry weight with the board."

Melnick sighed. "Okay, I'll be there."

While Hirschfield, Adler, and Davis were calling Los Angeles, Chicago, and St. Tropez, as well as several homes in the New York area, Mark Maged was telephoning his old friend and former law partner, Howard Holtzmann, the senior partner of the firm of Holtzmann, Wise & Shepard, which for decades had represented

Allen & Company. Herbert Allen's lawyer, Robert Werbel, was a partner in the firm, and Mark Maged had practiced there until he left to go into banking. Maged expressed surprise to Holtzmann that the Columbia Pictures situation had deteriorated so much. They discussed various ideas for getting the combatants to call a truce. In the course of the conversation, Maged told Holtzmann that the Columbia executive team was flying to New York the next day to try to confront the board before it had a chance to fire Hirschfield.

Later in the evening, Howard Holtzmann relayed this information to Herbert Allen and Robert Werbel.

The Mageds had planned a large party at their house in East Hampton for Monday evening, and even with the increasing rain, a lot of people showed up. Very few, however, knew that the constantly ringing telephone in the bedroom signaled preparations for the latest battle in a war for control of one of the nation's leading motion-picture companies. Like commanders alerting military units for airlift, Hirschfield, Davis, and Adler continued to make calls, as well as taking calls from people they had tried to reach earlier.

Herbert Allen and Matty Rosenhaus, meanwhile, were not reacting kindly to the news from Howard Holtzmann that the Columbia executives were assembling. It was suggested to Joe Fischer by phone Monday evening that "drumming up people to come in" was a violation of his responsibility to the company. (Fischer, who was spending the weekend at home in New Jersey, actually had played a minimal role in the recruitment, although he strongly favored it.) Matty Rosenhaus also telephoned Norman Levy, the studio's head of marketing and distribution, who was at home in Los Angeles, and told him it would be "improper" for him to come to New York—"a display of disloyalty."

"We can solve our own problems with Hirschfield," Rosenhaus said. "You have too much at stake, Norman, to get involved in this thing. It might hurt your career. I recommend that you not come."

Levy replied, "I've made my decision, Matty. I'm coming to New York, not as an act of disloyalty to the board, but in the hope of trying in some small way to make a contribution to the company in terms of Alan's problems."

By midnight in New York the rain had become torrential. By 3 A.M. it was leaking through the ceiling of Herbert Allen's apartment at the

Carlyle. Herbert summoned the night porter and together they placed garbage cans under the leaks. Fay Vincent, who on Friday had been tentatively offered Hirschfield's job, was due at Allen's apartment at 8 A.M. so that Herbert could take him to meet Rosenhaus. It was still raining when Vincent arrived.

"C'mon in, Fay," Herbert said. "If you get this job, I guarantee you'll live as well as I do." Vincent walked in and saw six streams of water flowing from the ceiling into six garbage cans in Herbert's elegant living room.

They were driven through the wet streets—deserted on that holiday morning—to the apartment of Matty Rosenhaus at the Pierre. By noon, Fay Vincent had Rosenhaus's blessing.

The East Hampton contingent drove into Manhattan that afternoon. Hirschfield, Adler, and Davis went to Hirschfield's office, along with Mark Maged, who suddenly had become an important adviser. They were met there by Robert Haines, Hirschfield's personal lawyer; Sidney Silberman, the proxy-fight specialist whom Hirschfield and Adler had been consulting; and Jonathan Rineheart, a Manhattan public-relations man. Hirschfield and Adler began removing sensitive material from their files and secreting it elsewhere in the building to guard against the possibility, however remote, that the entire executive team would be fired and their offices seized the next morning.

In St. Tropez, Dan Melnick had set his alarm for 6 A.M., five hours after his conversation with Adler. Leaving Marie-France at the villa, he set off for the Nice airport in his rented Mercedes. He was unfamiliar with the car and the road. While glancing about for a sign in the middle of a confusing intersection, he accidentally bumped another car. His gaze swung instantly from the cluster of signs to the other car, and he found himself looking at two irate police officers. Melnick had hit a police cruiser. The officers emerged from the cruiser shouting at Melnick. Knowing very little French, he got out of the Mercedes shouting, "*Faux pas! Faux pas!*" The policemen did not speak English. Although the damage was negligible, they ordered Melnick to pull off the road and laboriously inspected his driver's license, passport, and everything else in his wallet. Finally they let him go without so much as a written citation.

By the time he reached the Nice airport, his flight had left, but an accommodating Air France clerk helped him charter a private plane, which got him to Paris in time to catch his flight to New York. He was at JFK by four that afternoon, New York time, in his suite at the Sherry Netherland by 5:30, and in Alan Hirschfield's office by six.

The group at 711 Fifth Avenue considered each of Hirschfield's options—what he should do and say publicly and privately if he was fired and if he was not fired. Since Hirschfield and his advisers did not know precisely what the board would do—especially when confronted by the corporation's entire executive team—they could only make contingency plans. For the first time, Hirschfield confided to a wider group of people than just his lawyers and Allen Adler that he was considering a proxy fight. If he was fired the next day, he would have to mount the battle from outside the company— not a hopeless task but surely a daunting one.

Dan Melnick and Clive Davis telephoned Herbert Allen during the evening and learned for the first time that Herbert already knew that the executives were gathering. The board meeting was scheduled for ten o'clock Wednesday morning. If there were to be other meetings, they would have to be early. Herbert agreed to confer with Melnick and Davis at Melnick's suite at the Sherry at 6:30 A.M. It surely would be the earliest meeting in the history of show business.

Recalling that room service at the Sherry Netherland did not open until seven, Melnick walked over to a delicatessen on Sixth Avenue after the Tuesday night session broke up and purchased some instant coffee and orange juice.

SIXTY

The earliest meeting in the history of show business launched one of the most extraordinary days in the history of show business or any business. The heads of the operating divisions of major corporations—whether they make light bulbs, electric generators, and TV sets (in the case of General Electric); or Chevrolets, Buicks, and Pontiacs (in the case of General Motors); or motion pictures, television programs, and pinball machines (in the case of Columbia Pictures Industries)—normally spend most of their time following orders and implementing policy. It is very unusual for them as a group to defy their immediate boss, the corporation's chief executive officer. It is truly extraordinary for them to march en masse to headquarters and make demands upon the corporation's ultimate authority, the board of directors. *If* it had ever happened before Wednesday, July 5, 1978, it had happened very rarely.

The rain had passed and Manhattan glistened in the early morning sun. The temperature was just edging upward past sixty and a north breeze braced the few people in the quiet streets. It was a day that belonged in April, not July.

Herbert Allen and Clive Davis arrived at Melnick's suite at 6:30. Steaming cups of instant coffee were produced. Davis and Melnick told Allen that they wanted their mission to be constructive, not destructive, and that they wanted to help calm the strife, not inflame it further. But they were determined to see the board. The rest of the executives were gathering at Columbia's suite at the Drake Hotel five blocks away, waiting for word of when and where the meeting would be held.

Herbert knew that a confrontation between the board of directors and the executives, all in a room together, would be volatile and difficult to control. There probably would be displays of temper. There might even be a rash of resignations. But Herbert also knew that a refusal by the board to see the executives might have similar results. A refusal to meet would be regarded as deeply insulting, an act of high arrogance, and could be inflammatory. Herbert had given the dynamics of the moment a lot of thought over the weekend, and proceeded with what proved to be one of the more adept maneuvers of his business career.

"I want you fellows to be effective," he told Melnick and Davis, "and if you all come barging together into the board meeting and make a lot of demands, it won't be effective. The board will stiffen up and probably tell you to mind your own business. What you need to do to accomplish your purpose is to win them over. I'd like to see this thing settled, but some of these board members are awfully upset. We're all upset with Alan's letter. So what I suggest is that we do this in smaller groups. You divide yourself up into groups and each of us will see you individually. You can present your case, but it will be lower-key that way and you'll have a better chance of being effective.''

Davis and Melnick agreed.

Walking down Fifth a few minutes later, Herbert told Dan about Hirschfield's letter. Dan was sympathetic. It sounded to him as if Alan had been needlessly provocative and had exaggerated his grievances.

Although the dozen executives at the Drake were unanimous in their determination to confront the board and try to save Hirschfield, they felt very odd. They sensed the singular eccentricity of their unprecedented mission.

"It's bizarre, unreal, out of character, out of role, out of context, out of place," said Norman Horowitz, of the television division. "It's not as if we're trying to make a rational presentation with charts and graphs to try to convince them to buy or not buy another company. They won't even listen to a *rational* argument that Hirschfield is doing a good job. What we're doing isn't even based on business reality! It's based on—holy shit—this whole drama that's unfolded! We're talking about how to create a new drama to reverse the old drama! How do we deal with what's going on in Herbert Allen's head? How do we deal with what's going on dynamically with Matty?''

At 8 A.M., Davis and Melnick briefed the others and they adopted Herbert Allen's approach. It seemed reasonable—within the unreasonable setting. The executives divided into groups of three and at nine o'clock went to the Allen & Company offices where the board of directors, each in a separate office, awaited them. (Hirschfield, Fischer, and Adler did not participate.)

Through the morning, each in his own way, the division heads gave the directors the same message: We don't know everything that has transpired between you and Hirschfield, but whatever it is should be subordinated to the reality of Hirschfield's performance as president of the corporation. He may not be the most decisive executive in the annals of American business. He may have some annoying habits, such as not returning your phone calls. But he has presided in the last five years over one of the most dramatic turnarounds in history. He has brought talented people into this company. He has supported us in our individual businesses, each of which is doing well. Therefore, he should remain as president.

Furthermore, the executives said, two thieves do not mean that the company is "out of control." If you impose enough controls to prevent the last 1 percent of the larceny, you will create a police state, you will spend more money policing larceny than you now lose from larceny, and you will destroy people's ability to conduct business. Each of us can certify that his business is firmly under control. However, we have no objection to a study of the company's control systems, so long as the study is performed by a qualified and independent expert, and not by a man—Robert Stone—whom some of us know personally and will refuse to report to, and who we believe will be a disruptive force in the company.

Herbert Allen was uniformly cool, polite, and noncommittal toward each of the advocates. Matty Rosenhaus, however, while cordial toward the highest-ranking executives, Melnick and Davis, was angry and menacing toward those a step down the chain of command. Rosenhaus proclaimed that Hirschfield's letter to the board was one gigantic lie. Regarding the claim that the board had forced Hirschfield to reinstate Begelman, Rosenhaus declared: "Alan was free to do whatever he wanted without one bit of pressure from this board! He *chose* to bring David back! How dare you people come in here and say otherwise!"

Irwin Kramer as usual was belligerent. "This industry is full of selfish, spoiled, overpaid people, and most of them are replaceable," Kramer said. "I want you to know that I've got people I pay forty thousand dollars a year to, and they're happy to have the forty thousand dollars, and there isn't a man in this group here today who doesn't take home an income well into six figures, and—"

Norman Horowitz interrupted. "You want to fuck up Columbia's businesses, Irwin? Just send some of your forty-thousand-dollar people out to run them!"

The meetings broke up at noon, and everyone went to the eleventh floor—the directors to the board meeting, and the executives to await the results of the board meeting.

A nearly hysterical Matty Rosenhaus opened the board meeting by expressing the board's "outrage" at Hirschfield's letter.

"I'm sorry feelings are running so high," Hirschfield replied, "but you have to realize that I've taken a pretty good beating over the last nine months. I feel that what I said in my letter was totally accurate. If it sounded harsh, it certainly represented my thinking and my emotions at the time. It's hard to have no emotions after nine months of living through a nightmare."

Each of the directors then read aloud letters that they had written to Jaffe or directly to Hirschfield rebutting Hirschfield's letter.

Irwin Kramer: ". . . I am personally offended by Mr. Hirschfield's attack on me and his characterization of the exercise of my responsibility as a director and chairman of the audit committee as 'a studied program of harassment.' . . ."

Samuel Tedlow: ". . . I am allergic to veiled threats and ultimatums, and I doubt that they can contribute to the necessary atmosphere of good faith. Never before in the more than forty years that I have been in the business world have my motives or integrity ever been questioned. I find it exceedingly offensive and insulting to have it happen at this time. . . ."

Dan Lufkin: ". . . Sometimes I wish you'd just write/say what you feel rather than always posturing for legal effect, for the record, and in so doing weaving truths and half-truths together in ways to present misleading conclusions. Be that as it may, your letter was asinine—somewhere you've missed the point—the board is *very legitmately* concerned about the control/organizational structure of Columbia. And I feel correctly so. No one is trying to oust you—that's *why* it was expressly stated that the board wanted to give you a new contract and move down the road together, working for an improved Columbia. . . . What you are doing, Alan, and I am not even sure what it is that you are doing, leads to division and distrust—among management, among board members, among employees—and in my judgment—does severe damage to Columbia. Speaking frankly, as a friend, but also as a board member with serious public responsibility, I don't like it one bit."

Herbert Allen's reply naturally was the longest—an eight-page letter rebutting twenty-five passages in Hirschfield's letter that Herbert found objectionable. He concluded: ". . . I find it unfair, unwarranted, and most serious of all, untrue to imply that I have interfered in any way, shape, or form with Alan Hirschfield's ability to function as president. . . . Under the circumstances, the complaint of interference is an outrage! . . . Certainly all the demeaning, insulting, untrue, and outrageous statements about the board—and there are many in his letter—lead me to believe that he really does not wish to have us negotiate a new contract, and how under the circumstances can he expect the company to do so?''

Despite its profound anger, the board backed down and stopped short of firing Hirschfield. The sudden gathering of the executive group from two continents obviously had made a strong impression. The board also retreated from the Robert Stone issue, Herbert Allen acknowledging that the executives' opposition to Stone would "negate his effectiveness" in surveying the company's control systems. The directors voted instead to place the control study in the hands of Price Waterhouse and Samuel Tedlow, the least prominent member of the board.

Herbert Allen demanded, however, that Alan Hirschfield retract the letter he had sent to the board. Herbert insisted that the retraction be in writing and that it address specifically each allegation in the letter. Hirschfield, feeling victorious overall, and very relieved at not having been fired, agreed to "compose something more temperate."

After the meeting was adjourned, Hirschfield was jolted from his state of relief almost immediately when he found himself momentarily alone in Leo Jaffe's office with Matty Rosenhaus. Having barely held his temper during the board meeting, Rosenhaus exploded with rage:

"You're a liar! A liar! A liar!" he screamed at Hirschfield, his face flushed, spittle spewing from his mouth.

"Matty, calm down," Hirschfield said. "I'm going to write another letter, but I have a right to be emotional like everyone else."

"Liar! Liar!" Rosenhaus screamed.

Hirschfield walked down the hall to his own office where several of the executives awaited him.

"You asshole, why did you write that letter?" said Dan Melnick, who had not had a chance to confront Hirschfield since seeing the letter in Herbert Allen's office.

"Every word of it is true."

"Truth has nothing to do with this," Melnick declared. "It's truculent, and it could only inflame them."

"Why can't I be inflammatory once in a while. Why is only the board allowed to be inflammatory?"

"Alan, your *job* is at stake! We're trying to save your *job*. I'm schlepping back and forth from Europe to try to help save your *job*.

Now you owe it to us to cooperate. If you rescind the letter you won't be fired. So rescind the fucking letter.''

"They'll fire me anyway. They'll find some other excuse."

"Give them the benefit of the doubt. I understand the substantive points you're making and I'm not saying you're wrong. But this is no time to be trying to prove your cock is bigger than Herbert's. If taking back the letter can be a device for buying more time, and in the course of time, tempers and issues and egos can cool, then maybe we can get through it all.''

"For legal reasons," said Hirschfield, "I have to declare myself formally, on the record, on certain issues, or they can claim that I'm implicitly going along with them. But I've agreed to submit a more temperate letter to replace the other one, and I intend to do it.''

Later in the day, Herbert Allen and Matty Rosenhaus assured Robert Stone that he would be paid a fee for the study of Columbia's control system—$60,000—even though the board had decided, in the face of opposition by management, to have someone else conduct the study. Allen also said he would see that Stone was paid a salary, apart from the fee, until he had a permanent job.

Fay Vincent was put on hold.

The management group dispersed, gratified by their impact, but uneasy about the future. Dan Melnick was driven back to Kennedy, flew back to Paris, back to Nice, and drove his Mercedes back to St. Tropez, arriving about noon Thursday. He had been gone just over forty-eight hours.

"You are all insane," said Marie-France.

SIXTY-ONE

"You gotta retract that fuckin' letter," Marty Ransohoff said to Hirschfield early Thursday morning on the phone from California.

Having refused at the height of the Begelman dispute to carry any more messages between the combatants, Ransohoff had talked with Alan and Herbert only occasionally through the spring. As the crisis deepened through June, however, he was drawn back into the fray, and when he heard about Hirschfield's letter, his reaction was the same as Dan Melnick's: Whether the contents were true, false, or a combination, the letter was an unwise and unnecessary provocation.

"Alan, you gotta face up to the fact of who runs the company—who's got the tickets," Ransohoff declared. "You're nuthin' but a fuckin' employee, and if you don't face that soon, baby, you're gonna be in real trouble. I don't care how many bankers and Wall Street types are applauding you. They aren't even in this game. In reality, there are only two players in this game—you and the board. And the board runs the fuckin' company."

"I'm not totally without the ability to fight," Hirschfield said. "You should have seen what happened here yesterday."

"I know what happened there yesterday, and it's only temporary. That was no victory. All you won is a little time."

"That may be all I'll need. There are other people who own stock in this company, and who are capable of buying stock, besides Herbie and Matty," Hirschfield said.

"That's wishful thinking."

"We'll see."

Ransohoff was right about at least one thing. Hirschfield was proud of his good reputation among the bankers and Wall Street analysts who monitored the entertainment industry. He still hoped that these people could be marshaled against the Columbia board of directors—perhaps in a proxy fight. On the day of Ransohoff's call, Hirschfield kept a date with several of Wall Street's most prominent entertainment-industry analysts—Harold Vogel of Merrill Lynch; Lee Isgur of Paine, Webber, Mitchell Hutchins; and others. The analysts knew nothing of Hirschfield's letter to the board, the crisis over the weekend, and the confrontation on Wednesday. Hirschfield chose not to enlighten them or mention the possibility of a proxy fight. Instead, over lunch in a private dining room at Laurent, he stuck to generalities: Columbia's financial health and prospects couldn't be better. *Close Encounters* had nearly freed the company of debt and it likely would begin soon to pay cash dividends on its common stock for the first time since 1970. *California Suite* promised to be a very big picture; there had been problems with the ending of the film but they had been solved. As for Hirschfield's status at the company, the board of directors had committed itself to negotiating a new contract and he was hopeful that it would be completed soon.

Daily Variety appeared Friday with a page-one story which began: "Leo Jaffe, chairman of Columbia Pictures Industries, said today that negotiations with president and chief exec Alan Hirschfield on a contract renewal are continuing 'in good faith.'

"Jaffe added that he hopes talks will be concluded 'shortly' and further hopes that Hirschfield will be retained. Asked why all of Columbia's top divisional executives were in New York on Wednesday, Jaffe said that they were there for business meetings unrelated to Hirschfield's talks with the board."

Hirschfield guessed—there was no way to be sure—that the Fourth of July gambit had bought him perhaps two months within which to maneuver. The dog days of summer had arrived. The board members and everybody else in the company would be spending extended periods of time out of the city on vacation. Even Herbie Allen relaxed a little in the summer, and precipitous action seemed somewhat unlikely for the next several weeks. Hirschfield, therefore, gave himself until Labor Day to devise a solution.

The daily flow and range of telephone calls into Hirschfield's office did not abate just because the company was gripped by a crisis of control and management. Could Hirschfield get for William Demarest a print of an old film in which Demarest had appeared? He would try. Would he be willing to speak to a group of institutional investors to be assembled by the investment house of Bache Halsey

Stuart Shields in Boston on August 2? Yes. Could he arrange for his sister and her family to tour a working gold mine in Colorado? Yes. Would he be interested in purchasing some tax-exempt, New York State, A-rated bonds? No. Could he arrange to get two Barry Manilow tickets for a Wall Street friend? His secretary would take care of it.

On Monday, July 10, a report on Columbia Pictures Industries clattered out across the vast, international teletype network of Merrill Lynch, Pierce, Fenner & Smith. The nation's largest brokerage firm estimated that Columbia's earnings for the fiscal year just ended, which would not be computed for a month or two yet, had been about $5.50 per share of common stock, up more than 300 percent from the previous year. "The company has begun its fiscal 1979 year with a major film hit, *The Cheap Detective*, comparable in profitability to last summer's *The Deep* and, in our opinion, prospects seem favorable for continued long-term earnings growth in feature-film production, television syndication, recorded music, pinball machines, and TV commercial production," wrote Harold Vogel.

"We believe that there is now a somewhat heightened probability of renewal of [Alan Hirschfield's] contract, which has been in some doubt due to strong differences of opinion with significant stockholders on the board of directors. Such differences have arisen as a result of the well-publicized Begelman peculation. . . . If there is no renewal, we believe that a question of management stability, and ability to plan long-range growth strategy, would undoubtedly arise, thereby creating investor uncertainty and potential for pressure on the stock."

"AWAIT SMOKE SIGNAL ON ALAN HIRSCHFIELD: Columbia Shuns Daily Bulletins," headlined Wednesday's *Variety*. ". . . Hirschfield is given high marks by Wall Streeters," the paper noted. " 'He engineered the recovery,' says David Londoner, the widely respected entertainment-securities analyst for Wertheim & Co. 'He pulled off a whole bunch of brilliant things.' "

Alan and Berte had a long lunch at Quo Vadis on Thursday. They planned to leave with Laura the following week for Maine to visit Scott at camp, and then go on to Wyoming where Marc was at camp. They would be gone for a week or ten days and would return to Wyoming for a longer period in August. Alan, meanwhile, was looking forward to perhaps the most spectacular act of self-pampering he had ever indulged in: He was going out that weekend and buy himself a Ferrari. It would cost $35,000, but he could afford it, he had always wanted one, it had been a rough year, and he felt he deserved it. Berte agreed.

In his office, in his limo, and at home over the weekend, Hirschfield tried to draft a new letter to the board of directors. It was very difficult because he knew that anything fully acceptable to the board would be unacceptable to him. The process reminded him of all the unacceptable demands that had preceded it. If only he would reinstate Begelman, everything would be all right. . . . If only he would hire Bob Stone, the board would get off his back. . . . If only he would let Stone survey the financial control systems . . . If only he would retract his letter . . .

The difficulties of waging a proxy fight loomed larger, too. He and Adler continued their secret meetings with lawyer Sidney Silberman. Hirschfield, however, abhorred the prospect of fighting and losing, and he had to be willing to accept that risk.

Another voice from Wall Street was heard on Friday evening, July 14. Lee Isgur of Paine Webber Mitchell Hutchins, a large brokerage firm, appeared on PBS's *Wall Street Week* and said, "If the board of directors will stop arguing among themselves and renew the president's contract at Columbia Pictures, I think that's going to be a very attractive stock."

Unfortunately for Hirschfield, Wall Street was not a monolith. Wall Street included Herbert Allen, and Herbert Allen was contemptuous of much of the "analysis" of the entertainment business that was disseminated by the big Wall Street firms. Herbert was particularly irked by the comments that had flowed from Merrill Lynch, Wertheim, and Paine Webber that week. He had heard about the luncheon that Hirschfield had given at Laurent and he knew that those firms' analysts were among the guests. Hirschfield is supposed to be mending his fences inside the company, Herbert thought, and instead he's out campaigning for public support.

Hirschfield disseminated a four-page letter on Monday to Columbia Pictures Industries' twelve thousand stockholders commenting on the most recent executive appointments and the general state of the corporation. ". . . It is noteworthy that we enter the new fiscal year with more completed films, more productions in progress, and more projects in development than at any time in the past five years. . . . Columbia Pictures Industries' future era of growth will follow a very successful five-year period under the corporate-management team which joined the company five years ago. Our first goal was to rebuild the corporate financial base. Next, the company's management team was strengthened. We then accomplished diversification in order to stabilize earnings volatility. During this past fiscal year, now at a close, we believe the results of our efforts and planning have become evident. . . . Thank you for your support and cooperation.''

Leo Jaffe called on Tuesday to inquire about the status of Hirschfield's new letter to the board. Alan put him off. Clive Davis inquired about the letter on Wednesday. Alan put him off, too. He was preoccupied with the logistics of his trip to Maine and Wyoming starting the next afternoon. Fly to Boston. Tight connection to Portland, Maine. Rent a car. Back to Portland. Boston, Chicago, Denver. Private plane to Cody, Wyoming, just in time to see Marc ride in the camp rodeo parade.

Hirschfield spoke briefly to a Lehman Bros. investment banker about some potential deals for Columbia, to the Ferrari salesman about his new Ferrari, to Lee Isgur of Paine Webber to thank him for his comment on *Wall Street Week,* and to David Geffen, who called in from Malibu to see how things looked. Things looked relatively peaceful. Joe Fischer, who was leaving Wednesday afternoon for a few days in the Hamptons, commented on how quiet the company had been since the July 5 meetings two weeks earlier. Fischer said he thought the atmosphere might be improving slightly.

At 6:15 Hirschfield dropped in briefly to greet guests at a private screening of *The Eyes of Laura Mars* in the Columbia projection room, and then went home to help Berte pack for their trip.

SIXTY-TWO

The next morning—the morning of the day he was fired as the president of one of the world's leading movie companies—Alan Hirschfield shopped for a movie camera.

Wanting to take movies of Scott and Marc at their camps, he had compared prices advertised in the *Times* and decided to try the Camera Barn at Forty-fourth and Madison. As one who enjoyed tinkering with gadgets, Hirschfield took his time, anticipating only a few slow hours at the office followed by a trip to Maine. He examined several cameras and made a selection. Then he bought a new Nikon still-camera, a supplementary lens, a bag, and some film.

At about 10:30 he called his executive assistant, Lorraine Beekman. There was an urgent message. A meeting of the board of directors had been called for later in the day, and Herbert Allen was anxious to see Hirschfield as soon as possible. Alan said he would be in shortly.

He dawdled at the Camera Barn a little longer and then strolled up Madison and over to Fifth. It was hot and very humid—one of the most uncomfortable days of the summer. Just as Alan arrived at the office, Herbert called again and said that he and Dan Lufkin wanted to see Alan immediately. The three men conferred privately in the boardroom prior to the meeting of the full board of directors.

Herbert Allen had planned the firing with the utmost secrecy so that Hirschfield this time would not have a chance to pull any last-minute surprises. Fay Vincent had agreed to take Hirschfield's job. In addition to gaining the approval of Matty Rosenhaus, Vincent had passed the inspection of David Begelman's close friend Sy Weintraub, whom Herbert had sent to Washington to interview him. Vincent's salary would be well in excess of five times his annual pay of

$47,500 at the Securities and Exchange Commission and roughly twice what he had been making in private law practice. Having conferred with Herbert and attorney Bob Werbel frequently by phone, Vincent had flown up the night before, stayed at the Regency, and now was ensconced downstairs at Allen & Company. He had just been introduced to Irwin Kramer and Leo Jaffe for the first time. Werbel had polished the "firing script" that he had drafted for the board meeting two weeks earlier. A public-relations firm, Kekst & Company, had been retained to handle press announcements of Hirschfield's firing and Vincent's hiring. By Thursday morning, under tight security, the releases had been drafted, edited, typed, reproduced, and were ready for distribution to the media.

In the boardroom with Alan and Herbert, Dan Lufkin spoke first.

"We've been thinking very hard about everything, and we've decided things just can't go on any longer. For the good of the company, something's got to give, and it's got to be you. As long as you're here, this thing is just going to continue to fester. It's not going to solve itself."

"You've got the right dynamics," Hirschfield said, "but you're focusing on the wrong people. As long as the board keeps acting like it has been, we'll have problems. If I'm in your way, then just say so. But don't tell me the company can't run because I'm here. The company can't run because the board won't let it run."

"Well," Lufkin replied, "you're entitled to your opinion, but we feel the only solution is for you to leave."

Herbert Allen said: "This is the hardest conversation I've ever had to have. You know I've told you many times that we came to this company together and I'd always hoped that when we left, it would be together. But it's clearly not in the cards."

"It's clearly not in your cards, Herbert, but that's your decision," Hirschfield said.

"No, it's the board's decision. It's for the good of the company for you to resign."

"I'm not resigning. If you want to fire me, then you'll have to fire me."

"We wish you'd reconsider," Lufkin said. "It would cause less pain and anguish for everybody."

"I'm not resigning. I don't agree with what you're doing. I think it's a horrible injustice to me, and even worse, to the company and to some very loyal people. But it's your prerogative. I think this is what you've always wanted. I've been in your way. But I won't resign."

"Be that as it may, we have to move forward and do what we have to do," Herbert said. "It's too bad it had to end this way."

Benumbed, Hirschfield returned to his office and called Berte in Scarsdale, his father in Oklahoma City, Joe Fischer in Amagansett, and Bill Thompson in Boston. He was unable to reach his own lawyers, Haines and Silberman, but he supposed there was nothing they could do on the spur of the moment. He briefed other Columbia executives who were in the office, and then summoned Jonathan Rineheart, the public-relations man whom he had retained for such a contingency and who had been at the meeting in Hirschfield's office on the evening of the Fourth of July.

Matty Rosenhaus spoke first at the board of directors meeting. Sanctimonious to the last, he looked straight at Hirschfield and said, "I want you to know, Alan, that this is not something any of us wanted. It's a terrible, terrible day for Columbia, and for me personally, and for each of us personally. We had hoped to work this thing out, but it just wasn't meant to be. Nobody feels worse than I do. We've had our disagreements, but nobody ever wanted this day to come. It's a terrible, terrible day. It's a sad day for all of us, and I just want you to know that we all feel badly."

Hirschfield said nothing.

Rosenhaus began reading from a typed sheet, drafted by attorney Werbel and headed "Final Draft."

"WHEREAS, the Board of Directors of Columbia Pictures Industries Inc. has given extensive consideration to its management needs; and

"WHEREAS, in such context the Board of Columbia has been requested to consider renewal or extension of its existing employment arrangements with Alan J. Hirschfield; and

"WHEREAS, members of the Board have had extensive discussions on the matter and have duly deliberated thereon; and

"WHEREAS, upon deliberation thereof the Board considers adoption of the following resolutions to be in the best interests of Columbia and its stockholders;

"NOW, THEREFORE, IT IS HEREBY RESOLVED AS FOLLOWS:

"1. That Columbia not renew or extend its present employment arrangements with Mr. Hirschfield.

"2. That Mr. Hirschfield be and hereby is removed as President and Chief Executive Officer of Columbia and is relieved of all responsibilities as an employee of Columbia under his existing employment agreement with Columbia. . . ."

Herbert Allen seconded the motion.

Leo Jaffe denounced the firing as a "disaster and a disgrace."

The resolution carried 5-to-2 with Hirschfield and Jaffe voting against it.

Hirschfield wept briefly in the deserted hall outside the boardroom but composed himself and returned to his office. Most of the tears were shed by secretaries—those on the eleventh floor of 711 Fifth and those on the second floor of the Columbia building in Burbank as the word was flashed to the coast. The company executives for the most part sat in their offices in silence or spoke quietly with each other.

"I spoke to Dan Lufkin around two in the afternoon in the hall of the eleventh floor," Allen Adler wrote later in a memorandum. "I told him that the action that they were taking was wrong for the shareholders, for the management, and for the company, and did not represent the best interests of anyone but certain particular shareholders and directors. I asked him why he was involved in such a thing and he said 'there are certain things you do for friendship.' He then later tried to bathe his actions in the light of the overall long-term interest, but it was clear, and we refreshed each other on a previous conversation, where he said he had come on the board to protect Herbert Allen's interest and these are the things one did for a long-term friend. After the board meeting, Herbert Allen asked to see me for a few minutes and officially told me that Alan Hirschfield had been terminated. He told me that the board wanted everyone else to continue and that it would be best in the long run. I disagreed and said the same thing to him that I said to Lufkin. I mentioned to him that I thought it was improper that those of us in senior corporate management had not been consulted in any way. I told him that he had been operating on misinformation and erroneous 'facts' and that he was too far removed from the business to really know what had been going on. He seems to have the simpleminded view that the stock will go down, but what's the difference; the management will be upset, but they will get over it; and that he can say anything to the public and it's all right. My opinion is he has absolutely not considered the best interests of anyone but his own group.''

Adler's opinion, of course, was of negligible concern to Herbert Allen, who had never been particularly fond of the hot-tempered young *Cosmopolitan* Bachelor of the Month.

The corporate public-relations director, Jean Vagnini, whom the board of directors had long suspected of being a Hirschfield loyalist, was ordered to refer all press calls to Dan Lufkin. Vagnini's office was unceremoniously occupied by Allen attorney Werbel and by operatives of the board's PR firm, Kekst & Company. Vagnini, therefore, hurried to Hirschfield's office and used a telephone in his private bathroom—so as not to be seen by unfriendly witnesses—to arrange a press conference for him in a meeting room of the Gotham Hotel across the street. Vagnini and Jonathan Rineheart composed a press release which Hirschfield edited.

The board's announcement and Hirschfield's release arrived at news-media headquarters almost simultaneously and were on news wires across the country within minutes. The board's release said, ''It has recently become apparent that for Columbia to move forward to new levels of accomplishment, fresh leadership and greater management unity are required.'' In elaboration, Dan Lufkin added, ''This is a no-fault divorce. There were honest and sincere attempts to reach agreement.''

Werbel and the Kekst operatives monitored Hirschfield's press conference. ''The company is operating at the highest level of profitability in its history,'' Hirschfield said, his voice quavering slightly. ''. . . In light of this record, the only possible explanation for the board's action is that it is a direct consequence of the David Begelman affair, during which there were serious differences of opinion and judgment between certain members of the board and myself as to the proper resolution of the matter. It is now fully apparent that those differences can never be reconciled.''

After taking several questions, Hirschfield returned to the office for his new cameras and got in his limousine for the forty-minute ride to Scarsdale.

Still numb, he felt little except a vague sense of relief. Everything had happened in a flash—just like that.

Fired.

An unemployed mogul.

Ten months of ugliness, ten months of fighting, ten months of secret maneuvering—the most horrific months of his life. Was it possible that all of this had started with an IRS form and a forged check? To say it was farfetched was to understate the radical improbability of the whole affair. On the other hand, he had to acknowledge that if he and Herbert hadn't fought over Begelman, they might have clashed eventually over something else. In the end, the issue had become less important than the battle itself.

He could still mount a proxy fight from outside the company, but it would be much more difficult. Perhaps his vision of defeating Herbert had been a delusion from the beginning. All that effort he and Adler had spent on Jimmy Goldsmith, Time, Philip Morris, Penn Central, Mattel, Filmways, and the rest—wasted. Hirschfield had never really gotten properly organized to wage war on Herbert's level.

It was all a blur now, and in a strange way didn't seem to matter much, although he knew that it did matter. The most important business relationship of his life, and of his father's life, lay in ruins. He knew that he would continue to struggle against Herbert Allen, in one way or another, until all possibilities had been exhausted. There would be new dimensions of rage, recrimination, and depression. But the numbness of the moment kept him from feeling any of those things just yet. Instead, he felt oddly energetic, a little high.

Berte and Laura were waiting at home. They were numb, too, but their eyes were dry. He hugged them both.

"Are you all right?" Berte asked.

"I'm fine," Alan said. "Let's go to camp."

EPILOGUE

There was no mass resignation to protest the firing of Hirschfield. Despite their display of bravado two weeks earlier, the top Columbia executives were bound to the company by contract and would have jeopardized themselves financially by walking out abruptly. Many of them were men with families and big mortgages, and even though they were paid handsomely, they lived from paycheck to paycheck. Moreover, Herbert Allen and Fay Vincent asked them *very nicely* not to leave, and Hirschfield himself discouraged those who volunteered—and a few did—from rash action.

Hirschfield procrastinated through the rest of 1978 before deciding against waging a proxy fight for control of Columbia. Spurred by Allen Adler and other supporters, he conferred frequently with lawyer Sidney Silberman and potential financial backers, but finally concluded that victory was problematic and that he would hurt himself more by fighting and losing than by not fighting at all. He also retreated from another idea—starting his own motion-picture production company, a venture for which he could have obtained $150 million in credit from several banks and other sources. Even with that much money at his disposal, the company would have been relatively small, and Hirschfield aspired to bigger things.

At the beginning of 1979 he accepted an offer from his friend Steve Ross, the chief executive of Warner Communications, to become a consultant to Warner. Both men viewed the post as a temporary ''parking place'' that might lead to a permanent job. Although Hirschfield felt somewhat nostalgic at Warner—he had done a lot of investment banking for the company in the pre-Ross era of the sixties and had been financial vice president for a year—it became clear after a few months that there was no place for him in the upper echelon of the company. Warner was fully staffed if not overloaded with talented executives, some of whom felt threatened by Hirschfield's presence and potential ascendancy. He had no power, accomplished little, and suffered from depression, a delayed reaction to his experience at Columbia as much as a current reaction to the lack of opportunity at Warner. He brooded a lot, read a lot, spent some time with a psychiatrist, and recommended that his male friends read Daniel J. Levinson's *The Seasons of a Man's Life*, a sort of highbrow *Passages*.

After several months at Warner, Hirschfield got a lucky break. Alan Ladd, Jr., resigned as head of Twentieth Century-Fox's motion-picture unit, along with his top aides, after a dispute with corporate chairman Dennis Stanfill. Stanfill decided to hire Alan Hirschfield not only to replace Ladd but also to oversee Fox's other entertainment operations. By the middle of 1980, Hirschfield had brought to Fox dozens of his former Columbia colleagues, including Dan Melnick, Sherry Lansing, Allen Adler, Norman Levy, and Clive Davis. Lansing was named president of Fox productions, the first woman in the industry to hold such a high post.

Edgar Bronfman, the chairman of the Seagram liquor empire, sent a copy of *The Joys of Yiddish* to Fay Vincent shortly after Vincent accepted the presidency of Columbia Pictures Industries. Having been in and out of the movie business more than once, Bronfman thought that Vincent, as a staunch Roman Catholic from a conservative background, probably could use some help with elementary communication in the world of Hollywood. "At least the book can't hurt," Bronfman said, only half facetiously.

Herbert Allen meanwhile moved quickly to consolidate the spoils of his victory in the struggle with Hirschfield. Sy Weintraub, Begelman's close friend whose election to the Columbia board had been vehemently opposed by Hirschfield, joined the board. And Robert Stone, the stiff, ex-RCA officer whom Hirschfield and Allen had fought over so bitterly, was hired as Columbia's executive vice president and chief operating officer, the job Herbert had wanted him to have all along.

A number of Hirschfield's policies were continued, however. Columbia developed several methods for sharing the financial risk of picture-making with outside investors, a concept Hirschfield had pioneered. Vincent and Allen also had the good sense to retain Frank

Price, whom Hirschfield and Melnick had made head of motion-picture production. With the help of several films like *Kramer vs. Kramer* and *The China Syndrome*, which had been nurtured at Columbia by Hirschfield, Begelman, Melnick, and Lansing, Frank Price showed that he could run the Columbia studio just as well as he previously had run Universal's television arm. Price established good relationships with Fay Vincent (to whom he reported directly instead of through Robert Stone, despite Stone's highfalutin title) and with Ray Stark, whose power was underscored and enhanced by the firing of Hirschfield. Aside from the job itself, Frank Price felt that the two most attractive elements in the Columbia situation were the presence of Stark, whom Price considered the ablest producer in town, and the presence in the Columbia production pipeline of *Annie*, which Price believed held the potential of becoming the biggest movie musical in years.

Several films that Price himself squired, such as *The Blue Lagoon* and *Stir Crazy*, did well commercially. And the corporation's earnings also were aided substantially for years into the future by television syndication deals that Norman Horowitz, an important member of the Hirschfield team, had made before resigning as president of Columbia television distribution.* Horowitz was one of the many Columbia employees—ranging from top executives to secretaries—who left Columbia in the years after the firing of Hirschfield. In addition to those who resigned readily for new opportunities, others departed only after long periods of anxious procrastination and the eventual realization that they could not work effectively under Herbert Allen's new management team. And the new management naturally fired a sizable number of holdovers. The lives of many people, indeed entire families, were disrupted. Marriages were strained, and a few broke up. At the office and at home, in Los Angeles and New York, there were ugly scenes, loud denunciations, screaming telephone conversations, tears, and sleepless nights. The new Columbia management rewrote a lot of history. Having called Norman Levy, who headed motion-picture distribution and marketing, "the top executive in his field" while he still worked for Columbia, the company said less flattering things about him after he resigned to join Hirschfield at Fox.

---

*Norman Horowitz left to become president of PolyGram Television. a new company started by the PolyGram Group. the huge West German-Dutch entertainment conglomerate with extensive U.S. motion-picture and record interests.

*   *   *

Herbert Allen was able to relax a little. He took up with a new girl friend, Ann Reinking, a star of *Dancin'*, *All That Jazz*, and *Annie*. And Herbert made time for such things as the annual slow-pitch softball game mounted by his friend Ed Moose, the proprietor of the Washington Square Bar & Grill in San Francisco. In 1979 the team traveled to Paris to play a team of U.S. Embassy guards assembled by the proprietor of Le Moulin du Village, a restaurant near Maxim's. The game was played in the Bois de Boulogne, and Herbert was named the most valuable player.

But he soon was engulfed by continuing problems at Columbia. Kirk Kerkorian, the controlling shareholder of MGM, purchased a 25 percent interest in Columbia and tried to take control of it, too. After an extremely bitter and costly struggle, Kerkorian backed down, selling his block of stock to Columbia for a hefty profit of about $60 million. Columbia was out a lot of money but was rid of a pesky and unwanted suitor. During the fight, Begelman's friend Sy Weintraub was revealed as an ally of Kerkorian's and abruptly left the Columbia board of directors.

Weintraub had been a problem for Columbia ever since Herbert Allen had made him a member of the board in the wake of the firing of Hirschfield. Allen and Vincent had placed Weintraub in charge of all motion-picture and television operations on the coast but he had not performed up to expectations. Getting rid of him, however, posed a sensitive public-relations problem for both Columbia and Weintraub. Herbert Allen did not want it known that Columbia's management still was in disarray. And Sy Weintraub had become the company's most visible officer; he was going out with Barbara Walters and was being identified in gossip columns nationwide as her companion as well as a major force at Columbia Pictures. Naturally he did not want it known that he had been stripped of his power and supplanted by Frank Price.

To appease Weintraub, Allen and Vincent gave him the title of chairman of the executive committee. There were protracted disagreements over his contract. Then Herbert Allen began hearing whispers that Weintraub had become a secret agent for Kirk Kerkorian in the Columbia boardroom. William Forman, an elderly theater owner, an old friend of the Allens, and a major behind-the-scenes power in Hollywood for many years, telephoned Herbert one day in Sun Valley where Herbert was skiing and reported confidentially that Weintraub was working secretly with Kerkorian in an effort to seize control of Columbia. Shortly thereafter, Weintraub resigned from the Columbia board simultaneously with the public revelation of his alliance with Kerkorian. Weintraub sued Columbia, Columbia sued Weintraub, and invective filled lawyers' conference rooms on both coasts as the suits moved forward.

Warner Communications chairman Steve Ross, who had done business with Weintraub years earlier and did not hold him in high regard, took more than one opportunity to rib Herb Allen about his mistake in hiring Weintraub. "Why didn't you guys ask me about Weintraub—I could have told you," Allen quoted Ross as saying.

On Wednesday, June 27, 1979, David Begelman again stood before Burbank Municipal Court Judge Thomas C. Murphy, who a year earlier had fined him $5,000 and placed him on three years probation for felony grand theft. As part of his sentence, Begelman had produced a film, *Angel Death*, about the dangers of the drug PCP, or angel dust. After praising the film, Judge Murphy reduced the crime of which Begelman stood convicted from a felony to a misdemeanor. Then, to the consternation of the deputy district attorney in attendance, the judge entered a non-guilty plea to the reduced charges, dismissed the charges, and revoked the remaining two years of probation.

The judge said, ". . . he can go forward without the stigma of probation."

Begelman said, "My contrition is complete. It is not manufactured for the sake of expediency . . . and I understand the motivation that led me to commit the acts for which I have atoned."

The deputy district attorney expressed "outrage" and said, "It's very tough to explain to someone that the justice system treats everyone equally when they see something like this."

Back in partnership with his longtime associate Freddie Fields, Begelman spent much of the rest of the year producing his first motion picture for Columbia, a film entitled *Wholly Moses!*, starring Dudley Moore and Laraine Newman. Shot in a remote desert region north of Los Angeles, it was a biblical spoof and turned out to be an inept failure as a film. No one would know that, however, until it opened in mid-1980. And in December 1979, precisely two years after his abortive reinstatement as president of Columbia, David Begelman's career as a producer ended abruptly, and his restoration to the ranks of movie-industry royalty was completed, when he was

named to the presidency of Metro-Goldwyn-Mayer and commissioned to restore it to its heralded position in the Hollywood of L. B.
Mayer and Irving Thalberg. Just before the appointment was
announced, a joyous Begelman flew to New York and personally
told Herbert Allen and Matty Rosenhaus the good news. Liz Smith
and Rona Barrett broke the story, and the *Los Angeles Herald
Examiner* proclaimed BEGELMAN'S BACK AND MGM'S GOT HIM. When
David strolled into Ma Maison for lunch on the day the news came
out, several people stood and applauded, and he was surrounded by
hands to be shaken and cheeks to be bussed.

During the next six months Begelman hired several old colleagues
and friends from Columbia and elsewhere, and launched what MGM
called the most ambitious production program in its history. The
studio took a four-page, full-color advertisement in *Variety*, pictur-
ing forty stars and listing fifty-one movie projects in various stages
of development. The ad revived one of MGM's most famous old
slogans, "More stars than there are in Heaven."*

Over at Fox, Alan Hirschfield and Dennis Stanfill weren't getting
along well. Trouble had been predicted from the start. They were
men of vastly different personal styles: Stanfill, the starchy, severe
Annapolis graduate, known around Hollywood as the town *goy*, the
only major motion-picture executive who did not live in Beverly Hills
or environs (he lived in San Marino, near Pasadena); and Hirschfield,
the loose, playful Oklahoma Jew who wanted nothing more than to
make a lot of money and have a roaring good time doing it. Although
both men had come from Wall Street originally, they had come from the
opposite sides of the Street. In contrast to the entrepreneurial, rough-
and-tumble environment of Allen & Company, Dennis Stanfill's arena
had been old-line, blue-blooded, conservative Lehman Brothers.

Little that Hirschfield wanted to do at Twentieth Century-Fox
worked out, and he decided against moving his home and family to
Los Angeles. Fox tried and failed to acquire EMI. It tried and failed
to acquire Norman Lear's company, Tandem Productions. Hirschfield's
old pal Herb Siegel, the chairman of Chris-Craft Industries, raised
his stake in Fox to nearly 25 percent, making Dennis Stanfill very
nervous. To ward off the possibility of a hostile takeover, Stanfill

*With Begelman no longer available to produce *Annie*, Frank Price transferred the project to Ray Stark
and approved Stark's choice of John Huston to direct the picture. By the time of its opening in 1982
Annie had become Columbia's most expensive film since *Close Encounters*.

developed a plan to convert Fox into a privately owned corporation. But the banks, led by the First of Boston, refused to support the plan unless Stanfill guaranteed that Alan Hirschfield and the management team Hirschfield had assembled would be an integral part of the newly formed company. Stanfill scuttled the plan.

The two men's relationship deteriorated further when Harris Katleman, the flamboyant Hollywood figure whom Hirschfield had hired to rejuvenate Fox's ailing television operation, was charged with—and denied—cheating on his expense account. Dennis Stanfill, invoking the Begelman case and declaring that no chicanery would be tolerated at Fox, wanted to fire Katleman. Hirschfield, however, believed that the charges against Katleman were in no way comparable to Begelman's forgeries and embezzlements and insisted on keeping him.

The Katleman issue and the overall tension between Hirschfield and Stanfill were resolved when Denver oil baron Marvin Davis, who had made two unsuccessful attempts to buy the Oakland A's baseball team, purchased Twentieth Century-Fox for about $700 million and countermanded Stanfill's order that Harris Katleman be fired. Stanfill resigned. Davis named Alan Hirschfield chairman and chief executive officer of Fox. Stanfill began a lawsuit against Davis and Fox for breach of contract, which they denied.

In his office on the Fox lot, Hirschfield pasted a crown on his own photograph, along with the words, "It's good to be the king," a line from Mel Brooks's *History of the World, Part One*, which had just opened. It was a joke, of course, but it also was somewhat reminiscent of Alan's old naïveté. He wasn't the king. Marvin Davis was.*

Law enforcement authorities and the media continued to make much of the widespread allegations, originating with the Begelman affair, that Hollywood is rife with corruption. Los Angeles District Attorney John Van de Kamp established an "Entertainment Industry Task Force" and published a special telephone number that anyone could use to report embezzlements or other types of wrongdoing. During the first two years of the task force's existence it received more than six hundred calls, mostly from anonymous tipsters. A few major prosecutions resulted. A unit production manager at Universal pleaded

---

*Davis's purchase of Fox had been initiated by Ira Harris of Salomon Brothers, the investment banker who had put Hirschfield in touch with Jimmy Goldsmith in December 1977.

guilty to grand theft after he was caught putting his girl friend, an actress, on the payroll of a film in which she did not appear. The manager had forged the woman's name on time cards. An employee of Twentieth Century-Fox's film processing laboratory pleaded guilty to mail fraud and tax evasion in connection with the embezzlement of about $1.2 million. A Paramount employee pleaded no contest when charged with stealing $42,000 from that studio. The controller of the Academy of Motion Picture Arts and Sciences pleaded no contest to an allegation that he stole about $23,000 from the academy.

The DA's task force investigated allegations made by Jennifer Martin, an attorney for ABC-TV, that Leonard Goldberg, Aaron Spelling, and others diverted funds from the television series *Charlie's Angels* and thus defrauded the show's profit participants, who included Robert Wagner and Natalie Wood. The investigation took a year. It was marked by an odd press conference, featuring both the investigator and his targets, at which Goldberg and Spelling denied the charges and the deputy district attorney in charge of the investigation described the two producers as "completely cooperative" and "very respected members of the entertainment industry." In light of the tone of the press conference, it was no surprise when the case was dropped. "There is insufficient evidence to prove beyond a reasonable doubt that Aaron Spelling, Leonard Goldberg (or the others) are criminally responsible for conspiracy, grand theft, or embezzlement," said an eighty-one-page report prepared by the DA's office. Although District Attorney Van de Kamp assailed "shoddy business practices" and "murky contracts" in the entertainment industry, and raised questions about "fair dealing," he suggested that any disputes arising from the Spelling-Goldberg situation would be handled more appropriately through the civil courts than through criminal prosecution.*

Sixty Minutes did a story on "creative accounting" in the movie business. The *Los Angeles Times* published several lengthy articles on the same subject. Cliff Robertson appeared for an hour on Phil Donahue's television program, asserting, "We're trying to stop a corruption that has become malignant in our industry and grown every year." Along the way, the media cumulatively pointed out that nearly every major star in Hollywood, in addition to a lot of

---

*The district attorney's office also investigated the Harris Katleman case at Fox and found no grounds for prosecution, confirming Hirschfield's view that Katleman's conduct was not comparable to Begelman's.

directors and writers, had disputed studio accounting practices at one time or another and in some instances had begun lawsuits. Most cases were settled out of court.

A few people tried to take advantage of the sensitive climate to induce change in Hollywood business practices. Norman Horowitz, after resigning from Columbia to become president of PolyGram Television, published an open letter to the entertainment industry as a double-page advertisement in *Variety*. "The beginning of Poly-Gram Television represents a departure from the traditional values of the television business," Horowitz wrote. "In the coming years, there will be opportunities with PolyGram television . . . to depart from normal industry deals and begin anew, based on a concept of sharing. . . . I want to have a new approach to partnerships, not another new definition of net profits." Horowitz took three other double-page ads, each accompanied by a cartoon. "Have you ever owned a piece of a 'cop' show and ended up being 'robbed'?'' asked the first ad. The cartoon showed three Hollywood sharpies robbing a naïve script writer.

Despite the good intentions, Horowitz's ads were ineffectual. Although some people were angry and others privately applauded, most just smirked and shrugged. The ads, like a lot of the press coverage and the district attorney's activities, overlooked a crucial point. Hollywood is rife with corruption, all right, but the occasional embezzlement, fraud, cheating, and chiseling—as serious as they are—constitute symptoms of a more pervasive and subtle corruption, a corruption that is more difficult to combat than outright theft.

It is the corruption of power and arrogance. It is the corruption that inevitably pervades a large and glamorous institution when that institution is tightly controlled by a handful of people, and thousands upon thousands of other people are clamoring for entry.

Hollywood is as glamorous as it ever was, and the relatively few who strike it rich amount to a dangling lure that is irresistible to many others. Thus, hundreds of motion-picture ideas are presented for each one the studios produce and release. Hundreds of television ideas are presented for each one the networks put on the air. Hundreds of actors audition for each one chosen.

Such a radical power imbalance fosters overweening arrogance in some quarters. When not held in check, it can breed all manner of abuses, including the notion—sometimes subtle but always malignant—that anything goes, no one can stop it, and indeed no one cares. It was arrogance in part that led David Begelman to forge checks. It was arrogance in part that led the board of directors of Columbia Pictures Industries to believe that it could quietly investigate Begelman, quietly observe the legal niceties of quietly telling the SEC, and then restore Begelman to the studio presidency without anyone else's learning the details of what he had done, without a single executive or employee's getting upset, and without the press's spreading the whole affair across page one.

In more specific and tangible terms, the power imbalance and arrogance also result in employer-employee relationships that normally are weighted overwhelmingly in favor of the employer, giving rise to the "shoddy business practices" and "murky contracts" of which the district attorney spoke. In analyzing Hollywood's abuses, the truly sophisticated experts tend to focus not so much on the occasional instances of flagrant illegality as on the more prosaic standard terms and conditions of the average Hollywood contract—perfectly legal terms and conditions—that give the studio or the network enormous advantages over the actor, director, writer, or small production company. The powerful and arrogant few tend to take full advantage of every situation, and the lure of working in the industry is so strong that the fearful mass of prospective employees will sign just about anything to do so—often to their later regret. Hollywood is full of people who argue, *after* a film or TV series becomes a hit, that they deserve more money and are being cheated, when in fact they signed a legal contract—onerous and unfair perhaps, but legal nonetheless—that entitles them to no more money than they are getting.

And yet they keep coming. Would-be actors, directors, writers, producers—many with genuine talent—in far greater numbers than Hollywood can ever absorb. Hollywood always has been tough for newcomers. Even big companies that try their hand at the movie business often encounter difficulty. Time Incorporated, after deciding against acquiring all or part of Columbia Pictures in 1978, got into the motion-picture production business in 1979 by buying David Susskind's company, Talent Associates. Two years later, Time got out. "This isn't business, it's rocketry—nine out of ten fizzle," grumbled Time chairman Andrew Heiskell, who found that he disliked nearly everything about Hollywood, from what he considered excessive use of limousines to odd accounting practices.*

Only a small number of people and corporate entities are in such demand that they are able to force a righting of the power imbalance. They do so only for themselves, however, and even they remain dependent on the existing power structure—the studios, networks, and few big talent agencies and production companies that run the town. The two most visible symbols of the so-called "New Hollywood," Francis Ford Coppola and George Lucas, who never miss an opportunity to assail the traditional Hollywood "system," actually desire nothing more than to create studios of their own that they can control. Meanwhile, they must rely on the existing studios to distribute their films.

When Robert Redford, one of the very few truly powerful actors, accepted his Oscar as best director for *Ordinary People* at the Academy Awards ceremony in March 1981, he said, "It may not be too fashionable, but the fact is that I really do appreciate the support of Paramount Pictures—Charlie Bluhdorn, Barry Diller. They let us make the film the way we wanted to, and I'm very grateful for that." And when Warren Beatty was honored as best director for *Reds* in 1982, he said, "I want to name Mr. Barry Diller, who runs Paramount, . . . and Mr. Charles Bluhdorn, who runs Gulf & Western and God knows what else, and I want to say to you gentlemen that no matter how much we might have wanted to strangle each other from time to time, I think that your decision, taken in the great capitalistic tower of Gulf & Western, to finance a three-and-a-half hour romance which attempts to reveal for the first time just something of the beginnings of American socialism and American communism, reflects credit not only upon you; I think it reflects credit upon Hollywood and the movie business wherever that is, and I think it reflects more particular credit upon freedom of expression that we have in American society, and the lack of censorship we have from the government or the people who put up the money."

Redford (and implicitly Beatty) were right. It was not fashionable for an actor or director to thank the chief executive of the parent

---

*Time decided to concentrate on cable and pay television in which it had genuine expertise and exerted growing power in show business in its own right. (It owned one of the nation's largest cable systems, as well as Home Box Office, which maintained an ongoing relationship with Columbia Pictures.) Upon leaving Time, David Susskind made a production deal with David Begelman at MGM.

conglomerate and the head of the studio, but it was an accurate reflection of the realities of power.

"God, this is a tough town," Budd Schulberg's character Kit tells her companion in *What Makes Sammy Run?* . . . "Sometimes I think the three chief products this town turns out are moving pictures, ambition, and fear."

It was still true more than four decades after *Sammy* was written.

The Securities and Exchange Commission's investigation of Columbia Pictures dwindled and died. Aside from David Begelman's crimes, which already had been handled as an isolated issue by local Los Angeles authorities, the SEC found no evidence of federal law violations by anyone at Columbia. (Waging intense and brutal psychological warfare does not necessarily violate the law.) Specifically, the SEC found no evidence that Columbia Pictures Industries was "out of control" under Alan Hirschfeld's regime, as Dan Lufkin and Herbert Allen had asserted privately. Had the corporation been out of control it would have been in violation of federal securities laws, and the officers and directors could have been cited.

The few private lawsuits against Columbia did not amount to much either.

Nevertheless, Fay Vincent and Robert Stone (*Fortune* magazine named Stone one of "The Ten Toughest Bosses in America" in 1980) substantially increased Columbia's self-policing capability. Ilana Cytto, the ambitious young internal auditor, who was dubbed "Ilana Piranha" by certain studio people during the Audrey Lisner investigation, built an empire on the Lisner case. Her staff was increased from two to twenty-four over the next few years. In an interview with *The Hollywood Reporter* in 1981, Cytto said "my boys" will be auditing individual motion pictures and all of Columbia's new businesses, including home video.

Several people who figured directly or indirectly in the affairs of Columbia Pictures died in recent years:

• Serge Semenenko, 76, the deposed vice chairman of the First National Bank of Boston and the original "evil genius" of movie financing, who had been a longtime friend of Charlie Allen and Jack Warner and had aided the Allens' takeover of Columbia in 1973, of an unspecified illness at New York Hospital.

• James Wilmot, 68, the Columbia director who gave a Cadillac to Idi Amin, of cancer at his farm near Rochester, N.Y.

• Matty Rosenhaus, 69, the Geritol magnate and Columbia board member who called Alan Hirschfield "Iago," of a heart attack at the Pierre Hotel.

• Joyce Silvey, 39, the Beverly Hills police detective who forced the Cliff Robertson forgery to the attention of the top management of Columbia Pictures, of a heart attack in Los Angeles.

• Audrey Lisner's ex-husband Jerry, 46, the gangster, of eleven gunshot wounds, inflicted to his head and neck at close range by a person or persons unknown, at his home in Las Vegas. Once again under federal indictment, Lisner was believed to be secretly cooperating with an FBI investigation of certain of his compatriots.

Four years after Audrey Lisner's disappearance, opinion was divided on whether she was dead or alive. She had talked of suicide before leaving for Mexico. The Los Angeles police believed for a brief period in the summer of 1978 that a partially decomposed body found by a hiker in Griffith Park (Jane Doe No. 78) might be Audrey. Dental records, however, eliminated the possibility. At Christmas of 1979, Fay Vincent, Ilana Cytto, and a few other Columbia people received greeting cards made from a color snapshot of Audrey and bearing the words "A Prosperous New Year" and the printed signature "Audrey Lisner." Postmarked in Los Angeles, the cards created a stir and were turned over to the district attorney's office. Detectives laboriously traced them back to a former colleague of Audrey's with a droll sense of humor. In the summer of 1980, Ilana Cytto got a birthday card signed "Audrey." The card carried the word "LIBBER" and the rhyme: "Your hatred of men/Has your mind in a rut/Happy Birthday to you/You ignorant slut." The DA's office was unable to trace the card, which was postmarked in Santa Ana, California, a community just south of Los Angeles.

It is impossible to know how Filmways Incorporated would have fared if it had merged with Columbia Pictures in 1978. On its own, however, it fared badly and in 1982 was purchased by a group headed by Arthur Krim and Eric Pleskow, the former United Artists executives who had decided against affiliating with Columbia at the height of the Begelman scandal and instead had formed Orion Pictures under Warner Bros.'s aegis. . . . It is impossible to know how Mattel Incorporated would have performed as part of Columbia.

Remaining independent, it functioned unevenly, but in 1982 showed signs of steady growth in the burgeoning, highly competitive field of electronic games. . . . It is impossible to know whether IBM and Columbia would have succeeded as partners in laser-optical video discs. IBM went into business instead with MCA-Universal and Japan's Pioneer Electronic Corporation, and the joint venture did not work out. There were manufacturing snafus, and the market for video discs in general did not develop nearly so fast as the industry at large had anticipated. IBM and MCA retained their potentially valuable patents. . . . Philip Morris, after choosing not to acquire Columbia, purchased the Seven-Up Company, only to see Seven-Up's market share shrink.

Cliff Robertson was blacklisted for four years after reporting David Begelman's forgery. Finally Robertson was given a part in a film called *Brainstorm*, which proved to be Natalie Wood's last film before she drowned. As might have been predicted, Robertson found himself working on *Brainstorm* for MGM and David Begelman—a fact that Begelman did not allow to go unnoticed. Subsequently Robertson made a picture for Bob Fosse and another for Marty Ransohoff. Although gratified to be working again, Robertson was privately humiliated by the fact that he was being paid less than in the past. He also was embittered by a lack of success in raising money to finance a sequel to his Oscar-winning *Charly*. As for *Good Times, Bad Times*, the subject of the anonymous middle-of-the-night phone calls at the height of the Begelman furor, the picture still had not been made as of the middle of 1983.

In reflective moments, Begelman occasionally remarked to friends on the number of lives that had been affected directly or indirectly by the events the Cliff Robertson forgery had set in motion. The number surely was in the hundreds and perhaps the thousands. The entire entertainment community had been shaken. Four of the seven major studios—Columbia, Fox, MGM, and United Artists—had changed drastically, and a fifth, MCA-Universal, had suffered from Frank Price's move to Columbia. Only Warner and Paramount were essentially untouched. (Warner, however, was embarrassed by its own scandal. After a long investigation, culminating in a ten-count federal indictment for bribery and misappropriation of funds, Jay Emmett, one of the three members of the Office of the President under Chairman Steve Ross, pleaded guilty to two counts of defrauding Warner. The investigation concerned the financial collapse of the Westchester Premiere Theatre in which Warner had invested.)

Thwarted in his attempt to take control of Columbia Pictures, MGM's controlling shareholder Kirk Kerkorian bought United Artists. David Begelman was shifted from MGM to run UA, and Freddie Fields was brought in to head MGM's motion-picture program. Joe Fischer, after waiting in vain for Hirschfield to hire him at Fox (Hirschfield claimed Dennis Stanfilll wouldn't permit it), finally accepted an offer from Begelman to become the financial czar of both MGM and UA. Having never been terribly fond of Begelman, and having been a principal proponent of Columbia's firing him summarily in 1977 after the revelation of his crimes, Fischer found that his decision to accept Begelman's offer did not come easily. However, Fischer had been treated badly at Columbia after Hirschfield left—"promoted" to executive vice president and then stripped of most of his authority and responsibilities—and he yearned for a new challenge.

The slate of films Begelman developed at MGM, while including a few of high quality and originality (*Pennies from Heaven*), performed poorly at the box office, and MGM and UA in combination slid toward financial difficulty.* Kerkorian created a corporate parent called the MGM/UA Entertainment Company to take firm command of both studios. He named Frank Rothman, one of his longtime lawyers and the man who had defended David Begelman during the criminal prosecution, to run the new entity as chairman and chief executive officer. Joe Fischer was made president, Begelman's power declined, and in July 1982, Begelman was dismissed, only to move promptly across the MGM lot to head a new film production company financed in part by the Hunts of Dallas.

Herbert Allen had always said that if someone offered him a "ridiculous" price for Columbia Pictures he might sell it. Generally he defined "ridiculous" as somewhere between 50 percent and 100 percent above the current market price of the company's stock. In early 1982, the Coca-Cola Company offered what some observers considered a ridiculous price—cash and Coke stock with a total value of/between $700 million and $800 million, or about $70 a

---

*Meanwhile, Gladyce Begelman, along with her two coauthors, updated *New York on $500 a Day (Before Lunch)* and called the new version *New York on $1,000 a Day (Before Lunch)*.

Columbia share. (Columbia was trading at about $40 at the time.) On an original investment of $2.5 million, the Allens stood to make a profit on their interest in Columbia of more than $30 million, plus a multimillion-dollar investment-banking fee for handling the deal. Coke planned to let Columbia operate essentially autonomously, that is, under the control of Allen, Vincent, and Price. The deal would take months to conclude, and such deals occasionally fall through. Herbert Allen, however, seized the opportunity for a day in the limelight, something his publicity-shy father and uncle had never done in fifty years of deals of comparable magnitude. Herbert appeared on network television and was profiled by *Fortune* and other publications. The media were dazzled by the Coke merger and circulated some questionable propositions, as well as a number of outright errors. Herbert was portrayed as a financial wizard, even though others at Coke and Columbia had conceived the merger. *The New York Times* lavished praise, too, on Fay Vincent, saying, "He has guided the production of such blockbuster moneymakers as *Close Encounters of the Third Kind, The Deep,* and *Kramer vs. Kramer.*" Vincent, of course, had nothing to do with those films, all of which were made under Alan Hirschfield and David Begelman. But no one really begrudged Vincent and Allen the publicity. They had, after all, made a killing.* And the more interesting question was how soon the chairman of Coca-Cola, the good-humored, Cuban-born Roberto C. Goizueta, would "go Hollywood." A man with a taste for silk ascots and dark glasses, Goizueta had long been interested in getting Coke into show business.

At dawn on a cold, rainy Friday in the early spring of 1982, Alan Hirschfield boarded Twentieth Century-Fox's private jet at the Westchester County Airport for a flight to Los Angeles. He was accompanied by a business friend, a writer, a child, and the Hirschfield family dog, a black female poodle named Chauncey (after Chauncey Gardiner in *Being There*). The headwinds were strong, slowing the flight and necessitating a stop for fuel in Grand Island, Nebraska.

---

*Still holding about sixty thousand shares of Columbia stock, a fact he had not advertised, Alan Hirschfield did all right financially, too, making a profit of about $4 million on the Coke deal. Together with nearly $3 million he made a year earlier when Marvin Davis bought all the stock of Twentieth Century-Fox, the money unquestionably helped assuage the psychological traumas he had suffered. But its effect was limited. For the fights, of course, were never about money, always about power.

While there, Chauncey got loose and bolted for the open fields. There was a frantic chase across hundreds of yards of tarmac and prairie before she was trapped against a fence and returned to the plane. Another half hour was lost.

Hirschfield's limousine and senior West Coast secretary, Marce Raether, met the flight in Los Angeles, and since he was late for an already-convened luncheon meeting with Marvin Davis and Mickey Rudin, he was driven directly to the Fox commissary. Moving slowly through the Fox lot, the limousine came up behind production president Sherry Lansing, whom Hirschfield had appointed two years earlier and regarded very warmly.

"Female executives suck!" Hirschfield shouted as the limo eased past Lansing. She squealed with laughter, and everyone else within hearing range guffawed, too. Dennis Stanfill would have found the remark in bad taste, but Hirschfield could get by with such cracks. They were amusing coming from him. And they reflected the more relaxed atmosphere at Fox following Stanfill's departure. The studio was more stable than it had been in years. Hirschfield had signed a lucrative new four-year contract with Marvin Davis, and their relationship seemed good.

Nothing was absolutely certain, of course. It was uncertain whether Lansing, Melnick, Adler, or anyone else—even Hirschfield and Davis—would stay at Fox for the long term. There would be new opportunities, new problems, new feuds. Still, the laughter helped. There had been too little of it in recent years.

Hirschfield's personal life was more placid, too. His marriage had steadied, and he had finally moved his family to Los Angeles where he had leased a house with a tennis court and pool just north of Sunset near the Beverly Hills Hotel. Chauncey's arrival symbolized the completion of the move west. (The Hirschfields kept their place in Scarsdale, however, just in case.)

Although Alan Hirschfield and Herbert Allen encountered each other now and then and exchanged polite words, a genuine rapprochement seemed unlikely. Various Fox and Columbia officials sometimes talked business, but the personal wounds of 1977 and 1978 had not healed and neither Alan nor Herbert had any real desire to be friends again. When they talked of each other with other people, their words were still venomous.

It was Charlie Allen, not Herbert, who wanted peace. As he approached the eightieth year of his life, Charlie made small efforts to rekindle the warmth between the Hirschfield and Allen families. He occasionally telephoned Alan or his father, usually on a birthday or some other special occasion. But the warmth was superficial. Long after his son had been fired by Herbert Allen and the board of directors of Columbia Pictures, Norman Hirschfield remained deeply distressed.

"I think Charlie was wrong. There comes a time in life when you have to take a position, a stand. I was greatly disappointed in Charlie. He should have done it [stopped Herbert] out of friendship. He knew it hurt me. I was terribly depressed, physically ill. But you can't go through life with hatred. You'll destroy yourself. I won't destroy Herbert. I'll destroy myself. I'll never forget it, though."

NOTES

The primary source of the factual material in this book is hundreds of hours of interviews, many of them tape-recorded, which the author conducted with more than a hundred people who have detailed, firsthand knowledge of the subject. The author also has had access to the complete transcripts of sworn testimony taken by investigators for the U.S. Securities and Exchange Commission in the case titled *In the Matter of Columbia Pictures Industries Inc.*, Case No. HO-1076, from the following people:

Herbert Anthony Allen	John H. Mitchell
David Begelman	Clifford Parker Robertson III
Alan James Hirschfield	Raymond Otto Stark
Leo Jaffe	Robert Lewis Stone
Joseph R. Lipsher	John Patrick Veitch
Erwin Gerald Lipsky	Seymour Weintraub

The SEC testimony in most instances is consistent with interviewees' statements to the author.

The book employs voluminous documentary material—corporate records of various types including confidential minutes of meetings of the Columbia Pictures Industries board of directors, audit committee, and executive committee; reports of investigations by Price Waterhouse & Company, the certified public accounting firm; official police files and records of court proceedings, civil and criminal; analyses by investment firms; individuals' daily appointment calendars, telephone logs, and travel records; memoranda, letters, informal notes, and diaries; photographs; newspaper and magazine articles; and books.

Descriptions of physical settings are drawn in nearly every instance from the author's visits to the settings and his research into changes in the settings, if any, subsequent to the events described. References to weather and climatic conditions are taken from the daily records of the National Weather Service.

The author's basic interviewing method was to refresh the interviewee's memory by placing before him his appointment calendar, telephone log, and/or any other information about his activities on a particular day, and then to ask the interviewee to describe his actions, conversations, thoughts, and feelings, and those of other people to the extent that he had knowledge of them. This information was checked with other sources, e.g., other people involved in a particular meeting or conversation. The occasional conflicts in recollection were resolved by further interviewing and the marshaling of documentary material, and by the author's own knowledge, developed in the course of hundreds of hours of interviewing and verification, of which interviewees tended to have the best memories and most reliable records, and tended to tell the verifiable truth most consistently. If an interviewee's version checked out consistently well, when tested against others, it was given appropriate weight. If an interviewee exhibited poor memory, or tended to give vague answers, or answers that conflicted with multiple identical recollections of others, that, too, is reflected in the narrative. Certain remaining conflicts are footnoted in the text or cited below. Having thus assembled the facts, the author deemed it most efficient to tell the story without specific textual attribution of each fact to the source or sources of that fact.

Dialogue was reconstructed (except in a few instances when the author was present taking notes) by the same methods used to gather and check the facts in general, and is set forth on the same nonattributed basis. That is, the dialogue was reconstructed from many sources and the reader should not assume that the speaker of a line of dialogue is the author's only source, or even among the sources, of that line of dialogue. While the sources often include the speaker, they also often include other participants in the conversation, and in a few instances they include people who did not participate in the conversation but were reliably informed on it.

The author of course does not claim that the dialogue represents the exact words used by the characters at the time of the events described. He does assert, however, that the dialogue represents the best recollection of the most accurate interviewees, that it captures the essence and spirit of the conversations that are reconstructed, as well as the personalities and styles of the characters, and that it does so *more* accurately than paraphrase would. Human beings do not speak in paraphrase.

It is appropriate that sources and documentation supporting certain portions of the narrative be cited in specific detail. Those portions are delineated below.

EPIGRAPHS

John Huston: Lillian Ross, *Picture*, Rinehart & Company, Incorporated, New York, 1952, pp. 11–12.
David Chasman: Interview with the author.

CHAPTERS 1–5

The author has examined the Cliff Robertson check and all related correspondence and documentation, including memoranda prepared by the police departments of Los Angeles and Burbank, California.

Information on the *Red Baron* episode is contained in the files of *Cinerama Inc.* v. *Cliff Robertson and Robertson Associates*, C 17875, Superior Court of the State of California for the County of Los Angeles, 1972; Begelman affidavit, May 13, 1971; Robertson deposition, August 28, 1973.

CHAPTERS 6–9

Columbia's hit pictures of the 1970s: The studio also made some commercial failures such as *Nickelodeon* and *The Fortune* during the Hirschfield-Begelman era.

"Hollywood is a state of mind." The author does not claim exclusively to have conceived that phrase and notion. Explicitly and implicitly, others have stated the same or similar themes on occasion over many decades. It is attributed, for example, to Wilson Mizner, described as a wit, promoter, and gambler in the Hollywood of the 1920s, and quoted by Griffith, Mayer, and Bowser in their pictorial history, *The Movies*. In a broader sense, too, while the author accepts full responsibility for the analysis and reportage contained in this book, he gratefully acknowledges his debt to other writers who have helped shape his thinking. Strangely, those who write best about Hollywood seem to write least. A relatively small number of essays and articles by Joan Didion and Marie Brenner contain more insight into the subculture of the picture business than any nonfiction book of which the author is aware with the exception of Lillian Ross's *Picture* and John Gregory Dunne's *The Studio*. As for fiction, little of value has been published since the last novels about Hollywood by F. Scott Fitzgerald and Nathanael West, who have been dead for many years, and by Budd Schulberg and Norman Mailer, who fortunately are still with us.

L. B. Mayer and Nicholas Schenck: Article on Loew's Inc., *Fortune*, August 1939, reprinted in *The American Film Industry*, edited by Tino Balio, University of Wisconsin Press, 1976; Dore Schary, *Heyday*, Little, Brown and Company, Boston, 1979.

Beverly Hills statistics: Business licenses and other data on file with the Beverly Hills City Hall and Chamber of Commerce.

The most detailed explication of the Peter Choate transaction is contained in David Begelman's SEC testimony and accompanying exhibits.

CHAPTER 10

Herbert Allen's relationships with Jennifer O'Neil and Barbara Rucker are documented in several interviews and newspaper clippings.

Origin of "The Rabbit" as Ray Stark's nickname: Eugenia Sheppard interview with Fran Stark, *New York Herald Tribune*, reprinted in the *Los Angeles Times*, April 6, 1964; quotes reaffirmed by Sheppard in 1982. Fran Stark did not return a phone call seeking her confirmation.

Ray Stark's college career and early employment: Stark's SEC testimony; outline of Stark's biography released by Columbia Pictures, February 17, 1972.

Charles Allen and Serge Semenenko's role in the affairs of Warner Bros. and Jack Warner: *The Wall Street Journal* (hereafter *WSJ*), May 10, July 2, and 12, 1956; and March 21, 1957. Although Charles Allen technically was not a member of the original group headed by Semenenko that purchased Warner stock, Allen was an important financial adviser and subsequently did buy stock, owning 145,000 Warner shares by early 1957. Allen and Semenenko became Warner board members in July 1956.

Serge Semenenko's controversial and questionable role in the affairs of Warner Bros.: William M. Carley, "Unorthodox Banker," *WSJ*, July 17, 1967.

Semenenko's departure from the bank, *WSJ*, July 18, 1967.

Warner Bros.'s sale of its film library to Associated Artists Productions: *WSJ*, March 2, May 10, and July 30, 1956.

Chesler's association with Meyer Lansky and other gangsters and bookmakers, dating back to the 1940s: Hank Messick, *Syndicate Abroad*, The Macmillan Company, New York, Collier-Macmillan Ltd., London, 1969, especially pp. 64, 66, 74, 123, and 126. Further references in Messick, *The Beauties and the Beasts: the Mob in Show Business*, David McKay Company, Incorporated, New York, 1973, e.g., p. 208. (Neither book's authenticity was ever challenged by any person for whose background it is cited here as verification.) Further information on Chesler's relationships to Lansky is contained in the *Report of the Royal Commission of Inquiry into the Operation of the Business of Casinos in Freeport and in Nassau*, Nassau, Bahamas, published by Her Majesty's Stationery Office, London, 1967, p. 86 and other references.

Schwebel's criminal record: *WSJ*, February 16, 1961, May 1 and June 8, 1964; also Securities and Exchange Commission, Form 10, General Form for Registration of Securities, Seven Arts Productions Ltd., April 29, 1965, as amended, Item 11, p. 20, where Schwebel also is identified as the company's largest shareholder with 230,769 shares, or 10.14 percent of the common stock.

Associated Artists Productions board of directors: *Film Daily Yearbook of Motion Pictures*, 1957.

Stark's association with Associated Artists Productions in 1957; *The New York Times* (hereafter *NYT*), July 28, 1957.

Stark's association with Seven Arts Productions in 1957 and 1958:

NYT, April 4, 1958, reporting that Seven Arts Productions was founded in December 1957, as an "offshoot" of Associated Artists Productions.

Seven Arts officers and directors, 1961: Seven Arts Productions Ltd., annual report, year ended January 31, 1962.

Allen investment in Grand Bahama Port Authority Ltd.: Stanley Penn, "Meet Charlie Allen," *WSJ*, August 4, 1970, and previous articles by Penn.

Groves criminal record: *NYT*, February 22, 1941, and numerous subsequent *WSJ* and *Time* magazine articles; Messick, *Syndicate Abroad*, pp. 49–51.

Investments in Grand Bahama Development Co. by Stark, Hyman, Chesler, Seven Arts, and the Allens: Mentioned in opinion letter of Professor Louis Loss of the Harvard Law School to Eliot Hyman, June 4, 1964, filed as Exhibit 15.2 (a) with *Seven Arts Productions Ltd., Reorganization and Sale of Subordinated Notes, 1964*.

Agreement between Chesler and Stark that Chesler would purchase Seven Arts stock from Stark under certain conditions: Seven Arts's SEC Form 10 as amended, p. 13.

Seven Arts Productions Ltd.'s purchase of a 21 percent interest in Grand Bahama Development: Seven Arts annual report for the year ended January 31, 1962.

Groves's and Chesler's secret payments to Bahamian government officials: *Report of the Royal Commission of Inquiry*, 1967, numerous references; *WSJ*, several articles, e.g., August 4, 1970; Messick, *Syndicate Abroad*, several references.

Staffing the casino with Lansky associates after meeting with Lansky and other mobsters in Miami Beach: *Report of the Royal Commission of Inquiry*, p. 86 and other references; Messick, *Syndicate Abroad*, several references; *WSJ* report of Chesler's testimony to the royal commission, April 19, 1967.

(None of the foregoing should be construed as indicative of illegality or wrongdoing by Charles Allen, Ray Stark, or Eliot Hyman.)

Origin of Begelman and Stark's relationship; the clash over Streisand's contract: Both men's SEC testimony.

Luft testimony about Begelman and Garland: Luft deposition, April 16, 1969, taken in the case of *Judy Garland et al.* against *David Begelman et al.*, Supreme Court of the State of New York, County of New York, No. 16634/68, March 15, 1968.

Begelman's promise not to lie to Sam Cohn: Mark Singer, "Dealmaker," *The New Yorker*, January 11, 1982, p. 78. Begelman later claimed that Cohn had made the request of Begelman and Fields, not just of Begelman. Cohn said the exchange had been "jocular."

Chesler's departure from Seven Arts and the reorganization of the company are fully documented in Seven Arts's SEC Form 10 as amended, filed in 1965, and in related material collected under the title *Seven Arts Productions, Ltd.*, *Reorganization and Sale of Subordinated Notes, 1964*.

CHAPTERS 11–12

Alan Hirschfield's college activities: *The 1957 Sooner*, Yearbook of the University of Oklahoma.

Television and motion-picture audience statistics: Cobbett Steinberg, *TV Facts*, Facts on File Inc., New York, 1980, and *Reel Facts*, *The Movie Book of Records*, Vintage Books, A Division of Random House, New York, 1978.

The SEC's allegations against General Host, Allen & Company, Inc., and other defendants, and the settlement of the cases: *WSJ*, December 14, 1973, April 10, 1975, September 6, 1977.

Allen & Company Inc. performs services for Commonwealth United: *WSJ*, May 12, 1971.

SEC cases involving Kleiner, Bell & Co. and Burt S. Kleiner: *WSJ*, December 1, 1970, February 6, 1980, and Oct. 15, 1981.

The activities of Allen Manus: *WSJ*, May 2, 1979 and Oct. 15, 1981.

SEC charges against Del Coleman and others associated with Parvin-Dohrmann and settlement of the case: *WSJ*, October 17, 1969; December 16, 1970; Messick, *The Beauties and the Beasts*, pp. 237–241.

Controversy between Ray Stark and Seven Arts over Stark's relationship with Barbra Streisand: Information circulars and proxy statements for the mergers of Seven Arts and Warner Bros. (June 16, 1967, p. 43) and Warner Bros.-Seven Arts and Kinney National Service (May 16, 1969, p. 89). The "controversy" was settled "amicably," according to the 1969 document. Information in the two documents was supplemented by interviews.

Federal Trade Commission sanctions against the J. B. Williams Co.: *WSJ*, January 14, 1976.

SEC investigation of James Wilmot: *Time*, August 21, 1978.

Accounts of the September 23, 1977, board of directors meeting and all subsequent board meetings are based in part on the author's examination of the full minutes of each board meeting and related documents. Although the minutes are summaries and contain no actual dialogue, they do stand as the corporation's official and confidential record of the meetings and, at a minimum, provide a firm basis for further inquiry.

Frank Capra bases a character on Giannini: *Frank Capra, The Man and His Films*, edited by Richard Glatzer and John Raeburn, Ann Arbor Paperbacks, The University of Michigan Press, 1975, p. 29.

Considerable information on the role of banks and investment firms in the motion-picture industry is contained in Robert H. Stanley, *The Celluloid Empire*, Hastings House, New York, 1978; Tino Balio, *United Artists, The Company Built by the Stars*, University of Wisconsin Press, 1976; and *The American Film Industry*, edited by Tino Balio, University of Wisconsin Press, 1976.

The role of the First National Bank of Boston is described by William F. Thompson in an interview published by *Film Comment*, the Journal of the Film Society of Lincoln Center, September-October 1976, p. 20.

The most detailed explication of the Pierre Groleau embezzlement is contained in Begelman's SEC testimony and exhibits, and in memoranda prepared by the Burbank, California, police department.

Rona Barrett: Rona Barrett, *Miss Rona, An Autobiography*, Bantam Books, 1975.

The Wyman, Bautzer law firm later was renamed Wyman, Bautzer, Rothman, Kuchel & Silbert.

David Geffen's life: Julie Baumgold, "The Winning of Cher (and some other major achievements of David Geffen)," *Esquire*, February 1975; J. Curtis Sanburn, "David Geffen: Starting Over," *Gentlemen's Quarterly*, July 1981; Jennifer Allen, "What Makes David Geffen Run?," New York *Daily News*, February 25, 1981.

The seven major studios to which the author occasionally refers are Columbia, Metro-Goldwyn-Mayer, Paramount, Twentieth Century-

Fox, United Artists, Universal, and Warner Bros. Disney, although it is an important studio, is an exception to nearly every rule of Hollywood and is beyond the scope of this book.

The most detailed explication of the Martin Ritt embezzlement is contained in Begelman's SEC testimony and exhibits, and in memoranda prepared by the Burbank police.

CHAPTERS 23–36

Much of Gruenberger's interrogation of Begelman on November 7, 1977, was duplicated in less detail by the SEC's later questioning of Begelman.

One or more of Stark's loans to Begelman were verified or alluded to in the SEC testimony of Begelman, Stark, and Gerald Lipsky.

The author was present at the November 10, 1977, annual meeting, and at the November 15 premiere of *Close Encounters*.

Details of Berte Hirschfield's employment with E. J. Wolf & Associates Inc., are contained in letters from Leo Jaffe to Irwin Kramer and Alan Hirschfield, both dated Feb. 26, 1976, and from Weil, Gotshal & Manges to Irwin Kramer, dated May 15, 1978.

Northrup foreign payoffs scandal: *WSJ*, February 19, 1976.

The author was present at the all-day staff meeting November 28, 1977.

Ira Harris: "Ira Harris: Chicago's Big Dealmaker," *Business Week*, June 25, 1979.

Jimmy Goldsmith: William Mathewson, "Fighting Knight," *WSJ*, March 29, 1977.

Allan Carr's party for Gladyce Begelman was described by Andrew Tobias in "The Fall, Rise and Fall of David Begelman," *Esquire*, March 14, 1978. Tobias attended the party with an invited guest.

David Karr: Roy Rowan, "The Death of Dave Karr, and Other Mysteries," *Fortune*, December 3, 1979; Jeff Gerth, "U.S. Entrepreneur's Soviet Ties," *NYT*, October 5, 1979.

The December 20, 1977, *WSJ* article and subsequent *WSJ* articles cited here on Columbia Pictures were written by the author of this book.

Stark's call to Cliff Robertson on December 26, 1977, was described by Robertson in his SEC testimony.

Samples of Lucian Truscott's writing: Army career: *Harper's*, July 1974; Ali-Frazier fight: *The Village Voice*, March 18, 1971; Journalism: Monthly newsletter to the Alicia Patterson Foundation, May 1976. Truscott had a fellowship from the foundation that year to study his class at West Point. These samples are indicative of Truscott's style, personality, and approach to writing, but are not comprehensively representative of the total body of his journalism, which includes some creditable investigative reporting.

United Artists history: Balio, *United Artists*.

The author was the *WSJ* reporter who received the anonymous call about Berte Hirschfield.

The extract from Cliff Robertson's interrogation by Detective Elias and Deputy DA Lewis is taken from a transcript of the conversation.

Philip Morris details: Philip Morris Incorporated annual reports; "The Fortune 500," *Fortune*, May 8, 1978.

Judy Garland partially contradicts her letters: Deposition taken in the case of *Michael Sidney Luft* v. *Frances Gumm Luft, also known as Judy Garland*, Superior Court of the State of California for the County of Los Angeles, No. WED 4146, December 15, 1964.

The author was present at the security analysts' presentation, February 14, 1978.

Lucian Truscott's *New York Times Magazine* article: In addition to the mistakes noted in Chapter 46, the article contained other erroneous statements, including the following: that Charles Allen put up $11 million to buy RKO Pictures from Howard Hughes; that Villem Zwillinger brought Charles Allen into the movie business in 1953; that Eliot Hyman bought and sold RKO, and also bought and sold Monogram Pictures; that Zwillinger introduced Charles Allen to Hyman; that the 1948 decree requiring the studios to divest their theater chains was initiated by the SEC; that Charles Allen had an office on lower Broadway; that Columbia Pictures was a $100 million-plus corporation. (While technically correct, the low figure used in the last statement was highly misleading: according to Columbia's 1977 annual report, which was readily available to Truscott, the corporation's revenues were $391 million and its assets were $336 million.)

CHAPTERS 48–56

Nonpublic details of Begelman's deal with Columbia: Memorandum to corporate counsel Victor Kaufman, February 15, 1978, filed with board-meeting minutes.

Robert L. Stone: Hugh D. Menzies, "The Ten Toughest Bosses," *Fortune*, April 21, 1980; *WSJ*, March 22, 1977.

Herbert Allen's attitude toward Columbia's acquiring Filmways: On May 1, 1978, Allen wrote a letter to Hirschfield saying, "I think that this would be the proper time to acquire Filmways. . . ." On May 5, Hirschfield replied ". . . It sounds like an interesting idea to pursue. . . ." In view of subsequent developments, as well as the overall political climate within Columbia, it could be inferred that both letters were formalities and not entirely serious.

Discussion of the Mattel deal by Hirschfield, Spear, and Lufkin: Lufkin subsequently said that he had no genuine interest in being chief executive officer but may have offered to be a "straw horse" chief executive "to get the deal done." He said the talks were stymied by Art Spear's insistence on being chief executive.

Herbert Allen's objections to the Filmways and Mattel deals: Subsequently he said that both companies' asking prices had been too high, Rosenhaus disliked the toy business, the mode of payment Filmways had asked was unacceptable to Columbia, and Filmway's businesses did not "fit well" with Columbia's.

Robert Stone's talks with Herbert Allen: The account is based in large part on Stone's SEC testimony, which is generally consistent with Allen's testimony on this subject but more detailed and specific.

Audrey Lisner: The basic information on her alleged crimes is contained in the files of *The People of the State of California* v. *Audrey Bride Lisner*, Case No. A350655, Superior Court of the State of California for the County of Los Angeles. The author also was aided by the district attorney's *Affidavit for Search Warrant*, filed in support of Search Warrant No. 14799, signed June 7, 1978. The affidavit, which sets forth the details of Columbia's internal investigation by Ilana Cytto and Peter Gruenberger, was obtained from Columbia sources, as was extensive additional information on Lisner's background and activities.

Board meeting of June 22, 1978: Hirschfield later objected in writing to the accuracy of the board secretary's minutes of the meeting and subsequent board meetings. This book's account reflects those objections in instances where the author has determined that they have merit.

Price Waterhouse's analysis of Columbia's West Coast financial controls: In a six-page report dated February 24, 1978, Price Waterhouse said its investigation "disclosed no conditions that we believe to be material weaknesses" and emphasized that no "reasonable" control system can provide an "absolute" guarantee against circumvention by a "single individual within management with respect to the execution and recording of transactions." However, Price Waterhouse recommended thirteen procedural changes—most if not all of which Columbia implemented—to further reduce the possibility of embezzlement.

CHAPTERS 57–62

Begelman criminal proceeding: *The People of the State of California* v. *David Begelman*, Case No. A-586983, Superior Court of the State of California, County of Los Angeles, 1978.

Herbert Allen and Irwin Kramer's letters rebutting Hirschfield's letter of June 28, 1978: Further extracts follow:

Allen: ". . . The board is not 'out of control.' Without deprecating the 'management' members of the board, I am proud to say that the 'outside' board members are, without regard to their financial interest in the company, as purposeful, disciplined, honest and hard working a group as I have ever had the privilege of being associated with. I am forced to the conclusion that Mr. Hirschfield uses the term 'the board is out of control' because he feels that the board is out of his control and he cannot control the board. . . . It is not only factually incorrect but also grossly unfair to characterize the actions of the directors, taken in good faith, as 'vexatious and obstruent.' I for one have been available to the company generally, and to Mr. Hirschfield specifically, at a few moments' notice on a 24-hour-a-day basis. And Mr. Hirschfield has called on me on that basis—days, nights, telephone calls by him at 1:30 in the morning, telephone calls to me in Europe, the use of my home to negotiate with existing and proposed executives. And other directors have been similarly unstinting in their availability and output. . . ."

Kramer: ". . . as chairman of the audit committee of the board, my efforts have been extensive and intensive to make the audit committee more effective and responsive. It is only through hard

work of our committee, in the face of obstacles and delay, that we
have made progress in attaining our stated objectives. . . ."

Adler memorandum of meeting with Lufkin July 20, 1978: Lufkin
later said his remarks referred to his general motivation for joining
the Columbia board and not to the specific act of firing Hirschfield.

EPILOGUE

Clive Davis, Dan Melnick, and Allen Adler did not actually
become Fox employees. Columbia sold Davis's record company,
Arista, to Bertelsmann, a multinational media company based in
Germany. Davis remained the head of Arista, however, and established a production relationship with Fox. Dan Melnick moved his
production company from Columbia to Fox, and Adler, who had
learned by his middle thirties to control his temper and brashness,
went into partnership with Melnick. ·

Columbia's battle with Kerkorian is fully documented in *Tracinda
Corp.* v. *Columbia Pictures Industries Inc. et al.,* U.S. District
Court, District of Nevada, Las Vegas, Civ LV, No. 80–134 HEC,
1980–81.

Columbia's troubles with Sy Weintraub are documented in *Seymour
Weintraub* v. *Columbia Pictures Industries Inc.,* U.S. District Court,
Central District of California, No. 80 04047-WPG, 1980–81; Vincent deposition, August 10, 1981; Allen deposition, September 11,
1981; Weintraub deposition, August 24, 1981. Weintraub testified
that his service to Columbia was valuable and competent, and that
there was nothing wrong or improper about any of his dealings with
Kerkorian. Weintraub said that Vincent gave Weintraub a lesser title
in order to build up Vincent's own image as chief executive of the
corporation. Weintraub said of Vincent: "I believe his integrity at
times leaves something to be desired." Vincent said of Weintraub:
". . . obviously Sy was becoming apparently someone who, within
our midst and our board, was in the process of betraying us to
outside interests."

Allegations against Harris Katleman: Inquiries by Fox's internal
auditors and by Peat, Marwick, Mitchell & Co., the company's outside
auditors, revealed a number of "discrepancies" in Katleman's travel
and entertainment accounts for a trip to France in June 1980. Among
the discrepancies were the following: A $316.84 charge for a dinner
was supported by an American Express charge slip from a woman's

clothing store and hairdresser; two restaurant receipts, one for a dinner with Dionne Warwick and another for a dinner with Hal Linden, appeared to have been altered. Katleman's explanations were declared "inadequate" by the Fox auditors. Sources: Letter to John P. Meehan, Fox's vice president and controller, from Peat, Marwick, Mitchell, October 29, 1980; two memoranda to David Y. Handelman, Fox's senior vice president and general counsel, from Robert E. Younger, director of corporate audit, November 3 and 7, 1980.

Whatever the merits of the case against Katleman, and whether or not it was believed that expense-account discrepancies should have been grounds for dismissal, it was clear to insiders with full knowledge of the facts that Katleman's acts were not in the same category as David Begelman's forgeries and embezzlements. The district attorney's decision not to prosecute Katleman supported that assessment. However, a number of anti-Hirschfield people seized upon Hirschfield's defense of Katleman as proof that Hirschfield's ethics were inconsistent, and that his stance against David Begelman at Columbia had been hypocritical. These critics contended that the only consistency in Hirschfield's behavior was an attempt to use both the Begelman and Katleman episodes to increase his own power—at Columbia unsuccessfully, at Fox successfully.

Details of Entertainment Industry Task Force prosecutions: Letter to Jack Valenti, president of the Motion Picture Association of America, from District Attorney Van de Kamp, May 20, 1980.

Spelling-Goldberg investigation: James J. Ferruzzo, Deputy District Attorney, *Final Report: ABC/Spelling-Goldberg Productions Investigation*, December 2, 1980.

The circumstances and cause of Jerry Lisner's death: Official police and coroner's reports.

In 1982, Marvin Davis decided that Dan Melnick's production contract at Fox was too rich and instructed Alan Hirschfield to renegotiate it. After a protracted confrontation, culminating in the suicide of Melnick's lawyer, Norman Garey, Melnick left Fox to produce films for other studios. (Although there was no evidence that the confrontation was the cause of Garey's suicide, the clash apparently aggravated an existing mental illness.)

At the beginning of 1983, Sherry Lansing also departed Fox to form a film production partnership with Stanley Jaffe, the producer of *Kramer vs. Kramer, Taps,* and *Without A Trace*. Lansing never had been given sufficient authority at Fox to do her job properly.

INDEX